Fishes and the Break-up of Pangaea

Geological Society books refereeing procedures

The Society makes every effort to ensure that the scientific and production quality of its books matches that of its journals. Since 1997, all book proposals have been refereed by specialist reviewers as well as by the Society's Books Editorial Committee. If the referees identify weaknesses in the proposal, these must be addressed before the proposal is accepted.

Once the book is accepted, the Society Book Editors ensure that the volume editors follow strict guidelines on refereeing and quality control. We insist that individual papers can only be accepted after satisfactory review by two independent referees. The questions on the review forms are similar to those for *Journal of the Geological Society*. The referees' forms and comments must be available to the Society's Book Editors on request.

Although many of the books result from meetings, the editors are expected to commission papers that were not presented at the meeting to ensure that the book provides a balanced coverage of the subject. Being accepted for presentation at the meeting does not guarantee inclusion in the book.

More information about submitting a proposal and producing a book for the Society can be found on its web site: www.geolsoc.org.uk.

It is recommended that reference to all or part of this book should be made in one of the following ways:

CAVIN, L., LONGBOTTOM, A. & RICHTER, M. (eds) 2008. *Fishes and the Break-up of Pangaea*. Geological Society, London, Special Publications, **295**.

OTERO, O., VALENTIN, X. & GARCIA, G. 2008. Cretaceous characiform fishes (Teleostei: Ostariophysi) from Northern Tethys: description of new material from the Maastrichtian of Provence (Southern France) and palaeobiogeographical implications. *In*: CAVIN, L., LONGBOTTOM, A. & RICHTER, M. (eds) *Fishes and the Break-up of Pangaea*. Geological Society, London, Special Publications, **295**, 155–164.

GEOLOGICAL SOCIETY SPECIAL PUBLICATION NO. 295

Fishes and the Break-up of Pangaea

EDITED BY

L. CAVIN
Museum d'Histoire de Naturelle, Genève, Switzerland

A. LONGBOTTOM and M. RICHTER
Natural History Museum, UK

2008
Published by
The Geological Society
London

THE GEOLOGICAL SOCIETY

The Geological Society of London (GSL) was founded in 1807. It is the oldest national geological society in the world and the largest in Europe. It was incorporated under Royal Charter in 1825 and is Registered Charity 210161.

The Society is the UK national learned and professional society for geology with a worldwide Fellowship (FGS) of over 9000. The Society has the power to confer Chartered status on suitably qualified Fellows, and about 2000 of the Fellowship carry the title (CGeol). Chartered Geologists may also obtain the equivalent European title, European Geologist (EurGeol). One fifth of the Society's fellowship resides outside the UK. To find out more about the Society, log on to www.geolsoc.org.uk.

The Geological Society Publishing House (Bath, UK) produces the Society's international journals and books, and acts as European distributor for selected publications of the American Association of Petroleum Geologists (AAPG), the Indonesian Petroleum Association (IPA), the Geological Society of America (GSA), the Society for Sedimentary Geology (SEPM) and the Geologists' Association (GA). Joint marketing agreements ensure that GSL Fellows may purchase these societies' publications at a discount. The Society's online bookshop (accessible from www.geolsoc.org.uk) offers secure book purchasing with your credit or debit card.

To find out about joining the Society and benefiting from substantial discounts on publications of GSL and other societies worldwide, consult www.geolsoc.org.uk, or contact the Fellowship Department at: The Geological Society, Burlington House, Piccadilly, London W1J 0BG: Tel. +44 (0)20 7434 9944; Fax +44 (0)20 7439 8975; E-mail: enquiries@geolsoc.org.uk.

For information about the Society's meetings, consult *Events* on www.geolsoc.org.uk. To find out more about the Society's Corporate Affiliates Scheme, write to enquiries@geolsoc.org.uk.

Published by The Geological Society from:
The Geological Society Publishing House, Unit 7, Brassmill Enterprise Centre, Brassmill Lane, Bath BA1 3JN, UK

(*Orders*:   Tel. +44 (0)1225 445046, Fax +44 (0)1225 442836)
Online bookshop: www.geolsoc.org.uk/bookshop

The publishers make no representation, express or implied, with regard to the accuracy of the information contained in this book and cannot accept any legal responsibility for any errors or omissions that may be made.

British Library Cataloguing in Publication Data

A catalogue record for this book is available from the British Library.

ISBN 978-1-86239-248-9

Typeset by Techset Composition Ltd, Salisbury, UK

Printed by The Cromwell Press Ltd, Wiltshire, UK

Distributors

North America
For trade and institutional orders:
The Geological Society, c/o AIDC, 82 Winter Sport Lane, Williston, VT 05495, USA
Orders: Tel +1 800-972-9892
            Fax +1 802-864-7626
            E-mail: gsl.orders@aidcvt.com

For individual and corporate orders:
AAPG Bookstore, PO Box 979, Tulsa, OK 74101-0979, USA
Orders: Tel +1 918-584-2555
            Fax +1 918-560-2652
            E-mail: bookstore@aapg.org
            Website http://bookstore.aapg.org
India
Affiliated East-West Press Private Ltd, Marketing Division, G-1/16 Ansari Road, Darya Ganj, New Delhi 110 002, India
Orders: Tel +91 11 2327-9113/2326-4180
            Fax +91 11 2326-0538
            E-mail: affiliat@vsnl.com

Contents

Peter L. Forey

BRIAN GARDINER[1] & ALISON LONGBOTTOM[2]

[1]*Ringlee, Lindon Gardens, Leatherhead, Surrey KT22 7HB, UK*

[2]*Department of Palaeontology, Natural History Museum, Cromwell Road, London SW7 5BD, UK (e-mail: A.Longbottom@nhm.ac.uk)*

This book began with the desire by the editors to create a publication to honour Dr Peter Forey (Fig. 1) in recognition of his great contribution to fish systematics and palaeobiogeography. This preface gives a brief review of some of his accomplishments and a list of his publications to date. Peter Forey started his palaeontological career as a research student of Brian Gardiner at Queen Elizabeth College, University of London from 1968–1971.

His thesis on elopiform fishes was published in 1973 in the Bulletin of the British Museum (Natural History) (Geology supplement 10). That same year he produced what turned out to be a signal paper entitled 'Relationships of elopomorphs', which was published in 'Interrelationships of Fishes' (Greenwood, Miles & Patterson 1973). This was subsequently updated in 1996 by the paper Forey, Littlewood, Ritchie & Meyer, 'Interrelationships of elopomorph fishes', published in a new edition of 'Interrelationships of Fishes'.

These publications are still the standard works on fossil elopomorph comparative anatomy.

In 1972, sometime after graduation (during which period he had several jobs, including working for a security firm) he applied for, and secured, the position of Assistant professor in Zoology at the University of Alberta. He remained in this post until 1975 when he joined the fossil fish section in the Department of Palaeontology at the Natural History Museum, London. Here, working with Colin Patterson, he became one of the prime movers in getting phylogenetic systematics (or cladistics as it became called) accepted by the palaeontology community.

This new method for analysing phylogenies was being developed in the 1970s following the publication of a paper on phylogenetic systematics in English (Hennig 1966). The fossil fish section and other researchers from the Natural History Museum (including Peter, Colin, Chris Humphries (Botanist), Dick Vane-Wright (Entomologist) and, on occasion, Brian Gardiner and Gareth Nelson) had many fruitful discussions in a public house local to the museum, which became known as 'the Cladists Arms'. The cladistic methodology was viewed antagonistically by many palaeontologists at the time and finally a special session was set aside at the '26th Symposium of Vertebrate Palaeontology and Comparative Anatomy' held in 1978 at Reading University, England, to discuss the issue. The promotion of cladistics by the Natural History Museum speakers at this symposium led to some sharp exchanges in the pages of *Nature* journal (Halstead 1978; Halstead & White 1978; Gardiner et al. 1979). These discussions and disputes eventually led to the 1981 publication by Rosen, Forey, Patterson & Gardiner entitled 'Lungfishes, tetrapods, palaeontology and plesiomorphy'. On the face of it, this was a publication describing the anatomical details of the snouts of tetrapods, lobe-finned fishes and lungfishes, and their conclusion was that tetrapods were more closely related to the lungfish rather than other lobe-finned fishes (in particular the osteolepiforms), which was the accepted idea at that time. This caused quite a stir but mainly because

Fig. 1. Peter Forey.

From: CAVIN, L., LONGBOTTOM, A. & RICHTER, M. (eds) *Fishes and the Break-up of Pangaea.*
Geological Society, London, Special Publications, **295**, 1–6.
DOI: 10.1144/SP295.1   0305-8719/08/$15.00 © The Geological Society of London 2008.

Rosen *et al.* criticised the traditional methods of working out ancestor–descendant relationships, where it was deemed important that fossils played a large part. They again argued in strong terms for cladistic methodology where relationships should be inferred from extant forms alone without reference to fossils. Their apparent dismissal of fossils and contradiction of the accepted origins of tetrapods led to some very vitriolic reviews of their paper (especially Jarvik 1981) and they became known as 'the gang of four'.

The first use of this term in print has not been traced but it culminated with Henry Gee (1999) using it as a chapter heading in a book where he describes the history of the Rosen *et al.* 1981 paper and the reaction of the palaeontology community to it. Now that cladistic methodology is accepted it is difficult to understand the heated arguments and discussions that went on in the literature of the 1970s and 1980s, and Peter Forey's papers reflect this time of change.

Peter continued to champion cladistics and educate a new generation. Starting in 1983 with 'An Introduction to Cladistics', Peter has published many papers and books on cladistics and his most up-to-date contributions are a series of articles 'Cladistics for Palaeontologists' in the Palaeontology Newsletter (2005–2006) of the Palaeontological Association (UK). His background in lecturing also proved important for the development of cladistics at the Natural History Museum when in 1990 Peter, together with Chris Humphries, David Williams, Darrell Siebert and Ian Kitching, set up a course on cladistics for museum staff and MSc students and was one of the lead lecturers.

Undoubtedly Peter's other outstanding contributions have been on coelacanths (see Forey 1980, 1984*a*, 1988, 1989, 1990*b*, 1991*a*, 1991*c*) culminating in his book 'History of Coelacanth Fishes' (1998*c*). He is without doubt the world authority on coelacanths.

Peter has also published extensively on lungfishes, (e.g. Forey 1986), and their relationship to tetrapods (Forey *et al.* 1991).

Peter's other contributions to taxonomy concern the controversial PhyloCode, about which he published a description and commentary (see Forey 2001*c*, 2002*c*).

Peter has made valuable contributions to many other fields including palaeobiogeography (Forey 1981*a*, 1985*a*; Hilton & Forey 2005*b*). He has established himself as an outstanding teleost taxonomist with numerous publications throughout his career from the 1970s (Forey 1970, 1973*a*, 1973*b*–*c*, 1975, 1977) up to more recently (Forey & Patterson 2006). His extensive knowledge of fishes has been put to good use as he has, for many years, helped to identify the catches at the Alabama Deep Sea

Fig. 2. At the Alabama Deep Sea Fishing Rodeo (Dauphin Island, Alabama, USA), July 2002. From left to right: William E. Bemis, Peter Forey, and Lance Grande, with a Warsaw Grouper (*Epinephelus nigritus*, 2030 mm TL) that was landed during the fishing tournament. Photo: courtesy of L. Grande.

Fishing Rodeo and to select specimens for museum collections (Fig. 2). He has also made contributions to the study of more primitive fishes including on the origin of agnathans (Forey 1984*c*, 1995*a*, Forey & Janvier 1993, 1994, 1995*b*) and

Fig. 3. Peter Forey taking a short break from fossil collecting to make a study for a watercolour. At the Green River Formation, west of Kemmerer, Wyoming (USA), July 2003. Photo: E. J. Hilton.

on placoderms (Forey & Gardiner 1986). All of this is borne out by the fact that he has published over 114 peer-reviewed papers, 24 other articles and book reviews and written or contributed to 21 books and is still actively researching and writing. These are a lasting testimony to Peter Forey's accomplishments.

Throughout his career Peter's other major talent (as a gifted artist) has helped him to interpret and portray the complexities of fish morphology, as the beautiful illustrations in his papers show. Peter also paints watercolours and has exhibited and sold many paintings. His keenness extends to taking a sketchpad with him wherever he goes, even to the most remote (and some would say artistically-uninspiring) field areas (Fig. 3).

Peter's wide-ranging knowledge of and interest in fossil fishes and palaeobiogeography, and the inspiration his contributions have given to others, are acknowledged and reflected in the scope and subjects of the papers herein: this book is dedicated to him.

Alison Longbottom would like to thank Julien Kimmig for help compiling Peter Forey's bibliography.

References

GEE, H. 1999. *In search of Deep Time*. The Free Press, New York.
GREENWOOD, P. H., MILES, R. S. & PATTERSON, C. (eds) 1973. *Interrelationships of Fishes*. Acadamic Press, London.
HALSTEAD, L. B. 1978. The cladistic revolution–can it make the grade? *Nature*, **276**, 759–760.
HALSTEAD, L. B. & WHITE, E. I. 1979. A reply. *Nature*, **277**, 176.
HENNIG, W. 1966. *Phylogenetic Systematics*. Translated by: DWIGHT DAVIS, D. & RAINER ZANGERL. University of Illinois Press, Urbana.
JARVIK, E. 1981. Lungfishes, Tetrapods, Paleontology and Plesiomorphy. *Systematic Zoology*, **30**, 378–384.

Peter Forey Bibliography

AHLBERG, P. & FOREY, P. L. 1993. Therapsids and transformation series; discussion. *Nature*, **361**, 596–597.
BEMIS, W. E. & FOREY, P. L. 2001. Occipital structure and the posterior limit of the skull in actinopterygians. *In*: AHLBERG, P. (ed.) *Major events in early vertebrate evolution*. Systematics Association Special Volume series, **61**. Taylor & Francis, London, 350–369.
BEMIS, W. E., HILTON, E. J., BROWN, B., ARRINDDAL, R., RICHMOND, A. M., LITTLE, C. D., GRANDE, L., FOREY, P. L. & NELSON, G. J. 2004. Methods for preparing dry, partially articulated skeletons of osteichthyans with notes on making Ridewood dissections of the cranial skeleton. *Copeia*, **2004**, 603–609.
CAVIN, L. & FOREY, P. L. 2001. Osteology and systematic affinities of *Palaeonotopterus greenwoodi* Forey
1997 (Teleostei: Osteoglossomorpha). *Zoological Journal of the Linnean Society of London*, **133**, 25–52.
CAVIN, L. & FOREY, P. L. 2004. New Mawsoniid coelacanth (Sarcopterygii: Actinistia) remains from the Cretaceous of the Kem Kem Beds, Southern Morocco. *In*: ARRATIA, G. & TINTORI A. (eds) *Mesozoic fishes 3–Systematics, palaeoenvironments and biodiversity*. Dr F. Pfeil, Munich, 493–506.
CAVIN, L. & FOREY, P. L. 2007. Using ghost lineages to identify diversification events in the fossil record. *Biology Letters*, **3**, 201–204.
CAVIN, L., FOREY, P. L., BUFFETAUT, E. & TONG, H. 2005. Latest European coelacanth shows Gondwanan affinities. *Biology Letters*, 2005, 176–177.
CAVIN, L., FOREY, P. L. & LECUYER, C. 2007. Correlation between environment and Late Mesozoic ray-finned fish evolution. *Palaeogeography, Palaeoclimatology, Palaeoecology*, **245**, 353–367.
CHALONER, W. G., FOREY, P. L., GARDINER, B. G., HILL, A. J. & YOUNG, V. T. 1980. Devonian fish and plants from the Bokkeveld Series of South Africa. *Annals of the South African Museum*, **81**, 127–157.
CHENERY, S., WILLIAMS, T., ELLIOT, T., FOREY, P. L. & WERDELIN, L. 1996. Determination of rare earth elements in biological and mineral apatite by EPMA and LAMP-ICP-MS. *Mikrochimica Acta*, **Supplement 13**, 259–269.
CLOUTIER, R. & FOREY, P. L. 1991. Diversity of extinct and living actinistian fishes (Sacropterygii). *Environmental Biology of Fishes*. **32**, 59–74.
DONOGHUE, P. C. J. & FOREY, P. L. 1998. Conodont affinity, chordate phylogeny and the origin of vertebrate dermal skeleton. *Palaeontology Newsletter*, **39**, 7.
DONOGHUE, P. C. J., FOREY, P. L. & ALDRIDGE, R. J. 2000. Conodont affinity and chordate phylogeny. *Biological Reviews*, **75**, 191–251.
ELLIOT, T. A., FOREY, P. L. & WILLIAMS, C. T. 1995. Strontium isotopes and trace elements as palaeoenvironmental indicators in fossil fishes. *Terra Abstracts*, **7**, 237.
ELLIOT, T. A., FOREY, P. L., WILLIAMS, C. T. & WERDELIN, L. 1998. Application of the solubility profiling technique to Recent and fossil fish teeth. *Bulletin de la Société Géologique de France*, **169**, 443–451.
FOREY, P. L. 1970. A revision of the order Elopiformes (Pisces: Teleostei), University of London, PhD thesis.
FOREY, P. L. 1973a. A primitive clupeomorph fish from the Middle Cenomanian of Hakel, Lebanon. *Canadian Journal of Earth Sciences*, **10**, 1302–1318.
FOREY, P. L. 1973b. Relationships of elopomorphs. *In*: GREENWOOD, P. H., MILES, R. S. & PATTERSON, C. (eds) *Interrelationships of Fishes*. Academic Press, London, 351–368.
FOREY, P. L. 1973c. A revision of elopiform fishes, fossil and Recent. *Bulletin of the British Museum (Natural History) (Geology)*, **supplement 10**, 1–222.
FOREY, P. L. 1975. A fossil clupeomorph fish from the Albian of the Northwest Territories of Canada, with notes on cladistic relationships of clupeomorphs. *Journal of Zoology*, **175**, 151–177.
FOREY, P. L. 1977. The osteology of *Notelops* Woodward, *Rhacolepis* Agassiz and *Pachyrhizodus* Dixon (Pisces: Teleostei). *Bulletin of the British Museum (Natural History) (Geology)*, **28**, 123–204.

FOREY, P. L. 1980. *Latimeria*: a paradoxical fish. *Proceedings of the Royal Society of London*, **208**, 369–384.

FOREY, P. L. 1981a. Biogeography, Introduction. *In*: FOREY, P. L. (ed.) *The evolving Biosphere*. Cambridge University Press, Cambridge, 241–245.

FOREY, P. L. 1981b. The coelacanth *Rhabdoderma* in the Carboniferous of the British Isles. *Palaeontology*, **24**, 203–229.

FOREY, P. L. 1981c. *The Evolving Biosphere*. Cambridge University Press, Cambridge.

FOREY, P. L. 1982. Neontological analyses versus palaeontological stories. *In*: JOYSEY, K. A. & FRIDAY, A. E. (eds) *Problems of phylogenetic reconstruction*. The Systematics Association, Special Volume Series, **21**. Academic Press, London, 119–157.

FOREY, P. L. 1983. Introduction to cladistics. *In*: MINGZHENG, Z., MIMAN, Z. & XIABO, Y. (eds) *Translation of selected papers on cladistics*. Science Press, Beijing, 152–195.

FOREY, P. L. 1984a. The coelacanth as a living fossil. *In*: ELDREDGE, N. & STANLEY, S. M. (eds) *Living Fossils*. Springer Verlag, New York, 166–169.

FOREY, P. L. 1984b. L'origine des tétrapodes. *La Recherche*, **15**, 476–487.

FOREY, P. L. 1984c. Yet more reflections on Agnathan-Gnathostome relationships. *Journal of Vertebrate Paleontology*, **4**, 330–343.

FOREY, P. L. 1985a. Methods of palaeobiogeography. *Journal of the Open University Geological Society*, **6**, 3–9.

FOREY, P. L. 1985b. Obituary: Errol Ivor White, CBE, FRS, P-PLS (1901–1985). *The Linnean*, **1**, 28–32.

FOREY, P. L. 1986. Relationships of lungfishes. *In*: BEMIS, W. E., BURGGREN, W. W. & KEMP, N. E. (eds) *The biology and evolution of lungfishes*. Journal of Morphology, **Centennial supplement 1**, 75–91.

FOREY, P. L. 1987. The Downtonian ostracoderm *Sclerodus* Agassiz (Osteostraci; Tremataspididae). *Bulletin of the British Museum (Natural History) (Geology)*, **41**, 1–30.

FOREY, P. L. 1988. Golden Jubilee for the Coelacanth *Latimeria chalumnae*. *Nature*, **336**, 727–732.

FOREY, P. L. 1989. Le Coelacanthe. *La Recherche*, **20**, 1318–1326.

FOREY, P. L. 1990a. Cladistics. *In*: BRIGGS, D. E. & CROWTHER, P. R. (eds) *Palaeobiology: a synthesis*. Blackwell Scientific Publications, Oxford, 430–434.

FOREY, P. L. 1990b. The coelacanth fish: progress and prospects. *Science Progress*, **74**, 53–67.

FOREY, P. L. 1990c. An extraordinary Blue fish. *Endeavour*, **14**, 8–13.

FOREY, P. L. 1991a. Blood lines of the coelacanth. *Nature*, **351**, 347–348.

FOREY, P. L. 1991b. Des poissons aux tétrapodes. *In*: SABBAGH, C. (ed.) *On a marché sur la Terre*. Editions ICS. Museum National d'Histoire Naturelle, Paris, 31–36.

FOREY, P. L. 1991c. *Latimeria chalumnae* and its pedigree. *Enviromental Biology of Fishes*, **32**, 75–97.

FOREY, P. L. 1992a. Beetle shine in oily shale. Book review; Messel: An insight into the history of life and of the Earth by Schaal, S. & Zeigler, W. *New Scientist*, **136** (Dec.), 57.

FOREY, P. L. 1992b. Book review; Fish evolution and systematics: evidence from spermatozoa by Jamieson, B. G. M. *Trends in Ecology and Evolution*, **7**, 66–67.

FOREY, P. L. 1992c. Formal classification. *In*: FOREY, P. L., HUMPHRIES, C. J., KITCHING, I. J., SCOTLAND, R. W., SIEBERT, D. J. & WILLIAMS, D. M. (eds) *Cladistics: a practical course in systematics*. Systematics Association Publications, **10**. Oxford University Press, Oxford, 160–169.

FOREY, P. L. 1992d. Fossils and cladistic analysis. *In*: FOREY, P. L., HUMPHRIES, C. J., KITCHING, I. J., SCOTLAND, R. W., SIEBERT, D. J. & WILLIAMS, D. M. (eds) *Cladistics: a practical course in systematics*. Systematics Association Publications, **10**. Oxford University Press, Oxford, 124–136.

FOREY, P. L. 1994a. Book review; The Africa-South America connection by George, W. & Lavocat, R. *Journal of Biogeography*, **21**, 338–339.

FOREY, P. L. 1994b. Foreward. *In*: MINELLI, A. (ed.) *Biological Systematics: the state of the art*. Chapman & Hall, London.

FOREY, P. L. 1994c. Little comfort for advocates of saltational evolution and mass extinctions. Book review; Extinction and Phylogeny by NOVACEK, M. J. & WHEELER, Q. D. (eds); *Journal of Biogeography*, **21**, 353–356.

FOREY, P. L. 1995a. Agnathans Recent and fossil, and the origin of jawed vertebrates. *Reviews in Fish Biology and Fisheries*, **5**, 267–303.

FOREY, P. L. 1995b. Book review; Interpreting the hierarchy of nature by GRANDE, L. & RIEPPEL, O. (eds) *Journal of Vertebrate Paleontology*, **15**, 861–863.

FOREY, P. L. 1996a. Book review; Functional morphology in vertebrate paleontology by THOMASON, J. J. (ed.) *Biological Journal of the Linnean Society of London*, **58**, 245–246.

FOREY, P. L. 1996b. Nature read in tooth and jaw. Abstract. *Transactions of the Leicester Literary and Philosophical Society*, **90**, 41.

FOREY, P. L. 1997a. Book review; Early vertebrates: Monographs on geology and geophysics, number 33 by JANVIER, P. (ed.) *Historical Biology*, **12**, 299–300.

FOREY, P. L. 1997b. A Cretaceous notopterid (Pisces: Osteoglossomorpha) from Morocco. *South African Journal of Science*, **93**, 564–569.

FOREY, P. L. 1997c. New elopomorph teleosts from Namoura, Lebanon. *Journal of Vertebrate Paleontology*, **17**, 46.

FOREY, P. L. 1998a. Biogeography; a home from home for coelacanths. *Nature*, **395**, 319–320.

FOREY, P. L. 1998b. Book review; Molecular systematics of fishes by KOCHER, T. D. & STEPIEN, C. A. *Zoological Journal of the Linnean Society of London*, **125**, 513.

FOREY, P. L. 1998c. *History of the coelacanth fishes*. Chapman & Hall, London.

FOREY, P. L. 1998d. In Darwin's footsteps. Obituary of Colin Patterson. *The Guardian*.

FOREY, P. L. 1998e. Introduction. *In*: KITCHING, I. J., FOREY, P. L., HUMPHRIES, C. J. & WILLIAMS, D. M. (eds) *Cladistics: the theory and practice of parsimony analysis*. 2nd edn. Systematics Association

Publications, **11**. Oxford University Press, Oxford, 1–17.

FOREY, P. L. 1998*f*. Missing values. *In*: KITCHING, I. J., FOREY, P. L., HUMPHRIES, C. J. & WILLIAMS, D. M. (eds) *Cladistics: the theory and practice of parsimony analysis*. 2nd edn. Systematics Association Publications, **11**. Oxford University Press, Oxford, 79–89.

FOREY, P. L. 1998*g*. Obituary of Colin Patterson. *Systematics Association Newsletter*, **April**, 5–6.

FOREY, P. L. 1998*h*. Simultaneous and partitioned analysis. *In*: KITCHING, I. J., FOREY, P. L., HUMPHRIES, C. J. & WILLIAMS, D. M. (eds) *Cladistics: the theory and practice of parsimony analysis*. 2nd edn. Systematics Association Publications, **11**. Oxford University Press, Oxford, 152–168.

FOREY, P. L. 1998*i*. Two contributions in *Nature* on-line debate. 'The adequacy of the fossil record'. Moderated by Andrew Smith.

FOREY, P. L. 2000*a*. Global change and the fossil fish record; the relevance of systematics. *In*: CULVER, S. J. & RAWSON, P. (eds) *Biotic response to global change; the last 145 million years*. Cambridge University Press, Cambridge, 107–121.

FOREY, P. L. 2000*b*. Summary. *In*: FOREY, P. L., GARDINER, B. G. & HUMPHRIES, C. J. (eds) *Colin Patterson – His life*. **Special Issue 2**. The Linnean, Academic Press, London, 90–95.

FOREY, P. L. 2001*a*. Biological Systematics. *Palaeontology Newsletter*, **47**, 81–82.

FOREY, P. L. 2001*b*. Les fossiles et la systématique. *Biosystema*, **19**, 1–28.

FOREY, P. L. 2001*c*. The PhyloCode: description and commentary. *Bulletin of Zoological Nomenclature*, **58**, 81–96.

FOREY, P. L. 2001*d*. What's all this fuss about PhyloCode? *Palaeontology Newsletter*, **47**, 19–32.

FOREY, P. L. 2002*a*. Fossils, Phylogeny & form: analytical approach. *Palaeontology Newsletter*, **50**, 75–78.

FOREY, P. L. 2002*b*. A knotty problem of nomenclature. Book review; The poverty of the Linnean Hierarchy: A philosophical study of biological taxonomy by Ereshefsky, M. *Nature*, **415**, 839.

FOREY, P. L. 2002*c*. PhyloCode – pain, no gain. *Taxon*, **51**, 43–54.

FOREY, P. L. 2002*d*. Summary. *In*: MACLEOD, N. & FOREY, P. L. (eds) *Morphology, shape and phylogeny*. Taylor & Francis, London, 287–294.

FOREY, P. L. 2003. Book review; Genetics, Paleontology and Macroevolution by Levington, J. *Journal of Paleontology*, **77**, 199–200.

FOREY, P. L. 2004*a*. Cladistics and the coelacanth. *NHM Magazine*, **4**, 19–21.

FOREY, P. L. 2004*b*. Systematics and Palaeontology. *In*: WILLIAMS, D. M. & FOREY, P. L. (eds) *Milestones in Systematics*. The Systematics Association Special Volume Series, **67**. CRC Press, Boca Raton, 149–180.

FOREY, P. L. 2004*c*. A three-dimensional skull of a primitive clupeomorph fish from the Cenomanian English Chalk, and implications for the evolution of the clupeomorph acusticolateralis system. *In*: ARRATIA, G. & TINTORI, A. (eds) *Mesozoic fishes 3 Systematics, paleoenvironments and biodiversity*. Dr F. Pfeil, Munich, 405–427.

FOREY, P. L. 2005*a*. Biological radiations and speciation. *In*: SÉLLÉY, R. C., COCKS, L. R. M. & PLIMER, I. R. (eds) *Encyclopaedia of Geology; Volume 1*. Elsevier Academic Press, Oxford, 266–279.

FOREY, P. L. 2005*b*. Cladistics for Palaeontologists: Introduction. *Palaeontology Newsletter*, **60**, 26–37.

FOREY, P. L. 2005*c*. Jawless vertebrates. *In*: HILL, M. (ed.) *Encyclopedia of Science and Technology*, 9.

FOREY, P. L. 2005*d*. Naming the World: Is there anything left of Linnaeus. *Proceedings of the California Academy of Sciences*, **56**, 182–195.

FOREY, P. L. 2006*a*. Cladistics for Palaeontologists: Cladistic characters. *Palaeontology Newsletter*, **61**, 33–42.

FOREY, P. L. 2006*b*. Cladistics for Palaeontologists: Tree building. *Palaeontology Newsletter*, **62**, 43–59.

FOREY, P. L. 2006*c*. Cladistics: Optimisation. *Palaeontology Newsletter*, **63**, 26–35.

FOREY, P. L. 2007. Cladistics: Consensus trees and tree support. *Palaeontology Newsletter*, **64**, 23–34.

FOREY, P. L., AHLBERG, P. E., LUKSEVICS, E. & ZUPINS, I. 2000. A new coelacanth from the Middle Devonian of Latvia. *Journal of Vertebrate Paleontology*, **20**, 243–252.

FOREY, P. L. & CAVIN, L. 2007. A new species of *Cladocyclus* (Teleostei: Ichthyodectiformes) from the Cenomanian of Morocco. *Palaeontologia Electronica*, **10**, 10 p.

FOREY, P. L. & CLOUTIER, R. 1991. Literature relating to fossil coelacanths. *Enviromental Biology of Fishes*, **32**, 391–401.

FOREY, P. L. & FORTEY, R. A. 2001. Fossils in the reconstruction of phylogeny. *In*: BRIGGS, D. E. G. & CROWTHER, P. R. (eds) *Palaeobiology II*. Blackwell Science, Oxford, 515–519.

FOREY, P. L., FORTEY, R. A., KENRICK, P. & SMITH, A. B. 2004. Taxonomy and fossils; a critical appraisal. *Philosophical Transactions of the Royal Society of London, Biological Sciences*, **359**, 639–653.

FOREY, P. L. & GARDINER, B. G. 1973. A new dictyotypygid from the Cave Sandstone of Lesotho, southern Africa. *Paleontographica Africana*, **15**, 29–31.

FOREY, P. L. & GARDINER, B. G. 1981. J. A. Moy-Thomas and his association with the British Museum (Natural History). *Bulletin of the British Museum (Natural History) (Geology)*, **35**, 131–144.

FOREY, P. L. & GARDINER, B. G. 1986. Observations on *Ctenurella* Ptyctodontida and the classification of placoderm fishes. *Zoological Journal of the Linnean Society*, **86**, 43–74.

FOREY, P. L., GARDINER, B. G. & HUMPHRIES, C. J. 2000. Colin Patterson a celebration of his life. *The Linnean*, **Special Issue 2**, 1–96.

FOREY, P. L., GARDINER, B. G. & PATTERSON, C. 1991. The lungfish, the coelacanth and the cow revisited. *In*: SCHULTZE, H.-P. & TRUEB, L. (eds) *Origins of the higher groups of tetrapods: controversy and consensus*. Cornell University Press, Ithaca, 145–172.

FOREY, P. L. & GRANDE, L. 1998. An African twin to the Brazilian *Calamopleurus* (Actinopterygii: Amiidae). *Zoological Journal of the Linnean Society of London*, **123**, 1–17.

FOREY, P. L., HUMPHRIES, C. J., KITCHING, I. J., SCOTLAND, R. W., SIEBERT, D. J. & WILLIAMS, D. M. (eds) 1992. *Cladistics: a practical course in systematics.* Systematics Association Publications, **10**. Oxford University Press, Oxford.

FOREY, P. L., HUMPHRIES, C. J. & VANE-WRIGHT, R. I. 1994*a*. Preface. *In*: FOREY, P. L., HUMPHRIES, C. J. & VANE-WRIGHT, R. I. (eds) *Systematics and conservation evaluation.* The Systematics Association Special Volume Series, **50**. Oxford University Press, Oxford.

FOREY, P. L., HUMPHRIES, C. J. & VANE-WRIGHT, R. I. (eds) 1994*b*. *Systematics and conservation evaluation.* The Systematics Association Special Volume Series, **50**. Oxford University Press, Oxford.

FOREY, P. L. & JANVIER, P. 1993. Agnathans and the origin of jawed vertebrates. *Nature*, **361**, 129–134.

FOREY, P. L. & JANVIER, P. 1994. Evolution of the early vertebrates. *American Scientist*, **82**, 554–565.

FOREY, P. L. & JANVIER, P. 1995*a*. Early craniate radiations; should we rely on the fossil record? *Journal of Vertebrate Paleontology*, **15**, 29.

FOREY, P. L. & JANVIER, P. 1995*b*. Evolution of the early vertebrates. *American Scientist*, **82**, 554–565.

FOREY, P. L. & KITCHING, I. J. 1999. Experiments in coding multistate characters. *In*: SCOTLAND, R. & PENNINGTON, R. T. (eds) *Homology and systematics.* The Systematics Association Special Volume Series, **58**. Taylor & Francis, London, 54–80.

FOREY, P. L., LITTLEWOOD, D. T., RITCHIE, P. & MEYER, A. 1996. Interrelationships of elopomorph fishes. *In*: STIASSNY, M. L., PARENTI, L. R. & JOHNSON, G. D. (eds) *Interrelationships of fishes.* 2nd Edn. Academic Press, London, 175–191.

FOREY, P. L., LU, Y., PATTERSON, C. & DAVIES, C. E. 2003. Fossil fishes from the Cenomanian (Upper Cretaceous) of Namoura, Lebanon. *Journal of Systematic Palaeontology*, **1**, 227–330.

FOREY, P. L., MONOD, O. & PATTERSON, C. 1985. Fishes from the Akkuyu Formation (Tithonian), Western Taurus, Turkey. *Geobios*, **18**, 195–201.

FOREY, P. L. & PATTERSON, C. 2006. Description and systematic relationships of *Tomognathus*, an enigmatic fish from the English Chalk. *Journal of Systematic Palaeontology*, **4**, 157–184.

FOREY, P. L. & THOMSON, K. 1984. Essays presented to Dr. Bobb Schaeffer. *Journal of Vertebrate Paleontology*, **4**, 286–499.

FOREY, P. L. & WILLIAMS, D. M. 2004. Introduction. *In*: WILLIAMS, D. M. & FOREY, P. L. (eds) *Milestones in Systematics.* The Systematics Association Special Volume Series, **67**. CRC Press, Boca Raton, v–viii.

FOREY, P. L. & YOUNG, V. T. 1985. Acanthodian and coelacanth fishes from the Dinantian of Foulden, Berwickshire, Scotland. *Transactions of the Royal Society of Edinburgh: Earth Sciences*, **76**, 53–59.

FOREY, P. L. & YOUNG, V. T. 1985. Upper Stephanian fishes from the Puertallano Basin, Ciudad Real, Spain. *Anais da Faculdade de Ciencias do Porto*, **64**, 233–244.

FOREY, P. L. & YOUNG, V. T. 1999. Late Miocene fishes of the Emirate of Abu Dhabi, United Arab Emirates. *In*: WHYBROW, P. J. & HILL, A. (eds) *Fossil vertebrates of Arabia.* Yale University Press, New Haven, 120–135.

FOREY, P. L., YOUNG, V. T. & MCCLURE, H. A. 1992. Lower Devonian fishes from Saudi Arabia. *Bulletin of the British Museum (Natural History) (Geology)*, **48**, 25–43.

GARDINER, B. G., JANVIER, P., PATTERSON, C., FOREY, P. L., GREENWOOD, P. H., MILES, R. S. & JEFFERIES, R. P. S. 1979. The salmon, the lungfish and the cow: a reply. *Nature*, **277**, 175–176.

HILTON, E. & FOREY, P. L. 2005*a*. Contributions of Walter George Ridewood to systematic comparative anatomy, especially of the osteology of "lower" vertebrates. *Journal of Natural History*, **39**, 641–655.

HILTON, E. & FOREY, P. L. 2005*b*. Osteology, systematics & biogeography of fossil and living osteoglossid fishes (Teleostei, Osteoglossomorpha), with a description of new forms and a review of the biogeographic relationships of the clade members. *Journal of Vertebrate Paleontology*, **25**, 70.

KITCHING, I. J., FOREY, P. L., HUMPHRIES, C. J. & WILLIAMS, D. M. (eds) 1998. *Cladistics: the theory and practice of parsimony analysis.* 2nd edn. Systematics Association Publications, **11**. Oxford University Press, Oxford.

KITCHING, I. J., FOREY, P. L. & WILLIAMS, D. M. 2001. Cladistics. *In*: LEVIN, S. A. (ed.) *Encyclopedia of biodiversity.* Academic Press, San Diego, 677–692.

LUTHER, P. K., SQUIRE, J. & FOREY, P. L. 1996. Evolution of myosin filament arrangements in vertebrate skeletal muscle. *Journal of Morphology*, **229**, 325–335.

MACLEOD, N. & FOREY, P. L. 2002*a*. Introduction; morphology, shape and phylogenetics. *In*: MACLEOD, N. & FOREY, P. L. (eds) *Morphology, shape and phylogeny.* The Systematics Association Special Volume Series, **64**. Taylor & Francis, London, 1–7.

MACLEOD, N. & FOREY, P. L. (eds) 2002*b*. *Morphology, shape and phylogeny.* The Systematics Association Special Volume Series, **64**. Taylor & Francis, London.

MACLEOD, N., RAWSON, P. F., FOREY, P. L. *ET AL.* 1997. The Cretaceous-Tertiary biotic transition. *Journal of the Geological Society, London*, **154**, 265–292.

MILNER, A. C., FOREY, P. L., GREENWOOD, T. & WILLIAMS, C. T. 2001. Caveat emtor – fake fossils from the Far East. *Geology Today*, **17**, 52–58.

ROSEN, D. E., FOREY, P. L., GARDINER, B. G. & PATTERSON, C. 1981. Lungfishes, tetrapods, palaeontology and plesiomorphy. *Bulletin of the American Museum of Natural History*, **167**, 159–276.

SCHMITZ, B., ABERG, G., WERDELIN, L., FOREY, P. L. & BENDIX-ALMGREEN, S. E. 1991. $^{87}Sr/^{86}Sr$, Na, F, Sr & La in skeletal fish debris as a measure of the paleosalinity of fossil-fish habitats. *Bulletin of the Geological Society of America*, **103**, 786–794.

WERDELIN, L., SCHMITZ, B. & FOREY, P. L. 1992. Usefulness of Sr isotopes and the trace elements in the analysis of the paleosalinity of fossil-fish habitats. *Journal of Vertebrate Paleontology*, **12**, 59A.

WILLIAMS, D. M. & FOREY, P. L. (eds) 2004. *Milestones in Systematics.* The Systematics Association Special Volume Series, **67**. CRC Press, London.

Fishes and the Break-up of Pangaea: an introduction

LIONEL CAVIN[1], ALISON LONGBOTTOM[2] & MARTHA RICHTER[2]

[1]Department of Geology and Palaeontology, Muséum d'Histoire Naturelle, CP 6434, 1211 Genève 6, Switzerland (e-mail: lionel.cavin@ville-ge.ch)

[2]Natural History Museum, Department of Palaeontology, Cromwell Road, London SW7 5BD, UK

Abstract: There is general agreement that a tight relationship exists between evolutionary histories of living lineages and the shifting geography of the Earth during the Phanerozoic, but how to depict that link has been much disputed in recent decades. The issue is fundamental, as it involves two supposedly-irreconcilable paradigms for how we interpret past and present distributions: the Darwin–Wallace biogeographic paradigm that involves dispersal from centres of origin, and the vicariance paradigm. When dealing with extinct organisms, for which we have only sparse and fragmentary fossil remains, the limit between the two paradigms becomes blurred. Here, all available data about time (stratigraphy) and space (palaeogeography) need to be gathered in order to detect biogeographical signals.

Because of the incompleteness of the fossil record, the analyses may lead to storytelling style descriptions of biogeographic scenarios (phylogenies are often weakly supported, datings are frequently vague and occurrences are sparse). But these scenarios are always open to refutation if new fossils are found and, accordingly, are genuine scientific hypotheses. The Darwin–Wallace biogeographic paradigm and the vicariance paradigm have been described as the extreme points of a pendulum; in this book, examples of relationships between the evolutionary history of fish clades and the break-up of Pangaea are described using approaches that lie between these extreme points of the pendulum.

There have been many studies which construct biogeographic scenarios on the basis of Recent fish distributions. They deal mainly with primary freshwater fish faunas (Ribeiro 2006) or clades, such as osteoglossomorph subgroups (Nelson 1969; Kumazawa & Nishida 2000) or otophysans (Saitoh *et al.* 2003; Briggs 2005), because primary freshwater fishes are supposedly firmly confined to their continental environments. Distributions of marine fishes may also provide meaningful, although sometimes controversial, biogeographic patterns, as exemplified by the phylogenetic and biogeographic studies of notothenioids (Bargelloni *et al.* 2000) or cirrhitoids (Burridge 2000) for instance. Fossils are rarely included in these research programs, except as milestones providing minimum divergence ages by which to calibrate phylogenies. This caution comes from the weak reliability that most workers attribute to the fossil record, a criticism already put forward by Darwin some 150 years ago. But although some workers complain about the quality of the fossil record, others discover and describe new fossil fish occurrences and new taxa. Although much work remains to be done on the phylogenetic relationships of Recent and extinct fish clades, and to get better sampling of fossil fishes in Mesozoic and Cenozoic deposits worldwide, the amount of meaningful data is rapidly growing and the general picture is now better than ever. This volume aims at gathering together much of this available information on a large number of fish groups. However, far from exhausting the subject, our aim is to contribute to the furtherance of the debate.

In the Triassic, the close association of continental blocks allowed terrestrial and freshwater organisms to spread easily. **Richter & Toledo** show that a lungfish genus was widespread in the Triassic across most Southern continents and extended into Europe, and they suggest that its dispersal ability was determined by palaeoclimatic changes. At the infancy of the break-up of Pangaea, Laurasia split from Gondwana forming a marine route between the Tethys and the Pacific Ocean. **Arratia** finds evidence of this marine connection in the Late Jurassic by resolving the phylogenetic relationships of marine crossognathiforms. This reveals a sister-area relationship between Chile and Cuba, which together are the sister area of Germany. **Kriwet & Klug** suggest that shark assemblages were quite uniform in Europe in the Late Jurassic. Their analyses indicate that both vicariance and dispersal are required to explain the biogeographic pattern of Late Jurassic neoselachians. Marine vicariant events also affect coastal fishes, living on the

From: CAVIN, L., LONGBOTTOM, A. & RICHTER, M. (eds) *Fishes and the Break-up of Pangaea.*
Geological Society, London, Special Publications, **295**, 7–8.
DOI: 10.1144/SP295.2   0305-8719/08/$15.00 © The Geological Society of London 2008.

continental shelf, when they are tightly constrained by physical barriers. Barriers preventing fish dispersal include: marine currents, surface gradients of temperature and salinity, great water depths, and freshwater and sediment outflows from rivers. Examples of Early Cretaceous marine vicariance events involving ophiopsid taxa from the northern margin of the Gondwana and taxa from the southern margin of Laurasia in Western Tethys are detected by **Brito & Alvarado-Ortega**, a pattern also found for aspidorhynchids. The Early Cretaceous was a period when freshwater taxa were diversifying in biogeographical provinces that were becoming increasingly isolated from each other. This is the case for freshwater hybodonts in SE Asia, as **Cuny** shows, but also for a stem-group of Osteoglossomorpha in Eastern Asia, as **Wilson & Murray** show, and for an endemic Asian family of halecomorphs, the sinamiids. The late Early Cretaceous is also the time of the opening of the South Atlantic, and several freshwater or brackish fish taxa were clearly affected by this event: mawsoniid coelacanths, lepidosirenid lungfishes, a halecomorph and a paraclupeid among others. In the Late Cretaceous, both dispersal and vicariance events are detected. **Otero *et al.*** suggest that occurrences of characiforms in the Late Cretaceous of Europe may be the result of dispersals from Africa, and the same may be true for mawsoniid coelacanths. The Late Cretaceous witnessed connections between Eastern Asia and North America freshwater fishes as shown in polyodontids and in several lineages of osteoglossomorphs (although it remains difficult to discriminate between vicariance and dispersal events as pointed out by **Wilson & Murray**). In the Palaeogene, there are new examples of connections (dispersal or vicariances) between Asia and North America as **Chang & Chen** show with the catostomids. **Bonde** describes several marine osteoglossomorph taxa from the Palaeogene of Denmark, which makes the palaeobiogeographical scenario of this otherwise mainly freshwater lineage more complex.

The general pattern brought out (by analysing the relationships between evolutionary histories of fish lineages and the evolution of the geographical frameworks) using the fossil record does not differ significantly from the pattern that can be deduced from phylogenetic and distributional studies of Recent taxa. Inclusion of fossils provides a more colourful picture and unveils unexpected issues that would have been otherwise overlooked.

Many people were eager to contribute to such a volume as a personal thank you to Peter Forey. The editors would like to thank all the authors for their patience and co-operation during the compilation of the book and the many reviewers for their hard work and insightful comments. We also thank the Geological Society for accepting the project and Angharad Hills for her great patience and encouragement. Finally we would especially like to thank Peter Forey for his many years of friendship and mentoring to us all.

References

BARGELLONI, L., MARCATO, S., ZANE, L. & PATANELLO, T. 2000. Mitochondrial phylogeny of Notothenioids: a molecular approach to Antarctic fish evolution and biogeography. *Systematic Biology*, **49**, 114–129.

BRIGGS, J. C. 2005. The biogeography of otophysan fishes (Osteriophysi: Otophysi): a new appraisal. *Journal of Biogeography*, **32**, 287–294.

BURRIDGE, C. P. 2000. Biogeographic history of geminate cirrhitoids (Perciformes: Cirrhitoidea) with east-west allopatric distributions across southern Australia, based on molecular data. *Global Ecology & Biogeography*, **9**, 517–525.

KUMAZAWA, Y. & NISHIDA, M. 2000. Molecular phylogeny of Osteoglossoids: a new model for Gondwanian origin and plate tectonic transportation of the Asian Arowana. *Molecular Biology and Evolution*, **17**, 1869–1878.

NELSON, G. J. 1969. Infraorbital bones and their bearing on the phylogeny and geography of osteoglossomorph fishes. *American Museum Novitates*, **2394**, 1–37.

RIBEIRO, A. C. 2006. Tectonic history and the biogeography of the freshwater fishes from the coastal drainages of eastern Brazil: an example of faunal evolution associated with a divergent continental margin. *Neotropical Ichthyology*, **4**, 225–246.

SAITOH, K., MIYA, M., INOUE, J. G., ISHIGURO, N. B. & NISHIDA, M. 2003. Mitochondrial genomics of Ostariophysan fishes: perspectives on phylogeny and biogeography. *Journal of Molecular Evolution*, **56**, 464–472.

New eugeneodontid sharks from the Lower Triassic Sulphur Mountain Formation of Western Canada

RAOUL J. MUTTER[1] & ANDREW G. NEUMAN[2]

[1]*Department of Palaeontology, The Natural History Museum, Cromwell Road, London SW7 5BD, UK (e-mail: R.Mutter@nhm.ac.uk)*

[2]*Royal Tyrrell Museum of Palaeontology, P.O. Box, Drumheller, Alberta, T0J 0Y0, Canada (e-mail: Andrew.Neuman@gov.ab.ca)*

Abstract: Eugeneodontid sharks, previously believed to have become virtually extinct during the great end-Permian extinction event, are here shown to be diverse in the Early Triassic of western Canada. Although the specimens are probably predominantly Olenekian in age, they show an abundance similar to that of the Late Permian of East Greenland. Similar in size and morphology to their Palaeozoic predecessors, this diverse assemblage is seen to have a short duration within the Early Triassic. A number of identifiable dentitions and postcranial skeletal remains suggest the presence of at least two caseodontid species (*Caseodus varidentis* sp. nov. and *Fadenia uroclasmato* sp. nov.) and an edestoid (*Paredestus bricircum* gen. et sp. nov.) Many other specimens recovered from the Lower Triassic Vega-Phroso Siltstone Member (Sulphur Mountain Formation) at Wapiti Lake are too poorly preserved for identification but help demonstrate the major taxonomic problems in eugeneodontid systematics. We discuss the survival of this highly specialized group of 'sharks' and comment on their biogeographical distribution across the Permo-Triassic boundary.

The order Eugeneodontida *sensu* Zangerl, 1981 comprises 'Edestida' and 'Helicoprionida' *sensu* Moy-Thomas & Miles (1971). Well-preserved cranial material of eugeneodontid sharks was described by Zangerl in 1966. Descriptions of fragmentary dentitions have also been published over the past half century by Nielsen (1932, 1952), Bendix-Almgreen (1966, 1975a, 1975b, 1976) and Zangerl (1979, 1981). The highly specialized eugeneodontid sharks bear tooth whorls and are predominantly known from the Carboniferous and Permian. They are practically unknown from the Triassic. Zhang (1976) reported a partial tooth-whorl from the Lower Triassic of western China and one dentition fragment has been described from the (?earliest) Triassic of Greenland (Nielsen 1952).

The skeletons of all edestoids are believed to have been very poorly calcified, even at their latest stages in life, and the anatomy of crania, postcrania and dentitions can only be partly reconstructed by careful comparison of numerous fragmentary specimens. It is also assumed that the geologically younger (more advanced) members were less extensively calcified than the geologically older (more primitive) members (Zangerl 1981).

The taxonomic framework followed here was established by Zangerl (1981) who subdivided the order Eugeneodontida into two superfamilies each with two families (Superfamily Caseodontoidea Zangerl, 1981: Caseodontidae Zangerl, 1981 and Eugeneodontidae Zangerl, 1981; and Superfamily Edestoidea Hay, 1930: Agassizodontidae Zangerl, 1981 and Edestidae Jaekel, 1899). The superfamily Caseodontoidea comprises at least 10 genera, including the relatively well-known genera *Caseodus* and *Fadenia* (both Caseodontidae), and the superfamily Edestoidea comprises at least 12 genera including the relatively well-known agassizodontid *Sarcoprion*. The fossil record of the best-known members supports the currently proposed sister-group relationship between Caseodontoidea and Edestoidea (Zangerl 1981, p. 91), although the taxonomic framework and intrarelationships must be considered a working hypothesis.

The significance of Early Triassic eugeneodontid sharks

Here we describe the first articulated remains, partial dentitions and postcranial material of eugeneodontids definitely of Early Triassic age. Previous reports of eugeneodontids from the Triassic include only two poorly known species. *Parahelicampodus spaercki* Nielsen, 1952 from the Wordy Creek Formation of East Greenland is known from a single dentition fragment, and is the only species described as coming from the Lower Triassic of this area. The rock on which the specimen is located has been abraded, so we believe the

From: CAVIN, L., LONGBOTTOM, A. & RICHTER, M. (eds) *Fishes and the Break-up of Pangaea.*
Geological Society, London, Special Publications, **295**, 9–41.
DOI: 10.1144/SP295.3   0305-8719/08/$15.00 © The Geological Society of London 2008.

specimen could also be reworked from Permian rocks. All other eugeneodontid shark remains from East Greenland, including remains from the same locality as *P. spaercki*, are Late Palaeozoic in age. Additionally, recent re-investigation of the Wordy Creek Fm suggests that the most prolific fish assemblage (fish zone II and possibly other zones) described as Early Triassic in age, may in fact be Late Permian (Stemmerik *et al.* 2003).

Zhang (1976) described two *Helicampodus*-like dentition fragments from near Qubu in Dingri (Xian County) as *Sinohelicoprion quomolangma*. These finds may be Early Triassic in age but the specimens' taxonomic position is equivocal and in need of re-description (Chang & Jin 1996; Chang & Miao 2004).

Geological setting

The Wapiti Lake fossil site in Wapiti Lake Provincial Park (British Columbia) yields a remarkable 'Fossillagerstätte'. The site, normally referred to as 'Ganoid Ridge' or 'Ganoid Range', contains various localities where numerous fish fossils have been collected from outcrops of the Vega-Phroso Siltstone Member. Wapiti Lake and coeval localities contain the first Mesozoic strata yielding articulated eugeneodontids. The approximate Early Triassic age can be given with confidence, although a more precise dating is currently not possible for the various reasons outlined below. For a more detailed account of the geological setting and collecting sites in the Wapiti Lake locality, see Neuman & Mutter (2005). Over the past 20 years of extensive field work in this area, a great number of well-preserved fish specimens, collected from the slopes of the cirques on 'Ganoid Range', have been curated in Canadian museums and collections, and at AMNH (New York). Schaeffer & Mangus (1976) provided the first detailed account of the fish fauna from the Vega-Phroso Member of the Sulphur Mountain Fm. They concentrated on specimens mainly collected from the Ganoid Ridge – by far the most prolific of all fossil sites in British Columbia and Alberta. Neuman (1992) later outlined the fossil content of the two distinctive vertebrate faunas – Early Triassic and Middle Triassic in age respectively. The Laboratory for Vertebrate Paleontology of the University of Alberta (UALVP) in collaboration with the Royal Tyrrell Museum (TMP) recently undertook additional field work to expand their collection and undertake more detailed and systematic investigations of a suitable outcrop section (see Mutter & Neuman 2006).

Eugeneodontid remains from contemporaneous Alberta sites and horizons within the Sulphur Mountain Fm were first noted by Lambe (1916) as '*?Edestus* from the Permian of Alberta'. Neuman (1992) listed '?*Edestodus* Obruchev, 1953' as occurring in the Lower Triassic of the Sulphur Mountain Fm.

We now understand there are probably several different fish assemblages within the Lower Triassic of the Ganoid Range at Wapiti Lake, ranging from Induan to Ladinian in age (Neuman 1992; Neuman & Mutter 2005; Mutter & Neuman 2006). A single articulated hybodontoid specimen can be shown to be Olenekian in age (see below and Mutter *et al.* 2006). According to our present understanding, the eugeneodontid remains described here are most likely of early Olenekian (early Smithian) or slightly younger age. On the same block as the holotype specimen TMP 86.42.4 (*Fadenia uroclasmato* sp. nov.) is a specimen of *Helmolepis cyphognathus* Neuman & Mutter, 2005, corroborating the mid-Early Triassic age.

But no complete species lists have been compiled of *in situ* fossils in any measured section. It seems evident, however, that at least three major fish faunas (yielding articulated fish skeletons), currently termed 'fish assemblages', are stratigraphically distinct. Fragmentary fish fossils, brachiopods, bivalves, ammonoids and phyllocarids are preserved within and between the fish beds. Ammonoids and conodonts from the fish beds indicate an Induan to Olenekian age (Mutter & Neuman 2006). An ammonoid species, presumably coming from eugeneodontid-bearing concretions, is dated as Late Olenekian (Spathian; cf. *Xenoceltites subevolutus*, identification pers. comm., Hugo Bucher 2004).

Only a few fish remains are preserved in concretions, and the exact stratigraphic provenience of the majority of eugeneodontids from Wapiti Lake is unknown except for a single specimen, which has been recovered *in situ*. This single specimen recovered from systematic collecting activities in a section on top of the NW ridge of C-cirque (see Neuman 1992 or Mutter 2004 for specific sites) is an anterior body portion including the tail (specimen TMP 86.42.4) of *Fadenia uroclasmato* sp. nov., This specimen indicates an approximately Early Olenekian (Scythian) age.

Although the precise age of the majority of specimens is not yet determined, all specimens are Early Triassic in age. A single hybodontoid specimen (UALVP 19191) from Wapiti Lake, however, is Late Olenekian (Spathian) in age, as suggested by the conodont *Neospathodus homeri* (identification pers. comm., Mike Orchard 2004). Specimen TMP 86.42.4 (mentioned above) is the only *in-situ* specimen whose stratigraphic origin is reportedly Lower Olenekian (Upper Scythian). The calcareous concretions with fish remains, including the holotype of *Caseodus varidentis* sp. nov., are occasionally found in talus and are of uncertain stratigraphic origin. *Othoceras–Ophiceras*-like ammonite impressions are sometimes associated with flattened eugeneodontids preserved in darkish, slightly bituminous shales but no more precise age than Early Triassic can at present be attributed to the specimens found in scree.

The small actinopterygian *Helmolepis cyphognathus* Neuman & Mutter, 2005 is preserved in an immediately-underlying layer of specimen TMP 86.42.4 (*Fadenia uroclasmato* sp. nov.) and suggests an Early Triassic age (early Olenekian) of that particular specimen (Neuman & Mutter 2005). Specimen TMP 89.127.43 (Eugeneodontida gen. et sp. indet.) was collected high in the talus of D-cirque, either immediately below or above the 'marker bed' (see Mutter & Neuman 2006) and is hence also most probably mid-Early Triassic (early Olenekian; Smithian) in age. Specimen TMP 2001.15.03 (Eugeneodontida gen. et sp. indet.) is particularly interesting with regard to the stratigraphic provenance; it comes from the southernmost part of the Ganoid Ridge in 'Mount Becker'. Systematic rock samples in the same year and area yielded various Induan and Olenekian conodont samples ('Dienerian', 'Smithian', 'upper Smithian', '*c.* Smithian–Spathian Boundary' and 'Spathian' samples [pers. comm. Mike Orchard, Vancouver]). Specimen UALVP 46539 (described in open nomenclature) comes from high up in the talus of C-cirque just underneath the overturned section, which is the lowest part of the V–P Siltstone Member.

Neuman (1992) listed ?*Edestodus* in his first comprehensive faunal list of the Wapiti Lake fish material, but no detailed taxonomic study was possible at the time. Four of the eugeneodontid specimens now identifiable at the species level were recovered in recent field trips, and detailed investigation revealed that complementing parts and counterparts recovered on earlier field trips had been stored under different collection numbers. Some of these had been collected separately over the course of several years or stored in different collections. Here an attempt is made to include skeletal information of poorly preserved specimens and in particular, their cartilaginous elements. Very little is yet known about the eugeneodontid skeleton in general as it appeared to be often poorly calcified. Among the remains from the Canadian Rockies, however, we find almost every part of the eugeneodontid shark body reasonably well-calcified, even if poorly-preserved.

Material, methods and background of investigations

Most vertebrate fossils from Wapiti Lake are preserved in exceedingly hard siltstone, predominantly with low carbonate content, or in dark (slightly bituminous) and silty shales. All specimens investigated in this study come from Wapiti Lake Provincial Park, the 'Ganoid Ridge', where much of the lower part of the Sulphur Mountain Formation, the Vega-Phroso Siltstone Member, is exposed. Exact horizons, however, are not known for the majority of specimens and specific sites in the 'Ganoid Ridge' are referred to below as respective cirques (see sections below; Neuman 1992; Mutter 2004). All specimens are most probably Early Triassic in age, presumably early Olenekian ('Smithian').

Most specimens are dorso-ventrally flattened and preserved in parts and counterparts. Only minor preparation can be successfully carried out. Rubber peels were taken from specimens consisting of imprints alone. Some specimens, however, are preserved in 3D and are currently undergoing CT scanning. Specimens used for thin sectioning were embedded in resin and were ground using corundum powder.

Eugeneodontid sharks are predominantly known from isolated teeth and partial tooth-whorls. Numerous mesial and distal teeth have been reported but their taxonomic value is questionable, unknown or reportedly equivocal (e.g. Zangerl 1981). More complete skeletal remains and partially associated sharks are rare but known from a variety of Palaeozoic sites. The dental remains described from the Upper Permian of East Greenland (Nielsen 1952; Bendix-Almgreen 1976) come closest in stratigraphy and morphology to the material described here. The eugeneodontid material in the Geological Museum in Copenhagen, however, could not be located and investigated. Because of this, most cranial and postcranial remains are compared to isolated material held at the American Museum of Natural History (AMNH, New York) and the Natural History Museum (NHM, London). A list of comparative material used for this study is given in Appendix 1.

Comparison with skeletal material from the Carboniferous of East Greenland and from the Pennsylvanian Mazon Creek fauna and Logan quarry shales of Illinois and Indiana (Zangerl 1966, 1979) or from the Upper Devonian Cleveland Shale (Bendix-Almgreen 1976) is largely restricted to published accounts. However, the sample from Wapiti Lake shows a similar range of diversity as previously recorded from the Upper Permian of the Wordy Creek Fm of East Greenland with symphysial teeth assigned to three different genera. The little known Latin ending '-ad' is used in anatomical descriptions (e.g. laterad) to indicate the direction.

Institutional abbreviations

AMNH, American Museum of Natural History (New York, USA); BMNH, Natural History

Museum (London, UK); EOSUV, School of Earth and Ocean Sciences, University of Victoria (British Columbia, Canada); TMP, Royal Tyrrell Museum of Palaeontology (Drumheller AB, Canada); UAEAS, University of Alberta Earth and Atmospheric Sciences (Edmonton AB, Canada); UALVP, University of Alberta Laboratory for Vertebrate Paleontology (Edmonton AB, Canada).

Systematic palaeontology

Class Chondrichthyes Huxley, 1880
Subclass Elasmobranchii Bonaparte, 1838
Order Eugeneodontida Zangerl, 1981
Superfamily Caseodontoidea Zangerl, 1981
Family Caseodontidae Zangerl, 1981

Note: Zangerl (1981, p. 79) provides a comprehensive account of the family but refrains from providing observable caseodontid features in actual species. Apparently, the caseodontids (*Caseodus* Zangerl, 1981; *Romerodus* Zangerl, 1981; *Ornithoprion* Zangerl, 1966; *Fadenia* Nielsen, 1952 and *Erikodus* Nielsen, 1952) can only be characterized by tendencies resulting in fusion of haemal arch elements in the tail and 'more tumid or bulbous' teeth: these features are in contrast to other eugeneodontids who show acuminate teeth and symphyseal teeth with cutting blades (tips of tooth crowns) – but the structure of the caudal fins in these sharks is currently unknown. Abbreviations used in text and text-figures are given before the acknowledgements.

Genus Caseodus *Zangerl, 1981*

Type species. Caseodus basalis (Cope, 1894)

Diagnosis (emended from Zangerl [1981]). Teeth lacking strong crenulations in lingual wall of upper jaw teeth; notable variation; symphysial teeth not particularly enhanced; crown angle varying from 65 degrees in symphysial and up to 120 degrees in mesial teeth; structure of tooth whorl unknown.

Caseodus varidentis. *sp. nov.* Figures 1–8

Holotype. TMP 86.42.3 (from C-cirque).

Etymology. Vari- (from Latin, meaning 'different') and -*dentis* (from Latin, meaning 'tooth'), referring to the variable dentition.

Diagnosis. Small sharks, estimated body length 1 m to 1.5 m and fairly broad skull in dorsal view; ornamentation on dentition highly variable, consisting predominantly of blunt or pavement teeth; lower jaws fused at symphysis where crown shoulders in symphysial teeth meet at about 65° (acuminate, roof-shaped); mesial teeth with variably well developed central cusp (linguo-labially expanded, crowns enclose an angle of 100–120°); extensive crenulation at least in lateral teeth of lower jaw; mesial teeth in upper jaw probably lack ornament on labial wall (or ornament is poorly developed) but buttresses in almost all teeth conspicuously developed.

Description. Specimen TMP 86.42.3 is an almost complete, 3-D preserved neurocranium (Figs 1–2) in a concretion with the lower jaws and many teeth preserved *in situ* (Figs 1–6). The neurocranium slants from the occipital region toward the anterior region and possesses a very short postorbital portion. The tip of the rostrum and the extension of the lower jaws are missing, and only part of the ventral side of the neurocranium is exposed. Additional preparation could expose more of the ventral side of the skull if the exposed ventral and lateral sides are stabilized (Figs 1–6).

The preserved parts of the neurocranium measure 225 mm in length (from the posterior rim of the neurocranium to the anterior tip of the rostrum) and 200 mm in width. The skull is relatively broad. The entire dorsal surface of the neurocranium, including the rostrum, is covered by a shagreen of single or multiple lepidomoria. The supraorbital and central area of the skull are covered by single lepidomoria whereas the entire posterior portion of the skull is densely covered by multiple lepidomorial denticles. Distinctive, unique and unicuspid dermal denticles are preserved along the right postero-lateral rim of the neurocranium (inset of Fig. 2). These denticles measure at least 3 mm in length and are pointing forward. The latter region looks as if it was more strongly calcified and the surface, with scarce covering of denticles, appears to have also been underlain by uncalcified cartilage.

10 mm

Fig. 1. *Caseodus varidentis* sp. nov., holotype specimen TMP 86.42.3. The 3D preserved skull in dorsal view.

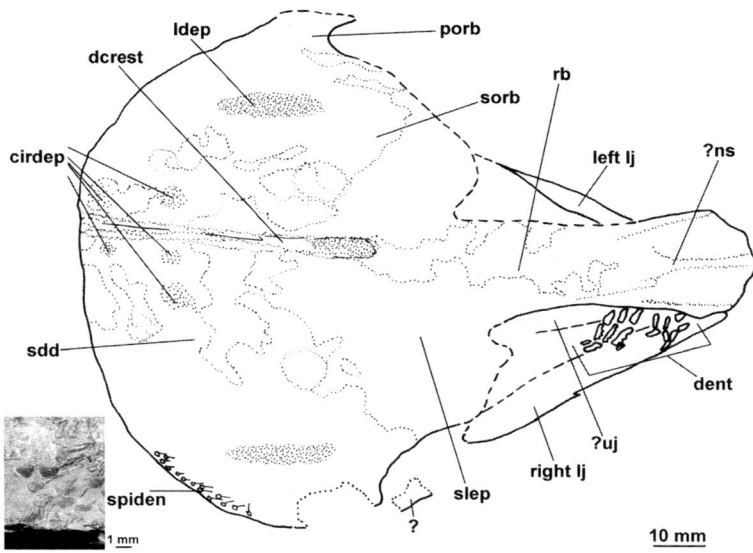

Fig. 2. *Caseodus varidentis* sp. nov., holotype specimen TMP 86.42.3. Line drawing of dorsal view of neurocranium and anterior portion of lower jaws. Note the inset with the unique, unicuspid denticles (spiden) covering, as preserved, delimited parts of the posterior region of the skull.

The rostral portion of the neurocranium is relatively massive and broad anteriorly and tapers slightly posteriad. The dorsal wall is slightly curved and extends into a conspicuous sagittal crest towards what appears to be the posterior border of the neurocranium. Paired, small,

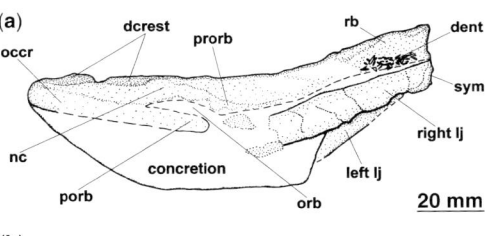

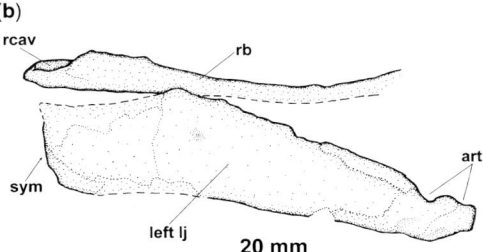

Fig. 3. *Caseodus varidentis* sp. nov., holotype specimen TMP 86.42.3. (**a**) neurocranium and right lower jaw in right lateral view, showing the partly scattered, partly *in-situ* dentition (close-up in Fig. 4). (**b**) left lower jaw and rostral tip of neurocranium.

median circular or oblong-lateral depressions are regularly arranged along both sides of the dorsal crest.

The dorso-anterior portion of the neurocranium is not as well calcified as the posterior portion. Only the supraorbital and the postorbital processes are thoroughly calcified. It is unclear what other parts of the neurocranium are preserved within the concretion.

The lower jaws (Figs 3–5) are deep anteriorly and fused at the symphysis, containing or adjoining a very well-calcified and massive tooth whorl (or symphysial tooth battery) of which only a couple of abraded tooth caps are ventrally exposed (in the apparent cartilage [symt in Fig. 5a], see also Fig. 6). The left lower jaw is much deeper anteriorly than the right lower jaw; a difference that probably resulted from dorso-ventral and slightly oblique compression of the skull. Both halves of the lower jaw taper posteriad and the left lower jaw shows a double-articulation area, either with the upper jaw, with the neurocranium or both (Fig. 3b).

There is no unequivocal evidence of upper jaws. The right upper anterior region of the dentition, however, is preserved partially *in situ* and is visible in ventral and in dorsal view (see 'dentition' below). This suggests that upper jaws might have been originally present (even if uncalcified) and reached anterior to the level of the symphysis, unless the upper tooth files were anchored in the neurocranium.

Fig. 4. *Caseodus varidentis* sp. nov., holotype specimen TMP 86.42.3. Lateral view of snout showing the dentition as preserved in the right lower and upper jaw.

Dentition. The smallest preserved teeth measure around 3 mm in width, whereas the largest ones (although fragmentarily preserved) can be estimated to have measured up to 25 mm in width. Strong heterodonty is present. Several dozen teeth are preserved, but only a small number of them are preserved in articulated tooth-files (Figs 4–6). Most teeth preserved are not found *in situ*, but are partially visible; embedded in matrix or irregularly scattered on top of each other. In general, most of these teeth are small (several millimetres), adding to the impression that the majority of tooth files were made up of smallish, blunt pavement teeth lacking a central cusp and cutting blades. Some of the teeth in distal tooth files are quite slender in occlusal and lateral views and have a conspicuous longitudinal crest. Others lack this crest entirely. There are several tooth files in mesial position. Two different mesial tooth files are preserved with tooth crown shoulders enclosing an angle of about 100–120°. These files show teeth oval in occlusal view and a pronounced central cusp, which is occasionally linguo-labially expanded or pyramidal in occlusal outline. The symphysial tooth whorl consists of teeth with an ornamented crown and a pointed-acuminate apex.

Even though articulation is variable, certain teeth can be assigned to their approximate position in the jaws. A variety of different teeth can be identified, differing only in the presence or absence of pronounced labial ridges and a central bulbous cusp (see in particular Fig. 6). Upper mesial teeth seem to have had smooth labial walls with no ornamentation in-between the conspicuous and well-spaced labial buttresses. Occasionally, strong and obliquely running crests are found. Conspicuous labial ridges and a vaulted central cusp are probably present in crowns of mesial or symphysial teeth in the upper jaw only. Some teeth, seemingly associated with the lower jaw, show very little of their buttresses and these may well be reduced in the majority of these teeth. However, since these teeth are embedded in matrix, it is possible that these features that are otherwise quite obvious are partly obscured. Symphysial teeth are well-separated, seemingly erupting from cartilage, and appear to have an acuminate cuspid tip with a weak sagittal ridge similar to specimen UALVP 46535 (see below), but the teeth are worn and no conspicuous blade (cutting edge of tooth crown) can be made out. The crowns of all teeth tend to be asymmetrical, and there is a tendency for large teeth to develop more numerous and irregular crenulations (compare Fig. 6a and b).

UALVP 46535. Specimen UALVP 46535 is a portion of the symphysial area of a lower jaw with 4 poorly preserved fragmentary teeth preserved *in situ* in the tooth whorl (Fig. 7). Several other partly-preserved teeth are present and are scattered beside the jaw elements. The majority of tooth fragments belong to teeth that were less than half the size of the teeth preserved in the tooth whorl. A cluster of several fragmentary teeth immediately to the left of the left ramus of the lower jaw seem to have been teeth from near the

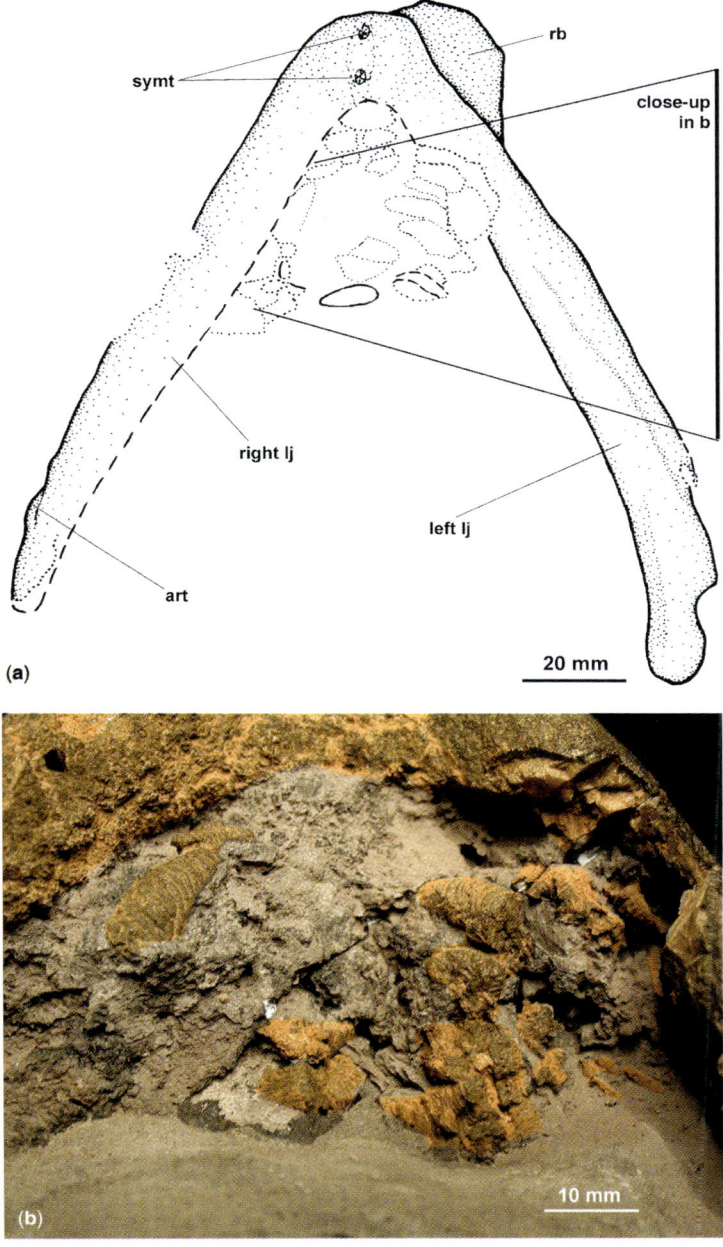

Fig. 5. *Caseodus varidentis* sp. nov., holotype specimen TMP 86.42.3. (**a**) sketch of the lower jaws in ventral view. (**b**) enlarged details of the preserved dentition of the lower jaw.

tooth whorl. The crowns of the teeth are stacked on top of each other, are rigidly connected to the cartilage and may represent non-functional teeth. The teeth of the partial tooth whorl show conspicuously dome-shaped crowns each with a prominent sagittal crest from which ridges descend vertically on both shoulders. The shoulders of each symphysial tooth crown meet at an angle of about 65–70°. Both crowns of the *in-situ* symphysial teeth and of the displaced stack of symphysial teeth show remnants

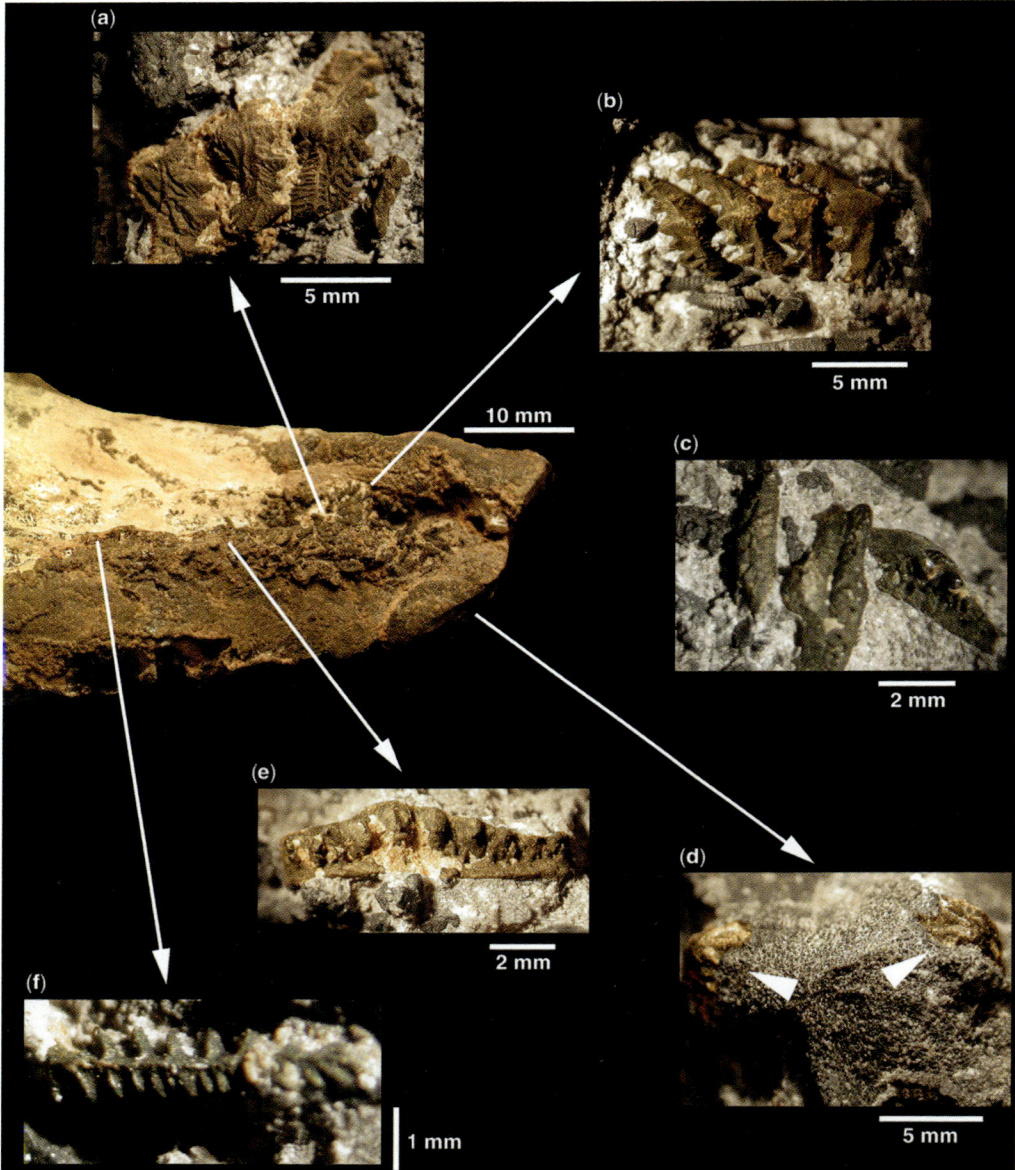

Fig. 6. *Caseodus varidentis* sp. nov; holotype specimen TMP 86.42.3. (**a**) mesio-lateral teeth in occlusal view presumably located in the lower jaw. (**b**) occlusal view of *in-situ* mesio-lateral teeth from the right upper jaw. (**c**) latero-distal teeth in basal view. (**d**) two symphysial teeth (arrows), somewhat abraded and partly buried in cartilage. (**e**) labial view of a distal tooth with slightly vaulted centre. (**f**) a bar-shaped distal tooth in occlusal view.

of a very well-developed, bulbous projection on the labial side. The blades (tips of tooth crowns) on symphysial teeth are richly but delicately crenulated, and one symphysial tooth shows a distinctive sagittal crest. A displaced cluster of ?lateral teeth (Fig. 7, dent) reveals that some functional teeth had a root that was as deep as or deeper than the crown.

Note: This specimen is associated with conodonts that could not yet be positively identified. The specimen may therefore provide valuable additional

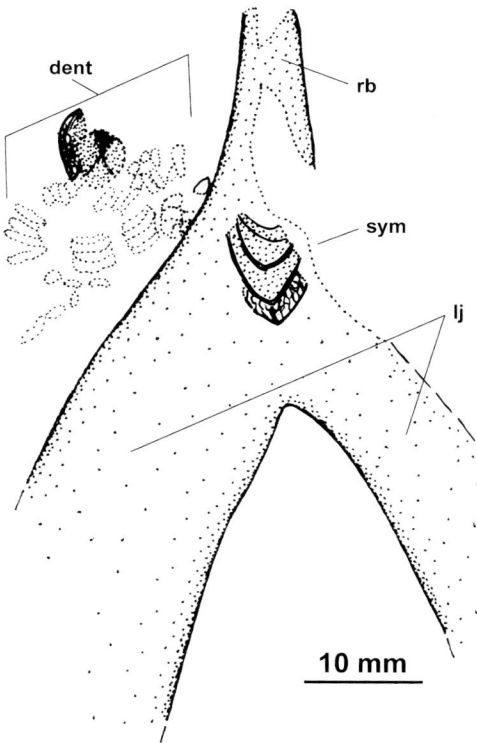

Fig. 7. *Caseodus varidentis* sp. nov., specimen UALVP 46535. Sketch of lower jaw symphysis with fragmentarily preserved tooth whorl and disarticulated mesio-lateral tooth families.

showing the two lower jaw rami *in situ*, an additional cartilaginous element between the lower jaw rami and several teeth, including the tooth whorl. However, the lower jaw rami meet at a less obtuse angle than in the latter specimen. In addition, there is a long, bar-shaped cartilage adjoining the anterior tip of the tooth whorl which appears to be a separate, median element of the lower jaw if compared to specimen UALVP 46535, where supposedly the same element – although more fragmentarily preserved – adjoins the anterior tip of the Meckel's cartilages.

The teeth on the jaw cartilages are broken away and difficult to interpret, but seem to match the general arrangement observed in UALVP 46535. Various tooth types are present but cannot be easily assigned to their original position.

UALVP 47003. Specimen UALVP 47003 is a concretion of a small fragment of a tooth whorl and adjoining lateral tooth files preserved in 3D (Fig. 8). This specimen closely matches the holotype specimen TMP 86.42.3 in body size. The orientation of the tooth-bearing cartilages is difficult to assess. The largest teeth (presumably the tooth whorl) are situated on a slightly elevated area on the cartilage. Somewhat smaller teeth can also be discerned immediately ?lateral to the symphysial tooth file. These teeth are relatively blunt and about half as large as teeth in the tooth whorl, diminishing gradually in size towards lateral positions. The cartilages comprising the tooth whorl are preserved as two oblique sections (Fig. 8a [2,3]) through the symphysial portion of the lower jaw in UALVP 47003. Sections through the anteriormost portion of this specimen reveals that symphysial teeth and tooth files in mesial position may look strikingly different.

All sections run obliquely through the tooth files and expose the basal (and partly apical) osteodentine and the apical orthodentine. The obliquely-cut symphysial tooth shows an acuminate crown in

information in future research to determine the relative age of this species and possibly other eugeneodontids.

TMP 86.42.1. Specimen TMP 86.42.1 (counterpart in the Royal British Columbia Museum, Victoria) is similar in overall morphology to UALVP 46535

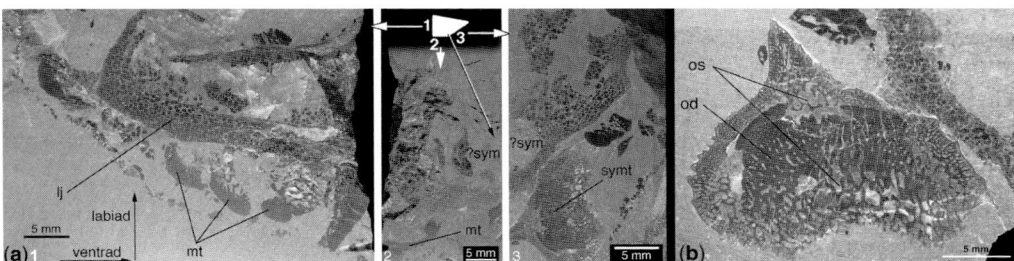

Fig. 8. *Caseodus varidentis* sp. nov., specimen UALVP 47003. (**a**) composite illustration of the obliquely cut lower jaws and the tooth whorl with indication of presumed cutting angles (outline of block with polished surfaces at top in [2]). (**b**) oblique cut through a symphysial tooth showing the extent of osteodentine (os) and orthodentine (od). Arrows point approximately in indicated directions.

antero-posterior view and is laterally flattened (Fig. 8b). The obliquely cut tooth clearly shows the remainder of the ornamentation of the tooth edge, probably consisting of cristae reaching fairly high up the tooth crown (Fig. 8b). Apical ornamentation in symphysial teeth can also be discerned in specimen TMP 86.42.1 but the extent of wear cannot be determined. Large vascular cavities are located relatively far apically in these teeth. The immediately adjoining mesial or mesio-lateral teeth are blunt with a slightly vaulted central cusp and show conspicuous linguo-labial projections (cut buttresses in section Fig. 8a[1]).

The thin sections also reveal that the majority of teeth and tooth files are covered by a quite dense layer of lepidomoria. Lepidomorial scales are not arranged in an obvious pattern but larger lepidomoria always lie interior to the smaller, single lepidomoria, suggesting that the denticles sank into the skin before and during decomposition of the soft tissue. (For a description of denticles, see below.)

Comparisons. The specimens TMP 86.42.1, UALVP 46535 and 47003 resemble the holotype in overall morphology and state of preservation and are thus most parsimoniously placed within the same species.

Compared to other caseodontids, *Caseodus varidentis* sp. nov. most closely resembles *Caseodus eatoni* Zangerl, 1981 in overall morphology but can readily be distinguished by tooth morphology. Of all teeth, only the distal teeth resemble each other in the two species, and these teeth are likely least significant with respect to taxonomy.

Ornamented blades, as in the symphysial teeth of *Caseodus varidentis* sp. nov., have not previously been described in any other caseodontid. The mesial teeth of the upper jaw most closely resemble the 'symphysial teeth' of *Caseodus basalis* Cope, 1894 – but the mesial teeth of *C. varidentis* sp. nov. have very strong crenulations. The symphysial teeth of specimen UA 46535, although somewhat more crenulated, resemble *C. basalis* (specimen FMNH PF 2500 in Zangerl [1981; fig. 91]) closely.

Genus Fadenia *Nielsen, 1932*

Type species. Fadenia crenulata *Nielsen, 1932*

Diagnosis (emended from Zangerl [1981]). Fusiform body shape; probably slender head (at least in some species); articulating area of upper jaw present and calcified; dentition consists of tumid and pavement teeth; symphysial teeth much enlarged, bulbous and tumid; pectoral fin with axially arranged elements but lacking proximal series of basals; ceratotrichia distally forked but this feature is questionably diagnostic (compare Bendix-Almgreen 1975*b*); haemapophysial and neurapophysial elements in caudal fin slender-triangular and variable in number (proximally fused to become very few elements).

Fadenia uroclasmato *sp. nov.* Figures 9–13.

Holotype specimen. TMP 86.42.4 (Figs 9–12). Tentatively referred specimens: TMP 87.42.11, UALVP 46526 (Fig. 13). Site: From D-ridge [holotype], others from C-cirque (see Neuman 1992).

Etymology. Clasmato- (from Greek, meaning 'fragment') and uro- (from Greek, meaning 'tail'), referring to the upper caudal fin lobe apically supported by several short, bar-shaped neurapophysial cartilages.

Diagnosis. The caudal fin is taken to be diagnostic of this new species: upper lobe consisting apically of a mosaic of small, long, asymmetrically triangular to diamond-shaped cartilages; proximal portion of the upper lobe supported by large triangular plates. The morphology of the caudal fin, however, shows strong affinities to the (yet undescribed) caudal fin of *Fadenia crenulata* Nielsen, 1932 from Permian strata of the Wordy Creek Formation in East Greenland (figured by Zangerl 1981, fig. 89D) and is intermediate in structure between *Caseodus* and *Fadenia*. If the tentatively referred specimens (UALVP 46526 and TMP 87.42.11) are correctly placed in *Fadenia uroclasmato* sp. nov., the diagnosis can be extended as follows: slender sharks of about 1 m body size and slender skull in dorsal view; moderate heterodonty, consisting predominantly of smallish, blunt pavement teeth; lateral teeth with extremely slender-oblong, asymmetrical and vaulted cusp; tooth whorl unknown.

Description. The holotype specimen TMP 86.42.4 consists of two major parts, showing the partial anterior body (Fig. 9) and an almost completely preserved caudal fin (Fig. 10). The remains of the anterior body comprise the jaws and most of the visceral skeleton elements and parts of the pectoral girdle and fins. Two large, rectangular to oval cartilages and a maximum of about 15 ceratotrichia are preserved. Two short, rod-shaped ?pectoral cartilages are present in front of the right pectoral fin. The outlines of a series of at least 5 branchial arches can be traced by the regular patches of pharyngeal teeth/denticles (Fig. 9, bas). Both lower jaws can be traced but the posterior end (articulation site) is set apart and appears to have been separately calcified. Alternatively, these portions may represent lateral flanges of the neurocranium, partly covered by the lower jaw elements. Only imprints of very slender, slightly curved '?upper jaws' are present immediately mesial to

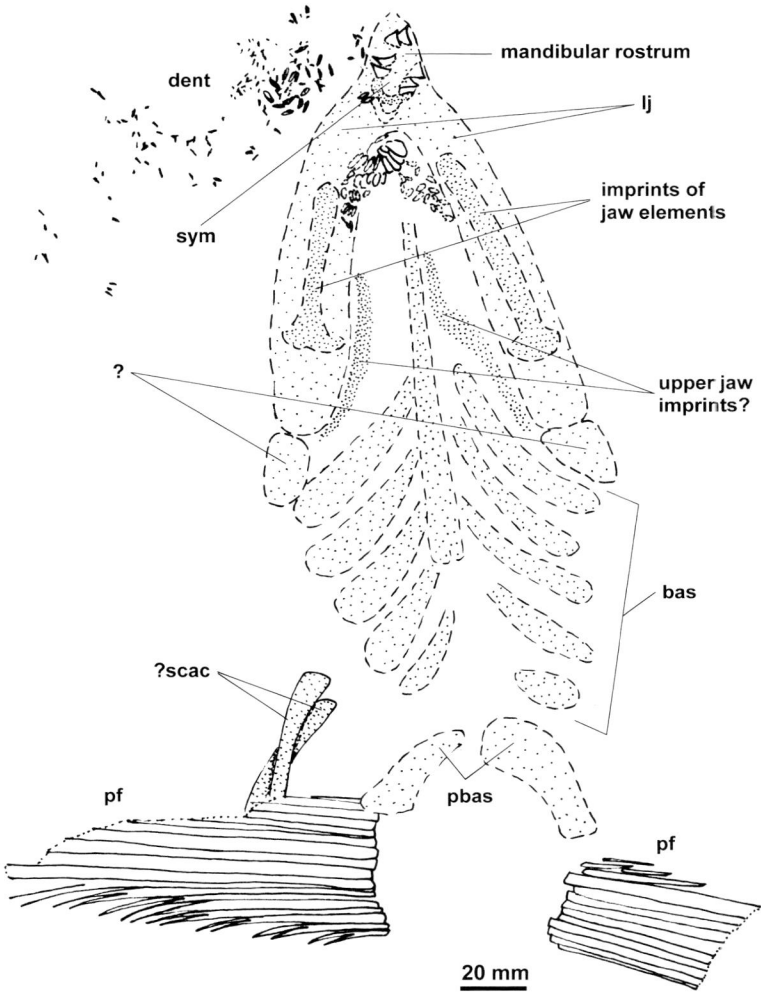

Fig. 9. *Fadenia uroclasmato* sp. nov., skull, visceral skeleton and pectoral fins as preserved in ore part of specimen TMP 86.42.4.

the lower jaws. Along the central portion of the lower jaws, relatively deep, slender-oblong depressions with a broadened posterior end can be found, which indicate the original presence of an additional cartilage supporting the lower jaw on each side. The mandibular rostrum is very short and contains the entire tooth whorl, which, although fragmentarily preserved, forms a near-complete circle.

The pectoral fin supports include oblong, calcified rods that are slightly curved distally. There are at least 12 rays in the left pectoral fin whereas the right pectoral contains 14 or 15 rays. Ray number 7 is the broadest in both fins. The rays increase in length up to ray number 9, which is

the first to fork clearly (the more anterior rays are less clearly preserved distally in this respect). Most of the support of the shoulder girdle is missing but there is one short (30 mm long) element ('rods that are slightly curved distally' mentioned above) on either side articulating with the pectorals and several smaller, rod-shaped elements that represent additional short rays of the fins. These are lined up anterior to the fins. Two extremely slender-oblong and curved elements (partly covered by the right pectoral fin) are interpreted as scapulocoracoids (Fig. 9, ?scac), although their shape is very unusual.

No cartilaginous elements of the branchial arches are preserved leaving only the outline of

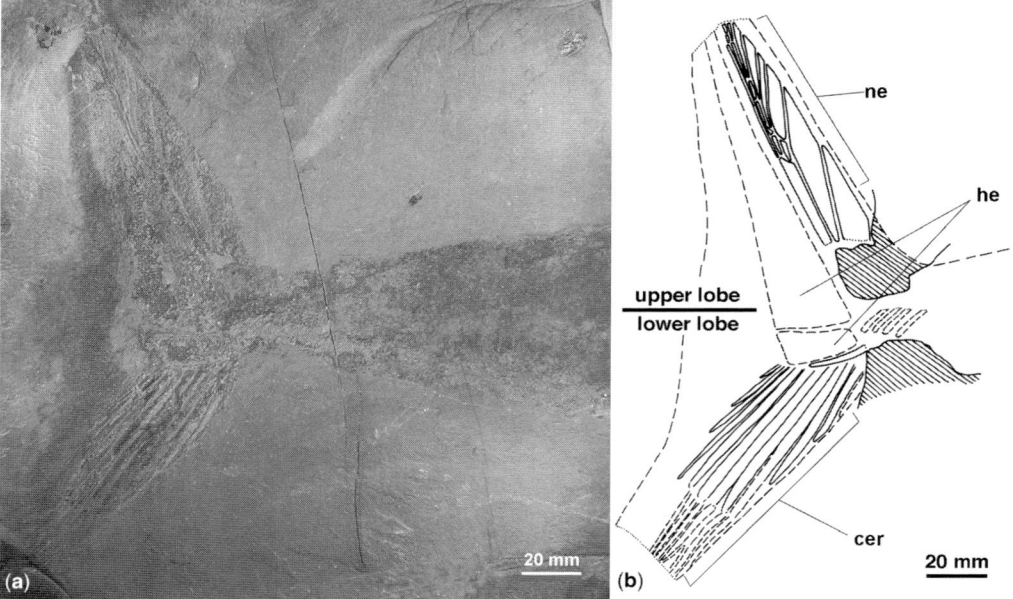

Fig. 10. (**a**) photograph and (**b**) sketch of the caudal fin of *Fadenia uroclasmato* sp. nov., as preserved in another part of specimen TMP 86.42.4. Note the similarity with *Fadenia crenulata* Nielsen, 1932 in the pattern of proximal fused neurapophysial cartilages. The relatively high counts of neurapophysial elements (ne) in the upper lobe are rather reminiscent of the genus *Caseodus*.

the basket. At least 5 branchial arches occur, which can be traced by the shagreen of branchial teeth lined up along the arches. There may have been a very short or rudimentary sixth arch present at least in the left side of the skull. Only an imprint of part of the basibranchial is visible. Apparently, there is a separate remnant of a cartilage abutting the posterior end of the lower jaw on either side and these may represent separate cartilages of the upper jaw articulating with the neurocranium and the lower jaws.

There are additional imprints of slightly curved cartilages of the visceral skeleton preserved between the lower jaws and these probably are the remainder of the upper jaws. Both lower jaws, including the proximal portion of the mandibular rostrum, show well-calcified prismatic cartilage around which numerous teeth are preserved partly *in situ* and partly scattered (see below).

The caudal fin is composed of a dozen slender, tapering and rod-shaped ceratotrichia in the lower lobe and a complex arrangement of triangular, diamond-shaped and rectangular haemapophysial and, in particular, neurapophysial cartilages in the upper lobe (Fig. 10). The rod-shaped elements in the lower lobe may be arranged in two series but the evidence is ambiguous. In the upper lobe, the smallest elements enclose the distal portion of the

notochord anteriorly whereas a single, large and triangular element supports the fin ventro-posteriorly. The anterior series of cartilages in the upper lobe decreases in size distally. In the caudal peduncle, the preservation is less perfect and definite calcifications cannot be unambiguously identified. However a short series of rod-shaped haemapophyses can be traced in front of the two uppermost, horizontally oriented elements of the lower lobe.

The dentition is very incomplete but a variety of different types of teeth are preserved. There is one fragmentarily-preserved, but almost complete, circle of a tooth whorl present in specimen TMP 86.42.4 (Figs 11–12). The tooth whorl is apparently situated at the anterior tip of the lower jaw symphysis and on the mandibular rostrum. The largest completely preserved tooth measures 6 mm in length but there are several broken teeth suggesting a maximum tooth length of 8–10 mm. As far as visibly preserved, there are several tooth batteries with enlarged teeth situated near the symphysis (either from the upper or lower jaw).

These teeth are very poorly preserved but do not seem to form a whorl-like series and are instead regular tooth families, including teeth with blunt crowns lacking the smooth and acuminate blade of the symphysial teeth in the lower jaw. Although the crowns in the tooth whorl are very

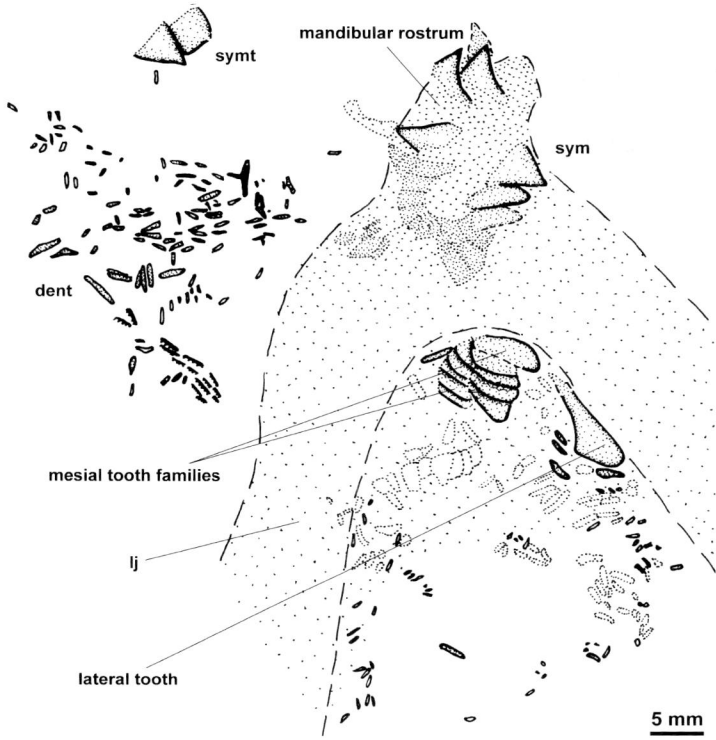

Fig. 11. Close-up of specimen TMP 86.42.4, *Fadenia uroclasmato* sp. nov., showing the disarticulated dentition and much of the symphysial tooth whorl *in situ*.

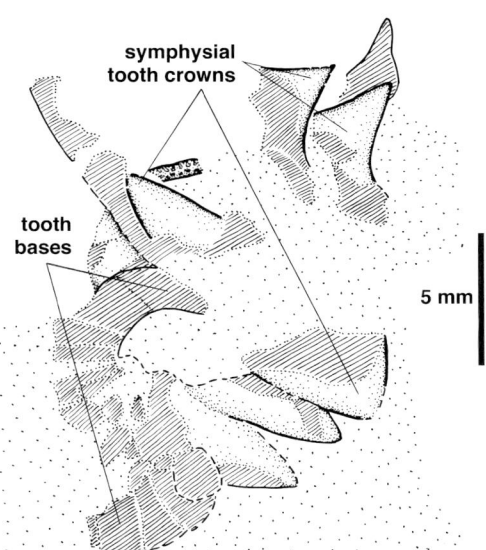

Fig. 12. Close-up of the symphysial tooth whorl of specimen TMP 86.42.4, *Fadenia uroclasmato* sp. nov., describing a disrupted, but almost complete, circle.

fragmentarily-preserved, these teeth show evidence that there is no significant increase in tooth size from older to younger teeth, as in contrast in *Paredestus* gen. nov. (UALVP 46579), and the roots form a single, solidly-fused, small and tightly curled basis fused to the mandibular rostrum (Figs 11–12). The exact orientation of the roots is indeterminable as their outline cannot be followed. Their depth measures about half the length of the crowns. The shape of the crown is remarkably similar to *Paredestus bricircum* gen. et sp. nov. but the blade is not recurved and serration (again poorly preserved in one tooth) may have occurred on the lingual edge of the blade rather than on the labial edge.

Tentatively referred specimens (UALVP 46526, TMP 87.42.11). Specimen UALVP 46526 (Fig. 13a, b) is an anterior body section with two pectoral fins, vague outlines and surface depressions of the dorsoventrally flattened neurocranium, the sclerotic rings, part of the branchial skeleton with several arches and part of the tooth-bearing jaws including a distinctive, asymmetrical lateral tooth family. Only five to seven teeth are

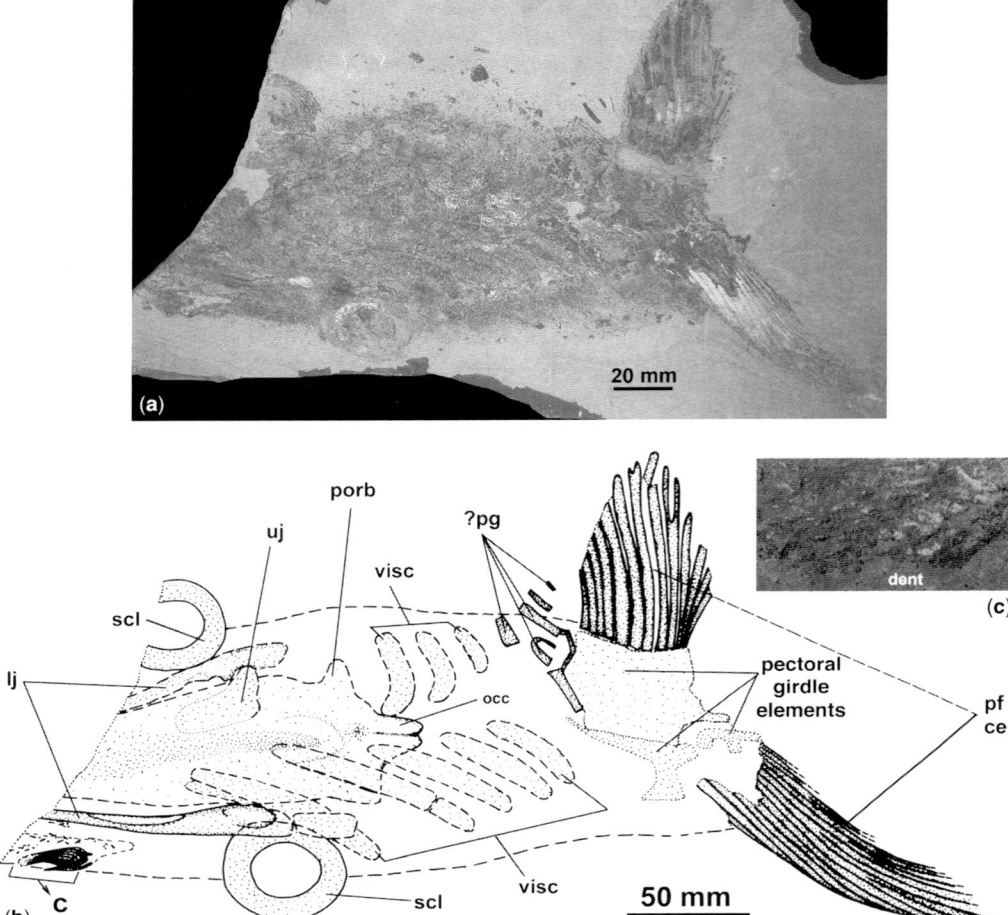

Fig. 13. cf. *Fadenia uroclasmato* sp. nov., specimen UALVP 46526. (**a**) photograph and (**b**) line-drawing of the entire specimen. (**c**) close-up of the partly preserved dentition, an asymmetrical lateral tooth family.

visible. The weathered lateral teeth are very slender, oblong and are conspicuously vaulted with their highest elevation shifted towards the distal shoulder.

Several skeletal elements of the anterior body half are preserved: the neurocranium is seen in ventral view with patches of elongated denticles clustered in several distinctive areas. This shark specimen was quite slender anteriorly, including an oblong head and slender lower jaws. Accordingly, the neurocranium is relatively slender and elongate. Only the occipital region is well-preserved and shows lateral processes situated far posteriorly and a deeply cleft occipital process in ventral view. The supraorbital rim of the neurocranium appears to be located far posteriorly, roughly

in the vicinity of the preserved sclerotic rings revealing a reinforced outer rim. The sclerotic rings are solid and well-calcified, evidence of very large eye-sockets and, thus, large eyes. The visceral skeleton is partly calcified including the very slender, oblong lower jaws and the left ?upper jaw, which appears to be reduced to a small element articulating with the posterior neurocranium. Alternatively, it may be only partly-preserved or partly-calcified. Branchial arches can be traced in outline, due to preservation of pharyngeal teeth, and they number at least five on either side. Poor evidence of a sixth arch is present between arches 1 and 2 and underneath arch 1 of the right body half. Several unidentifiable but well-calcified, bar-shaped elements are preserved immediately in front of the fin region and are therefore interpreted as the remainder of supporting elements of the pectoral girdle. Two partial fins with ceratotrichia and a single basal cartilage are preserved. Despite their strikingly different outlines, the preserved fins are taken to represent the two pectoral fins, both consisting of at least one dozen branched rays. Alternatively, the more anteriorly situated fin may be interpreted as a dorsal fin due to the ceratotrichia being slightly re-curved at their tips. However, branching ceratotrichia are not known to occur in the dorsal fin of any other shark.

The dentition is heavily weathered and difficult to interpret. There are at least two lateral tooth families, one of which is clearly larger, centrally vaulted and quite asymmetrical (Fig. 13c). The extended shoulders of these larger teeth point anteriad. The teeth probably appear more asymmetrical because they are heavily weathered and obliquely embedded. These lateral teeth, however, taper much more abruptly toward the distal (than toward the proximal) shoulder of the crown. A tooth family of much smaller and non-vaulted teeth adjoin anteriorly. A number of tiny, blunt teeth lacking a vaulted main cusp are preserved. However, the state of preservation of those lateral size and latero-distal teeth does not allow any further assessment than that they formed a pavement in lateral and distal positions.

Provisionally referred specimen: in specimen TMP 87.42.11 (collected in C-cirque), the pectoral fin also shows about 15 ceratotrichia, many of which are distally branched. The base of the pectoral fin is supported by a slender-triangular, tripod-like structure that may be equivalent to several, short, bar-shaped elements as preserved in disarticulation in the holotype specimen.

Comparisons. This new species resembles specimen UALVP 38822 (+part UALVP 46536 [*Fadenia* sp. indet.]) in overall anatomy of the preserved anterior postcranial region but the diagnostic significance of these features is not currently settled (see below and Fig. 13).

The caudal fin is intermediate in morphology between the genus *Caseodus* and the (undescribed) line drawing of a caudal fin of *Fadenia crenulata* figured by Zangerl (1981, fig. 89C) following a sketch drawn by S. E. Bendix-Almgreen (preliminary drawing erroneously attributed to E. Nielsen [pers. comm. H.-P. Schultze, 2004]). The upper lobes of the caudal fin differ in composition of the supporting cartilages.

Fadenia *sp. Figure 14.*

Specimen. UALVP 38822 (+part UALVP 46536), 46532, 47016 (from C-cirque and R-cirque).

Description. Specimen UALVP 38822 (+part UALVP 46536, superimposed view in Fig. 14) comes from R-cirque (south wall) and consists of several parts and counterparts collected separately during several field trips. The pieces belong undoubtedly to one individual and only differ in degree of weathering. A composite sketch of parts and superimposed counterparts is shown in

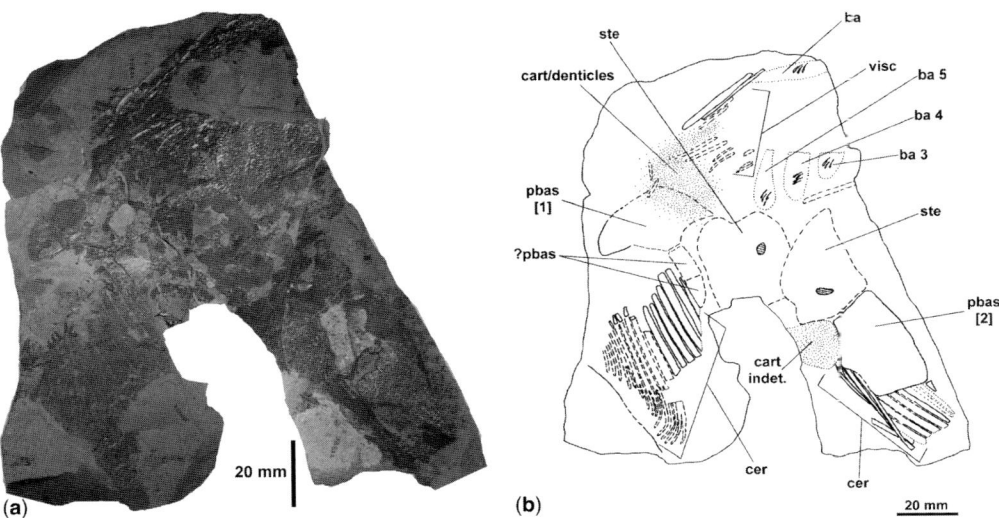

Fig. 14. *Fadenia* sp., composite photograph (**a**) and line-drawing (**b**) of several parts and counterparts superimposed as preserved in specimen UALVP 38822 (+UALVP 46536). Major parts of the pectoral girdle are visible: the pectoral fins, branchial arches, dermal denticles and unidentifiable cartilaginous 'elements'.

Figure 14b. Some parts are heavily weathered but show interesting features mainly as imprints of cartilages and *in situ* pharyngeal teeth on the remnants of the posterior visceral arches (ba3-5), arranged in gently curved rows in the posterior throat region. The structure of the pharyngeal teeth/denticles is identical with those figured in specimen UALVP 17936 (Eugeneodontida gen. et sp. indet.). Some of the pharyngeal teeth on arch 3 look like the one displayed in Figure 22, with a prominent central spike-like cusp and short lateral cusps, whereas most of the other teeth show 7 slender-oblong cusps projecting from a well-developed base. Slender and elongate, bar-shaped visceral elements are scattered between the clusters of pharyngeal teeth. Adjacent to what is interpreted to have been the hyoid-visceral area, are four large elements (one of which is very poorly preserved) that must have represented parts of the shoulder girdle. The two elements of the left pectoral fin enclose a number of small, fragmentarily-preserved elements but it is not clear whether they were fractured post-mortem or actually represent small elements close to the base of the pectoral fin (Fig. 14b, ?pbas). The four large cartilages are probably separate elements of the pectoral girdle (basal and sternal cartilages). These elements are roughly square, thin plates with rounded edges. Two elements (pbas [1] and [2] in Fig. 14b) that are larger than the slender, oblong and distal ceratotrichia, are preserved adjacent to the basal cartilage of the right pectoral fin (view as in Fig. 14). Some of the ceratotrichia of both pectoral fins are preserved with their proximal portions intact. None of the ceratotrichia are jointed but

at least 5 distal radials of the right pectoral fin are distally branched. The basal cartilage of the left pectoral fin (view as in Fig. 14) is fragmentarily-preserved but actually shows part of the articulation with the enlarged proximal basal cartilages (?pbas).

UALVP 47016. Figures 15–16. Specimen UALVP 47016 reveals numerous teeth including the tip of a symphysial tooth crown. In overall morphology, the remnants of the skull resemble *Fadenia uroclasmato* sp. nov. The slender tip is also reminiscent of tips of teeth of *Sarcoprion edax* Nielsen, 1952 (plate 7) but the state of preservation does not allow adequate comparison and assignment at the species level.

Note: This specimen probably represents a new species but its overall poor preservation does not allow us to establish diagnostic features with confidence (see Figs 15–16). Only two tips of symphysial teeth are preserved partly as imprints and these show almost smooth and laterally flattened high-acuminate cusps (Fig. 16a). Mesial teeth are moderately vaulted and distal teeth may lack prominent labial buttresses altogether (Fig. 16b, c). The dermal denticles preserved along with the cartilage and the oral teeth, however, are reminiscent of caseodontids, and this specimen is provisionally assigned to *Fadenia* sp.

The specimen also shows the mid-portion of the neurocranium (including the broad supraorbital rim) and numerous 'durophagous' teeth on the ventro-lateral margins. These teeth are fairly large and lack a main cusp, sharing a very prominent crenulation. The tooth whorl is not preserved but

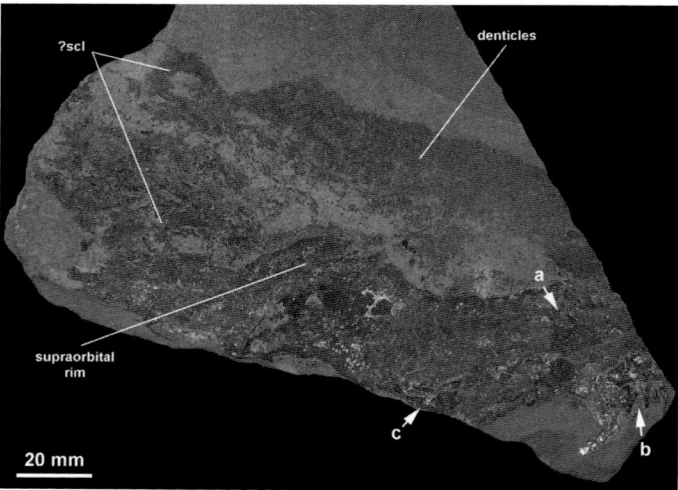

Fig. 15. *?Fadenia* sp.; a cranial portion associated with dermal denticles as preserved in specimen UALVP 47016. The lower case letters refer to close-ups Figure 16a, b and c.

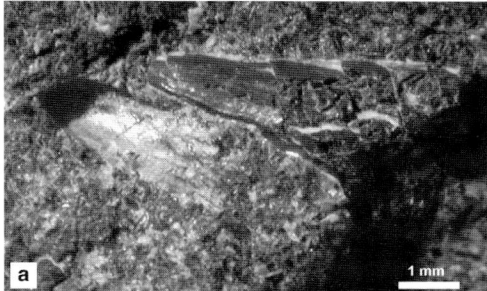

Fig. 16. Close-up of exposed teeth as preserved in *Fadenia* sp., specimen UALVP 47016. (**a**) blades (tips) of symphysial teeth; left blade as imprint, right blade broken. (**b**) broken mesial teeth (arrow: note the vaulted central portion of the crown). (**c**) flat distal teeth.

the scattered fragments of high-acuminate teeth are almost perfectly smooth showing very few and faint crenulations. Judging from the preserved fragments of symphysial teeth, it appears they have a long, slender and acuminate blade (tip), which is sagittal in orientation and their ornamentation consists of oblong, fine ridges running down the blade. The precise outlines of none of these teeth can be restored, because most exposed parts are broken off. The majority of distal teeth are very long and flat (Fig. 16c).

UALVP 46532. Specimen UALVP 46532 (Fig. 17) is a relatively complete large pectoral fin tentatively

referred to *Fadenia* (see Discussion). This fin shows the characteristic distal branching in the numerous – at least 19 – ceratotrichia. In general, the midportion of the anterior elements are broadest but the ceratotrichia also broaden toward the distal tip of the fin, where some of the radials fork just before adjoining the border of the fin.

Caseodontidae *gen. et sp. indet.* Figure 18.

Specimens. TMP 88.98.100, ?TMP 86.154.94, ?TMP 95.114.8 (collected in C-cirque and D-cirque).

Description. TMP 88.98.100: Specimen TMP 88.98.100 (from D-cirque talus along south wall) is a disarticulated head region of a small, presumably juvenile edestid which is not further identifiable. The cartilaginous remains represent the neurocranium, rostrum and presumably, the upper jaw, but details of respective cartilages could not be assigned to specific skull elements. This specimen shows a series of distal teeth (Fig. 18), but these are not readily comparable with those of other specimens due to their small size and the presumably young age of the specimen.

Tentatively referred: Specimen TMP 86.154.94 (C-cirque from talus slope) is a portion of the postcranial skeleton showing a fin articulation that is not further identifiable and TMP 95.114.8 (collected from talus low below a fold containing Palaeozoic to Lower Triassic rock) is an unidentified cranial fragment with numerous and small durophagous teeth that do not show any features that allow assignment of the specimen to a lower taxonomic rank.

Superfamily Edestoidea Hay, 1930
?Family Edestidae Zangerl, 1981
Genus *Paredestus* gen. nov.

Type species. Paredestus bricircum gen. et sp. nov. *Diagnosis.* See below.

Etymology. Par- (from Latin, meaning 'to bring forth'). The name *Paredestus* refers to the affinities with the genus *Edestus* Leidy, 1855
Paredestus bricircum gen. et sp. nov. Figure 19.

Holotype and single preserved specimen. UALVP 46579 (from C-cirque).

Etymology. Bri- (from Latin, meaning 'short') and circ- (from Latin, meaning 'wheel'), referring to the small tooth whorl consisting of very few teeth.

Diagnosis. Very short symphysial tooth whorl with teeth rapidly increasing in size; edges in symphysial

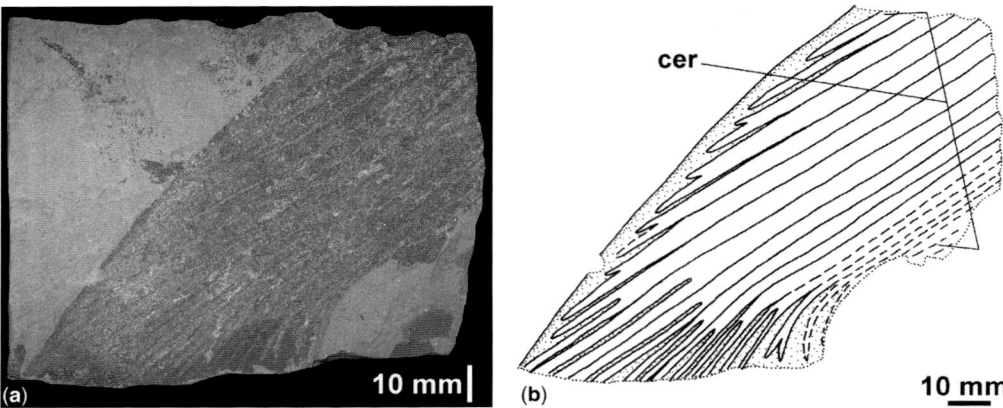

Fig. 17. Photograph (**a**) and sketch (**b**) of ?*Fadenia* sp., pectoral fin of specimen UALVP 46532. Note the distally branched (anterior and posterior) ceratotrichia (cer).

teeth possibly serrated; roots of symphysial teeth directed posteriad; mesial teeth with variably and moderately vaulted cusp; oblong pavement teeth are blunt showing a pronounced longitudinal crest.

Description. The partial jaw UALVP 46579 (Fig. 19) shows very informative views of the symphysial tooth whorl in the lower jaw and the adjacent tooth files – presumably mesio-lateral teeth. The former teeth show the general arrangement characteristic of tooth whorls – arranged in a half-circle, sharing the site of root attachment and apparently completely fused roots. As far as visible (parts of the teeth are covered by other teeth and a shagreen of denticles), the tooth crowns of teeth in the tooth whorl are largest proximally and smallest towards the anterior tip of the lower jaw. The roots are poorly-preserved and the crowns are partially fragmented but intact. The crowns are broad but acuminate and are clearly delimited from the joined roots, although swinging gently posteriad with the basally expanded portion. Although imperfectly preserved, weathered and partly covered, the crowns clearly show a rounded lateral wall in lateral

Fig. 18. Caseodontidae gen. et sp. indet., specimen TMP 88.98.100. Gently vaulted, long distal teeth in lingual view.

aspect and the second hindmost preserved tooth of the tooth whorl shows a serrated sagittal edge above the posterior 'saddle' of the root. It appears that the serration in the second tooth from the right is due to weathering (see Fig. 19c).

The roots on the symphysial teeth are broken off and poorly preserved but appear to have extended posteriorly at an oblique angle to the axis of the tooth crown – as is common in edestids.

In contrast to the teeth of the tooth whorl that show entirely smooth tooth crowns, teeth of the mesial tooth files are unicuspid teeth with a conspicuously broadened middle portion (or cusp) with a more or less blunt apex and extensive crenulation (Fig. 19). One sagittal and one transverse crest respectively divide these teeth into four discernible sectors, and numerous crenulations, partly branching, run down the apex. The transverse crest is faintly but better developed than in symphysial teeth. A large number of flat teeth lacking main cusps but showing prominent crenulations and a pronounced longitudinal crest are distributed over the slab and seem to have represented a pavement dentition lining the ventral wall of the neurocranium or an (unpreserved, ?cartilaginous) upper jaw element merged with the neurocranium, against which the symphysial teeth may have abraded. As far as discernible, the crown ornament is much more prominent on the labial wall of the crowns than on the lingual wall. In addition to the numerous (?upper) pavement teeth, there are at least two additional tooth families with enlarged teeth.

Comparisons. The mesial and lateral teeth preserved along with the symphysial teeth show little affinities with other known eugeneodontid dentitions but the overall pattern in dental morphology and variation is remotely similar to a number of

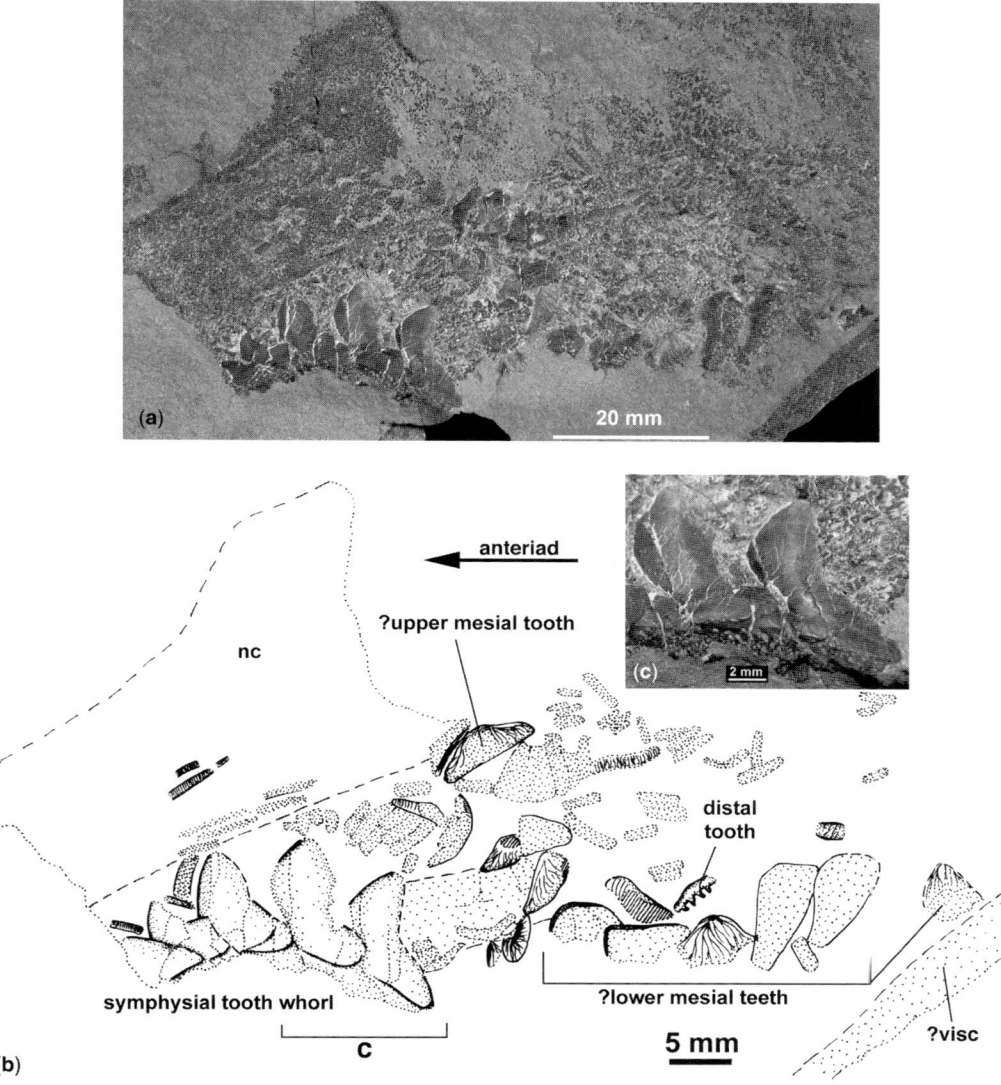

Fig. 19. (**a**) photograph and (**b**) line drawing of *Paredestus bricircum* gen. et sp. nov., specimen UALVP 46579. Note the teeth in the symphysial tooth whorl decrease in size rapidly anteriad. (**c**) close-up of the partly preserved symphysial tooth whorl. Arrow points anteriad.

other edestoids. The central vaulting of teeth, interpreted as being mesial, is reminiscent of the genus *Agassizodus* St. John & Worthen, 1875. The morphology and root orientation, however, are interpretive due to the poor preservation and the crowns show similarity with the edestid *Helicampodus* Branson, 1935 and *Sinohelicoprion* Zhang, 1976 (which may be closer to *Helicampodus*; see Chang & Miao 2004) in outline and gross morphology. With reservation, the latter taxon may therefore also be alternatively placed within Edestidae Jaekel, 1899 (*sensu* Zangerl 1981). The pattern

of a half-circle symphysial tooth whorl abrading against upper pavement teeth in *Paredestus bricircum* gen. et sp. nov. is also reminiscent of *Sarcoprion edax* Nielsen, 1952.

Eugeneodontida *gen. et sp. indet.*

Figures 20–26.

The specimens have been collected in C-cirque (except for TMP 89.127.43 [D-cirque]), but do not allow assignment to any recognized species.

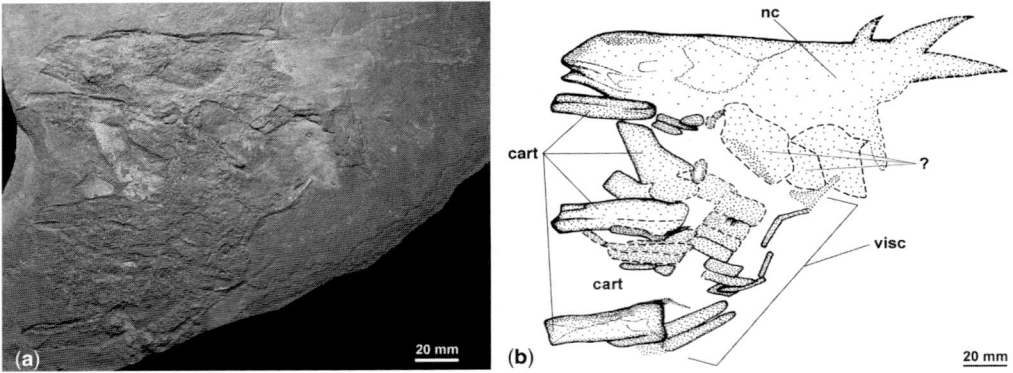

Fig. 20. (a) photograph and (b) sketch of specimen TMP 86.42.2 (+TMP 95.118.1; Eugeneodontida gen. et sp. indet.); parts of the visceral skeleton associated with the neurocranium. The counterpart TMP 95.118.1 was discovered 10 years after collection of TMP 86.42.2 in the same slope of C-cirque and shows nicely disarticulated elements in fine preservation. The lack of dental remains prevents more definite assignment and comparison with other eugeneodontids.

Description.

TMP 86.42.2: This specimen (TMP 95.118.1 is part of the same individual) is preserved in several parts and counterparts in ventral view and its estimated standard length is about 1 m (Fig. 20). The large slab shows major, disarticulated elements of the rostrum and the visceral skeleton associated with a partial fin in part and counterpart (the presumed dorsal fin does not necessarily belong to the same specimen and hence is not shown in Fig. 20). This dorsal fin resembles specimen TMP 89.131.2 (see

Fig. 21. Isolate patches of dermal denticles (and pharyngeal 'teeth') as preserved in Eugeneodontida gen. et sp. indet. (a) specimen UALVP 22108 (type I denticles): these denticles occur quite spaced and similar lepidomorial scales cover large areas. (b and c), specimen UALVP 17936 (type II denticles): these denticles, visible in ventral view, were probably pharyngeal teeth or gill-raker like teeth found only in the gill area (b = anterior view; c = posterior view).

Fig. 22. Eugeneodontida gen. et sp. nov., anterior view of flattened and weathered, raker-like teeth with broad and spike-like extended central cusp as preserved in specimen UALVP 17937.

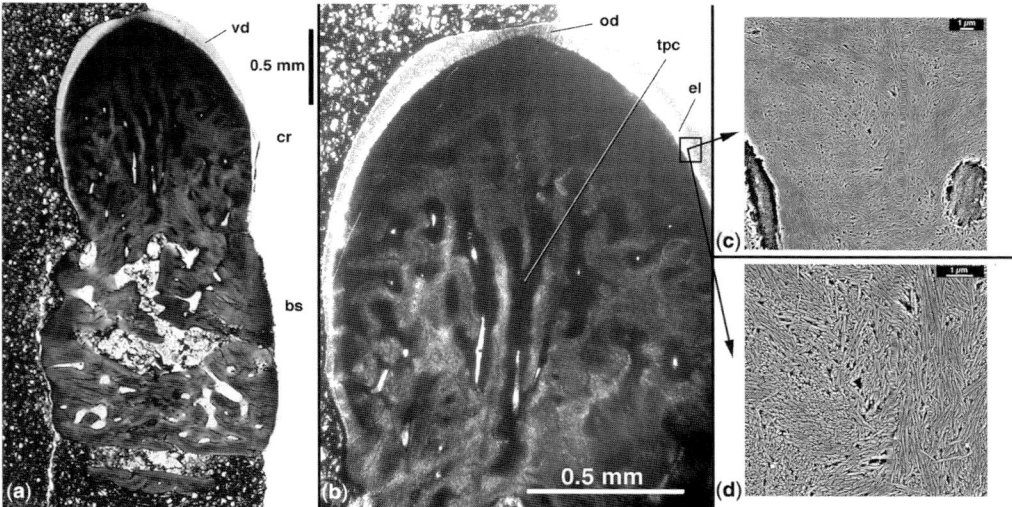

Fig. 23. Eugeneodontida gen. et sp. indet., tooth ultrastructures as preserved in an isolated tooth in specimen TMP 98.127.43. (**a** and **b**, close-up), tooth basis (bs) and crown (cr) histology is predominantly osteodont (developed as a tubular pulp cavity, tpc) with an apically restricted band of orthodentine (od) reaching into the enameloid layer (el). (**c** and **d**, close-up; section etched 5 seconds in 5% HCl), the thick tooth enameloid is composed of cross-bundled fibres of slender crystals in well-defined orientation.

below: 'Specimens showing fin girdles and fins') in having similarly arranged ceratotrichia. The imprints of anterior neurocranial 'projections' of the neurocranium are reminiscent of *Caseodus* sp.

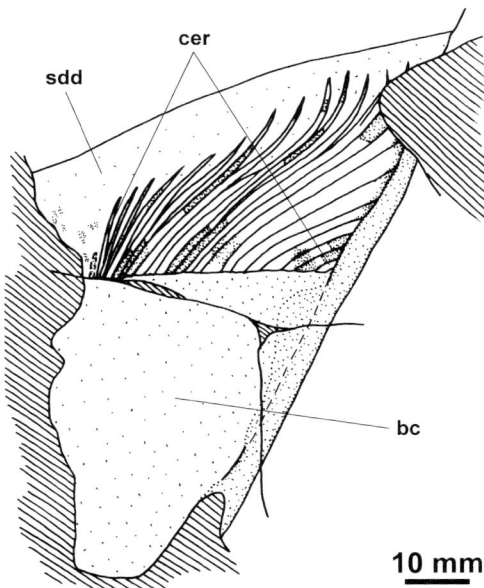

Fig. 24. Eugeneodontida gen. et sp. indet., sketch of the basal cartilage and the dorsal fin of specimen UALVP 17928.

(see Zangerl 1981, fig. 84B, C). The disarticulated head and visceral region can, at present, not be unambiguously interpreted and we were unable to identify some of the elements preserved as vague imprints due to lack of suitable comparative material. The preserved parts clearly show symmetrical arrangement of rather small and ridged elements, triangular or rectangular in outline, that are suggestive of parts of calcified visceral cartilages (mandibular and hyal elements).

UALVP 22108. Specimen UALVP 22108 (Fig. 21a) shows reasonably well-preserved denticles ('type I'). The state of preservation of the denticles does at present not allow to recognize distinctive features (see 'Discussion' below). The multiple lepidomorial scales (*sensu* Stensiö 1962) displayed using this specimen are quite uniform and flat, and they cover major parts of the body as is seen in various other specimens.

UALVP 17936. Specimen UALVP 17936 (Fig. 21b–c) shows favourably preserved 'pharyngeal teeth' (denticles 'type II') in sharply delimited areas originally probably covering much of the branchial arches. Type II–denticles (or pharyngeal teeth/denticles) are seemingly more variable among specimens but depending on their orientation, these denticles may look quite different in anterior (Fig. 21b) and posterior view (Fig. 21c). Type II–denticles are easily identified by the 6–8

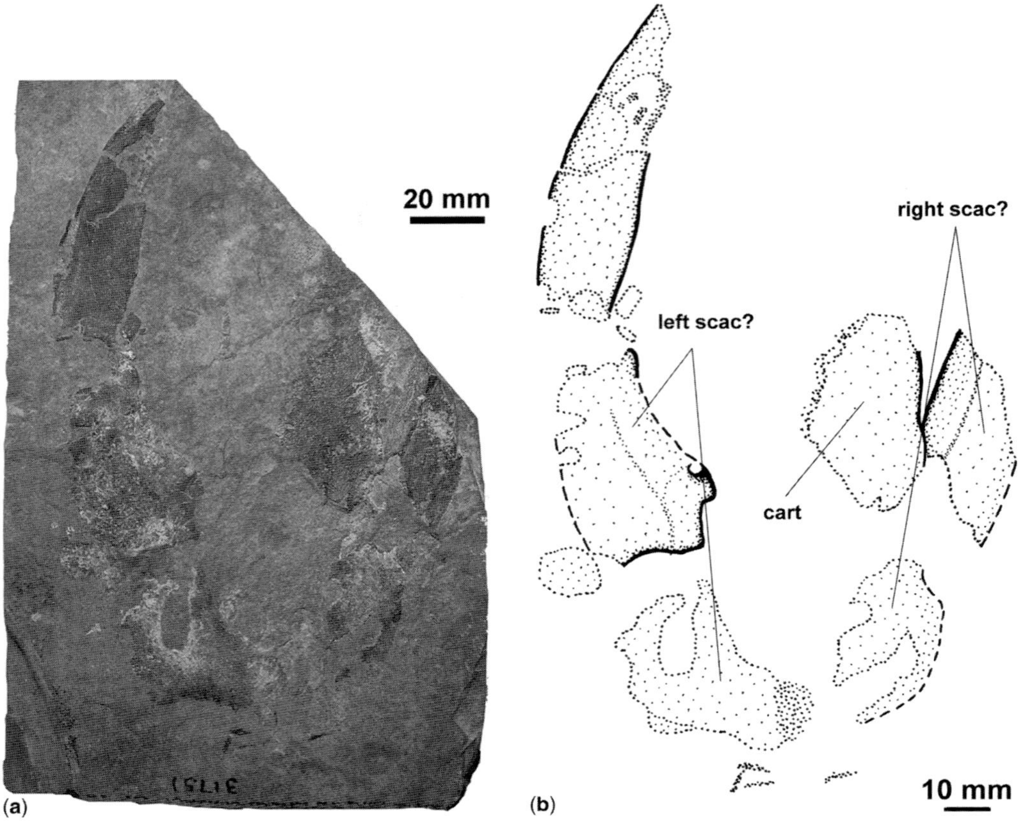

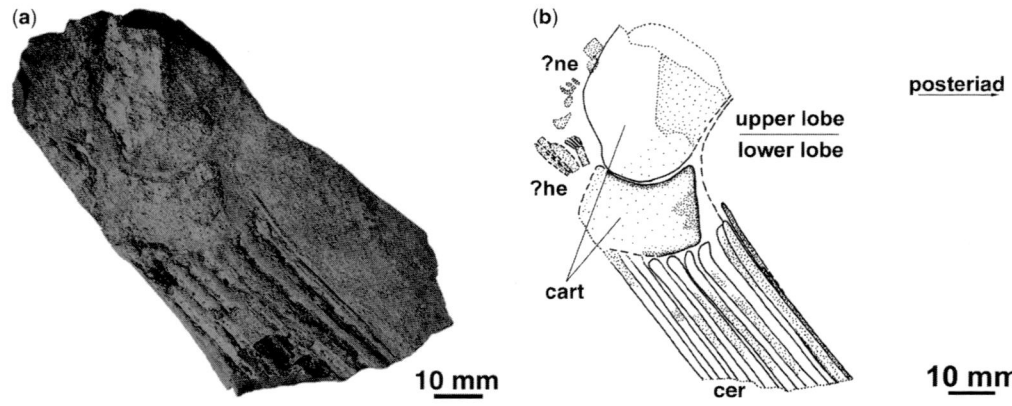

Fig. 25. Eugeneodontida gen. et sp. indet. (**a**) Photograph and (**b**) sketch of the relatively large, weathered ?pectoral girdle elements as preserved in specimen UALVP 31751.

Fig. 26. Eugeneodontida gen. et sp. indet. (**a**) photograph and (**b**) sketch of imprints of a portion of probable caudal fin as preserved in specimen TMP 95.118.2.

long and acuminate cusps radiating from the basal plate which bulges out anteriad and posteriad, and which is apically re-curved. The central cusps may be considerably extended in some specimens but the evidence also suggests that the excessive length of the central cusp may be due to embedding and preservation in favourable aspect, because the denticles' morphology may look strikingly different when flattened, weathered or seen in different views (compare also specimen UALVP 17937 [Fig. 22]).

TMP 89.127.43: A thin section through the crown shoulder of an isolated mesio-lateral tooth (TMP 89.127.43 (Fig. 23) reveals that the root is larger than the crown and highly vascularized. The crown is oval-shaped in cross-section, consists of tubular pulp cavities (tpc), orthodentine (od) entering the enameloid (el) and an outermost thin layer of apical vitrodentine (vd; according to terminology of Zangerl 1981). The enameloid-vitrodentine layer is much more thickly developed apically than on the crown shoulders but covers the entire crown.

Tooth histology in eugeneodontids is hence apparently primitive in being osteodont with a distinctly restricted apical band of orthodentine penetrating the enameloid layer. The thick tooth enameloid is composed of cross-bundled fibres of slender crystals in irregular but well-defined orientation (Fig. 23c, d). The thin apical layer we identify here as Zangerl's vitrodentine, has been considered synonymous with the enameloid layer by Bendix-Almgreen (1983).

Specimens showing fin girdles and fins

The fin in specimen TMP 95.118.1 has ceratotrichia reminiscent in organization but slightly smaller in number than specimen TMP 89.131.2. Both specimens represent portions of dorsal fins. Specimen UALVP 17928 shows an almost completely preserved dorsal fin and its supporting cartilage (Fig. 24). The cartilage supporting the fin is only partly preserved but is clearly deeper than long. There were at least 22 ceratotrichia, of which most are preserved as imprints. The rays are all gently curved, increase in width posteriad and taper to a point. The anterior rays are all re-curved whereas the more posterior ones are rather s-shaped.

Specimen UALVP 31751 (Fig. 25) shows the weathered scapulocoracoids of both halves of the pectoral girdle, seen in lateral (external) view and an additional, unidentified cartilage beside the right scapulocoracoid. The slender scapulocoracoids are sickle-shaped and have an acuminate apical tip. The apical portion appears most thoroughly calcified with a prominent thick anterior border. The middle and distal portions are slightly

detached from each other and this may indicate originally poor calcification. The middle portions share postero-external surfaces developed as thickened rims that probably served as articulation sites for the pectoral fin's basal cartilage and its radials. The distal portions are thin cartilages and are very weakly-calcified. Scattered in-between the elements are small to tiny shreds, fragments and imprints of additional, unidentifiable cartilages.

Specimen UALVP 17930 is probably a fragment of the central portion of the main shoulder girdle element, the scapulacoracoid but this element and the following specimens can not be more precisely identified at present. Specimen TMP 86.154.94 is a portion of the postcranial skeleton showing a fin articulation and TMP 2001.15.03 is part of a caudal fin.

Specimen TMP 95.118.2 (Fig. 26; collected from middle of C-cirque directly below quarry) shows imprints of the lower lobe of a partially preserved caudal fin, associated with smeared shagreens of dermal denticles. At least 7 ceratotrichia and 2-calcified cartilages are preserved as imprints, the surface is largely broken or weathered. The most proximal element is slender, oblong and abuts (with its knob-like head) the proximal, concave face of the distally adjoining second cartilage. The latter element has the shape of an arched rectangle and articulates distally with at least 7 extremely slender rays, composed almost entirely of prismatic cartilage. The ?anterior rim is delimited by several (only partly-preserved) narrow ridges, also consisting of prismatic cartilage. Beside these elements, there are also a number of more fragmentary cartilages preserved immediately posterior to the large cartilages (basal elements?), but their outlines and shapes are too poorly-preserved to allow identification.

The dermal denticles are minute, often smeared or broken but the smallest ones are rounded or diamond-shaped in outline, flat and bear several (4–7) antero-posteriorly running ridges. Slightly larger, thicker denticles with entirely smooth surfaces are also present.

?Eugeneodontida *gen. et sp. indet.* The following specimens are tentatively referred to eugeneodontids. Specimen UALVP 46684 probably represents the snout tip of a rostral cartilage of a shark, possibly an edestoid. Thin section through the posteriormost portion reveals the prismatic cartilage only, not associated with dermal denticles. However, on the same slab is an edestoid tooth fragment associated with coelacanth remains (scale and fin ray).

Specimen TMP 95.114.8 is a cranial fragment with numerous 'durophagous' teeth that do not show any features that allow assignment to a recognized group. However, the blunt crown morphology and their large number clearly suggest eugeneodontid affinities, although many teeth are almost completely buried in matrix in various views.

Specimen UALVP 46533 shows the distal portion of a partial ?pectoral fin. The tips of the 3 ceratotrichia taper distally and there are narrow gaps in between as in other specimens referred to eugeneodontids (see above).

Specimen TMP 89.131.2 (collected from talus in C-cirque) appears to be a dorsal fin as it possesses at least 21 slender ceratotrichia, each one progressively thickening in width posteriad while tapering distally. They are all jointed ventrally by the dorsal cartilage. The specimen is badly weathered and is mainly preserved as an imprint. The scales are badly weathered and smeared but both types of denticles observed are comparable to specimen TMP 95.118.2.

Description in open nomenclature

Eugeneodontida *gen. et sp. indet. (unnamed eugeneodontid, Fig. 27).*

Specimen UALVP 46539 (from C-cirque): This specimen is part of a thick slab of brownish weathered, compact siltstone with a partial, disarticulated dentition showing many partially preserved teeth and their peculiar features in various aspects. The labial side of some lateral teeth has about a dozen very pronounced large ridges (Fig. 27a), whereas the lingual side shows a much more shallow

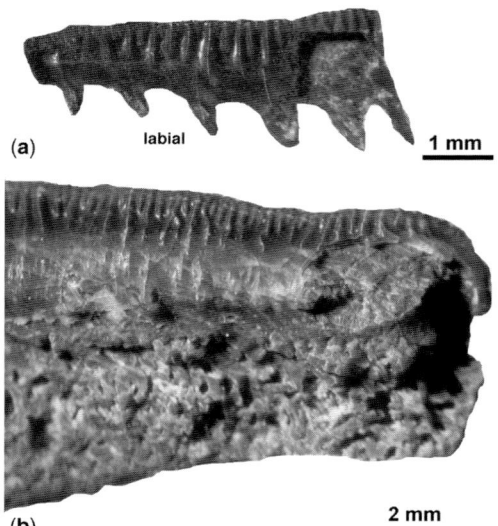

(a)   labial   1 mm

(b)   2 mm

Fig. 27. Unnamed eugeneodontid (possibly a caseodontoid), specimen UALVP 46539. (**a**) smaller distal tooth crown in occlusal view with a smooth labial wall. (**b**) fragment of a larger lateral tooth in lingual view.

ornament that is distantly reminiscent of tooth crowns of acrodontids (Fig. 27b). No conspicuous longitudinal crest along the tooth shoulder is developed. The visible teeth range in length from a few millimetres to about 25 mm. The large lateral teeth are highly ornamented lingually, whereas distal teeth are asymmetrical and almost devoid of any ornament.

Comparisons. The range of tooth variation in this specimen is close to that observed in *Caseodus varidentis* sp. nov. but the significance and variation in lower v. upper dentitions is not known in any other eugeneodontid taxon and we therefore refrain from assigning this specimen to the same taxon.

This specimen also stands out in its type of preservation. The teeth are widely scattered across the bedding plane on top of this single (approximately 15 cm thick) siltstone slab – suggesting a different postmortem depositional history than all other eugeneodontid specimens recovered to date from Wapiti Lake.

Discussion of comparisons with described taxa

Dentitions and teeth

Eugeneodontid taxa reported from the Induan–Olenekian of Wapiti Lake display an astonishing diversity. These new specimens exhibit body sizes comparable to some of the latest Palaeozoic members of that group, and suggest eugeneodontids may have represented some of the largest marine predators during the Early Triassic. This contrasts with the occurrence of dwarfism during the marine Early Triassic – occurring in vertebrates and invertebrates (Wignall & Benton 1999; Twitchett 2001; Hautmann & Nützel 2005; Mutter 2005). However, compared to their Palaeozoic predecessors, the tooth whorls of these Triassic forms are only of moderate size and often half-circles (not spiral-shaped, cf., e.g., spirals of *Helicoprion* Karpinsky, 1899), suggesting that differing feeding adaptations prevailed among the Early Mesozoic members.

The actual extent of reduction of the upper jaw in Late Palaeozoic caseodontids has been suggested by Zangerl (1981). It is not clear what role the possible upper jaw elements played in eugeneodontids, and there is currently no unequivocal evidence of a completely-calcified upper jaw of the length of the lower jaw in any eugeneodontid specimen from Wapiti Lake. *Caseodus varidentis* sp. nov. and *Paredestus bricircum* gen. et sp. nov. yield evidence of partial *in-situ* tooth files that are most parsimoniously reconstructed as located in an upper jaw element. However, we are unable to identify additional jaw cartilages in this position. The anterior upper jaw was probably adapted to accommodate the modified jaw action using the lower jaw symphysial dentition in a specialized feeding strategy. In contrast, the lateral and distal posterior (lower and upper) jaw regions were well adapted to durophagous feeding habits. The variable degree of calcification in these remains does to some degree support the view of Zangerl (1981) that the lack of preserved skeletal remains in Late Palaeozoic forms could be due to lack of calcification, but we find no support for an evolutionary process favouring loss of calcification towards the end of the Palaeozoic. It is likely that partial calcification of head and anterior skeleton was also imperative for functions of jaws and associated levers in support of the presumed partly durophagous feeding habit. It is unclear whether the absence of anterior jaw elements is due to fusion, loss or lack of calcification (or a combination of these states) in the eugeneodontids studied here.

The assessment of individual tooth variation within a single lower v. upper tooth family or entire jaw dentition is problematic. However, it seems that heterodonty has previously been greatly underestimated. For instance, teeth of the same specimen show varying degrees of crown ornamentation, development of buttresses, tooth size, angle between crown shoulders and complex crown morphology.

The central vaulting in mesial teeth may have diagnostic significance in addition to, or even instead of, a 'smooth lingual wall' (cf. Zidek 1976). *Paredestus bricircum* gen. et sp. nov. (specimen UALVP 46579) remotely resembles *Edestus giganteus* Newberry, 1888 (specimen AMNH 225) in overall morphology of the tooth crown. Tooth file curvature is stronger in the crown in the former taxon and edges and roots are poorly preserved. In *Paredestus bricircum* gen. et sp. nov., the anterior teeth in the file are strikingly small but the curvature and size of the tooth whorl seemingly rules out the specimen being a juvenile individual. Unfortunately, the only cranial material available for comparison with the material described here is *Ornithoprion hertwigi* Zangerl, 1966. Cranial morphology of the latter species does not match the cranial morphology of the new specimens: the jaws of this species are particularly massive, long and peculiarly shaped.

The postulated synonymy of *Campodus* de Koninck, 1844 and *Agassizodus* St. John & Worthen, 1875 (hinted at by Zangerl 1981, p. 77) cannot yet be resolved. In contrast, specimen TMP 86.42.3 further complicates the matter by providing evidence for intradental variation in *Caseodus* with the upper jaw dentition lacking lingual crenulations, considered to be typical for the genus *Campodus*. However, teeth assigned to *Campodus* do show other assumingly diagnostic features that distinguish this genus from all other eugeneodontids: the coarse ridges bulge out on both lingual and labial walls, all teeth are remarkably uniform (AMNH 8853) and rather *Orodus*-like in lingual and labial outline.

The holotype of *Campodus variabilis* is a purported 'symphysial row of teeth' from the Upper Carboniferous Coal Measures of Cedar Creek, Nebraska (USA). Remarkably similar teeth occur in mesial or near symphysial position in the holotype of *Caseodus varidentis* sp. nov. (although the crown shoulders in these teeth enclose a much greater angle) and these teeth belong in the same dentition together with completely differently shaped lateral teeth.

Unfortunately, only a few teeth of *Fadenia* have been found and are described here – but, nevertheless, the new caseodontid *Caseodus varidentis* sp. nov. clearly reveals affinities in its dentition to the former genus. For instance, the large lateral teeth of *Fadenia gigas* Eaton, 1962 from the Lower Pennsylvanian of the Upper Cherokee Shale (Lexington Coal) in Lucas (Henry County, Missouri, USA), come close in overall morphology to the respective tooth file in the holotype of *Caseodus varidentis* sp. nov.

Variation in the dentition found in *Caseodus varidentis* sp. nov. holotype specimen TMP 86.42.3 is comparable in range to the variation in *Fadenia crenulata* as illustrated by Nielsen (1932, pls 2-6), although teeth of the former species show more extensive crenulation. Crowns of *Fadenia crenulata* are less massively developed linguo-labially and have less extremely vaulted central cusps in lateral tooth files.

The slant of the root and lower portion of the crown in *Paredestus* gen. nov. are of ambiguous morphology but of crucial importance with respect to the genus' systematic position. The orientation of the root is interpretive (namely posteriad) and not similar to other geologically young taxa such as the agassizodontid *Sarcoprion edax* Nielsen, 1952 (see below). The symphysial teeth are broad but less widely separated than in *Edestus* Leidy, 1855. In *Edestus heinrichi* Newberry & Worthen, 1870 the teeth are similar in being closely positioned but differ greatly in many respects, including shape of the tooth crown. The orientation of the root slant and the affinities of this genus to both superfamilies of edestoids are therefore interpreted with caution. In edestoids, no similar-sized mesial and lateral teeth beside the tooth whorl are known and all other teeth in the dentition are of pavement-type and much smaller than teeth in the tooth whorl (see also Nielsen [1952] below). All previously described edestoids are quite unlike *Paredestus* gen. nov. in this respect. *Helicampodus kokeni* Branson, 1935, *Lestrodus* Obruchev, 1953, *Helicoprion* (see Bendix-Almgreen [1966] and Zangerl [1981]) and various other 'true' edestids match the crown morphology and possibly the root organization by pointing posteriad (Fig. 19), but differ in lower crown morphology and in being more tightly joined. The 'helicoprionid' fragmentary tooth whorl, '*Sinohelicoprion*' (cf. *Helicampodus*) *qomolangma* Zhang, 1976 (the only other unquestioned Early Triassic eugeneodontid) from western China, looks remarkably similar to the abovementioned four taxa and its taxonomic status is in need of re-assessment (see also Chang & Miao 2004). Some of the poorly-preserved eugeneodontid tooth crowns such as the one in specimen UALVP 46539 (described here in open nomenclature), come close to '*Sinohelicoprion*' (cf. *Helicampodus*) *Qomolangma* (Zhang 1976).

Nielsen (1952) described various edestoids from the Upper Permian Wordy Creek Fm of East Greenland, but except for *Fadenia crenulata*, none of the edestoids closely resemble the material recovered from Wapiti Lake. In fact, we have found no evidence of agassizodontid edestoids. This is surprising, as the Greenland eugeneodontids are stratigraphically close to the Wapiti Lake sample. In particular, no agassizodontid remains comparable in root morphology to *Sarcoprion edax* Nielsen, 1952, and represented by several specimens from Greenland, can be positively identified in the Wapiti Lake sample. The edestid *Paredestus bricircum* gen. et sp. nov. comes close in symphysial and anterior tooth file morphology but unambiguously possesses enlarged mesial teeth, too.

As discussed above, some of the features that are believed to be diagnostic for eugeneodontid teeth are probably linked to functional needs and the position of the teeth in the dentition. For example, we identify as such the strong buttresses combined with smooth crown surfaces both in labial and in lingual walls respectively in upper jaw teeth of *Caseodus varidentis* sp. nov. Also, the varying angle between the tooth crown shoulders in symphysial and mesial teeth of the same species and the general dissimilarities in tooth crowns in upper and lower jaws of eugeneodontids prevent us from reconstructing dentitions with confidence. It seems likely that some isolated tooth files described in the literature as 'symphysial tooth whorls', may in fact be near-symphysial (=mesial) tooth files in the symphysis of the lower or the upper jaw. 'Genuine' symphysial tooth whorls are always found anterior to these symphysial teeth and often on an extended or separate rostral cartilage adjoining the lower jaw

symphysis. The distance between the lower jaw symphysis and the tooth whorl may differ considerably between eugeneodontid taxa, and isolated tooth whorls should ideally be preserved on the rostral cartilage or as near-complete tooth batteries to be justifiably identified as such. In at least some caseodontoids such as *Caseodus* or *Fadenia*, the mandibular rostrum may be reduced or absent and/or tooth whorls may be flanked by transitional mesio-symphysial tooth files. It is also conceivable, that agassizodontid edestoids such as *Sarcoprion* and *Agassizodus* differ in lacking the mesial/symphysial tooth type found in the lower jaw symphysis of caseodontoids, because teeth of the tooth whorl in the former taxa are greatly enlarged if compared to all other tooth types found in the same dentition.

Cranial and postcranial skeleton

Zangerl (1966) reconstructed *Ornithoprion hertwigi* with six gill arches but in 1981 he revised his reconstruction of the gill basket to having only five arches. The evidence from Wapiti Lake eugeneodontids is also unclear in this respect and there may have been a sixth gill arch preserved beneath the first ray in *Fadenia uroclasmato* sp. nov. even though we can see only five gill arches clearly developed in specimen UALVP 46526 (Fig. 13). This alternative interpretation would also be supported by the large gap between neurocranium and shoulder girdle (cf. Zangerl [1979, p. 457]).

Pectoral fins are preserved in several of the specimens in association with remains of *Fadenia* but there is also an isolated fin (Figs 14, 17). All are assigned to *Fadenia* primarily on the basis of the branching ceratotrichia (cer). This feature is highlighted by Bendix-Almgreen (1976) and listed by Zangerl (1981) as diagnostic of *Fadenia*. However, Bendix-Almgreen (1975b) showed that distally forked rays and similarly organized pectoral girdles also occur in other, not closely related groups of sharks including several species of *Cladoselache*. However, the branching occurs in *Fadenia* in posterior and anterior rays, and the branching in anterior rays is not known in any other shark.

Dermal denticles

There are three different kinds of denticles found in the eugeneodontids from Wapiti Lake, each showing a varying distribution and abundance. The denticles located in the posterior head region consist of a single ?anteriorly projecting cusp that do not resemble any other denticle currently known (see inset Fig. 2). The second kind of denticles are of 'classic' lepidomorial shape (single or multiple elements; primary and secondary *sensu* Stensiö

1962). These 'type I' denticles appear in many body regions, are abundant, and resemble a general type of lepidomorial aggregate found in many chondrichthyans that are not closely related such as *Eugeneodus* Zangerl, 1981 and *Orodus* Agassíz, 1844 (see Fig. 21a; compare Zangerl 1981).

The third kind of denticles (see Fig. 21b, c and Fig. 22, 'type II' denticles) have not been described previously in eugeneodontids. They are pharyngeal or raker-like-teeth (or specialized denticles) apparently sitting on and restricted to visceral elements.

Conclusions

The youngest record of eugeneodontid sharks

The remains described here are the first articulated eugeneodontids recovered from any Triassic strata and likely represent one or several assemblages possibly spanning a few million years in time (Induan–Olenekian; early Smithian [possibly Griesbachian] to Spathian). Few of the specimens were recovered *in situ* but there is convincing evidence (from data collection and lithology) that all specimens weathered out of Lower Triassic (not Upper Palaeozoic) rock. For instance, conodont samples of late Induan and early Olenekian (Dienerian to Smithian) ages were taken from the same area where specimen TMP 2001.15.03 was found, and specimen TMP 89.127.43 was collected high in the talus of D-cirque, in which locality there are no Palaeozoic rocks present in the overturned section.

Several lineages of eugeneodontids hence survived the end-Palaeozoic crisis and are recovered in astonishing diversity from the Vega-Phroso Siltstone Member at Wapiti Lake. Helicoprionid-type spirals and agassizodontids, widely spread in the Permian, are apparently absent from this assemblage. All species are of similar body size to their latest Palaeozoic relatives. However, the current state of eugeneodontid taxonomy and systematics is still unsatisfactory. The present paper adds to an already biased picture, in which most species and genera are almost exclusively known by fragmentary dental remains, and the genus *Fadenia* yields information based predominantly on non-dental material.

Many skeletal elements cannot yet be identified and assigned to a distinctive species because of the lack of adequate comparative material and because the taxonomic significance of differences in dental v. skeletal features cannot yet be assessed. More complete specimens are needed to improve the current taxonomic concept.

A wide variety of eugeneodontid dentitions evolved in the Late Palaeozoic. However, the fact that almost all taxa are established on the basis of very fragmentary material must not be underestimated. As outlined above, the probable dental variation present in lower v. upper jaws and the individual, intraspecific and interspecific variation in teeth is just beginning to be explored.

Teeth preserved in partial view and reported 'features' in isolated material must be interpreted with caution. In general, features in teeth, other than symphysial tooth whorls and mesial teeth, presumably bear less diagnostic significance. The entire tooth battery may show a strikingly different organization in different taxa but such assessment must await the discovery of more completely articulated dentitions. According to the present taxonomic concept and our study, a wide variety of dental 'architectures' may indeed have existed in spite of a comparatively uniform postcranial skeleton. The pectoral girdle is apparently variably developed and may consist of broad plates and slender-oblong scapulocoracoids (cf. Figs 9, 13, 14 and 25). The caudal fin skeleton appears to yield diagnostic features in the degree of fusion of haemapophysial v. neurapophysial elements in caseodontids. Unfortunately, this information has not yet been seen in association with differences established on the basis of diagnostic dental features.

The fact that none of the specimens recovered from Wapiti Lake can be referred to previously described species reflects the incompleteness of the group's fossil record across the Permo-Triassic boundary and also evokes important corollaries on future taxonomic work. First, a re-investigation of the most completely preserved dentitions is needed to establish diagnostic features. Second, crania should be examined closely, because it is likely that eugeneodontids possessed, among other characters, either a relatively broad or a slender skull together with differing types of dentitions (cf. e.g. Figs 2 and 13). Third, caudal fin skeletons add to our knowledge in only a few species. This area may contribute significantly to the improvement of diagnoses, despite the generally assumed absence of diagnostic features in the postcranium (see also Zangerl [1981]).

Dental variation, jaw reconstruction and jaw suspension

Due to the rarity and fragmentary state of preservation of eugeneodontid sharks, almost all aspects of dental variation, including monognath or dignath heterodonty, individual, intraspecific and interspecific variation and upper jaw anatomy, are poorly known. According to this study, major differences can be expected to occur in the arrangement and morphology of upper and lower jaw dentition in eugeneodontids. The most complete dentition of *Caseodus varidentis* sp. nov. (in holotype specimen TMP 86.42.3) shows striking discrepancy in degree of tooth surface crenulation (ornament) in upper and lower dentition. The upper jaw can be traced in radiographs of *Caseodus basalis* and *Eugeneodus richardsoni* (see Zangerl, 1981, fig. 32) and appears to be anteriorly reduced yet firmly attached to the neurocranium. Zangerl (1981; p. 26) refrains from using the term 'hyostylic' and suggests the caseodontoid condition is derived, but in a different way than in neoselachians. Following Zangerl's (1981; p. 24–26) interpretation of upper jaw morphology and jaw suspension, the lower symphysial tooth whorl would actually not act against teeth of the palato-quadrate but against teeth of an additional anterior cartilage in the upper jaw or against teeth embedded in the ventral surface of the rostral tip of the neurocranium. *Fadenia uroclasmato* sp. nov. may have upper jaws not fused with the neurocranium (compare Fig. 9). The holotype specimen TMP 86.42.3 of *Caseosus varidentis* sp. nov. suggests that relatively large mesial teeth occur in the upper dentition immediately behind the tooth whorl but we currently lack enough information on upper jaw structure in *Caseodus varidentis* sp. nov. to comment on the reconstruction provided by Zangerl (1981). Further study of the internal structure of the skull of TMP 86.42.3 may reveal in more detail how the caseodontoid jaw suspension was constructed.

In any case, the generally accepted reconstruction of the upper jaw/tooth whorl as a functional 'tin-opener', suggests a solid (dental) anatagonist for the lower jaw symphysial tooth whorl. As outlined in the Discussion, we can only assume upper jaw elements were either absent, weakly calcified (thus, not preserved) or firmly integrated into the neurocranium.

Implications for the end-Permian extinction event and palaeobiogeographic considerations

The Permo-Triassic boundary has long been held as the turning point in environmental history due to magmatic events, palaeoclimatic change, seawater isotope changes, magnetic polarity shift and proposed biota extinctions (e.g. Veevers *et al.* 1994). The discovery of this group of elasmobranchs in surprising diversity in the open marine Early Triassic is set against this global picture. While many marine clades dwindled or became extinct towards the boundary, the presence of eugeneodontids in the Early Triassic of western Canada in relatively high diversity suggests this group was much less affected by the major environmental turning point than previously believed. Investigation and comparison of *Parahelicampodus spaercki* Nielsen, 1952 and *Fadenia crenulata* Nielsen, 1952 from Kap Stosch, East Greenland, and 'cf. *Helicampodus qomolangma*' (Zhang, 1976) from Dingri (Xian County), should be the next, highly valuable studies to further explore this phenomenon. There is no sign of extinction or decrease in body size of the group as a whole: it has been suggested this would have occurred during the recovery phase due to dwarfism (Twitchett 2001) and has recently been shown for an isolated group of stem actinopterygians (Mutter 2005) and was documented in clams (Hautman & Nützel 2005). Although the evidence does not yet allow precise assessment of relative diversity of this particular group during the entire Permo-Triassic turnover, these new findings support the view that the marine end-Permian extinction event was highly selective.

Palaeonisciform fishes are also represented by several isolated lineages in the Triassic (Mutter 2003), and some other fish groups do not conform with the end-Permian extinction scenario. For example, actinistia may or may not peak in diversity in the Early Triassic (compare Forey 1998 and Schultze 2004). Although it is true for many fish groups that a major faunal change took place across the Permo-Triassic boundary, we lack accurate dating for many of these fossil sites and are still unable to trace and reconstruct the events leading to faunal turnover in a temporal sequence during the Early Triassic. Establishing reliable time-control is essential for understanding and reconstructing relevant historic events.

The reconstruction of outlines of Pangaean 'subcontinents' and borders of Triassic marine habitats and their interconnections is problematic, eventhough continental plate movements following the break-up of the super-continent Pangaea (at the beginning of the Jurassic) are fairly well understood. It is generally assumed that (according to the theoretical computer fit, in which the relevant coastlines of today's continents are displayed to match perfectly) there were no apparent seaways present, for instance, between the Americas and Africa or that there was no passage between the Proto-Atlantic and the west coast of central America connecting marine realms of the southern and northern hemisphere. The fact that we find similar faunal assemblages in both hemispheres ('cosmopolitan' taxa) very early in the Triassic, is normally explained as rapid dispersal events in impoverished habitats following the great extinction event (recovery process). Palaeoichthyology is capable of providing important contributions to more accurate delineation of ancient coastlines, because fish fossils are ubiquitous and often identifiable once a taxonomical framework is in place. In addition, certain Late Palaeozoic–Early Mesozoic sharks were stenohaline (eugeneodonts), euryhaline (some hybodonts) or occured predominantly in freshwaters (xenacanths) and are hence excellent indicators for palaeoenvironments.

But should we continue to observe a rising number of 'Lazarus taxa' in ever earlier stages in the Early Triassic, we may be forced to think about alternative explanations for the 'reappearance' of taxa and will have to attempt a quantification of the Early Triassic sedimentation rates and their bearing on the rock and fossil gap. Recent research confirmed that the Induan represents an extremely short timeframe (see Ogg 2004) during which a smaller volume of sedimentary rock, and hence fossil preservation, may be expected.

The pre-break-up phase of Pangaea, the Triassic, is particularly interesting because it spans a timeframe that holds a key to understanding Mesozoic and even extant biotic diversity. From today's perspective it seems improbable that global environmental changes on the scale of the Permo-Triassic boundary event or the Jurassic Pangaea break-up event have been paralleled by an event comparable in significance during the Triassic. Turnovers in faunal composition also occurred during the Triassic, and the causes for these allegedly minor changes may no longer be negligible for reconstruction of the Triassic recovery scenario. Establishing a temporal sequence of small-scale (non-global) environmental changes is a necessity in identifying more localized 'turning points' in Pangaean history that clearly pre- or clearly post-date the Permo-Triassic boundary. Only this data will provide a more detailed scenario of Late Palaeozoic/Early Mesozoic palaeobiogeography and disappearance of certain groups of vertebrates.

It may be concluded that although environmental and faunal changes occurred during the Triassic at a smaller scale, these events may not necessarily have had a less severe effect on the faunal turnover.

The importance of including detailed alpha-taxonomical studies of Lower Triassic fish remains when interpreting the scenario of the Permo-Triassic faunal turnover can hardly be overestimated because the assessment of changing diversity is always based on taxonomy and not on the fossil record itself. It is likely that poorly-preserved fish groups such as eugeneodontids tend to be overlooked due to the lack of an established taxonomical framework. From this perspective, the eugeneodontids are an extraordinary example, because not only has their stratigraphical

distribution been underestimated, but also their diversity and geographical occurrence – apparently mainly due to the lack of appropriate preservation (poor calcification and fragmentary condition). Eugeneodontids are most probably strictly marine and highly specialized fishes that are now known to co-occur in astonishing diversity across the Permo-Triassic boundary in the eastern Panthalassa and in the Proto-Atlantic. The single find in the eastern Palaeo-Tethys (cf. *Helicampodus*? From Dingri, Xian County) further expands the eugeneodontids' strato-palaeogeographic distribution. Future investigation of the undescribed eugeneodontid material from the Permo-Triassic of East Greenland may significantly amend our comprehension of palaeobiology of these sharks. It is also possible that Permo-Triassic eugeneodontid oral teeth remain unidentified in various collections because their dental remains were previously not expected to occur in the Smithian and because their minute distal and some of their lateral teeth are not easily distinguished from other, non-eugeneodontid shark teeth.

Apart from the serious difficulties in accurate dating of classical Late Permian and Early Triassic fish sites, as discussed above, there are a number of other uncertainties linked to that particular fossil record in general (e.g. hiatuses, reworking and sampling) and to taxonomy and phylogeny of organisms across the Permo-Triassic biotic boundary transition. These problems are reminiscent of those encountered when interpreting the Cretaceous–Tertiary biotic transition (see MacLeod *et al.* 1997).

In the case of relatively high faunal diversity in a geographically remote area and in stratigraphically close proximity to the boundary, a peak in diversity would be interpreted as a biotic refugium following the extinction event (see e.g. Cope *et al.* 2005). This scenario would be likely to change with a more complete record at hand and does not explain the occurrence of archaic, taxonomically diverse sharks in an open marine habitat during the early Olenekian.

Abbreviations used in text and text-figures

art, articulating area of lower jaw; ba(s), branchial arch(es); bc, basal cartilage; bs, base or root (of tooth or denticle); cart, unidentifiable cartilaginous element(s); cer, ceratotrichia; cirdep, circular depressions; cr, crown (of tooth or denticle); dcrest, dorsal crest; dent, dentition; el, enameloid layer; he, haemapophysial elements; mt, mesial tooth family; nc, neurocranium; ne, neurapophysial elements; ns, nasal septum; ldep, lateral depression; lj, lower jaw; ne, elements; occr, occipital rim of neurocranium; od, orthodentine; orb, orbit; os, osteodentine; pbas, basal element of pectoral girdle; pf, pectoral fin; pg, pectoral girdle; porb, postorbital process (of the neuocranium); prorb, preorbital process; rb, rostral bar; rcav; superficial rostro-nasal cavities; scac, scapulocoracoid; scl, sclerotic ring; sdd, shagreen of dermal denticles; slep, single lepidomorial denticles; sorb, supraorbital process (of the neurocranium); spiden, denticles with elongate central cusp (on the neurocranium); ste, sternal element; sym; symphysial area of lower jaws; symt, symphysial tooth of the lower jaw; tpc, tubular pulp cavity; uj, upper jaw; vd, vitrodentine; visc, visceral elements.

We acknowledge review and critical comments by C. Underwood, M. Richter and A. Longbottom. Numerous colleagues helped with collection of specimens and with field and lab assistance: M. Johns (Pacific PaleoQuest, Brentwood Bay), L. Pyle (EOSUV), B. Chatterton, S. Gibb and R. McKellar (UAEAS), J. Bruner, T. Bullard, A. Lindoe, M. V. H. Wilson (UALVP), many staff and volunteers of the RTMP, P. McClafferty and Y. Mutter. Thin sections were made by D. Resultay (UAEAS). Financial support was received with research and travel grants from following foundations: SNF (81ZH-68466 and PA002-109021), J. de Giacomi (Swiss Academy of Sciences, travel grant), R. L. Thyll-Dürr, Arlesheim (research grant), Theodore Roosevelt Fund, New York, USA (research grant), Zürcher Universitätsverein (FAN grant: all to RJM) and NSERC grant (to Mark VH Wilson, UALVP). Transport of fossils was kindly arranged and partly sponsored by Veritas Energy Services Ltd. (Ed Schreuder, Calgary), and TMP supported part of the field trips and CT studies. The final stage of this research was supported by a Marie Curie Intra-European Fellowships within the 6th European Community Framework Programme (MEIF-CT-2006-023691).

Appendix 1

Additional material studied

This list contains important specimens housed at AMNH and BMNH used for comparison

Agassizodus variabilis (Newberry & Worthen, 1870): AMNH 6662 from upper Pennsylvanian, Holt Shale - Virgil Series, quarry Kaser Bros & Bartlett, Iowa (section of jaw). AMNH 6663 from the Pennsylvanian of Wea Shales, quarry Papillion, Nebraska, USA (disarticulated jaws with scattered teeth, shoulder girdle element). AMNH 6664 from the middle Pennsylvanian, Greenfield, (quarry) Stark-Shale Missourian, Iowa, USA (shagreen of denticles).

Agassizodus sp.: AMNH 19623 from the ?Carboniferous Oolagh Formation, locality Dewey Cement, Tolsa, Oklahoma, USA (Gilmore collection, 'Itano nr. 5') (a tooth fragment). Also: unlabelled specimen, in the Cope Collection AMNH from the Lower Permian Red Beds, Texas, USA (7 teeth).

Campodus agassizianus de Koninck, 1844: BMNH P. 28754 (part of type) from the Lower Carboniferous of Chockier near Liège, Belgium (disarticulated distal teeth in concretion).

Campodus rectangulus Trautschold, 1879: BMNH P. 7053/4 from the ?Middle/Upper Carboniferous of Myachkovo, Moscow, Russia (4 fragmentary teeth).

Campodus variabilis Newberry & Worthen, 1870: BMNH P. 9673/4 from the Upper Carboniferous Coal Measures in Cedar Creek, Nebraska, USA (casts of ?symphysial and other tooth files).

?Campodus sp.: AMNH 7084 from Upper Coal Measures, Cedar Creek, Nebraska, USA (cast of partial symphysial tooth whorl). AMNH 8853 from U. Pennsylvanian, near Topeka, Kansas, USA – same species comes also from Osaga County, Kansas (dentition of left lower jaw in place). Unlabelled specimen AMNH from Black Hills, Powder River, South Dakota, USA (broken lateral tooth file with 4 teeth).

Campodus sp.: BMNH P. 12931 from the Lower Carboniferous (Pendleside Beds) of High Greenwood, Hardcastle Croggs Valley in Sowerby, West Riding, Yorks, UK (isolated mesial and lateral teeth embedded in various views).

Campyloprion ivanovi (Karpinsky, 1922): BMNH P. 37767/8 from the Upper Carboniferous (C$_3$, Ghzhel stage) of Rusavkino (near Moscow), Russia (casts of partial tooth whorls). See also Eastman (1902).

Edestus giganteus Newberry, 1888: AMNH 225 (holotype) from the Pennsylvanian (Coal Measures) of Illinois, USA (symphysial teeth).

Edestus heinrichi Newberry & Worthen, 1870: AMNH 488 (cast of holotype) from Pennsylvanian, Coal Measures, Belleville, Illinois (symphysial teeth). BMNH P. 2231/2, 3151, 4795 and unlabelled BMNH specimens from the Upper Carboniferous of Coal Measures, Belville, Illinois, USA (casts of lower symphysial tooth whorls and isolate fragmentary teeth).

Edestus karpinskii Missuna, 1908: BMNH P. 37770 from the Upper Carboniferous (C$_2$; Myachkovian) near Kolomna, Moscow District, Russia (cast of holotype, a fragmentary symphysial tooth whorl).

Edestus newtoni Woodward, 1917 [*Lestrodus* Obruchev, 1953]: BMNH P. 12362 from the ?Upper Carboniferous of the Millstone Grit, Brockholes, Yorks, UK (3 tooth fragments *in situ*).

Edestus protospirata (Trautschold, 1888): BMNH P. 37769 from the Upper Carboniferous (C$_2$; Myatchkovo horizon) of Akishino, River Oka, Ryazansk District, Russia (cast of symphysial tooth whorl). See also Obruchev (1951).

Edestus sp.: BMNH P. 16195 from the Lower Devonian near Bundenbach, Hunsrück Shale, Rhenish Prussia, Germany (almost complete, obliquely flattened tooth whorl).

Fadenia gigas Eaton, 1962: AMNH 8780 (cast of holotype) from Lower Pennsylvanian, U. Cherokee Shale (Lexington Coal), Lucas, Henry County, Missouri, USA (2 casts of symphysial teeth).

Helicoprion bessonowi Karpinsky, 1899: AMNH 7212 from the Permo-Carboniferous of Artinsk Fm, Krasnoufimsk, Ural, Russia (cast of holotype of symphysial tooth whorl; AMNH 7213 is another cotype). BMNH P. 9693/4, 15640-3 from the Lower Permian (P_A^h – Artinskian-Divia Beds), quarry near Krasnoufimsk, Stonspits, west of Divia-Gora, Russia (quarter of tooth whorl and casts of tooth whorls).

Helicoprion davisi Woodward, 1886: BMNH P. 5122 from the Lower Permian of Gascoyne District, West Australia (cast of holotype – partial tooth whorl).

Helicoprion ferrieri Hay, 1907 (in Hay [1909]) (*Lissoprion ferrieri* Hay, 1907): AMNH 7549 (cotype) from the Permo-Carboniferous, near Montpellier, Bear Lake, Idaho, USA (fragment of symphysial tooth file, for name see Romer [1960]). BMNH P. 47782/3 from the Middle Permian Phosphoria Fm of Waterloo Mine, Montpelier Canyon, SE Idaho, USA (casts of symphysial tooth whorls)

Ornithoprion hertwigi Zangerl, 1966: unlabelled remains AMNH from Bradfield quarry (small quarry prepared for the 9th International Carboniferous Congress, May 1979, at Urbana, Illinois; location: along Highway 41; $\frac{1}{8}$ mile up the highway from discovery site of Mecca Quarry Shale, just south of Section line 29, T15 N, R8W; Wabash Township; Parke County, Indiana, USA), Mecca Quarry Shales, Kansas, USA, and found in 1979 (lower jaw, tail and unidentified remains). BMNH P. 62284/5 and unlabelled specimens BMNH from the Upper Carboniferous (Westphalian D) of the Carbondale Fm, Bethel Quarry, Pike County, Indiana, USA (various skeletal remains, unprepared).

Ornithoprion nevadensis Wheeler, 1938: BMNH P. 22976 from the Lower Permian of Koipato Fm, University of Nevada locality 28, Rochester District, Lovelock quadrangle, Pershing County, Nevada, USA (cast of symphysial tooth whorl).

'*Orodus variabilis*' Newberry, 1875: AMNH 11545 (cotype) from the ?Carboniferous of Waverly Group, Vanceburg County, USA (1 tooth, 1 tooth fragment) and numerous BMNH teeth, not referred to in the paper.

Unidentified eugeneodontids (?*Caseodus*): unlabelled specimens AMNH from Ace Hill quarry, Upper Permian, Queen-Hill Shale-Virgilian (scattered teeth and imprints with partial jaws) and (also AMNH) from Mecca Quarry Shales (Liverpool cyclothem; Linton Formation; Des Moines Series), Westphalian Upper C (or Lower D), Pennsylvanian localities, Indiana, USA (neurocranium and posterior visceral elements?).

References

AGASSIZ, J. L. R. 1833–44. *Recherches sur les poissons fossiles.* Petitpierre, Neuchâtel et Soleure, 5 vols, 1–1420.

BENDIX-ALMGREEN, S. E. 1966. New investigations on *Helicoprion* from the Phosphoria Formation of south-east Idaho, U.S.A. *Det Kongelige Danske Videnskabernes Selskab*, **14**, 1–54, 15 pls.

BENDIX-ALMGREEN, S. E. 1975a. Palaeovertebrate faunas of Greenland. *In*: ESCHER, A. & WATT, W. S. (eds) *Geology of Greenland.* The Geological Survey of Greenland, Copenhagen, 536–573.

BENDIX-ALMGREEN, S. E. 1975b. The paired fins and shoulder girdle in *Cladoselache*, their morphology and phyletic significance. Problèmes actuels de paléontology – évolution des vértebrés. *Colloque international C.N.R.S.* **218**(1973), 111–123, 4 pls.

BENDIX-ALMGREEN, S. E. 1976. Fossil fishes from the marine late Paleozoic of Holm Land-Amdrup Land, north-east Greenland. *Meddelelser om Grønland.* **195**, 1–38, 2 pls.

BENDIX-ALMGREEN, S. E. 1983. *Carcharodon megalodon* from the Upper Miocene from Denmark, with comments on elasmobranch tooth enameloid: coronoin. *Bulletin of the Geological Society of Denmark*, **32**, 1–32.

BONAPARTE, C. L. 1838 Synopsis vertebratorum systematis. *Nuovi Annali delle Scienze naturali (Bologna)*, **2**, 105–133.

BRANSON, C. C. 1935. A labyrinthodont from the Lower Gondwana of Kahmir and a new edestid from the Permian of the Salt Range. *Memoirs of the Connecticut Academy of Arts and Sciences*, **9**, 19–26, 2 pls.

CHANG, M.-M. & JIN, F. 1996. Mesozoic fish faunas of China. *In*: ARRATIA, G. & VIOHL, G. (eds) *Mesozoic Fishes 1 – Systematics and Palaeoecology.* Dr F. Pfeil, Munich, 461–478.

CHANG, M. & MIAO, D. 2004. An overview of Mesozoic fishes in Asia. *In*: ARRATIA, G. & TINTORI, A. (eds) *Mesozoic Fishes 3 – Systematics, Paleoenvironment and Biodiversity.* Dr F. Pfeil, Munich, 535–563.

COPE, E. D. 1894 New and little known Paleozoic and Mesozoic fishes. *Journal of the Academy of Natural Sciences of Philadelphia*, **2**, 427–448, 18 pls.

COPE, K. H., UTGAARD, J. E., MASTERS, J. M. & FELDMANN, M. 2005. The fauna of the Clayton Formation (Paleocene, Danian) of southern Illinois: a case of K/T survivorship and Danian recovery. *Bulletin of the Mizunami Fossil Museum*, **32**, 97–108.

EASTMAN, C. R. 1902. On *Campyloprion*, a new form of *Edestus*-like dentition. *Geological Magazine*, **4**, 148–152, pl. 8.

EATON, T. H., JR. 1962. Teeth of edestid sharks. *University of Kansas Publications Museum of Natural History*, **12**, 349–362.

FOREY, P. L. 1998. History of coelacanth fishes. Chapman & Hall, London, 419 pp.

HAUTMANN, M. & NÜTZEL, A. 2005. First record of a heterodont bivalve (Mollusca) from the Early Triassic: palaeoecological significance and implications for the 'Lazarus problem'. *Palaeontology*, **48**, 1131–1138.

HAY, O. P. 1907. A new genus and species of fossil shark related to *Edestus* Leidy. *Science, New Series*, **26**, 22–24.

HAY, O. P. 1909. On the nature of *Edestus* and related genera, with description of one new genus and three new species. *Proceedings of the United States National Museum*, **37**(1699), 43–61.

HAY, O. P. 1930. Second bibliography and catalogue of the fossil Vertebrata of North America. *Publications Carnegie Institution, Washington*, **390**. 2 vols i–viii + 1–916 (1929); i–xiv + 1–1074 (1930).

HUXLEY, T. 1880. On the application of the laws of evolution to the arrangement of the Vertebrata, and more particularly of the Mammalia. *Proceedings of the Zoological Society of London*, **1880**, 649–662.

JAEKEL, O. 1899. Ueber die Organisation der Petalodonten. *Zeitschrift der deutschen geologischen Gesellschaft*, **51**, 258–298, pls 14–15.

KARPINSKY, A. 1899. Ueber die Reste von Edestiden und die neue Gattung *Helicoprion*. *Verhandlungen der kaiserlichen Russischen Mineralogischen Gesellschaft, Serie 2*, **36**, 1–111.

KARPINSKY, A. P. 1922. *Helicoprion ivanovi* n. sp. *Bulletin of the Academy of Sciences, St. Petersburg*, **16**, 369–378.

DE KONINCK, L. G. 1844. *Description des animaux fossiles que se trouvent dans le terrain carbonifère de Belgique*, 1–4, Liège. i–iv + 1–716, atlas, 60 pls.

LAMBE, L. M. 1916. Report of the vertebrate palaeontologist. *Geologial Survey of Canada, Summary Report*, 1915, 193–198.

LEIDY, J. 1855. Indications of five species, with two new genera, of extinct Fishes. *Proceedings of the Academy of Natural Sciences of Philadelphia*, **7**, 414.

MACLEOD, N., RAWSON, P. F., FOREY, P. L. ET AL. 1997. The Cretaceous–Tertiary biotic transition. *Journal of the Geological Society*, **154**, 265–292.

MISSUNA, A. 1908. Ueber eine neue *Edestus*-Art aus den Karbon-Ablagerungen der Umgebungen von Kolomna. *Bulletin of the Society of Naturalists, Moscow (new series)*, **21**, 529–535.

MOY-THOMAS, J. A. & MILES, R. S. 1971. *Palaeozoic Fishes*. (2nd ed.) Chapman & Hall, London.

MUTTER, R. J. 2003. Reinvestigation of the Early Triassic ichthyofauna of the Sulphur Mountain Formation (BC, Canada). *Canadian Paleontology Conference Proceedings*, **1**, 32–36.

MUTTER, R. J. 2004. Fossile Fische aus den kanadischen Rocky Mountains. *Vierteljahrsschrift der Naturforschenden Gesellschaft in Zürich*, **149**, 51–58.

MUTTER, R. J. 2005. Re-assessment of the genus *Helmolepis* Stensiö 1932 (Actinopterygii: Platysiagidae) and the Evolution of Platysiagids in the Early-Middle Triassic. *Swiss Journal of Geosciences*, **98**, 271–280.

MUTTER, R. J. & NEUMAN, A. G. 2006. An enigmatic chondrichthyan with Palaeozoic affinities from the Lower Triassic of western Canada. *Acta Palaeontologica Polonica*, **51**, 271–282.

MUTTER, R. J., NEUMAN, A. G. & DE BLANGER, K. 2006. Elasmobranchs from the Lower Triassic Sulphur Mountain Formation near Wapiti Lake (BC, Canada). *Zoological Journal of the Linnean Society*, **149**, 309–337.

NEUMAN, A. G. 1992. Lower and Middle Triassic Sulphur Mountain Formation Wapiti Lake, British Columbia: summary of geology and fauna. *Contributions to Natural Science, Royal British Columbia Provincial Museum*, **16**, 1–12.

NEUMAN, A. G. & MUTTER, R. J. 2005. *Helmolepis cyphognathus*, sp. nov., a new platysiagid actinopterygian from the Lower Triassic Sulphur Mountain Formation (British Columbia, Canada). *Canadian Journal of Earth Sciences*, **42**, 25–36.

NEWBERRY, J. S. 1875. Description of fossil fishes. *Geological Survey of Ohio*, **2**, 1–64.

NEWBERRY, J. S. 1888. On the structure and relations of *Edestus*, with a description of a gigantic new species. *Annals of the New York Academy of Sciences*, **4**, 113–122, pls. 4–6.

NEWBERRY, J. S. & WORTHEN, A. H. 1870. Descriptions of fossil vertebrates. *Geological Survey of Illinois*, **1870**, 347–374.

NIELSEN, E. 1932. Permo-Carboniferous fishes from East Greenland. *Meddelelser om Grønland*, **86**, 1–63, 16 pls.

NIELSEN, E. 1952. On new or little known Edestidae from the Permian and Triassic of East Greenland. *Palaeozoologica Groenlandica*, **6**, 1–55, 13 pls.

OBRUCHEV, D. M. 1951. A new discovery of *Edestus protospirata* Trautschold. *Doklady Akademii Nauk SSSR*, **81**, 273–276, 1 pl. [in Russian.]

OBRUCHEV, D. V. 1953. Studies on edestids and the works of A. P. Karpinski. U.S.S.R. Academy of Sciences. *Works of the Palaeontological Institute Publications*, **45**, 1–86 [in Russian.]

OGG, J. G. 2004. Chapter 17 – The Triassic Period. *In*: GRADSTEIN, F. M., OGG, J. G. & SMITH, A. G. (eds) *A Geologic Time Scale*. Cambridge University Press, Cambridge, 271–306.

ROMER, A. S. 1960. *Bradyodonti*. McGraw-Hill. *Encyclopaedia Science and Technology*, **2**, 315–316.

SCHAEFFER, B. & MANGUS, M. 1976. An Early Triassic fish assemblage from British Columbia. *Bulletin of the American Museum of Natural History*, **156**, 517–563.

SCHULTZE, H.-P. 2004. Mesozoic sarcopterygians. *In*: ARRATIA, G. & TINTORI, A. (eds) *Mesozoic Fishes 3 – Systematics, Paleoenvironment and Biodiversity*. Dr F. Pfeil, Munich, 463–492.

STEMMERIK, L., BENDIX-ALMGREEN, S. E. & PIASECKI, S. 2003. The Permian-Triassic boundary in central East Greenland: past and present views. *Bulletin of the Geological Society of Denmark*, **48**, 159–167.

STENSIÖ, E. 1962. Origine et nature des écailles placoïdes et des dents. Problèmes actuels de paléontologie – évolution des vertébrés. *Colloques internationaux du centre national de la recherche scientifique*, **104**, 75–85.

ST JOHN, O. H. & WORTHEN, A. H. 1875. Descriptions of fossil fishes. *Geological Survey of Illinois*, **6**, 245–488.

TRAUTSCHOLD, H. 1879. Die Kalkbrüche von Mjatschkowa – Eine Biographie des oberen Bergkalks. *Nouveaux Mémoires de la Société Impériale des Naturalistes de Moscou*, **14**, 3–82.

TRAUTSCHOLD, H. A. 1888. Ueber *Edestus protopirata*, Trd. *Zeitschrift der deutschen geologischen Gesellschaft*, **40**, 750–753.

TWITCHETT, R. J. 2001 Incompleteness of the Permian-Triassic fossil record: a consequence of productivity decline? *Geological Journal*, **36**, 341–353.

VEEVERS, J. J., CONAGHAN, P. J. & SHAW, S. E. 1994. Turning point in Pangean environmental history at the Permian/Triassic (P/Tr) boundary. *In*: KLEIN, G. D. (ed.) Pangea: Paleoclimate, Tectonics, and Sedimentation During Accretion, Zenith, and Breakup of a Supercontinent. Boulder, Colorado, *Geological Society of America Special Paper*, **288**, 187–196.

WHEELER, H. E. 1938. Paleogeographic significance of *Helicoprion* in Nevada and California. *Proceedings of the Geological Society of America*, **1937**, 298.

WIGNALL, P. B. & BENTON, M. J. 1999. Lazarus taxa and fossil abundance at times of biotic crisis. *Journal of the Geological Society, London*, **156**, 453–456.

WOODWARD, H. 1886. On a remarkable ichthyodorulite from the Carboniferous series, Gascoyne, Western Australia. *Geological Magazine*, **3**, 1–7, 1 pl.

WOODWARD, A. S. 1917. On a new species of *Edestus* from the Upper Carboniferous of Yorkshire. *Quarterly Journal of the Geological Society*, **7**, 1–5.

ZANGERL, R. 1966. A new shark of the family Edestidae, *Ornithoprion hertwigi* from the Pennsylvanian Mecca and Logan Quarry shales of Indiana. *Fieldiana (Geology)*, **16**, 1–43.

ZANGERL, R. 1979. New chondrichthyans from the Mazon Creek fauna (Pennsylvanian) of Illinois. *In*: NITECKI, M. H. (ed.) *Mazon Creek Fossils*. Academic Press, New York, 449–500.

ZANGERL, R. 1981. Chondrichthyes I - Paleozoic Elasmobranchii. *In*: SCHULTZE, H.-P. (ed.) *Handbook of Paleoichthyology*. Gustav Fischer Verlag, Stuttgart, i–iii + 1–115.

ZHANG, M. 1976. A new helicoprionid shark from Xizang. *Scientia Geologica Sinica*, **10**, 332–336, pl. 2 [in Chinese with English summary.]

ZIDEK, J. 1976. Oklahoma Paleontology – Part V: Chondrichthyes. *Oklahoma Geology Series*, **36**, 175–192.

The first Triassic lungfish from South America (Santa Maria Formation, Paraná Basin) and its bearing on geological correlations within Pangaea

M. RICHTER[1] & C. E. V. TOLEDO[2]

[1]*Natural History Museum, Department of Palaeontology, Cromwell Road, London SW7 5BD, UK (e-mail: M.Richter@nhm.ac.uk)*

[2]*Universidade Estadual Paulista – UNESP/IGCE, CP 178, CEP 13506-900 Rio Claro, Brazil (e-mail: cetoledo@rc.unesp.br)*

Abstract: The Triassic fish faunas of the Southern Hemisphere are only known from a few sedimentary basins and the most productive sites are those from the Karoo Supergroup, in South Africa and the Sydney Basin of Australia. A single lungfish tooth plate ascribed to *Ptychoceratodus* cf. *philippsi* was recovered from Late Triassic (Carnian) red beds of southern Brazil and is described herein. This find extends to South America the palaeogeographic distribution of the genus, which occurs in the Early Triassic of Australia and South Africa and the Middle/Late Triassic of Europe and Late Triassic of Madagascar and India. The presence of this dipnoan solely in the uppermost part of the Santa Maria Formation suggests that the migration of *Ptychoceratodus* towards the Paraná Basin began not before the late Induan/early Olenekian (late Early Triassic). At that time, more humid (monsoonal) conditions prevailed in what is now southern Brazil, compared to semi-arid/desert conditions that dominated the Late Permian and possibly the earliest Early Triassic (the latter presumably not represented in the Paraná Basin).

The Mesozoic fish record of South America has been recently revised by López-Arbarello (2004). Triassic lungfishes from Gondwana are known from Africa, Australia, Antarctica, India and Madagascar and comprise isolated tooth plates, fragments of jaw, some cranial bones and some complete specimens.

The first occurrence of Triassic lungfish in Brazil comes from the Santa Maria Formation, Rio Grande do Sul State and, except for the single tooth plate described herein, and a doubtful tooth plate fragment illustrated by Beltan *et al.* (1987), the Triassic record of lungfishes in South America is barren.

This is the second find only of Dipnoiformes in the State of Rio Grande do Sul. Previously, Palaeozoic lungfish remains (gnathorhizid tooth plates) from that state were reported by Richter & Langer (1998) in the Late Permian Rio do Rasto Formation. Further gnathorhizid remains come from the Late Permian Corumbataí Formation of São Paulo State (Toledo & Bertini 2005) also in southern Brazil.

The lungfish tooth plate was collected from red beds of the Santa Maria Formation at a recently discovered site in São João do Polêsine, State of Rio Grande do Sul (Fig. 1). Perez & Malabarba (2002) have described actinopterygian and chondrichthyan remains from this locality. This formation is best known for its Middle to Late Triassic tetrapod fauna (e.g. Barberena *et al.* 1985, 1991; Langer *et al.* 1999; Rubert & Schultz 2004) associated with plant remains of the *Dicroidium–Thinfeldia* flora (Bortoluzzi *et al.* 1983; see also McLoughlin 2001).

This is the first discovery of an association of Dipnoiformes, lower actinopterygians and possible amphibians within the Late Triassic Rosário do Sul Group. The deposits apparently represent a new biofacies within that geological unity, since no previously described site has yielded a similar association. Additionally to the tooth plate, fragmentary bones belonging to dipnoans and, a lower jaw of a large predator bearing massive labyrinthodont tusks, were collected at the site, but are yet to be described.

Fish remains preliminarily ascribed to palaeonisciforms and Perleidiformes associated with conchostracans and *Dicroidium* have been described by Lima *et al.* (1984) from claystones of the Passo das Tropas Member of the Santa Maria Formation. A similar association, but including amphibian and archosaurian remains, was described by Mancuso (2003) for the lacustrine black shales of Los Rastros Formation in the Ischigualasto–Villa Unión Basin of Argentina. No dipnoan remains have so far been reported from the Los Rastros Formation, nor from Chile, where Triassic fishes (Perleidiformes) occur in the marine sequences of Quebrada San Pedrito (Arratia & Schultze 1999).

From: CAVIN, L., LONGBOTTOM, A. & RICHTER, M. (eds) *Fishes and the Break-up of Pangaea*
Geological Society, London, Special Publications, **295**, 43–54.
DOI: 10.1144/SP295.4   0305-8719/08/$15.00 © The Geological Society of London 2008.

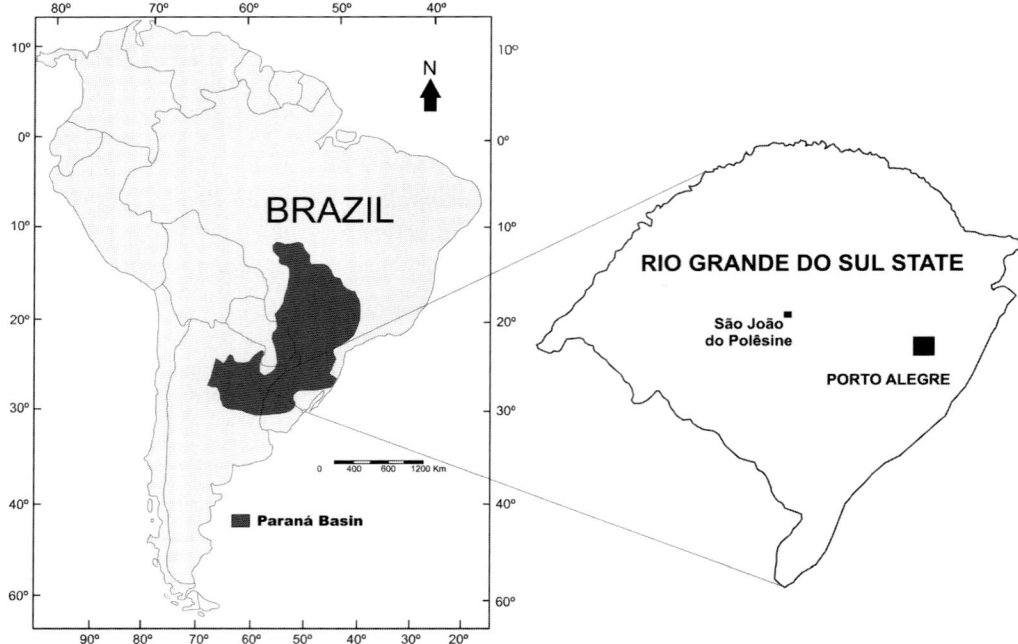

Fig. 1. Collecting site of specimen FZB/RS PV 3464, *Ptychoceratodus* cf. *philippsi*, in strata of the Santa Maria Formation in São João do Polêsine, southern Brazil.

The dipnoan from the Santa Maria Formation is, therefore, also the first Triassic record of this group, or any sarcopterygian fish of this age in South America. The main aim of this paper is to describe the tooth plate from the Santa Maria Formation and discuss the worldwide distribution of dipnoans during the Triassic period.

The Santa Maria Super-sequence and its connections to Africa

The name 'Santa Maria Beds' was proposed by Moraes Rego (1930) for siltstones and claystones within a dominantly sandy section within the Paraná Basin that occur in the central region of the State of Rio Grande do Sul, southern Brazil. These beds known today as the Santa Maria Formation, correspond to the middle part of the Rosário do Sul Group (Andreis *et al.* 1980), which includes the overlying Caturrita Formation (Rhaetic/Jurassic) and the underlying Sanga do Cabral Formation (Early Triassic).

The intracratonic Paraná Basin developed during the Palaeozoic and its deposits cover a wide area of southern Brazil, Uruguay, NE Argentina, Paraguay and also Western Namibia (Milani & Zalán 1997). According to Zerfass *et al.* (2005), the Santa Maria Formation belongs within the third-order Santa Maria Super-sequence, which is palaeogeographically connected to similar

strata deposited between the Ladinian and the Rhaetic in Namibia and South Africa. The Santa Maria Super-sequence is chrono-correlated with the South African Waterberg, Mid–Zambezi and Cabora–Bassa rift basins that were controlled by reactivated faults of the Damara–Katanga–Mozambique Mobile Belt during the Triassic. The Mesozoic fluvial and deltaic rocks of southern Brazil show a dominantly northeastward palaeo-current trend (Zerfass *et al.* 2003).

Zerfass *et al.* (2005) suggested a Sinemurian age for the Santa Maria 3 Sequence, assuming synchronicity with the African side. The palaeogeographic connections between Triassic deposits of south Brazil and South Africa were discussed by Zerfass *et al.* (2003, 2005), Langer (2005a, b) and others. Until the Permo-Triassic, the Paraná deposits covered a large area of southern Brazil, Uruguay, northeastern Argentina, Paraguay and also Western Namibia (Lavina 1991; Milani *et al.* 1998; Stollhoffen *et al.* 2000). However, an extensive NW–SE fracture system affected the Paraná Basin from the Palaeozoic until the Cretaceous, displacing blocks vertically and making it difficult to correlate the outcropping sites of the Santa Maria Formation.

Recent studies in southern Brazil by Zerfass *et al.* (2005) identified anastomosed faults and kinematic indicators like slickside lineations (striae and mineral fibres), conjugate shears, drag folds and displacement markers, all of which show that this region shares the same fracture pattern found in Namibian and South African sequences. This indicates that this wide region was affected by similar extensional faults (rift phase) started during the Early Triassic that eventually led to the opening of the southern Atlantic Ocean in the Early Cretaceous (Aptian).

Palaeoenvironment of the Santa Maria Formation

Rosa *et al.* (2004) studied the differences in litho and biofacies of alluvial deposits within the Santa Maria Formation. They found evidence that the sedimentation was controlled by meandering rivers with large flood plains that were affected by seasonal variations in the water table. As well as sequences representing canal and flood plain deposits, they were able to recognize levels within the Santa Maria Formation with palaeosoils and others with mud-cracks, so sub-aerial exposure of the ground was not infrequent. They suggested that the Santa Maria red beds were deposited in a palaeoenvironment similar to present day salt pan Etosha in Namibia (Buch & Rose 1996). In this large and depressed region, seasonal rains create a large but shallow lake that breaks into smaller alkaline lakes towards the dry season.

This interpretation is in agreement with computer-generated models of the Ladinian–Carnian climate based on geological studies of the northern hemisphere. Mutti & Weissert (1995) pointed out that Pangaea was divided symmetrically about the palaeoequator and this would be ideal condition for monsoonal circulation.

Biostratigraphy of the Santa Maria Formation

The biozonation of the tetrapod traditional 'local faunas' (Barberena *et al.* 1985; Schultz *et al.* 2000) from distinct localities is still in a state of flux (see also Abdala *et al.* 2001). A new correlation horizon based on ictidosaurid reptiles has been identified recently (Rubert & Schultz 2004) in the overlying Caturrita Formation (Carnian–Norian). In contrast with the meandering system recognized for the Santa Maria Formation, the sequence they have described was deposited by braided rivers, which is evidence of tectonic reactivation and at least periodical, plentiful rainfall (see Mutti & Weissert 1995).

Contrary to the situation in eastern Gondwana, the climate in southern Brazil was dry/arid during the Late Permian/Early Triassic (see Dias-da-Silva *et al.* 2004) but during the time of deposition of the Sanga do Cabral (late

Induan/early Olenekian) and the Santa Maria Formation (Middle to Late Triassic), it became more humid, favouring a diverse amphibian fauna.

A correlation table of Triassic deposits within Pangaea based on vertebrates remains largely tentative. According to Zerfass (pers. comm., 2006), the deposits in São João do Polêsine that yielded the dipnoan tooth plate, are stratigraphically above the level with rhynchosaurs, still within the Alemoa Member of the Santa Maria Formation, but below the strata containing small cynodonts and conifers (Caturrita Formation).

The sequence under consideration falls approximately within or after the 'Adamanian' (latest Carnian) Land-Vertebrate Faunachron (LVF) of Lucas (1998), which corresponds in time to the Blue Mesa Member of the Petrified Forest Formation in Arizona, the Lossiemouth Sandstone Formation in Scotland and the Ischigualasto Formation in Argentina. The Triassic Molteno and Elliot formations in South Africa were considered problematic for correlation (Lucas & Hancox 2001) and there are no studies correlating the *Ptychoceratodus*-bearing strata with South American sequences, although Kemp (1996) includes the Orange Free State locality in the *Cynognathus* Zone (upper Early Triassic).

Schultz (2005) has recently discussed the major problems in the biostratigraphic record of African and South American tetrapod faunas and argued that on the basis of tetrapods, the Ischigualasto–Santa Maria assemblages are undoubtly Late Carnian. Correlation charts of South American tetrapod faunas are given in Figures 2 and 3.

Langer (2005*b*) has also argued that Lucas' LVFs were not defined on the basis of a type assemblage and that many of the referred sequences comprise dubious index fossils; therefore its adoption could lead to misinterpretation of the duration and correct correlation between the faunal associations. He advocated instead, that an Ischigualaschian faunachron, based on the first appearance of the rhynchosaur *Hyperodapedon* and the first appearance of the dicynodont *Jachaleria*, is a more reliable tool for correlations within Pangaea. Considering the stratigraphic position of the collecting site, the dipnoan dental plate from the Santa Maria Formation falls within this faunachron, but it could potentially still be found in earlier sequences, possibly in the Early Triassic Sanga do Cabral Formation.

Systematic palaeontology

Order Dipnoiformes Müller 1845
Family Ptychoceratodontidae Martin 1982
Genus *Ptychoceratodus* Jaekel 1926
Ptychoceratodus cf. *philippsi* (Agassiz 1838).
  (Figs 4, 5d)

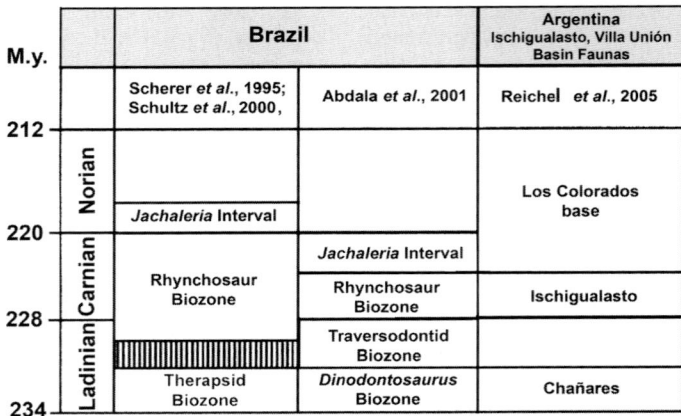

Fig. 2. Combined lithostratigraphic and biostratigraphic scheme for Middle to Late Triassic strata of south-western South America, based on Reichel *et al.* (2005). Specimen FZB/RS 3464, ascribed to *Ptychoceratodus* cf. *philippsi*, comes from an under-explored short sequence laying above the Rhynchosaur Biozone and bellow the *Jachaleria* Interval within the Alemoa Member of the Santa Maria Formation (Zerfass, pers. comm. 2006). The 'Jachaleria' interval may be unsustainable (C. L. Schultz, 2006, pers. comm.)

1838 *Ceratodus philippsi* Agassiz, p. 135, Tab. 19, Fig. 17
1887–1890 *C. phillipsi* Zittel, p.133
1891 *C. phillipsi* Woodward, p. 269–270
1908 *C. ornatus* Broom, p. 253–254, pl. 12, Fig. 4
1980 *C. gypsatus* Dziewa, p. 147–149, Fig. 3

1982 *Ceratodus* cf. *C. philipsi* Kemp, p. 13–34, Tab. 2
1982 '*Ptychoceratodus*' *philipsi* Martin, p. 612
1983 *Ptychoceratodus philipsi* Monod *et al.* Figs. 3, 3c
1984 '*Ptychoceratodus*' *phillipsi* Martin, p. 238

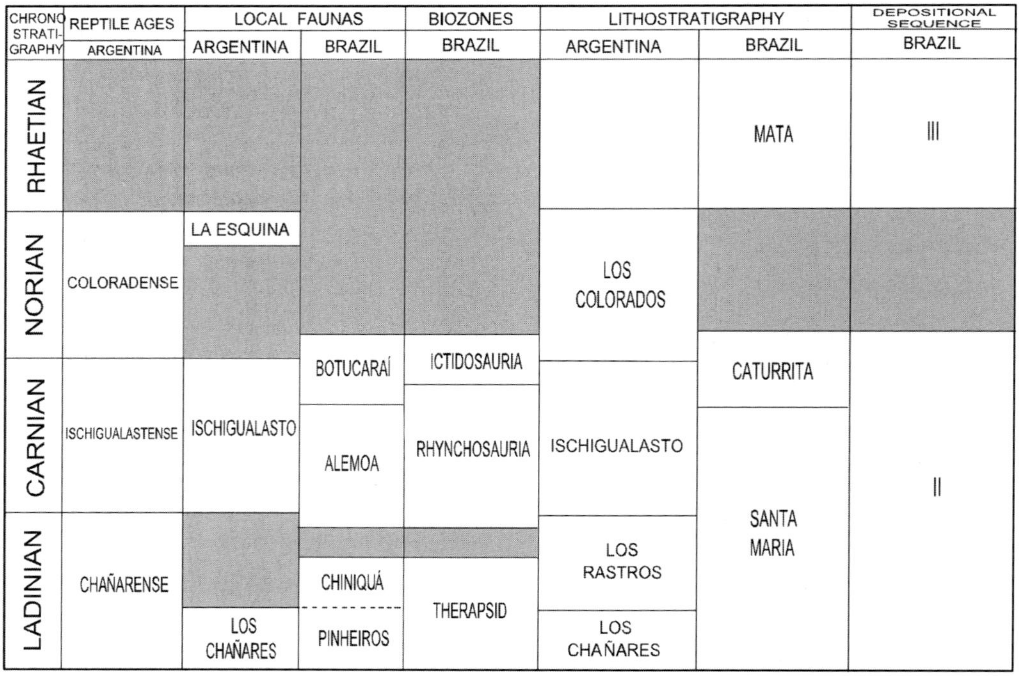

CHRONOSTRATI-GRAPHY	REPTILE AGES	LOCAL FAUNAS		BIOZONES	LITHOSTRATIGRAPHY		DEPOSITIONAL SEQUENCE
	ARGENTINA	ARGENTINA	BRAZIL	BRAZIL	ARGENTINA	BRAZIL	BRAZIL
RHAETIAN						MATA	III
NORIAN	COLORADENSE	LA ESQUINA			LOS COLORADOS	CATURRITA	
CARNIAN	ISCHIGUALASTENSE	ISCHIGUALASTO	BOTUCARAÍ	ICTIDOSAURIA	ISCHIGUALASTO		II
CARNIAN			ALEMOA	RHYNCHOSAURIA		SANTA MARIA	
LADINIAN	CHAÑARENSE		CHINIQUÁ		LOS RASTROS		
LADINIAN		LOS CHAÑARES	PINHEIROS	THERAPSID	LOS CHAÑARES		

Fig. 3. Triassic chronostratigraphy of southern South America (from Rubert & Schultz 2004).

Fig. 4. Pterygoid tooth plate of *Ptychoceratodus* cf. *philippsi* (FZB/RS PV 3464) from the Santa Maria Formation (Carnian) of Brazil. (**a**) labio-occlusal view. Arrows indicate position of ridges, including 1, 4 and 5, which are broken. Petrodentine canals indicated 'den'; (**b**) medial view; (**c**) view of fractured anteriormost ridge showing canals in the petrodentine canals -'den'; (**d**) lingual view of second and third ridges showing unworn denticles (arrows); (**e**) view of occlusal face, showing the denticle-free area of the grinding surface of the plate; (**f**) basal view showing remains of the bone to which the plate is attached. Scale bars = 5 mm.

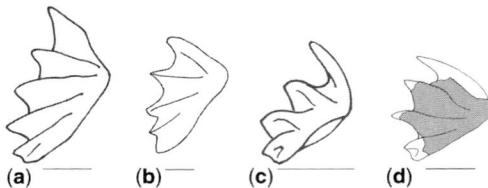

Fig. 5. Outline of upper tooth plates from right side of: (**a**) *Ptychoceratodus serratus* from Europe; (**b**) *P. philippsi* from Australia; (**c**) *P. rectangulus* from Germany (line drawing based on pl. 4, fig. 2 of Linck 1936) and; (**d**) tentative reconstruction of *P.* cf. *philippsi* based on specimen FZB/RS PV 3464 from the Santa Maria Formation, Carnian from Brazil. Darkened area indicates actual extent of preservation of the plate (see Fig. 3a). Scales: a = 30 mm; b = 10 mm; c = 10 mm; d = 10 mm.

1991 *Ceratodus* cf. *C. phillipsi* (partim) Kemp, p. 470, 472
1992 *C. philippsi* Schultze, p. 276–277
1992 ? *C. ornatus* Schultze, p. 270–271
1996 *Ptychoceratodus philippsi* Kemp p. 411, figs. 1–3
See also Schultze (1992) for a comprehensive synonymy list.

Ptychoceratodus philippsi dental plates diagnosis. (according to Kemp, 1996): Tooth plates high crowned with restricted pulp cavity and ridges originating anteriorly; punctuations simple and arranged without pattern; occlusal tubercles absent; crest of ridge 1 curved in upper jaw tooth plates and straight in the lower jaw; slope on ridge 1 present in both jaws; enamel to bone junction on the laial face of both jaws is straight; upper and lower tooth plates close but not contiguous in the midline.

Lectotype. SMNS 55260, skull bones and associated lower jaw tooth plate (Kemp 1996, fig. 1).

Note: Martin *et al.* (1999) claim that the holotype described by Agassiz (1838) is not lost, but housed in the Museum of Natural History in Neuchâtel.

Type locality and horizon of lectotype. Winnaarsbaken Farm, Orange Free State, South Africa, Channel Bonebed, *Cynognathus* Zone, upper Early Triassic (Kemp 1996).

Material. At Fundação Zoobotânica do Rio Grande do Sul in Porto Alegre, under registration number FZB(RS) PV 3464. Fragmentary upper (pterygoid) right tooth plate (Fig. 4).

Collecting locality and horizon. Ravine at 'Sítio Buriol' (Buriol mini-farm) in the municipality of São João do Polêsine, Rio Grande do Sul State, Brazil. Co-ordinates: 29°39′34.5″S and 53°25′47.5″W.

Red beds of the Alemoa Member, topmost Santa Maria Formation, Rosário do Sul Group, Late Triassic (Carnian).

Description. The fragmentary tooth plate FZB/RS 3464, measuring 16 mm in length and 15 mm in width is of a generalized triangular design with ridges originating anteriorly (Fig. 4a; 5d). The specimen corresponds to an upper (pterygoid) tooth plate from the right side of the fish. Although badly broken, it shows the remains of five high ridges (Fig. 4a) bearing sharp crests and deep furrows (Fig. 4b–d). The ridges are made up of petrodentine whose canals can be seen in broken surfaces of some ridges (Fig. 4a, c); each ridge bears a single row of unworn denticles lingually (Fig. 4d), outside the occlusal area. Each denticle is placed between two growth lines. The biting (worn) area is confined to the medial side of the occlusal area (Fig. 4e), away from the deep, labial furrows. The dental plate is attached to the fragmentary pterygoid (Fig. 4f). The angle between ridges is approximately 20°.

The plate original length is estimated in *c.* 20 mm, which falls inside the known range of the dental plates sizes of the most complete specimens of *P. philippsi* available (from Australia and South Africa), a species whose tooth plate is estimated to have reached 70 mm in length. The angle between ridges in the Brazilian fossil is likewise acute.

Systematic comparisons. The dental plate from Brazil bears resemblance with *Ptychoceratodus* cf. *philippsi*, a species found in Europe, Australia, Africa, India and Madagascar. The tooth plates of this species have five ridges in the upper jaw and four in the lower. According to Kemp (1996) the last ridge in *P. philippsi* is almost parallel to the lingual face; the tooth plates are high crowned with a restricted pulp cavity and ridges originating anteriorly, punctuations simple and arranged without pattern; denticles absent on occlusal surface; medio-lingual keel present; medial edge of both jaws forms a wide curve; crest of ridge 1 curved in upper jaw tooth plates and straight in lower jaws; slope on ridge 1 present in both jaws; enamel to bone junction on the basal face of both jaws is straight; pterygopalatine process present; pterygopalatine sulcus shallow; prearticular sulcus double (anterior sulcus vestigial), upper and lower tooth plates close but not contiguous in the midline. Tooth plates and associated jaw bones are short and strong, triangular in outline, with high ridges and with a narrow occlusal surface.

We found strong similarities between the Brazilian material and the South African *Ptychoceratodus phillipsi* described by Kemp (1996). However, Martin *et al.* (1999) suggested that the small dental plates described by Kemp may not belong to that species; they claim that the dental plates of juvenile specimens of different species are more similar than the plates of adult individuals of distinct species (see also Martin 1982).

P. philippsi differs from *Ptychoceratodus serratus* (Schultze 1981) and *Ptychoceratodus retangulus* (Linck 1936) from Europe in characters of jaws, dental plates and skull bone pattern. A comparison of pterygoid tooth plates of *P. philippsi*, *P. serratus* and *P. rectangulus* and the dental plate from the Santa Maria Formation in Brazil is provided (Fig. 5).

P. hislopianus (Oldham 1878) re-described and figured by Martin *et al.* 1999 from Maleri Formation, of Madagascar has large tooth plates with the labial part of the ridges not crushing, five cutting radiating ridges, the inner angle obtuse; the lingual edge straight or slightly curved, contrary to the Brazilian material. Some denticles are present on the labial unworn part of the ridge of small, young tooth plates and the first notch is broad (see Martin *et al.* 1999).

P. acutus (Priem 1924) differs from the tooth plate described here by having large tooth plates, with the ridges being sharp and straight (see Martin *et al.* 1999).

However, the systematic affinities of isolated ceratodontid/ptychoceratodid-type tooth plates, which are abundant worldwide, remain largely tentative or unresolved. Kemp (2002) studied the development of the dental plates of the extant species *Neoceratodus forsteri* from Australia and observed that the shape of the upper and lower tooth plates changes during the life time of the specimens reared in her laboratory. The dental plates in early stages of ontogenetic development consists of separate sharp cusps that merge later on with one another and with the underlying bone to form the tooth plates.

Morphogenesis, according to that author, "involves changes in every dimension, area, depth, angles between ridges, number of ridges, and number of cusps" (Kemp 2002, p. 231). If this is true for this extant species, it is reasonable to assume that the same wide range of unstable parameters were also present in extinct species of many lungfishes. For instance, the biometry of the ridges of the tooth plates (see Vorobyeva & Minikh 1968) or, ratios of length and breadth have not been useful to separate Australian extinct and extant Neoceratodontidae species (Kemp 1997). As Kemp pointed out, "angles (between ridges) are not valid taxonomic characters, unless derived from a large statistical sample (...) and

cusps, or denticles, at the labial extremities of the ridges are equally invalid as taxonomic determinants. All lungfishes with tooth plates based on radiating ridges have cusped or denticulated tooth plates at some stage in the life cycle and the structures are part of the continuing growth process of all." (Kemp 1997, p. 731).

Systematic comparisons of the fragmentary dental plate from Brazil are therefore hindered by these difficulties and the identification of the single specimen available is accordingly provisional at the species level.

World-record of *Ptychoceratodus* and remarks on some related dipnoan genera from the Triassic

The palaeogeographic distribution of the genus *Ptychoceratodus* (Fig. 6) includes records from the Early, Middle and Late Triassic. Below is an overview of the main sites where *Ptychoceratodus* tooth plates have been found.

Europe

Large dipnoans belonging to the genus *Ptychoceratodus* were first described from the Middle Triassic of Europe (Switzerland) as *Cerctodus serratus* (Agassiz 1838), but the holotype is apparently lost. Schultze (1981) studied well-preserved lungfish material from the Keuper (Middle/Late Triassic) of Germany and ascribed it to *Ptychoceratodus serratus*, providing an extensive list of synonyms and comparisons for related materials found in Germany, Russia, Madagascar and Australia.

P. serratus pterygoid (upper) tooth plates (Fig. 4a) have 5 high ridges and prearticular (lower) plates have 5, with the posterior-most one being flatter (Schultze 1981, fig. 10). Both Schultze (1981) and Kemp (1996) recognize as valid the species *Ptychoceratodus rectangulus* (Linck 1936), from the Late Triassic ('mittlerer Keuper')

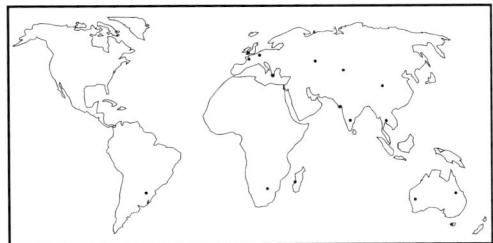

Fig. 6. Distribution of the Triassic genus *Ptychoceratodus* based on Martin (1982), Monod *et al.* (1983), Martin *et al.* (1999), Kemp (1996) and Lopez-Arbarello (2004).

of Germany, known from skull roof bones and many tooth plates.

Africa

The Triassic record of lungfishes in Africa comprises the ceratodontids *Arganodus atlantis, Ceratodus arganensis* and *Microceratodus angolensis* (Teixeira 1954; Martin 1979; Marshall 1986). *Arganodus atlantis*, from the Late Triassic Morocco, was described by Martin (1979) but considered by Kemp (1998) to be as synonymous with *Asiatoceratodus*. The latter genus is also present in the Cretaceous of NE Brazil (Dutra & Malabarba 2001; Castro *et al.* 2004).

Northern Angola and the Karoo Supergroup (Cassanga Series, Early Triassic) yielded another apparently diverse, but poorly known fauna including the dipnoan *Microceratodus* (Murray 2000). Another Triassic locality at Farm Vaalbank, near Burgersdorp, Orange Free State (Early Triassic; upper Beaufort Series) produced a single taxa, namely *Ptychoceratodus philippsi* (Kemp 1996).

According to Antunes *et al.* (1990), dipnoans are represented in the Early Triassic of Angola by a single taxon, namely *Ceratodus angolensis* described by Teixeira (1949) and re-described and assigned to *Microceratodus* by Teixeira (1954). Teixeira (1978) ascribed this small lungfish, known by complete specimens, to *Microceratodus angolensis*. *Microceratodus*, according to Antunes *et al.* (1990) based on the skull roofs, is close to the ancestry of the genus *Neoceratodus*.

Madagascar

The Triassic lungfish fauna from Madagascar comprises *Paraceratodus germaini* and *Beltanodus ambilobensis* (Marshall 1986; Antunes *et al.* 1990; Beltan 1996); *Ptychoceratodus* cf. *hislopianus* and *P. acutus* (Martin *et al.* 1999).

According to Martin *et al.* (1999), *Ptychoceratodus* cf. *hislopianus* from Madagascar has five cutting ridges arranged in a radiating pattern and the inner angle between ridges is clearly obtuse. An obtuse inner angle is also recorded for *P. ornatus* (Early Triassic–South Africa). However, the interrelationship of *P. ornatus* with the species from India and Madagascar is not clear.

Martin *et al.* (1999) reported on two *Ptychoceratodus* species from Madagascar, namely *Ptychoceratodus* cf. *hislopianus* and *Ptychoceratodus acutus*. The former was described on the basis of the 5th ridge being always longer than the 4th as in the Indian material; the latter has four radiating, cutting ridges, the ridges being straight and the lingual edge slightly curved. The inner angle is obtuse. *Ptychoceratodus* cf. *hislopianus* and

P. acutus from the Late Triassic of Madagascar are closely related to *P. hislopianus* and to *P. virapa*, respectively, both from the continental Late Triassic of India (Martin *et al.* 1999).

No associated tooth plates are known for *Microceratodus angolensis* and *Paraceratodus germaini* (Triassic, SW Madagascar) and *Beltanodus ambilobensis* (Early Triassic, northern Madagascar) is known only by one isolated calvarium (Schultze 1981; Kemp, 1994).

India

The first record of *Ceratodus* from the Maleri Formation was established by Oldham (1859) with four species, *Ceratodus hislopianus, C. hunterianus, C. virapa* and *C. oblongus*. Miall (1878) considered the first three species valid, but not the last one. Jain *et al.* (1964) suggested that there are only two species of *Ceratodus* from the same geological unit, without naming them.

Jain (1968) described vomerine teeth of *Ceratodus* from the Maleri Formation (Late Triassic) of Deccan, two of the specimens probably representing new species.

Marshall (1986) recognized only one species of ceratodont from India, *Ceratodus hislopianus* (Late Triassic); Martin *et al.* (1999) reviewed the Indian material, ascribing previously described species to *Ptychoceratodus hislopianus* and *P. virapa*; *Ceratodus hunterianus* and *Ceratodus oblongus* were considered *nomina dubia*.

Australia

Australia has a good record of lungfish, showing the evolution from the Early Devonian (*Dipnorhynchus* – marine) to the Holocene (*Neoceratodus forsteri* – fresh water) (Ritchie 1981). The best-known Triassic fish faunas of Australia are those from the Sydney Basin. Three major faunas have been reported from that basin; these are, in stratigraphic order, the Gosford, Brookvale and St Peter's faunas. The Gosford fauna comes from the Narabeen Group, which is of Early Triassic age; the Brookvale fauna is derived from the Hawkesbury Group, which is dated as Anisian, and the St Peter's fauna is found in the Wianamatta Group of late Anisian age (Balme 1990). The genus *Gosfordia* is known from Gosford and Brookvale. As noted by Kemp (1991), ceratodont dipnoans are known from all three of these faunas.

The record of Triassic lungfish from Australia includes the families Sagenodontidae, Gnathorhizidae, Ceratodontidae, Neoceratodontidae and Ptychoceratodontidae (Kemp 1996, 1997). These include one indeterminate genus (Turner 1982); *Ceratodus formosus, Ceratodus avus* and *Gosfordia truncata* (Marshall 1986; Antunes *et al.* 1990; Long *et al.* 1982; Kemp 1994); *Ceratodus* cf. *C. phillipsi* and *Ceratodus* cf. *C. tiguidensis* (Long *et al.* 1982; Kemp 1996); *Aphelodus anapes* and *Namatozodia pitikanta* (Kemp 1993); *Ariguna formosa* (Kemp 1994) and *Archaeoceratodus avus* (Kemp 1997).

Other Triassic fish localities are not so well known, but some of them have yielded *Ptychoceratodus philippsi*, e.g., the Early Triassic of the Arcadia Formation of the Rewan Group in Queensland, the Knocklofty Formation of the Tasmania Basin, and the marine Blina Shale of the Canning Basin in Western Australia (Kemp 1996). This occurrence extends the geographic range of *Ptychoceratodus* to the Southern Hemisphere, and its stratigraphic range from the Middle to the Early Triassic.

According to Kemp (1996), *Ceratodus* cf. *C. philippsi* belongs to the genus *Ptychoceratodus*. The occurrences of *Ptychoceratodus philippsi* in the South Hemisphere are older than in Europe, since the occurrences in Australia and South Africa are just above the Permo-Triassic boundary (Kemp 1996).

Antarctica

Only a single lungfish tooth plate, provisionally referred to *Ceratodus*, is known from the Triassic of Antarctica (Young 1991). It comes from the lower part of the Fremouw Formation of Early Triassic age, which is well known for its fauna of amphibians and reptiles. According to Dziewa (1980), the material corresponds to a single fragmentary dental plate, showing three ridges, all sharply crested.

Conclusions

The fossil described herein represents one of the youngest recorded of the genus *Ptychoceratodus* worldwide and the first record of the family Ptychoceratodontidae in South America. This is also the first record of a Triassic dipnoiformes anywhere in this continent.

The single tooth plate found in the Santa Maria Formation is a valuable addition to the Mesozoic vertebrate fauna of southern Brazil. Although *Ptychoceratodus philippsi* occurs in assumed Early Triassic strata of South Africa (Kemp 1996) this information cannot be readily utilized to date the strata that have yielded *Ptychoceratodus* cf. *philippsi* from southern Brazil. In the absence of Lower Mesozoic rocks suitable for radiometric studies in southern Brazil (volcanic rocks are Late Jurassic/Early Cretaceous), correlation between Triassic deposits within this western part of Pangaea is mostly based on tetrapod biostratigraphy. The

sequence yielding *Ptychoceratodus* in Brazil corresponds to the Late Triassic (Carnian) Ischigualastian faunachron (see Langer 2005*b*).

There is also strong indication of substantial climate change from arid/desert conditions at the end of the Permian, towards the beginning of the sedimentation of the Santa Maria Formation (Ladinian). A monsoonal climate similar to the northern hemisphere (Mutti & Weissert 1995) affected the most recent deposits of this formation (Carnian), where *Ptychoceratodus* was collected. Substantial geological and palaeontological ancillary data point to the red beds stratigraphically above the rhynchosaurids level in Rio Grande do Sul, where the fossil was found, as being Late Triassic (Carnian/Norian) in age (see Zerfass *et al.* 2003, 2005).

The palaeogeographic distribution of *Ptychoceratodus* suggests an early radiation in the Early Triassic from Eastern Gondwanan areas of the Pangaea (Australia, Tasmania and South Africa) northwards (Europe, where it is represented by *P. serratus*). The *Ptychoceratodus* specimen found in the Late Triassic Santa Maria Formation suggests that this genus is a late arrival in South America.

The distribution of one group of spiders in geographically distant regions of Pangaea during the Late Triassic provides an example of a Pangaea-wide radiation of a non-vertebrate fauna possibly encouraged by similar climatic conditions (Selden *et al.* 1999). They described the oldest world record (Carnian) of fossil spiders from South Africa and the USA (Virginia) and correlated the Molteno Formation with the Cow Branch Formation.

Ptychoceratodus is considered the sister-group of *Gnathorhiza* (see Schultze & Chorn 1997) and gnathorhizids were present in the Paraná basin during the Late Permian (Richter & Langer 1998; Toledo & Bertini 2005). The presence of *Ptychoceratodus* in all continents (except Antarctica), suggests that this was one of the most successful Triassic dipnoan lineages.

There is no indication of marine sedimentation during the whole of the Triassic along present-day coastal Brazil, nor along the coast of South Africa. This indicates that this region of Pangaea remained united during this period. McLoughlin (2001) produced a comprehensive account of floristic changes from Late Palaeozoic to Mesozoic in that and other Gondwanan regions and provided a scheme for continental breakup episodes (*op. cit.*, p. 279). Continental drift-related basalts linked to the opening of the southern Atlantic Ocean have been radiometrically dated as Late Jurassic to Early Cretaceous (135–105 Ma). As with all known post-Devonian lungfish, the *Ptychoceratodus* tooth plate was found in freshwater deposits. The presence of this fish in the Late Triassic of Brazil contributes further strong biostratigraphic evidence that South America was joined with Africa and other Gondwanan continents at least until the Carnian.

MR is grateful to J. Ferigolo and A.-M. Ribeiro (Fundação Zoobotânica do Rio Grande do Sul) for the loan of the specimens described in this paper and for geological information about the collecting site. H. Zerfass has also provided valuable geological information and J. Kimmig helped with German translations. The initial study of the material was undertaken while MR was based at the Federal University of Rio de Janeiro supported by the National Council for Scientific and Technologic Development, Brazil (CNPq, proc. 30.5384/85–6); comparative studies were undertaken at the Natural History Museum in London and at UNESP/Rio Claro. CEVT is grateful to Dr. M. Borsuk–Bialynicka (Polish Academy of Science) for the comparative material from Poland and to FAPESP (Fundação de Amparo a Pesquisa do Estado de São Paulo, grant 01/12575–0).

References

ABDALA, N. F., RIBEIRO, A. M. & SCHULTZ, C. L. 2001. A rich cynodont fauna of Santa Cruz do Sul, Santa maria Formation (Middle-Late Triassic), southern Brazil. *Neues Jahrbuch für Geologie und Paläontologie Monstschefte*, **2001**, 669–687.

AGASSIZ, L. 1838. *Recherches sur les Poissons Fossiles.* Petitpierre, Neuchâtel, vol. 3, 73–140, pls.

ANDREIS, R. R., BOSSI, G. E. & MONTARDO, D. K. 1980. O Grupo Rosário do Sul (Triássico) no Rio Grande do Sul. *In*: Brazilian Congress of Geology, **31**, Camboriú. *Anais*, **2**, 659–673.

ANTUNES, M. T., MAISEY, J. G., MARQUES, M. M., SCHAEFFER, B. & THOMSON, K. S. 1990. Triassic fishes from the Cassange Depression (R. P. de Angola). *Ciências da Terra, Número Especial*, **1**, 1–64.

ARRATIA, G. & SCHULTZE, H.-P. 1999. Mesozoic Fishes from Chile. *In*: ARRATIA, G. & SCHULTZE, H.-P. (eds) *Mesozoic Fishes 2 – Systematics and Fossil Record.* Verlag Dr F. Pfeil, 565–593.

BALME, B. E. 1990. Australian Phanerozoic Timescales, 7. Triassic. Biostratigraphic charts and explanatory notes. *Bureau of Mineralogical Resources Records*, **37**, 1–28.

BARBERENA, M. C., ARAÚJO, D. C., LAVINA, E. L. & AZEVEDO, A. K. 1985. O estado atual de conhecimento sobre os tetrapodes permianos e triássicos do Brasil meridional. *In*: *MME–DNPM, Coletânea de Trabalhos Paleontológicos, série Geologia*, 27, 21–28.

BARBERENA, M. C., ARAÚJO, D. C., LAVINA, E. L. & FACCINI, U. F. 1991. The evidence for close apleofaunistic affinity between South America and Africa. *In*: *7th Gondwana Symposium, São Paulo, Proceedings*, 455–467.

BELTAN, L. 1996. Overview of systematics, paleobiology, and paleoecology of Triassic fishes of northwestern Madagascar. *In*: ARRATIA, G. & VIOHL, G. (eds) *Mesozoic Fishes – Systematics and Paleoecology.* Verlag Dr F. Pfeil, 479–500.

BELTAN, L., FRENEIX, S., JANVIER, P. & LOPEZ-PAULSEN, O. 1987. La faune triasique de la formation de Vitiacua dans la region de Villamontes (Department de Chuquisaca, Bolivie). *Neues Jahrbuch für Geologie und Paläontologie, Monatshefte*, **2**, 99–115.

BORTOLUZZI, C. A., GUERRA-SOMMER, M. & CAZZULO-KLEPZIG, M. 1983. Tafoflora triássica da Formação Santa Maria, RS, Brasil: I – equisetales, ginkgoales, coniferales e pteriodophylla. *In*: *MME–DNPM, Coletânea de Trabalhos Paleontológicos, Série Geologia*, **27**, 539–549.

BROOM, R. 1908. The fossil fishes of the Upper Karroo beds of South Africa. *Annals of the South African Museum*, **7**, 251–269.

BUCH, M. W. & ROSE, D. 1996. Mineralogy and geochemistry of the sediments of the Etosha Pan region in northern Namibia: A reconstruction of the depositional environment. *Journal of African Earth Sciences*, **22**, 355–378.

CASTRO, D. F., TOLEDO, C. E. V., SOUZA, E. P. & MEDEIROS, M. A. 2004. Nova ocorrência de *Asiatoceratodus* (Osteichthyes, Dipnoiformes) na Formação Alcântara, eo-Cenomaniano da Bacia de São Luís, MA, Brasil. *Revista Brasileira de Paleontologia*, **7**, 245–248.

DIAS-DA-SILVA, S., MARSICANO, C. & SCHULTZ, C. L. 2004. Early Triassic Temnospondyl Skull Fragments From Southern South America (Paraná Basin, Brazil). *Revista Brasileira de Paleontologia*, **8**, 165–172.

DUTRA, M. F. A. & MALABARBA, C. S. L. 2001. Peixes do Albiano–Cenomaniano do Grupo Itapecuru no Estado do Maranhão, Brasil. *In*: ROSSETTI, D. F., GÓES, A. M. & TRUCKENBRODT, W. (eds) *O Cretáceo da Bacia de São Luís-Grajaú.* Museu Paraense Emílio Goeldi, Belém (Coleção Friedrich Katzer), 191–208.

DZIEWA, T. J. 1980. Note on a dipnoan fish from the Triassic of Antarctica. *Journal of Paleontology*, **54**, 488–490.

JAEKEL, O. 1926. Zur Morphologie der Gebisse und Zähne. Vjschr. Zahnheilkde, 217–242, Berlin.

JAIN, S. L. 1968. Vomerine teeth of *Ceratodus* from the Maleri Formation (Upper Triassic, Deccan, India). *Journal of Paleontology*, **42**, 96–99.

JAIN, S. L., ROBINSON, P. L. & ROY CHOWDHURY, T. 1964. A new vertebrate fauna from the Triassic of the Deccan, India. *Quarterly Journal of the Geological Society, London*, **120**, 115–124.

KEMP, A. 1982. Australian Mesozoic and Cenozoic lungfish. *In*: RICH, P. V. & THOMSON, E. M. (eds) *The Fossil Vertebrate Record of Australia.* Clayton (Monash University Press), 133–143.

KEMP, A. 1991. Australian Mesozoic and Cenozoic lungfish. *In*: VICKERS-RICH, P., MONAGHAN, J. M., BAIRD, R. F. & RICH, T. (eds) *Vertebrate Palaeontology of Australasia*, 465–496.

KEMP, A. 1993. Problematic Triassic Dipnoans from Australia. *In*: LUCAS, S. G. & MORALES, M. (eds) *The Non-marine Triassic. New Mexico Museum of Natural History & Science Bulletin*, **3**, 223–227.

KEMP, A. 1994. Australian Triassic Lungfish Skulls. *Journal of Paleontology*, **68**, 647–654.

KEMP, A. 1996. Triassic lungfish from Gondwana. *In*: ARRATIA, G. & VIOHL, G. (eds) *Mesozoic Fishes – Systematics and Paleoecology*, 409–416.

KEMP, A. 1997. A revision of Australian Mesozoic and Cenozoic lungfish of the family Neoceratodontidae (Osteichthyes: Dipnoi), with a description of four new species. *Journal of Paleontology*, **71**, 713–733.

KEMP, A. 1998. Skulls of post-Palaeozoic lungfish. *Journal of Vertebrate Paleontology*, **18**, 43–63.

KEMP, A. 2002. Growth and hard tissue remodeling in the dentition of the Australian lungfish, *Neoceratodus forsteri* (Osteichthyes: Dipnoi). *Journal of Zoology, London*, **257**, 219–235.

LANGER, M. C. 2005a. Studies on continental Late Triassic tetrapod biochronology. I. The type locality of *Saturnalia tupiniquim* and the faunal succession in south Brazil. *Journal of South American Earth Sciences*, **19**, 205–218.

LANGER, M. C. 2005b. Studies on continental Late Triassic tetrapod biochronology. II. The Ischigualastian and a Carnian global correlation. *Journal of South American Earth Sciences*, **19**, 219–239.

LANGER, M. C., ABDALA, N. F., RICHTER, M. & BENTON, M. 1999. A sauropodomorph dinosaur from the Upper Triassic (Carnian) of South-Brazil. *Comptes Rendus de l'Academie de Sciences*, Paris, **329**, 511–517.

LAVINA, E. L. 1991. Geologia sedimentar e paleogeografia do Neopermiano e Eotriássico (intervalo Kazaniano-Scythiano) da Bacia do Paraná. PhD thesis, Universidade Federal do Rio Grande do Sul, Post-Graduate Course on Geosciences.

LIMA, M. C. S. L., RICHTER, M. & LAVINA, E. L. 1984. Paleoictiologia da Formação Santa Maria (Grupo Rosário do Sul), Triássico, RS, Brasil. *In*: *Congresso Brasileiro de Geologia, 33°, Rio de Janeiro, Sociedade Brasileira de Geologia*. Anais, **1**, 563–577.

LINCK, O. 1936. Ein Lebensraum von *Ceratodus* im Stubensandstein des Strombergs mit *Ceratodus rectangulus* n.sp. und anderen Arten. *Jahreshefte des Vereins für vateraländische Naturkunde in Württemberg*, **92**, 45–68.

LONG, J., TURNER, S. & KEMP, A. 1982. Contributions to Australian Fossil Fish Bioestratigraphy. *In*: *The Fossil Vertebrate Record of Australasia*, Monash University, Victoria, 119–143.

LÓPEZ-ARBARELLO, A. 2004. The record of Mesozoic fishes from Gondwana (excluding India and Madagascar). *In*: ARRATIA, G. & TINTORI, A. (eds) *Mesozoic Fishes 3 — Systematics, Paleoenvironments and Biodiversity*, 597–624.

LUCAS, S. G. 1998. Global Triassic tetrapod biostratigraphy and biochronology. *Palaeogeography, Palaeoclimatology, Palaeoecology*, **143**, 345–382.

LUCAS, S. G. & HANCOX, P. J. 2001. Tetrapod-based correlation of the nonmarine upper Triassic of southern Africa. *Albertiana*, **25**, 5–9.

MANCUSO, A. C. 2003. Continental fish taphonomy: a case study in the Triassic of Argentina. *Journal of South American Earth Sciences*, **16**, 275–286.

MARSHALL, C. R. 1986. A list of Fossil and Extant Dipnoans. *Journal of Morphology Supplement*, **1**, 15–23.

MARTIN, M. 1979. *Arganodus atlantis* et *Ceratodus arganensis*, deux nouveaux Dipneustes du Trias supérieur continental marocain. *Comptes Rendus de l'Academie de Sciences, Paris*, **289**, 89–92.

MARTIN, M. 1982. Nouvelles donnes sur la phylogenie et la systématique des dipneustes postpaleozoiques. *Comptes Rendus de l'Academie de Sciences, Paris*, **294**, 611–614.

MARTIN, M. 1984. Revision des Argonocontides et des Neoceratodontides (Dipnoi: Ceratoontiformes) du Crétacé africain. *Neues Jahrbuch für Geologie und Paläontologie, Abheilung*, **169**, 225–260.

MARTIN, M., BARBIERI, L. & CUNY, G. 1999. The Madagascan Mesozoic Ptychoceratodontids (Dipnoi) systematic relationships and paleobiogeographical significance. *Oryctos*, **2**, 3–16.

MCLOUGHLIN, S. 2001. The breakup history of Gondwana and its impact on pre-Cenozoic floristic provincialism. *Australasian Journal of Botany*, **49**, 271–300.

MIALL, L. C. 1878. On the genus *Ceratodus*, with special reference to the fossil teeth found at Maledi, Central India. *Memoirs of the Geological Survey of India, Paleontologia Indica, Series IV*, **1**(2), 9–17.

MILANI, E. J. & ZALÁN, P. V. 1997. An outline of geology and petroleum systems of the Paleozoic interior basins of South America. *Episodes*, **22**, 199–205.

MILANI, E. J., FACCINI, U. F., SCHERER, C. M., ARAÚJO, L. M. & CUPERTINO, J. A. 1998. Sequences and stratigraphic hierarchy of the Paraná Basin (Ordovician to Cretaceous), Southern Brazil. *Boletin IG-USP*, **29**, 125–173.

MONOD, O., MESHUR, M., MARTIN, M. & LYS, M. 1983. Découverte de dipneustes triasiques (Ceratodontiformes, Dipnoi) dans la formation de Cenger ("Arkoses rouges") du Taurus lycien (Turquie occidentale). *Géobios*, **16**, 161–168.

MORAES REGO, L. F. 1930. A geologia do petróleo no Estado de São Paulo. Rio de Janeiro. *Boletim Serviço Geológico Mineralógico do Brasil*, **6**, 1–110.

MÜLLER, J. 1845. Über den Bau und die Grenzen der Ganoiden und über das natürliche System der Fische. *Abhandlungen der Akademie der Wissenschaften zu Berlin*, **1844**, 117–216.

MURRAY, A. M. 2000. The Palaeozoic, Mesozoic and Early Cenozoic fishes of Africa. *Fish and Fisheries*, **1**, 111–145.

MUTTI, M. & WEISSERT, H. 1995. Triassic monsoonal climate and its signature in Ladinian-Carnian carbonate platforms (Southern Alps, Italy). *Journal of Sedimentary Research*, **B65**(3), 557–367.

OLDHAM, T. 1859. On some fossil fish-teeth of the genus *Ceratodus* from Maledi, south of Nagpur. *Memories of the Geological Survey of India*, **1**, 295–309.

PEREZ, P. A. & MALABARBA, M. C. S. L. 2002. A Triassic freshwater fish fauna from the Parana Basin, in southern Brazil. *Revista Brasileira de Paleontologia*, **4**, 27–33.

PRIEM, F. 1924. Paléontologie de Madagascar: une composante venue de Laurasie est-elle-envisageable? *In*: LOURENCO, W. C. (ed.) *Biogéographie de Madagascar*, Orstom, Paris, 27–35.

REICHEL, M., SCHULTZ, C. L. & PEREIRA, V. P. 2005. Diagenetic pattern of vertebrate fossils from the Traversodontidae Biozone, Santa Maria Formation (Triassic), southern Brazil. *Revista Brasileira de Paleontologia*, **8**, 173–180.

RICHTER, M. & LANGER, M. C. 1998. Fish remains from the Upper Permian Rio do Rasto Formation (Paraná Basin) of southern Brazil. *Journal of African Earth Sciences*, **27**, 158–159.

RITCHIE, A. 1981. First complete specimen of the Dipnoan *Gosfordia truncata* Woodward from the Triassic of New South Wales. *Records of The Australian Museum*, **33**, 606–616.

ROSA, A. A. S. DA, PIMENTEL, N. L. V. & FACCINI, U. F. 2004. Paleoalterações e Carbonatos em depósitos aluviais na região de Santa maria, Triássico Médio a Superior do Sul do Brasil. *Pesquisas em Geociências*, **31**, 3–16.

RUBERT, R. R. & SCHULTZ, C. L. 2004. Um novo horizonte de correlação para o Triássico Superior do Rio Grande do Sul. *Pesquisas em Geociências*, **31**, 71–88.

SCHULTZ, C. L. 2005. Biostratigraphy of the non-marine Triassic: Is a global correlation based on tetrapod faunas possible? *In*: KOUTSOUKOS, E. (ed.) *Applied Stratigraphy*. Springer, 123–145.

SCHULTZ, C. L., SCHERER, C. M. S. & BARBERENA, M. C. 2000. Biostratigraphy of southern Brazilian Middle/Upper Triassic. *Revista Brasileira de Geociências*, **30**, 491–494.

SCHULTZE, H.-P. 1981. Das Schädeldach eines ceratodontiden Lungfishes aus der Trias Süddeutschlands (Dipnoi, Pisces). *Stuttgarter Beiträge zur Naturkunde*, **B(70)**, 1–31.

SCHULTZE, H.-P. 1992. Dipnoi. *In*: WESTPHAL, F. (ed.) *Fossilium Catalogus 1. Animalia*. Kugler Publications, 1–464.

SCHULTZE, H.-P. & CHORN, 1997. The Permo-Carbonifeorus genus *Sagenodus* and the beginning of modern lungfish. *Contributions to Zoology*, **67**, 9–70.

SELDEN, P. A., ANDERSON, J. M., ANDERSON, H. M. & FRASER, N. 1999. Fossil araneomorph from the Triassic of South Africa and Virginia. *The Journal of Arachnology*, **27**, 401–414.

STOLLHOFFEN, H., STANISTREET, I. G., ROHN, R., HOLZFÖRSTER, R. & WANKE, A. 2000. The Gai-As lake system, Northern Namibia and Brazil. *In*: GIERLOWSKI-KORDESCH, E. H. & KELTS, K. R. (eds) Lake basins through space and time. *AAPG Studies in Geology*, **46**, 87–108.

TEIXEIRA, 1949. La faune de poissons du Karroo de l'Angola et du Congo Belge. *Boletim do Museu e Laboratorio de Mineralogia e Geologia, Faculdade de Ciências da Universidade de Lisboa, Classe Ciências*, **7**, 55–60.

TEIXEIRA, 1954. Sur un Ceratodontidé du Karroo de l'Angola. *Memórias da Academia de Ciências, Lisboa*, **7**, 55–60.

TEIXEIRA, C. 1978. Les poissons fossiles du Karroo de l'Angola. Reconhecimento científico de Angola: Estudos de Geologia, de Paleontologia e de Micologia. *Publicação do II Centenário da Academia de Ciências de Lisboa*, Lisboa, 275–300.

TOLEDO, C. E. V. & BERTINI, R. J. 2005. Occurrences of the fossil Dipnoiformes in Brazil and its stratigraphic and chronological distributions. *Revista Brasileira de Paleontologia*, **8**, 47–56.

TURNER, S. 1982. A catalogue of fossil fish in Queensland. *Memories of the Queensland Museum*, **20**, 599–611.

VOROBYEVA, E. I. & MINIKH, M. G. 1968. Experimental application of biometry to the study of ceratodontid dental plates. *Palaeontological Journal*, **2**, 217–227.

WADE, R. T. 1935. *The Triassic Fishes of Brookvale, New South Wales*. British Museum (Natural History), London.

WOODWARD, A. S. 1891. *Catalogue of the Fossil Fishes in the British Museum (Natural History)*. Part II. London.

YOUNG, G. C. 1991. Fossil fishes from Antarctica. *In*: TINGEY, R. J. (ed.) *The Geology of Antarctica*. Oxford Monographs in Geology and Geophysics, 538–567.

ZERFASS, H., LAVINA, E. L., GARCIA, C. L., FACCINI, U. F. & CHEMALE, F., JR. 2003. Sequence stratigraphy of continental Triassic strata of southernmost Brazil: a contribution to Southeastern Gondwana palaeogeography and palaeoclimate. *Sedimentary Geology*, **161**, 85–105.

ZERFASS, H., CHEMALE, F., JR. & LAVINA, E. L. 2005. Tectonic control of the Triassic Santa Maria Supersequence of the Paraná Basin, Southern Brazil, and its correlation to the Waterberg Basin, Namibia. *Gondwana Research*, **8**, 163–176.

ZITTEL, K. A. 1887–1890. *Handbuch der Paläontologie. 1, Paläozoologie. 3, Band Vertebrata*. Oldenbourg, München, Leipzig.

Diversity and biogeography patterns of Late Jurassic neoselachians (Chondrichthyes: Elasmobranchii)

JÜRGEN KRIWET & STEFANIE KLUG

Museum of Natural History, Humboldt–University of Berlin, Invalidenstr. 43, 10115 Berlin, Germany (e-mail: juergen.kriwet@museum.hu-berlin.de)

Abstract: The regional diversity and biogeographic patterns of Late Jurassic neoselachians at genus level in Europe were analysed based on samples and an extensive literature survey of about 40 localities ranging from the Oxfordian to Tithonian. The simple completeness metric (SCM) displays a quite good fossil record of neoselachians in the Late Jurassic with a peak in the Kimmeridgian. The origination, extinction, diversification and turnover rates were calculated for every stage and indicate that background origination occurred in the Oxfordian and Kimmeridgian with no disappearance of genera. In the Tithonian, background extinction is the main factor for neoselachian diversity decline. The decline in neoselachian diversity at the end of the Jurassic is most probably related to reduced habitats in the course of major regression events, establishment of physical barriers, and climatic changes. Faunal assemblages are quite uniform and mostly agree well with the contemporaneous palaeogeographic situation. Our analyses indicate that both vicariance and dispersal were important processes in the biogeographic pattern of Late Jurassic neoselachians.

The fossil history of neoselachians ranges back to the Early Triassic (Thies 1982) although rare findings in Palaeozoic sediments might be assigned to neoselachians (e.g. Duffin & Ward 1983; Turner & Young 1987). A first major radiation event is ascertainable in the Early Jurassic (Maisey *et al.* 2004) with subsequent diversity increases in the Middle to Late Jurassic (e.g. Candoni 1993; Thies 1983, 1989, 1993; Cuny 1998; Underwood 2002; Kriwet 2003; Kriwet & Klug 2004). Batoids have a quite long fossil record and first appeared in the Early Jurassic (e.g. Delsate & Candoni 2001). However, their systematic position is still discussed despite a general consensus that they form a monophyletic group. Analyses based on morphological data suggest that batoids are positioned high within squalomorphs (orbitostylic sharks of Maisey 1984) (e.g. Shirai 1992, 1996; de Carvalho 1996), whereas molecular data place batoids as sister group to sharks (e.g. Douady *et al.* 2003).

The Jurassic thus heralds the first major neoselachian radiation event (Maisey *et al.* 2004) and it was then that many modern groups (e.g. Hexanchiformes, Heterodontiformes, Squatiniformes, Orectolobiformes, Carcharhiniformes, Rajiformes), with the exception of Squaliformes and Lamniformes (e.g. Kriwet & Klug 2004; Musick *et al.* 2004), had their first appearance in the fossil record. However, most of these records consist of isolated teeth. The oldest skeletal remains of neoselachians are known from Early Jurassic deposits of England and southern Germany with few taxa of extinct groups (e.g. Synechodontiformes)

(e.g. Klug & Kriwet 2006*a*). Conversely, Late Jurassic limestones of southern Germany yielded numerous skeletons of many modern groups making this time interval important for addressing evolutionary issues and might provide important insights into the processes underlying the evolution of neoselachians.

Late Jurassic marine fish communities of Europe are mostly dominated by neritic-water, often presumed bottom-dwelling sharks and rays. However, trophic guild and ecomorphology reconstructions indicate that they occupied different habitats and that it might be possible to identify allochthonous and autochthonous taxa within the different localities (Klug & Kriwet 2006*b*).

Diversity and zoogeography are closely connected concepts for understanding the adaptive radiation of organisms. Historical biogeography (palaeobiogeography) is one of the two major disciplines in zoogeography and is used to explain past distribution patterns of biota. This approach analyses the occurrence of animals, often at various taxonomic levels, over large spatial scales and involves zoogeographic mechanisms over long temporal scales (Briggs 1995). Most workers use a traditional approach in historical biogeography, which identifies and describes the allopatric distribution of closely-related taxa in different areas to reconstruct places of origins, migration abilities of the organisms under study, and the nature of the available dispersal routes and barriers (e.g. Simpson 1943). The disjunct distribution pattern of organisms was previously explained by dispersal, which means that a given species spreads actively across

From: CAVIN, L., LONGBOTTOM, A. & RICHTER, M. (eds) *Fishes and the Break-up of Pangaea*.
Geological Society, London, Special Publications, **295**, 55–70.
DOI: 10.1144/SP295.5   0305-8719/08/$15.00 © The Geological Society of London 2008.

an existing barrier to colonize another area. Consequently, dispersal requires active swimming of taxa, which depends on the vagility of these taxa (Musick *et al.* 2004).

The theory of plate tectonics suggests that splitting of continents leading to vicariance biogeography is another important factor in subdividing and isolating populations (e.g. Croizat 1964; Nelson & Platnick 1981; Nelson & Rosen 1981; Forey *et al.* 1992). In this scenario, the barrier and the allopatric taxa are of equal age. In the dispersal model, conversely, the barrier is older than the allopatric taxa (Mooi & Gill 2002). However, the processes underlying the distribution of extinct neoselachians has never been analysed up to now.

The intention of this paper is to analyse the diversity and historical biogeography of neoselachian sharks during the Late Jurassic. The focus is on European occurrences, because there are few Late Jurassic neoselachian occurrences outside Europe: Argentina (Cione 1999), Ethiopia (Goodwin *et al.* 1999), Somalia (D'Erasmo 1960) and Tanzania (Arratia *et al.* 2002).

Methods

Data used for this study were largely extracted from published literature, personal observations and unpublished data (e.g. Kimmeridgian and Tithonian of north-eastern Spain, Guimarota and SW Portugal) or unpublished theses (e.g. Mudroch 2001). Each taxon reported in a locality constitutes a taxonomic occurrence in the database. Individual abundance data were omitted from the present analyses because of the heterogenous nature of data (isolated teeth, complete skeletons). Consequently, resampling analyses (e.g. rarefaction) were not conducted here. The palaeobiogeographic interpretations presented here are based only on taxonomic data resolved at the genus level (35 genera) because of low ratios of species-level identified occurrences (only 42%) (Appendix 1). Although no revision of taxa is presented here, a considerable synonymization of taxa was conducted to reduce the taxonomic noise considerably. For instance *Squalogaleus* is considered a junior synonym of *Protospinax* (de Carvalho & Maisey 1996). Taxonomic problems related to the identity of Late Jurassic batoids are beyond the scope of this study and we consider all batoids from southern Germany to belong to *Asterodermus*. All squatinoid remains from Jurassic deposits are transferred here to *Pseudorhina* (de Carvalho *et al.* in review). *Palaeocarcharias*, which is generally considered to be an early representative of lamniform sharks is considered here to be the sister group of orectolobiforms and lamniforms (unpublished data).

We used 120 actual and additional 12 Lazarus occurrences, resulting in 132 total Late Jurassic occurrences. Lazarus occurrences were identified by scrutinizing all Jurassic and Cretaceous records of the taxon under consideration. Thirteen taxa are considered endemic here. The occurrences of Late Jurassic taxa in the Early and Middle Jurassic (13) were used to infer the extinction rate at the end of the Middle Jurassic.

This indicates that: (1) neoselachians in the Late Jurassic are still underexplored and their true diversity is far from being completely known and (2) neoselachian occurrences are usually reported on rather large spatial and temporal scales (e.g. most citations from the 19th and beginning of 20th century) (see also Underwood 2006).

The standing diversity (alpha diversity) of Late Jurassic neoselachians was calculated by raw counts of species numbers. It was not possible to employ species richness and diversity measures (e.g. Shannon/Wiener information function), because those calculate species abundance in relation to the number of individuals. The beta diversity as used here characterizes the taxonomic differentiation between different localities and regions. The more different the faunal compositions are, the higher is the beta diversity, following the simple formula: beta diversity = global diversity/ local diversity (e.g. Schluter & Ricklefs 1993).

Here, faunal similarities are based on qualitative (presence/absence) data and were calculated using the Jaccard coefficient of Community and the Simpson Index. The Dice Coincidence Index, which gives double weight to presence data but is otherwise redundant with the more widely applied Jaccard coefficient (Sepkoski 1988), is excluded because it is useless if the species number (diversity) is very low in one region compared to the other; the number of endemic species of the region with lower diversity is consequently zero resulting in no positive conclusion of the analysis. The Simple Matching coefficient is also excluded here because it reveals incoherent values in comparison with the other coefficients. Experience has shown that the results for the other used coefficients are quite similar. The mean value was calculated from both coefficients for each area pair.

There is a plethora of methods for establishing historical biogeographic patterns and testing hypotheses have proliferated over the last 30 years, e.g. hierarchical phenetic algorithms method (multivariate data analyses), dispersalism, phylogenetic biogeography, panbiogeography, and cladistic biogeography (for a detailed review see Morone & Crisci 1995). Cladistic approaches that are applied to palaeobiogeography to get testable hypotheses can be divided into two different groups; parsimony analysis of endemism (PAE, cladistic biogeography) and phylogenetic biogeography. In this study, the parsimony analysis of endemism (PAE) is used. This approach treats the taxa of a defined area as its taxonomic characters. The method is rather similar to phylogenetic analysis using cladistic principles; shared characters among taxa suggest common ancestry in phylogenetic, shared taxa among areas suggest Recent common ancestry for localities (Rosen 1988; Rosen & Smith 1988).

Although PAE is not phylogenetic biogeography because it does not employ robust phylogenetic hypothesis for the taxa under consideration, it is actually preferable, since it makes no assumptions about the evolutionary relationships of the taxa (Waggoner 1999). In fact, no phylogenetic hypothesis for Jurassic neoselachians is available. It also ignores taxa endemic to only one locality as autapomorphies and removes possible sources of uncertainties from the analysis in this way. Here, we performed PAE for the Oxfordian, Kimmeridgian, and Tithonian to interpret the history of space occupancy by taxa through time, testing the assumption that subsequent dispersal has not obliterated the vicariant pattern and that extinctions are random.

The rates of origination $[r_o = (1/D) \times (S/t)]$, extinction $[r_e = (1/D) \times (E/t)]$, diversification $(r_d = r_o - r_e)$, and recovery $(r_t = r_o + r_e)$ following Sepkoski (1978) and Lasker (1978) were calculated to establish the diversity patterns of neoselachians in the Late Jurassic of Europe. 'D' indicates the number of taxa present in a specific interval, 'S' the number of taxa originations, 'E' the number of taxa losses, and 't' the time interval in Ma.

Singleton taxa (those occurring only in the Oxfordian, Kimmeridgian, or Tithonian) introduce unacceptable biases and were omitted from these analyses to reduce the noise and to obtain more realistic biological signals.

The simple completeness metric (SCM) of Benton (1987) is used to assess the diversity dynamics and completeness of the fossil record for genera. The 68% and 95% confidence intervals were calculated according to Raup (1991). The errors of 95% and 68% binominal confidence intervals are given to obtain a measure about the significance of these values.

Localities

About 40 different localities yielding remains of Late Jurassic neoselachians are forming the base for this study (Appendix 1) (e.g. Bigot 1896; Sauvage 1902; Saint-Seine 1949; D'Erasmo 1960; Schweizer 1964; Thies 1983; Duffin 1993a, b; Candoni 1993, 1994, 1995; Cavin et al. 1995; Duffin & Thies 1987; Kriwet 1997, 1998, 2004;

Thies & Candoni 1998; Leidner & Thies 1999; Böttcher & Duffin 2000; Mudroch 2001. Underwood 2002; Kriwet & Klug 2004; collections of the authors). Localities were combined into areas to facilitate the palaeobiogeographic analyses (Fig. 1): area A: SW Germany (e.g. Buchsteige, Mahlstetten, Nusplingen, Reichenbach, and Stuifen); area B: SE Germany (e.g. Blumenberg, Eichstätt, Kelheim, Solnhofen, etc.); area C: N Germany (Lower Saxony Basin; e.g. Hainholz, Hirschkopf, Hozen, Holzmühle, Oker, Uppen; all near Hanover); area D: S England (mainly Ringstead region); area E: N and NW France (e.g. Boulogne-sur-Mer, Calvados, Octeville, Paris basin); area F: W France (e.g. Chassiron, Lot-et-Garonne); area G: E France (only Cerin); area H: Switzerland; area I: north-eastern Spain (e.g. Barranco-de-las-Estacas, Calanda, Frías de Albarracin, Moscardon, Rafales, Tosos, Viruella); area K: Portugal (e.g. Guimarota, Santa Cruz); and area L: Italy.

The localities combined into areas share the same palaeogeographic position and generally similar depositional areas except for Mahlstetten, which is more pronouncedly open marine compared to Nusplingen, which represents a lagoonal setting. This arrangement, however, is the most useful for the purposes of this paper, because consideration of neoselachian ecomorphotypes and ecologies is beyond the scope of this study and will presented somewhere else. A major problem of such analyses are taphonomic biases. This applies especially to those localities were complete skeletons were found (e.g. Nusplingen, Solnhofen) but no bulk sampling and processing methods for obtaining additional, isolated teeth of neoselachians were conducted. Consequently, the taxonomic diversity of these localities is considered to be incompletely known. Diversity analyses require the exclusion of such localities to minimize the monographic effects.

However, excluding these localities from the current study would result in a blurred picture of Late Jurassic neoselachian diversity. Consequently, these occurrences were left in the analyses until more material and improved methods are available.

Results and discussion

Fossil record

The quality of the fossil record of organisms has been debated considerably in the last decades. While many analyses have been carried out to assess the quality of the fossil record of tetrapods, assumptions on the completeness of the fossil record of neoselachians are scarce and generally ambiguous. Shirai (1996) assumes that the fossil record of neoselachians is incomplete, whereas

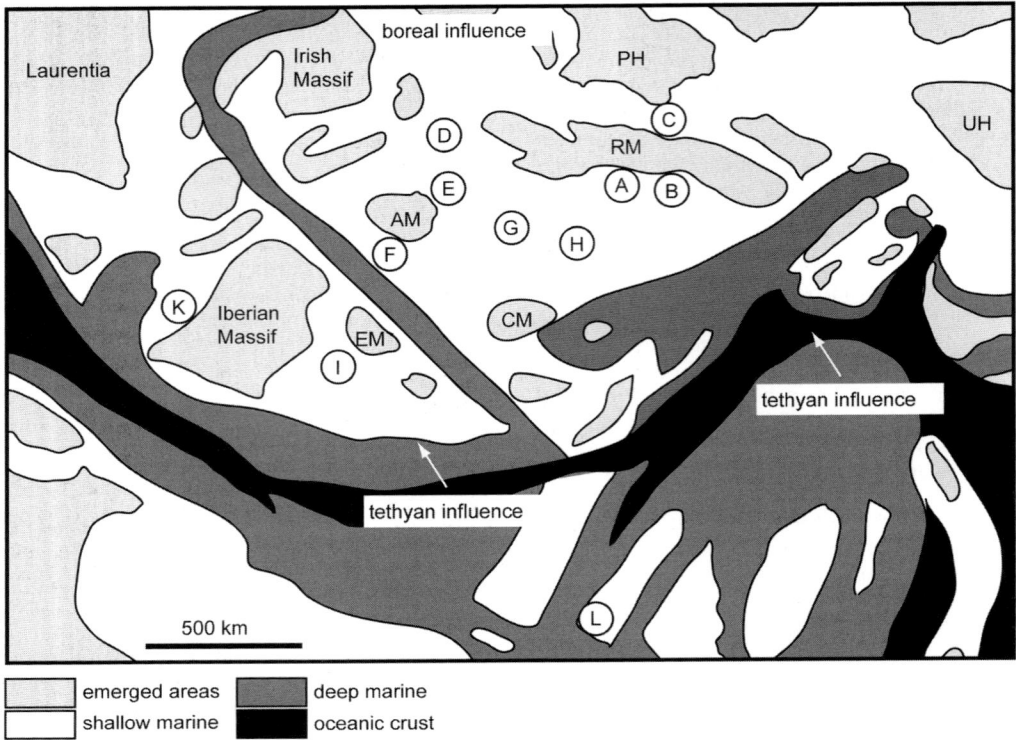

Fig. 1. Late Jurassic palaeogeographic map showing location of study areas. Letters relate to areas **A**: south-western Germany; **B**: south-eastern Germany (Solnhofen area); **C**: northern Germany; **D**: southern England; **E**: northern France; **F**: western France; **G**: eastern France (Cerin); **H**: Switzerland; **I**: north-eastern Spain; **K**: Portugal; **L**: Italy. Abbreviations are: EM, Ebro Massif, Am, Armorican Massif; CM, Central Massif; PH, Pompekjian Height; RM, Rhenish Massif; UH, Ukrainia. Map modified from Ziegler (1988).

Maisey *et al.* (2004) concluded that the fossil record of neoselachians might not be too poor when molecular phylogenies are tested against the stratigraphic distribution of taxa. However, morphology-based phylogenies indicate relatively large gaps in the fossil record (Maisey *et al.* 2004), as is also exemplified for squaliforms by Adnet & Cappetta (2001). The only analysis available using the simple completeness metric to infer the quality of the fossil record of neoselachians is that of Kriwet & Benton (2004), who concluded that their fossil record across the K/T boundary (Maastrichtian = 94% and Danian = 85%) is undeniably good although several groups were heavily affected by the extinction event(s).

The fossil record of modern sharks (neoselachians) consists predominantly of isolated teeth and dates back at least to the Early Triassic, some 250 million years ago (Cuny *et al.* 1998). Prior to the Jurassic, the fossil record of neoselachians is very poor, with most fossils having uncertain phylogenetic positions (Cuny *et al.* 1998). The first

unequivocal neoselachian remain is known from the Lower Triassic of Turkey (Thies 1982), although the lineage is believed to have originated in the Palaeozoic (Duffin & Ward 1983; Turner & Young 1987; Cuny & Benton 1999). Neoselachians were remarkably diverse already by the Middle Jurassic (e.g. Kriwet 2003; Underwood & Ward 2004). This supports the interpretation that a major radiation event must have occurred in the Early Jurassic that heralds the first appearance of many groups that display tooth morphologies similar to those seen in extant taxa (e.g. Thies 1983, 1989; Candoni 1993; de Carvalho 1996; Cuny *et al.* 1998; Kriwet 2003; Maisey *et al.* 2004; Underwood & Ward 2004). From the Early Jurassic, several articulated or partially preserved skeletons of basal neoselachians have been recorded providing insights into the skeletal morphology of basal galeomorph neoselachians (e.g. Duffin & Ward 1993; Klug & Kriwet 2006a).

All major clades of modern neoselachians, with the exception of Squaliformes and Lamniformes, are seemingly present in the Late Jurassic (e.g. Schweizer 1964; Capetta 1987; Thies 1992; Duffin & Ward 1993; Cavin et al. 1995; Kriwet & Klug 2004). The famous localities of Nusplingen, Eichstätt, Solnhofen, and Kelheim yielded numerous articulated skeletons of neoselachians that provide a lot of new information on the evolution of characters within neoselachians (e.g. Schweizer 1964; Kriwet & Klug 2004; Kriwet 2008; de Carvalho et al. 2008). During the latest Jurassic and beginning of the Cretaceous, neoselachians rapidly diversified and in the late Early Cretaceous, shark faunas of 'truly' modern character appeared. However, the fossil record from the uppermost Jurassic and Early Cretaceous continues to be incomplete (e.g. Kriwet 1999; Rees 2005; Underwood 2006). This is related to collecting-biases and lack of suitable sediments to obtain microteeth faunas. The colonization of pelagic environments during the Cretaceous presumably represented one of the major steps in the evolution of modern sharks. Simultaneously to the radiation of modern sharks, the numbers of hybodonts (their plesiomorphic sister group) declined, and eventually this group of sharks vanished at the end of the Cretaceous.

Late Cretaceous neoselachian skeletons are only known from the Late Cretaceous of England and the limestone deposits of Lebanon (e.g. Duffin & Ward 1993; Cappetta 1980a, b). These assemblages include members of all major lineages including the only known fossil skeletons of squaliform neoselachians. This material, although already described, never has been analysed in terms of diversity measures and has not yet been included in phylogenetic analyses.

Here, we calculated the simple completeness metric (SCM) for all neoselachian genera and all Late Jurassic stages although this measure might not give a perfect measure of the relative incompleteness of the fossil record (Benton 1987). This approach, nevertheless, is advantageous because it disregards cladogenetic events but includes those taxa that must have been present in a certain stage but have not been recorded from the fossil record (Lazarus taxa). We excluded stratigraphic singletons (defined as genera occurring in only one stratigraphic stage) in all analyses to minimize the monographic effects (e.g. Upper Jurassic selachians from the Solnhofen area). The SCM for all stages analysed are shown in Table 1. The evidence of a good fossil record of neoselachians in the Late Jurassic of Europe is compelling and surprisingly good. It is best in the Kimmeridgian (SCM = 95%) despite the comparably high number of singleton occurrences (Kimmeridgian = 33%). In the Tithonian, the fossil record still is very good (SCM = 79%) (with 17% singletons), the

Table 1. *Completeness of the fossil record (SCM) of Late Jurassic neoselachians measured by stratigraphic stages and by occurrences of genera and corresponding errors of 68% and 95% binominal confidence intervals. Singletons were excluded*

	SCM	95%–CI	68%–CI
Oxfordian	61.11%	22.29%	11.74%
Kimmeridgian	95.00%	7.39%	5.40%
Tithonian	78.95%	17.14%	9.60%

Oxfordian, conversely, displays the worst fossil record (SCM = 61%).

For comparison, we calculated the fossil record of several neoselachian groups excluding singletons. The results indicate that the quality of individual neoselachian groups is not as good as that for time intervals and/or assemblages (e.g. Squaliformes: c. 50%).

Standing diversity

The standing diversity (defined in the original sense as number of species) including and excluding Lazarus-taxa of Late Jurassic neoselachians is shown in Figure 2 based on published and unpublished information. The pattern of the standing diversity is quite similar in all three stages when excluding singletons. The lowest diversity is found in the Oxfordian and correlates with a quite low SCM (see above), whereas the highest diversity occurs in the Kimmeridgian. The Tithonian displays a decline of diversity and the diversity of neoselachians gradually diminishes towards the middle Cretaceous (Kriwet, unpublished data). The decrease of neoselachians at the end of the Jurassic and the beginning of the Cretaceous might reflect an extinction event with subsequent low recovery rates.

Early Cretaceous selachian faunas are known from many localities in Europe, but the majority of these assemblages are derived from non-marine deposits and include almost exclusively hybodont sharks (e.g. Patterson 1966; Ansorge 1990; Rees 2002; Underwood & Rees 2002). Neoselachians are known only from a few localities (Biddle 1988; Canudo et al. 1995; Cappetta 1990; Kriwet 1999; Leriche 1910; Underwood et al. 1999; Thies 1979, 1981; Ward & Thies 1987) and are mostly represented by lamniform and batoid taxa probably indicating marginal marine settings. There are no open marine neoselachian records from the Berriasian (Rees 2002. Underwood & Rees 2002). Despite these persuasive records, our understanding of Early Cretaceous neoselachian

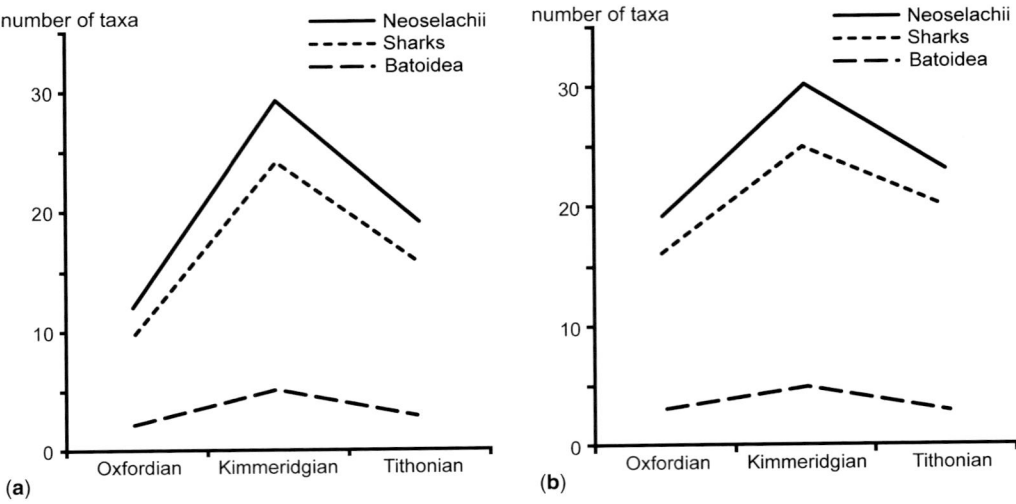

Fig. 2. Patterns of diversification and standing diversity of neoselachians in general, sharks and batoids, and neoselachians in general including (**a**) and excluding (**b**) Lazarus taxa on generic level in the Late Jurassic (in terms of taxa present per stratigraphic range).

diversity is still very inadequate and has not yet been analysed. However, equalizing the diversity curves from the Jurassic and Late Cretaceous (e.g. those provided by Underwood (2006)) indicates that the diversity of Early Cretaceous neoselachians was much higher. We hypothesize that there was no significant extinction event at the end of the Jurassic and the lack of evidence is probably more the result of collecting-biases and the absence of suitable sediments for recovering microvertebrate remains (such as selachian teeth).

Extinctions, originations, diversification and turnover rates

We evaluated the disappearance, origination, diversification, and recovery rates of Late Jurassic neoselachians to scrutinize their diversity patterns at genus level. The rates and corresponding values at the 95% and 68% confidence intervals are depicted in Table 2.

At the end of the Middle Jurassic, 3.6% of genera vanished. As little as 2% of new

Table 2. Total rates of extinction (r_e), origination (r_o), diversification (r_d) and turnover (r_t) at genus level excluding singletons for the Oxfordian, Kimmeridgian and Tithonian, and the corresponding errors of 68% and 95% binominal confidence intervals for these rates. The large errors of 95% binominal confidence intervals prevent a conclusive statement and indicate the need for further research

	Rates of origination			Rates of extinction		
	r_o	95% CI	68% CI	r_e	95% CI	68% CI
Oxfordian	+/−2.02%	+/−9.45%	+/−3.94%	+/−0.00%	+/−0.00%	+/−0.00%
Kimmeridgian	+/−2.04%	+/−8.85%	+/−3.68%	+/−0.00%	+/−0.00%	+/−0.00%
Tithonian	+/−0.00%	+/−0.00%	+/−0.00%	+/−0.99%	+/−6.57%	+/−2.05%
	Rates of diversification			Rates of recovery		
	r_d	95% CI	68% CI	r_t	95% CI	68% CI
Oxfordian	+/−2.02%	+/−9.45%	+/−3.94%	+/−2.02%	+/−9.45%	+/−3.94%
Kimmeridgian	+/−2.04%	+/−8.85%	+/−3.68%	+/−2.04%	+/−8.85%	+/−3.68%
Tithonian	+/−0.99%	+/−6.57%	+/−2.05%	+/−0.99%	+/−6.57%	+/−2.05%

neoselachian genera have evolved in the Oxfordian and Kimmeridgian respectively. Although almost no data for comparison exist, the scales are remarkable considering the comparably higher origination rate of neoselachians in the Danian after the K/T boundary extinction event (Kriwet & Benton 2004). Consequently, the Late Jurassic values are deemed to represent common background origination rates for neoselachians. No background extinctions are recognized in the Oxfordian and Kimmeridgian. Conversely, no neoselachian genus had its first appearance in the Tithonian but little background extinction (total rates of extinction = 1%) is detectable by our analyses. The diversification and turnover rates in the Oxfordian and Kimmeridgian are the same as the corresponding origination rates and as the corresponding extinction rate in the Tithonian. Background originations and extinctions are linked to small-scale events acting on a local and regional rather than a global scale. Background extinction also might be related to migrations of taxa into other regions or to community shifts because of climatic changes. We assume that the palaeogeographic setting and distribution of facies were quite stable on a regional scale because of the comparably small origination and extinction rates. However, small scale changes in diversity and in origination rate also might be related to the surface area of outcrops (e.g. Peters & Foote 2001). Unfortunately, insufficient data on outcrop area and number of formations for all three Late Jurassic stages are available so that it is not possible to standardize the data.

Beta diversity

Faunal similarities are based on regional faunas reported from all samples within the study area and the three stratigraphic intervals considered. They were calculated employing the Jaccard coefficient of Community and the Simpson Index. Faunal similarities range from 0.16 to 1.00 in the Oxfordian, from 0.08 to 0.92 in the Kimmeridgian, and from 0.07 to 0.59 in the Tithonian (Figs 3–5). Low similarities are attributed to the occurrence of rare taxa, incomplete sampling and small sample sizes.

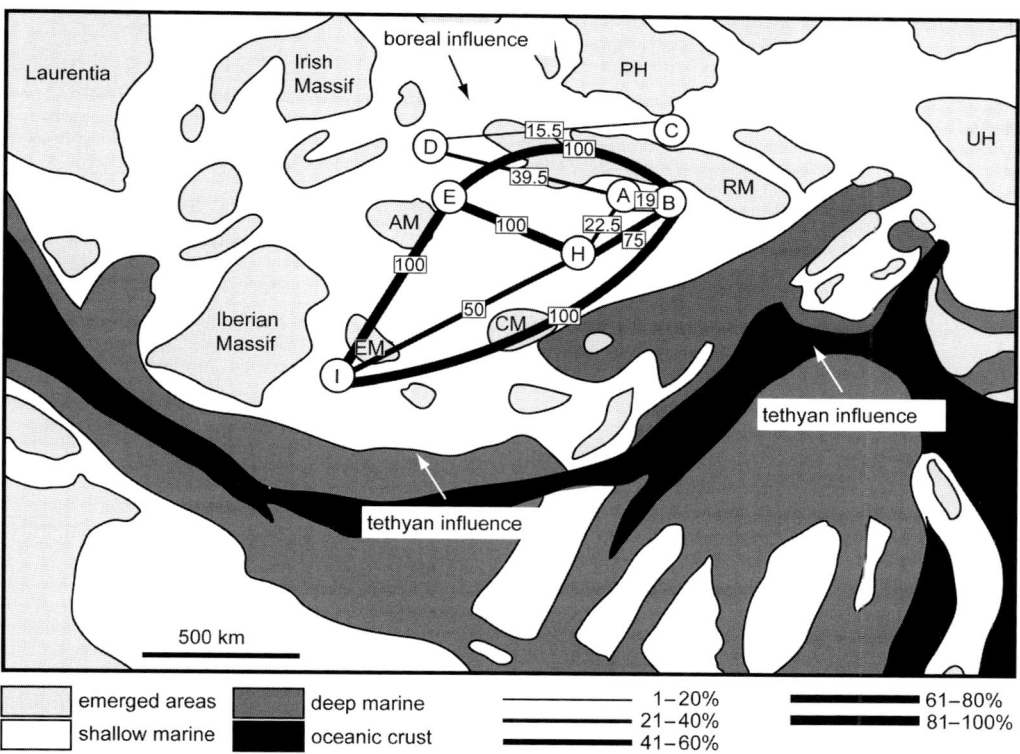

Fig. 3. Link diagram demonstrating the faunal affinities of Oxfordian neoselachians between areas (%). Legend same as in Figure 1.

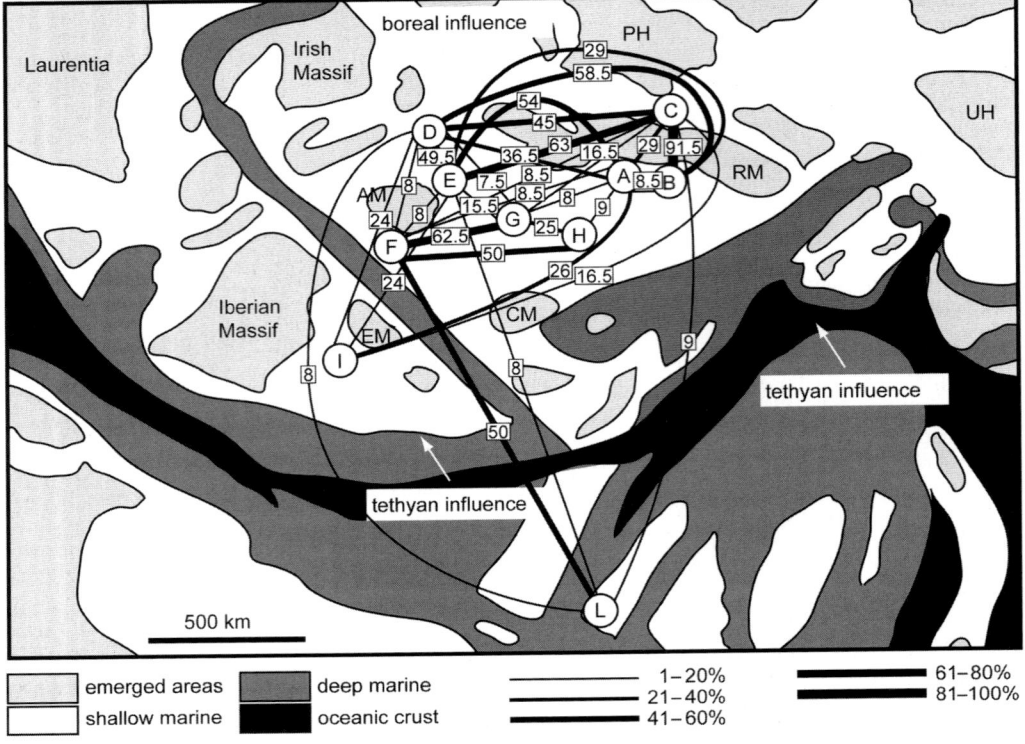

Fig. 4. Link diagram demonstrating the faunal affinities of Kimmeridgian neoselachians between areas (%).
Legend same as in Figure 1.

In the Oxfordian, neoselachian faunas bear the impression of a relatively uniform composition. The highest similarities are between southern England and northern France, southern England and north-eastern Spain, northern France and Switzerland, and northern France and north-eastern Spain (Fig. 3). The apparent uniformity is certainly related to the absence of important physical barriers. The lowest similarity is found between southern England and northern Germany, which is especially remarkable considering the geographic proximity. The differences between southern England plus northern Germany and the remaining areas might indicate boreal influences.

In the Kimmeridgian, the neoselachian faunas still are very uniform, especially in central Europe (Fig. 4). Boreal influences seem to have no impact on the faunal compositions. During this time, south-eastern Germany and northern Germany share the greatest similarity despite the fact that south-western Germany is more closely located and southern Germany is separated from northern Germany by the Rhenish Massif. The faunal similarities between south-western Germany, and

southern England and south-eastern Germany and southern England are quite good (0.37 and 0.59 respectively). The similarities between the faunas situated in the epicontinental shallow sea covering most of central Europe and those that are separated by deep marine trenches are generally low as expected. The only exception is western France and Italy with 0.50. However, this represents an artificial bias because of very small sample sizes.

The Tithonian displays the least faunal similarities because of restricted numbers of areas and neoselachian occurrences (Fig. 5). The best match exists, remarkably, between northern Germany and western France (0.59). The smallest similarity is recorded for south-eastern Germany and northern Germany (0.07); there seems to be no tethyal influence. The pattern is most likely related to collecting-biases and many still unidentified taxa.

The overall similarity patterns agree well, more or less, with the palaeogeographic situation in the Late Jurassic. We consider the deep marine trench (caused by the Bay of Biscaya Rift in the Kimmeridgian between the Iberian Peninsula and

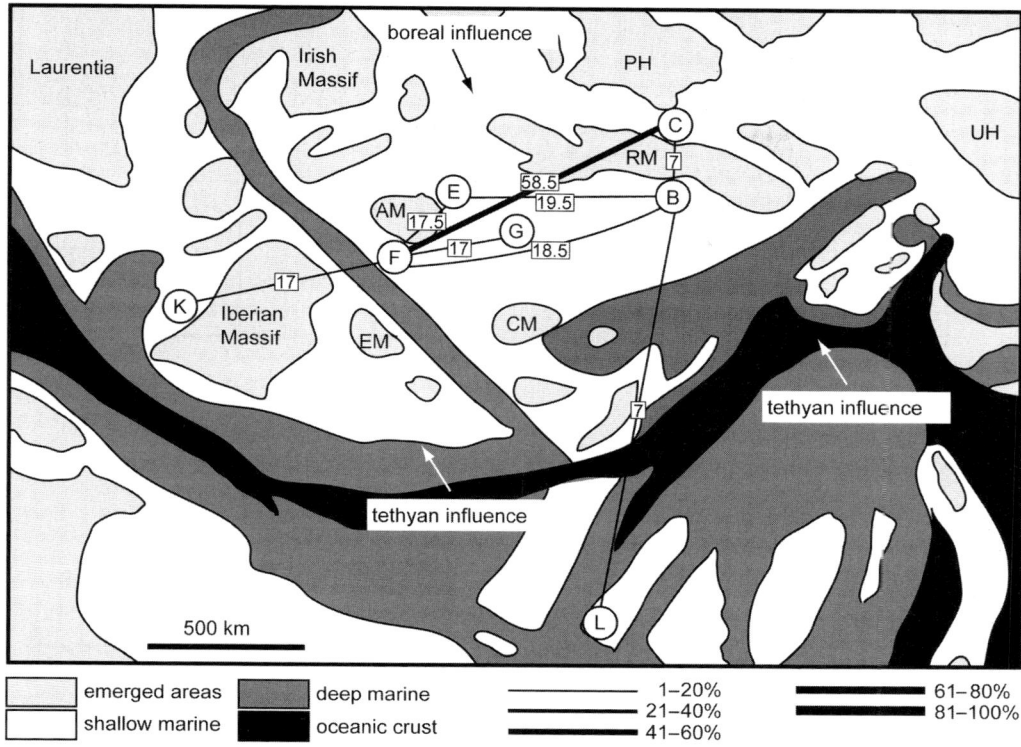

Fig. 5. Link diagram demonstrating the faunal affinities of Tithonian neoselachians between areas (%). Legend same as in Figure 1.

central Europe) a barrier preventing faunal exchanges, which resulted in vicariance speciation events during its establishment. These vicariant patterns are expressed by pronounced dissimilarities between Iberian and central European faunas at species level (Kriwet 1997, 1998, 2004). There are no pronounced differences between northern and southern areas in central Europe indicating that there were no separate boreal and tethyal faunas as for several invertebrate groups.

Parsimony analyses of endemism and area cladograms

Parsimony analyses of endemicity assume that it is not necessary to establish taxon relationships but only geographic occurrences, that vicariance is the most important mechanism producing the distribution of taxa and that the historical relationships among areas are internested (Brooks & van Veller 2003). Here, we conducted four separate parsimony analyses of endemicity for the Oxfordian, Kimmeridgian, Tithonian, and Late Jurassic respectively.

Singleton occurrences were included and all analyses were performed with PAUP version 4.0b10 using heuristic search options and randomizing the entering order of the areas 100 times. The PAE generated 2 most parsimonious trees (MPTs) for the Oxfordian, ten for the Kimmeridgian, 1 for the Tithonian and 2 for the Late Jurassic. The results are shown in Figure 6. The area cladograms show very low resolutions for the different stages with many polytomies. In the Oxfordian (Fig. 6a), the consensus tree has two main groupings representing faunistic blocks in central Europe. North-eastern Spain belongs to a clade comprising south-eastern Germany, northern and north-western France and Switzerland. In the Kimmeridgian, only a single but major faunistic block exists (Fig. 6b). North-eastern Spain represents the basal sister to four central European areas. The low similarity of north-eastern Spain to central European areas expressed by this cladogram and the subsequent cladogram for the Tithonian (Fig. 6c), and the unresolved position of Portugal and Italy in all three stages, is related to the palaeogeographic constellation of barriers. The area

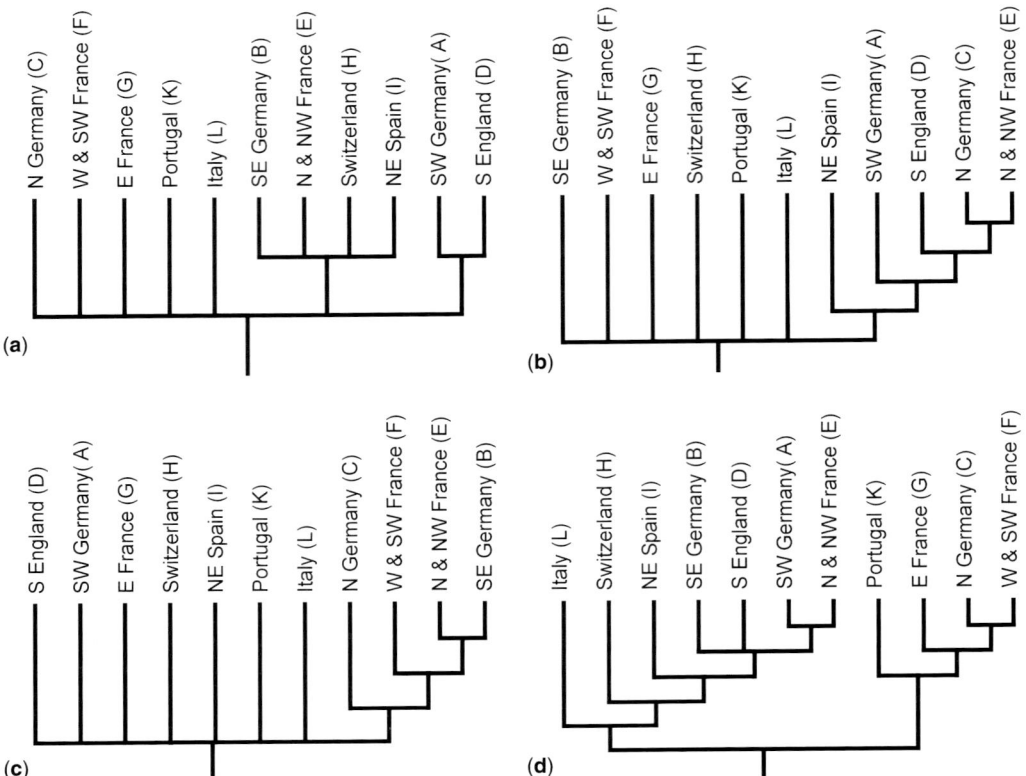

Fig. 6. Strict consensus trees for PAE results for Late Jurassic neoselachians from raw data. (**a**) strict consensus tree of 2 most parsimonious trees (MPTs) of Oxfordian endemicity patterns. Tree length: 15, CI: 0.80, RI: 0.63, HI: 0.20; (**b**) strict consensus tree of ten MPTs of Kimmeridgian endemicity patterns. Tree length: 38, CI: 0.76, RI: 0.73, HI: 0.24; (**c**) strict consensus tree of single MPT of Tithonian endemicity patterns. Tree length: 24, CI: 0.97, RI: 0.50, HI: 0.21; (**d**) strict consensus tree of 2 MPTs of combined Late Jurassic endemicity patterns. Tree length: 53, CI: 0.66, RI: 0.65, HI: 0.34.

cladogram combining all data and all three stages into a single analysis resulted in two major faunistic blocks (Fig. 6d). It is especially intriguing that Portugal is part of a block consisting of eastern France, northern Germany and western France but does not belong to an assemblage including north-eastern Spain. The quite erratic area relationships in comparison with the actual occurrence of areas is most likely the result of incomplete sampling (although the SCM scales are quite good), taxonomic problems and, most notably, the inability of the method to detect dispersal patterns.

Conclusions

The purpose of this study was to gain better insights into the distribution and faunal relationships of Late Jurassic neoselachians. It is obvious from this and similar studies (e.g. Underwood 2006) that the

taxonomic concepts are not very accurate and a lot of taxonomic information is based on publications from the 19th or the beginning of the 20th century. Consequently, a revision of Jurassic and Early Cretaceous neoselachian taxa is urgently needed. The taxonomic concepts are generally based on isolated teeth, because complete skeletons are very rare. However, the value of tooth morphologies and their inter- and intraspecific variability is not established. Consequently, convergent evolutions in tooth morphologies remain undetected and result in lumping of different taxa. In addition, several Late Jurassic faunas (e.g. Portugal, Spain, northern Germany, Poland) are currently studied by us and probably will contribute to our understanding of early neoselachian diversification.

The preservation of neoselachian remains is very heterogeneous. Generally, fossil neoselachians are only known from their teeth and similar hardparts. However, some localities (e.g. Nusplingen,

Solnhofen area, Cerin) yielded articulated skeletons introducing monographic effects into all analyses (e.g. the well-described Solnhofen area neoselachians; Appendix 2). In addition, bulk sampling methods have not been applied to most Late Jurassic shark tooth bearing deposits (e.g. Solnhofen area, Switzerland, Italy) and the knowledge of Late Jurassic neoselachians from those areas is based on surface collected big teeth (e.g. those of *Sphenodus*).

Consequently, the limited data sets and inaccurate faunal descriptions continue to form a serious problem in analysing past diversity and biogeographic patterns of sharks. Some of the problems could be corrected by employing rigorous phylogenetic methods using cladistic principles to form a testable basis of neoselachian interrelationships. For this, different data sets (e.g. dental and skeletal characters must be combined using different approaches). The resulting phylogenetic hypotheses might provide better insights into the biogeographic history of neoselachian distributions in the Late Jurassic than these parsimony analyses of endemism. Nevertheless, it is also possible to infer distributional and diversity patterns from the data available and to interpret this in a non-phylogenetic framework. According to all data from this study, we consider the distribution of Late Jurassic neoselachians in Europe to be the result of vicariance and occasional subsequent endemisms (e.g. composition of Portuguese and Spanish assemblages in the Kimmeridgian), but also dispersal events. Consequently, the parsimony analyses of endemism, which assume vicariance being the predominant process for organism distributions, fails to provide an accurate sketch of faunal and area relationships.

Benthic and small neoselachians, such as squatinids, orectolobiforms, and batoids generally display the least geographic ranges and highest endemisms during the Jurassic. This is in good accordance with results proposed by Musick *et al.* (2004) indicating that the mode of life (benthic vs. pelagic) and the habitat controls the range size of neoselachians. Larger taxa, such as *Paraorthacodus*, may have had larger range sizes. However, not enough data are available to test this hypothesis.

The Tethys certainly was a centre of origin for modern neoselachians and the break-up of Pangaea may have been important in their diversification related to vicariant patterns. Dispersal, conversely, was certainly important in larger, more vagile taxa but also those that were small and coastal.

The diversity fluctuations observed in the three Late Jurassic stages are related to normal background originations (Oxfordian, Kimmeridgian) and background extinctions (Tithonian) operating at genus level. The neoselachian diversity decline

at the end of the Jurassic is therefore not related to an extinction event at the Jurassic–Cretaceous boundary but most probably the expression of missing sediments for finding marine organisms, because the Berriasian was a time of major regressions (Ziegler 1990). However, the lowermost Early Cretaceous is a time of increased diversification amongst non-marine and brackish hybodont sharks (e.g. *Lonchidion*).

The comparable large errors of 95% binominal confidence intervals are similar to those established by Kriwet & Benton (2004) for the diversity fluctuations of neoselachians across the K/T boundary and indicate the need for further research into the taxonomy and stratigraphic distribution of neoselachians.

During the Late Jurassic, an obvious reduction in neoselachian biogeographic diversification is apparent: from two assemblages (northern boreal influenced and uniform central European groupings) in the Oxfordian to a relatively uniform composition in the Kimmeridgian. Data for the Tithonian are not significant but are more likely related to the beginning of the latest Jurassic regression. The degree of endemism, as expressed by the area cladograms, is lowest in the Oxfordian and increases continuously towards the Tithonian.

The fairly uniform faunal compositions, especially in the Kimmeridgian, are certainly related to a fairly uniform palaeoclimate during the Late Jurassic (which was warm and humid, with sea level high stands and the absence of important physical barriers in central and northern Europe; e.g. Haq *et al.* 1938; Rawson & Riley 1982; Ziegler 1990). The opening of the Bay of Biscaya Rift certainly had great influence on the ocean currents and acted as a physical barrier that reduced the possibilities of faunal exchanges (as expressed by comparable small faunal similarities between the Iberian Peninsula and central Europe).

Latest Jurassic neoselachians display the least endemisms. These findings are opposite to those exemplified by invertebrates, which display a distinctive differentiation into Boreal and Tethyan realms in the Tithonian (e.g. Mutterlose *et al.* 2003). Endemic marine biotas are considered characteristic for this time interval and endemism was favoured by restricted epicontinental seas supporting *in-situ* evolution. Reasons for minor provincialisms in neoselachians during this time might be changed marine currents or taphonomic biases. The faunal similarities between Portugal and central Europe (NW France, NW Germany) in the Tithonian are related to the occurrence of small epipelagic carcharhiniform sharks that were able to cross deeper marine areas.

Appendix 1

Distribution of Late Jurassic neoselachians in Europe.

	E/M Jurassic	Oxfordian	Kimmeridgian	Tithonian
'Eonotidanus'	X	D	A	B
Asterodermus			C	B
Belemnobatis	X	*	A, E, F, G, H	E
Carcharhiniformes new			C	
Cantioscyllium	X	*	D	
Cretorectolobus etc	X	*	D	*
Heterodontus		D	D, B	B
Leiribatos			**K**	
Macrourogaleus				**B**
Notidanoides	X	B, E, H, I	A	B
Orectolobiformes nov.			**A**	
Orectolobiformes nov.				**B**
Orectolobiformes nov.			**D**	
Orectolobiformes nov.		**C**		
Orectolobiformes nov.			**C**	
Orectolobiformes nov.			**I**	
Orectolobiformes nov.				**E**
Palaeobrachaelurus	X	*	A, E	*
Palaeocarcharias				**B**
Palaeoscyllium	X	C, D	A, C, D, E, I	B
Paracestracion	X	C	A, B, D, C, E	B, E, F
Paraorthacodus	X	*	A, E	B
Phorcynis	X	*	G	B, C, F
Proscylliid?			**E**	
Protospinax	X	A, C	A, C, D, E, I	B, F
Pseudorhina (Squatina s.l.)		A, D	A, C, D, E, G, K, I	A, E, F
Pseudospinax	X	*	D	*
Rajiformes nov.			**K**	
Rajiformes nov.			C, E	
Scyliorhinidae nov.			**K**	
Spathobatis	X	C	C, D, E, G	F, K
Sphenodus	X	A, H	C, D, E, F, L	B, L
Pseudorhina		A, D	A, D, E, I	B, E
Synechodus	X	A, D	A, C, D, E	B, E
Welcommia	X	F	*	*

area A SW Germany	area F W & SW France	area L Italy
area B SE Germany	area G E France (Cerin)	*Lazarus
area C N Germany	area H Switzerland	**bold** endemic
area D S England	area I NE Spain	
area E N & NW France	area K Portugal	

Appendix 2

Updated list of neoselachians from the Solnhofen area. Data from Kriwet & Klug (2004), Kriwet (2008) and de Carvalho *et al.* (2008).

Hexanchiformes: *Notidanoides muensteri*, '*Eonotidanus*' *serratus*

Protospinacidae, order inc. sed.: *Protospinax annectans*

Synechodontiformes: *Sphenodus nitidus*, *Paraorthacodus* sp., *Synechodus* sp.

Squatiniformes: *Pseudorhina alifera*

Heterodontiformes: *Pracestracion falcifer*, *Heterodonts zitteli*, *Heterodonts semirugosus* (only isolated teeth known from Kehlheim)

Orectolobiformes: *Phorcynis catulina*, Orectoloboidae gen. nov. sp. nov.

Carcharhiniformes: *Palaeoscyllium formosum*, *Macrourogaleus hassei*

Lamniformes: *Palaeocarcharias stromeri*

Batoidea: *Asterodermus platypterus*

This paper is dedicated to Peter Forey for his contributions to our knowledge of the evolution and taxonomy of extinct fishes. We thank L. Cavin for his patience while preparing this paper. C. J. Underwood and J. Rees are acknowledged for sharing their knowledge of Mesozoic neoselachians with us. We also thank W. Kiessling (Berlin) for providing the computer program to calculate confidence intervals. We especially thank C. J. Duffin and C. J. Underwood for their constructive reviews. This study is a project on the systematics and diversity of Mesozoic neoselachians, which is supported by the German Research Foundation (DFG) under contract numbers KR 2307/1-1 and KR 2307/3-1.

References

ADNET, S. & CAPPETTA, H. 2001. A palaeontological and phylogenetical analysis of squaliform sharks (Chondrichthyes: Squaliformes) based on dental characters. *Lethaia*, **34**, 234–248.

ANSORGE, J. 1990. Fischreste (Selachii, Actinopterygii) aus der Wealdentonscholle von Lobber Ort (Münchgut/Rügen/DDR). *Paläontologische Zeitschrift*, **64**, 133–144.

ARRATIA, G., KRIWET, J. & HEINRICH, W.-D. 2002. Selachians and actinopterygians from the Upper Jurassic of Tendaguru, Tanzania. *Mitteilungen des Museums für Naturkunde Berlin, Geowissenschaftliche Reihe*, **5**, 207–230.

BENTON, M. J. 1987. The History of the Biosphere – Equilibrium and Nonequilibrium Models of Global Diversity. *Trends in Ecology and Evolution*, **2**, 153–156.

BIDDLE, J. P. 1988. Contribution à l'étude des sélaciens du Crétacé du Bassin de Paris. Découverte de quelques nouvelles espèce associées à une faune de type wealdien dans le Barrémien supérieur (Crétacé inférieur) des environs de Troyes (Aube). *Publications, Musée de Saint-Dizier*, **2**, 1–22.

BIGOT, A. 1896. Catalogue des sélaciens jurassiques du Calvados et de l'Orne. *Bulletin de la Société linnéenne de Normandie*, **10**(4), 7–13.

BÖTTCHER, R. & DUFFIN, C. J. 2000. The neoselachian shark *Sphenodus* from the Late Kimmeridgian (Late Jurassic) of Nusplingen and Egesheim (Baden-Württemberg, Germany). *Stuttgarter Beiträge zur Naturkunde, Serie B (Geologie und Paläontologie)*, **283**, 1–31.

BRIGGS, J. C. 1995. Global biogeography. *In*: WIGNALL, P. (ed.) *Developments in Palaeontology and Stratigraphy*, **14**, 1–452.

BROOKS, D. R. & VAN VELLER, M. P. G. 2003. Critique of parsimony analysis of endemicity as a method of historical biogeography. *Journal of Biogeography*, **30**, 819–825.

CANDONI, L. 1993. Découverte de *Parasymbolus octevillensis* gen. et sp. nov. (Scyliorhinidae: Elasmobranchii) dans le Kimméridgien de Normandie, France. *Professional Paper of Belgian Geological Survey* **264**, 147–156.

CANDONI, L. 1994. *Parasymbolus octevillensis* Candoni 1993 (Scyliorhinidae Elasmobranchii) dans le Kimméridgien. *Bulletin trimestriel de la Société Géologique de Normandie et Amis Muséum du Havre*, **81**, 47–53.

CANDONI, L. 1995. Deux faunes inédites de sélaciens dans le Jurassique terminal français – premiers résultats stratigraphiques. *Bulletin trimestriel de la Société Géologique de Normandie et Amis Muséum du Havre*, **82**, 29–49.

CANUDO, J. I., CUENCA-BESCÓS, G. & RUIZ-OMENACA, J. I. 1995. Tiburones y rayas (Chondrichthyes, Elasmobranchii) del Barremiense superior (Cretacico inferior) de Vallipón (Castellote, Teruel). *Beca del Museo de Mas de las Matas Ano*, **1995**, 35–57.

CAPPETTA, H. 1980a. Les sélaciens du Crétacé supérieur du Liban. I. Requins. *Palaeontographica Abteilung A*, **168**, 69–148.

CAPPETTA, H. 1980b. Les sélaciens du Crétacé supérieur du Liban. II. Batoides. *Palaeontographica Abteilung A*, **168**, 149–229.

CAPPETTA, H. 1987. Chondrichthyes II. Mesozoic and Cenozoic Elasmobranchii. *In*: SCHULTZE, H.-P. (ed.) *Handbook of Paleoichthyology, 3B*. Gustav Fischer Verlag, 1–193.

CAPPETTA, H. 1990. Hexanchiforme nouveau (Neoselachii) du Crétacé inférieur du sud de la France. *Palaeovertebrata*, **20**, 33–54.

CAVIN, L., CAPPETTA, H. & SERET, B. 1995. Révision de *Blemnobatis morinicus* (Sauvage, 1873) du Portlandien du Boulonnais (Pas-de-Calais, France). Comparaison avec quelques Rhinobatidae Jurassiques. *Geologica et Palaeontologica*, **29**, 245–267.

CIONE, A. L. 1999. First report of a Jurassic ray outside of Europe. *In*: ARRATIA, G. & SCHULTZE, H.-P. (eds) *Mesozoic Fishes 2 – Systematics and Fossil Record*. Dr F. Pfeil, Munich, 21–28.

CROIZAT, L. 1964. *Space, Time, Form: The Biological Synthesis*. L. Croizat, Caracas, Venezuela.

CUNY, G. 1998. Primitive neoselachian sharks: a survey. *Oryctos*, **1**, 3–21.

CUNY, G. & BENTON, M. 1999. Early radiation of the neoselachian sharks in Western Europe. *Geobios*, **32**, 193–204.

CUNY, G., MARTIN, M., RAUSCHER, R. & MAZIN, J. M. 1998. A new neoselachian shark from the Upper Triassic of Grozon (Jura, France). *Geological Magazine*, **135**, 657–668.

DE CARVALHO, M. R. 1996. Higher-level elasmobranch phylogeny, basal squaleans, and paraphyly. *In*: STIASSNY, M. L. J., PARENTI, L. R. & JOHNSON, G. D. (eds) *Interrelationships of Fishes*. Academic Press San Diego, 35–63.

DE CARVALHO, M. R. & MAISEY, J. G. 1996. Phylogenetic relationships of the Upper Jurassic shark *Protospinax* Woodward 1919 (Chondrichthyes: Elasmobranchii). *In*: ARRATIA, G. & VIOHL, G. (eds) *Mesozoic Fishes – Systematics and Paleoecology*. Dr F. Pfeil, Munich, 9–49.

DE CARVALHO, M. R., KRIWET, J. & THIES, D. 2008. Anatomical revision of Late Jurassic angelsharks (Chondrichthyes: Squatinidae). *In*: ARRATIA, G., SCHULTZE, H.-P. & WILSON, M. V. H. (eds) *Mesozoic Fishes, 4*. Dr F. Pfeil, Munich (in press).

DELSATE, D. & CANDONI, L. 2001. Description de nouveaux morphotypes dentaires de Batomorphii toarciens (Jurassique inférieur) du Bassin de Paris: Archaeobatidae nov. fam. *Bulletin de la Société Naturelle de Luxembourg*, **102**, 131–143.

D'ERASMO, G. 1960. Nuovi avanzi ittiolitici della 'serie di Lugh' in Somalia conservati nel Museo Geologico di Firenze. *Palaeontographica Italica*, **55**, 1–23.

DOUADY, D. J., DOSAY, M., SHIVJI, M. S. & STANHOPE, M. J. 2003. Molecular phylogenetic evidence refuting the hypothesis of Batoidea (rays and skates) as derived sharks. *Molecular Phylogenetics and Evolution*, **26**, 215–221.

DUFFIN, C. J. 1993a. New records of Late Jurassic sharks teeth from Southern Germany. *Stuttgarter Beiträge für Naturkunde, Serie B (Geologie und Paläontologie)*, **193**, 1–13.

DUFFIN, C. J. 1993b. The palaeospinacid shark 'Synechodus' jurensis Schweizer, 1964 from the Late Jurassic of Germany. *Professional Paper of Belgian Geological Survey*, **264**, 157–174.

DUFFIN, C. J. & THIES, D. 1987. Hybodont shark teeth from the Kimmeridgian (Late Jurassic) of northwest Germany. *Geologica et Palaeontologica*, **31**, 235–356.

DUFFIN, C. J. & WARD, D. J. 1983. Teeth of a new Neoselachian shark from the British Lower Jurassic. *Palaeontology*, **26**, 839–844.

DUFFIN, C. J. & WARD, D.J. 1993. The Early Jurassic Palaeospinacid sharks of Lyme Regis, southern England. *Belgian Geological Survey Professional Paper*, **264**, 53–102.

FOREY, P. L., HUMPHRIES, C. J., KITCHING, I. J., SCOTLAND, R. W., SIEBERT, D. J. & WILLIAMS, D. 1992. Cladistics. A practical course in systematics. *The Systematics Association Publication*, **10**, 1–191.

GOODWIN, M. B., CLEMENS, W. A., HUTCHINSON, J. H., WOOD, C. B., ZAVADA, M. S., KEMP, A., DUFFIN, C. J. & SCHAFF, C. R. 1999. Mesozoic continental vertebrates with associated palynostratigraphic dates from the Northwestern Ethiopian Plateau. *Journal of Vertebrate Paleontology*, **19**, 728–741.

GREGOR, C. B. 1985. The mass-age distribution of Phanerozoic sediments. *In*: SNELLING, N. J. (ed.) *The Chronology of the Geologic Record*. Geological Society of America, Memoir **10**, Boulder, 284–289.

HAQ, B. U., HARDENBOL, J. & VAIL, P. R. 1988. Mesozoic and Cenozoic chronostratigraphy and cycles of sea-level change. *SEPM Special Publication*, **42**, 71–108.

KLUG, S. & KRIWET, J. 2006a. Anatomy and systematics of the Early Jurassic neoselachian shark *Synechodus smith-woodwardi* (Fraas, 1896) from southern Germany. *Neues Jahrbuch für Geologie und Paläontologie, Monatshefte*, **2006**(4), 193–211.

KLUG, S. & KRIWET, J. 2006b. Diversity and biogeography patterns of Late Jurassic neoselachians (Chondrichthyes, Elasmobranchii). *Berichte – Reports des Instituts für Geowissenschaften, Christian-Albrechts-Universität*, **22**, 50.

KRIWET, J. 1997. Beitrag zur Kenntnis der Fischfauna des Oberjura (unteres Kimmeridgium) der Kohlengrube Guimarota bei Leiria, Mittel-Portugal: 2. Neoselachii (Pisces, Elasmobranchii). *Berliner geowissenschaftliche Abhandlungen, Reihe E*, **25**, 293–301.

KRIWET, J. 1998. Late Jurassic elasmobranch and actinopterygian fishes from Portugal and Spain. *Cuadernos de Geología Ibérica*, **24**, 241–260.

KRIWET, J. 1999. Neoselachier (Pisces, Elasmobranchii) aus der Unterkreide (unteres Barremium) von Galve und Alcaine (Spanien, Provinz Teruel). *Palaeo Ichthyologica*, **9**, 113–142.

KRIWET, J. 2003. Neoselachian remains (Chondrichthyes, Elasmobranchii) from the Middle Jurassic of SW Germany and NW Poland. *Acta Palaeontologia Polonica*, **48**, 583–594.

KRIWET, J. 2004. Late Jurassic selachians (Chondrichthyes: Hybodontiformes, Neoselachii) from Central Portugal. *Neues Jahrbuch für Geologie und Paläontologie, Monatshefte*, **2004**(4), 233–256.

KRIWET, J. 2008. A Late Jurassic carpetshark (Neoselachii, Orectolobiformes) from southern Germany. *In*: ARRATIA, G., SCHULTZE, H.-P. & WILSON, M. V. H. (eds) *Mesozoic Fishes, 4*. Dr F. Pfeil, Munich (in press).

KRIWET, J. & BENTON, M. J. 2004. Neoselachian (Chondrichthyes, Elasmobranchii) diversity across the K/T boundary. *Palaeogeography, Palaeoclimatology, Palaeoecology*, **214**, 181–194.

KRIWET, J. & KLUG, S. 2004. Late Jurassic selachians (Chondrichthyes, Elasmobranchii) from southern Germans: Re-evaluation on taxonomy and diversity. *Zitteliana*, **A44**, 67–95.

LASKER, H. R. 1978. Measurement of taxonomic evolution – preservational consequences. *Paleobiology*, **4**(2), 135–149.

LEIDNER, A. & THIES, D. 1999. Placoid scales and oral teeth of Late Jurassic elasmobranches from Europe. *In*: ARRATIA, G. & SCHULTZE, H.-P. (eds) *Mesozoic Fishes 2 – Systematics and Fossil Record*. Dr F. Pfeil, Munich, 29–40.

LERICHE, M. 1910. Sur quelques Poissons du Crétacé du Bassin de Paris. *Bulletin de la Société Géologique de France*, **10**, 455–471.

MAISEY, J. G. 1984. Higher elasmobranch phylogeny and biostratigraphy. *Zoological Journal of the Linnean Society*, **82**, 33–54.

MAISEY, J. G., NAYLOR, G. J. P. & WARD, D. J. 2004. Mesozoic elasmobranchs, neoselachian phylogeny and the rise of modern elasmobranch diversity. *In*: ARRATIA, G. & TINTORI, A. (eds) *Mesozoic Fishes 3 – Systematics, Paleoenvironments and Biodiversity*. Dr F. Pfeil, Munich, 17–56.

MOOI, R. D. & GILL, A. C. 2002. Historical biogeography of fishes. *In*: HART, P. S. B. & REYNOLDS, J. D. (eds) *Handbook of Fish Biology and Fisheries, Vol. I*. Blackwell Science, Oxford, 43–68.

MORONE, J. J. & CRISCI, J. V. 1995. Historical biogeography: introduction and methods. *Annual Review of Ecology, Evolution, and Systematics*, **26**, 373–401.

MUDROCH, A. 2001. *Fischzähne aus dem Oberjura Nordwesteuropas – Systematik, Biogeochemie und Palökologie*. PhD Thesis, University of Hanover.

MUSICK, J. A., HARBIN, M. M. & COMPAGNO, L. J. V. 2004. Historical zoogeography of the Selachii. *In*: CARRIER, J. C., MUSICK, J. A. & HEITHAUS, M. R. (eds) *Biology of Sharks and their Relatives*. CRC Press, Boca Raton, FL, 33–78.

MUTTERLOSE, J., BRUMSACK, H., FLÖGEL, S., HAY, W., KLEIN, C., LANGROCK, U., LIPINSKI, M., RICKEN, W., SÖDING, E., STEIN, R. & SWIENTEK, O. 2003. The Greenland-Norwegian Seaway: A key area for understanding Late Jurassic to Early Cretaceous paleoenvironments. *Paleoceanography*, **18**, 1–26.

NELSON, G. & PLATNICK, N. I. 1981. *Systematics and biogeography: Cladistics and vicariance*. Columbia University Press, New York.

NELSON, G. & ROSEN, D. E. 1981. *Vicariance Biogeography: A Critique*. Columbia University press, New York.

PATTERSON, C. 1966. British Wealden Sharks. *Bulletin of the British Museum (Natural History), Geology*, **11**, 283–350.

PETERS, S. E. & FOOTE, M. 2001. Biodiversity in the Phanerozoic: a reinterpretation. *Paleobiology*, **27**, 583–601.

RAUP, D. M. 1991. The future of analytical paleobiology. *Short Courses in Paleontology*, **4**, 207–216.

RAWSON, P. F. & RILEY, L. A. 1982. Latest Jurassic-Early Cretaceous events and the 'late Cimmerian unconformity' in North Sea area. *AAPG Bulletin*, **66**, 2628–2648.

REES, J. 2002. Shark fauna and depositional environment of the earliest Cretaceous Vitaback Clays at Eriksdal, southern Sweden. *Transactions of the Royal Society of Edinburgh, Earth Sciences*, **93**, 59–71.

REES, J. 2005. Neoselachian shark and ray teeth from the Valanginian, Lower Cretaceous, of Wawal. *Palaeontology*, **48**, 209–221.

ROSEN, B. R. 1988. From fossils to earth history: applied historical biogeography. In: MYERS, A. A. & GILLERS, P. S. (eds) *Analytical Biogeography*. Chapman & Hall, London, 437–481.

ROSEN, B. R. & SMITH, A. B. 1988. Tectonics from fossils? Analysis of reef-coral and sea-urchin distribution from late Cretaceous to Recent, using a new method. Gondwana and Tethys. In: AUDLEY-CHARLES, M. G. & HALLAM, A. (eds) *Geological Society Special Publication*, **37**, Clarendon Press, Oxford.

SAINT-SEINE, P. DE. 1949. Les poisons des calcaires lithographiques de Cerin (Ain). *Nouvelles Archives du Muséum d'Histoire Naturelle de Lyon*, **2**, 159–276.

SAUVAGE, H.-É. 1902. Recherches sur les vertébrés du Kimmeridgien supérieur de Fumel (Lot-et-Garonne). *Mémoires de la Société Géologique de France (Paléontologie)*, **25**, 1–32.

SCHLUTER, D. & RICKLEFS, R. E. 1993. Convergence and the regional component of species diversity. In: RICKLEFS, R. E. & SCHLUTER, D. (eds) *Species Diversity in Ecological Communities*. University of Chicago Press, Chicago, 230–240.

SCHWEIZER, R. 1964. Elasmobranchier und Holocephalen aus den Nusplinger Plattenkalken. *Palaeontographica Abteilung A*, **123**, 58–110.

SEPKOSKI, J. J., JR. 1978. Kinetic-Model of phanerozoic taxonomic diverstiy. 1. Analysis of marine orders. *Paleobiology*, **4**, 223–251.

SEPKOSKI, J. J., JR. 1988. Alpha, beta or gamma: Where does all the diversity go? *Paleobiology*, **14**, 221–235.

SHIRAI, S. 1992. Phylogenetic relationships of the angel sharks, with comments on elasmobranch phylogeny (Chondrichthyes, Squatinidae). *Copeia*, **1992**, 505–518.

SHIRAI, S. 1996. Phylogenetic interrelationships of Neoselachians (Chondrichthyes: Euselachii). In:

STIASSEY, M. L. J., PARENTI, L. R. & JOHNSON, G. D. (eds) *Interrelationships of Fishes*. Academic Press, San Diego, 9–34.

SIMPSON, G. G. 1943. Mammals and the nature of continents. *American Journal of Science*, **241**, 1–31.

SMITH, A. B., GALE, A. S. & MONKS, N. E. A. 2001. Sea-level change and rock-record bias in the Cretaceous: a problem for extinction and biodiversity studies. *Paleobiology*, **27**, 241–253.

THIES, D. 1979. Selachierzähne aus der nordwestdeutschen Unterkreide. *International Union of Geological Sciences, Series A*, **6**, 211–222.

THIES, D. 1981. Vier neue Neoselachier-Haiarten aus der NW-deutschen Unterkreide. *Neues Jahrbuch für Geologie und Paläontologie, Monatshefte*, **1981**(8), 475–486.

THIES, D. 1982. A neoselachian shark tooth from the Lower Triassic of the Kocaeli (=Bithynian) Peninsula, W Turkey. *Neues Jahrbuch für Geologie und Paläontologie, Monatshefte*, **1982**(5), 272–278.

THIES, D. 1983. Jurazeitliche Neoselachier aus Deutschland und S-England (Jurassic Neoselachians from Germany and S-England). *Courier Forschungs-Institut Senckenberg*, **58**, 1–116.

THIES, D. 1989. Some problematical shark teeth (Chondrichthyes: Neoselachii) from the early and middle Jurassic of Germany. *Paläontologische Zeitschrift*, **63**, 103–117.

THIES, D. 1992. A new species of *Palaeospinax* (Chondrichthyes, Neoselachii) from the Lower Jurassic *Posidonia* Shale of Southern Germany. *Paläontologische Zeitschrift*, **63**, 137–146.

THIES, D. 1993. New evidence of *Annea* and *Jurobatos*, two rare neoselachians (Pisces: Chondrichthyes) from the Jurassic of Europe. *Professional Paper of Belgian Geological Survey*, **264**, 137–146.

THIES, D. & CANDONI, L. 1998. *Corysodon* Saint-Seine 1949 – a valid genus of Mesozoic neoselachian sharks. *Geologica et Palaeontologica*, **32**, 221–233.

TURNER, S. & YOUNG, G. C. 1987. Shark teeth from the Early-Middle Devonian Cravens Peak Beds, Georgina Basin, Queensland. *Alcheringa*, **11**, 233–244.

UNDERWOOD, C. J. 2002. Sharks, rays and a chimaeroid from the Kimmeridgian (Late Jurassic) of Ringstead, Southern England. *Palaeontology*, **45**, 297–325.

UNDERWOOD, C. J. 2006. Diversification of the Neoselachii (Chondrichthyes) during the Jurassic and Cretaceous. *Paleobiology*, **32**, 215–235.

UNDERWOOD, C. J. & REES, J. 2002. Selachian faunas from the lowermost Cretaceous Purbeck Group of Dorset, southern England. *Special Papers in Palaeontology*, **68**, 83–101.

UNDERWOOD, & WARD, D. J. 2004. Neoselachian sharks and rays from the British Bathonian (Middle Jurassic). *Palaeontology*, **47**, 447–501.

UNDERWOOD, C. J., MITCHELL, S. F. & VELTKAMP, K. J. 1999. Shark and ray teeth from the Hauterivian (Lower Cretaceous) of north-east England. *Palaeontology*, **42**, 287–302.

WAGGONER, B. 1999. Biogeographic analyses of the Ediacara biota: a conflict with paleotectonic reconstructions. *Paleobiology*, **25**, 440–458.

WARD, D. J. & THIES, D. 1987. Hexanchid shark teeth (Neoselachii, Vertebrata) from the Lower Cretaceous of Germany and England. *Mesozoic Research*, **1**, 89–106.

WILKINSON, B. H. & WALKER, J. C. G. 1989. Phanerozoic cycling of sedimentary carbonate. *American Journal of Science*, **289**, 525–548.

WOLD, C. N. & HAY, W. W. 1990. Estimating ancient sediment fluxes. *American Journal of Science*, **290**(9), 1069–1089.

ZIEGLER, P. A. 1990. *Geological Atlas of Western and Central Europe*. Elsevier, Amsterdam.

The varasichthyid and other crossognathiform fishes, and the Break-up of Pangaea

GLORIA ARRATIA

Biodiversity Research Center, The University of Kansas, Dyche Hall, Lawrence, Kansas 66045-7561, USA (e-mail: garratia@ku.edu)

Abstract: Crossognathiforms have been traditionally considered typical marine Cretaceous forms widely represented in the Northern Hemisphere and by a few members in Brazil. During the last 30 years they have been interpreted as Teleostei *incertae sedis*, clupeocephalans or a non-monophyletic group. New evidence indicates that the Oxfordian taxon *Chongichthys* (previously considered a Teleostei *incertae sedis* or a clupeocephalan), the Late Jurassic family Varasichthyidae (interpreted as basal teleosts), and the crossognathoids and pachyrhizodontoids form a clade here recognized as the Crossognathiformes. Varasichthyids are the sister group of a clade including *Chongichthys* (at the base) and crossognathoids + pachyrhizodontoids. The Crossognathiformes (including Varasichthyidae and *Chongichthys*) are basal teleosts placed between the Late Jurassic basal genera *Tharsis* and *Ascalabos* in one tree or between *Ascalabos* and the ichthyodectiforms in the second tree. The position of elopomorphs as the most basal extant teleosts is confirmed. A new interpretation of the phylogenetic position of the clade [*Humbertia* + [*Erichalcis* + [*Leptolepides* + *Orthogonikleithrum*]]], at the base of clupeocephalans, is suggested.

The presence of the Late Jurassic varasichthyids (e.g. *Domeykos*) in South America (Chile) and Central America (Cuba; *Luisichthys*), and *Chongichthys* (Chile), and of the Late Jurassic genera *Ascalabos* and *Tharsis* and the ichthyodectiforms (e.g. *Allothrissops*) in Europe (e.g. Germany) allows the proposal of a sister-area relationship between Chile and Cuba, which was the sister area of Germany during the Late Jurassic. The Late Jurassic connection between the Palaeopacific (Chilean region) and the Tethys Sea (southern Germany) was through the newly formed Central Atlantic Ocean (Cuban region) as a result of the break up of Pangaea and separation of North America, South America and Africa.

The Crossognathiformes is an extinct fish order, erected by Taverne (1989) to contain the crossognathoids and the pachyrhizodontoids, and is considered a typical Cretaceous taxon. The history of the group is complicated since several families and numerous genera and species have been described over the last century, most of which are now considered synonyms (see for instance Agassiz 1841; Dixon 1850; Pictet 1858; Cope 1872; Loomis 1900; Woodward 1901; Forey 1977; Patterson & Rosen 1977; Teller-Marshall & Bardack 1978; Taverne 1980, 1989; Patterson 1993).

Currently, crossognathoids are known from one family, two genera and three species, all recovered in localities in the Northern Hemisphere: *Crossognathus sabaudianus* from the Lower Cretaceous of France (Vallentigny), Germany (e.g. Helgoland, Hildesheim), and France (Voirons) (Taverne 1989; Patterson 1993), *Crossognathus danubiensis* from the Lower Cretaceous of Romania (Cavin & Grigorescu 2005), and *Apsopelix anglicus* from North America (e.g. Colorado, Kansas, S Dakota), England, and France (Teller-Marshall & Bardack 1978). The oldest known crossognathiforms are the specimens of *Crossognathus* recovered in Voirons, Barremian age. In contrast, pachyrhizodontoids are known from many species placed in at least two families, i.e. Notelopidae and Pachyrhizodontidae, with a wide geographical and temporal distribution. The oldest pachyrhizodontoids are known from the Aptian of Brazil (e.g. *Notelops brama* and *Rhacolepis buccalis*) (see Agassiz 1833–1844; Jordan & Branner 1908; Silva Santos & Valença 1968; Dunkle 1940; Forey 1977; Maisey 1991*a*, *b*) and the youngest from the Paleogene (Lutetian) of Monte Bolca (*Platinx macropterus*) (Taverne 1980; Patterson 1993).

The monophyly of the Crossognathiformes *sensu* Taverne (1989) is supported by few unique characters mainly associated with head morphology. However, Cavin (2001) in his study of a new pachyrhizodontoid, *Goulmimichthys arambourgi*, from the Upper Cretaceous of Morocco, questioned the monophyly of crossognathiforms. Cavin (2001, p. 530, 533) suggested that crossognathoids are not closely related to pachyrhizodontoids, but possibly related to varasichthyids. A possible sister-group relationship was proposed by Cavin & Grigorescu (2005, p. 5, 14).

From: CAVIN, L., LONGBOTTOM, A. & RICHTER, M. (eds) *Fishes and the Break-up of Pangaea*. Geological Society, London, Special Publications, **295**, 71–92. DOI: 10.1144/SP295.6   0305-8719/08/$15.00 © The Geological Society of London 2008.

The Upper Jurassic of Chile is known from some remarkably well-preserved fishes, among which the teleosts are the best represented (for details, see Arratia & Schultze 1999). Among the Jurassic Chilean teleosts three groups deserve attention here: the family Varasichthyidae, a teleost *incertae sedis*, *Chongichthys dentatus*, from the Oxfordian of the Cordillera de Domeyko, northern Chile, and an undetermined pachyrhizodontoid from the Upper Jurassic of Termas del Flaco, central Chile.

The monophyletic family Varasichthyidae is known from four marine genera (*Bobbichthys*, *Domeykos*, *Protoclupea*, and *Varasichthys*) from the Oxfordian of northern Chile and one marine genus (*Luisichthys*) from the Upper Jurassic of Cuba (Arratia 1981, 1994, 1997; Arratia & Schultze 1985). The phylogenetic position of the family is between the European marine genera *Tharsis* and *Ascalabos* (among basal teleosts) (Arratia 1996, 1997, 1999), and this seems to be correct if the primitive morphological pattern of the group is considered. In contrast, the monotypic family Chongichthyidae is known from one marine genus, *Chongichthys*, with a very distinct morphology that is still incompletely known (Arratia 1982, 1997). Previous studies have given an unresolved phylogenetic position of *Chongichthys* among Teleostei or among the so-called clupeocephalans (Arratia 1982; Arratia 1997, fig. 102). While *Chongichthys* is well known (from the neurocranium, external skull bones, and the vertebral column and its associated elements), the undetermined pachyrhizodontoid recovered in the Upper Jurassic of central Chile is known only from disarticulated head bones and a caudal skeleton showing an hypural plate probably formed by the fusion of three hypurals (Arratia & Schultze 1999, fig. 17).

The goal of this paper is to test whether varasichthyids and *Chongichthys* are crossognathiforms or not, and to assess the paleogeographical implications of these fishes.

Methods and material

The phylogenetic relationships of varasichthyids, *Chongichthys*, and crossognathiforms are studied using cladistic principles (Hennig 1966). The phylogenetic analyses in this study were conducted using PAUP (Phylogenetic Analysis Using Parsimony) software (version 4.0b10) of D. L. Swofford (2005) on a Macintosh computer. All characters are treated as unweighted, unordered, and considered to be simple and independent of one another (Appendix 1). Most characters and taxa from previous study are used (Arratia 2000, appendix 1). Two taxa, the Late Jurassic *Ascalabothrissops* and *Tischlingerichthys*, were deleted because

of their numerous missing characters. Four characters were deleted (Arratia 2000, characters 38, 120, 134 and 147) because of partial-overlap with other characters or ambiguous description. A few characters were modified from their original presentation; these changes are identified in the list of characters (see Appendix 1). The coding of *Apsopelix anglicus*, *Crossognathus sabaudianus*, *Chongichthys dentatus*, *Goulmimichthys arambourgi*, *Notelops brama*, and *Rhacolepis buccalis* were added to the data matrix, as well as seven additional characters (188 to 194) (Appendix 2). Nine genera are included in the outgroup (*Amia*, the aspidorhynchiforms *Aspidorhynchus*, *Belonostomus*, and *Vinctifer*, the lepisosteiforms *Lepisosteus* and *Obaichthys*, the pycnodontiform *Mesturus*, and the pachycormiforms *Hypsocormus* and *Pachycormus*).

For the coding of the additional taxa added to Arratia's (2000) matrix, the following literature was used:

Apsopelix anglicus: Teller-Marshall & Bardack (1978), Patterson & Rosen (1977), and my own observations on specimens deposited at FMNH and KUVP.

Chongichthys dentatus: Arratia (1982, 1986, 1997) and observations on uncatalogued material recently collected by Arratia and H.-P. Schultze in northern Chile.

Crossognathus sabaudianus: Wenz (1965), Patterson & Rosen (1977), and Taverne (1989).

Goulmimichthys arambourgi: Cavin (2001).

Notelops brama: Forey (1977), and Maisey (1991*b*).

Rhacolepis buccalis: Forey (1977), and Maisey (1991*a*).

For additional material included in this study see Arratia (1999, p. 269–273).

Abbreviations

Institutional abbreviations. FMNH, Field Museum of Natural History, Chicago, Illinois, U.S.A.; KUVP, Vertebrate Paleontological Collection of the Natural History Museum, The University of Kansas, Lawrence, Kansas, U.S.A.

Anatomical abbreviations. ang, angular; ant, antorbital; ANT, anterior; ant + io1, fused antorbital and infraorbital 1; asph, autosphenotic; boc, basioccipital; br.r, branchiostegal rays; bsp, basisphenoid; cfr?, caudal fin rays?; cl, cleithrum; de, dentary; d.sct, dorsal caudal scute; dsph, dermosphenotic; E1–4, epurals 1–4; ep, epiotic; exc, extrascapula; exo, exoccipital; f.i.c.a, foramen for internal carotid artery; f.o.n.a, foramen for orbital artery; H1 + 2 + 3?, fused hypurals 1, 2 and 3?; H3–11, hypurals 3–11; hs2, haemal spine of preural centrum 2; hyd, hypural diasteme; ic, intercalar; io1–5, infraorbital bones 1–5; io4 + 5, fused infraorbital bones 4 and 5; iop, interopercle; lj, lower jaw; met, mesethmoid; mx, maxilla; na, nasal bone; naPU1, neural arch of preural centrum 1; naU1, neural arch of first ural centrum; nsPU2–4, neural spine of preural centra 2–4; op, opercle; op.p, opercular process of the hyomandibula; orb, orbitosphenoid; pa[= fr], parietal bone [= frontal bone of traditional terminology]; par, parasphenoid; pcl, postcleithrum; PH, parhypural; pmx, premaxilla; pop, preopercle; ppa[= pa], postparietal bone [= parietal bone of traditional terminology]; pro, prootic; pt, pterotic; p.t.f.c, posterior opening of jugular canal; PR1, 20, principal caudal rays 1, 20; ptt, posttemporal bone; PU1, preural centrum 1; qu, quadrate; rar, retroarticular; rep.r, reduced epaxial caudal ray; scl, supracleithrum; sct, scute; smx, supramaxilla; smx1–2, supramaxillae 1–2; sob, suborbital bone; soc, supraoccipital; sop, subopercle; sup, supraorbital bone; sy, symplectic; U?, ural centrum?; U2, second ural centrum; U + H1–2, ural centrum fused to hypurals 1 and 2; UN1–6, uroneurals 1–6; v.sct, ventral caudal scute; I, foramen for olfactory tract; III, foramen for oculomotor nerve; V, foramen for trigeminal nerve; VI, foramen for abducens nerve; VII, foramen for hyomandibular trunk of facial nerve; IX, foramen for glossopharyngeal nerve; X, foramen for vagus nerve.

Varasichthyid and crossognathiform characters

A possible close relationship between varasichthyids and crossognathoids was suggested by Cavin (2001, p. 530) based on the following characters: (1) a foramen for the vagus nerve placed in the posterolateral face of the exoccipital alone; (2) parasphenoid extending posterior to basioccipital; (3) atrophied premaxilla; (4) ventroposterior region of preopercle broadly expanded; and (5) absence of fringing fulcra in median fins. Some varasichthyids and crossognathoids have about 10 hypurals, six unoneurals, and the first uroneurals reach preural centrum 3. Cavin & Grigorescu (2005, p. 14) added a few more features to the list of potential synapomorphies, e.g. edentulous parasphenoid, trigeminal foramen opening into the orbit and presence of numerous tubules and grooves in the preopercular canal.

Although the five varasichthyid genera share the synapomorphies of the family (see Arratia 1994, 1997, 1999), there are some major morphological differences between them: it is difficult to put forward generalizations concerning the whole group. All of them share several homoplastic features and two uniquely derived features e.g. the presence of numerous long branches of the preopercular sensory canal almost reaching the ventral and postero-ventral margins of the broadly expanded ventral limb of the preopercle (Arratia 1994, text-fig. 4A–D; Arratia 1997, fig. 88A), and the unique pattern of circuli in the cycloid scales (Arratia 1997, fig. 6A–C). Among varasichthyids, *Varasichthys ariasi* (Fig. 1a) is the best known; the morphological information of the species includes almost the whole skeleton, even the neurocranium and its foramina for cranial nerves.

A comparison between varasichthyids and crossognathoids shows several similarities, but also some interesting differences. For instance:

(1) The foramen for the vagus nerve located on the exoccipital alone (Fig. 2a) is shared by varasichthyids and crossognathoids. This feature is shared by varasichthyids and more advanced teleosts in the phylogenetic hypothesis of Arratia (1999: fig. 19, character 25, state [1]), a phylogenetic position that it is more basal than the clupeocephalan phylogenetic level suggested by Taverne (1989). See phylogenetic analysis, character 21[1] below.

(2) The position of the trigeminal foramen opening into the orbit is an interesting feature that deserves more attention. According to the published evidence that is confirmed here (varasichthyid prootics were checked again), a trigeminal foramen anteriorly-placed, and apparently opening into the orbit, is found in *Domeykos* and *Luisichthys*, but not in *Varasichthys* (where the foramen is laterally-placed) (Arratia 1994, text-fig. 3A, C, E).

(3) The parasphenoid of *Varasichthys ariasi* extends posterior to the basioccipital (Fig. 2A); a similar condition was described and illustrated for the crossognathoid *Apsopelix anglicus* by Teller-Marshall & Bardack (1978, fig. 3; pers. obser. in material deposited at KUVP and FMNH). However, this is not a synapomorphy of Varasichthyidae because the parasphenoid is short in *Domeykos* as well as in *Luisichthys* (see Arratia, 1994: text-fig. 3A, C, E). The presence of a long parasphenoid extending posterior to the basioccipital in *Varasichthys ariasi* and *Apsopelix anglicus* may be interpreted as independently acquired in both taxa. See phylogenetic analysis, character 11[2].

(4) An edentulous parasphenoid is apparently the condition present in all varasichthyids, but this feature is not unique to varasichthyids and crossognathoids. It is also found in other crossognathiforms and in a variety of teleosts. See phylogenetic analysis, character 10[1].

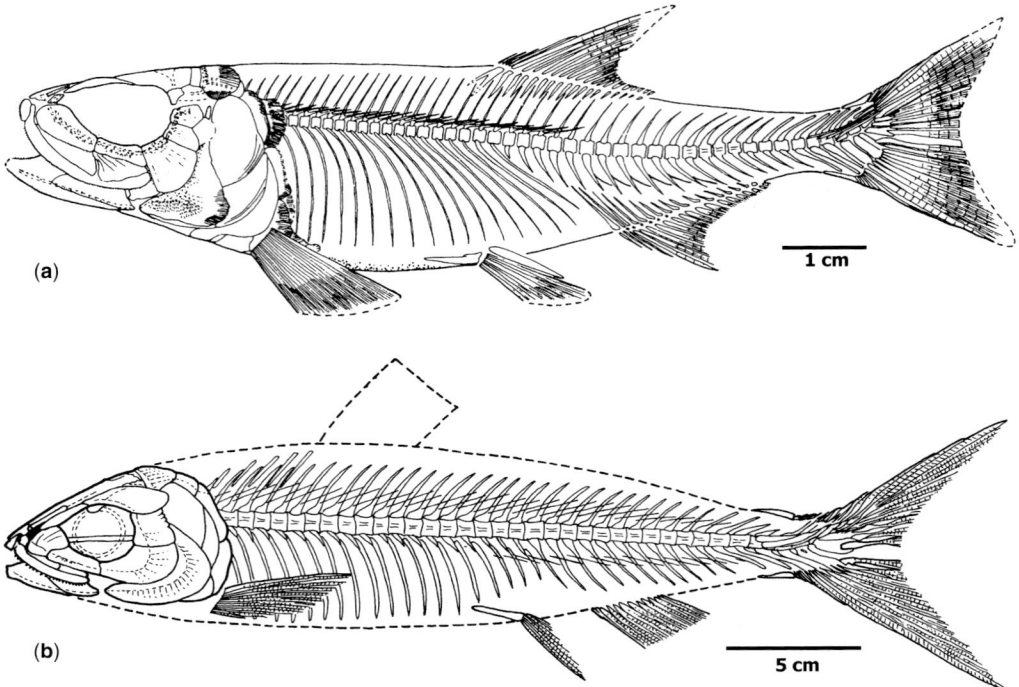

Fig. 1. Restorations in lateral views. (**a**) *Varasichthys ariasi* (after Arratia 1996); (**b**) *Crossognathus sabaudianus* (slightly modified from Taverne 1989).

(5) The premaxilla of crossognathoids (Fig. 3b) is very small, and it has been misinterpreted sometimes because of its small size (Teller-Marshall & Bardack 1978). In addition, it is placed between the anterior border of the maxillary blade and the very short, anterior articulatory process of the maxilla, so that both premaxillae lie below the middle region of the mesethmoid (see Taverne 1989, fig. 4). The premaxilla of *Apsopelix* is still unknown. Among varasichthyids, the premaxilla is known only in *Varasichthys ariasi*. The premaxilla of *Varasichthys ariasi* is small, triangular-shaped (Fig. 3a), slightly elongated, and mostly placed below the elongated articulatory process of the maxilla. Thus, only a small section of the maxilla is placed below the mesethmoid. This is a pattern similar to that found in other primitive forms, e.g. *Pholidophorus bechei, Leptolepis coryphaenoides, Ascalabos,* and *Tharsis* (Arratia 1996, fig. 1D: Arratia 1997, figs. 5, 15, 16; pers. obser.).

(6) There is a large extrascapular bone (Fig. 3b) in crossognathoids. A large bone is also

present in varasichthyids (Fig. 3a) as well as in other crossognathiforms. See below phylogenetic analysis, character 189[1].

(7) The presence of a ventro-posteriorly expanded preopercular bone with many long preopercular sensory tubules is a synapomorphy of Varasichthyidae. Although crossognathoids and the elopiforms have a preopercular bone that is expanded posteriorly, the shape of the preopercle in crossognathiforms, elopiforms, and varasichthyids differs in the three groups. In crossognathoids and elopiforms the preopercle is broadly expanded posteriorly and its dorsal limb does not narrow dorsally as in varasichthyids (cf. Fig. 3a and 3b). In addition, the position and orientation of the preopercle in varasichthyids and crossognathoids are different. Grooves are not associated with the preopercular sensory canal in varasichthyids; the surface of the bone is smooth.

(8) The absence of fringing fulcra in median fins is a feature shared by varasichthyids, crossognathoids, pachyrhizodontoids as well as most other teleosts above the level of *Tharsis* (Arratia, 1999, figs 19, 20, character

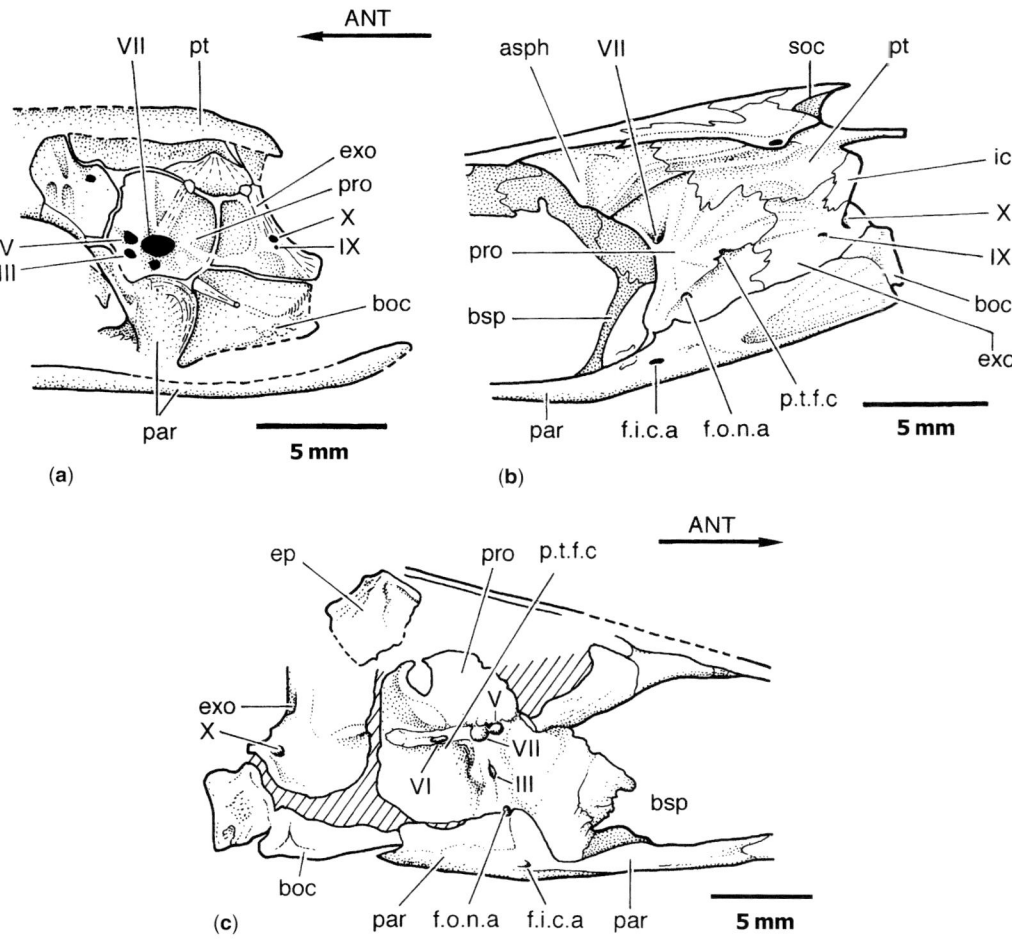

Fig. 2. Braincases in lateral views. (**a**) *Varasichthys ariasi* (slightly modified from Arratia 1981); (**b**) *Rhacolepis buccalis* (slightly modified from Forey 1977); (**c**) *Chongichthys dentatus* (slightly modified from Arratia 1982).

172[1]). Apparently, all crossognathiforms also lack basal fulcra. However, the dorsal elements illustrated for *Crossognathus sabaudianus* by Patterson & Rosen (1977, fig. 21) resemble a series of dorsal basal fulcra instead of procurrent rays. Unfortunately, this is a difficult feature to observe in these fishes because caudal fin rays are often incomplete or poorly preserved.

(9) The caudal skeletons of varasichthyids and crossognathoids (Fig. 4a, b) as well as those of some other basal teleosts share some primitive teleostean features such as the large number of uroneurals and hypurals (see phylogenetic analysis, characters 118 and 124). However, both groups differ in the position of the anteriormost uroneurals in relation to

the lateral surfaces of the centra (resembling the ichthyodectiform pattern present in crossognathoids, as noted by Patterson & Rosen 1977; see below, character 120), the unfused (in varasichthyids) *versus* fused (in crossognathoids) condition of hypurals 1 and 2 (see below, character 164), the presence of a broad hypural diasteme in varasichthyids (missing in crossognathoids, see below, character 128), and the length of the neural spines or preural centra 1–3 (see phylogenetic analysis, characters 105 and 106).

Certainly, there are morphological similarities between varasichthyids and *Crossognathus* as Cavin (2001) and Cavin & Grigorescu (2005) correctly noted. However, there are very few

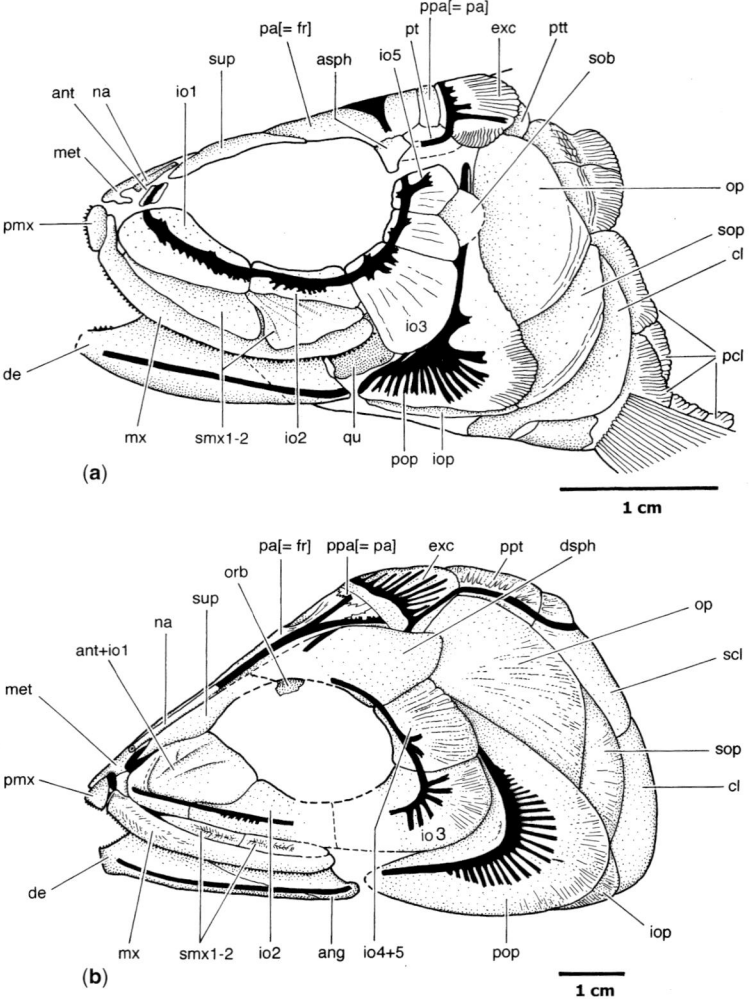

Fig. 3. Heads in lateral views. (**a**) *Varasichthys ariasi* (modified from Arratia 1984); (**b**) *Crossognathus sabaudianus* (modified from Taverne 1989).

similarities between varasichthyids and *Apsopelix anglicus*. Despite these overall similarities, varasichthyids do not present the crossognathiform synapomorphies of Taverne (1989). For instance, varasichthyids do not share their unique features of the circumorbital series of bones with crossognathoids; i.e. the presence of a complete circumorbital ring with no space between bones as is found in crossognathiforms. In varasichthyids, the antorbital and infraorbital 1 are separate elements of 'normal' size, and not fused as in crossognathiforms (cf. Fig. 3a and 3b). In varasichthyids, the complete circumorbital series is known only from *Varasichthys ariasi* and the series (see Fig. 3a) forms an incomplete ring, the so-called

'archaic' teleostean type of Taverne (1989), and is similar to that in *Leptolepis coryphaenoides* and other basal teleosts. The dermosphenotic is a large, well-developed bone in crossognathoids; the dermosphenotic is unknown in varasichthyids, but the preserved circumorbital bones do not suggest that the bone was large, as in crossognathoids. In crossognathoids the posterior infraorbital bones are large, elongate and extend over the anterior margin of the preopercle, whereas the bones are comparatively smaller (cf. Fig. 3a and 3b) in varasichthyids and similar to those in *Leptolepis coryphaenoides* and other primitive teleosts (see Arratia 1996, fig. 1D; Arratia 1997, figs. 5, 15, 26, 40).

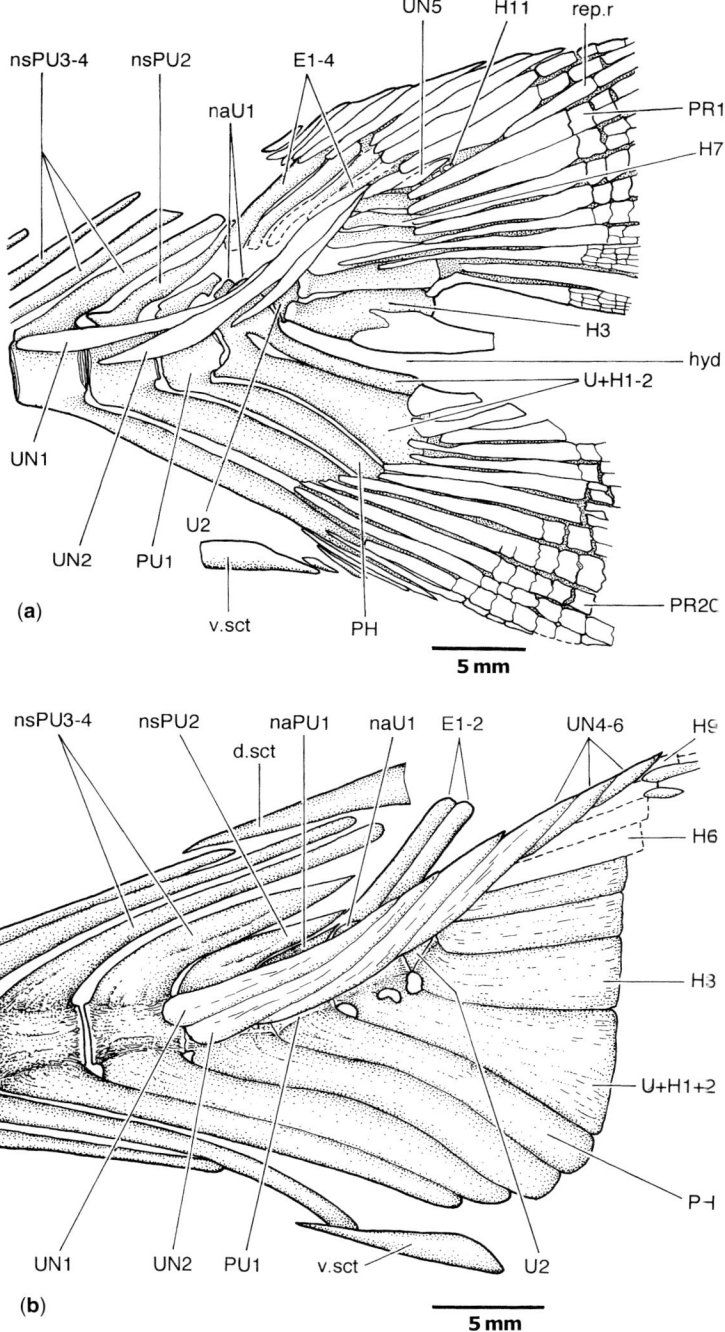

Fig. 4. Caudal skeletons in lateral views. (**a**) *Domeykos profetaensis* (slightly modified from Arratia 1984); (**b**) *Crossognathus sabaudianus* (modified from Taverne 1989).

There are other major differences between varasichthyids and crossognathoids. The two supramaxillary bones present in varasichthyids are well-developed as in other primitive teleosts. In contrast, the supramaxillary bones in crossognathoids are narrower than in varasichthyids (cf. Fig. 3a and 3b). Varasichthyids have a series of epineural bones in the abdominal region and a few epipleurals, whereas a complete series of dorsal and ventral intermuscular bones are present along the caudal region in crossognathoids (cf. Fig. 1a and 1b). Although the caudal skeleton is incompletely known in crossognathoids as well as in varasichthyids, there are important differences in the number of epurals and the hypural series. Hypurals 1 and 2 (Fig. 4b) are fused into one element in crossognathoids, which is a synapomorphy of crossognathiforms (Taverne 1989). Hypurals 1 and 2 are distinct elements in varasichthyids (Fig. 4a). Separate hypurals is the primitive condition for teleosts.

Chongichthyidae and crossognathiforms

The monotypic family Chongichthyidae was erected by Arratia (1982) to contain a newly-described species from the Oxfordian of northern Chile, *Chongichthys dentatus*, which was left as Teleostei *incertae sedis*. *C. dentatus* is incompletely known (Fig. 5a). For instance, the caudal fin is lacking in all specimens and the infraorbital series is incompletely preserved. New material with partially-preserved orbital bones and complete opercular series permitted Arratia (1986) to partially complete the description of the head. *Chongichthys* appears in an unresolved position among clupeocephalans in Arratia's (1997, fig. 102) phylogenetic hypothesis.

A general comparison between *C. dentatus* and crossognathiforms shows that there are apparently more morphological similarities between *Chongichthys* and the pachyrhizodontoids than between *Chongichthys* and the crossognathoids (cf. Figs 1b, 3b and 5a, b, 6a, b). For instance, the posterior series of infraorbital bones is composed of elongated bones in *Chongichthys*, extending over the preopercle, in a pattern similar to that found in *Rhacolepis buccalis* (cf. Fig. 6a and 6b) among pachyrhizodontoids (see Forey 1977, figs 6, 30; Maisey 1991*a*, p. 250; Maisey, 1991*b*, p. 262). However, the bone that is interpreted as infraorbital 3 in *Chongichthys* is comparatively much larger than the bone interpreted as infraorbital 2+3 in *Rhacolepis bucalis* by Forey (1977). The interpretation of the infraorbital bones is different in Maisey (1991*b*) where *Notelops* is described as having

only three infraorbitals and *Rhacolepis* four infraorbital bones (Maisey 1991*a*). The new material that was recently collected in northern Chile does not allow clarification of the composition of the complete circumorbital series in *Chongichthys*, so that the limit between infraorbital bones 1 and 2 remains unclear.

The preopercle of *Chongichthys dentatus* lacks the broad posterior expansion present in crossognathoids (cf. Fig. 6a and 6b) and in *Pachyrhizodus megalops* (Forey 1977, fig. 30). The shape of the preopercle of *Chongichthys* differs from that of *Notelops brama* and *Rhacolepis buccalis* (Forey 1977, figs 6, 20; Maisey 1991*a*, p. 250; Maisey 1991*b*, p. 262). However, the pattern of the branches of the preopercular sensory canal is similar in the three taxa.

The pattern of epineural bones, as processes of the neural arches of the abdominal vertebrae of *Chongichthys*, resembles that in *Notelops* and *Rhacolepis* and is unlike the pattern in crossognathoids (cf. Figs 1b and 5a, b). However, *Chongichthys* has few epipleural bones associated with the first caudal vertebrae. Epipleural bones are absent in both *Notelops* and *Rhacolepis* according to the descriptions and restorations by Forey (1977).

Chongichthys dentatus presents two large postparietal bones (the so-called parietals of traditional terminology) that are slightly separated caudally by a small supraoccipital bone bearing a small short supraoccipital crest (Arratia 1986, text-fig. 13A). A similar condition is found in *Notelops brama* (Forey 1977). However, the supraoccipital extends rostrad, completely separating both postparietal bones in *Racolepis buccalis*. The parietal branch of the supraorbital sensory canal extends into the postparietal bone in *Chongichthys* unlike the condition in pachyrhizodontoids where the branch ends in the parietal bone (so-called frontal of traditional terminology).

Additionally, anterior and middle pit-lines are present in *Chongichthys* unlike the condition found in *Rhacolepis* and *Notelops*. Anterior and middle pit-lines have not been reported in pachyrhizodontoids. The pattern of the supraorbital canal and pit-lines found in *Chongichthys* corresponds to the primitive pattern found in basal teleosts such as *Leptolepis coryphaenoides*, *Ascalabos voithii*, and others (see Arratia 1997, figs 5, 12).

The neurocranium of *Chongichthys*, as far as the preservation permits, shows major differences from that of pachyrhizodontoids (Forey 1977, figs 2, 13; cf. Fig. 2a, 2b and 2c); for instance, in the curvature of the parasphenoid and its posterior extension under the basioccipital, and the development and relationships of the prootic to other cranial bones.

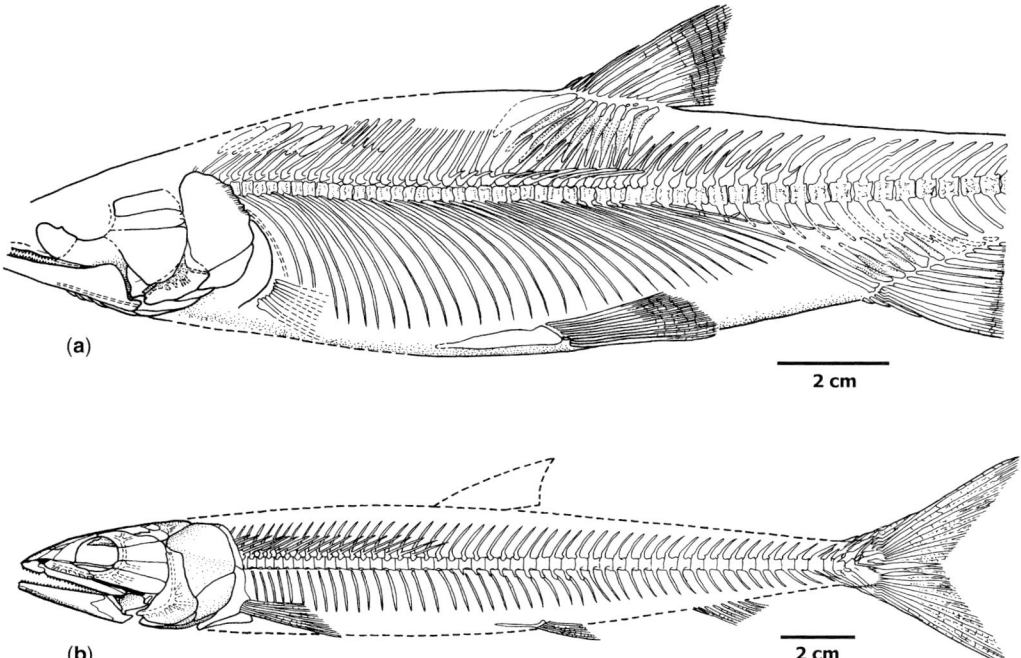

Fig. 5. Restorations in lateral view. (**a**) *Chongichthys dentatus* (modified from Arratia 1997). (**b**) *Rhacolepis buccalis* (slightly modified from Forey 1977).

Phylogenetic analysis

A phylogenetic analysis was performed to study the phylogenetic relationships of fishes previously included within the crossognathiforms, of *Chongichthys*, and varasichthyids as well as other teleosts. This analysis is based on 194 unordered and unweighted characters (Appendix 1) and 51 taxa. The trees are rooted using user-specified outgroup methods, but there is no difference in the topology of the ingroup when using different outgroup methods. There are numerous characters coded with a question mark due to incomplete preservation. For instance, the caudal skeleton of *Chongichthys* is still unknown.

The strict consensus tree of the two most parsimonious trees (MPT) has 681 evolutionary steps (Fig. 7). The consistency index (CI) is 0.4038 and the CI excluding uninformative characters is 0.4035. The nodes of non-teleostean fishes (outgroup) are represented by numbers and those of the teleosts with letters. For a complete list of characters supporting nodes see Arratia (2000, fig. 21).

Node D corresponds to the trichotomy including *Ascalabos*, a clade comprising varasichthyids, *Chongichthys*, crossognathoids and pachyrhizodontoids,

and all other teleosts. The trichotomy is due to the fact that *Ascalabos* changes position in both topologies, because three characters (14[2], 39[0], and 137[1]) may have different interpretations in both trees. For characters supporting Nodes D to D6, see Figure 7. Character 39[0] is a reversal at this node that is interpreted by PAUP as homoplastic; however, the preopercular process at the posterior margin of the hyomandibula is absent in all fishes – for which the condition is known – at Node D. It is interpreted as uniquely derived at this node.

Node D1 comprises two clades and represents the Crossognathiformes. This node is supported by six characters (in the two most parsimonious trees). Most characters are homoplastic, with the exception of character 189[1] (presence of a large, well-developed extrascapular bone extending caudally close to the posterior margin of opercle), which appears as uniquely derived in the two trees. Character 110[1], neural arch of first ural centrum reduced or absent, is interpreted as homoplastic because it is present in crossognathiforms, but also in other clades (see Node J). A similar situation is found for character 188[1] concerning the bones framing the post-temporal fossa.

Node D2 corresponds to the branching of the Jurassic varasichthyids and is supported by 10

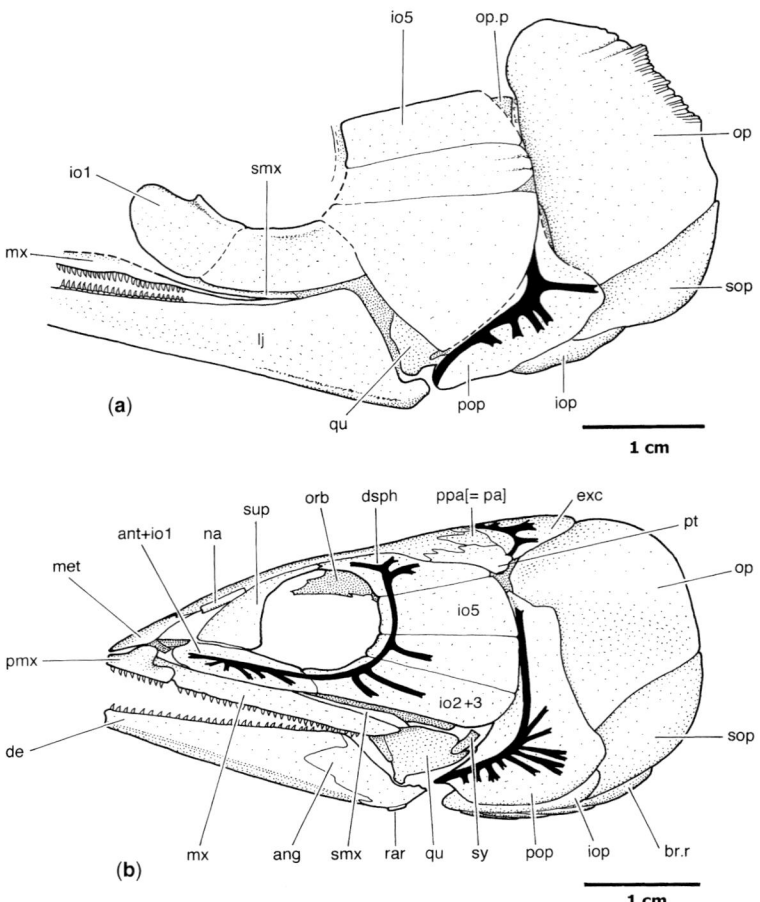

Fig. 6. Heads in lateral views. (**a**) *Chongichthys dentatus* (modified from Arratia 1997). (**b**) *Rhacolepis buccalis* (modified from Forey 1977).

characters in the two topologies. Two of them are uniquely derived (65[1] and 149[1]). In addition it should be noted that characters 89[1] (four or more postcleithra) and 93[1] (an elongate bony pelvic axillary process) are uniquely derived at this phylogenetic level. Character 161[1] supports the monophyly of the family only in one topology. The results confirm the monophyly of the Vara-sichthyidae (Arratia 1994, 1997, 1999) and the basal position of the group among teleosts. For internal nodes within Varasichthyidae see Arratia (1997, fig. 21; 1999, figs 19, 20; 2000, fig. 21).

Node D3 corresponds to the branching of a clade including the Oxfordian *Chongichthys* at the base plus all the Cretaceous crossognathiforms included in the cladistic analysis. This node is supported by 15 characters in both topologies, three of which are uniquely derived (164[2], 190[1], and 191[1])

at this level. However, characters 164[2] (fused first two hypurals and ural centrum), 190[1] (circumorbital ring completely closed, no space between bones), and 191[1] (a very large, well-developed dermosphenotic) are still unknown in *Chongichthys* and are coded with question marks (Appendix 2); consequently, PAUP assumes their presence in *Chongichthys*. Similar assumptions are made for five characters of the caudal skeleton.

Node D4 corresponds to the branching of *Note-lops* plus other Cretaceous crossognathiforms and is supported by five homoplastic characters in both trees. Character 95[1] – dorsal fin origin anterior to that of anal fin – is uniquely derived at this level, but this character is interpreted as homoplastic by PAUP because it is also found in other fishes included in the cladistic analysis (see Fig. 7, Node I). The branching of crossognathids

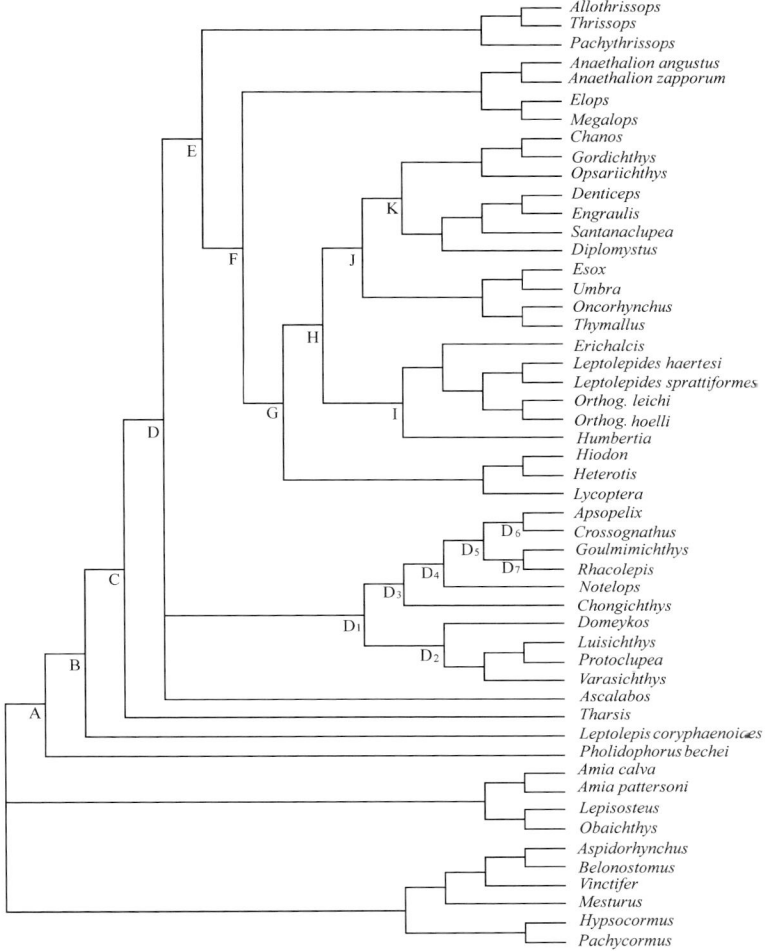

Fig. 7. Hypothesis of phylogenetic relationships of some fossil and basal teleosts. Consensus tree of two most parsimonious trees at 681 evolutionary steps (using 194 characters; for characters and their coding see Appendices 1 and 2). Characters interpreted as uniquely-derived are indicated with an asterisk (*). Only the characters for Nodes D to D6, E, F, G, H, and J are listed here. For other nodes see Arratia (2000, fig. 21). **Node D:** 14[2], 39[0]*, and 137[1]. *Node D_1* (Crossognathiformes): 21[1], 47[1], 110[1], 136[1], 188[1], and 189[1]*. *Node D_2* (Varasichthyidae): 65[1]*, 87[1], 89[1], 92[1], 93[1], 128[1], 138[0], 139[1], 149[1]*, and 150[1]. *Node D_3* (unnamed clade): 26[1], 33[1], 46[0], 48[0], 50[0], 96[1], 108[1], 116[2], 118[2], 123[2], 164[2]*, 190[1]*, 191[1]*, 192[1], and 193[1]. *Node D_4:* 7[1], 11[1], 30[1], 84[0], and 95[1]*. *Node D_5:* 35[1], 48[2], 55[1], 64[1], and 141[1]. *Node D_6:* 7[0], 11[2]*, 46[1], 84[2], 86[1], 123[1], and 184[1]*. *Node D_7:* 30[0], 87[1], 101[1], 124[1], 136[0], and 194[1]. **Node E** (ichthyodectiforms plus more advanced teleosts): 21[1], 26[1], and 128[1]. **Node F** (elopomorphs plus more advanced teleosts): 50[0], 56[1], 57[1], 59[1]*, 60[1], 84[2], 100[2], 118[3], 121[3], 122[2], 123[2], 124[1], 133[2], 136[1], 141[1], 142[0], 169[1]*, and 177[1]. **Node G** (osteoglossomorphs plus more advanced teleosts): 24[1], 48[0], 51[1]*, 55[1], 60[2], 105[1], 133[3], and 143[1]. **Node H** (clupeocephalans): 47[1], 48[2], 56[2], 57[0], 61[1]*, 62[1], 33[1], 108[1], 109[1], 119[2], and 130[1]. **Node I:** 34[1]*, 99[2], 103[1], and 133[2]. **Node J:** 36[1]*, 86[1], 110[1], 118[4], 119[3], 122[3], 123[3], and 194[1]. **Node K** (ostarioclupeomorphs): 28[1]*, 74[1], 100[2], 126[0], and 130[0].

and pachyrhizodontids stands at Node D5 and is supported by five homoplastic features in the two topologies.

Crossognathus and *Apsopelix* form a sister group (Node D6) supported by seven homoplastic characters. Two characters (11[2] and 184[1]), that are interpreted by PAUP as homoplastic, may be considered unique at this phylogenetic level. Character 11[2] – long parasphenoid extending posterior to the basioccipital bone – is also present in

Varasichthys ariasi. Character 184[1] – presence of *c*. 40 vertebrae – is present in the Jurassic genus *Ascalabos* (see Fig. 7, Nodes D and D6).

Goulmimichthys and *Rhacolepis* are sister groups (Node D7). Six homoplastic features support this node.

The consensus tree shows a resolved topology concerning the positions of the ichthyodectiforms, elopomorphs, osteoglossomorphs, and the sister-group relationship clupeomorphs + ostariophysans (above Node D in Fig. 7) that are identical to those in Arratia (1999, 2000); however, there is a major change at Node H (clupeocephalans, see Fig. 7). The clade [*Humbertia* + [*Erichalcis* + [*Leptolepides* + *Orthogonikleithrus*]]] that in previous hypotheses appeared as the sister group of the esociforms plus salmonids, has now a basal position among clupeocephalans. Node H is supported by 11 characters, two of which are uniquely-derived (61[1] and 130[1]). The first character concerns branchial arches; they are well known in recent forms only, so that the PAUP assumes that this character was also present in the fossil clade that now appears at the base of clupeocephalans. The second character (130[1], presence of stegural) is unique at the base of the clade with a reversal at node K (absence of stegural).

The two parsimonious trees that resulted from the cladistic analysis differ only in the position of *Ascalabos* in relation to the crossognathiforms and *Tharsis*. In MPT 1, *Tharsis* stands close to the base, followed by the crossognathiforms and then *Ascalabos* plus more advanced teleosts. In MPT 2, *Ascalabos* appears in an intermediate position between *Tharsis* and the crossognathiforms plus more advanced teleosts. The changes in position of *Ascalabos* result in the unresolved trichotomy shown by the consensus tree at Node D (Fig. 7). The unresolved position of *Ascalabos* in this study is not surprising since the genus changes position in other phylogenetic studies, e.g. as the sister group of Varasichthyidae (Arratia 1996) or above the phylogenetic level of Varasichthyidae (Arratia 1997, 1999). The unresolved position of *Ascalabos* may be explained by the fact that many characters are still unknown. Recent findings of well-preserved specimens in the Solnhofen Limestones will permit a more complete description of the genus (Arratia in prep.).

Final comments and conclusions

According to the results of the phylogenetic analysis, the crossognathiforms of Taverne (1989), including crossognathoids and pachyrhizodontoids, are monophyletic. Nevertheless, the clade interpreted here as Crossognathiformes has a different content because it includes the Jurassic family Varasichthyidae and the Jurassic genus *Chongichthys* in addition to the Cretaceous crossognathiforms and pachyrhizodontoids.

Members of the family Varasichthyidae, *Chongichthys*, crossognathoids, and pachyrhizodontoids form a monophyletic clade in the phylogenetic analysis (Fig. 7).

The clade is supported by one unique character, the presence of a large, well-developed extrascapular bone. Homoplastic characters supporting the monophyly of Crossognathiformes are: the presence of a large, roofed posttemporal fossa framed by the epiotic, pterotic, exoccipital, and intercalar; the retroarticular bone excluded from the joint facet for the quadrate; a reduced neural arch over 'first' ural centrum; and proximity of the dorsal procurrent rays to neural spines, epurals, and posterior uroneurals. The presence of an atrophied or reduced neural arch on the 'first' ural centrum was used by Taverne (1989) to support the placement of his new order Crossognathiformes among clupeocephalans. As shown here, as well as by Arratia (1999), the presence of an atrophied or reduced neural arch on the 'first' ural centrum is not unique to clupeocephalans because it is present at other phylogenetic levels among teleosts. PAUP interprets the presence of the foramen for the vagus nerve placed in the posterolateral face of the exoccipital alone as a synapomorphy at this level (Fig. 7, Node D1), and then again at the level of the ichthyodectiforms and more advanced teleosts (Fig. 7, Node E) because the information is missing in *Ascalabos*. It is more parsimonious to interpret this feature as a synapomorphy, at the level of Crossognathiformes and more advanced teleosts, than to assume that it has been acquired twice in the evolution of teleosts. This interpretation should be tested when information on the braincase of *Ascalabos* becomes available.

The addition of *Chongichthys* to the phylogenetic analysis has proven to be important because *Chongichthys* appears as the primitive sister group of phachyrhizodontoids + crossognathoids (Fig. 7, Node D3, unnamed clade) according to the present evidence (based on the morphology of the head and body without caudal fin and caudal skeleton). Following this interpretation, *Chongichthys* is the oldest known crossognathiform, extending the age range of the group to the Oxfordian, early Late Jurassic. This is not now an isolated finding: new material recently collected in the Upper Jurassic of Bavaria, Germany, seems to be a crossognathiform-like fish (Arratia and Tischlinger in prep.). The caudal skeleton and skull bones collected in the Upper Jurassic of Termas del Flaco, Chile, showing fusion of hypurals 1 and 2 (and a possible third?) (see Fig. 8) can be added

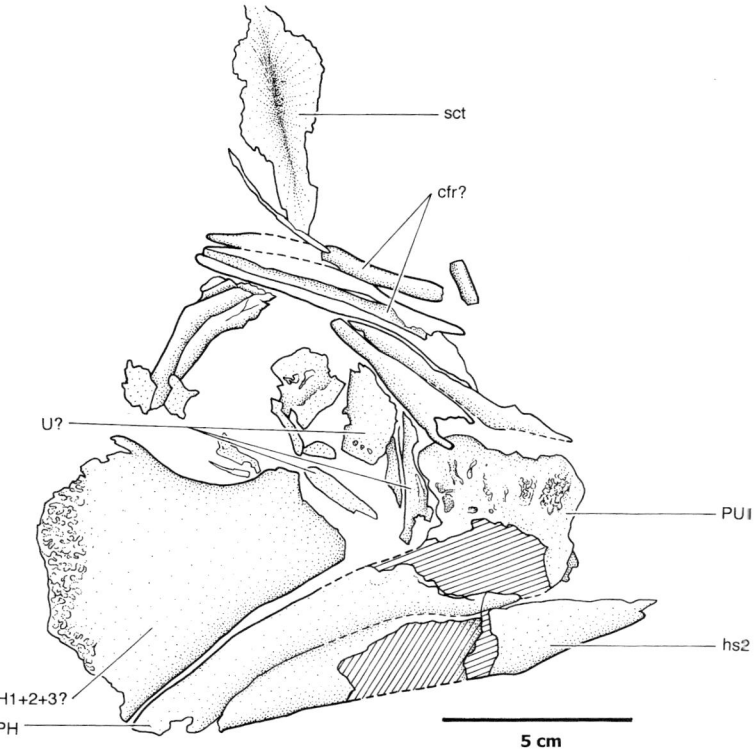

Fig. 8. Undetermined pachyrhizodontoid from the Upper Jurassic of Termas del Flaco, Chile. Incomplete caudal skeleton in lateral view (after Arratia & Schultze 1999).

to the evidence presented above, as further support of the presence of crossognathiforms in the Upper Jurassic of South America. The fusion between hypurals 1 and 2 and the 'first' ural centrum is a synapomorphy of crossognathoids and pachyrhizodontoids and possibly also *Chongichthys* (character 168[2]; Fig. 7, Node D3). The material belongs to an indeterminate pachyrhizodontoid according to Arratia & Schultze (1999).

Pachyrhizodontoids were left as Teleostei *incertae sedis* by Forey (1977) because some of the derived character states shown by these fishes are comparable to protacanthopterygian euteleosts. However, Forey (1977) preferred not to assign the fishes to the euteleosts because euteleosts were, and still are, incompletely known at the basal level. Later, the crossognathiforms, including the pachyrhizodontoids, were interpreted as clupeocephalans by Taverne (1989) (see comments above). Maisey (1991a, b) did not recognize Taverne's (1989) crossognathiform taxon and assigned the pachyrhizodontoids *Rhacolepis* and *Notelops* to the Elopomorpha. The groups under study here are phylogenetically distant from Elopomorpha

(represented by the elopiforms here; Fig. 7, Node F1) as well as from the clupeocephalans of Patterson & Rosen 1977; Fig. 7, Node H).

The new interpretation of *Chongichthys* from the lower Upper Jurassic (Oxfordian) of South America, as a primitive crossognathiform and the new finding of a crossognathiform-like fish in the Upper Jurassic (Tithonian) of southern Germany leads to interesting questions about the origin and early diversification of the group. Crossognathiforms were considered up to now as typical marine Cretaceous forms. The new information presented here clearly illustrates the necessity of more field work, not only in South America but in Europe and North America as well, to collect more specimens so that some of the incompletely known morphological features of crossognathiforms can be clarified.

For instance, the orbital region that seems to be quite specialized in crossognathiforms leaves open questions. Is the antorbital bone lost in crossognathoids and pachyrhizodontoids or fused to infraorbital 1 or fused to the supraorbital bone? Is there an independent infraorbital 2, or is the bone absent, or is the bone fused to another infraorbital bone? Are the enlarged posterior infraorbitals the result of fusion of bones or the result of the expansion and development of a few bones? Is there a large dermosphenotic in varasichthyids? There are also open questions about the vertebral column and intermuscular bones as well as the structure of the paired girdles and paired and unpaired fins (e.g. position of fins, shape of fins) including the caudal skeleton (e.g. number of uroneurals and its patterns, number of hypurals, epurals). Probably, a better knowledge of the oldest Jurassic forms (e.g. varasichthyids and *Chongichthys*) will help to answer some of these questions. Certainly, further comparative studies and the finding of well-preserved specimens will help to answer these questions.

Finally, there are a few other interesting results that merit further comment. The inclusion of new taxa (e.g. a few Cretaceous crossognathiforms), the addition of new characters and deletion or modification of others have no effect in the phylogenetic position of elopomorphs as the most basal extant taxon (see Fig. 7, Node F) and confirm other phylogenetic hypotheses based on fossil and extant forms (e.g. Arratia 1991, 1996, 1997, 1999; Shen 1996; Li & Wilson 1999). The new phylogenetic hypothesis does show a major difference in the topology above the Ichthyodectiformes in comparison to Arratia's (1997, 1999, 2000) phylogenetic hypotheses. The euteleostean clade comprising [*Humbertia* + [*Erichalcis* + [*Leptolepides* + *Orthogonikleithrus*]]], that was previously interpreted as a sister group of esociforms and salmonids, is now placed in a basal position among clupeocephalans. This is probably the result of the addition of several crossognathiform taxa that changes previous interpretations concerning the distribution of certain characters among teleosts, and also the addition of a few new characters.

Biogeographic comments

According to Arratia's (1994, text-fig. 8) phylogenetic results, the sister area of the Cordillera de Domeyko, in northern Chile, is the Sierra de Vinales, in Cuba. The sister area of the two American sister areas is Bavaria in southern Germany (Arratia 1994, text-fig. 11). This biogeographic interpretation was based on the phylogenetic relationships between the Chilean varasichthyids (*Domeykos*, *Protoclupea* and *Varasichthys*) and the Cuban genus *Luisichthys*. The Jurassic family Varasichthyidae, now as part of the Crossognathiformes, is placed in the cladogram between the Jurassic European genera *Tharsis* and *Ascalabos* or *Ascalabos* and the Jurassic European

ichthyodectiforms (*Allothrissops*, *Pachythrissops*, and *Thrissops*). Connection of these areas through the Tethys seaway seems probable. This sister-area relationship (based on varasichthyids) is evidence for a connection by the Tethys seaway between fish faunas of South America (Chile), Central America (Cuba), and Europe (southern Germany) during the Late Jurassic. A marine corridor (Hispanic or Caribbean corridor) has been postulated between the Western Tethys (European Tethys) and the East Pacific (west of South America) during the Late Jurassic (e.g. Hallam 1977, 1983); however, new marine corridors arose as a consequence of the fragmentation of Laurasia and Gondwana (Hallam 1983; Scotese 1987; Riccardi 1991). More recent studies show that already in the Oxfordian, and as result of the fragmentation of Pangaea, the Central Atlantic Ocean was opened as North America was moving to the northwest, away from South America. Thus, the Central Atlantic Ocean was a corridor between the Palaeopacific and the Tethys Sea (Stampfli & Borel 2002; see also www.scotese.com). Late Jurassic marine vertebrates that could have used this corridor include fishes (e.g. varasichthyids and crossognathiforms) and crocodiles. *Metriorhynchus* and *Geosaurus* (Gasparini 1992) have been reported from the Upper Jurassic of South America and Europe.

The presence of pachyrhizodontoids in the Lower Cretaceous of Brazil and of crossognathoids in the Lower Cretaceous of Europe supports a connection between the Tethys Sea and the South Atlantic – the Central Atlantic was used as a corridor between both. Recently, it has been proposed that the marine fish radiation was very important during the 'mid'-Cretaceous, especially in the Tethys Sea, which may have been the centre of origin of some clades (Cavin *et al.* 2007). It can be added that the Tethys and the Palaeopacific were also very important in the late Middle Jurassic–Late Jurassic, as the centre of origin of some clades (e.g. crossognathiforms, elopiforms; Arratia 2004 and results presented here), a time when some teleostean clades began to radiate.

I am grateful to L. Cavin for stimulating my curiosity about varasichthyids and crossognathiforms, a project that now will be expanded by the inclusion of other Late Jurassic taxa, and for his comments on this manuscript. I thank H.-P. Schultze and E. Wiley for comments and discussion on phylogenetic interpretations and methodologies, J. Chorn for improving the style of the manuscript, and L. Grande and L. Martin for facilities to study material under their care. Special thanks to P. Forey and L. Taverne for granting their permission to re-draw and modify some of their published figures. The support of grants 5118–93 of the National Geographic Society, NSF AToL 37870, and of a research fellowship from the Field Museum of Natural History are greatly appreciated.

Appendix 1: List of characters

The phylogenetic relationships of certain teleosts (Fig. 7) are based on the features listed below that are mostly from Arratia (2000). Numbers in brackets correspond to the character number in Arratia (2000). [0] represents the plesiomorphic character state and [1], [2], [3] and [4] the apomorphic character states. The outgroup used to polarize characters includes *Amia calva* and *A. pattersoni*, *Aspidorhynchus*, *Belonostomus*, *Hypsocormus*, *Lepisosteus*, *Mesturus*, *Obaichthys*, *Pachycormus*, and *Vinctifer*.

(1) Ethmopalatine ossification in the floor of the nasal capsule articulating with autopalatine: absent [0]; present [1].

(2) Two paired endoskeletal ethmoidal ossifications: absent [0]; present [1].

(3) Postparietal (= so-called parietal) bones: independent [0]; fused to each other [1]; fused with other skull bones [2].

(4) Supraoccipital bone: absent [0]; present [1] (modified from Arratia 2000).

(5) Basisphenoid: present [0]; absent [1].

(6) Sutures between cartilage bones in the braincase retained throughout life, rather than being lost ontogenetically: absent [0]; present [1] (Patterson & Rosen 1977).

(7) Suture between parietal bones (= so-called frontals) smooth (*sutura armonica*): present [0]; absent [1].

(8) Large orbitosphenoid bone: absent [0]; present [1].

(9) Orbitosphenoid partially or completely reaching the parasphenoid ventrally: absent [0]; present [1].

(10) Parasphenoid: with small teeth [0]; toothless [1]; with large teeth [2].

(11) Parasphenoid: short, just reaching the basioccipital [0]; long, almost reaching the posterior margin of basioccipital [1]; long, extending posterior to basioccipital [2] (modified from Arratia 2000).

(12) Ossified aortic canal: present [0]; absent [1].

(13) Canals for occipital arteries in basioccipital bone: present [0]; absent [1].

(14) Spiracular canal: well-developed [0]; greatly reduced [1]; absent [2].

(15) Anterior myodome: as a median compartment [0]; paired [1]; absent [2].

(16) Posterior myodome: bone-enclosed [0]; opens posteriorly [1] (Patterson 1977).

(17) *Recessus lateralis*: absent [0]; present [1].

(18) Otophysic connection involving a diverticulum of the swimbladder that penetrates the exoccipital and extends into the prootic within the lateral wall of the braincase: absent [0]; present [1] (Patterson & Rosen 1977; Grande 1985).

(19) Pre-epiotic fossa: absent [0]; present [1].

(20) Foramen for glossopharyngeal nerve in exoccipital: absent [0]; present [1] (Patterson & Rosen 1977).

(21) Foramen for vagus nerve placed in posterolateral face of exoccipital alone: absent [0]; present [1].

(22) Cephalic sensory canal components: continuous [0]; interrupted between them [1].

(23) Cephalic sensory canals with: branched tubules [0]; simple tubules [1]; reduced tubules [2].

(24) Antorbital bone: carrying a portion of the infraorbital canal [0]; without sensory canal [1] (modified from Arratia 2000).

(25) An ethmoidal commissure that penetrates and passes through the whole width of a broad mesethmoid: absent [0]; present [1].

(26) Middle pit-line groove crossing the dermopterotic (or pterotic): present [0]; absent [1].

(27) Supratemporal commissure (primitively) passing through postparietals or through postparietals (= so-called parietal) and supraoccipital: absent [0]; present [1] (Patterson & Rosen 1977; Grande 1985).

(28) Ankylosis or fusion between the mesial extrascapula and postparietal alone or postparietal (= so-called parietal) and supraoccipital: absent [0]; present [1] (Arratia & Gayet 1995; modified from Lecointre & Nelson 1996).

(29) A narrow tube-like infraorbital 1 or a broad antorbital plus infraorbital 1 combined with enlarged bone(s) representing the third and fourth and/or fourth and fifth of other teleosts: absent [0]; present [1].

(30) Fourth and fifth infraorbital bones: separate [0]; fused forming an expanded bone [1].

(31) Suborbital bone(s): one or more [0]; none [1].

(32) Supraorbital bone(s): two or more [0]; one [1]; none [2]; fused with other bone forming the supraorbito-dermosphenotic [3].

(33) Large supraorbital bone with expanded anteroventral portion: absent [0]; present [1].

(34) Comma-shaped antorbital bone: absent [0]; present [1].

(35) Toothed dermopalatine bone(s): present [0]; absent [1].

(36) Autopalatine bone: ossifies late in ontogeny [0]; ossifies early in ontogeny [1] (Arratia & Schultze 1991).

(37) Elongation of suspensorium: 'normal', no special elongation [0]; parasagittal elongation due to separation between quadrate and hyomandibula and elongation of symplectic [1] (Fink & Fink 1981; Arratia 1992); partial elongation due to enlargement of quadrate and symplectic and the separation between the long and

narrow ventral part of the hyomandibula and symplectic [2] (modified from Arratia 2000).

(38) Elongation of the suspensorium due to the ventro-posterior inclination of the hyomandibula: absent [0]; present [1].

(39) Hyomandibular bone with a preopercular process at its posterior margin: absent [0]; present [1].

(40) Elongate jaws bearing numerous villiform teeth: absent [0]; present [1].

(41) Upper and lower jaws: with teeth [0]; without teeth [1].

(42) Very broad, concave-convex premaxilla: absent [0]; present [1] (Poyato-Ariza 1996).

(43) Articular process of maxilla very long and irregularly shaped: absent [0]; present [1].

(44) Dentated maxilla: present [0]; absent [1]; other condition, maxilla and infraorbital bones fused [2].

(45) Supramaxilla(ae): dorsal to the dorsal margin of maxilla [0]; placed posterior to maxilla [1] (modified from Arratia 1999, 2000).

(46) Quadrate-mandibular articulation: posterior to orbit [0]; placed below the posterior half of orbit [1]; below anterior half of orbit [2]; anterior to orbit [3].

(47) Retroarticular bone: included in the joint facet for quadrate [0]; excluded from the joint facet for quadrate [1]; retroarticular bone absent [2].

(48) Articular bone: not fused to angular and retroarticular [0]; fused with angular and retroarticular bones [1]; fused with angular [2]; partially-fused with anguloretroarticular late in ontogeny [3].

(49) Postarticular process of lower jaw: poorly-developed [0]; well-developed [1].

(50) Notch in the deep dorsal ascending margin of the dentary: absent [0]; present [1].

(51) Posterior opening of the mandibular sensory canal: placed medial or posterior [0]; placed lateral to the angular portion of the jaw [1].

(52) Posterior section of the mandibular canal: present [0]; absent [1].

(53) Mandibular canal enclosed in bone along the whole lower jaw: present [0]; absent [1].

(54) Elongate posteroventral process of quadrate: absent [0]; present [1] (Arratia & Schultze 1991).

(55) Gular plate: present [0]; absent [1].

(56) Hyoidean artery: not piercing the hypohyals [0]; piercing the hypohyals [1]; piercing ventral hypohyal [2].

(57) Basibranchials 1–3 and basihyal cartilages overlain by median tooth plate(s): absent [0]; present [1] (Lauder & Liem 1993).

(58) Branchial spiracle: absent [0]; present [1].

(59) Pharyngobranchials: two ossified elements and a cartilaginous one bearing tooth plate(s) [0]; three ossified elements and a cartilaginous one bearing tooth plate(s) [1];

another condition: pharyngobranchials 1 and 4 missing [2].

(60) Pharyngobranchial 1 in large individuals: rod-like or elongate [0]; with a bony, broad base articulating with epibranchial 1 and bearing a short dorsal process [1]; with a cartilaginous or bony narrow base, keeping mainly or only the elongate ossified dorsal process [2]; pharyngobranchial 1 absent [3].

(61) Tooth-plate of last pharyngobranchial bone formed by: confluence of many tooth-plates [0]; growth of one tooth-plate [1]; cartilaginous pharyngobranchial 4 of teleosts missing [2].

(62) Tooth-plates associated with pharyngobranchials 1–3: absent [0]; present [1]; another condition: pharyngobranchial 1 absent [2].

(63) Suprapreopercle: absent [0]; present [1].

(64) Ventroposterior region of preopercle: narrow or slightly expanded [0]; broadly expanded [1].

(65) Preopercular sensory canal with many tubules in ventral limb reaching ventral and ventroposterior margin of the bone: absent [0]; present [1].

(66) Preopercular sensory canal with four or fewer short and simple tubules placed in the ventral limb of the bone: absent [0]; present [1].

(67) Distinctively enlarged preopercle: absent [0]; present [1].

(68) Irregular parallelogram, or oval, or kidney-shaped opercular bone: absent [0]; present [1] (Li & Wilson 1996).

(69) *Opisthocoelus* centra with a convex articular surface and a concave posterior articular surface: absent [0]; present [1].

(70) Each vertebral centrum of the caudal region of adult individuals formed by: mineralized chordacentrum and arcocentra [0]; chordacentrum and basal part of arcocentra surrounded by autocentrum [1]; basal part of arcocentra surrounded by autocentrum [2].

(71) Midcaudal vertebral autocentra: absent [0]; thin and smooth [1]; thick and sculptured [2]; thick and smooth [3] (modified from Arratia 1991, 1997).

(72) Autocentrum of midcaudal vertebrae: absent [0]; without cavities for adipose tissue [1]; with cavities for adipose tissue [2].

(73) Midcaudal autocentra: absent [0]; not constricting the notochord [1]; strongly constricting the notochord [2].

(74) Neural arches of the abdominal region: not fused to the centra [0]; fused, except for the first five or six [1]; fused to the autocentra [2].

(75) Dorso-medial portions of the anterior neural arches expanded and abutting against each other and the posterior margin of the exoccipital; absent [0]; present [1] (Fink & Fink 1981, 1996).

(76) Neural arches of most abdominal vertebrae: with separate halves of the neural arch [0]; with fused halves of the neural arch forming a median neural spine [1].

(77) Supradorsal cartilages in abdominal vertebrae: present [0]; absent [1].

(78) Anterior pleural rib, on third vertebra, is distinctly larger than the next few ribs: absent [0]; present [1] (Fink & Fink 1981, 1996).

(79) Neural spines of caudal region: paired [0]; unpaired [1].

(80) Interhaemal bones: present [0]; absent [1].

(81) The first supraneural anterior to the neural spine of vertebra 1 develops independently, and the remainders differentiate in rostral and caudal gradients from a focus midway between the occiput and dorsal fin origin: absent [0]; present [1] (Johnson & Patterson 1996).

(82) In adult individuals, elongate, solid epineural processes of neural arch: absent [0]; present [1]; another condition: a separate bone joined to the neural arch by a ligament [2].

(83) In adult individuals, last epineural processes of neural arch belonging to caudal vertebrae: absent [0]; present [1].

(84) Epipleural intermuscular bones: absent [0]; few bones in the anterior caudal region [1]; many bones developed in the abdominal and anterior caudal region [2].

(85) Complex epipleural bones: absent [0]; present [1].

(86) Series of dorsal intermuscular bones throughout caudal region: absent [0]; present [1].

(87) Supracleithrum with main lateral line emerging: at its upper half [0]; at its most posteroventral margin [1]; lateral line not running through the supracleithrum [2].

(88) Postsupracleithrum(-ra): absent [0]; present [1].

(89) Postcleithra: three or two [0]; four or more [1]; none [2].

(90) Coracoid bone enlarged ventrally meeting its fellow in a midventral coracoid symphysis: absent [0]; present [1] (Patterson & Rosen 1977).

(91) Pectoral propterygium fused with first pectoral ray: absent [0]; present [1] (Jessen 1972; Patterson 1977).

(92) Pectoral axillary process: absent [0]; present; formed by small bony elements [1]; present; formed by an elongate bony element [2]; present; formed by modified scales [3].

(93) Pelvic axillary process: absent [0]; present; formed by an elongate bone [1]; present; formed by a combination of bony element(s) and modified scales [2]; present; formed by modified scales [3].

(94) Dorsal and anal fins posteriorly placed: absent [0]; present [1].

(95) Dorsal fin origin anterior to that of pelvic fin: absent [0]; present [1].

(96) Dorsal and anal fins acuminate: absent [0]; present [1].

(97) Anal fin long, falcate, opposed by a short, remote dorsal fin: absent [0]; present [1] (Patterson & Rosen 1977).

(98) First anal pterygiophore placed posterior to fourth or fifth haemal spine: absent [0]; present [1].

(99) Preural vertebrae (without preural centrum 1) of adult individuals with haemal arches; autogenous [0]; laterally fused to their respective autocentra [1]; not fused laterally to their autocentra [2].

(100) Parhypural (in adults) with haemal arch: autogenous [0]; laterally fused to its autocentrum [1]; laterally not fused to its autocentrum [2].

(101) Hypurapophysis: absent [0]; present [1].

(102) Neural spine of vertebrae 5–3 distally expanded by fine anterior and posterior membranous outgrowths; absent [0]; present [1].

(103) Neural spines of at least preural vertebrae 4–2 with membranous outgrowths and leaf-like: absent [0]; present [1].

(104) Neural spine of preural vertebra 3: inclined toward the horizontal at an angle of less than 45° in relation to the dorsal margin of the centra [0]; inclined toward the horizontal at an angle of over 45° [1].

(105) Neural spine of preural centrum 2: shorter than neural spine of preural centrum 3 [0]; as long as neural spine of preural centrum 3 [1]; neural spine absent [2].

(106) Neural spine of preural centrum 1: rudimentary or short [0]; long, close to, or reaching the dorsal margin of the body [1]; absent [2].

(107) Neural arch on preural centrum 1: present [0]; absent or atrophic [1].

(108) Neural spine of ural centra 1 and 2 or 'first' ural centrum: present [0]; absent [1]; other condition: preural centrum 1 fused with ural centrum(-ra) [2].

(109) Neural arch of ural centra 1 and 2 or 'first' ural centrum: present [0]; absent [1]; other condition: fusion of elements [2].

(110) Neural arch over 'first' ural centrum: complete [0]; reduced [1]; other condition: fusion of elements [2].

(111) A mass of cartilage, or uroneural cartilage, apparently originated by fusion of cartilaginous neural arches: absent [0]; present [1].

(112) A compound neural arch formed in a mas of cartilage over preural centrum 1 and ural centra: absent [0]; present [1] (modified from Patterson & Rosen 1977).

(113) Ural centra (originated only) as expansion of the dorsal arcualia: absent [0]; present [1] (Schultze & Arratia 1986, 1989).

(114) 'First' ural centrum corresponds to: two separate centra or fusion of ural centra 1 and 2 [0]; ural centrum 2 only [1]; ural centrum(a) fuses to preural centrum 1 [2]; all elements fused [3].

(115) 'Second' ural centrum corresponds to: ural centrum 2 [0]; two or more separate centra or fusion of ural centra [1]; ural centrum 4 [2]; all elements fused [3] (modified from Arratia 2000).

(116) Number of epurals: five or more [0]; three or four [1]; two [2]; one [3]; none [4].

(117) Some preural neural arches modified as uroneural-like bones: absent [0]; present [1].

(118) Number of ural neural arches modified as uroneurals: none [0]; seven or more [1]; six [2]; five or four [3]; three or less [4].

(119) All uroneurals inclined towards the horizontal, one besides the other: no uroneural present [0]; present [1]; absent [2]; other condition: less than two uppermost uroneurals present [3].

(120) Six or seven uroneurals, the first three or four extending antero-ventrally to cover the entire lateral surface of the first, second and third preural centra: absent [0]; present [0].

(121) Uppermost three uroneurals forming a series that overlaps and lies at an angle to the longer anterior ones: no uroneural present [0]; absent [1]; present [2]; other condition: less than three uppermost uroneurals [3] (modified from Patterson & Rosen 1977).

(122) First uroneural reaches: no uroneural present [0]; preural centrum 4 or 3 [1]; preural centrum 2 [2]; preural centrum 1 [3]; reaching no preural centrum [4].

(123) Two uroneurals, rather than three or four, extending forward beyond the 'second' ural centrum: no uroneural present [0]; absent [1]; present [2]; other condition: one uroneural present [3] (modified from Patterson & Rosen 1977).

(124) Number of hypurals in adult individuals: ten, nine or eight [0]; seven or less [1]; all hypurals fused [2].

(125) Only hypural 2 fused with 'first' ural centrum: absent [0]; present [1].

(126) Bases of hypurals 1 and 2: not joined by cartilage in any growth stage [0]; joined by cartilage (and/ or bone) in some growth stage [1].

(127) Both hypurals 1 and 2 associated by fusion or articulation with a 'compound centrum', apparently formed by preural centrum 1 and ural centrum(a): absent [0]; present [1]; fusion of elements [2].

(128) A space or diasteme between hypurals 2 and 3: absent [0]; present [1]; other condition: fusion of elements [2].

(129) First uroneural fused with a 'compound centrum' apparently formed by preural centrum 1 and ural centrum(a): absent [0]; present [1].

(130) Stegural: absent [0]; present [1].

(131) Membranous outgrowth of stegural covering laterally the ventral tips of epurals: absent [0]; present [1].

(132) Median caudal cartilages: absent [0]; present [1].

(133) Urodermals and 'urodermals': more than two urodermals present [0]; two 'urodermals' [1]; one 'urodermal' [2]; none [3].

(134) Three or more fringing fulcra preceding the first principal caudal ray: present [0]; absent [1].

(135) Both epaxial and hypaxial basal fulcra: present [0]; absent [1].

(136) Proximity of the fulcra or dorsal precurrent rays to: epurals and posterior uroneurals [0]; neural spines, epurals, and posterior uroneurals [1]; absence of structures [2].

(137) Long dorsal segmented precurrent rays; absent [0]; present [1].

(138) Number of principal caudal rays: twenty or more [0]; nineteen [1]; less than nineteen [2].

(139) Lower lobe of the caudal fin with: no well-defined ventral lobe [0]; more than nine principal rays [1]; nine principal rays [2]; less than nine principal rays [3].

(140) Branched rays of the caudal fin: more than 16 [0]; 16 or less [1].

(141) Bases of the dorsalmost principal rays of the caudal fin crossing obliquely over the entire upper hypural series (save the last); present [0]; absent [1].

(142) Dorsal processes of the bases of the innermost principal caudal rays of upper lobe: absent [0]; present [1].

(143) Principal caudal rays with elongate segments and with: Z-like or step-like segmentation [0]; straight segmentation [1] (modified from Arratia 1991, 1996, 1997).

(144) One or more abdominal scutes, each of a single element which crosses the ventral midline of the fish: absent [0]; present [1].

(145) Dorsal scute(s) preceding caudal fin: present [0]; absent [1].

(146) Amioid-type of scales or scales with radial structures (*sensu* Schultze 1996): absent [0]; present [1].

(147) Lepidosteoid-type of scales (*sensu* Schultze 1996): absent [0]; present [1].

(148) Cycloid scales: absent [0]; present [1]; other condition: without scales [2].

(149) Cycloid scales posterior to the pectoral girdle with circuli crossed by transverse lines in the middle field: absent [0]; present [1]; other condition: without scales [2].

(150) Cycloid scales with crenulate posterior margin: absent [0]; present [1]; other condition: without scales [2].

(151) Leptocephalous larva: absent [0]; present [1].

(152) Separation between olfactory organ and eye: narrow [0]; broad [1].

(153) Primary olfactory lamellae bearing secondary lamellae: present [0]; absent [1].

(154) Adipose fin: absent [0]; present [1].

(155) Primary bite between parasphenoid and basihyal: absent [0]; present [1] (Li & Wilson 1996).

(156) Intestine coiling to left of stomach: absent [0]; present [1] (Nelson 1969).

(157) Posterior margin of maxilla: concave or at least notched [0]; convexly rounded or straight [1]; sharp [2] (modified from Grande & Bemis 1998).

(158) Symplectic: articulates with lower jaw [0]; does not articulate withy lower jaw [1] (Patterson 1973).

(159) Solid perichondrally ossified diplospondylous centra in adult individuals: absent [0]; present [1].

(160) Posterior margin of caudal fin convexly rounded: absent [0]; [present [1].

(161) Number of ossified ural neural arches: more than two [0]; two [1]; one or none [2].

(162) Arrangements of hypurals and caudal fin rays: each hypural normally articulates with one caudal ray [0]; each hypural normally articulates with a few caudal rays [1]; fusion of hypurals [2] (modified from Grande & Bemis 1998).

(163) Number of ural centra (in adults): more than two [0]; two or one [1]; no ural centra [2] (modified from Patterson 1977; Pinna 1996).

(164) First two hypurals supported by a single centrum: absent [0]; present [1]; fusion of elements [2] (modified from Patterson 1977; Pinna 1996).

(165) Only ural neural arches modified as uroneurals: absent [0]; present [1] (modified from Patterson 1973, 1977; Pinna 1996).

(166) Two ossified hypohyals: absent [0]; present [1] (Arratia & Schultze 1990).

(167) Urohyal formed as an unpaired tendon-bone: absent [0]; present [1] (Arratia & Schultze 1990; Pinna 1996).

(168) Hyoidean artery: not piercing the hypohyal(s) [0]; piercing one or both hypohyals (Arratia & Schultze 1990; Pinna 1996).

(169) Independent endoskeletal basihyal: absent [0]; present [1]; other condition [2].

(170) Premaxilla: without mobility [0]; with certain mobility [1]; mobile [2] (modified from Patterson & Rosen 1977; Pinna 1996).

(171) Coronoid bones in lower jaw: present [0]; absent [1] (Patterson 1977; Pinna 1996).

(172) Surangular bone in lower jaw: present [0]; absent [1].

(173) Posterior myodome: not extending into basioccipital (e.g. in prootic) [0]; extending in basioccipital [1]; absent [2] (modified from Patterson 1977; Pinna 1996).

(174) Vomer (in adults): paired [0]; unpaired [1] (modified from Patterson 1977; Pinna 1996).

(175) Parietal bones (=so-called frontals): not distinct broadening between anterior and posterior parts [0]; distinctly broader posteriorly, but long

and narrow anteriorly [1]; fused to other cranial bones [2] (Arratia & Schultze 1987; Pinna 1996).

(176) Craniotemporal muscle: absent [0]; present [1] (Stiassny 1986; Pinna 1996).

(177) Accessory nasal sacs: absent [0]; present [1] (Chen & Arratia 1994; Pinna 1995).

(178) Four proximal pectoral radials: absent [0]; present [1] (Jessen 1972; Patterson 1977; Pinna 1996).

(179) Premaxillae forming a rostral tube that projects into the ethmoidal region: absent [0]; present [1] (Brito 1997).

(180) Presence of toothed predentary: absent [0]; present [1] (Brito 1997).

(181) Very posterior position of the preopercular sensory canal in a peculiarly shaped preopercle: absent [0]; present [1] (Brito 1997).

(182) Interopercular bone: present [0]; absent [1] (Brito 1997; Arratia 1999).

(183) An occipital process formed by fusion of intercalary and autopterotic: absent [0]; present [1] (Brito 1997).

(184) Approximately 40 vertebrae (including preural centrum 1): absent [0]; present [1].

(185) Narrow, elongate neural and haemal arches placed at the dorsal and middle regions of each centrum: absent [0]; present [1]

(186) Large compound rostrodermethmoid meeting the parietal bones (=so-called frontals) posteriorly, and separating the paired premaxillae and nasal bones: absent [0]; present [1] (Mainwaring 1978).

(187) Pectoral fin scythe-like and rays branching at their extreme ends: absent [0]; present [1] (Mainwaring 1978).

The seven additional characters, unique to this paper are:

(188) Large, roofed posttemporal fossa framed by the epiotic, pterotic, exoccipital and intercalar: absent [0]; present [1].

(189) Large, well-developed extrascapular bone extending caudally close to the posterior margin of opercle: absent [0]; present [1].

(190) Circumorbital ring: incompletely closed [0]; completely closed ring, no space left between bones [1].

(191) Dermosphenotic: small [0]; very large, well-developed bone [1].

(192) Independent antorbital bone: present [0]; absent [1].

(193) Posterior infraorbital bones: small and not overlapping or slightly overlapping the anterior margin of preopercle [0]; expanded posterior infraorbitals overlapping the anterior margin of preopercle [1].

(194) Condition of skull roof: mediopostparietal [0]; lateropostparietal [1] (Cavin 2001, but following the terminology based on homologization of skull roof bones).

Appendix 2: Matrix

Data matrix of 51 taxa representing 194 characters belonging to fossil and extant taxa is available online at http://www.geolsoc.org.uk/SUP18314. Outgroup taxa: *Amia calva* and *A. pattersoni, Aspidorhynchus, Belonostomus, Hypsocormus, Lepisosteus, Mesturus, Obaichthys, Pachycormus,* and *Vinctifer*. 0, plesiomorphic state; 1–4, apomorphic states; ?, unclear owing to preservation of specimens; —, non-applicable. Abbreviations: angustu, *angustus*; bech., *bechei*; coryp., *coryphaenoides*; Lept, *Leptolepides*; zapporu, *zapforum*. (The MacClade file containing the matrix can be obtained directly from the author.)

References

AGASSIZ, L. 1833–1844. *Recherches sur les Poissons Fossiles.* 5 vols., Petitpierre, Neuchâtel et Soleure, Switzerland.

ARRATIA, G. 1981. *Varasichthys ariasi* n. gen. et sp. from the Upper Jurassic of Chile (Pisces, Teleostei: Varasichthyidae). *Palaeontographica Abteilung A,* **175**, 107–139.

ARRATIA, G. 1982. *Chongichthys dentatus,* new genus and species from the Late Jurassic of Chile (Pisces, Teleostei: Chongichthyidae, new family). *Journal of Vertebrate Paleontology,* **2**, 133–149.

ARRATIA, G. 1986. New Jurassic fishes of Cordillera de Domeyko, Northern Chile. *Palaeontographica Abteilung A,* **192**, 75–91.

ARRATIA, G. 1991. The caudal skeleton of Jurassic teleosts; a phylogenetic analysis. *In:* CHANG, M.-M., LIU, Y.-H. & ZHANG, G.-R. (eds) *Early Vertebrates and Related Problems in Evolutionary Biology.* Science Press, Beijing, 249–340.

ARRATIA, G. 1992. Development and variation of the suspensorium of primitive Catfishes (Teleostei: Ostariophysi) and their phylogenetic relationships. *Bonner Zoologische Monographien,* **32**, 1–149.

ARRATIA, G. 1994. Phylogenetic and paleobiogeographic relationships of the varasichthyid group (Teleostei) from the Late Jurassic of Central and South America. *Revista Geológica de Chile,* **21**, 119–165.

ARRATIA, G. 1996. Reassessment of the phylogenetic relationships of certain Jurassic teleosts and their implications on teleostean phylogeny. *In:* ARRATIA, G. & VIOHL, G. (eds) *Mesozoic Fishes – Systematics and Paleoecology.* Dr F. Pfeil, Munich, 219–242.

ARRATIA, G. 1997. Basal teleosts and teleostean phylogeny. *Palaeo Ichthyologica,* **7**, 1–168.

ARRATIA, G. 1999. The monophyly of Teleostei and stem-group teleosts. Consensus and disagreements. *In:* ARRATIA, G. & SCHULTZE, H.-P. (eds) *Mesozoic Fishes 2 – Systematics and Fossil Record.* Dr F. Pfeil, Munich, 265–334.

ARRATIA, G. 2000. Remarkable teleostean fishes from the Late Jurassic of southern Germany and their phylogenetic relationships. *Mitteilungen aus dem Museum für Naturkube in Berlin, Geowissenschaftliche Reihe,* **3**, 137–179.

ARRATIA, G. 2004. Mesozoic halecostomes and the early radiation of teleosts. *In:* ARRATIA, G. & TINTORI, A. (eds) *Mesozoic Fishes 3 – Systematics, Paleoenvironments and Biodiversity.* Dr F. Pfeil, Munich, 279–315.

ARRATIA, G. & GAYET, M. 1995. Sensory canals and related bones of Tertiary siluriform crania from Bolivia and North America and comparison with Recent form. *Journal of Vertebrate Paleontology,* **15**, 482–505.

ARRATIA, G. & SCHULTZE, H.-P. 1985. Late Jurassic teleosts (Actinopterygii, Pisces) from Northern Chile and Cuba. *Palaeontographica Abteilung A,* **189**, 29–61.

ARRATIA, G. & SCHULTZE, H.-P. 1987. A new halecostome (Actinopterygii, Osteichthyes) from the Late Jurassic of Chile and its relationships. *Dakoterra,* **3**, 1–13.

ARRATIA, G. & SCHULTZE, H.-P. 1990. The urohyal: Development and homology within osteichthyans. *Journal of Morphology,* **203**, 247–382.

ARRATIA, G. & SCHULTZE, H.-P. 1991. Development and homology of the palatoquadrate in osteichthyans. *Journal of Morphology,* **208**, 1–81.

ARRATIA, G. & SCHULTZE, H.-P. 1999. Mesozoic fishes from Chile. *In:* ARRATIA, G. & SCHULTZE, H.-P. (eds) *Mesozoic Fishes 2 – Systematics and Fossil Record.* Dr F. Pfeil, Munich, 565–593.

BRITO, P. 1997. Révision des Aspidorhynchidae (Pisces: Actinopterygii) du Mésozoïque: ostéologie, relations phylogénétiques, données environnementales et biogéographiques. *Geodiversitas,* **19**, 681–772.

CAVIN, L. 2001. Osteology and phylogenetic relationships of the teleost *Goulmimichthys arambourgi* Cavin, 1995, from the Upper Cretaceous of Goulmima, Morocco. *Eclogae geologicae Helvetiae,* **94**, 509–535.

CAVIN, L. & GRIGORESCU, D. 2005. A new *Crossognathus* (Actinopterygii–Teleostei) from the Lower Cretaceous of Romania with comments on Crossognathidae relationships. *Geodiversitas,* **27**, 5–16.

CAVIN, L., FOREY, P. & LÉCUYER, C. 2007. Correlation between environment and Late Mesozoic ray-finned fish evolution. *Palaeogeography, Palaeoclimatology, Palaeoecology,* **245**, 353–367.

CHEN, X.-Y. & ARRATIA, G. 1994. Olfactory organ in Acipenseriformes and comparison with other actinopterygians: patterns of diversity. *Journal of Morphology,* **222**, 241–267.

COPE, E. D. 1872. On the families of fishes of the Cretaceous formation in Kansas. *Proceedings of the American Philosophical Society, Philadelphia,* **12**, 327–357.

DE SILVA SANTOS, R. & VALENÇA, J. G. 1968. A formação Santana e sua paleoictiofauna. *Anais de la Academia Brasileira de Ciencias, Rio de Janeiro,* **40**, 339–360.

DIXON, D. H. 1850. *The Geology and Fossils of the Tertiary and Cretaceous Formations of Sussex.* F. Dixon, London.

DUNKLE, D. H. 1940. The cranial osteology of *Notelops brama* (Agassiz), an elopid from the Cretaceous of Brazil. *Looydia,* **3**, 157–190.

FINK, S. & FINK, W. 1981. Interrelationships of ostario-physan fishes (Teleostei). *Zoological Journal of the Linnean Society, London*, **72**, 297–358.

FINK, S. & FINK, W. 1996. Interrelationships of ostario-physan fishes. *In*: STIASSNY, M. L. J., PARENTI, L. R. & JOHNSON, D. G. (eds) *Interrelationships of Fishes*. Academic Press, San Diego, 209–249.

FOREY, L. P. 1977. The osteology of *Notelops* Woodward, *Rhacolepis* Agassiz and *Pachyrhizodus* Dixon (Pisces: Teleostei). *Bulletin of the British Museum of Natural History, Geology*, **28**, 125–204.

GASPARINI, Z. 1992. Marine reptiles of the Circum-Pacific region. *In*: WESTERMAN, G. (ed.) *The Jurassic Circum-Pacific, World and Regional Geology*, **3**, 361–364.

GRANDE, L. 1985. Recent and fossil clupeomorph fishes with materials for revision of the subgroups of clupeids. *Bulletin of the American Museum of Natural History*, **181**, 231–272.

GRANDE, L. & BEMIS, W. 1998. A comprehensive phylogenetic study of amiid fishes (Amiidae) based on comparative skeletal anatomy. An empirical search for interconnected patterns of natural history. *Journal of Vertebrate Paleontology*, **18**, **suppl. 1**, 1–609.

HALLAM, A. 1977. Biogeographic evidence bearing on the creation of Atlantic seaway in the Jurassic. *In*: WEST, R. (ed.) *Paleontology and Plate Tectonics*, Milwauke Public Museum, Special Publication in Biology and Geology, **2**, 23–34.

HALLAM, A. 1983. Early and mid-Jurassic molluscan biogeography and the establishment of the Central Atlantic seaway. *Palaeogeography, Palaeoclimatology, Palaeoecology*, **43**, 181–193.

HENNIG, W. 1966. *Phylogenetic Systematics*. University of Illinois Press, Urbana, Chicago, London.

JESSEN, H. 1972. Schultergürtel und Pectoralflosse bei Actinopterygiern. *Fossils and Strata*, **1**, 1–101.

JOHNSON, G. D. & PATTERSON, C. 1996. Relationships of lower euteleost fishes. *In*: STIASSNY, M. L. J., PARENTI, L. R. & JOHNSON, D. G. (eds) *Interrelationships of Fishes*. Academic Press, San Diego, 251–332.

JORDAN, D. S. & BRANNER, J. C. 1908. The Cretaceous fishes of Ceará, Brazil. *Smithsonian Miscellaneous Collections, Washington*, **52**, 1–30.

LAUDER, G. V. & LIEM, K. 1993. The evolution and interrelationships of the actinopterygian fishes. *Bulletin of the Museum of Comparative Zoology, Harvard University*, **150**, 95–197.

LECOINTRE, G. & NELSON, G. J. 1996. Clupeomorpha, sister group of Ostariophysi. *In*: STIASSNY, M. L. J., PARENTI, L. R. & JOHNSON, D. G. (eds) *Interrelationships of Fishes*. Academic Press, San Diego, 193–207.

LI, G.-Q. & WILSON, M. V. H. 1996. Phylogeny of Osteoglossomorpha. *In*: STIASSNY, M. L. J., PARENTI, L. R. & JOHNSON, D. G. (eds) *Interrelationships of Fishes*. Academic Press, San Diego, 163–174.

LI, G.-Q. & WILSON, M. V. H. 1999. Early divergence of Hiodontiformes *sensu stricto* in East Asia and phylogeny of some Mesozoic teleosts from China. *In*: ARRATIA, G. & SCHULTZE, H.-P. (eds) *Mesozoic Fishes 2 – Systematics and Fossil Record*. Dr F. Pfeil, Munich, 369–384.

LOOMIS, F. 1900. Die Anatomie und die Verwandtschaft der Ganoid- und Knochen Fische aus der Kreide-Formation von Kansas. *Palaeontographica*, **46**, 213–284, pls. 19–27.

MAISEY, J. 1991*a*. *Rhacolepis* Agassiz, 1841 *In*: MAISEY, J. (ed.) *Santana Fossils, An Illustrated Atlas*. T.F.H. Publications, Inc., Neptune City, 248–257.

MAISEY, J. 1991*b*. *Notelops* Woodward, 1901. *In*: MAISEY, J. (ed.) *Santana Fossils, An Illustrated Atlas*. T.F.H. Publications, Inc., Neptune City, 258–271.

MAINWARING, A. J. 1978. *Anatomical and Systematic Revision of the Pachycormidae, a Family of Mesozoic Fossil Fishes*. PhD Thesis, Westfield College, London.

NELSON, G. J. 1969. Infraorbital bones and their bearing on the phylogeny and geography of osteoglossomorph fishes. *American Museum Novitates*, **2394**, 1–37.

PATTERSON, C. 1973. Interrelationships of holosteans. *In*: GREENWOOD, P. H., MILES, R. S. & PATTERSON, C. (eds) *Interrelationships of Fishes. Zoological Journal on the Linnean Society* **Suppl. 1**, 233–305.

PATTERSON, C. 1977. The contribution of paleontology to teleostean phylogeny. *In*: HECHT, P. C., GOODY, P. C. & HECHT, B. M. (eds) *Major Patterns in Vertebrate Evolution*, Plenum Press, New York, 579–643.

PATTERSON, C. 1993. Osteichthyes: Teleostei. *In*: BENTON, M. (ed.) *The Fossil Record*. Chapman & Hall, London, 621–663.

PATTERSON, C. & ROSEN, D. E. 1977. Review of the ichthyodectiform and other Mesozcic teleost fishes and the theory and practice of classifying fossils. *Bulletin of the American Museum of Natural History*, **158**, 83–172.

PINNA, M. DE. 1996. Teleostean monophyly. *In*: STIASSNY, M. L. J., PARENTI, L. R. & JOHNSON, D. G. (eds) *Interrelationships of Fishes*. Academic Press, San Diego, 147–162.

PICTET, F. J. 1858. Description des fossiles contenus dans le terrain néocomian des Voirons. Troisième partie. *Matériaux pour la paléontologie suisse, ou recueil des monographies sur les fossiles du Jura et des Alpes, série 2*, **no. 1**.

POYATO-ARIZA, F. J. 1996. A revision of the ostariophysan family Chanidae, with special reference to the Mesozoic forms. *Palaeo Ichthyologica*, **6**, 5–52.

RICCARDI, A. 1991. Jurassic and Cretaceous marine connections between the southeast Pacific and Tethys. *Palaeogeography, Palaeoclimatology, Palaeoecology*, **87**, 155–189.

SCHULTZE, H.-P. 1996. The scales of Mesozoic actinopterygians. *In*: ARRATIA, G. & VIOHL, G. (eds) *Mesozoic Fishes – Systematics and Paleoecology*. Dr F. Pfeil, Munich, 243–259.

SCHULTZE, H.-P. & ARRATIA, G. 1986. Reevaluation of the caudal skeleton of actinopterygian fishes. I. *Lepisosteus* and *Amia*. *Journal of Morphology*, **195**, 257–303.

SCHULTZE, H.-P. & ARRATIA, G. 1989. The composition of the caudal skeleton of teleosts (Actinopterygii, Osteichthyes). *Zoological Journal of the Linnean Society*, **97**, 189–231.

SCOTESE, C. 1987. *Atlas of Mesozoic Plate Tectonic Reconstruction*. Global Section, Shell Developmental Company, Houston, Texas.

SHEN, M. 1996. Fossil osteoglossomorphs from East Asia and their implications for teleostean phylogeny.

In: ARRATIA, G. & VIOHL, G. (eds) *Mesozoic Fishes – Systematics and Paleoecology*. Dr F. Pfeil, München, 261–272.

STAMPFLI, G. M. & BOREL, G. G. 2002. A plate tectonic model for the Paleozoic and Mesozoic constrained by dynamic plate boundaries and restored synthetic oceanic isochrones. *Earth and Planetary Science Letters*, **196**, 17–33.

STIASSNY, M. L. J. 1986. The limits and relationships of the acanthomorph teleosts. *Journal of Zoology*, **B1**, 411–460.

SWOFFORD, D. L. 2005. *PAUP*: Phylogenetic analysis using parsimony (*and other methods), version 4.0 Beta*. Sinauer Associates, Sunderland, Massachusetts.

TAVERNE, L. 1980. Ostéologie et position systématique du genre *Platinx* (Pisces, Teleostei) de l'éocène du Monte Bolca (Italie). *Academie Royale de Belgique, Bulletin de la Classe des Sciences, 5, série*, **66**, 873–889.

TAVERNE, L. 1989. *Crossognathus* Pictet, 1858 du Cretacé inférieur de l'Europe et systématique, paleozoogeographie et biologie des Crossognathiformes nov. ord. (Téléostéens) du Cretacé et du Tertiare. *Palaeontographica Abteilung A*, **207**, 79–105.

TELLER-MARSHALL, S. & BARDACK, D. 1978. The morphology and relationships of the Cretaceous teleost *Apsopelix*. *Fieldiana, Geology*, **41**, 1–35.

WENZ, S. 1965. Les poissons albiens de Vallentigny (Aube). *Annales de Paléontologie, Paris*, **51**, 3–23.

WOODWARD, A. S. 1901. *Catalogue of the Fossil Fishes in the British Museum (Natural History), 4*. British Museum (Natural History), London.

Hybodont sharks from the lower Cretaceous Khok Kruat Formation of Thailand, and hybodont diversity during the Early Cretaceous

G. CUNY[1,5,*], V. SUTEETHORN[2], S. KAMHA[3] & E. BUFFETAUT[4]

[1*]Corresponding author. The Natural History Museum of Denmark, Øster Voldgade 5–7, 1350 Copenhagen K, Denmark (e mail:gilles@snm.ku.dk)

[2]Department of Mineral Resources, Rama VI Road, Bangkok 10400, Thailand

[3]Department of Biology, Mahasarakham University, Tambon Khamriang, Amphur Kantarawichai, Mahasarakham 44150, Thailand

[4]Centre National de la Recherche Scientifique, UMR 5125, 16 cour du Liégat, 75013 Paris, France

[5]UMR 5125 of the CNRS and Université Lyon–1, 7 rue Dubois, 69622 Villeurbanne cedex, France

Abstract: Isolated teeth of five hybodont species are described from the Khok Kruat Formation (Aptian): *Hybodus aequitridentatus* nov. sp., *Heteroptychodus steinmanni*, *Thaiodus ruchae*, *Khoratodus foreyi* nov. gen. et nov. sp., and *Acrorhizodus khoratensis*. A new family, Thaiodontidae is also erected for *Thaiodus* and *Khoratodus*. Two species are recognized inside the genus *Heteroptychodus*, *H. steinmanni* and *H. chuvalovi* nov. comb. These sharks show a wide range of diet and many of them appear to be restricted to a freshwater environment and thus are probably endemic to the Khorat Plateau. However, *Thaiodus* and *Heteroptychodus* are also found in deltaic and/or marine environments outside Thailand, but are nevertheless restricted to the Asian continent. It seems that the appearance of three different palaeobiogeographical provinces (Europe, Asia and Africa–South America) around the Tethys during the Early Cretaceous led to the highest diversity at the generic level in the history of hybodont sharks.

During the last 20 years, the Khok Kruat Formation (Aptian) has yielded a rich fauna of continental vertebrates in the northeastern part of Thailand (Fig. 1). These faunas include dinosaurs, known from both fossil bones (Buffetaut *et al.* 2005) and footprints (Le Loeuff *et al.* 2005), pterosaurs, turtles (Tong *et al.* 2005), crocodiles, isolated teeth and scales of actinopterygians, as well as a rich hybodont fauna (Cappetta *et al.* 1990, 2006; Cuny *et al.* 2003, 2004*b*, 2005). The teeth of actinopterygians appear to be rarer than those of hybodonts, and are dominated by unusual teeth showing a well developed 'wing' behind the acrodine cap (Fig. 2). Such teeth are of unclear taxonomic affinities. The fish scales are, on the other hand, of Semionotiformes form and more abundant than teeth. Many of the hybodont sharks have not yet been named and this is the aim of the present work, as well as to provide new information on those hybodonts already described. The description of the Khok Kruat fauna adds to the known diversity of hybodont sharks during the Early Cretaceous. Indeed, these sharks seem to reach a maximum diversity at this time, and it is also the aim of the present article to better understand this phenomenon.

To protect the fossiliferous sites, their exact locations are not provided in this article. For scientific purposes, these locations can be obtained on request from the second author.

Material and method

1,200 kilograms of fine grained red and white sandstone from the Khok Pha Suam locality (Si Muang Mai District, Ubon Ratchathani Province) have been screen-washed using 0.5 and 1.7 mm mesh-sized sieves. In addition, larger teeth were obtained by surface collecting. Specimens from San Ram (Khon Kaen Province) were mainly obtained by surface collecting from fine-grained red sandstone. Nearly 200 kg of sediments were also collected for screen-washing, but they yielded only a few teeth. Teeth collected from Ban Sapan Hin (Nakhon Ratchasima Province) are rather large teeth, around 20 mm mesio-distally, all belonging to the genus *Thaiodus*, and found in a very hard red sandstone. Only one tooth has been freed from this matrix using formic acid diluted in water (10% formic acid, 90% water).

From: CAVIN, L., LONGBOTTOM, A. & RICHTER, M. (eds) *Fishes and the Break-up of Pangaea.* Geological Society, London, Special Publications, **295**, 93–107.
DOI: 10.1144/SP295.7   0305-8719/08/$15.00 © The Geological Society of London 2008.

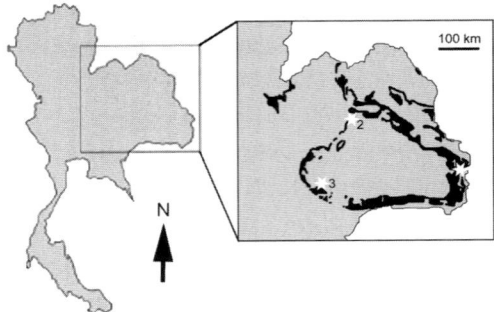

Fig. 1. Map of northeastern Thailand showing outcrops of the Khok Kruat Formation (in black). White stars indicate the locations of the fossiliferous sites: 1: Khok Pha Suam; 2: San Ram; 3: Ban Sapan Hin and Ban Khok Kruat (these two sites are only 1500 m from each other).

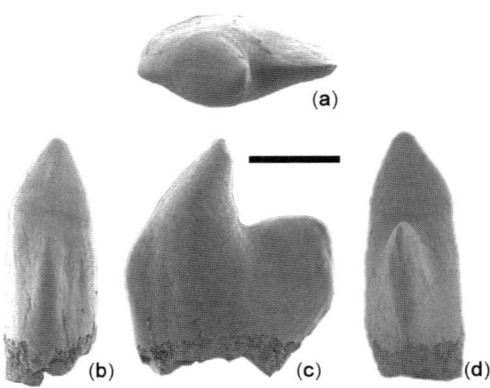

Fig. 2. Actinopterygian 'winged-teeth' from Khok Pha Suam in (**a**) apical, (**b**) labial, (**c**) mesial or distal, and (**d**) lingual views. Scale bar: 1 mm.

The fossils from Khok Pha Suam and San Ram are housed at the Siridhorn Museum Centre (TF numbers) in Sahatsakhan, Kalasin Province, while those from Ban Sapan Hin are housed at the Museum of Petrified Wood and Mineral Resources (NRRU numbers), Nakhon Ratchasima, Nakhon Ratchasima Province.

Geological settings

The Khok Kruat Formation belongs to the Khorat Group, which is a set of freshwater sandstones, clays and limestones deposited during the Mesozoic in NE Thailand (and parts of adjacent Laos and Cambodia). It ranges in age from the Late Jurassic (Phu Kradung Formation) to the Cenomanian (Maha Sarakham Formation), and its total thickness is nearly 3200 m. These deposits were laid down after the collision of the Shan-Tai (=Sibumasu) terrane with the Indochina block (Metcalfe 1996; Charusiri *et al.* 1997; Racey *et al.* 1997*a*). The Khorat Group has yielded a succession of non-marine vertebrate assemblages (Fig. 3; Buffetaut & Suteethorn 1998) but the stratigraphy and palaeoecology of its different formations is still poorly known (Racey *et al.* 1994, 1996, 1997*b*; Metcalfe 1998). The age of the Khok Kruat Formation is however fairly well constrained by biostratigraphical evidence. The occurrence of the peculiar freshwater hybodont shark *Thaiodus ruchae*, which is also known from the Aptian–Albian Takena Formation of Tibet, suggests a similar age for the Khok Kruat Formation (Cappetta *et al.* 1990). In addition, palynomorphs indicating an Aptian age have been reported from its upper part (Sattayarak *et al.* 1991; Racey *et al.* 1996). An Aptian age is therefore well-supported. The Khok Kruat Formation mainly consists of red siltstones, sandstones and conglomerates, indicative of a predominantly fluvial depositional environment (Racey *et al.* 1996).

Systematic description

Class Chondrichthyes Huxley
Subclass Elasmobranchii Bonaparte
Order Hybodontiformes Maisey
Family Hybodontidae Owen
Subfamily Hybodontinae Owen *sensu* Maisey, 1989
Genus *Hybodus* Agassiz

Hybodus aequitridentatus sp. nov.

Hybodus sp. A, Cuny *et al.* 2003, p. 51–52, fig. 1A–C.
Hybodus sp. A, Cuny et al. 2004*b*, fig. 1A–C.
'*Hybodus*' sp., Cuny *et al.* 2005, p. 589.
Hybodus? sp., Cappetta *et al.* 2006, p. 549–550, text-fig. 5.

Derivation of name. From the Latin *aequi*, the same, *tri*, three and *dens*, tooth, referring to the same size of the main cusp and the first pair of lateral cusplets.

Material. More than 170 partial teeth (including TF 7645), with only one being reasonably complete (TF 7644), which is here designated the holotype.

Type locality. Khok Pha Suam, Ubon Ratchathani Province, northeastern Thailand.

Type stratum. Khok Kruat Formation, Khorat Group, Aptian.

Other occurrences. One tooth has been found at San Ram.

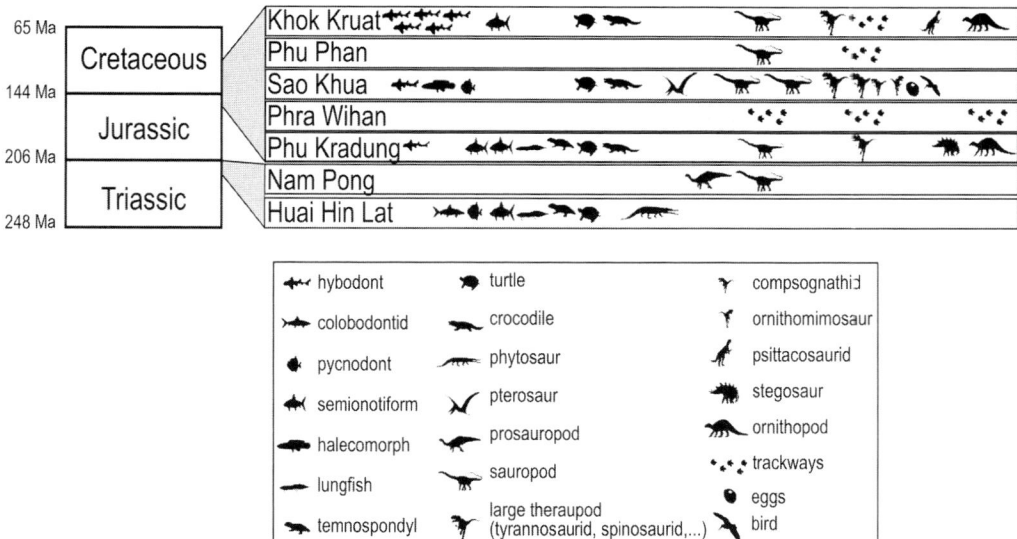

Fig. 3. Distribution of fossil vertebrates in the non-marine Mesozoic Formations of Thailand. Chart by Lionel Cavin.

Diagnosis. Teeth quite large, attaining 20 mm mesio-distally, showing low, blunt cusps, the first pair of lateral cusplets being almost the same size as the main cusp in anterior teeth; crown ornamented by a dense pattern of fine anastomosed ridges; neither labial nor lingual nodes on crown; root ana-ulacorhize, massive, rectangular in basal, labial and lingual views, with a row of enlarged foramina at the base of the lingual and labial surfaces.

Description. The holotype is the largest tooth, being 19.5 mm mesio-distally, 4 mm labio-lingually and 6 mm high at the level of the main cusp. All the teeth show a low main cusp flanked by up to two pairs of lateral cusplets (Fig. 4a-c). The first pair may be almost as high as the main cusp, while the second pair is half that height. One incomplete tooth (TF 7645) shows a minute accessory cusplet on the labial face of the main cusp, near the valley separating the main cusp from a lateral cusplet (Fig. 4d). As this was recorded in no other teeth, this is probably due to some anomaly in the development of this tooth. The crown is ornamented by a dense pattern of fine anastomosed ridges that cover the whole crown, except the lingual shoulder which is smooth. There is a moderately-developed longitudinal crest that is interrupted at the tip of each cusp and cusplets, although this may be the result of wear. There is no labial node at the base of the crown, but very rarely faint lingual nodes may be seen near the mesial or distal extremities of the crown. When preserved, the root is nearly

as high as the crown and is not projected lingually. The basal face is flat. The whole root is perforated by a multitude of foramina randomly distributed with the addition of a row of large foramina at the base of the root, crossing it labio-lingually.

As this species is known from only one complete tooth, tooth variation is difficult to assess. The ornamentation pattern shows no obvious variation. It is possible that some teeth might have possessed three pairs of lateral cusplets, but in some tooth fragments it is difficult to know if it is three lateral cusplets, or the main cusp flanked by two lateral cusplet, which are preserved. The only complete crown, apart from the holotype that is preserved in our collection, shows only two pairs of lateral cusplets. However, the first pair of lateral cusplets is only half the height of the main cusp. No crown fragments show cusps that are bent distally, which seems to indicate that this species has a weak monognathic heterodonty (the latter appears to be marked only by a reduction of the height of the first pair of lateral cusplets). There is no indication of a dignathic heterodonty. Only one tooth fragment shows a crown shoulder extended mesially or distally, which is bent lingually. Normally, the crown shoulder is very short after the last lateral cusplet.

Discussion. Teeth with very different morphologies have been ascribed to the genus *Hybodus*, and there is to date no diagnosis of the genus based on tooth morphology. This genus is thus best regarded as a

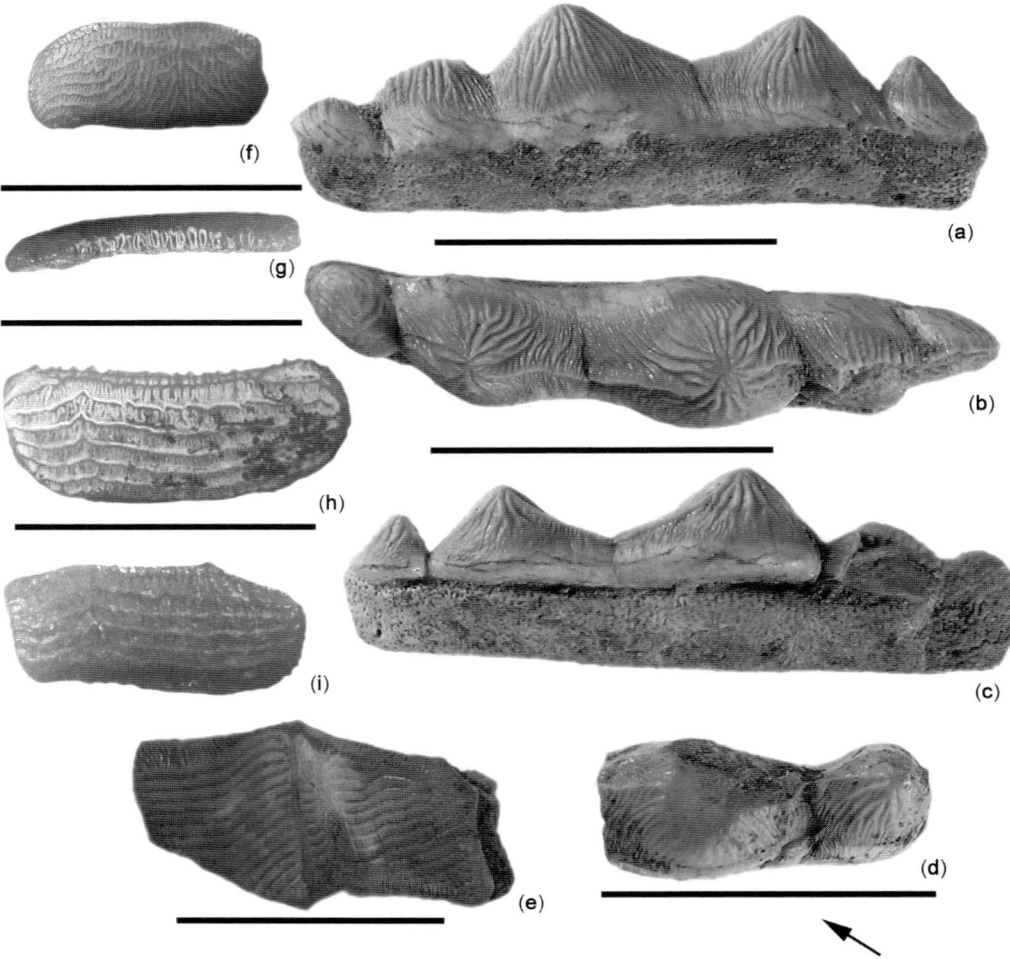

Fig. 4. (a–c), Holotype of *Hybodus aequitridentatus* (TF 7644) in (a) labial; (b) apical; and (c) lingual views. (**d**) tooth of *Hybodus aequitridentatus* (TF 7645) in apical view. The arrow indicates the position of a labial accessory cusplet. (**e**) Pathological tooth of *Heteroptychodus steinmanni* (TF 7679) in apical view. (**f–i**) Teeth of *Heteroptychodus chuvalovi* from the Aptian of Mongolia in (f, h–i) apical view. (f), 115/12178; (h), 113/12178 (holotype); and (i) 114/12178. (g) lingual view of 114/12178. All scale bars: 10 mm.

form genus for the time being (Underwood & Rees 2002). *Hybodus reticulatus* Agassiz, 1836, the type species for *Hybodus*, possesses a high and slender main cusp with well-developed cutting edges and ornamented by seldom branching vertical ridges which rarely reach the cusp apices (Delsate *et al.* 2002), a morphology quite different from that of *H. aequitridentatus*. However, these two species share a circular cross-section of the cusps and the absence of labial nodes (Delsate *et al.* 2002; Underwood & Rees 2002), so the teeth from Thailand are provisionally attributed to the genus *Hybodus*, pending a revision of *H. aequitridentatus*.

The density of the ornamentation of the teeth from Thailand is reminiscent of that of *Polyacrodus (Hybodus) brevicostatus* from the Wealden of Britain (Patterson 1966). However, the teeth from Thailand are easily distinguished from those of *P. brevicostatus* by the much better-developed main cusp and lateral cusplets and the absence of labial and lingual nodes at the base of the crown. It is the presence of well-developed labial and lingual nodes that probably justifies the placing of the species *P. brevicostatus* into the genus *Polyacrodus*, but this genus is also badly defined at present, and the precise generic attribution of

P. brevicostatus remains quite unclear (Cappetta 1987). Duffin (*in* Goodwin *et al.* 1999) considered it to be *Hybodus brevicostatus* while Underwood and Rees (2002) put it into the genus *Polyacrodus*. Due to the absence of labial and lingual nodes in the teeth, the species from Thailand is probably not closely-related to *P. brevicostatus*. The teeth from Thailand also show an ornamentation quite similar to those of *Hybodus* sp. described from the Upper Jurassic of Ethiopia (Goodwin *et al.* 1999), but are easily distinguished from the latter on the basis of a higher first pair of lateral cusplets and the absence of fine, short non-branching ridges on the longitudinal crest in *H. aequitridentatus*. The ridges reaching the longitudinal crest in *H. aequitridentatus* are not as short as in the teeth from Ethiopia, and they are often anastomosed (Cappetta *et al.* 2006, text-fig 5).

Family Ptychodontidae Jaekel
Genus *Heteroptychodus* Yabe & Obata

Heteroptychodus steinmanni *Yabe & Obata*

Heteroptychodus steinmanni Yabe & Obata 1930, figs. 6–8.
Heteroptychodus sp. Tanimoto & Tanaka 1998, figs. 1–2.
Heteroptychodus steinmanni Cuny *et al.* 2003, fig. 1G–K, fig. 4E–F.
Heteroptychodus steinmanni Cuny *et al.* 2004*b*, fig. 1G–K, fig. 2E–F.
Heteroptychodus steinmanni Cuny *et al.* 2006, fig. 4A–H.
Heteroptychodus aff. steinmanni Cappetta *et al.* 2006, p. 550–552, text-fig. 6–7.

Material. More than 170 partial teeth from Khok Pha Suam, including TF 7647–50 and TF 7679, plus four teeth probably belonging to juveniles (including TF 7655). Some teeth were also found at San Ram, and more than 150 teeth were also retrieved from the Sao Khua Formation (Fig. 3), including TF 7675, 7676 and 7678 (Cuny *et al.* 2005, 2006).

Occurrences. These teeth have a large stratigraphic distribution, having been found at various localities in the Phu Kradung, Sao Khua and Khok Kruat Formations, occurring therefore from the Late Jurassic up to the Aptian.

Phu Kradung Formation. Several fragmentary teeth from Khum Phok (Mukdahan Province). Teeth of *Heteroptychodus* were also found on the SE and NW coasts of the island of Ko Kut, but were misidentified as possibly belonging to *Bdellodus* (Buffetaut & Ingavat 1983). The outcrops belong probably to the Phu Kradung Formation.

Sao Khua Formation. Phu Phan Thong, Phu Wat, Ban Huai Dua and Huai Lao Yang (Nong Bua Lamphu Province); Phu Wiang 1A (Khon Kaen Province); Phu Kum Khao and Phu Mai Paw (Kalasin Province); Phu Phok and Phu Noi (Sakhon Nakhon Province); Non Liam (Chaiya Phum Province).

Khok Kruat Formation. Khok Pha Suam (Ubon Ratchathani Province); San Ram (Khon Kaen Province).

Pathological tooth. The teeth of *Heteroptychodus steinmanni* from Thailand were described in detail elsewhere (Cuny *et al.* 2003, 2005; Cappetta *et al.* 2006), except for a pathological tooth recently found by one of us (KS) in Khok Pha Suam (TF 7679). This arched tooth shows a deep groove in the enameloid on top of the apex of the crown, and on one side of the crown, the mesio-distal ridges are interrupted by irregular, anastomosed ridges, with a labio-lingual general direction (Fig. 4e, 5). Arched teeth were interpreted by Cuny *et al.* (2003) as anterior teeth. This pathological tooth may be the result of an injury in the anterior part of the mouth of the shark, which disturbed the normal development of the tooth. Examples of such disturbances are well-documented in both modern and fossil neoselachian sharks (Hubbell 1996; Becker *et al.* 2000).

Discussion. *Heteroptychodus steinmanni* represents the most common hybodont species found in the Khorat Group. Its teeth show significant morphological variation, with teeth possessing from 3–25

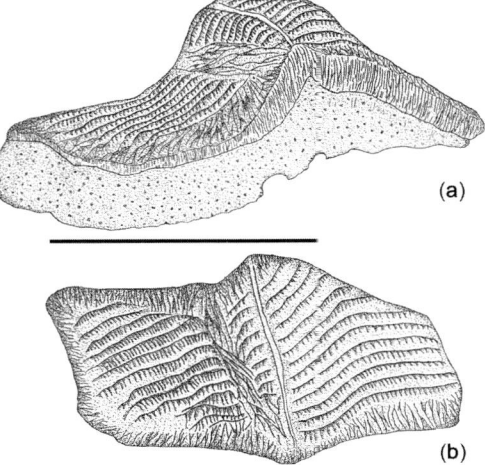

Fig. 5. Pathological tooth of *Heteroptychodus steinmanni* (TF 7679) in (**a**) disto-lingual view; (**b**) apical view. Scale bar: 10 mm.

mesio-distal ridges. The largest teeth, thus possessing the highest number of ridges, were found in the Sao Khua Formation (Cuny et al. 2006). This morphological variation encompasses the variation observed among the type specimen (Yabe & Obata 1930) and other teeth found in Japan (Tanimoto & Tanaka 1998). There is, therefore, no evidence that the teeth from Japan and Thailand belong to more than a single species and they are all ascribed to H. steinmanni. However, Heteroptychodus is not a monospecific genus.

Hybodont teeth attributed to the genus Asiadontus were reported from the Aptian–Albian of Kyrgyzstan and Mongolia (Nessov 1997), and they are strikingly similar to those of Heteroptychodus. One of us (GC) had the opportunity to study the teeth of Asiadontus chuvalovi, Nessov, Glückman & Mertiniene from Mongolia at the Zoological Institute of the Russian Academy of Sciences in St Petersburg (numbers 113/12178 [holotype], 114/12178, and 115/12178), and these teeth show an ornamentation pattern typical of Heteroptychodus, consisting of numerous mesio-distal ridges, each showing numerous short perpendicular ridges. However, these teeth appear slightly different from those of Japan and Thailand. The mesiodistal ridges on the apical face show well developed chevrons in the ornamentation (Fig. 4f-h), and the lingual face of the crown shows strong vertical ridges (Fig. 4i). The teeth from Mongolia should, therefore, be considered as a separate species of Heteroptychodus, H. chuvalovi nov. comb., and Asiadontus becomes a junior synonym of Heteroptychodus. As we have had no possibility as yet to examine the teeth from Kyrgyzstan, their specific status should be considered as uncertain for the time being. Large teeth of Heteroptychodus steinmanni from the Sao Khua Formation sometimes show very faint chevrons in the ornamentation on their apical face (TF 7678), but they are never as developed as in the Mongolian teeth (Fig. 6a).

Several teeth from Khok Pha Suam and Phu Phan Thong were attributed to juveniles based on the fact that they lack the short ridges perpendicular to the main mesio-distal ridges (Cuny et al. 2003, 2006) and have very few main mesio-distal ridges. One of these teeth (TF 7655), found at Khok Pha Suam, is however unusual because it shows one cusp on each of the mesio-distal ridges (Fig. 6b–c). If we compare this situation with modern sharks possessing a grinding dentition, Reif (1976) has documented that the juveniles of the modern Heterodontus show a dentition that is not as durophagous as that of the adult. It is, therefore, reasonable to think that this may have also been true of some Mesozoic hybodonts, because they had the same mechanical constraints that prevent small juvenile specimens strengthening their jaws in order to cope with high

compressive forces. However, similar cusps, to the best knowledge of the authors, have never been reported in the juveniles of hybodonts possessing a grinding dentition.

This tooth measures only 1.8 mm mesiodistally, while the largest teeth can reach 20 mm, and its size is in accordance with the hypothesis that it belongs to a very young individual. It might be possible that these cusps fused together later during ontogeny, and that they formed the apical arched part of the crown of anterior teeth of adults. Like the cusps in TF 7655, these arched parts are not in a central position in the teeth of adults (Cuny et al. 2003). This could explain why some other small teeth from juveniles found at Khok Pha Suam do not show any cusp (Cuny et al. 2006), possibly because they are posterior teeth. The attribution of TF 7655 to a juvenile Heteroptychodus must however be considered tentative for the time being, considering the absence of more material supporting the hypothesis proposed above. Teeth of juveniles are indeed very rare in the samples, although this could be related to an identification problem. The deposits are of high energy, and most of the teeth recovered so far are broken. The lack of the comb-like ornamentation in juveniles, so typical of the teeth from adults, and their small size make the identification of fragmentary teeth of juveniles quite difficult.

Family Thaiodontidae nov. fam.

Diagnosis. Hybodontiformes possessing asymmetric teeth with an occlusal crest displaced lingually; teeth elongated mesio-distally; ornamentation, if present, limited to the upper half of the crown; teeth from the same file narrowly interlocked.

Derivation of name. From Thaiodus, the first described genus belonging to the family.

Genus Thaiodus Cappetta et al., 1990
Thaiodus ruchae Cappetta et al., 1990
Thaiodus ruchae Cappetta et al., 1990, figs. 1–2.
Thaiodus ruchae Cuny et al., 2003, fig. 1D–F.
Thaiodus ruchae Cuny et al., 2004b, fig. 1D–F.
Thaiodus ruchae Cappetta et al. 2006, text-figs. 2–4.

Material. More than 300 partial teeth, 9 with the root preserved.

Occurrences. Khok Pha Suam and San Ram (Ubon Ratchathani Province); Ban Khok Kruat and Ban Sapan Hin (Nakhon Ratchasima Province).

Discussion. Teeth of Thaiodus ruchae have been described in detail elsewhere (Cappetta et al. 1990, 2006; Cuny et al. 2003). These teeth were

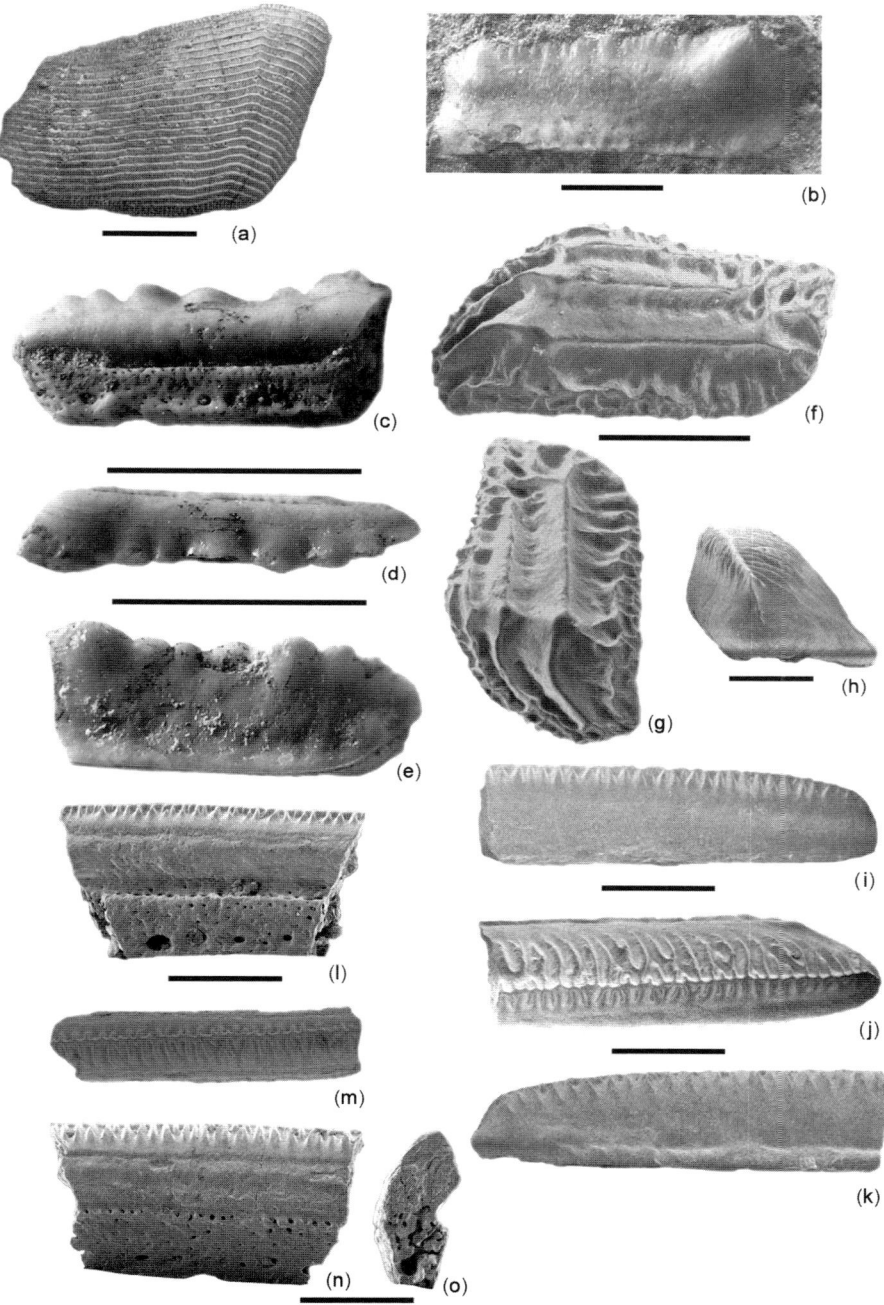

Fig. 6. (a) Lateral tooth of *Heteroptychodus steinmanni* (TF 7678) from Ban Huai Dua (Nong Bua Lamphu Province, Sao Khua Formation) in apical view; (b) Posterior tooth of *Thaiodus ruchae* (NRRU-A1733) in labial view; (c–e), Tooth of *Thaiodus ruchae* (TF 9016) in (c) lingual; (d) apical; (e) labial views. (f–g) Tooth from a possible juvenile *Heteroptychodus steinmanni* (TF 7655) in (f), apical; (g) mesio-apical views. (h–k), Tooth of *Khoratodus foreyi* (TF 7659) in (h) mesial or distal; (i) labial; (j) apical; (k) lingual views. (l–o), Holotype of *Khoratodus foreyi* (TF 7680) in (l) lingual; (m) apical; (n) labial; (o) mesial or distal views. Scale bars: (a, d–g) 5 mm; (b–c, h–j, l–o) 1 mm; (k) 0.5 mm.

originally described as possessing a convex labial face, and a concave lingual face, flared basally (Cappetta *et al.* 1990); this led Cuny *et al.* (2003) to consider *Thaiodus* as possibly belonging to the Steinbachodontidae. However, on the basis of a single tooth with the root preserved, Cappetta *et al.* (2006) have reversed the orientation of these teeth. Since then, two more teeth from Khok Pha Suam (including TF 9016, fig. 6d–f), and seven from Ban Sapan Hin have been found with their roots preserved. In labial view, the crown completely overhangs the root (Fig. 6f, Cappetta *et al.* 2006, text-fig. 2A). In the teeth from Ban Sapan Hin, being preserved in hard sandstone, the root can only be seen in lingual view, and it is likely that more teeth, exposed only in labial view, have their roots preserved. The root never exceeds half the height of the crown, and always shows a row of enlarged foramina at the base of the basal face. These new finds confirm the new orientation of the teeth. It is thus clear that Cuny *et al.* (2003) were wrong in tentatively assigning *Thaiodus* to the Steinbachodontidae.

Cappetta *et al.* (1990, 2006) assign this genus to the family Hybodontidae, but without justification. Although the orientation of the teeth has been changed, this genus shows no characteristic of this family, and we think it would be better considered as belonging to a family of its own together with *Khoratodus foreyi* (see below).

One recent find from Ban Sapan Hin also allows a better understanding of the heterodonty pattern in this genus. The tooth NRRU–A1733 is 18 mm long mesio-distally and 6 mm high. It is still embedded in the matrix, and thus only the labial face can be observed. This tooth is very asymmetric, with the main cusp being situated on the mesial end of the crown, while the distal end shows a faint cusplet (Fig. 6g). Both the main cusp and the distal cusplet are serrated. In between the two, there are 15 serrated denticles. The main cusp is ornamented at its apex by a few short ridges. This tooth probably represents a posterior tooth, as anterior teeth are more symmetric with a main cusp situated centrally (Cappetta *et al.* 1990; Cuny *et al.* 2003), although it is not possible in the present state of our knowledge to decide whether it is an upper or a lower tooth. It is nearly as long mesio-distally as the other probable anterior teeth, collected from the same red sandstone at Ban Sapan Hin by the Museum of Petrified Wood and Mineral Resources' staff, one of us (GC) has measured in the collection of this Museum. Twenty one complete teeth were measured, excluding NRRU–A1733, and the resulting mean mesio-distal length was 22 mm, the shortest being 17 mm, and the longest 27 mm (Table 1). This would seem to indicate that *Thaiodus* possessed posterior teeth that became extremely asymmetric, but without showing a significant reduction in size. It is, of course, possible that NRRU–A1733

Table 1. *Main characteristics of the complete teeth of* Thaiodus ruchae *kept at the Museum of Petrified Wood and Mineral Resources in Nakhon Ratchasima*

Tooth number	Mesio-distal width (mm)	Ornamenting ridges
No number	22	yes
No number	17	yes
No number	25	yes
No number	23	yes
No number	25	yes
NRRU-A781	25	no
No number	21	yes
NRRU-A1914	20	yes
NRRU-A1916	21	no
No number	27	yes
No number	20	yes
No number	24	?
No number	24	yes
NRRU-A1035	20	yes
NRRU-A1359	18	no
NRRU-A1666	24	yes
NRRU-A1742	20	yes
NRRU-A1736	27	yes
NRRU-A1732	17	no
NRRU-A1733	18	yes
NRRU-A1743	22	no
NRRU-A1734	24	no

belonged to a very large shark, and that the smaller posterior teeth of *Thaiodus* were not recovered at Ban Sapan Hin, but this seems extremely unlikely. Unfortunately, most of the teeth from the Khok Pha Suam locality are incomplete, and the monognathic heterodonty pattern of the genus cannot be assessed from the teeth from this site.

The teeth from Ban Sapan Hin also show some variation in the ornamentation of the crown. Some teeth have ridges ornamenting their cusps, and some teeth show smooth cusps. These changes in ornamentation appear to be independent of the size of the teeth, which could be indicative of a dignathic heterodonty as well.

The heterodonty pattern observed in the teeth from Ban Sapan Hin is very different from that described in typical Hybodontidae, such as *Egertonodus basanus* and *Hybodus hauffianus* (Maisey 1983; Duffin 1997). In these species, the posterior teeth show a regular reduction in size, and do not become as asymmetrical as in *Thaiodus*. The heterodonty pattern is also different to that observed in some Lonchidiidae, like *Lissodus humblei* where the posterior teeth become asymmetrical, but also longer mesio-distally than the anterior teeth (Duffin 2001*b*). This reinforces the idea that *Thaiodus* is not a Hybodontidae, but belongs in a family of its own.

Genus *Khoratodus* nov. gen.

Derivation of name. From the Khorat Plateau, where the specimens were found, and *odous*, tooth in Greek.

Type species. Khoratodus foreyi nov. sp.

Diagnosis. Small teeth; asymmetric labio-lingually with a longitudinal crest displaced lingually; mesio-distal length at least six times the labio-lingual width; zigzag-shaped longitudinal crest; crown apex ornamented by branching ridges not reaching the base of the crown; root anaulacorhize with a basal row of enlarged foramina; teeth within the same file closely interlocked.

Khoratodus foreyi *nov. gen. et nov. sp.*

New genus and species #1 Cuny *et al.* 2003
 p. 57–58, fig. 4A–D
New genus and species #1 Cuny *et al.* 2004*b*,
 fig. 2A–D
New genus and species #1 Cuny *et al.* 2005,
 p. 589

Derivation of name. In honour of Peter Forey, for his enormous contribution to palaeoichthyology, and to whom this volume is dedicated.

Material. More than 100 fragmentary teeth, including TF 7659 and the holotype TF 7680.

Type locality. Khok Pha Suam, Ubon Ratchathani Province, northeastern Thailand.

Type stratum. Khok Kruat Formation, Khorat Group, Aptian.

Diagnosis. Same as for genus.

Description. The teeth of this genus are very elongated and rod shaped. Their labio-lingual width is generally about 1 mm although one tooth is 2.5 mm wide. The maximum mesio-distal length is unknown as no complete teeth have been found yet but it is at least six times the width in TF 7659. The teeth show a low coronal profile with a well-developed, zigzag-shaped longitudinal crest (Fig. 6i). Ridges originate from the longitudinal crest, often branching, but they do not reach the base of the crown (Fig. 6h, j). The crown is asymmetric with a short and convex lingual face while the labial face is flared basally although remaining slightly convex (Fig. 6k): as a result the longitudinal crest is displaced lingually. There is a faint basal groove on the labial face. At the mesial and distal ends of the teeth, there is a short basal bulge on the lingual face.

Only one tooth, the holotype TF 7680, has the root preserved, but lacks both the mesial and distal extremities (Fig. 6l–m). The root is anaulacorhize and two-thirds the height of the crown. It is slightly projected lingually (Fig. 7). On the lingual face, there is a row of basal, enlarged foramina. The lingual crown/root junction forms a wide and deep groove, where the labial face of the crown of the preceding tooth in the file probably fits. The teeth within a file were therefore interlocked.

Discussion. When first described (Cuny *et al.* 2003), these teeth were interpreted as having a longitudinal crest displaced labially, in comparison to *Thaiodus ruchae*. Since then, the orientation of the teeth of *T. ruchae* has been changed (Cappetta *et al.* 2006). The recent find of TF 7680 shows that *Khoratodus* also possesses teeth with a longitudinal crest displaced lingually. As noted before (Cuny *et al.* 2003), the crown of the teeth of *Thaiodus* and *Khoratodus* show common features in addition to their asymmetry: they are both elongated mesio-distally, and, when present, the ornamentation is restricted to the upper half of the crown. The new discoveries also show common features of the root with a similar vascularization pattern, and the same deep groove on the lingual face at the root/crown junction for the teeth to interlock (Cappetta *et al.* 2006). Such features are quite unusual among hybodonts, especially the interlocking system, and these two genera are therefore included in a new family, the Thaiodontidae, which, so far, appears to be restricted to Asia. The interlocking system of the

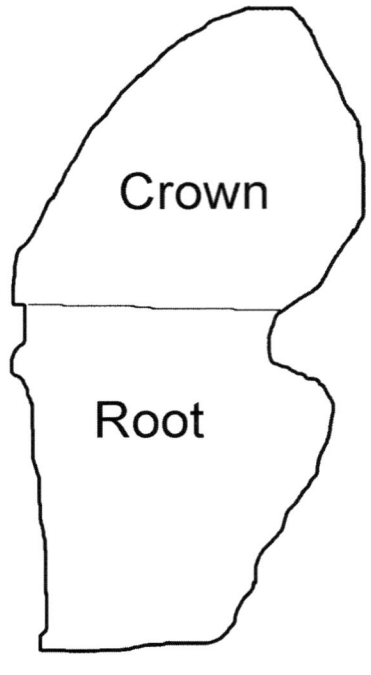

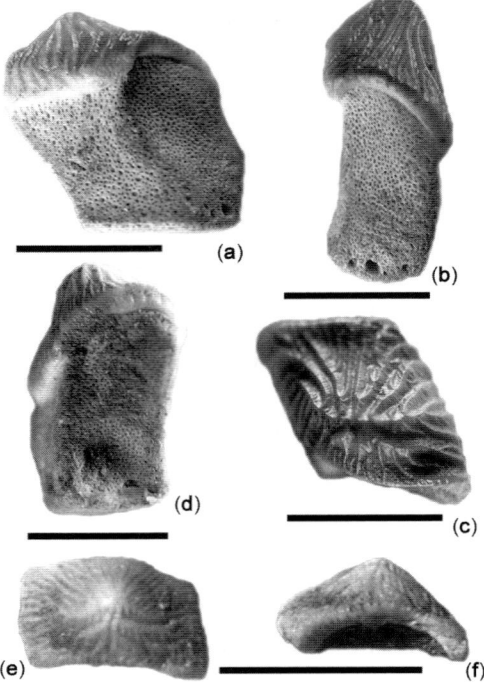

Fig. 7. Outline of a transverse section of the holotype of *Khoratodus foreyi* (TF 7680). Labial face to the left. Scale bar: 0.1 mm.

Fig. 8. (**a–d**), Posterior tooth of *Acrorhizodus khoratensis* (TF 7653) in (a) mesio-lingual or disto-lingual; (b), lingual; (c), apical; (d) labial views. (**e–f**) Tooth of a possible new hybodont taxon (TF 7651) in (e) apical, and (f) lingual views. All scale bars: 5 mm.

teeth probably provided this shark with a very efficient crushing dentition.

Family *incertae sedis*

Acrorhizodus khoratensis *Cappetta et al. 2006*

New genus and species #2 Cuny *et al.* 2003, fig. 4G–I.
New genus and species #2 Cuny *et al.* 2004*b*, fig. 2G–I.
New genus and species #2 Cuny *et al.* 2005, p. 589.

Material. More than 30 teeth including TF 7653 (Fig. 8a–d) and TF 7657.

Occurrences. Khok Pha Suam, Ubon Ratchathani Province, Khok Kruat Formation.

Description. In apical view, the crown is broadly rectangular with a slightly convex labial outline and a slightly concave lingual one. In TF 7657, the best-preserved tooth, the crown is 5 mm mesio-distally and 4 mm labio-lingually. The largest complete crown is 9 mm mesio-distally and 5 mm labio-lingually (Cuny *et al.* 2003). There is a blunt cusp on the labial side that is almost as wide as the crown. The crown is ornamented with a dense pattern of primary anastomosed ridges originating

from the longitudinal crest, which is U-shaped in apical view. These primary ridges attain the base of the crown. On large unworn teeth, there are short, secondary ridges originating from both sides of the primary ridges on most of their length. On the lingual face of the crown, inside the U made by the longitudinal crest, the primary ridges are parallel to each other and orientated labio-lingually. On the labial, distal and mesial faces, outside the U made by the longitudinal crest, the primary ridges show a radiating pattern. In mesial or distal view, the labial face is slightly convex while the lingual face is strongly concave and flared basally.

Posterior teeth are parallelogram-shaped (including TF 7653 and TF 7654, Fig. 8c) with a tendency to be wider than long. The longitudinal crest loses its U-shape and becomes straighter.

The root is preserved in six teeth, including TF 7653, TF 7654, and TF 7657, and is 1.5–2 times the height of the crown (Fig. 8a, b, d). It is perforated by a multitude of randomly distributed foramina. There is a rather irregular basal row of enlarged foramina, the central one always being the largest. The basal face is rectangular in shape and flat. The root is orientated lingually, with a convex labial face and a concave lingual face. The crown slightly overhangs the root lingually.

Discussion. Cuny *et al.* (2003) described a new genus and species #3 from Khok Pha Suam. However, Jan Rees (Karlstad University), in his review of the present article, as well as Cappetta *et al.* (2006) emitted doubts concerning the validity of this genus. Indeed, a careful reappraisal of the material at hand shows that at least some of the teeth included by Cuny *et al.* (2003) into their new genus and species #3 are more likely to represent posterior teeth of *Acrorhizodus khoratensis* (Fig. 8 a–d). However, among the ten teeth originally ascribed to the new genus and species #3, there is still one (TF 7651, Fig. 8e–f), which does not fit *Acrorhizodus khoratensis*.

This tooth has a rectangular outline in apical view, being mesio-distally longer than labio-lingually wide. The crown is ornamented with a dense pattern of radiating, often anastomosing ridges. The ridges all originate from the longitudinal crest and reach the base of the crown. The longitudinal crest is not very well-developed. On the lingual side of the cusp, two pairs of ridges become parallel to the longitudinal crest. The longitudinal crest and some main ridges show short, non-branching ridges perpendicular to them, a pattern similar to that seen in *Heteroptychodus* and *Isanodus* (Cuny *et al.* 2003, 2006). In labial and lingual view, the base of the crown is arched (Fig. 8f). There is no preserved root.

Acrorhizodus is characterized by teeth possessing a U-shaped longitudinal crest, except in the posterior teeth, and a lingual ornamentation made of ridges orientated labio-lingually (which is a very different ornamentation pattern from that seen in TF 7651, where the ornamentation is mainly orientated mesio-distally).

Several characteristics of this tooth are reminiscent of the teeth of *Heteroptychodus*: the parallelogram to rectangular shape of the crown, the presence of some ridges parallel to the longitudinal crest, the presence of short ridges perpendicular to the main ridges, and a crown that is arched in lingual and labial view. However, the hypothesis of a relationship with *Heteroptychodus* is difficult to ascertain. It is therefore likely that there is an additional taxon present among the Khok Kruat hybodont fauna, but too few teeth have been collected so far to allow a precise identification and characterization of this possible new taxon.

Discussion

The hybodonts from the Khok Kruat Formation show adaptations towards various diets. *Hybodus aequitridentatus* and *Acrorhizodus khoratensis* were probably opportunistic feeders, but the low cusps of their teeth indicate some specialization towards rather hard-shelled prey (Cappetta *et al.* 2006). *Heteroptychodus* and *Khoratodus* possess flat teeth which indicate a specialization towards durophagy. Finally, the serrated teeth of *Thaiodus* would usually indicate feeding on large prey. However, the teeth are very low and show double serration. This latter character is also found in some species of *Squalicorax* and *Galeocerdo*, which also possess rather low, pitched teeth (Cappetta 1987). These two sharks possess similar feeding mechanics, and are known scavengers (Shimada & Cicimurri 2005) with teeth capable of cutting through very tough material (Frazetta 1988). The teeth of *Thaiodus* are strongly interlocked (Cappetta *et al.* 2006), which would also made them capable of cutting through tough material. It is therefore possible that *Thaiodus* was an occasional scavenger, with a wide range of diet similar to that of *Galeocerdo* or *Squalicorax*.

Hybodont sharks thus represented an important and diverse component of the freshwater ecosystems of the Khorat Plateau during the Aptian, with many species showing an adaptation towards durophagy. As mentioned in the introduction, teeth of osteichthyans are not common in the Khok Kruat Formation, and one may notice the lack of button-shaped *Lepidotes* teeth in this Formation, which are otherwise very common worldwide at that time. The lack of durophagous Semionotiformes in Thailand may thus have favoured the development of durophagous hybodont sharks in the freshwater ecosystems of Thailand during the Aptian. The Semionotiformes which have been so far collected in Thailand in the Upper Jurassic–Lower Cretaceous Phu Kradung Formation show indeed no adaptation towards durophagy (Cavin *et al.* 2003; Cavin & Suteethorn 2006).

Hybodus aequitridentatus, *Khoratodus foreyi*, and *Acrorhizodus khoratensis* are so far found only in the Khok Pha Suam and San Ram localities. They were probably freshwater sharks, which partly explains their apparent endemism. *Thaiodus* on the other hand is known both from the Khorat Plateau and Tibet, where it has been found in a deltaic environment (Cappetta *et al.* 1990). This shark was therefore able to tolerate some changes in salinity. Finally, *Heteroptychodus* has the largest distribution, both geographically and stratigraphically, having been recorded in Thailand, Japan, Kyrgyzstan, and Mongolia (Yabe & Obata 1930; Nessov 1997; Tanimoto & Tanaka 1998). *Heteroptychodus steinmanni* ranges from the Late Jurassic to the Aptian in Thailand, and from the Berriasian to the Hauterivian in Japan (Goto *et al.* 1996;

Tanimoto & Tanaka 1998), and *H. chuvalovi* seems to be restricted to the Aptian (Averianov & Skutschas 2000). Moreover *Heteroptychodus* has been found in marine sediments in Kyrgyzstan as *Asiadontus* (Averianov & Skutschas 2000). The record of *Heteroptychodus* and *Thaiodus* in marine and deltaic environments demonstrates that not all the hybodont sharks from Thailand were restricted to freshwater. However, these sharks are unknown outside Asia and were thus probably unable to face open water. They possibly followed the coastline and invaded several freshwater systems around the continent. A similar strategy is seen today among the sawfish *Pristis perotteti*, which has colonized several lakes along the Atlantic coast of Central and South America (Thorson 1982). The ray *Himantura chaophraya*, which is found in several rivers from Thailand in the North to Australia in the South (Last & Stevens 1994) is another example of such a mode of life.

The peculiar freshwater sharks of the Khok Kruat Formation may represent the result of endemic evolution from a basal stock that became isolated from the assemblages of other land masses at an early period. The presence of the Lonchidiidae *Parvodus* and *Lonchidion*, in the older Sao Khua Formation seems to indicate a European origin for the Thai hybodonts. It is possible that they reached Thailand following the coast sometime in the Jurassic and then settled in freshwater environments where they diversified (Cuny *et al.* 2006). The Lonchidiidae were later replaced in Thailand by more endemic hybodonts (Cuny *et al.* 2003, 2006), which may suggest that the link with Europe was cut sometime during the Early Cretaceous. The reason for the disappearance of the Lonchidiidae in Thailand remains unclear in the present state of our knowledge.

The hybodont fauna from the Khok Kruat Formation appears therefore to be a fauna of specialized hybodonts that have developed an array of different dentitions, from grinding to cutting, and are endemic to the Asian continent. Interestingly enough, a very similar pattern in hybodont sharks can be observed in South America and Africa. The hybodont faunas from these two continents in the Early Cretaceous are represented mainly by endemic taxa found in freshwater or shallow coastal waters: *Priohybodus arambourgi*, *Tribodus limae*, *Tribodus tunisiensis*, *Diabodus tataouinensis*, and *Pororhiza molimbaensis* (D'Erasmo 1960; Tabaste 1963; Casier 1969; Brito & Ferreira 1989; Brito 1992; Maisey & de Carvalho 1997; Goodwin *et al.* 1999; Duffin 2001*a*; Perea *et al.* 2001; Cuny *et al.* 2004*a*). In contrast, the Early Cretaceous hybodonts from Europe include only one endemic genus, *Hylaeobatis*, although *Vectiselachos* may also have been restricted to Europe

(Rees & Underwood 2002; Underwood & Rees 2002). Most of the European hybodont faunas consist of genera known at least since the Jurassic (*Hybodus*, *Lissodus*, *Lonchidion*, *Polyacrodus* and *Parvodus*), with many of them showing a worldwide distribution (*Hybodus*, *Lissodus*, *Lonchidion* and *Polyacrodus*), although the precise taxonomic status of *Hybodus* and *Polyacrodus* remain unclear, and they may be polyphyletic (Cappetta 1987; Underwood & Rees 2002). However, the presence of *Egertonodus basanus* in the Lower Cretaceous of Morocco and in the Lower Cretaceous of Europe (Duffin & Sigogneau-Russell 1993) indicates that there was some connection between the European and North African hybodont faunas.

The presence of *Parvodus* in Thailand seems to favour a European origin for at least part of the Asian fauna, including the *Heteroptychodus* lineage (Cuny *et al.* 2006). Similarly, '*Hybodus*' *ensis*, which shows some serration at the base of the main cusp of its teeth (Underwood & Rees 2002), might indicate a European origin for the African lineage leading to *Priohybodus*. Europe might thus have represented the centre of origin for the Asian and the Africa–South American hybodont faunas. However, both Asia and the Africa–South American continent show a very scarce hybodont fossil record from the Jurassic, and the timing of the inter-continental migrations remains unknown. Moreover, there has been much more research activity during the last two centuries in Europe than in Asia, Africa, or South America. This difference in research activities may also biased our understanding of the evolution of these faunas through time.

The appearance during the Early Cretaceous of these three palaeobiogeographical provinces: Europe, Asia, and Africa–South America (which have mainly freshwater and coastal waters sharks, each possessing a very different hybodont fauna) led to an unprecedented diversification of these animals that reached a peak of diversity at the generic level. Indeed, 11 genera of hybodont sharks are known from the Triassic (*Acrodus*, *Asteracanthus*, *Diplolonchidion*, *Donguzodus*, *Hybodus*, *Lissodus*, *Lonchidion*, *Palaeobates*, *Polyacrodus*, *Reticulodus*, and *Steinbachodus*, Cappetta 1987; Minikh 2001; Murry & Kirby 2002; Heckert 2004. (*Doratodus*, *Pseudodalatias*, and *Vallisia* are not considered to be hybodont sharks; Cuny & Benton 1999). Ten genera are known from the Jurassic (*Acrodus*, *Asteracanthus*, *Bdellodus*, *Egertonodus*, *Hybodus*, *Lissodus*, *Lonchidion*, *Parvodus*, *Polyacrodus*, and *Priohybodus*) (Cappetta 1987; Maisey 1987; Rees & Underwood 2002). Twenty hybodont genera have been found in the Cretaceous (*Acrodus*, *Acrorhizodus*, *Asteracanthus*, *Bahariyodon*, *Egertonodus*, *Heteroptychodus*, *Hybodus*,

Hylaeobatis, Isanodus, Khoratodus, Lissodus, Lonchidion, Parvodus, Polyacrodus, Pororhiza, Priohybodus, Ptychodus, Thaiodus, Tribodus and *Vectiselachos*) (Cappetta 1987; Brito & Ferreira 1989; Duffin 2001*b*; Rees & Underwood 2002; Cappetta *et al.* 2006; Cuny *et al.* 2006). It is also during the Late Jurassic – Early Cretaceous that hybodonts developed a cutting dentition for the first time in their history. Interestingly, they developed such a dentition in three different patterns, according to different patterns: *Thaiodus* in Asia and *Pororhiza* in Africa developed low, serrated teeth, which may indicate a scavenging specialization, while *Priohybodus* developed high, triangular, serrated teeth, well-adapted for the consumption of large, soft prey.

Conclusions

The Khok Kruat Formation yields a diverse fauna of freshwater hybodont sharks, containing five different genera and species. *Hybodus aequitridentatus*, *Khoratodus foreyi*, and *Acrorhizodus khoratensis* are restricted to Thailand, while *Heteroptychodus steinmanni* and *Thaiodus ruchae* are restricted to Thailand, Japan, and Tibet. A second species of *Heteroptychodus*, *H. chuvalovi*, occurs in Mongolia, and perhaps in Kyrgyzstan. This Asian fauna greatly improves the known diversity of hybodont sharks during the Early Cretaceous. The appearance of three palaeobiogeographical provinces (Asia, Europe and Africa–South America) around the Tethys led to maximum diversity of hybodont sharks at a generic level during the Early Cretaceous, when they mainly inhabited freshwater environments and coastal waters.

This work was supported by the Danish Natural Science Research Council and the TRF–CNRS Special Program for Biodiversity Research and Training Programme (BRT/BIOTEC/NSTDA) Grant BRT R-245007, as well as by the Carlsberg Foundation, the Department of Mineral Resources in Bangkok, the University of Maha Sarakham, the Jurassic foundation, the CNRS ECLIPSE programme, and the Institut National des Sciences de l'Univers from the CNRS. We would also like to thank all the people who took part in field work, including P. Bunchalee, L. Cavin, S. Chitsing, J. Claude, U. Deesri, T. Katisart, S. Khansubha, K. Lauprasert, J. Le Loeuff, M. Philippe, T. Saenyamoon, C. Souillat, P. Srisuk, S. Suteethorn, H. Tong and S. Trisivakul. We are indebted to P. Jintasakul (Museum of Petrified Wood and Mineral Resources, Nakhon Ratchasima) for allowing us access to the collections under his care, as well as to N. Boonchai for all the help provided to one of us (GC) during his stay there. We are also indebted to P. Srisuk for allowing us access to his private collection, and to A. Averianov (Zoological Institute of the Russian Academy of Sciences, St. Petersburg) for his warm welcome in St. Petersburg, and for giving one of us (GC) access to the *Asiadontus* teeth from Mongolia. Finally, comments from A. Longbottom (Natural History Museum, London) and J. Rees (Karlstad University) greatly improved the first version of this article.

References

AGASSIZ, L. 1836. *Recherches sur les poissons fossiles, tome 3 contenant l'histoire de l'ordre des Placoïdes.* Imprimerie de Petitpierre, Neufchâtel.

AVERIANOV, A. & SKUTSCHAS, P. 2000. A eutherian mammal from the Early Cretaceous of Russia and biostratigraphy of the Asian Early Cretaceous vertebrate assemblages. *Lethaia*, **33**, 330–340.

BECKER, M. A., CHAMBERLAIN, J. A. & STOFFER, P. W. 2000. Pathologic tooth deformities in modern and fossil chondrichthyans: a consequence of feeding-related injury. *Lethaia*, **33**, 103–118.

BRITO, P. M. 1992. Nouvelles données sur l'anatomie et la position systématique de *Tribodus limae* Brito & Ferreira, 1989 (Chondrichthyes: Elasmobranchii) du Crétacé inférieur de la Chapada do Araripe (N.–E. Brésil). *Géobios*, **M.S. 14**, 143–150.

BRITO, P. M. & FERREIRA, P. L. N. 1989. The first hybodont shark, *Tribodus limae* n.g., n.sp., from the Lower Cretaceous of Chapada do Araripe (North-East Brazil). *Anais da Academia Brasileira de Ciencias*, **61**, 53–57.

BUFFETAUT, E. & INGAVAT, R. 1985. Vertebrates from the continental Jurassic of Thailand. *Coordinating Committee for Geoscience Programmes in East and Southeast Asia Technical Bulletin*, **16**, 68–75.

BUFFETAUT, E. & SUTEETHORN, V. 1998. The biogeographical significance of the Mesozoic vertebrates from Thailand. *In*: HALL, R. & HOLLOWAY, J. D. (eds) *Biogeography and Geological Evolution of SE Asia.* Backhuys Publishers, Leiden, 83–90.

BUFFETAUT, E., SUTEETHORN, V., LE LOEUFF, J., KHANSUBHA, S., TONG, H. & WONGKO, K. 2005. The dinosaur fauna from the Khok Kruat Formation (Early Cretaceous) of Thailand. *International Conference on Geology, Geotechnology and Mineral Resources of Indochina (GEOINDO 2005).* Khon Kaen University, Khon Kaen, 575–581.

CAPPETTA, H. 1987. Chondrichthyes II. Mesozoic and Cenozoic Elasmobranchii. *Handbook of Paleoichthyology*, **3B**, Gustav Fischer Verlag, Stuttgart, 193pp.

CAPPETTA, H., BUFFETAUT, E. & SUTEETHORN, V. 1990. A new hybodont from the Lower Cretaceous of Thailand. *Neues Jahrbuch für Geologie und Paläontologie Monatshefte*, **1990**, 659–666.

CAPPETTA, H., BUFFETAUT, E., CUNY, G. & SUTEETHORN, V. 2006. A new elasmobranch assemblage from the Lower Cretaceous of Thailand. *Palaeontology*, **49**, 547–555.

CASIER, E. 1969. Addenda aux connaissances sur la faune ichthyologique de la serie de Bokungu (Congo). *Annales du Musée royal de l'Afrique Centrale–Tervuren, Belgique, Série 8 – Sciences géologiques*, **62**, 1–20.

CAVIN, L. & SUTEETHORN, V. 2006. A new semionotiform (Actinopterygii: Neopterygii) from Upper

Jurassic – Lower Cretaceous deposits of North-East Thailand, with comments on the relationships of Semionotiforms. *Palaeontology*, **49**, 339–353.

CAVIN, L., SUTEETHORN, V., KHANSUBHA, S., BUFFETAUT, E. & TONG, H. 2003. A new semionotid (Actinopterygii: Neopterygii) from the Late Jurassic–Early Cretaceous of Thailand. *Comptes Rendus Palevol*, **2**, 291–297.

CHARUSIRI, P., KOSUWAN, S. & IMSAMUT, S. 1997. Tectonic evolution of Thailand: from Bunopas (1981) to a new scenario. *Proceedings of the International Conference on Stratigraphy and tectonic evolution of Southeast Asia and the South Pacific.* Bangkok, **1**, 414–420.

CUNY, G. & BENTON, M. J. 1999. Early radiation of the neoselachian sharks in Western Europe. *Geobios*, **32**, 193–204.

CUNY, G., SUTEETHORN, V., BUFFETAUT, E. & PHILIPPE, M. 2003. Hybodont sharks from the Mesozoic Khorat Group of Thailand. *Mahasarakham University Journal*, **22**, 49–68.

CUNY, G., OUAJA, M., SRARFI, D., SCHMITZ, L., BUFFETAUT, E. & BENTON, M. J. 2004*a*. Fossil sharks from the Early Cretaceous of Tunisia. *Revue de Paléobiologie*, **9**, 127–142.

CUNY, G., SUTEETHORN, V. & BUFFETAUT, E. 2004*b*. Freshwater hybodont sharks from the Lower Cretaceous of Thailand. *In*: MARTIN, R. A. & MACKINLAY, D. (eds) *International Congress on the Biology of Fish, Biology and Conservation of freshwater Elasmobranchs Symposium Proceedings.* American Fisheries Society, 15–26.

CUNY, G., SUTEETHORN, V. & KAMHA, S. 2005. A review of the hybodont sharks from the Mesozoic of Thailand. *Proceedings of the International Conference on Geology, Geotechnology and Mineral Resources of Indochina (GEOINDO 2005).* Khon Kaen University, Khon Kaen, 588–593.

CUNY, G., SUTEETHORN, V., KAMHA, S., BUFFETAUT, E. & PHILIPPE, M. 2006. A new hybodont shark assemblage from the Lower Cretaceous of Thailand. *Historical Biology*, **18**, 21–31.

DELSATE, D., DUFFIN, C. J. & WEIS, R. 2002. A new microvertebrate fauna from the Middle Hettangian (early Jurassic) of Fontenoille (province of Luxembourg, South Belgium). *Memoirs of the Geological Survey of Belgium*, **48**, 1–84.

DUFFIN, C. J. 1997. The dentition of *Hybodus hauffianus* Fraas, 1895 (Toarcian, Early Jurassic). *Stuttgarter Beiträge zur Naturkunde Serie B (Geologie und Paläontologie)*, **256**, 1–22.

DUFFIN, C. J. 2001*a*. The hybodont shark, *Priohybodus* d'Erasmo 1960 (Early Cretaceous, northern Africa). *Zoological Journal of the Linnean Society*, **133**, 303–308.

DUFFIN, C. J. 2001*b*. Synopsis of the selachian genus *Lissodus* Brough, 1935. *Neues Jahrbuch für Geologie und Paläontologie Abhandlungen*, **221**, 145–218.

DUFFIN, C. J. & SIGOGNEAU-RUSSELL, D. 1993. Fossil shark teeth from the Early Cretaceous of Anoual, Morocco. *Belgian Geological Survey, Professional Paper*, **264**, 175–190.

D'ERASMO, G. 1960. Nuovi avanci ittiolitici della 'serie di Lugh' i Somalia conservati nel Museo Geologico di Firenze. *Palaeontographia italica*, **55**, 1–23.

FRAZZETTA, T.H., 1988. The mechanics of cutting and the form of shark teeth (Chondrichthyes: Elasmobranchii). *Zoomorphology*, **108**; 93–107.

GOODWIN, M. B., CLEMENS, W. A., HUTCHINSON, J. H., WOOD, C. G., ZAVADA, M. S., KEMP, A., DUFFIN, C. J. & SCHAFF, C. R. 1999. Mesozoic continental vertebrates with associated palynostratigraphic dates from the northwestern Ethiopian plateau. *Journal of Vertebrate Paleontology*, **19**, 728–741.

GOTO, M., UYENO, T. & YABUMOTO, Y. 1996. Summary of Mesozoic elasmobranch remains from Japan. *In*: ARRATIA, G. & VIOHL, G. (eds) *Mesozoic fishes – Systematics and Paleoecology.* Dr F. Pfeil, Munich, 73–82.

HECKERT, A. B. 2004. Late Triassic microvertebrates from the lower Chinle Group (Otischalkian–Adamanian: Carnian), southwestern U.S.A. *New Mexico Museum of Natural History & Science Bulletin*, **27**, 1–170.

HUBBELL, G. 1996. Using tooth structure to determine the evolutionary history of the white shark. *In*: KLIMLEY, A. P. & AINLEY, D. G. (eds) *Great white sharks, the biology of* Carcharodon carcharias. Academic Press, San Diego, 9–18.

LAST, P. R. & STEVENS, J. D. 1994. *Sharks and rays of Australia.* CSIRO, Australia.

LE LOEUFF, J., SAENYAMOON, T., SUTEETHORN, V., KHANSUBHA, S. & BUFFETAUT, E. 2005. Vertebrate footprints of South East Asia (Thailand and Laos): a review. *International Conference on Geology, Geotechnology and Mineral Resources of Indochina (GEOINDO 2005).* Khon Kaen University, Khon Kaen, 582–587.

MAISEY, J. G. 1983. Cranial anatomy of *Hybodus basanus* Egerton from the Lower Cretaceous of England. *American Museum Novitates*, **2758**, 1–64.

MAISEY, J. G. 1987. Cranial anatomy of the Lower Jurassic shark *Hybodus reticulatus* (Chondrichthyes: Elasmobranchii), with comments on hybodontid systematics. *American Museum Novitates*, **2878**, 1–39.

MAISEY, J. G. 1989. *Hamiltonichthys mapesi*, g. and sp. nov. (Chondrichthyes: Elasmobranchii), from the Upper Pennsylvanian of Kansas. *American Museum Novitates*, **2931**, 1–42.

MAISEY, J. G. & DE CARVALHO, M. R. 1997. A new look at old sharks. *Nature*, **385**, 779–780.

METCALFE, I. 1996. Pre-Cretaceous evolution of SE Asian terranes. *In*: HALL, R. & BLUNDELL, D. J. (eds) *Tectonic evolution of SE Asia.* Geological Society, London, Special Publications, **106**, 97–122.

METCALFE, I. 1998. Palaeozoic and Mesozoic geological evolution of the SE Asian region: multidisciplinary constraints and implications for biogeography. *In*: HALL, R. & HOLLOWAY, J. D. (eds) *Biogeography and geological evolution of Southeast Asia.* Backhuys publishing, Leiden, 25–41.

MINIKH, A. V. 2001. Sharks from the Triassic of European Russia. *Transactions of the Scientific Research Geological Institute of the N.G. Chernyshevskii Saratov State University, New Series*, **8**, 46–54 [in Russian].

MURRY, P. A. & KIRBY, R. E. 2002. A new hybodont shark from the Chinle and Bull Canyon formations, Arizona, Utah and New Mexico. *In*: HECKERT, A. B. & LUCAS, S. G. (eds) *Upper Triassic*

Stratigraphy and Paleontology. New Mexico Museum of Natural History and Science Bulletin, **21**, 87–106.

NESSOV, L. A. 1997. *Cretaceous Nonmarine vertebrates of Northern Eurasia.* University of Saint Petersburg, Institute of Earth Crust, Saint Petersburg.

PATTERSON, C. 1966. British Wealden sharks. *Bulletin of the British Museum (Natural History), Geology*, **11**, 283–350.

PEREA, D., UBILLA, M., ROJAS, A. & GOSO, C. A. 2001. The West Gondwanan occurrence of the hybodontid shark *Priohybodus*, and the Late Jurassic–Early Cretaceous age of the Tacuarembo Formation, Uruguay. *Palaeontology*, **44**, 1227–1235.

RACEY, A., GOODALL, J. G. S., LOVE, M. A., POLACHAN, S. & JONES, P. D. 1994. New age data for the Mesozoic Khorat Group of northeastern Thailand. *In*: ANGSUWATHANA, P., WONGWANICH, T., TANSATHIEN, W., WONGSOMAK, S. & TULYATID, J. (eds) *Proceedings of the International Symposium on Stratigraphic Correlation of Southeast Asia.* Department of Mineral Resources, Bangkok, 245–252.

RACEY, A., LOVE, M. A., CANHAM, A. C., GOODALL, J. G. S., POLACHAN, S. & JONES, P. D. 1996. Stratigraphy and reservoir potential of the Mesozoic Khorat Group, NE Thailand. Part 1: Stratigraphy and sedimentary evolution. *Journal of Petroleum Geology*, **19**, 5–40.

RACEY, A., STOKES, R. B., LOVATT-SMITH, P. & LOVE, M. A. 1997*a*. Late Jurassic collision in Northern Thailand and significance of the Khorat Group. *Proceedings of the International Conference on Stratigraphy and tectonic evolution of Southeast Asia and the South Pacific.* Department of Mineral Resources, Bangkok, **1**, 412–413.

RACEY, A., DUDDY, I. R. & LOVE, M. A. 1997*b*. Apatite fission track analysis of Mesozoic red beds from northeastern Thailand and western Laos. *Proceedings of the International Conference on Stratigraphy and tectonic evolution of Southeast Asia and the South Pacific.* Department of Mineral Resources, Bangkok, **1**, 200–209.

REES, J. & UNDERWOOD, C. J. 2002. The status of the shark genus *Lissodus* Brough, 1935, and the position of nominal *Lissodus* species within the Hybodontoidea (selachii). *Journal of Vertebrate Paleontology*, **22**, 471–479.

REIF, W.-E. 1976. Morphogenesis, pattern formation and function of the dentition of *Heterodontus. Zoomorphologie*, **83**, 1–47.

SATTAYARAK, N., SRIGULAWONG, S. & PATARAMETHA, M. 1991. Subsurface stratigraphy of the non-marine Khorat Group, northeastern Thailand. *GEOSEA VII Abstracts*, Bangkok, **36**.

SHIMADA, K. & CICIMURRI, D. J. 2005. Skeletal anatomy of the Late Cretaceous shark, *Squalicorax* (Neoselachii: Anacoracidae). *Paläontologische Zeitschrift*, **79**, 241–261.

TABASTE, N. 1963. Etude de restes de poissons du Crétacé saharien. *Mémoire IFAN*, **58**, 437–485.

TANIMOTO, M. & TANAKA, S. 1998. *Heteroptychodus* sp. (Chondrichthyes) from the Lower Cretaceous Matsuo Group of Arashima, Toba City, Mie Prefecture, Southwest Japan. *Chigakukenkyu*, **47**, 37–40.

THORSON, T. B. 1982. Life history implications of a tagging study of the largetooth sawfish, *Pristis perotteti*, in the Lake Nicaragua–Río San Juan system. *Environmental Biology of Fishes*, **7**, 207–228.

TONG, H., SUTEETHORN, V., CLAUDE, J., BUFFETAUT, E. & JINTASAKUL, P. 2005. The turtle fauna from the Khok Kruat Formation (Early Cretaceous) of Thailand. *International Conference on Geology, Geotechnology and Mineral Resources of Indochina (GEOINDO 2005).* Khon Kaen University, Khon Kaen, 610–614.

UNDERWOOD, C. J. & REES, J. 2002. Selachian faunas from the lowermost Cretaceous Purbeck Group of Dorset, Southern England. *Special Papers in Palaeontology*, **68**, 83–101.

YABE, H. & OBATA, T. 1930. On some fossil fishes from the Cretaceous of Japan. *Japanese Journal of Geology and Geography*, **8**, 1–8.

New occurrence of *Mawsonia* (Sarcopterygii: Actinistia) from the Early Cretaceous of the Sanfranciscana Basin, Minas Gerais, southeastern Brazil

MARISE S. S. DE CARVALHO[1] & JOHN G. MAISEY[2]

[1]*CPRM–Servico Geológico do Brasil-DEGEO-DIPALE, Avenida Pasteur, 404, Praia Vermelha, 22292–040 Rio de Janeiro, RJ, Brazil*

[2]*Division of Paleontology, American Museum of Natural History, 79th Street and Central Park West, New York, NY 10024-5192, USA (e-mail: maisey@amnh.org)*

Abstract: The Cretaceous actinistian *Mawsonia* is represented by more than 360 dissociated, but well-preserved, bones obtained from the Areado Group in the Sanfranciscana Basin of Minas Gerais, Brazil. These are among the oldest records of *Mawsonia* (Berriasian, Lower Neocomian) and include previously undescribed or poorly known skeletal elements (e.g. splenial, dentary, autopalatine, zygals). The new material is referred to the type species, *M. gigas*. Morphological variation in the sample blurs some of the distinctions formerly drawn between nominal species of *Mawsonia*, and species level diversity in the genus is difficult to establish. *Mawsonia libangiensis*, *M. libyca*, and *M. brasiliensis* are considered to be junior subjective synonyms of *M. gigas*. *Mawsonia gigas* probably appeared prior to the separation of S America and Africa and became widespread throughout much of western Gondwana (including parts of Africa), even surviving briefly on both continents following their separation. *Mawsonia tegamensis* is a morphologically distinctive Late Cretaceous African species with no evident fossil record in Brazil and which probably arose by vicariant speciation following isolation of a local *Mawsonia* population during the later stages of rifting between Northern Africa and the rest of Western Gondwana. Similarities between *Axelrodichthys*, *Lualabaea* (here regarded as Early Cretaceous in age) and recently described fossils from Morocco, Niger, and Madagascar suggest the presence of a second endemic Cretaceous mawsoniid lineage in northeastern Brazil and Africa.

Mawsonia is an extinct non-marine actinistian (coelacanth) genus that has been credited in the past with considerable biogeographical interest. It was apparently restricted to continental and estuarine palaeoenvironments of Western Gondwana (Maranhão, Ceará, Alagoas, Bahia, and Minas Gerais in Brazil; Morocco, Algeria, Egypt, Niger, and the Democratic Republic of Congo in Africa), and its first occurrences predate the late Aptian seaway between Africa and South America, while its later occurrences are on both sides of the seaway (Wenz 1980; Maisey 2000). *Mawsonia* is also the largest known actinistian, with some individuals reaching an estimated length of several meters. The most complete remains of *Mawsonia* described in the literature are from Brazil, and include articulated skulls, postcranial skeletons, and even complete skeletons, from the Neocomian of Bahia and the Albian of Ceará (Woodward 1908; Carvalho 1982; Maisey 1986; Yabumoto 2002). Unfortunately, the majority of *Mawsonia* records, on both sides of the Atlantic, consist of extremely fragmentary material. This makes it difficult to compare and evaluate it phylogenetically.

In 1995, the geologists Geraldo Norberto C. Sgarbi (Universidade Federal de Minas Gerais) and José Eloi G. Campos (Universidade de Brasilia) discovered fossil bone fragments in ferruginous Early Cretaceous shales belonging to the Areado Group of the Sanfranciscana Basin, State of Minas Gerais, Brazil. Although these shales are widely exposed on low hummocks and hills, the fossil material described here came from a fairly small area covering a few hundred square meters, on the Fazenda Teresa, near Olhos d'Água do Oeste and about 40 km from the town of João Pinheiro, located in the northwestern part of the state (Fig. 1). Initially, the bones were thought to be crocodilian, but Diogenes de Almeida Campos (DNPM) subsequently recognized them as coelacanth remains, referable to the genus *Mawsonia*. Additional material (including approximately 360 disarticulated elements from the skull, cheek, jaws, hyoid arch, and pectoral fins) was collected from 1997–1999 by the authors, students and researchers of the UFRJ-DG. The coelacanth bones are associated with fin spines and cephalic spines of hybodont sharks, amiiform vertebrae, bones and teeth, semionotid scales and vertebrae,

From: CAVIN, L., LONGBOTTOM, A. & RICHTER, M. (eds) *Fishes and the Break-up of Pangaea.*
Geological Society, London, Special Publications, **295**, 109–144.
DOI: 10.1144/SP295.8   0305-8719/08/$15.00 © The Geological Society of London 2008.

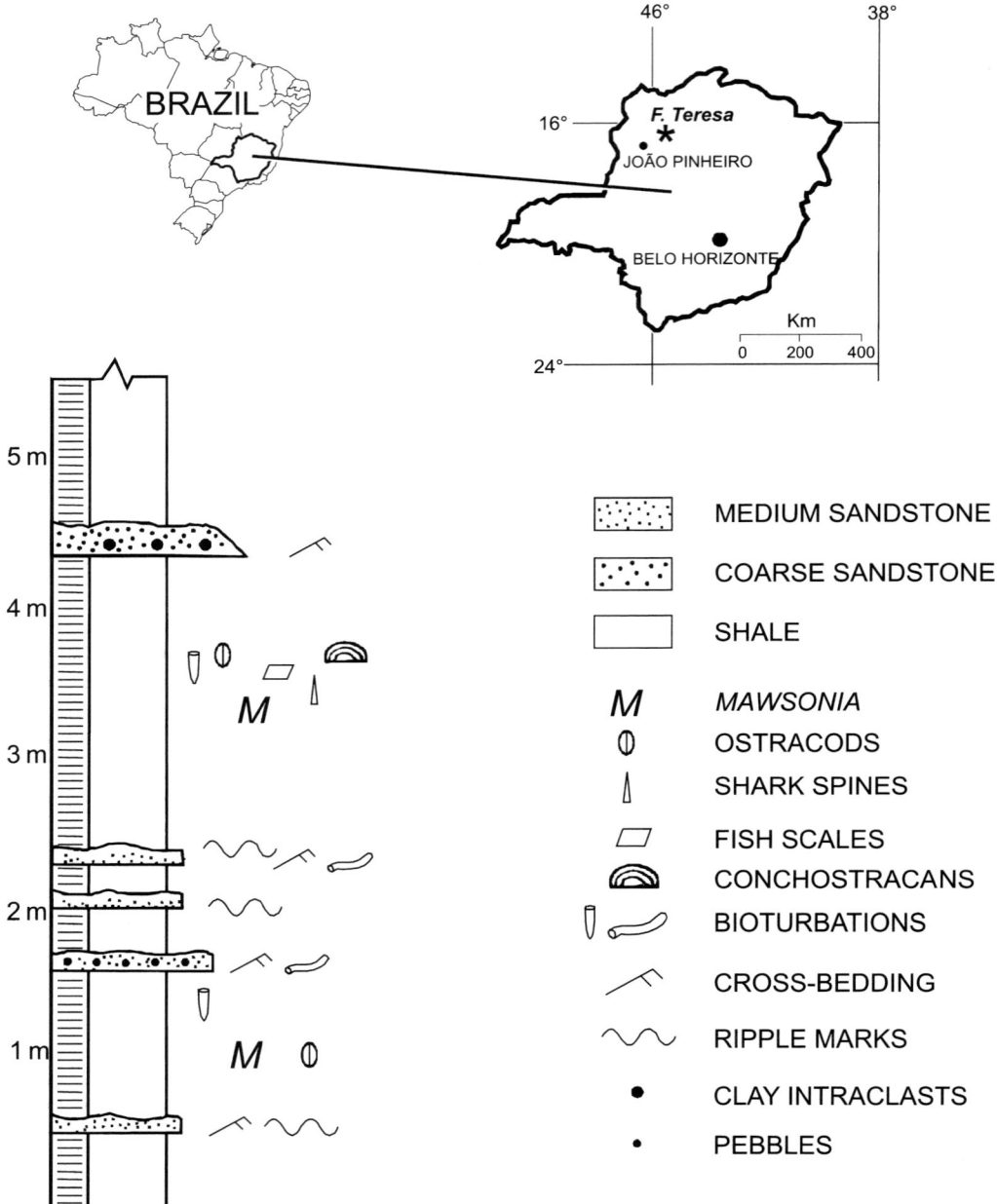

Fig. 1. Map of the collecting area and local stratigraphic sequence at Fazenda Teresa, Sanfranciscana Basin, Minas Gerais, Brazil.

conchostracans, ostracods and bioturbation structures. Although the sample is undoubtedly biased toward larger surface-picked elements, no lungfish toothplates or tetrapod bones were found.

Otherwise, the general aspect of the assemblage is fairly typical for early Cretaceous non-marine deposits in western Gondwana, particularly those from Africa (Maisey 2000). This new occurrence is the most southerly record of *Mawsonia* known to date, and the sample represents many different individuals of varying sizes.

The material is now deposited in two different institutions; Museu de Ciências da Terra, Departamento Nacional da Produção Mineral, Rio de Janeiro (catalog prefix MCT), and the Universidade Federal do Rio de Janeiro, Departamento de Geologia (catalog prefix UFRJ-DG). All the elements are well-preserved in 3D and are essentially free of matrix, providing an opportunity to investigate morphological variation in large samples of skeletal elements from a single locality (although no meristic analyses were attempted). Almost all the specimens collected were isolated bones, apart from a partial parietonasal shield and an operculum associated with parts of a shoulder girdle. Many of the bone fragments recovered could be reunited with others, suggesting that they were freshly broken at the outcrop and that further excavation might reveal more complete remains. Besides the large number of individual specimens, the Sanfranciscana Basin material also includes skeletal elements of *Mawsonia* that have rarely been documented before, including the splenial, dentary, autopalatine and numerous zygals.

Stratigraphy of the Sanfranciscana Basin

The Sanfranciscana Basin lies within the Abaeté depression, which is separated from the Bauru depression farther west by the Alto Paranaiba Axis (Hasui & Haralyi 1991). The Abaeté depression contains an important Early Cretaceous sequence; the Areado Formation, which has customarily been divided into the Abaeté, Quiricó, and Três Barras members. From a sequence-stratigraphic viewpoint, however, these members probably represent proximal and median facies of an alluvial fan overlapping with a sedimentary complex of lacustrine origin; followed by closure of the lacustrine system and replacement by a braided alluvial plain and aeolian dune fields. Within the southern portion of the Sanfranciscana Basin, the lowest part of the sequence consists of reddish lacustrine shales and aeolian sandstones deposited in arid and warm conditions during the Late Jurassic and Early Cretaceous.

Dinosaur footprints have been recorded in sandstones near João Pinheiro (Kattah 1994; Carvalho & Kattah 1998). The middle part of the sequence consists of reddish bioturbated shales (the source of the coelacanth bones described here), plus fin spines of hybodont sharks, ganoid scales, conchostracans and ostracods are indicative of a non-marine environment including *Pattersoncypris*, *Darwinula*, *Ilyocypris* and *Cypridea*; Delicio *et al.* 1998;

Carvalho & Maisey 1998; Carvalho 2002). These shales are intercalated with siltstones and sandstones both with ripple marks, cross bedding and pebbles, all probably deposited within a flood plain at the margin of a lake. The precise stratigraphic level of the *Mawsonia*-bearing horizon is uncertain, but overlying strata contain ostracods of Barremian age (Do Carmo *et al.* 2004) as well as the Barremian–early Aptian palynomorph *Transitoripollis crisopolensis*. However, other palynological data suggest that at least part of the sequence lies close to the Barremian–Aptian boundary (notably a high *Afropollis* count and the presence of other angiosperm pollen that appear at the Barremian–Aptian boundary; Arai *et al.* 1995).

The upper part of the Areado Group consists of sandstones intercalated with shales containing freshwater fishes including *Dastilbe moraesi* and *Laeliichthys ancestralis* (Scorza & Silva Santos 1955; Silva Santos 1985), which are regarded as Aptian because *Dastilbe* is well known from Cretaceous deposits elsewhere in Brazil. Other fossils from this part of the sequence include charophytes, gymnosperms (e.g. *Araucarioxylon*, *Podozamites*, *Brachyphylum*), angiosperms (*Paraleptaspis*, *Nymphaeites*), conchostracans and ostracods (Barbosa 1965).

Materials

Specimens from the Sanfranciscana Basin were catalogued in groups according to bone type, with the institutional prefix followed by catalog number, specimen letter (listed alphabetically), and suffix 'P' (Palaeontology Collection); e.g., 10 postparietals were catalogued under MCT 1384a-j-P, and another 10 under UFRJ-DG356a-j-P. This approach was adopted so that future finds could be assigned to the appropriate groups without generating additional numbers. The following list represents material catalogued as of June 2006.

MCT 1364a-P; Basisphenoid and posterior parietal
MCT 1364b-h-P; UFRJ-DG 341a-e-P; basisphenoid
MCT 1365a-p-P; UFRJ-DG 342a-n-P; parasphenoid
MCT 1366a-d-P; UFRJ-DG 343a-d-P; parietal and
  supraorbital
MCT 1367-P supraorbital; MCT 1368-P; lachrymojugal
MCT 1369a-h-P; UFRJ-DG 300-P; 344a-g-P; operculum
MCT 1370a-t-P; UFRJ-DG 345a-u-P; angular
MCT 1371a-f-P; UFRJ-DG 346a-d-P; splenial
MCT 1372a-f-P; UFRJ-DG 347a-e-P; dentary
MCT 1373a-g-P; UFRJ-DG 348a-c-P; articular
MCT 1374a-h-P; UFRJ-DG 349a-f-F; posterior coronoid
MCT 1375-P; gular
MCT 1376a-b-P; UFRJ-DG 350-a-b-P; autopalatine
MCT 1377a-m-P; UFRJ-DG 351a-m-P; pterygoid
MCT 1378a-k-P; UFRJ-DG 352a-k-P; metapterygoid

MCT 1379a-k-P; UFRJ-DG 353a-j-P; quadrate
MCT 1380a-j-P; UFRJ-DG 354a-i-P; prootic
MCT 1381-P; UFRJ-DG 362-P; basioccipital
MCT 1382-P; supraoccipital
MCT 1383a-j-P; UFRJ-DG 355a-j-P; zygal
MCT 1384a-j-P; UFRJ-DG 356a-j-P; postparietal
MCT 1385a-o-P; UFRJ-DG 357a-n-P; supratemporal
MCT 1386a-e-P; UFRJ-DG 358a-d-P; extrascapular
MCT 1387a-f-P; UFRJ-DG 359a-e-P; ceratobranchial
MCT 1388a-h-P; UFRJ-DG 360a-f-P; cleithrum
MCT 1389-P; UFRJ-DG 361a-b-P; scapulocoracoid

Other Brazilian mawsoniid material examined included the following:

Araripe Basin; *Axelrodichthys araripensis*: AMNH 11759, AMNH 11760, AMNH 12209–12213, MCT 1131-P; *Mawsonia* cf. *M. gigas*: AMNH 11758, AMNH 12216, 12217, 12218; *Mawsonia gigas*: UFRJ-DG 277-P; UFRJ-DG 278-P, UFRJ-DG 299-P.
Recôncavo Basin; *Mawsonia gigas*: DGM 1040-P to 1047-P.
Tucano Basin; *Mawsonia gigas*: DGM 1038-P, 1039-P, DGM 1048-P.
Grajaú Basin; *Mawsonia gigas*: MN 4532-V; *Axelrodichthys araripensis*: UFRJ-DG 220-P.
São Luís Basin; *Mawsonia gigas*: UFRJ-DG 143-P; UFRJ-DG 312-P; UFRJ-DG 313-P; UFRJ-DG 319-P; UFRJ-DG 340-P.

Anatomical abbreviations:

ant ap	anterior apophysis
ant pr	antotic process
desc pr	descending process of postparietal
Ent	entopterygoid
ext	extrascapular
gr d	groove for dentary
gr md c	groove for mandibular sensory canal
mpt	metapterygoid
ot can	otic sensory canal
pit	depression in basisphenoid for pituitary
post pa	posterior parietal
ppa	postparietal
pr con	processus connectens
q	quadrate
s ent	suture for entopterygoid
stt	supratemporal

Institutional abbreviations:

AMNH – American Museum of Natural History, New York
BMNH – The Natural History Museum, London
DGM-DNPM – Divisão de Geológia e Mineralogia, Departamento Nacional da Produção Mineral, Rio de Janeiro
MCTer/DNPM-RJ – Museu de Ciências da Terra, Departamento Nacional da Produção Mineral, Rio de Janeiro

UFRJ-DG – Universidade Federal do Rio de Janeiro, Departamento de Geológia
MDE – Musée de Dinosaures, Espéraza, France.

Systematic palaeontology

Class Osteichthyes
Subclass Sarcopterygii
Infraclass Actinistia
Order Coelacanthiformes
Suborder Latimerioidei Schultze, 1993
Family Mawsoniidae Schultze, 1993
Mawsonia Woodward *in* Mawson & Woodward, 1907

Emended diagnosis. Mawsoniid fish of large size (including the largest known actinistians); head large and deep, with very thick dermal bones ornamented with coarse rugosities (often obscuring sensory canals) and with prominent ridges on the operculum, angular and gular; postparietal shield short and broad, parallel-sided posteriorly; two extrascapulars firmly sutured into postparietal shield and resembling an additional pair of postparietals; no median extrascapular; parietonasal shield narrow, generally more than twice as long as postparietal shield, convex dorsally in transverse and lateral view, and lacking pores; two pairs of elongate parietals present; Snout composed of a mosaic of star-shaped ossicles; lateral rostral extremely slender anteriorly, extending well in front of eye and angled dorsally at its anterior tip; Preorbital absent; sclerotic plates absent; tectal and supraorbital series as wide as parietonasal series, but containing comparatively few elements (usually six); posterior parietal usually meets posteriormost 3 supraorbitals; supratemporal lacks descending process; cheek bones in contact with each other; lachrymojugal elongate and slender, reaching the tectal series, with the infraorbital sensory canal located in its ventral margin; postorbital with splint-like process directed anteriorly; squamosal large, quadrangular, forming major element of cheek; lateral ethmoid of braincase with very pronounced posterodorsal process which contacts undersurface of skull roof; basisphenoid stout, with prominent, parallel-sided antotic process; palatoquadrate with very shallow anterior limb of pterygoid, bearing a single strengthening ridge on its lateral surface; autopalatine small; principal coronoid of lower jaw with a small sutural surface contacting mid-region of angular, markedly saddle-shaped in lateral view with the posterior limb considerably higher; extensive area of overlap between dentary and angular; dentary elongate and slender anteriorly; pit-lines open via small pores in the dentary and larger ones in the angular.

Type Species. Mawsonia gigas Woodward *in* Mawson & Woodward, 1907.

1891 'Pterosaurian' Woodward; p. 314, fig. 2.
1896 'Pterodactyl' Woodward; p. 255, fig. A–C.
1907 *Mawsonia gigas* Woodward *in* Mawson & Woodward; p. 134, Plate 7, Plate 8, fig. 1–6.
1908 *Mawsonia minor* Woodward; 358, Plate 42, fig. 1–3.
1935 *Mawsonia libyca* Weiler; p. 11, fig-text 1, Plate 1, fig. 5–10, 12, 17–29, 31–34, 42–46, 50–52; Plate 2, fig. 4, 9, 27, 35–36; Plate 3, fig. 1–6, 11, 13, 18.
1961 *Mawsonia ubangiana* Casier; p. 23, fig. 4b, 5b, 6, 8b, 9b; Plate 2, Plate 3, fig. 1–2.
1969 *Mawsonia ubangiensis* Casier; p. 16, Plate 2, fig. 2.
1982 *Mawsonia gigas* Woodward. Carvalho; p. 522, Plate 2–8.
1986 *Mawsonia* cf. *M. gigas* Woodward. Maisey; p. 3, fig. 1–11.
1991 *Mawsonia* cf. *M. gigas* Woodward. Maisey; p. 317.
1998 *Mawsonia gigas* Woodward. Forey; p. 327.
1998 *Mawsonia ubangiensis* Casier. Forey; p. 328.
1998 *Mawsonia libyca* Weiler. Forey; p. 328.
1998 *Mawsonia* sp. Carvalho & Maisey; p. 32A.
2001 *Mawsonia* cf. *M. gigas* Woodward. Dutra & Malabarba; p. 204, fig. 6C.
2001 *Mawsonia* sp. Medeiros & Schultz; p. 216, fig. 4D.
2002 *Mawsonia brasiliensis* Yabumoto; p. 343, fig. 1–4.

Holotype. BMNH P 10355, incomplete skull and associated bones from jaw, plus a series of isolated bones including the parietal, quadrate, articular, angular, coronoid, pterygoid and gular.

Paratypes. BMNH P 10356, right postparietal; BMNH P 10357, right operculum.

Type locality. Almeida Brandão, Salvador, Bahia, NE Brazil.

Horizon. Candeias Formation, Early Cretaceous (Neocomian).

Emended diagnosis. Large species in which the quadrate condyle can be up to 110 mm across; ornament of coarse rugosities arranged in strong longitudinal ridges on the parietals, postparietals and angular; anterior foramen for otic sensory canal of the postparietal located close to the anterior apophysis; Pre-operculum as large as or larger than squamosal, but does not meet lachrymojugal; triangular operculum ornamented with delicate ridges radiating outward from growth centre; pelvic fin located level with the first dorsal fin; caudal fin length approximately one-third overall length.

Description. The large sample of isolated bones at our disposal provides the first opportunity to investigate morphological variation within an apparently monospecific population of *Mawsonia* from the Early Cretaceous, and to compare the sample with the type and other nominal species of the genus. Rather than presenting a tedious monographic description of all the bones, attention will be focussed on certain elements and features that seem to have bearing on the systematics of these large and spectacular non-marine coelacanths. However, numerous specimens will be illustrated in order to document the variability within the sample. *Mawsonia* specimens from the Santana Formation of Brazil, in which the head skeleton is relatively complete, were used extensively as a guide to identify isolated skull elements in the new material (including AMNH11758, originally referred to *Mawsonia* cf. *M. gigas*; Maisey 1986; *M. brasiliensis*; Yabumoto 2002; and another large undescribed specimen in the Museu Nacional).

Specimens of *M. gigas* from other Brazilian localities were also compared, including recently-discovered material from Bahia and Maranhão, but a description of that material is beyond the scope of this paper. Comparisons were also made between *Mawsonia* and *Axelrodichthys* (resolved cladistically as the sister taxon of *Mawsonia*; Forey 1998). These forms are readily distinguished by differences in the shape and proportions of the skull roof, presence (*Axelrodichthys*) or absence (*Mawsonia*) of a median extrascapular, cheek bone arrangement and differences in the articulation between the basisphenoid and metapterygoid (Maisey 1986).

Parietonasal shield. One of the most complete specimens in the sample represents the posterior part of the ethmosphenoid region from a moderately small individual (MCT 1364a-P; Fig. 2d–f). The specimen agrees in most respects with a more complete ethmosphenoid of *M.* cf. *M. gigas* (Fig. 2a–c), and it is also very similar to the parietonasal shield in the holotype of *M. brasiliensis* (Yabumoto 2002). Although the ornament of ridges and grooves differs in these specimens, its expression also varies within the Sanfranciscana Basin posterior parietals and does not seem to be size-related. Six isolated and incomplete parietals were identified, the largest of which is *c.* 60 mm long (Fig. 3), although it was not possible to distinguish between anterior and posterior parietals. In two specimens the parietal and supraorbital bones are still associated (MCT 1366d–P; Fig. 3a–b, UFRJ–DG 343d–P; Fig. 3c–c) and parietal

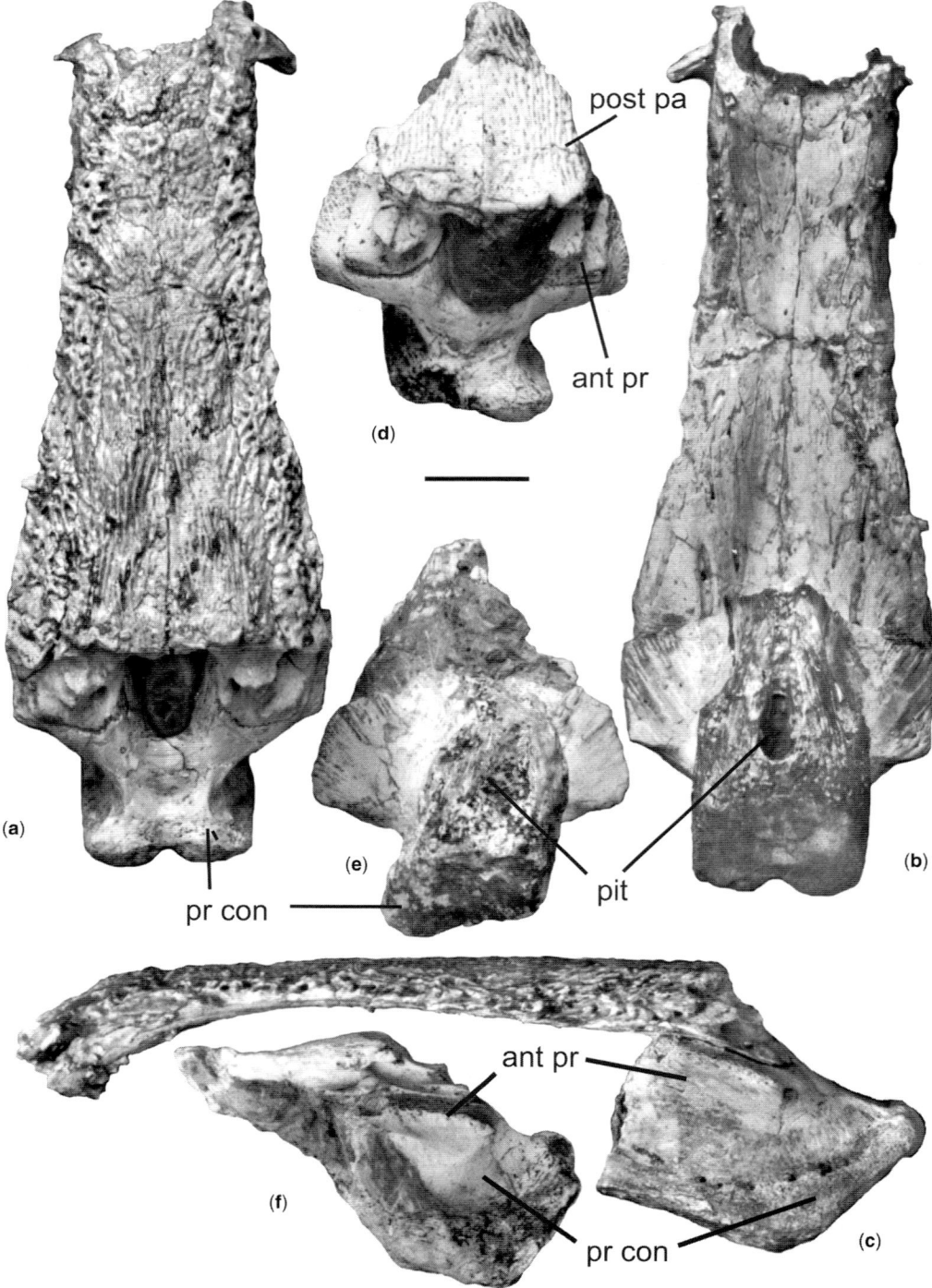

Fig. 2. (a–c), acid-prepared parietonasal shield and basisphenoid of *Mawsonia* cf. *M. gigas* Woodward (AMNH 11758, from the Santana Formation, Araripe Basin); (d–f), corresponding views of the most complete Sanfranciscana Basin specimen, referred here to *Mawsonia gigas* (MCT 1364a-P). (a–d) dorsal view; (b–e) ventral view; (c–f) left lateral view. Anterior to top in orientation (a–b, d–e) and to left (c, f). Scale bar = 10 mm.

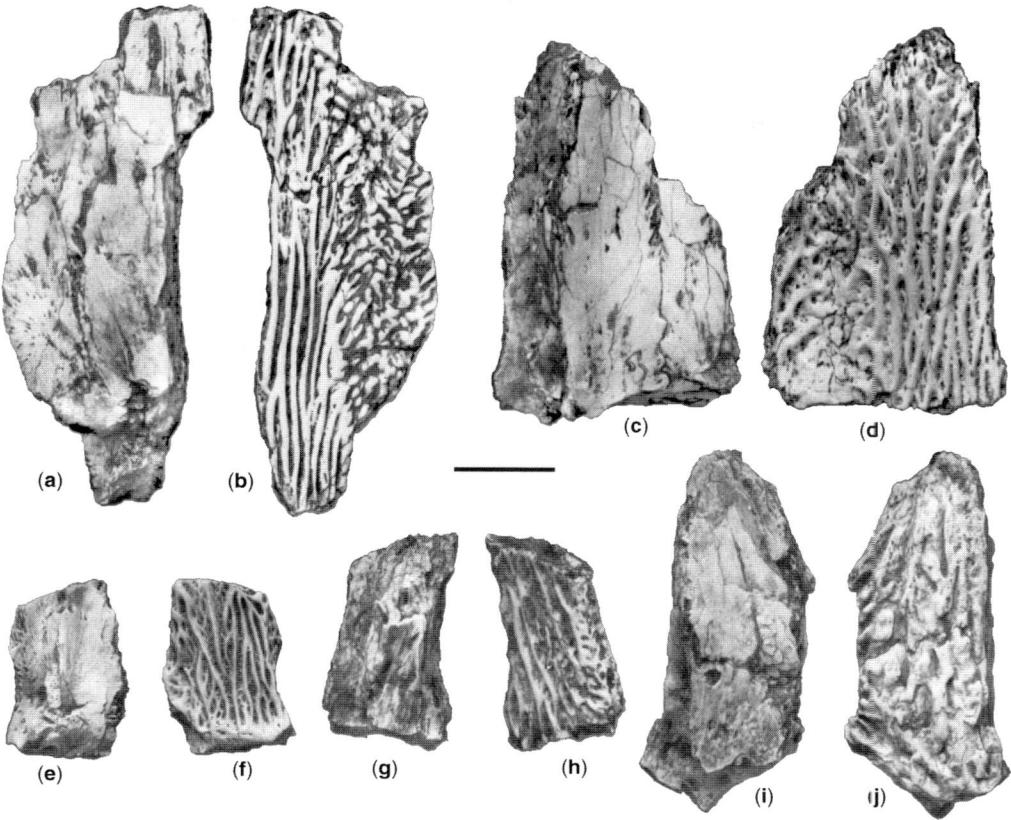

Fig. 3. *Mawsonia gigas* parietals (**a–h**) and supraorbitals (**i–j**) from the Sanfranciscana Basin. (a–b) left parietal MCT 1366c-P; (c–d) right? parietal fragment UFRJ-DG 343-d-P; (e–f) parietal fragment UFRJ-DG 343-c-P; (g–h) parietal fragment UFRJ-DG 343-b-P; (i–j) parietal fragment MCT 1367-P. Anterior to top in (a–d); orientation uncertain in other views. Scale bar = 10 mm.

fragments are still attached to some of the basisphenoids. Two associated supraorbitals were also found (MCT 1367–P; Fig. 3i–j). The posterior parietal descending process and the basisphenoid are tightly associated even in broken specimens.

The posterior parietals in MCT 1364a–P are narrow, as in *Mawsonia* cf. *M. gigas* from the Santana Formation and the holotype of *M. brasiliensis* (Maisey 1986; Yabumoto 2002). In all the Santana Formation specimens examined, the supraorbitals do not extend appreciably beyond the lateral margins of the posterior parietal, and it is thought that the Sanfransicana *Mawsonia* is similar. In *M. tegamensis* the posterior parietals are comparatively wide and the supraorbitals do not extend behind them (Wenz 1975). However, in specimens referred to *M. lavocati*, there may be a deep notch between the posterior parietal and

supraorbital (Cavin & Forey 2004). According to Wenz (1981) *M. lavocati* and *M. tegamensis* differ in the proportion and ornamentation of bones forming the median series. All the parietals in our sample are ornamented with sub-parallel ridges that frequently branch and merge, and the supraorbital ornament is more reticulated (e.g. Fig. 3b, d, j).

Wenz (1975) noted that the lateral margins of the parietals in *Mawsonia tegamensis* are occupied by a cavity that, together with a corresponding space in the medial margin of the supraorbitals, produces a tube for the supraorbital sensory canal. The same arrangement is found in *M.* cf. *M. gigas* and may be characteristic of the genus.

Basisphenoid. MCT 1364a–P is an almost complete basisphenoid, still attached to the posterior parietals (Fig. 2d–f). Its antotic process is triangular in shape and is sutured dorsally to the descending process of the posterior parietal, as in *Mawsonia* cf. *M. gigas* (Fig. 2a–c). The antotic process is strongly ridged and probably forms the insertion of the anterior adductor mandibulae muscle. The lateral surface of the antotic process is fairly smooth and straight, and the ventral surface of the basisphenoid contains a large pit (somewhat abraded in MCT 1364a–P) that probably contained the pituitary. In posterior view, the foramen of the superficial ophthalmic nerve is located near the base of the parietal descending process. The processus connectens is well-developed on either side of the basisphenoid, and passes posteriorly into the sphenoid condyles. These are large and are positioned close together. The ventral surface of the basisphenoid is strongly rounded from side to side.

Twelve other incomplete basisphenoids were also found, most of which are broken in the hypophysial region and show only the sphenoid condyles and the processus connectens (Fig. 4). The largest fragment (representing only the sphenoid condyles and processus connectens; MCT 1364f–P; Fig. 4d) is approximately 68 mm wide. Four other fragmentary basisphenoids (not illustrated here) represent parts of the antotic process, with a

sutural surface for the descending process of the posterior parietal (fragments of which are sometimes attached).

The antotic process in the Sanfranciscana Basin basisphenoids is virtually identical to that of *Mawsonia* cf. *M. gigas* (Maisey 1986), but in other Brazilian material referred to *M. gigas* the basisphenoid is poorly-preserved and the shape of the antotic process has not been determined. The basisphenoid has also not been described to *M. libyca* or *M. ubangiensis* and is poorly known in *M. tegamensis* and *M. lavocati* (Wenz 1975, 1981; Carvalho 1982). In *Mawsonia* sp. from Niger, the antotic process is slightly larger than in *M. gigas*, and its lateral margin is not as straight (Wenz 1981, fig. 4).

Parasphenoid. Although more than 30 parasphenoid fragments of various sizes were recovered, they provide little morphological information and none are illustrated here. Parasphenoid teeth seem to be confined to a small patch anteriorly, and are invariably small and closely spaced as in *Mawsonia lavocati, M. lybica* and *M. tegamensis*. Above the toothed area, some of the fragments show a distinct zone with strong ridges, presumably representing

Fig. 4. *Mawsonia gigas* sphenoid condyles from broken basisphenoids, Sanfranciscana Basin. All dorsal views, anterior to top. (**a**) MCT 1364g-P; (**b**) UFRJ-DG 341-d-P; (**c**) UFRJ-DG 341a-P; (**d**) MCT 1364f-P; (**e**) MCT 1364e-P. Scale bar = 10 mm.

the sutural surface for the lateral ethmoids (e.g. MCT 1365e–P).

Postparietal shield. The postparietal shield is one of the better known parts of the head in *Mawsonia*, and is one of the few skeletal components that can be compared in several nominal species. The best-preserved example is an acid prepared specimen from the Santana Formation (Maisey 1986; AMNH 11758; see Fig. 5a). In the Sanfranciscana Basin sample, 20 postparietals (nine from the right side, 11 from the left), 29 supratemporals (13 right, 16 left), and nine extrascapulars have been identified. All the specimens are fragmentary but their dimensions differ greatly and they clearly represent a suite of individuals covering a wide size range.

In general, the morphology and ornament of the postparietals in our sample are typical for *Mawsonia* (Figs 5–7). The external face of the bone is entirely ornamented by ramifying ridges separated by pronounced grooves, and there is a well-developed descending process on its ventral surface. A large anterior foramen for the otic lateral line canal is present on the anterior margin of the postparietal.

In the largest Sanfranciscana Basin postparietal (UFRJ-DG 356g–P; Fig. 7), the otic canal foramen is located some distance posterolaterally from the anterior apophysis, as in the holotype of *M. gigas* (BMNH P10356), *M. lavocati* and *M. libyca*. In other Sanfranciscana Basin specimens, the canal is much closer to the anterior apophysis, as in *M.* aff. *tegamensis* (Wenz 1975), *M.* cf. *M. gigas* (Maisey 1986), and *M. brasiliensis* (Yabumoto 2002). The proximity of the otic canal foramen to the anterior apophysis therefore varies within our sample and seems unreliable as a systematic character. Also in UFRJ-DG 356g–P, the anterior apophysis is not connected by a bony bridge to the descending process arc. This bridge is also absent in several other specimens (e.g., MCT 1384-i-P; Fig. 5c, MCT 1384-b-P; Fig. 6e), but is present in some (Figs 5g; 6a, c). Forey (1998) noted comparable variation between two specimens of *M. gigas* in the BMNH collection. Presence or absence of the bridge therefore seems to be an unreliable criterion for species recognition (cf. Wenz 1981). Our sample suggests that this variation is unrelated to size and may simply reflect differences between individuals or genders.

Casier (1961) found two anterior apophyses on the anterior margin of the postparietal in *M. gigas*, but identified only one in *M. ubangiensis*. Only one is present in most Sanfranciscana Basin postparietals (e.g. UFRJ-DG356a-P; MCT.1384b-P; Fig. 6d, f), but some have two (e.g. UFRJ-DJ

356g-P; indicated by asterisks in Fig. 7). This difference probably arises as a result of differential ossification of the apophysis and is probably not a systematically useful character in *Mawsonia*.

According to Casier (1961), the postparietal in the type specimen of *M. gigas* is ornamented by parallel ridges close to the anterior process, but these were absent in his specimen of *M. ubangiensis*. However, there is considerable variation in the pattern and intensity of ornament of this region in the Sanfranciscana Basin postparietals, suggesting that it is also not a systematically useful character in *Mawsonia*.

Other variation is also observed in the Sanfranciscana Basin postparietals. In some specimens, the anterior apophysis projects in front of the bone as Casier (1961) reported in *M. ubangiensis*, but in others it is represented only by a low prominence (as he showed in *M. gigas*; Casier 1961, Fig. 4; cf. Figs 5–7 here). In many specimens, the ornamented external lamina extends up to, or even overhangs the base of the anterior apophysis, as in *M. gigas*, *M.* cf. *M. gigas*, *M. ubangiensis*, and *M. tegamensis*, but in some specimens the external lamina terminates some distance behind the apophysis, exposing an area of vascular bone normally covered by the external lamina (Fig. 7). Thus, there is considerable variation in the relative position of the otic canal foramen and the anterior apophysis, in the number and size of anterior processes of the postparietal, the relative forward projection of the anterior apophysis, and in the anterior extent of the dorsal lamina above the process. These features consequently do not seem to offer reliable criteria for distinguishing between species of *Mawsonia*.

The postparietals from the Sanfranciscana Basin have a continuous transverse median branch of the otic sensory canal. The opening for this branch is readily observed within the sutural surface at the midline. A similar branch is also present in *Mawsonia* cf. *M. gigas* (Maisey 1986, fig. 3), as well as in *M. tegamensis* (Wenz 1975, fig. 1), but Casier (1961) did not identify it in *M. ubangiensis* or in the holotype of *M. gigas*, and a median branch is apparently absent in *M. lavocati* (Wenz 1981). The arrangement of the otic sensory canal in the holotype of *Mawsonia gigas* is unknown. In *Latimeria*, a median branch is present, but it divides into anterior and posterior canals that emerge onto the surface of the bone close to the dorsal midline (Forey 1998, fig. 3.1), rather than passing entirely through the bone as in *Mawsonia*. It is therefore possible that the median branch of the otic canal passed through the postparietal in some *Mawsonia* individuals but not in others, but the systematic significance of this variation is unclear.

Nineteen incomplete prootics were collected, of which 13 are from the left side and 6 are from the right (Fig. 8). In all respects that we could

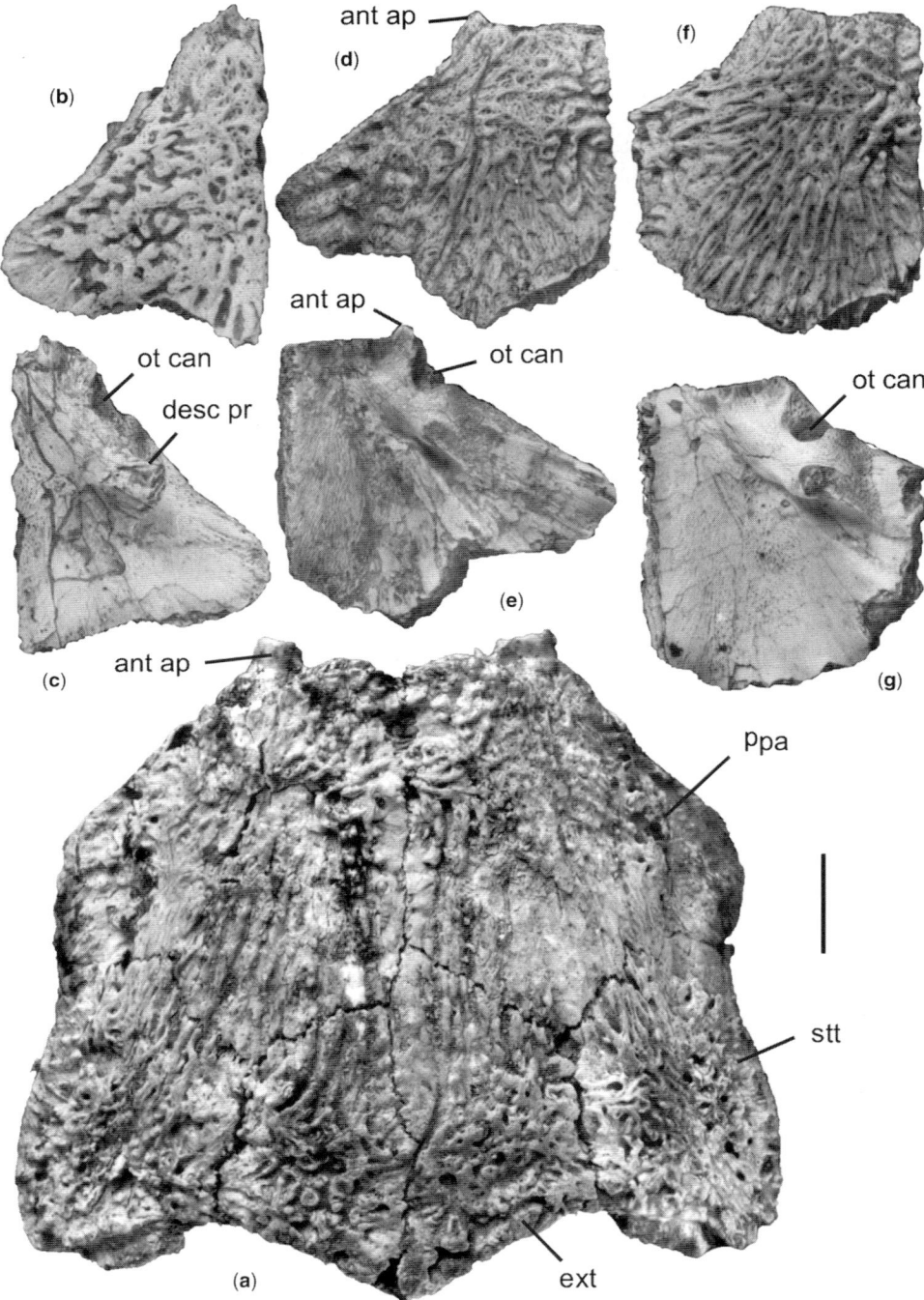

Fig. 5. (**a**) Complete acid-prepared postparietal shield from *Mawsonia* cf. *M. gigas* (AMNH 11758, Santana Formation, Araripe Basin), dorsal view. (**b–g**) *Mawsonia gigas* from the Sanfranciscana Basin, left postparietals in dorsal (b, d, f) and ventral (c, e, g) views. (b–c) MCT 1384i-P; (d–e) UFRJ 356h-P; (f–g) UFRJ-DG 356j-P. Anterior to top in all views. Scale bar = 10 mm.

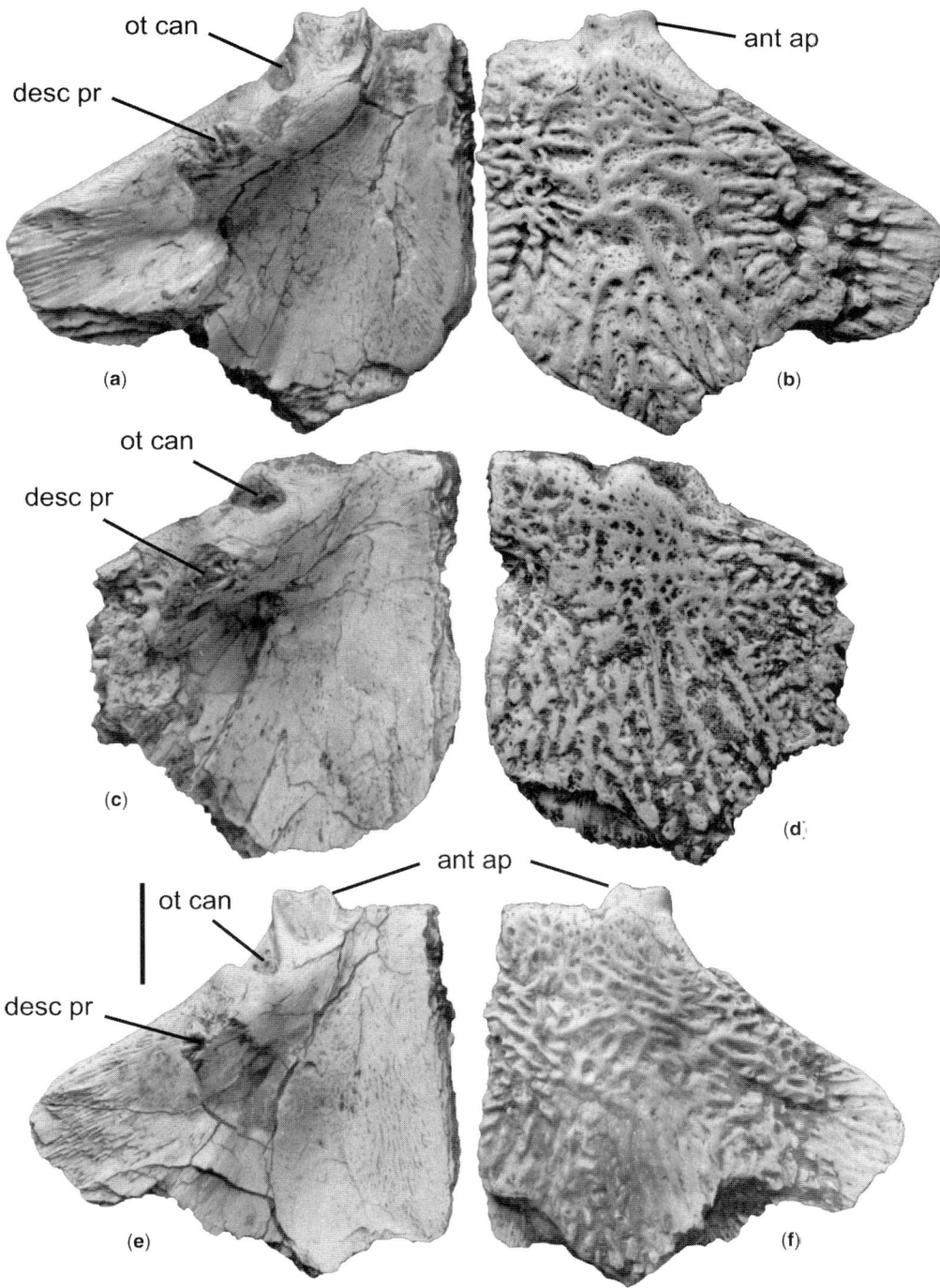

Fig. 6. *Mawsonia gigas* from the Sanfranciscana Basin, right postparietals, anterior to top, in ventral (**a, c, e**) and dorsal (**b, d, f**) views. (a–b) MCT 1384a-P; (c–d) UFRJ-DG 356a-P; (e–f) MCT 1384b-P. Scale bar = 10 mm.

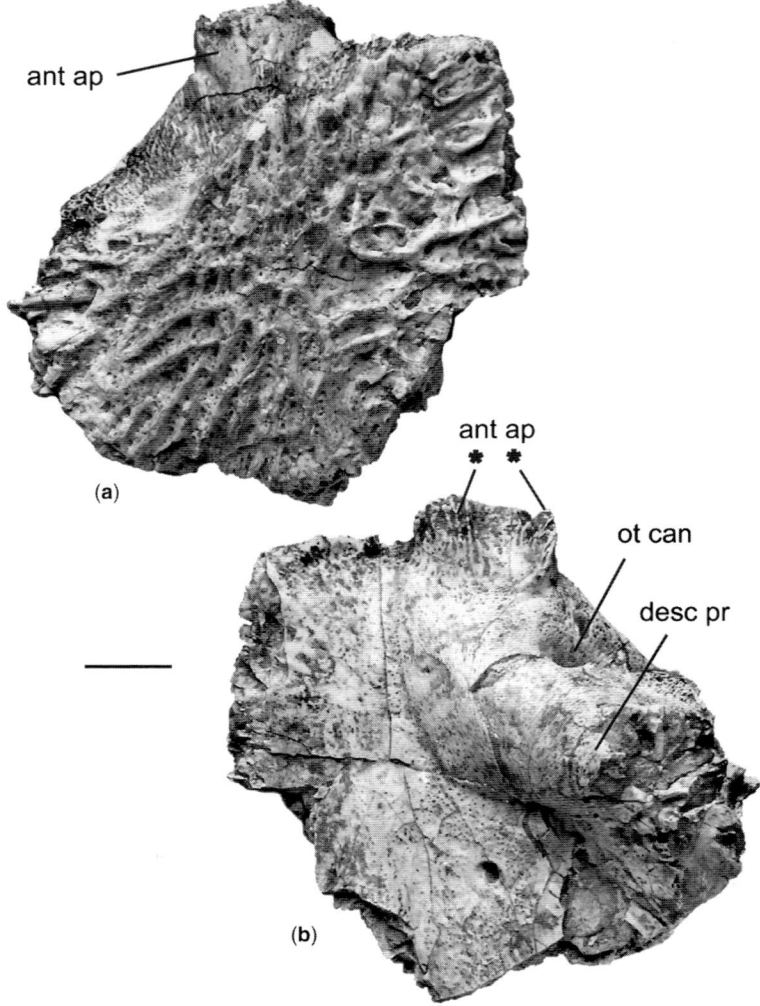

Fig. 7. *Mawsonia gigas* left postparietal from Sanfranciscana Basin, UFRJ-DG 356g-P (the largest specimen recovered), anterior to top. (**a**) dorsal view; (**b**) ventral view. Scale bar = 10 mm.

observe, the prootics are identical to those of *Mawsonia* cf. *M. gigas* from the Santana Formation (the only other form in which these have been described; Maisey 1986).

The supratemporals are distinctive bones that contribute to the rounded posterolateral margin of the postparietal shield (Fig. 9). As in other mawsoniids, the extrascapulars form an integral part of the postparietal shield and are strongly sutured to the postparietal and supratemporal (Fig. 10). All the extrascapulars in the Sanfranciscana Basin material are paired and asymmetrical and only a single pair was probably present. The largest extrascapular is approximately 40 × 40 mm.

Cheek bones and operculo-gular region. No postorbitals, squamosals, spiraculars, suboperculae or pre-operculae were found (perhaps for preservational reasons, since these bones tend to be rather thin and delicate) and only a single fragmentary lachrymojugal was identified. A single gular fragment was also found, 55 mm long and 25 mm wide.

Numerous thick and strongly ornamented fragments of operculae were identified in the Sanfranciscana Basin sample, some of which are shown here (Fig. 11). The operculum apparently resembles that of other *Mawsonia* species, with a thick anterior margin and a well-developed internal attachment

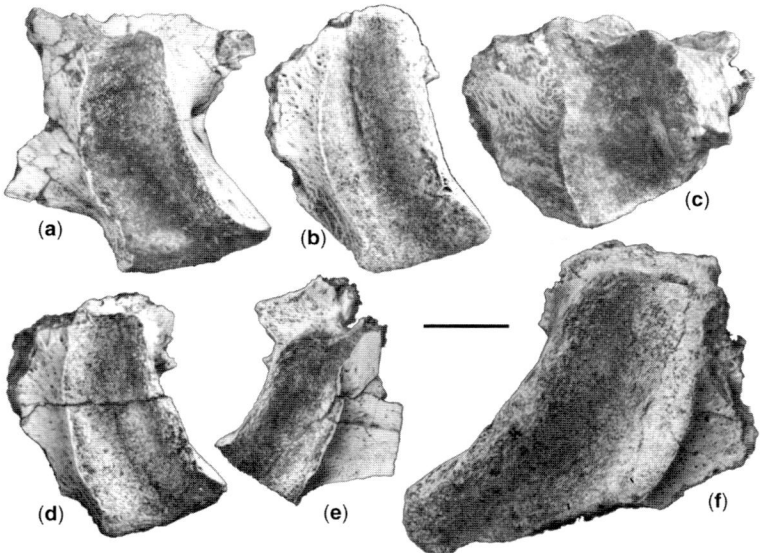

Fig. 8. *Mawsonia gigas* incomplete prootics from the Sanfranciscana Basin (mostly the articular surface for the basisphenoid), all in medial view. (**a–d**) left prootics; (a) MCT 1380a-P; (b) MCT 1380b-P; (c) UFRJ-DG 354c-P; (d) MCT 1380c-P. (**e–f**) right pro-otics; (e) UFRJ-DG 354g-P; (f) MCT 1380g-P. Scale bar = 10 mm.

surface for the hyomandibula. The ornament pattern in our material seems very similar to that in the paratype of *M. gigas* (Mawson & Woodward 1907), with delicate radiating ridges that become slightly coarser and reticulated on the anterodorsal region of the operculum (overlying the point of attachment to the hyomandibula).

As in other *Mawsonia* spp., the external surface of the operculum has two distinct regions, with a smooth or slightly pitted area overlying the centre of growth, and a more distal region ornamented by radiating ridges. However, the relative extent of these two areas and the emphasis of the ornament are apparently quite variable in *Mawsonia*. For example, in specimens referred to *M. gigas* from Bahia, the external surface above the growth centre is commonly smooth and comparatively small; ridges arising near here are fine but become much more coarse as they radiate across the bone (Carvalho 1982, pl. 2). Woodward (1908) described the opercular ornament in *M. minor* as very fine radiating ridges, but this may simply represent an ontogenetic difference (Carvalho 1982). The opercular ridges are also fine and weak in the holotype of *M. brasiliensis*, suggesting that this individual was not fully grown. In that specimen, about one-third of the operculum surface behind the growth centre is pitted rather than ridged (Yabumoto 2002, fig. 3). In *M.* cf. *M. gigas* from the Santana Formation, the pitted area is confined to the dorsal margin of the operculum, and the

remainder of the operculum is covered in fine ridges (Maisey 1986, fig. 8). In *M. tegamensis*, the opercular ornament is comparatively coarse, with an extensive network of reticulated ridges extending from the growth center over approximately half the bone surface area, and with radiating ridges more distally (sometimes interconnected transversely; Wenz 1975, pl. 5, fig. 4). In *M. libyca*, the outer surface above the growth center is unpitted and smooth, but most of the bone is covered by pronounced ridges, which extend radially from the growth center toward the margins. In *Axelrodichthys*, the operculum is ornamented by fine, radiating ridges, but the area overling the growth centre is smooth.

Palate. No complete palates were recovered, but numerous fragmentary quadrates, pterygoids and metapterygoids were identified. All the fragments are morphologically similar to an almost complete acid-prepared palate of *Mawsonia* cf. *M. gigas* described by Maisey (1986; fig. 12a, b).

Quadrate. Isolated quadrate condyles are among the most distinctive and abundant elements in the sample, because their characteristic biconvex articular surfaces are robust and therefore more readily-preserved. At least 21 quadrate condyles are present in our sample, divided more or less equally among left and right elements (Figs 12c, d, 13). Some of the left and right elements agree

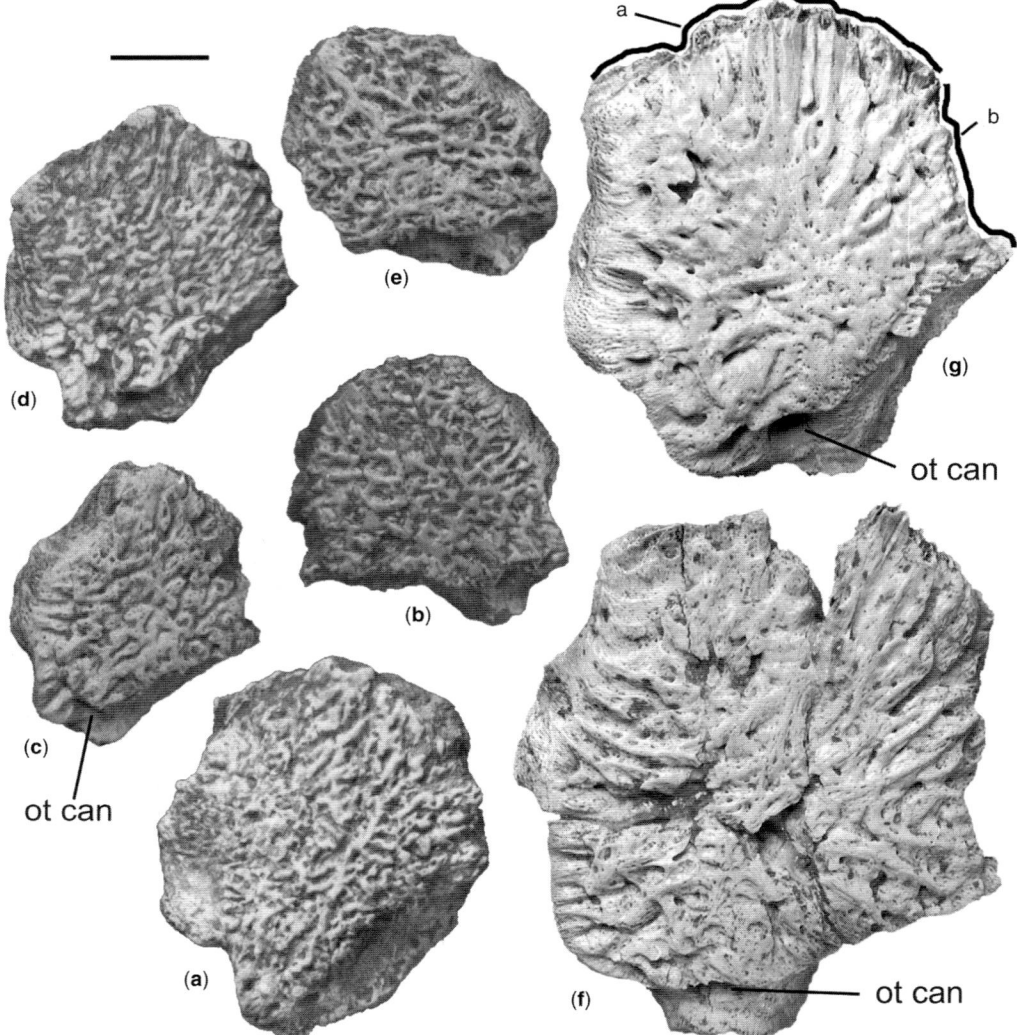

Fig. 9. *Mawsonia gigas* supratemporals from the Sanfranciscana Basin, anterior to top. (**a, c–d, f–g**) left supratemporals; (**b, e**) right supratemporal. (a) MCT 1385d-P; (b) MCT 1385h-P; (c) UFRJ-DG 357c-P; (d) MCT 1385c-P; (e) UFRJ-DG 357i-P; (f) UFRJ-DG 357a-P; (g) MCT 1385b-P. a = suture with posterior parietal; b = suture with extrascapular. Scale bar = 10 mm.

closely in size and may come from single individuals, but none could be reliably matched. The condylar heads display considerable size range, with a maximum anteroposterior length (measured from front to back across the biconvex surface) ranging from 11–31 mm. The minimum individual size represented by the Sanfranciscana Basin *Mawsonia* quadrates was estimated using the holotype of *M. brasiliensis* from the Santana Formation (an almost complete individual) as a guide. That specimen is *c.* 1435 mm overall length (Yabumoto

2002), and its quadrate condyle is *c.* 25 mm long. On that basis, our smallest specimen (MCT 1379h-P, condyle length 11 mm; Fig. 13g) represents an individual *c.* 630 mm overall length, which closely approximates the length of the type specimen of *M. minor* (said to be *c.* 600 mm long; Woodward 1908). Our largest examples (UFRJ-DG 353d-P, MCT 1379n-P; left and right elements both with a condyle length of 31 mm, possibly from a single individual; Fig. 13d, n) represent an overall body length of *c.* 1.8 m. In

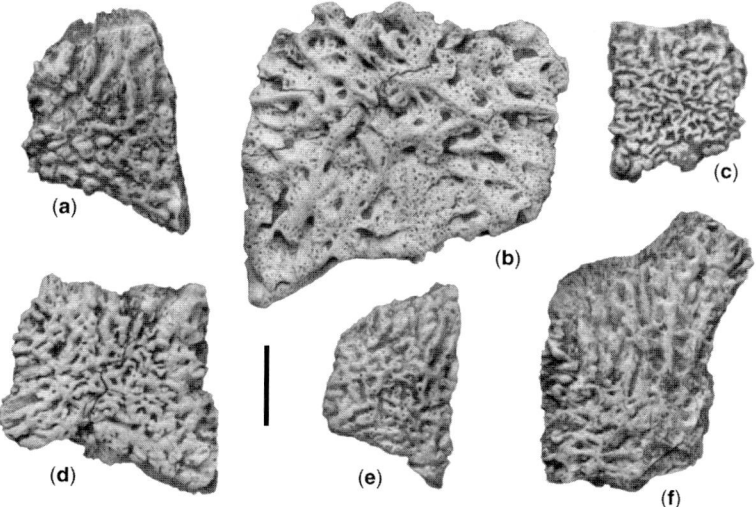

Fig. 10. *Mawsonia gigas* extrascapulars from the Sanfranciscana Basin, anterior to top. (**a, d, e**) left extrascapula; (**b, c, f**) right extrascapular. (a) MCT 1386d-P; (b) UFRJ-DG 358a-P; (c) UFRJ-DG 358b-P; (d) MCT 1386e-P; (e) MCT 1386a-P; (f) UFRJ-DG 358c-P. Scale bar = 10 mm.

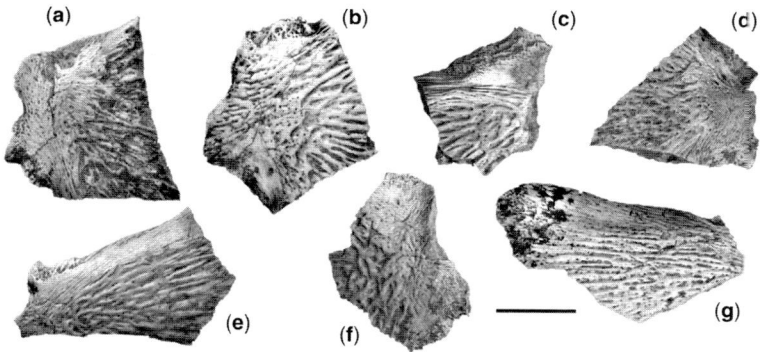

Fig. 11. *Mawsonia gigas* operculum fragments from the Sanfranciscana Basin, showing variation in the ornament pattern above the growth centre, dorsal to top. (**a–b, e**) left operculum, (**c–d, f–g**) right operculum. (a) MCT 1369b-P; (b) MCT 1369d-P; (c) UFRJ-DG344b-P; (d) MCT 1369e-P; (e) MCT 1369a-P; (f) UFRJ-DG 344a-P; (g) MCT 1369f-P. Scale bar = 10 mm.

comparison, the largest known *Mawsonia* quadrate from Brazil (DGM 1.048-P from the Neocomian of Bahia, with a condyle length of 110 mm) represents an individual with an estimated overall length of *c.* 6.3 m (20.8 ft), i.e. about ten times the length of the smallest Sanfranciscana Basin specimen and over three times the size of the largest one.

The ascending shaft of the quadrate has a deep cleft, with a rough, spongy sutural surface anteriorly, suggesting that its sutural contact with the pterygoid was very strong. The pterygoid extended

ventrally almost to the base of the quadrate, usually terminating on its mesial surface just above the anterior part of the condyle (e.g. Fig. 13j, t, u; indicated by an arrow), but occasionally extending just below the condylar margin anteriorly (e.g. Fig. 13d, n–p, s).

Metapterygoid. Twenty-two metapterygoids have been identified in our sample, although only the upper articular surface is preserved (Fig. 14). The mesial surface of the metapterygoid has a broad, strongly ridge sutural contact with the lateral face of the pterygoid below the articular

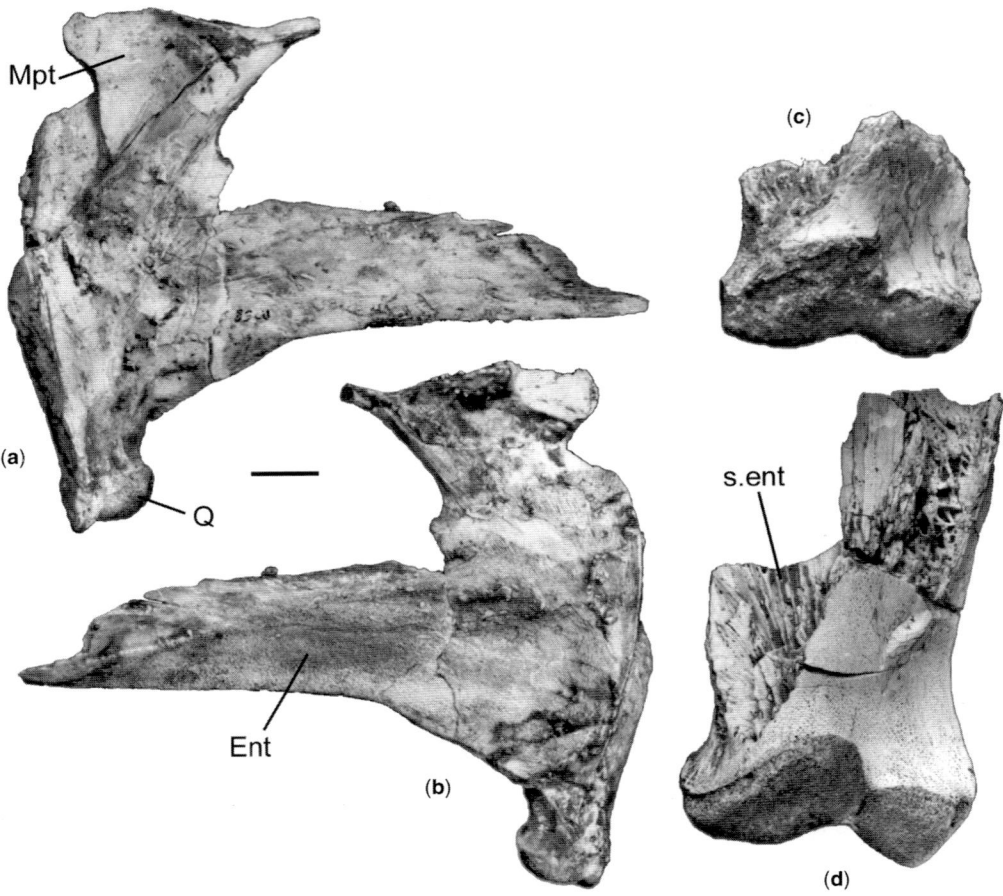

Fig. 12. (a–b) *Mawsonia* cf. *M. gigas* (AMNH 11758, Santana Formation, Araripe Basin) complete acid-prepared palatoquadrate; (a) lateral surface; (b) mesial surface. (c–d) *Mawsonia gigas* right quadrate condyles from Sanfranciscana Basin, both in mesial view. (a) MCT 1379a-P; (d) MCT 1379b-P. Scale bar = 10 mm.

region, providing a means for the left and right elements to be determined. As with the quadrates, almost equal numbers of left and right metapterygoids were collected, and the sample clearly represent a wide individual size range (although it is difficult to obtain precise dimensions because the anterior and posterior tips of the articular surfaces are frequently broken). In the smallest Sanfranciscana Basin metapterygoids (Fig. 14a, b), the preserved part of the articular surface is c. 11 mm long, but was probably 30% longer when complete (cf. the complete articular surface of the metapterygoid in *Mawsonia* cf. *M. gigas* from the Santana Formation is c. 25 mm long; Fig. 12a, b).

Pterygoid. The pterygoid elements did not reveal any characters of systematic interest and none is

illustrated here. Twenty-six tooth-covered fragments were recovered, but in most cases the margins are not preserved. However, one somewhat oval-shaped fragment resembles the posterior part of the pterygoid in *Mawsonia* cf. *M. gigas* from the Santana Formation, and other more slender pieces probably represent the pterygoid anterior process. The pterygoid teeth are small, densely spaced, and have a pebbly appearance; they are somewhat coarser than in *M.* cf. *M. gigas*, where the pterygoid teeth are more granular.

No ectopterygoids were identified in the sample. Four autopalatine fragments were identified but are too incomplete for illustration. The autopalatine is known only in *Mawsonia* cf. *M. gigas* (Maisey 1986, fig. 10), where it has a comparatively deep posterior part and a short, narrow dorsal process. The autopalatine in *Axelrodichthys araripensis* is

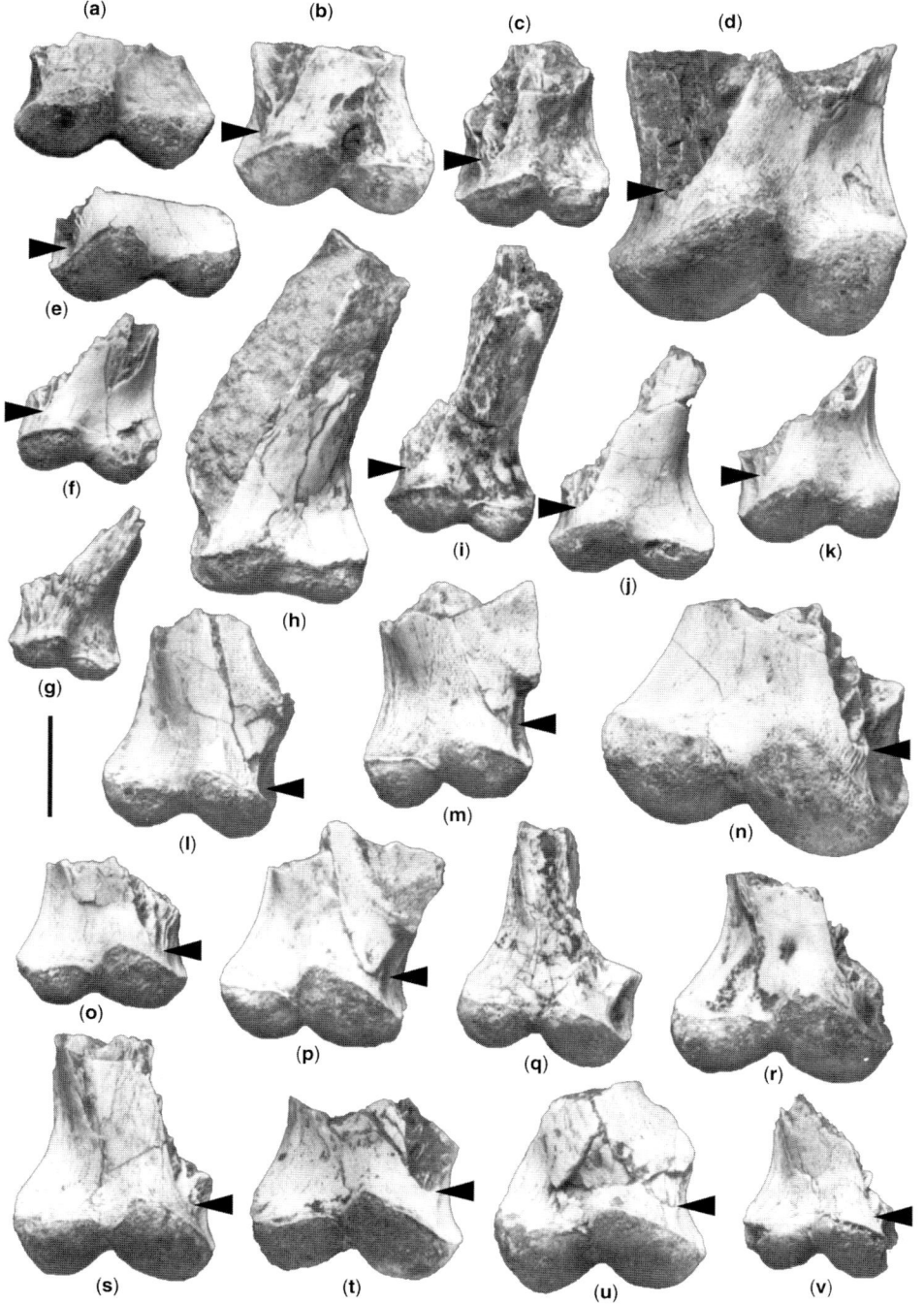

Fig. 13. *Mawsonia gigas* quadrate condyles from the Sanfranciscana Basin, all in mesial view. Arrowheads indicate lowest point of suture with entopterygoid. (**a–k**) right condyles; (a) UFRJ-DG 353b-P; (b) UFRJ-DG 353e-P; (c) MCT 1379e-P; (d) UFRJ-DG 353d-P; (e) UFRJ-DG 353c-P; (f) MCT 1379d-P; (g) MCT 1379h-P; (h) MCT 1379c-P; (i) MCT 1379f-P; (j) UFRJ-DG 353a-P; (k) MCT 1379g-P. (**l–v**) left condyles; (l) MCT 1379l-P; (m) MCT 1379k-P; (n) MCT 1379n-P; (o) UFRJ-DG 353f-P; (p) MCT 1379j-P; (q) UFRJ-DG 353j-P; (r) UFRJ-DG 353i-?; (s) MCT 1379m-P; (t) UFRJ-DG 353g-P; (u) UFRJ-DG 353k-P; (v) UFRJ-DG 353h-P. Scale bar = 10 mm.

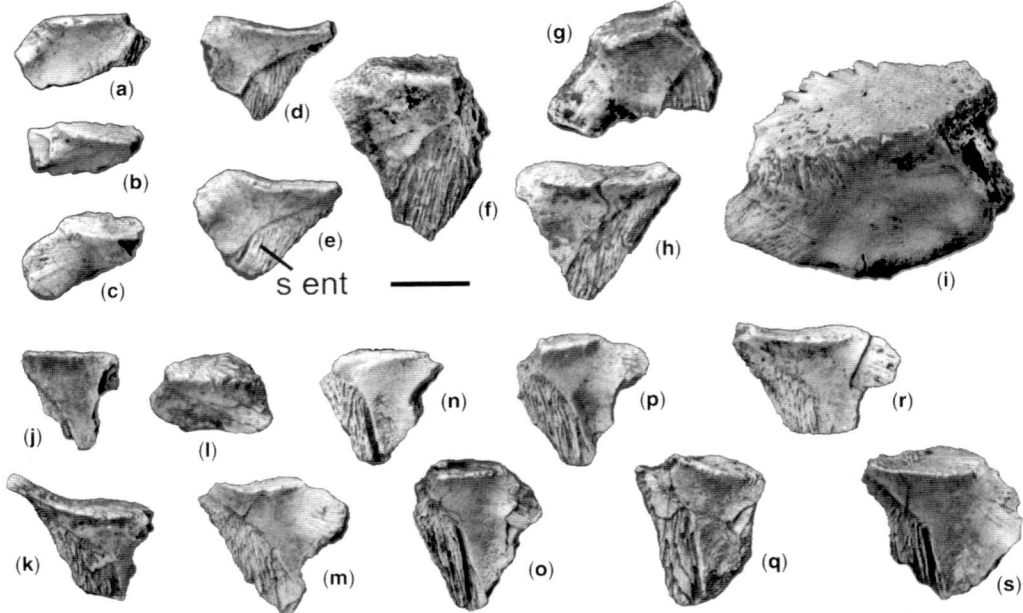

s ent

Fig. 14. *Mawsonia gigas* metapterygoids from the Sanfranciscana Basin, all in mesial view. (**a**–**i**) right metapterygoids; (a) UFRJ-DG 352a-P; (b) UFRJ-DG 352b-P; (c) UFRJ-DG 352c-P; (d) UFRJ-DG 352f-P; (e) UFRJ-DG 352d-P; (f) MCT 1378b-P; (g) UFRJ-DG 352e-P; (h) MCT 1378a-P; (i) MCT 1378c-P. (**j**–**s**) left metapterygoids; (j) UFRJ-DG 352g-P; (k) MCT 1378k-P; (l) UFRJ-DG 352h-P; (m) MCT 1378g-P; (n) UFRJ-DG 352i-P; (o) MCT 1378j-P; (p) UFRJ-DG 352j-P; (q) MCT 1378i-P; (r) MCT 1378h-P; (s) MCT 1378f-P. Scale bar = 10 mm.

more slender posteriorly, and its dorsal process is comparatively broad at the base (Maisey 1986, fig. 26).

Lower jaw. Numerous fragments of the lower jaw were recovered, including at least 42 incomplete angulars (evenly divided into left and right elements, although it was not possible to identify matched pairs) plus numerous isolated subtriangular dorsal processes. Parts of 10 splenials, 11 dentaries, 14 posterior coronoids and 10 articulars were also found.

The angulars of *Mawsonia* are easily identified by their heavy rugose ornament, with pronounced ridges arranged radially and longitudinally, sometimes forming a reticulate pattern with short connecting branches. The most complete angular is MCT 1370c-P (Fig. 15a, b). It is *c.* 95 mm long and has a maximum depth of 25 mm just anterior to its mid point (at the dorsal process). There is a distinct suture surface for the principal coronoid (a comparatively unusual feature among actinistians, possibly representing a synapomorphy of *Mawsonia* and *Axelrodichthys*; Forey 1998). A deep groove forms the overlap surface for the dentary at the anterior end of the angular. Sensory

canal pores arranged along the lateral surface separate an ornamented upper part from a smooth lower one. The gulars probably overlapped the smooth area as in *M. brasiliensis* (Yabumoto 2002, figs 3, 4). The mesial surface of the angular is concave, with a deep Meckelian fossa anteriorly and an adductor fossa farther posteriorly.

The centre of growth of the angular in *Mawsonia* is only evident on the mesial surface of the bone, within the contact surface for the pre-articular, and its position relative to the dorsal process of the angular is variable (Forey 1998, fig. 5.11). Although the angulars in our sample are fragmentary, the position of the centre of growth relative to the dorsal process was ascertained in several specimens (indicated by a dot in Fig. 15). In some specimens, the dorsal process lies far anteriorly to the centre of growth (e.g. MCT 1379h-P; Fig. 15c) as Forey (1998) showed in *M. gigas* (BMNH P.10360), but in other examples the apex is closer to the growth center (e.g. MCT 1370m-P; Fig. 15f), as in the angulars of *M. tegamensis* and *M. lavocati* (Tabaste 1963; Wenz 1981). The extent of ornament on the external surface of the angular also varies in the Sanfranciscana Basin specimens. In some, the rugose ornament extends

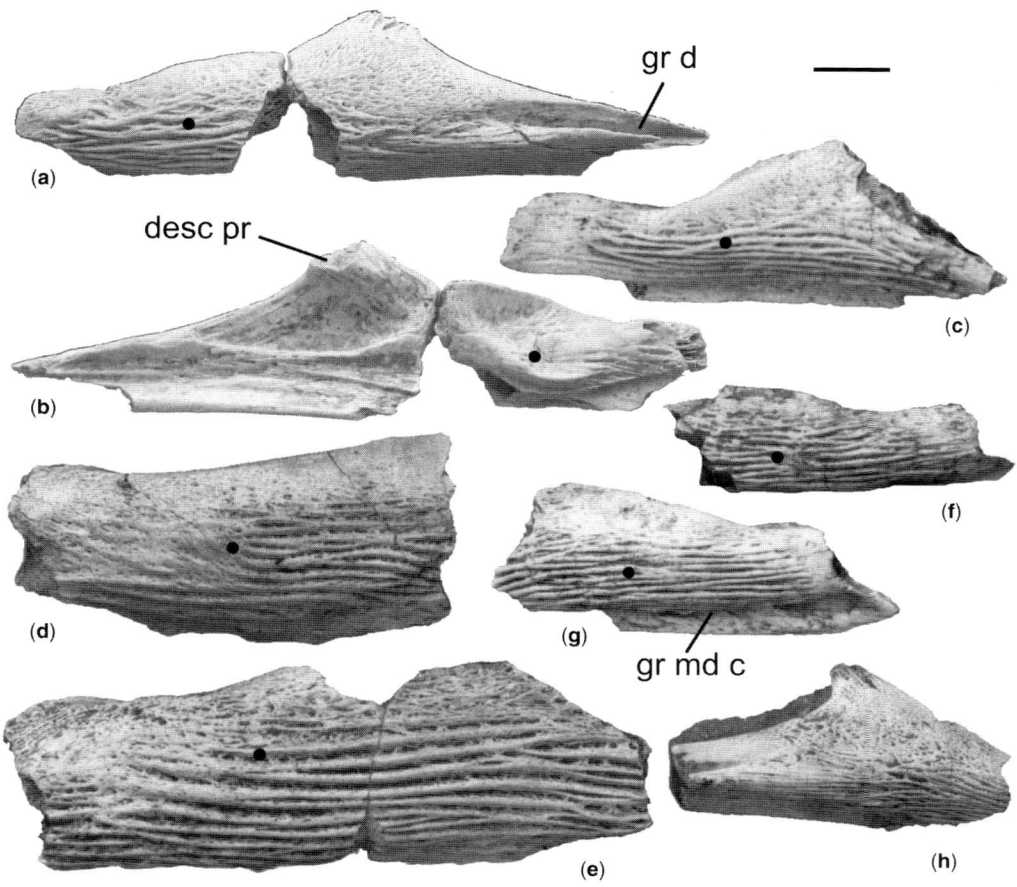

Fig. 15. *Mawsonia gigas* angulars from the Sanfranciscana Basin. (**a–b**) MCT 1370c-P, right angular; (a) lateral view; (b) mesial view. (**c–e**) fragments of right angular, anterior to right; (c) MCT 1370h-P; (d) MCT 1370a-P; (e) MCT 1370b-P. (**f–h**) fragments of left angular, anterior to left; (f) MCT 1370m-P; (g) UFRJ-DG 345m-F; (h) MCT 1370o-P. Position of growth centre (where determined) is indicated by a black dot. Scale bar = 10 mm.

posteriorly as far as the growth centre but rapidly fades above and behind it (e.g. Fig. 15c–e), whereas in others the ornament continues above and behind the growth centre (e.g. Fig. 15g). The dorsal margin of the angular also displays some variation in shape; in some specimens, it is gently inclined from the apex of the dorsal process to the adductor fossa, as in *M. gigas* and *M. lavocati* (e.g. Fig. 15c, f), but in others it is slightly concave and/or more steeply inclined anteriorly (e.g. Fig. 15h). The angulars included in the Sanfranciscana Basin material therefore display considerable variation in the location of the growth center, the extent and strength of the rugose ornament, and the shape of the dorsal process. Since the material is so fragmentary, however, the significance of this variation is uncertain.

Isolated principal coronoids recovered from the Sanfranciscana Basin (Fig. 16a–c) show a strong sutural surface for the dorsal process of the angular. The principal coronoid is very similar to those of *Mawsonia tegamensis* (Wenz 1975, pl. V, fig. 3) and *M.* cf. *M. gigas* (Fig. 16d).

Dentaries are mostly represented only by their anterior extremities and the anterior part of the adductor fossa (Fig. 16e–i). In both *Mawsonia brasiliensis* and *Axelrodichthys araripensis*, there is an anteroposteriorly elongated fenestra in the floor of the adductor fossa, formed below the suture between the dentary and pre-articular. The anterior part of this fenestra can be also seen in some of the Sanfranciscana Basin dentary fragments (e.g. UFRJ-DG 347e-P, Fig. 16h; MCT 1372f-P, Fig. 16i). In *M. brasiliensis*, the posterior

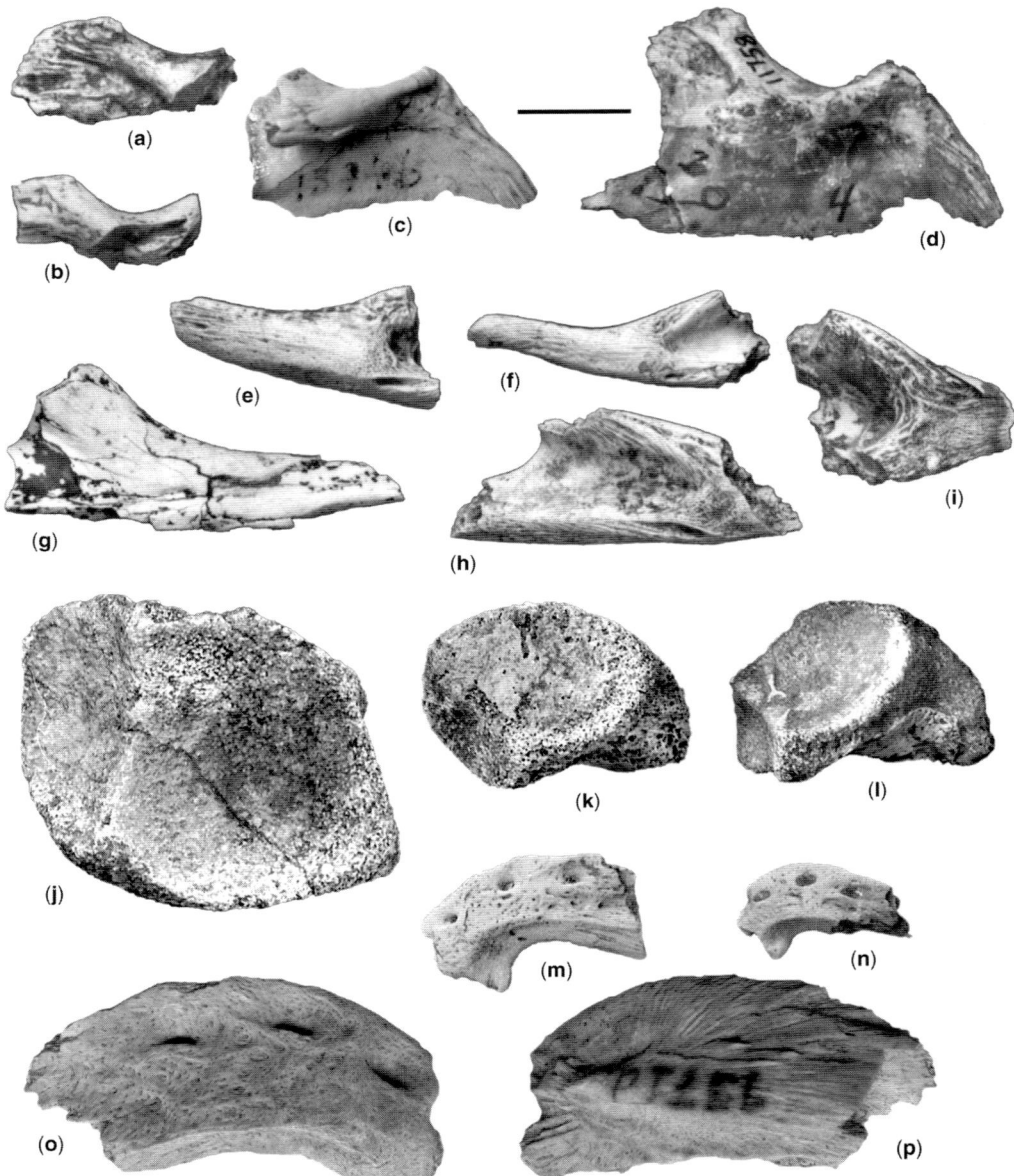

Fig. 16. (a–c) Right principal coronoids from the Sanfranciscana Basin, lateral view; (a) UFRJ-DG 349c-P; (b) MCT 1374d-P; (c) MCT 1374b-P. (**d**) right principal coronoid from *Mawsonia* cf. *M. gigas* (AMNH 11758, Santana Formation, Araripe Basin) for comparison, lateral view. (**e–i**) anterior part of dentary from the Sanfranciscana Basin, lateral view; (e–f) left dentary; (g–i) right dentary. (e) MCT 1372a-P; (f) UFRJ-DG 347b-P; (g) MCT 1372e-P; (h) UFRJ-DG 347e-P; (i) MCT 1372f-P. (**j–l**) isolated articulars from the Sanfranciscana Basin; (j) left articular MCT 1373b-P; (k) right articular MCT 1373a-P; (l) right articular UFRJ-DG 348a-P. (**m–p**) isolated splenials from the Sanfranciscana Basin; (m) left splenial MCT 1371b-P, lateral view; (n) left splenial MCT 1371c-P, lateral view; (o–p), right? splenial MCT 1371d-P (o = lateral view, p = medial view). Scale bar = 10 mm.

end of the fenestra is obscured by the angular in lateral view (Yabumoto 2002, fig. 3), whereas in *A. araripensis* it is completely exposed (Maisey 1986, fig. 26). The condition cannot been definitively determined in the Sanfranciscana Basin material, but the anterior part of the most complete angular (Fig. 15a, b) is considerably longer than in *A. araripensis* and probably overlapped the posterior part of the fenestra, as in *M. brasiliensis*. The anterior tip of the Sanfranciscana Basin dentaries are slender and elongated, again as in *M. brasiliensis* and unlike *A. araripensis*, in which the dentary is comparatively short and blunt anteriorly.

Several isolated articulars were recovered. These are large and composed of somewhat spongy cancellous bone (Fig. 16j–l). The articular has a characteristically biconcave facet for the articular surfaces of the quadrate condyle, as in actinistians generally.

The splenials have a series of sensory pores along their outer surface, but since all the examples are broken it is not possible to determine their original length or how many sensory pores they contained (only three are evident in many of the fragments; Fig. 16m–p). The splenial in other *Mawsonia* is poorly known except in the holotype of *M. brasilienis*, where it is quite long and contains at least 5 or 6 sensory pores along its lower surface (Yabumoto 2002, fig. 4). By contrast, the splenial in *Axelrodichthys araripensis* is comparatively short and contains only 3 or 4 pores (Maisey 1986, fig. 26). The Sanfranciscana Basin splenials have a smooth narrow lower margin below the row of pores. This surface was probably not overlapped by the gulars, and in the holotype of *Mawsonia brasiliensis* the gulars only reach the posterior ends of the splenials (Yabumoto 2002, fig. 4). The gulars also just reach the splenials in *A. araripensis* (Maisey 1986, fig. 26).

Zygals and occipital bones. Zygal bones are highly distinctive lunate or semicircular chondral ossifications of the neurocranium that surround and support the unconstricted notochord in the otic region. In *Latimeria*, the zygals include a single anazygal dorsally, which articulates with the sphenoid condyles of the basisphenoid, and two catazygals ventrally (anterior and posterior); these occupy the basicranial fenestra and are entirely free from each other and other neurocranial bones (Millot & Anthony 1958; Forey 1998). Additional chondral bones of the otico-occipital region in *Latimeria* (largely surrounded by cartilage) include a narrow U-shaped basioccipital, small paired exoccipitals associated with the glossopharyngeal foramen and a small supraoccipital above the foramen magnum.

Zygals have rarely been described in fossil actinistians but are known in *Laugia*, *Macropoma*, *Rhabdoderma*, *Sassenia*, and *Whiteia* (Forey 1998). These bones are well developed in *Mawsonia* (they were referred to as 'arcual bones' in Maisey [1986, p. 7] but were not described). Zygals, basioccipitals and supraoccipitals are present in some acid-prepared neurocrania of *M.* cf. *M. gigas*; (Fig. 17a–d), which provided a basis for identifying isolated zygal and occipital bones from the Sanfranciscana Basin. Zygals have also been described in an undetermined mawsoniid from Morocco (Cavin & Forey 2004; MDE F36). The exoccipitals in *Mawsonia* and *Axelrodichthys* may not have ossified, and zygals apparently did not ossify in *Axelrodichthys*.

Anazygals from the Sanfranciscana Basin range in width from 10–16 mm (Fig. 17e–g), but no large ones were found. The bones are morphologically similar to the corresponding element in *Mawsonia* cf. *M. gigas* (Fig. 17c) and in MDE F36 from Morocco (Cavin & Forey 2004, figs 1, 2).

Anterior catazygals from the Sanfranciscana Basin display a far greater size range (Fig. 17i–n). Two are very large (approximately 55 mm wide and 20 mm high), and the smallest are *c.* 20 mm wide and 10 mm high. The anterior catazygal has a butterfly-shaped outline, with rounded margins showing a radial arrangement of the underlying spongy bone. They closely resemble the anterior catazygal in *Mawsonia* cf. *M. gigas* (Fig. 17b). Cavin & Forey (2004) did not find an anterior catazygal in MDE F36, and the bone has not been described in other mawsoniids.

The posterior catazygal is shaped like an orange segment, and complete specimens range in width between 16–25 mm, and the largest broken specimen had an estimated original width of approximately 41 mm (Fig. 17o–t). The bone is notably wider than long, resembling the posterior catazygal in *Mawsonia* cf. *M. gigas* (Fig. 17a). By contrast, the posterior catazygal in MDE F36 from Morocco is slightly longer than wide, with a trapezoidal outline. The posterior catazygal is unknown in other mawsoniids.

Only two incomplete basioccipitals were found, the largest of which is approximately 25 mm wide and 30 mm deep (Fig. 17h). These resemble the basioccipital in *Mawsonia* cf. *M. gigas* from Araripe (Fig. 17d) in having an extensive area of spongy bone that extends below the concave finished surface. The basioccipital in MDE F36 from Morocco is incompletely-preserved with no spongy bone below its concave surface (Cavin & Forey 2004, figs 1, 2).

A single broken supraoccipital fragment was also collected, but has not been illustrated here. The supraoccipital is known in *Mawsonia*

130   M. S. S. DE CARVALHO & J. G. MAISEY

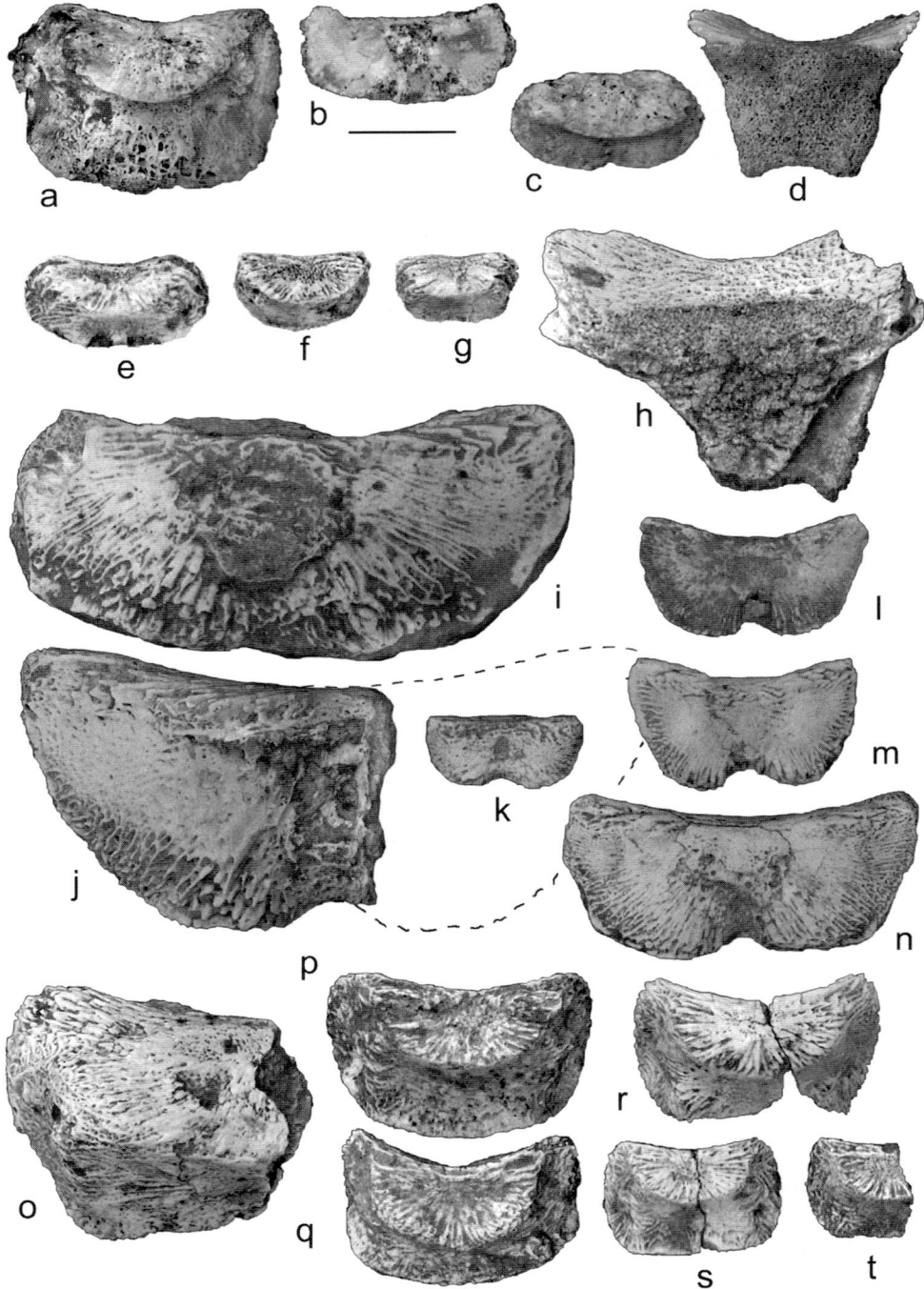

Fig. 17. *Mawsonia* zygals and occipital bones. (**a–d**) acid-prepared zygals and basioccipital from *Mawsonia* cf. *M. gigas* (AMNH 11758, Santana Formation, Araripe Basin); (a) posterior catazygal; (b) anterior catazygal; (c) anazygal; (d) basioccipital. (**e–t**) Sanfranciscana Basin specimens. (e–g) anazygals; (e) MCT 1383a-P; (f) MCT 1383b-P; (g) UFRJ-DG 355a-P. (h) basioccipital UFRJ-DG 362-P. (i–n) anterior catazygals; (i) UFRJ-DG 355c-P; (j) UFRJ-DG 355d-P; (k) UFRJ-DG 355e-P; (l) UFRJ-DG 355f-P; (m) MCT 1383d-P; (n) MCT 1383c-P. (o–t) posterior catazygals; (o) UFRJ-DG 355g-P; (p) UFRJ-DG 355h-P; (q) UFRJ-DG 355j-P; (r) UFRJ-DG 355j-P; (s) MCT 1383g-P; (t) MCT 1383h-P. Scale bar = 10 mm.

cf. *M. gigas* from Araripe (Maisey 1986, fig. 6), *M. tegamensis* (Wenz 1975, pl. 1, fig. 1b), and MDE F36 from Morocco (Cavin & Forey 2004). In *M.* cf. *M. gigas*, the basioccipital is not sutured to the postparietal shield; instead, the dorsal surface of the supraoccipital is flat and was separated from the overlying extrascapulars by a narrow space. The supraoccipital has a deep inverted V-shape in posterior view, with a smooth finished ventral surface. Only the dorsal part of the supraoccipital can be seen in the specimen of *M. tegamensis* figured by Wenz (1975 pl. 1), but it seems to agree with that of *M.* cf. *M. gigas* in shape and its position relative to the postparietal shield. The supraoccipital in the Mawsoniidae indet. from Morocco has not been illustrated, but from the description (Cavin & Forey 2004, p. 496) it seems similar to that in *M.* cf. *M. gigas*. The supraoccipital has not been described in

Axelrodichthys araripensis but is exposed in several acid prepared specimens, where it resembles that of *M.* cf. *M. gigas*.

Postcranial elements. A few postcranial bones were identified including visceral arch elements, some of which are parallel-sided and others broadly expanded, plus scapulocoracoids and fin axial mesomeres (probably from the pectoral fin). None of these bones has been described in other *Mawsonia* material, but comparison with *Mawsonia* cf. *M. gigas* from the Santana Formation suggests that the parallel-sided visceral arch fragments may be ceratobranchials, and the more expanded ones may be ceratohyals (Fig. 18a–e). The scapulocoracoids and fin mesomeres closely resemble those described in *Latimeria* (Fig. 18f–k).

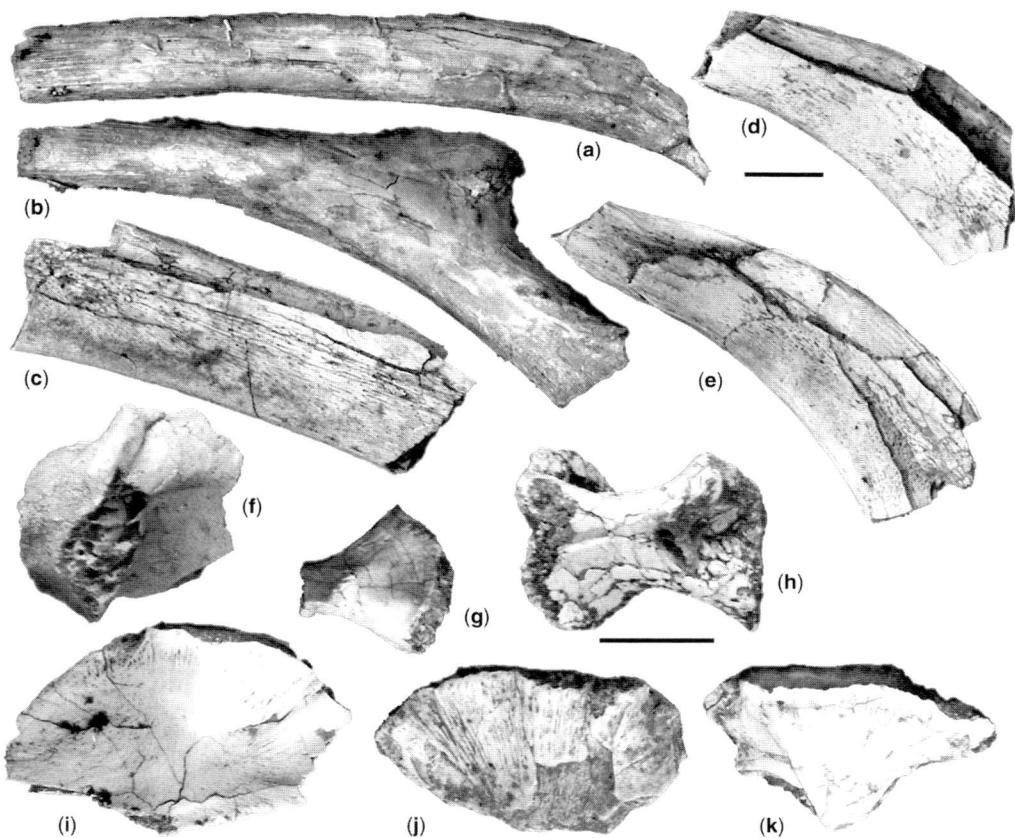

Fig. 18. (a–e) *Mawsonia* visceral arch elements; (a–b) from *Mawsonia* cf. *M. gigas* (AMNH 11758, Santana Formation, Araripe Basin); (a) ceratobranchial; (b) ceratohyal. (c–e) from Sanfranciscana Basin; (c) ?ceratobranchial MCT 1387a-P; (d) ?ceratohyal UFRJ-DG 359b-P; (e) ?ceratohyal UFRJ-DG 359a-P. (**f–h**) scapulocoracoids; (f) UFRJ-DG 361b-P; (g) UFRJ-DG 361a-P; (h) UFRJ-DG 359d-P. (**i–k**), axial mesomeres; (i) MCT 1392a-P; (j) MCT 1392b-P; (k) MCT 1392c-P. Scale bars = 10 mm (upper bar for a–e, lower bar for remainder).

Discussion

Occurrences of Mawsonia

Since *Mawsonia* was first discovered in Neocomian strata of the Recôncavo Basin, Bahia (Mawson & Woodward 1907) there have been numerous other findings in Brazil (Figs 19, 20). Several articulated specimens of *Mawsonia* (including postcranial skeletons) were collected on Itaparica Island, in the Baía de Todos Santos (W of Bahia) and were referred to the type species (Carvalho 1982). All the Recôncavo Basin material comes from the Neocomian Candeias or Maracangalha formations (Rio da Serra local Brazilian Stage; Caixeta *et al.* 1994). *Mawsonia* is also known from the Tucano Basin of Bahia (Carvalho 2002) and from the Morro do Barro Formation of the Almada Basin, near the Municipality of Ilhéus, Bahia (Carvalho 1982; Netto *et al.* 1994), including the holotype of *M. minor* (Woodward 1908). *Mawsonia* is also known from the Araripe Basin of Ceará, including articulated specimens from the Santana Formation (Albian; Campos & Wenz 1982; Maisey 1986; Yabumoto 2002) and the older and very fragmentary remains from the Brejo Santo Formation (Berriasian; Brito *et al.* 1994; Malabarba & Garcia 2000). Isolated *Mawsonia* bones are also

known from the Icó Formation, Iguatu Basin of Ceará (Neocomian), which was deposited in a continental environment (Rio da Serra local Brazilian Stage; Ponte Filho 1994); from the Itapecuru Formation (an Albian continental sequence in the Grajaú Basin of Maranhão; Dutra & Malabarba 2001); from the Alcântara Formation (a Cenomanian continental sequence on Cajual Island, in the São Luís Basin of Maranhão; Carvalho 2002); and from the Areado Group (a continental Berriasian sequence) in the Sanfranciscana Basin of Minas Gerais (described herein). In addition, a caudal fin referred to *Mawsonia* is known from the Barremian Morro do Chaves Member of the Coqueiro Seco Formation in the Alagoas Basin (Maffizzoni 1998). Thus, Brazilian records of *Mawsonia* range in age from the late Hauterivian–early Barremian to the Cenomanian, spanning all but the earliest stages of active rifting and crustal extension related to the final tectonic separation of northern South America from Africa (including the establishment of a permanent equatorial seaway between the South Atlantic and Caribbean Tethys during the Aptian; Maisey 2000).

In Africa, *Mawsonia* was first reported from the Baharija Formation (Cenomanian) of Egypt (*M. libyca*; Weiler 1935). Although the original material was destroyed during the Second World

Fig. 19. Occurrences of *Mawsonia* in the Cretaceous of Brazil. Base map modified from Schobbenhaus *et al.* 1984.

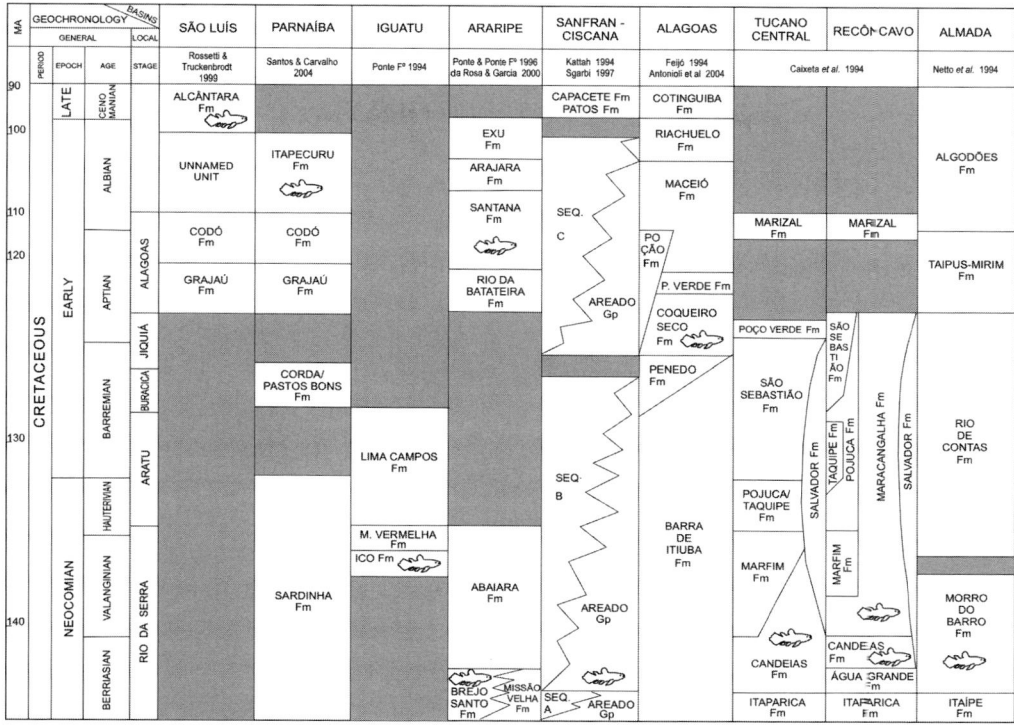

Fig. 20. Stratigraphic occurrences of *Mawsonia* in the Cretaceous of Brazil (indicated by small coelacanth outline).

War, recent excavations in Egypt have produced new material that is under study elsewhere (Grandstaff 2002). *Mawsonia* was subsequently described from the ?Neocomian of Ubangi, Democratic Republic of Congo (*M. ubangiensis* Casier 1961); from Niger, including Upper Neocomian–Barremian remains near In Gall, Aptian remains from the Tegama Series of Gadoufaoua (*M. tegamensis* Wenz 1975), and Albian remains from In Abangarit (Wenz 1981). Angular bones referred to *Mawsonia lavocati* were documented from the Albian of Gara Samani, Algeria (Wenz 1981). The holotype of *M. lavocati* is an isolated angular from the Kem Kem beds of Gara Sba, Morocco, but several partial skulls and dissociated bones have also been referred to this species (Tabaste 1963; Wenz 1981; Cavin & Forey 2004; Yabumoto & Uyeno 2005). The *Mawsonia*-bearing part of the Kem Kem sequence contains elasmobranchs that are considered to be Cenomanian in age (Sereno *et al.* 1996). New mawsoniid remains from the Kem Kem beds described by Cavin & Forey (2004) include a postparietal shield that includes paired and median extrascapulars (as in *Axelrodichthys*) and an ethmosphenoid region identified as cf. *Mawsonia lavocati*, but whose proportions

and concave profile in lateral view seem more in agreement with *Axelrodichthys* than *Mawsonia*. African records of *Mawsonia* are therefore broadly identical in age to those from Brazil, extending from the Neocomian–Barremian to the Cenomanian. The temporal range of *Mawsonia* thus encompasses much of the tectonic episode during which Brazil finally separated from NW Africa, and some of its occurrences on both sides of the Atlantic lie within regions that were tectonically active at that time (Maisey 2000).

Axelrodichthys is morphologically similar to *Mawsonia* (Maisey 1986), and these two forms are closely-related (Forey 1998). Both occur in the Santana Formation (Albian) of Brazil, and *Axelrodichthys* has also been found in the underlying Crato Formation (?Aptian; Brito & Martill 1999). We can also report a specimen of *A. araripensis* from the Albian Itapecuru Formation of the Grajau Basin (Maranhão State). Gottfried *et al.* (2004) referred an isolated median extrascapular from the late Cretaceous (?Santonian/Coniacian) of Madagascar to *Axelrodichthys*, as well as the posterior part of a mawsoniid postparietal shield (also with a median extrascapular) from the Aptian of Ingal, Niger. A late Jurassic (Kimmeridgian) age has been suggested for the Lualaba Series in which *Lualabaea lerichei* occurs (Forey 1998), but according to Sgarbi (2000) these deposits are of early Cretaceous age. The Lualaba Series has been correlated with the Areado Group of the Sanfranciscana Basin and the sequences share important sedimentological similarities (Chaves 1991). *Axelrodichthys* and *Lualabaea* may therefore be much closer in age than was previously thought and they are very similar morphologically. Thus, Cretaceous mawsoniids with a median extrascapular occur both in Brazil and Africa, and their stratigraphic ranges are congruent but less evenly balanced than *Mawsonia*; in Brazil the occurrences are restricted to the Aptian and Albian, whereas they are much wider in Africa (possibly beginning in the late Jurassic, but at least from the Early Cretaceous to the Santonian or Coniacian). The Brazilian occurrences are more or less contemporaneous with the development of a permanent equatorial seaway between Tethys and the South Atlantic, whereas the African records begin earlier (spanning the rift/crustal extension episodes) and end later (the material from Madagascar represents the last known occurrence of mawsoniids; Gottfried *et al.* 2004).

Morphological comparisons. From Brazil, the parietonasal shield is known in *Mawsonia gigas*, *M.* cf. *M. gigas*, *M. brasiliensis* and *Axelrodichthys araripensis* from Brazil, and from Africa it is known in *M. tegamensis*, specimens referred to *M. lavocati* (Cavin & Forey 2004; Yabumoto & Uyeno 2005) and *Lualabaea lerichei* (Saint-Seine 1955). Only the posterior parietal has been described in *M. libyca*, and the parietonasal shield is unknown in *M. ubangiensis*. The holotype of *Mawsonia gigas* includes an incomplete posterior parietal that has a prominent bevelled margin and is ornamented with longitudinal ridges (Mawson & Woodward 1907).

Unfortunately, the parietals are not known in *M. gigas* from Recôncavo (Carvalho 1982), but specimens referred to *M. gigas* from the Tucano and Grajaú Basins have posterior parietals with the same ornamentation pattern as the holotype (Carvalho 2002). Parietal ornament in *Mawsonia libyca* consists of longitudinal ridges similar to those in *M. gigas* (Weiler 1935). In *M.* cf. *M. gigas* from the Santana Formation, the parietal situated more posteriorly is larger than the anterior one and has a wavy posterior margin (Maisey 1986). By contrast, in *M. tegamensis* the anterior and posterior parietals are more equal in length (Wenz 1975).

In *Mawsonia tegamensis* (Wenz 1975, fig. 1), the posterior parietals make contact with supraorbitals 1–3 (with 1 posteriormost), and the anterior

parietals contact supraorbitals 3–5 (the anteriormost of which contacts the posterior nasal and could be identified as a tectal, but for the purposes of this discussion the distinction is moot). In the parietonasal shield of *Mawsonia* cf. *M. gigas* described by Maisey (1986, fig. 1C), the posterior parietals also contact supraorbitals 1–3, and the anterior parietals contact supraorbitals 3–5. In the holotype of *M. brasiliensis*, the right posterior parietal meets supraorbitals 1–4 and the anterior parietal meets supraorbitals 4–6 (the arrangement on the left side is unknown; Yabumoto 2002, fig. 2). In an incomplete parietonasal shield referred to *M. lavocati* by Cavin & Forey (2004, fig. 5), each posterior parietal again contacts supraorbitals 1–3. In another specimen referred to *M. lavocati* (Yabumoto & Uyeno 2005), the right posterior parietal contacts supraorbitals 1–3, but the left one only meets supraorbitals 1 and 2. Collectively, these observations suggest that the posterior parietal in *Mawsonia* usually contacts supraorbitals 1–3, but because of individual variation, 2–4 supraorbitals may meet the posterior parietal. In *Axelrodichthys araripensis*, however, the posterior parietal typically meets only supraorbitals 1 and 2, and the anterior parietal meets supraorbitals 2–4; i.e. the number of supraorbitals arrayed along the margins of the parietals is clearly less than in *Mawsonia*. The number and arrangement of supraorbitals is unknown in *Lualabaea lerichei*.

In *Mawsonia* cf. *M. gigas* and the holotype of *M. brasiliensis*, the parietonasal shield tapers anteriorly to a point approximately mid-way along the anterior parietal, then becomes almost parallel-sided (Maisey 1986, fig. 1C; Yabumoto 2002, fig. 2). However, in *M. tegamensis* and specimens referred to *M. lavocati*, the posterior part of the parietonasal shield is parallel-sided (Wenz 1975, fig. 1; Cavin & Forey 2004, fig. 5; Yabumoto & Uyeno 2005). The parietonasal shield in *Axelrodichthys araripensis* is also parallel-sided posteriorly and tapered anteriorly (Maisey 1986, figs 17, 18). In *M. lavocati*, the parietonasal shield attains its maximum width at the level of the anterior parietal, where the supraorbitals are slightly expanded laterally. By contrast, in *M.* cf. *M. gigas* and *M. brasiliensis*, the parietonasal shield is widest posteriorly. The postparietal shield in *Lualabaea lerichei* also seems to be widest posteriorly (Saint-Seine 1955, pl. III).

The posterior margins of supraorbital 1 and the posterior parietal are aligned transversely in *Mawsonia tegamensis*, *M.* cf. *M. gigas* and the holotype of *M. brasiliensis*, forming an almost straight posterior border to the parietonasal shield. In specimens referred to *M. lavocati*, however, the posterior border of the shield is notched between the posterior parietal and supraorbital 1, and the posterior parietals are convex posteriorly (e.g. Cavin & Forey 2004, fig. 5A). A similar notch is present between the postparietal and supraorbital 1 in *Axelrodichthys araripensis* (Maisey 1986, fig. 18A). The arrangement is uncertain in *Lualabaea lerichei*.

The profile of the parietonasal shield in lateral view displays some variation in mawsoniids, although it has rarely been observed and can be difficult or even impossible to determine in specimens that have been crushed. In *Mawsonia* cf. *M. gigas* the profile is slightly convex (Maisey 1986, fig. 1B), and the holotype of *M. brasiliensis* has an almost straight profile dorsally (Yabumoto 2002, fig. 3). By contrast, the profile in specimens referred to *M. lavocati* is markedly concave, as in *Axelrodichthys araripensis* and many other actinistians (Wenz 1975, fig. 2; Cavin & Forey 2004, fig. 6A; Yabumoto & Uyeno 2005).

In *Mawsonia gigas* from Bahia, the parasphenoid is long and slender, and the posterior portion of its dorsal face is excavated by a longitudinal canal (Mawson & Woodward 1907; Carvalho 1982), but its teeth are unknown. The dorsal surface of the parasphenoid in *M.* cf. *M. gigas* forms a deep V-shaped gutter posteriorly, above the posterior part of the toothed area (AMNH 12215). The anterior part of the parasphenoid has not been described in *M.* cf. *M. gigas* and it is unknown whether a dorsal median keel is present here or in *M. brasiliensis*. A keel extends almost to the posterior end of the toothed area in a parasphenoid attributed to *M. lavocati* (Wenz 1981, pl. IB). A keel is also present in a parasphenoid fragment of *M. libyca* (Weiler 1935). In *M. libyca*, the parasphenoid has numerous small teeth, a dorsal median keel, and lateral expansions (Weiler 1935; Wenz 1981). In *Mawsonia lavocati* and *M. tegamensis*, the parasphenoid is slightly constricted along its length, but lacks lateral expansions on the toothed area. In *Axelrodichthys araripensis*, the parasphenoid has a median dorsal keel only anteriorly. Farther posteriorly, its dorsal surface forms a broad gutter similar to that shown by Wenz (1981, fig. 1, section d) in *M. lavocati*, rather than a deep V-shaped gutter as in *M.* cf. *M. gigas*.

The postparietal shield is known in several mawsoniids from Africa and Brazil. Casier (1961) provided a detailed discussion of postparietal morphology in *Mawsonia* and considered that several features were systematically important, including: the position of the anterior foramen of the otic lateral line canal relative to the anterior apophysis; the position and size of the anterior apophysis; the number and extent of anterior processes formed on the anterior margin above the apophysis; and the curvature and ornament of the entire postparietal shield. According to Casier (1961), the foramen for the otic canal is located on the lateral margin of the postparietal in both *M. ubangiensis* and *M. gigas*, but the opening lies much farther from the anterior apophysis in *M. gigas*. Specimens referred to *M. lavocati* and *M. libyca*, the apophysis is apparently located in the middle of the anterior margin (Weiler 1935; Tabaste 1963; Wenz 1981), but it is situated laterally in the undetermined Moroccan mawsoniid described by Cavin & Forey (2004, fig. 3). Yabumoto (2002) claimed that *M. brasiliensis* and *M. gigas* differ in the position of the otic canal foramen relative to the anterior apophysis. Furthermore, according to Wenz (1975), this foramen lies much closer to the apophysis in *M.* aff. *tegamensis* than in either *M. gigas* or *M. ubangiensis*. Casier (1961) also distinguished *M. gigas* from *M. ubangiensis* on the basis of the number of anterior processes along the anterior margin of the postparietal (two in *M. gigas*, one in *M. ubangiensis*), and by supposed differences in the ornamentation and convexity of the postparietal shield. Wenz (1981) found a bony bridge between the anterior apophysis and descending process of the postparietal in *M. tegamensis* but not in *M. lavocati*, and suggested that this may represent a distinguishing feature.

These supposed differences are based on observations of very few specimens, whereas the Sanfranciscana Basin material represents a very large sample of individuals and reveals considerable variation, especially in postparietal morphology. Of those differences identified by Casier (1961) in *M. gigas* and *M. ubangiensis*, the position of the anterior foramen for the otic lateral line canal relative to the anterior apophysis varies within the Sanfranciscana Basin postparietals, and the location, size and number of the anterior apophyses along the anterior margin of the ornamented region is also variable (Figs 5–7). Additionally, the extent of the ornamented region on the postparietal anteriorly is highly variable, extending above the base of the anterior apophysis in some specimens but failing to reach it in others. Presence of a bony bridge (*sensu* Wenz 1981) between the anterior apophysis and descending process is variable in the Sanfranciscana Basin *Mawsonia* postparietals, as well as in *M. gigas* from Bahia (Forey 1998).

Certain features of the postparietal shield may nevertheless have systematic and phylogenetic importance. For example, the parietal shield is somewhat broad for its length in *M. tegamensis*, but is comparatively narrower in other mawsoniids. The presence and extent of the median branch of the otic lateral line canal in mawsoniids seems to be variable, although no clear distribution pattern is discernible and we suspect that Casier's (1961) reconstruction of the canal in *M. gigas* (and perhaps in *M. ubangiensis*) is inaccurate in not depicting a median branch. The anterior apophyses are located closer to the midline in *A. araripensis* than in most fossils referred to *Mawsonia* (except for *M. libyca*, where they seem to be comparatively close together; Weiler 1935; Cavin & Forey 2004, fig. 4C). The anterior apophyses have not been observed in *Lualabaea lerichei* but, judging from the shape of its postparietal anterior border, they were probably positioned as close to the midline as in *A. araripensis*. The anterior apophyses are widely separated in the undetermined mawsoniid MDE F36 from Morocco described by Cavin & Forey (2004).

The supratemporals in MDE F36 (Cavin & Forey 2004, fig. 3) have more divergent supratemporal lateral margins than in *Axelrodichthys araripensis*, *M. gigas* and *M. tegamensis*, although the supratemporal margins are also divergent in *L. lerichei*. Isolated supratemporals from the Sanfranciscana Basin are not appreciably wider posteriorly than anteriorly, suggesting that the lateral margins of the postparietal shield were no more divergent than in *M. gigas* or *M. tegamensis*. The shape of the supratemporal in *Lualabaea lerichei* is uncertain as its margin seems to be overlain by the operculum in the holotype (Saint-Seine 1955, pl.I).

Many forms referred to *Mawsonia* possess a single large pair of extrascapulars in the postparietal shield (e.g. Wenz 1975; Maisey 1986; Yabumoto 2002). An additional median extrascapular is present in *Lualabaea lerichei*, *Axelrodichthys araripensis* and in a mawsoniid referred to *Axelrodichthys* from Niger (Saint-Seine 1955; Maisey 1986; Gottfried *et al.* 2004, fig. 2B). A large median extrascapular is also present in MDE F36 from Morocco, although the right paired extrascapular is either vestigial or absent (Cavin & Forey 2004). The median extrascapular is narrower than the paired elements posteriorly in *A. araripensis*, but is wider than them in *L. lerichei* and MDE F36. The width of the paired extrascapulars cannot be determined in the mawsoniid from Niger, and it is unknown whether the median extrascapular from Madagascar described by Gottfried *et al.* (2004, fig. 2A) was accompanied by paired extrascapulars. Both of the median extrascapulars described by Gottfried *et al.* (2004) are strongly ornamented by anteriorly radiating ridges, whereas the ornament of the median extrascapular in *A. araripensis* is comparatively subdued. Anteriorly radiating ridges also seem to be absent in MDE F36. The strongly ornamented median extrascapulars described by Gottfried *et al.* (2004) are sufficiently distinct to suggest that they may pertain to one or more new mawsoniid species. Only the anterior margin of the median extrascapular is preserved in the holotype of *Lualabaea lerichei*, but it appears to have strong ridges that may radiate from a growth center farther posteriorly (Saint-Seine 1955, pl. I).

Opercular ornament is much finer in smaller Sanfranciscana Basin specimens than in larger ones. Two concentric ornamented fields are present on the operculum of *Mawsonia* and its sister taxon *Axelrodichthys*; a smooth or pitted proximal area, and a more distal region with radial ridges. The proximal area in *M. tegamensis* is quite extensive and covered with rugose ornament, and the radial pattern is only developed farther distally (Wenz 1975, pl. I, pl. V, fig. 4). In *Mawsonia* from Brazil, the initial radial ridges are always fine, and the ridges either remain fine or may become much heavier distally. By contrast, in both *M. tegamensis* and *M. libyca*, the radial ridges are strong over their entire length. In *Lualabaea lerichei*, the entire operculum (including the proximal area) appears to be covered by comparatively fine radial ridges (Saint-Seine 1955, pl. 1), similar to those in *A. araripensis* (Maisey 1986, figs 13B, 22A). The operculum is not known in *M. ubangiensis*.

Although the angular in *Mawsonia* is quite variable in shape and is known in several nominal species, assumptions that species can be recognized by differences in angular morphology are probably unjustified (Wenz 1975; Forey 1998). As shown earlier, the angular bones from the Sanfranciscana Basin display considerable individual variation in shape, proportions and ornament, suggesting that these features are not systematically informative.

In mawsoniids, the dentary is known only in *Mawsonia brasiliensis*, *Axelrodichthys* and *Lualabaea lerichei*. The anterior part of the Sanfranciscana Basin dentaries are elongated, as in *M. brasiliensis*. However, the dentary in *A. araripensis* lacks an anterior elongation (Maisey 1986). The anterior shape of the dentary is uncertain in *L. lerichei* (Saint-Seine 1955).

Complete postorbitals are known only in *Mawsonia tegamensis*, *M.* cf. *M. gigas* and *M. brasiliensis*. The postorbital in these forms is distinctive in having an anterior process extending above the dorsal margin of the lachrymojugal. In *M. tegamensis* described by Wenz (1975), the anterior process is comparatively deep and may have reached the supraorbital series. By contrast, in *M.* cf. *M. gigas* and *M. brasiliensis* the anterior process is splint-like and does not reach the supraorbitals (Maisey 1986; Yabumoto 2002). The postorbital lacks an anterior process in *Axelrodichthys araripensis* (Maisey 1986). The postorbital is unknown in *Lualabaea lerichei*, but Saint-Seine (1955, p. 9) noted the presence of 'les os sous orbitaires', one of which may include the postorbital.

The lachrymojugal in *Mawsonia tegamensis*, *M*. cf. *M. gigas*, and *M. brasiliensis* has a very distinctive morphology that may characterize the genus (Wenz 1975; Maisey 1986; Yabumoto 2002). The bone is greatly elongated anteroposteriorly, with a J-shaped upturned anterior end that may be constricted below the eye, and sensory pores are typically absent. In *M*. cf. *M. gigas* and *M. brasiliensis*, the anterior part of the lachrymojugal is not expanded and in *M. tegamensis* it is only slightly expanded. By contrast, in *Axelrodichthys araripensis*, the anterior part of the lachrymojugal is considerably expanded (Maisey 1986, fig. 26; Forey 1998, fig. 4.17). According to Forey (1998), the lachrymojugal is expanded anteriorly only in actinistians lacking a preorbital bone, but it is sometimes narrow even where the preorbital is absent (as in *Mawsonia*). The lachrymojugal in *L. lerichei* is elongated anteroposteriorly, but its precise shape is uncertain (Saint-Seine 1955, pls. I, III).

A pre-operculum is present in *Mawsonia tegamensis* (Wenz 1975, fig. 1, 'préopercule inferieur'), but according to Clément (2005) the bone is absent in a large undescribed *Mawsonia* skull from Morocco. The preoperculum has not been described in *M. gigas* or in *M*. cf. *M. gigas*, but one is present in the holotype of *M. brasiliensis* (Yabumoto 2002, fig. 3), and one has also been observed in a large undescribed head of *Mawsonia* from the Santana Formation. Although Clément (2005) coded absence/presence of a pre-operculum as uncertain in *Mawsonia*, it is undoubtedly present both in African and Brazilian specimens and its occasional absence is probably a taphonomic or preservational feature. Consequently, the preoperculum in *Mawsonia* should be coded as present in future phylogenetic studies of actinistians. A small pre-operculum is also present in *Axelrodichthys araripensis* but apparently did not contact the squamosal, although there seems to be contact between the squamosal and postorbital (Maisey 1986, fig. 14; Forey 1998, fig. 4.17). By contrast, in *M. brasiliensis* (Yabumoto 2002) and an undescribed *Mawsonia* skull from the Santana Formation, the pre-operculum, squamosal, and postorbital form a continuous arcade. Forey (1998) suggested that the cheek bones in *Lualabaea* are reduced and probably did not contact each other, but it is uncertain whether a preoperculum was present.

Ossified zygals are known in *Mawsonia* cf. *M. gigas* and MDE F36 from Morocco (Maisey 1986; Cavin & Forey 2004) as well as in the Sanfranciscana Basin material. Their wider distribution among mawsoniids is largely unknown, although they apparently did not ossify in *Axelrodichthys araripensis*.

Systematics of Mawsonia. There is little agreement in the literature as to how many *Mawsonia* species are valid. Cloutier & Forey (1991) recognized five species (*M. gigas* Woodward 1907; *M. libyca* Weiler 1935; *M. ubangiensis* Casier 1961; *M. lavocati* Tabaste 1963; and *M. tegamensis* Wenz 1975). Yabumoto (2002) accepted that number but added a sixth species, *M. brasiliensis*, which was distinguished on the basis of the position of the otic canal fossa (supposedly different from *M. ubangiensis*), the shape of the anterior end of the angular (less elevated than in *M. lavocati*, more concave than in *M. libyca*) and the proportions of the parietonasal and postparietal shields (different from *M. tegamensis*). Unfortunately, such differences cannot be compared across all the taxa, and many of the features (especially postparietal and angular morphology) are highly variable in the Sanfranciscana Basin material.

Ever since *Mawsonia* was first described (Mawson & Woodward 1907), all the material discovered subsequently from Brazil has either been referred to the type species or is considered close to it (Carvalho 1982; Campos & Wenz 1982; Maisey 1986; Brito *et al.* 1994; Carvalho & Maisey 1998; Maffizzoni 1998; Medeiros & Schultz 2001; Carvalho 2002). The only other nominal Brazilian species are *M. minor* Woodward, 1908 and *M. brasiliensis* Yabomuto, 2002. *M. minor* is probably a juvenile specimen of *M. gigas* (Carvalho 1982), and *M. brasiliensis* is also very similar to *M. gigas* and may be synonymous. Until now, *M. gigas* had not been formally recognized from Africa, from where four supposedly distinct nominal species have been erected (*M. libyca* Weiler 1935; *M. ubangiensis* Casier 1961; *M. lavocati* Tabaste 1963; and *M. tegamensis* Wenz 1981). Unfortunately, complete or articulated skeletal remains of *Mawsonia* are extremely rare and some of the African species are founded upon fragmentary material, placing severe constraints on the extent to which these nominal species can be compared with each other. Bones such as the angular and postparietal are known in several forms and have therefore tended to carry greater weight in systematic comparisons than they probably deserve (e.g. Weiler 1935; Casier 1961; Tabaste 1963). We do not claim to have improved this situation significantly. However, by documenting a large sample of bones from numerous individuals, we have at least established that morphological variation within a presumably single population could easily account for *some* of the differences that have been used in the past to distinguish between *some* of the nominal species.

We can find no convincing morphological features to allow recognition of more than a single species of *Mawsonia* in Brazil the type species

M. gigas Woodward (*in* Mawson & Woodward 1907). Furthermore, we are not convinced that *M. ubangiensis* from Africa is morphologically distinguishable from *M. gigas*, and we therefore regard it as a subjective junior synonym of the type species. The African *M. tegamensis* differs from *M. gigas* in having a comparatively wide parietonasal and postparietal shield and perhaps also in its postorbital morphology.

The systematic status of *Mawsonia lavocati* is problematic. The holotype is an angular (Tabaste 1963), but Wenz (1981), Cavin & Forey (2004) and Yabumoto & Uyeno (2005) have all referred parts of various skulls to this species. Some of those specimens resemble *Axelrodichthys* from Brazil, although the shape of the angular described originally by Tabaste (1963) is more like that of *M.* cf. *M. gigas* than *Axelrodichthys araripensis*. It is possible that two different mawsoniids are present in these Moroccan deposits. Unfortunately, no reliable diagnostic features for *M. lavocati* are evident in the type specimen, and the species should be considered a *nomen vanum*. Better preserved Moroccan mawsoniid material should perhaps be referred to new taxa for which more adequate diagnoses can be formulated.

Mawsonia libyca is another problematic species, because the type and original referred specimens were unfortunately destroyed during World War II, and the species is *incertae sedis* until a lectotype is erected. Given the presence of two distinct mawsoniid taxa in the Santana Formation of Brazil and the possible existence of two taxa in Moroccan deposits, considerable care needs to be exercised in lectotype selection for *M. libyca* since the Egyptian mawsoniids may also include more than one taxon.

Phylogenetic relationships and biogeography. Recent discoveries of mawsoniid fossils in both Brazil and Africa have considerably improved our knowledge of these enigmatic forms, but have also raised important questions surrounding their interrelationships. The material described in the present work has blurred some of the traditional distinctions between supposedly different species of *Mawsonia*, while new fossils from Morocco suggest new character combinations among Cretaceous mawsoniids (Cavin & Forey 2004; Yabumoto & Uyeno 2005). We can only conclude that the current systematic treatment of mawsoniids is inadequate and that a thorough revision of these forms is needed.

Unfortunately, these conclusions leave little scope for biogeographical investigation of *Mawsonia*, despite its tantalizing geographic and temporal contemporaneity with tectonic events associated with the break-up of western Gondwana

(Maisey 2000). The first appearance of the genus (and of the type species, in its present broadened concept) is within Berriasian pre-rift and early syn-rift stratigraphic sequences of the Eastern Brazilian Rift Sytem (EBRIS) in NE Brazil, and in contemporaneous syn-rift sequences of central and NW Africa (Fig. 21). Its Aptian–Albian occurrences are in syn-rift and post-rift sequences in both Africa and Brazil, and fall largely within the same geographical area as before (Fig. 22), but its latest (Cenomanian) records are mostly African, where they extend well beyond the rift basins associated with EBRIS in Africa and Brazil (Fig. 23).

Mawsonia tegamensis may represent a distinct mid-Cretaceous lineage which was apparently restricted to NW Africa, and this form was contemporary with the early and mid-Aptian tectonic events related to the separation of Africa and South America. Tectonic events within EBRIS that would eventually result in the separation of present-day Africa and South America were initiated in the late Jurassic–Berriasian (155–145 Ma), but rifting along the Equatorial Branch between NW Africa and NW Brazil and along the Benue Trough between NW and western equatorial Africa only began in the early and mid-Aptian (*c.* 125–115 Ma). A contemporaneous switch from active rifting to passive drifting occurred within EBRIS rift basins belonging to the Recôncavo–Tucano–Jatobá trend of NE Brazil. The most significant tectonic consequence of these events was the separation of NW Africa from NE Brazil, which remained attached to the rest of South America instead of splitting from it along with the rest of Africa (Maisey 2000).

These events provide an empirical maximum theoretical age for the isolation of a *Mawsonia* population within NW Africa. Rifting along the Benue Trough between NW and western Africa stopped during the Late Cretaceous, but the trough then became occupied by a temporary seaway between the South Atlantic and eastern (Mediterranean) Tethys (Gee 1988). Northwestern Africa was thus tectonically and/or geographically separated from both South America and the remainder of Africa throughout the mid-and Late Cretaceous (i.e. the time-frame during which *M. tegamensis* lived), and fluvial and lacustrine systems within that region may have been sufficiently isolated geographically to have provided opportunities for vicariant speciation that may have led to the appearance of *M. tegamensis*. Furthermore, the temporary epicontinental seaway also effectively separated Late Cretaceous populations of *Mawsonia* in NW Africa from those in Egypt, but it is unknown whether this had any impact on mawsoniid distribution.

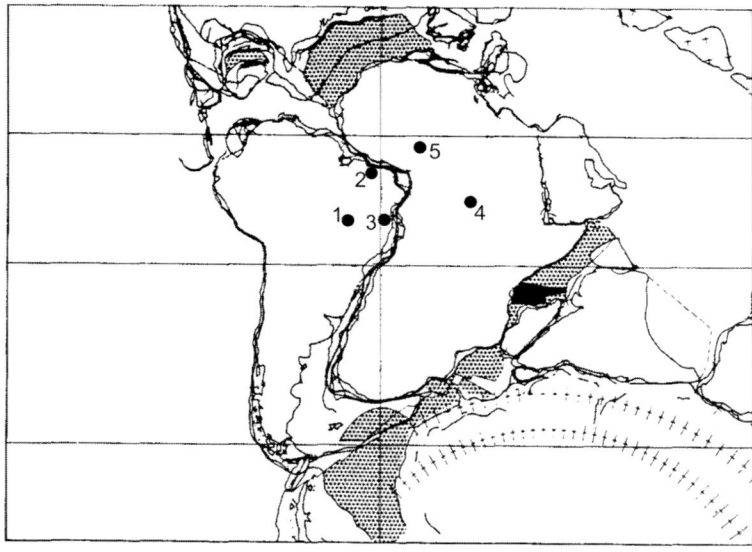

			NEOCOMIAN			BARRE-MIAN
			BERRIA-SIAN	VALAN-GINIAN	HAUTE-RIVIAN	
AFRICA	NIGER	5 - *M.* sp.	▓		▓	▓
	DEM. REP. CONGO	4 - *M. ubangiensis*	▓		▓	
SOUTH AMERICA	BRAZIL	3 - *M. gigas* (BA)	▓	▓		
		2 - *M.* cf.—*M.gigas* (CE)	▓	▓		
		1 - *M. gigas* (MG)	▓			

Fig. 21. Distribution of *Mawsonia* in the earliest Cretaceous (Neocomian–Barremian). Base map modified from Scotese *et al.* (1988).

Axelrodichthys-like mawsoniids also seem to have been distributed fairly widely across western Gondwana during the Cretaceous (although their temporal range in Brazil seems more restricted than in Africa; see earlier). At present, it is uncertain whether these forms represent a second Gondwanan mawsoniid lineage, or whether their evolutionary relationships can be correlated with tectonic events related to the separation of Africa and Brazil. *Lualabaea lerichei* is almost certainly a mawsoniid and resembles *Axelrodichthys* more than *Mawsonia*, but its phylogenetic relationships and stratigraphic age are in need of better resolution.

Cladistically, *Diplurus* and *Chinlea* are sister taxa to mawsoniids (Cloutier & Forey 1991; Forey 1998), but these forms are known only from Triassic non-marine deposits of North America (Schaeffer 1952, 1967). The intervening history of freshwater actinistians is largely unknown, but the Gondwanan distribution of Cretaceous mawsoniids seems at odds with the known distribution of the Triassic forms unless the earlier Mesozoic tectonic histories of these regions are considered. The sedimentary basins in which *Diplurus* occurs are located along the tectonic line of separation between eastern North America and Morocco, so Triassic relatives of *Diplurus* (perhaps including 'stem mawsoniids') conceivably existed in NW Africa. Following the break-up of this region, freshwater actinistians have no Jurassic or Cretaceous record in North America and presumably became extinct, but they were apparently more successful in western Gondwana (where they became fairly

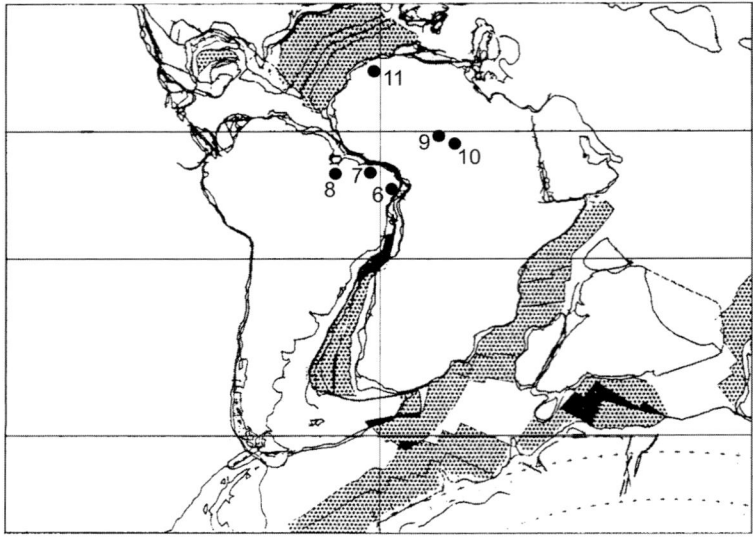

			APTIAN	ALBIAN
AFRICA	ALGERIA	11 - *M. lavocati*		▓
	NIGER	10 - *M. lavocati* 9 - *M. tegamensis*	▓	▓
SOUTH AMERICA	BRAZIL	8 - *M. gigas* (MA)		▓
		7 - *M. cf.– M. gigas; M. brasiliensis* (CE)		▓
		6 - *M. sp.* (AL)	▓	▓

Fig. 22. Distribution of *Mawsonia* in the Aptian–Albian. Base map modified from Scotese *et al.* (1988).

widespread and abundant). Following the Cretaceous separation of Brazil from western Africa, they survived on both sides of the South Atlantic (albeit only briefly in Brazil).

Conclusions

1. The *Mawsonia* material from the Areado Formation represents numerous individuals of various sizes. Although the remains are dominated by skull bones, other parts of the skeleton are also represented, suggesting there has been little post-mortem disturbance or taphonomic sorting. It is suggested that the sample probably represents a single population of a single species, and that morphological variations noted within the sample probably reflect individual differences among that population. The majority of individuals from the Sanfranciscana Basin represent comparatively small individuals (2 m or less), which is considerably smaller than the largest known *Mawsonia*.

2. Morphological variations observed in the Sanfranciscana Basin material have important implications for many of the characters that were used in the past to distinguish between putative species of *Mawsonia*, particularly in the postparietal shield and lower jaw. No characters were found to distinguish the Sanfranciscana Basin material from the type species, first described from Bahia, Brazil (Mawson & Woodward 1907). Based on the present analysis, other Brazilian material (e.g. *in* Maisey 1986; Dutra & Malabarba 2001; Medeiros & Schultz 2001; Yabumoto 2002) cannot be distinguished confidently from the type species.

3. *Mawsonia gigas* has not been recognized previously from Africa, but it is contended here that at least two nominal African species, *Mawsonia libyca* (Weiler 1935) and *Mawsonia*

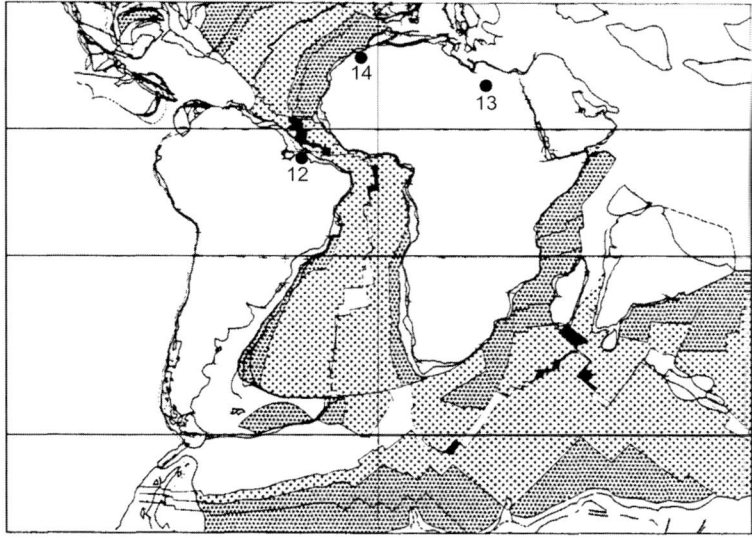

			CENOMANIAN
AFRICA	MOROCCO	14 - *M. lavocati*	
	EGYPT	13 - *M. libyca*	
SOUTH AMERICA	BRAZIL	12 - *M. gigas* (MA)	

Fig. 23. Distribution of *Mawsonia* in the Cenomanian. Base map modified from Scotese *et al.* (1988).

ubangiensis (Casier 1961) are probably synonymous with the type species. Our findings expand the pre-Atlantic seaway records of *M. gigas* from NW South America into southern Brazil and parts of Africa (including *M. ubangiensis*). Post-seaway (Albian) occurrences of *M. gigas* include those from the Santana and Itapecuru Formations of Brazil and *M. libyca* from Africa. We consider the Late Cretaceous *M. tegamensis* from NW Africa may be sufficiently distinct to merit retaining it as a separate species. It may have evolved following tectonic activity that tended to isolate NW Africa from the rest of W Gondwana during the mid-Cretaceous. Some Moroccan mawsoniids share features with *Axelrodichthys* and should perhaps be removed from *Mawsonia*, and it is possible that *Axelrodichthys*-like mawsoniids formed a

distinct lineage that was endemic to the northern part of W Gondwana during the Late Cretaceous, although rifting along the equatorial seaway had by then separated NE Brazil from NW Africa.

4. *Mawsonia* systematics is still very poorly resolved and clearly is in need of major revision. At the present time only two species (*M. gigas*, *M. tegamensis*) are recognized on the basis of credible morphological evidence. Some nominal species (e.g. *M. ubangiensis*, *M. brasiliensis*) are regarded here as junior subjective synonyms of *M. gigas*, and one species (*M. lavocati*) is so poorly established that it should be considered a *nomen vanum*. Some specimens referred in the past to *M. lavocati* resemble *Axelrodichthys* and probably do not belong in *Mawsonia*. Many of the morphological differences used in the past to

distinguish between species of *Mawsonia* may have no systematic value. Moreover, some newly discovered mawsoniid fossils do not fit easily into a conventional classification scheme (Cavin & Forey 2004). Such discoveries show that improved understanding of mawsoniid phylogeny and biogeography will only emerge as more complete material becomes available and as intrapopulational variation becomes better understood.

We dedicate this paper to Peter Forey in recognition of his outstanding work on fossil fishes, especially actinistians. MSSC thanks the Companhia de Pesquisas de Recursos Minerais, Serviço Geológico do Brasil for providing funds for the senior author to visit the American Museum of Natural History in New York, and the Superintendência Regional de Belo Horizonte for field support in Minas Gerais. Funding for fieldwork by JGM in Brazil was provided by the American Museum of Natural History. We give special thanks to Dr Ismar de Souza Carvalho (Universidade Federal do Rio de Janeiro), Dr R. de Cassia Tardin Cassab and D. de Almeida Campos (Departamento Nacional de Produção Mineral), M. E. Carvalho M. Santos, Dr V. Gallo (Universidade Estadual do Rio de Janeiro), V. M. M. da Fonseca (Museu Nacional, Universidade Federal do Rio de Janeiro), Dr M. da Glória Pires de Carvalho, L. Meeker and C. Tarka (American Museum of Natural History), G. N. Sgarbi (Universidade Federal de Minas Gerais), M. S. de Carvalho for photography, and colleagues at the Companhia de Pesquisas de Recursos Minerais for supplying the diagrams and maps. We also thank G. Clément for his thorough review of the original version of this paper and for his many suggestions for improvement.

References

ARAI, M., HASHIMOTO, A. T. & UESUGUI, N. 1995. Significado cronoestratigráfico da associação microfloristica do Cretáceo Inferior do Brasil. *Boletim de Geociências da Petrobrás*, **3**, 87–103.

BARBOSA, O. 1965. Série Bambuí. *In*: Congresso Brasileiro de Geologia 19, Rio de Janeiro, 1965, Simpôsio das Formações Eo-Paleozõicas do Brasil. *Anais Sociedade Brasileira de Geologia*, 1–11.

BRITO, P. M. & MARTILL, D. 1999. Discovery of a juvenile Coelacanth in the Lower Cretaceous, Crato Formation, Northeastern Brazil. *Cybium*, **23**, 311–314.

BRITO, P. M., BERTINI, R. J., MARTILL, D. M. & SALLES, L. O. 1994. Vertebrate fauna from the Missão Velha Formation (Lower Cretaceous NE, Brazil). *In*: *Simpósio sobre o Cretáceo do Brasil*, Rio Claro. Universidade do Estado de São Paulo, 139–140.

CAIXETA, J. M., BUENO, G. V., MAGNAVITA, L. P. & FEIJO, F. J. 1994. Bacias do Recôncavo, Tucano e Jatobá. *Boletim de Geociências da Petrobras*, **8**, 163–172.

CAMPOS, D. A. & WENZ, S. 1982. Première découverte de Coelacanthes dans le Crétacé inférieur de la Chapada do Araripe (Brésil). *Comptes Rendus de l'Académie des Sciences, Paris*, **294**, 1151–1154.

CARVALHO, I. S. & KATTAH, S. S. 1998. As pegadas fósseis do Paleodeserto da Bacia Sanfrancisco (Jurássico Superior-Cretáceo Inferior, Minas Gerais). *Anais da Academia Brasileira de Ciências*, **70**, 53–67.

CARVALHO, M. S. S. 1982. O gênero *Mawsonia* na ictiofáunula do Cretáceo do estado da Bahia. *Anais da Academia Brasileira de Ciências*, **54**, 519–539.

CARVALHO, M. S. S. 2002. *O gênero* Mawsonia *(Sarcopterygii, Actinistia), no Cretáceo das bacias Sanfrancisco, Tucano, Araripe, Parnaíba e São Luís*. Rio de Janeiro. PhD Thesis, Universidade Federal do Rio de Janeiro.

CARVALHO, M. S. S. & MAISEY, J. G. 1998. Early Cretaceous fresh water actinistians from the interior of Brazil. *Journal of Vertebrate Paleontology, Abstracts of Papers*, **18a**, 32.

CASIER, E. 1961. Matériaux pour la faune ichthyologique Eocritacique du Congo. *Annales du Musée Royal de l'Afrique Centrale, Série 8, Sciences Géologiques*, **39**, 1–96.

CASIER, E. 1969. Addenda aux connaissances sur la faune ichthyologique de la Serie de Bokungu (Congo). *Annales du Musée Royal de l'Afrique Centrale, Série 8, Sciences Géologiques*, **62**, 1–20.

CAVIN, L. & FOREY, P. L. 2004. New mawsoniid coelacanth (Sarcopterygii: Actinistia) remains from the Cretaceous of the Kem Kem beds, Southern Morocco. *In*: ARRATIA, G. & TINTORI, A. (eds) *Mesozoic Fishes 3 - Systematics, Paleoenvironments and Biodiversity*. F. Pfeil, Munich, 493–506.

CHAVES, M. L. de S. C. 1991. Sequências cretácicas e mineralizações diamantiferas no Brasil central e Africa central meridionel, Considerações preliminares. *Geociências*, **10**, 231–245.

CLÉMENT, G. 2005. A new coelacanth (Actinistia, Sarcopterygii) from the Jurassic of France, and the question of the closest relative fossil to *Latimeria*. *Journal of Vertebrate Paleontology*, **25**, 481–491.

CLOUTIER, R. & FOREY, P. L. 1991. Diversity of extinct and living actinistian fishes (Sarcopterygii). *Environmental Biology of Fishes*, **32**, 59–74.

DELICIO, M. P., BARBOSA, E. M., COIMBRA, J. C. & VILELLA, R. A. 1998. Ocorrência de conchostráceos e ostracodes em sedimentos pós-paleozóicos da Bacia Alto Sanfrancisco-Olhos d'Água, noroeste de Minas Gerais. *Acta Geologica Leopoldensia*, **21**, 13–20.

DO CARMO, D. A., TOMASI, H. Z. & OLIVEIRA, S. B. S. G. 2004. Taxonomia e Distribuição Estratigráfica dos Ostracodes da Formação Quiricó, Grupo Areado (Cretáceo Inferior) Bacia Sanfrancisco, Brasil. *Revista Brasileira de Paleontologia*, **7**, 139–149.

DUTRA, M. F. A. & MALABARBA, M. C. S. L. 2001. Peixes do Albiano-Cenomaniano do Grupo Itapecuru no estado do Maranhão, Brasil. *In*: ROSSETTI, D. F., GÓES, A. M. & TRUCKENBRODT, T. W. (eds) *O Cretáceo na Bacia de São Luís-Grajaú*. Friedrich Katzer, Belém, 191–208.

FOREY, P. L. 1998. *History of the Coelacanth Fishes*. London, Chapman & Hall.

GEE, H. 1988. Cretaceous unity and diversity. *Nature, London*, **332**, 487.

GOTTFRIED, M. D., ROGERS, R. R. & ROGERS, K. C. 2004. First record of late Cretaceous coelacanths from Madagascar. *In*: ARRATIA, G., WILSON, M. V. H. & CLOUTIER, R. (eds) *Recent advances in the origin and early radiation of vertebrates*. Dr. F. Pfeil, Munich, 687–691.

GRANDSTAFF, B. S. 2002. New specimens of *Mawsonia* (Actinistia: Coelacanthiformes) from the Cenomanian (Late Cretaceous) of Bahariya Oasis, Western Desert, Egypt. *Journal of Vertebrate Paleontology, Abstracts of Papers*, **22**, 32.

HASUI, Y. & HARALYI, N. I. 1991. Aspectos lito-estruturais e geofisicos do soerguimento do Alto Parnaíba. *Geociências, Sao Paulo*, **10**, 57–77.

KATTAH, S. S. 1994. A ocorrência de pegadas de dinossauros no Grupo Areado, porção meridional da Bacia Sanfrancisco, oeste de Minas Gerais. *Anais da Academia Brasileira de Ciências, Rio de Janeiro*, **66**, 181–187.

MAFFIZZONI, A. F. 1998. A coelacanthia of the Brazilian eoaptian. *Asociación Paleontológica del Golfo San jorge: Correlaciones del mesozoico en al atlantico Sur. Project 381* (IGCP-IUGS), Comodoro Rivadavia, **1**, 19–20.

MAISEY, J. G. 1986. Coelacanths from the Lower Cretaceous of Brazil. *American Museum Novitates*, **2866**, 1–30.

MAISEY, J. G. 1991. *Mawsonia. In*: MAISEY, J. G. (ed.) *Santana Fossils; an illustrated atlas*. Neptune, New Jersey, TFH Publications, 317–323.

MAISEY, J. G. 2000. Continental break-up and the distribution of fishes in Western Gondwana during the Early Cretaceous. *Cretaceous Research*, **21**, 281–314.

MALABARBA, M. C. & GARCIA, A. J. V. 2000. Actinistian remains from the Lowermost Cretaceous of the Araripe Basin, Northeastern Brazil. *Comunicações do Museu de Ciências e Tecnologia da Pontifícia Universidade Católica do Rio Grande do Sul, Porto Alegre*, **13**, 177–199.

MAWSON, J. & WOODWARD, A. S. 1907. On the cretaceous formation of Bahia (Brazil) and on vertebrate fossils collected therein. *Quarterly Journal of the Geological Society*, **63**, 128–139.

MEDEIROS, M. A. & SCHULTZ, C. L. 2001. Uma paleocomunidade de vertebrados do Cretáceo Médio, Bacia de São Luís. *In*: ROSSETTI, D. F., GÓES, A. M. & TRUCKENBRODT, T. W. (eds) *O Cretáceo na Bacia de São Luís-Grajaú*. Friedrich Katzer, Belém, 209–221.

MILLOT, J. & ANTHONY, J. 1958. *Anatomie de Latimeria chalumnae. 1. Squelette et muscles*. Paris, Centre National de la Recherche Scientifique.

NETTO, A. S. T., WANDERLEY FILHO, J. R. & FEIJÓ, F. J. 1994. Bacias de Jacuípe, Camamu e Almada. *Boletim de Geociências Petrobras*, **8**, 173–184.

PONTE FILHO, F. C. 1994. Sistemas deposicionais nas bacias sedimentares do Iguatu: Estado do Ceará. *In*: DIAS-BRITO, D., PONTE, F. C., DE CASTRO, J. C., PERINOTO, J. A. J. & BERTINI, R. J. (eds) *Simpósio sobre o Cretáceo do Brasil, Rio Claro*. Universidade do Estado de São Paulo, 141–146.

SAINT-SEINE, P. DE 1955. Poissons fossiles de l'étage de Stanleyville (Congo belge). Première partie; la faune des argiles et schistes bitumineux. *Annales du Musée Royal du Congo belge, Série 8, Sciences Géologiques*, **14**, 1–126.

SCHAEFFER, B. 1952. The Triassic coelacanth fish *Diplurus*, with observations on the evolution of the Coelacanthini. *Bulletin of the American Museum of Natural History*, **99**, 29–78.

SCHAEFFER, B. 1967. Late Triassic fishes from the western United States. *Bulletin of the American Museum of Natural History*, **135**, 287–342.

SCHOBBENHAUS, C., CAMPOS, D. A., DERZE, G. R. & ASMUS, H. E. 1984. *Geologia do Brasil. Texto explicativo do mapa geológico do Brasil e da área oceânica adjacente depósitos minerais; escala 1:2,500,000*. Brasília, Departamento Nacional da Produção Mineral.

SCHULTZE, H.-P. 1993. Osteichthyes: Sarcopterygii. *In*: BENTON, M. J. (ed.) *The Fossil Record 2*. London, Chapman & Hall, 657–663.

SCORZA, E. P. & SILVA SANTOS, R. 1955. Ocorrência de folhelho fossilífero cretácico no município de Presidente Olegário, Minas Gerais, Brasil. *Divisão de Geologia e Mineralogia, Boletim*, **155**, 1–27.

SCOTESE, C. R., GAHAGAN, L. M. & LARSON, R. L. 1988. Plate tectonic reconstructions of the Cretaceous and Cenozoic ocean basins. *Tectonophysics*, **155**, 27–48.

SERENO, P. C., DUTHEIL, D. B., IAROCHENE, M., LARSSON, H. C. E., LYON, G. H., MAGWENE, P. M., SIDOR, C. A., VARRICCHIO, D. J. & WILSON, J. A. 1996. Predatory dinosaurs from the Sahara and late Cretaceous faunal differentiation. *Science*, **272**, 986–991.

SGARBI, G. N. C. 2000. The Cretaceous Sanfranciscana Basin, eastern plateau of Brazil. *Revista Brasileira de Geociências*, **30**, 450–452.

SILVA SANTOS, R. 1985. *Laeliichthys ancestralis*, novo gênero e espécie de Osteoglossiformes do Aptiano da Formação Areado, Estado de Minas Gerais, Brasil. *Coletânea de Trabalhos Paleontológicos*, **27**, 161–167.

TABASTE, N. 1963. Étude de restes de poissons du Crétacé Saharien. Mélanges Ichthyologiques à la mémoire d'Achille Valenciennes. *Mémoire de l'Institut Fondamental d'Afrique Noire, Mélanges Ichthyologiques*, **68**, 437–485.

WEILER, W. 1935. Ergebnisse der Forschungsreisen Prof. E. Stromers in den Wüsten Aegyptens. II. Wirbeltierreste der Baharije-Stufe (unterstes Cenoman). 16. Neue Untersuchungen an den Fischresten. *Abhandlungen der Bayerischen Akademie der Wissenschaften, Mathematisch-Naturwissenschaftliche Abteilung*, **32**, 1–57.

WENZ, S. 1975. Un nouveau Coelacanthidé du Crétacé Inférieur du Niger, remarques sur la fusion des os dermiques. *In*: Colloques Internationaux du Centre National de la Recherche Scientifique, Paris, 1973. *Problèmes actuels de Paléontologie (Evolution des Vertébrés)*. Centre National de la Recherche Scientifique, 175–190.

WENZ, S. 1980. A propos du genre *Mawsonia*, Coelacanthe géant du Crétacé Inférieur d'Afrique et du Brésil. *Mémoire de la Société Géologique de France*, **139**, 187–190.

WENZ, S. 1981. Un Coelacanthe géant, *Mawsonia lavocati* Tabaste, de l'Albien-base du Cénomanien du sud Marocain. *Annales de Paléontologie (Vertébrés)*, **67**, 1–20.

WOODWARD, A. S. 1891. Evidence of the occurrence of pterosaurians and plesiosaurians in the Cretaceous of Brazil, collected by Joseph Mawson. *Annals and Magazine of Natural History*, **6**, 132–136.

WOODWARD, A. S. 1896. On the quadrate bone of a gigantic pterodactyl, discovered by Joseph Mawson in the Cretaceous of Bahia. *Annals and Magazine of Natural History, N. ser.*, **17**, 255–257.

WOODWARD, A. S. 1908. On some fossil fishes discovered by Prof. Ennes de Souza in the Cretaceous Formation at Ilhéos (State of Bahia), Brazil. *Quarterly Journal of the Geological Society of London*, **64**, 358–362.

YABUMOTO, Y. 2002. A new coelacanth from the Early Cretaceous of Brazil (Sarcopterygii, Actinistia). *Paleontological Research*, **6**, 343–350.

YABUMOTO, Y. & UYENO, T. 2005. New materials of a Cretaceous coelacanth, *Mawsonia lavocati* Tabaste from Morocco. *Bulletin of the National Science Museum, Series C (Geology & Paleontology)*, **31**, 39–49.

A new species of *Placidichthys* (Halecomorphi: Ionoscopiformes) from the Lower Cretaceous Marizal Formation, northeastern Brazil, with a review of the biogeographical distribution of the Ophiopsidae

PAULO M. BRITO & JESÚS ALVARADO-ORTEGA

Departamento de Biologia Animal e Vegetal, Universidade do Estado do Rio de Janeiro,
Rua São Francisco Xavier 524, Rio de Janeiro, RJ 20559-900, Brazil
(e-mail: pbritopaleo@yahoo.com.br)

Abstract: A new halecomorph fish is described from the Early Cretaceous Marizal Formation of Tucano Basin. This new material is identified as a new species of *Placidichthys, P. tucanensis* sp. nov. based on the absence of an anal fin, the lower number of flank scales in the caudal region, the slender shape of the body, and body proportions. *Placidichthys tucanensis* sp. nov. increases the distribution and diversity of ophiopsids in the western part of the Tethys Sea, being distributed along the epicontinental seas of Gondwana.

Placidichthys is considered the sister-taxon of the exclusively Cretaceous taxa *Teoichthys* + *Macrepistius* from the western Tethys. These groups show a discernible geographical distribution pattern with *Placidichthys* known only from the Southern margin of the Tethys region (South America), whilst *Teoichthys* and *Macrepistius* are known only from North America and possibly Europe.

Early Cretaceous fossil fishes from the Marizal Formation were first discovered in the 1950s and early 1960s when the Tucano Basin, in the NE part of the State of Bahia, Brazil, was surveyed for hydrocarbons (I. M. Brito 2000, pers. comm.). R. S. Santos of the Departamento Nacional de Produção Mineral, studied some of this material and described two nominal taxa, *Clupavus brasiliensis* and *Vinctifer longirostris*, and reported the occurrence of other groups, such as the macrosemiids (= ophiopsids), amiids, chirocentrids (= ichthyodectiforms), and chanids (Santos 1985, 1990). Recently, a third nominal species discovered in such pioneer collections was described as *Britoichthys marizalensis* Figueiredo, 2004.

The Tucano Basin covers an area of approximately 40000 km^2, within which the Marizal Formation crops out extensively (Brito 1979) (Fig. 1). New palaeontological prospections in the basin were undertaken during 1985 and 1986 by the first author and during 2004–2005 by the staff of the 'Laboratory of Ichthyology, Time, and Space' of the Universidade do Estado do Rio de Janeiro. During these expeditions, over 700 fossil fish were collected from the Marizal Formation, providing the most complete specimens of previously described species, as well as a number of new actinopterygian taxa (their descriptions are in progress).

The first mention of an ophiopsid from South America was made by Santos & Valença (1968), who cited a specimen from the Santana Formation as *Ophiopsis cretaceous*, which is *nomen nudum*.

However, examining this specimen (see also Maisey 1991, p. 169), we were unable to find any diagnostic character to place it within the ophiopsids (Brito 2000). The presence of ophiopsids in South America thus remained unproven until *Placidichthys bidorsalis* Brito, 2000 (Fig. 2a and b) (from the Crato and Santana formations, of the Araripe Basin, NE Brazil) was recognized as an ophiopsid. Originally, this species was described as a single member of an uncertain family within the Order Ionoscopiformes *sensu* Grande & Bemis (1998) due to its singular dorsal fin divided into two parts. Recently, Alvarado-Ortega & Espinosa-Arrubarrena (2008) investigated the interrelationships of the ionoscopiforms and recognized two monophyletic clades, Ophiopsidae and Ionoscopidae. Based on certain characters, (including body shape and presence of rhomboidal scales) they suggested that *Placidichthys* belongs within Ophiopsidae, a view also accepted by Brito (2006).

In the present paper we describe a new species of *Placidichthys* from the Marizal Formation, which is clearly distinguishable from the type species. This new taxon increases the geographic distribution and diversity of ophiopsids in the western Tethys.

Systematic palaeontology

Division Holostei *sensu* Huxley, 1861
Subdivision Halecomorphi Cope, 1872
Order Ionoscopiformes *sensu* Grande & Bemis, 1998

From: CAVIN, L., LONGBOTTOM, A. & RICHTER, M. (eds) *Fishes and the Break-up of Pangaea.*
Geological Society, London, Special Publications, **295**, 145–154.
DOI: 10.1144/SP295.9   0305-8719/08/$15.00 © The Geological Society of London 2008.

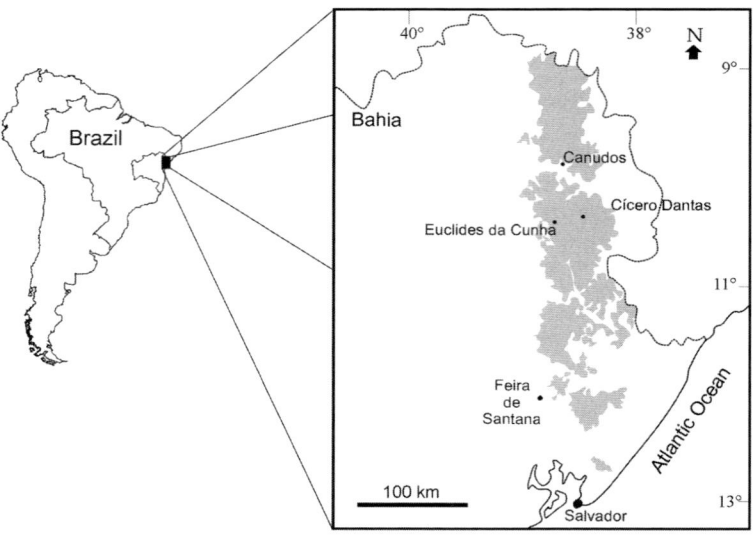

Fig. 1. Outcropping area of the Marizal Formation (in grey) in the Tucano Basin, State of Bahia, northeastern Brazil.

Family Ophiopsidae Bartram, 1975
Genus *Placidichthys* Brito, 2000

Type species. Placidichthys bidorsalis Brito, 2000.

Placidichthys tucanensis *sp. nov.*

Holotype. Universidade do Estado do Rio de Janeiro: UERJ-PMB 92. A nearly complete specimen missing most of the anterior part of the skull (Fig. 3).

Additional material. Universidade do Estado do Rio de Janeiro: UERJ-PMB 90, UERJ-PMB 91a and b; Departamento Nacional de Produção Mineral: DGM 981-P, DGM 981b-P DGM 982-P, and DGM 983-P.

Locality and horizon. The type locality is of Early Cretaceous age (?Aptian), Marizal Formation, in the Tucano Basin, State of Bahia, Northeastern

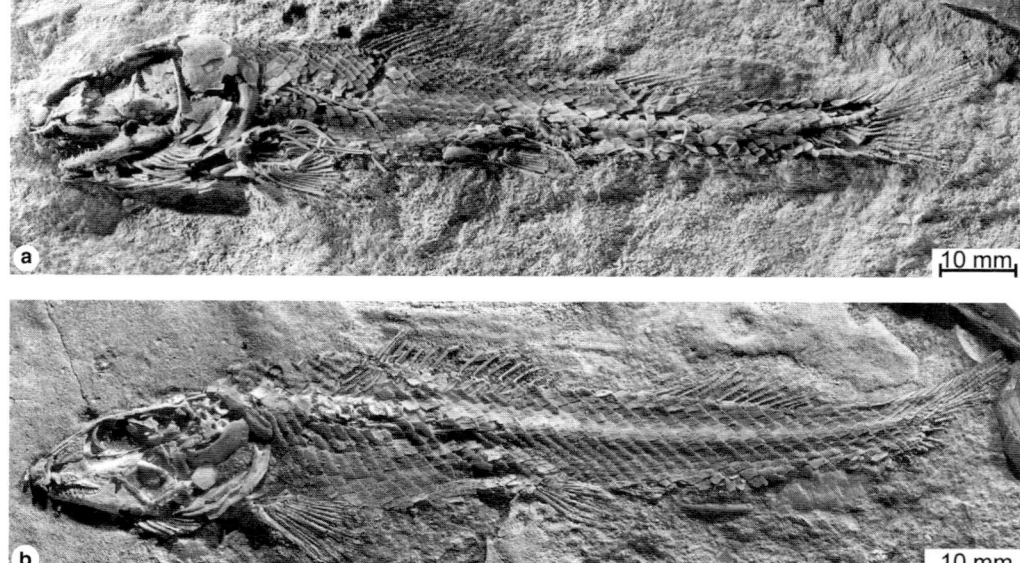

Fig. 2. *Placidichthys bidorsalis* from the Santana Formation, Brazil. (**a**) Holotype MPSC-P 288a. (**b**) Paratype (inverted), UERJ-PMB 300a.

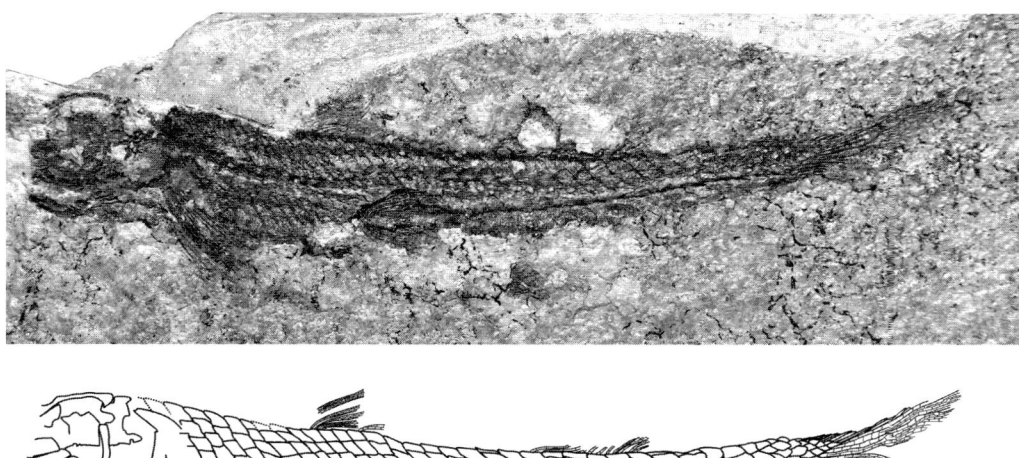

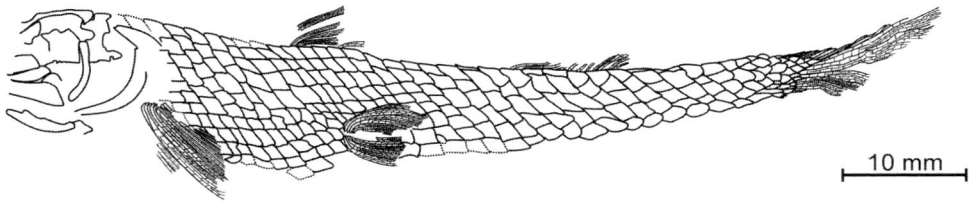

Fig. 3. UERJ-PMB92, holotype of *Placidichthys tucanensis* sp. nov., from the Early Cretaceous (?Aptian) Marizal Formation, Tucano Basin, State of Bahia, northeastern Brazil.

Brazil, at a quarry near the town of Euclides da Cunha. Other specimens were collected from near the Town of Cícero Dantas (Fig. 1).

The strata here are thought to be lagoonal, probably deposited under mixohaline conditions perhaps with intermittent marine connections. The associated fauna is dominated by the teleosts *Clupavus brasiliensis* and *Britoichthys marizalensis*, but also includes *Vinctifer longirostris* and ichthyodectiforms. Rare gastropods and numerous pleocyemata shrimps (Roxo 1940; Beurlen 1950) have also been reported.

Diagnosis. Placidichthys tucanensis sp. nov. differs from the type species, by the following combination of characters: the absence of anal fin; fewer flank scales in the caudal region (4 or 5 in *P. tucanensis* versus 8 or 9 in *P. bidorsalis*); a relatively slender body shape; a post-pelvic portion of body longer.

Etymology. Tucanensis, after the Tucano Basin, where the species occurs.

Description. The holotype of *Placidichthys tucanensis*, sp. nov. is small, with an estimated standard length of 54 mm. The length of the missing part of the head is estimated based on incomplete specimens UERJ-PMB 90 and UERJ-PMB 91(Fig. 4), as well as, on complete specimens of *P. bidorsalis* (see Fig. 2a and b). The body of *P. tucanensis* sp. nov. is more elongated and much more slender than that of *P. bidorsalis*.

Skull. Most of the skull is missing in the holotype. However, the skull roof is exposed partially in dorsal view in specimens DGM 981 and UERJ- PMB91.

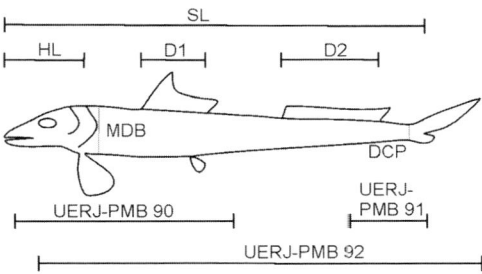

Specimen	Measurements (in mm.)
UERJ-PMB 90	HL, 9.3; D1, 5.0.
UERJ-PMB 91	DCP, 3.3.
UERJ-PMB 92	SL, 54.(estimated); DCP, 2.7; MDB, 7.1.
DGM-P 981 a and b	DCP, 2.5.
DGM-P 982 a and b	DCP, 4.2.
DGM-P 983	DCP, 1.5.

Fig. 4. Measurements of *Placidichthys tucanensis* sp. nov (also see Table 1). SL, standard length; HL, head length; D1, length of dorsal fin 1; D2, length of dorsal fin 2; MDB, maximum depth of the body; DCP, depth of caudal peduncle. The body shape of *P. tucanensis* sp. nov was based on the specimens UERJ-PMB 92 (holotype), UERJ-PMB 90 and UERJ-PMB 91.

The rostral region appears to be relatively slender, with its lateral processes directed caudally. The nasals are large and slightly convex (Fig. 5). The frontals consist of paired and median components. They are wider in the postorbital region of the orbits and posteriorly are sutured to the parietals, which are not easily discernible on their posterior and lateral margins in our material.

The dermosphenotic is preserved in specimen UERJ-PMB92. It makes up the posterior corner of the orbit and, as in *Placidichthys bidorsalis*, seems to be sutured to the skull roof.

The preopercular is crescent-shaped, long and narrow and a sensory canal extends along its entire length. The opercular is slightly deeper than wide, subopercular and interopercular are subtriangular. The gular plate is seen in lateral view in the holotype. A few broken branchiostegal rays are preserved. They are very elongate and thin bones.

The maxilla is long and narrow and, as in the type species, it appears to terminate posterior to the middle of the orbit. The dentary is long and slender. Its posterior part bears an insipient coronoid process.

Except for the hyomandibular, which is a prominent bone, the suspensorium and pterygoid series, although present in the holotype, are not easily

discernible. The quadrate and symplectic are partially visible as impressions in specimen UERJ-PMB 91-b. The quadrate is fan shaped with a well-developed condyle, and the symplectic also has a well-developed condyle. The orientation of these two condyles indicates a double jaw articulation.

Caudal fin. The caudal fin is deeply forked with a considerably longer upper lobe compared to the lower lobe as in *P. bidorsalis*. The upper lobe has six or seven basal fulcra plus at least nine principal rays. The lower lobe has at least two basal fulcra and seven principal rays. The caudal endoskeleton is not preserved.

Paired fins. The posttemporal is elongated with a rounded posterior margin. The supracleithrum is large and elongate; the bone contacts anteriorly the posterolateral corner of the post-temporal and ventrally overlaps the cleithrum. The dorsal limb of cleithrum is more developed than the ventral one. Eleven or 12 pectoral rays are preserved (Fig. 6). As in the type species, the pectoral fin margin is convex. The pelvic bone is elongated and somewhat hourglass in shape. Six to seven pelvic fin rays were counted. There are no fulcra on the anterior border of the paired fins.

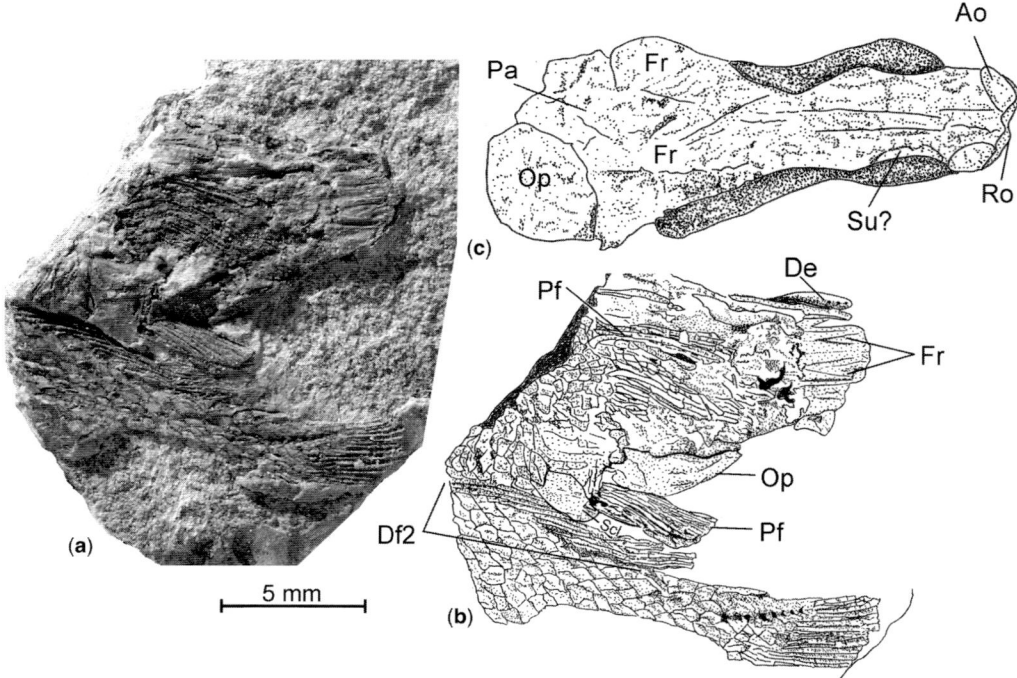

Fig. 5. *Placidichthys tucanensis* from the Marizal Formation. (**a**) and (**b**), DGM 981-P: (**c**) DGM 981b-P. Ao, antorbital: De, dentary: Df2, second dorsal fin; Fr, frontal; Op, opercular; Pa, parietal; Pf, pectoral fin; Ro, rostral; Su, supraorbital.

Dorsal fins. Although incompletely preserved, it is clear that the dorsal fin is subdivided, as in *P. bidorsalis*, (Fig. 2a and b). Its anterior part contains at least 10 rays; whereas the posterior part has about 12 rays. No trace of an anal fin was found in any of the specimens examined. This absence is confirmed by the constant pattern of the scales in the region where the anal fin is expected. The absence of an anal fin is very rare within halecomorphs and is unique within ophiopsids. Absence of the anal fin has been reported in the macrosemiid *Aphanepygus* (Bassani 1879; Bartram 1977).

Squamation. There are at least 41 lateral rows of ganoid-type scales from the supracleithrum to the base of the axial lobe of the caudal fin. The anterior-most scales are deeper than wide; the caudal scales are diamond-shaped.

There is a marked difference in the number of flank scales in the caudal region between *P. tucanensis* and *P. bidorsalis*. The new species presents 4 to 5 flank scales, whilst there are 8 or 9 in the type species.

Discussion

A double jaw articulation is considered as a halecomorph synapomorphy. The presence of ganoid-type scales, from the supracleithrum to the base of the axial lobe of the caudal fin, the deeply forked caudal fin with a considerably longer upper lobe and the presence of a very long dorsal fin divided in two led us to assign the new taxon to *Placidichthys*. Table 1 summarizes the differences between the two species of *Placidichthys*. It is worth noticing that *P. tucanensis* sp. nov. is characterized by its slender body shape and absence of anal fin.

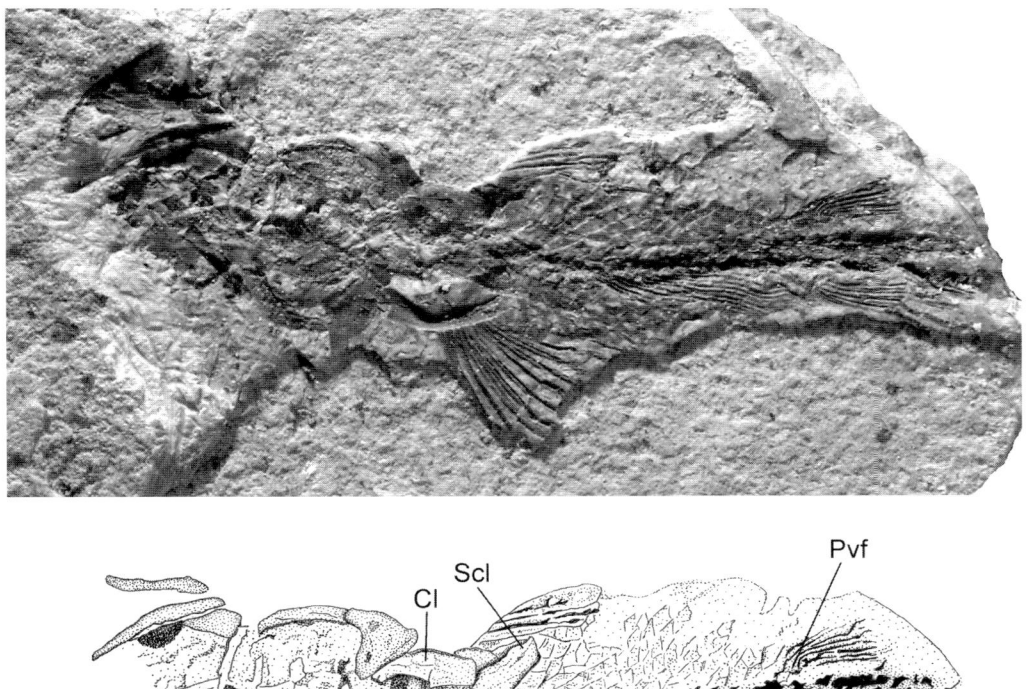

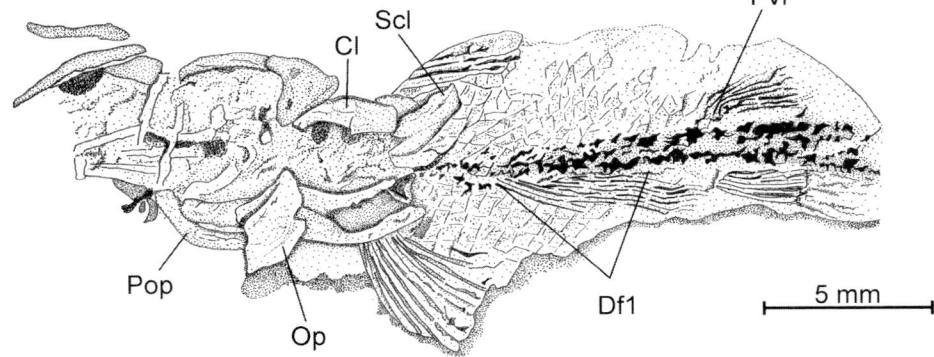

Fig. 6. *Placidichthys tucanensis*, UERJ-PMB 91 from the Marizal Formation. Cl, cleithrum; Df1, first dorsal fin; Op, opercle; Pop, preopercle; Pvf, pelvic fin; Scl, supracleithrum.

Table 1. *Comparison between* Placidichthys *species*

Measurements taken	*Placidichthys bidorsalis*	*Placidichthys tucanensis* sp. nov.
SL (including from anterior nasal tip to most posterior scale)	121.6 mm (based on complete specimens)	54 (estimated)
HL as % of SL	24.6	17
MDB as % of SL	18.9 (just behind the head)	13–14
DCP as % of SL	7.8 (just behind the second dorsal fin)	5
PD1 as % of SL	36.75–56.3	33–48
PV as % of SL	65.5	45
PD2 as % of SL	65–82.2	68–91
PA as % of SL	64–67	Without anal fin
PCFR	14–15	11–12
D1R	16	More than 9
D2R	12–13	More than 7
PVRF	6–7	6–7
AFR	4	Without anal fin
CFR	9U + 7L	4U + 7L
Scale lines on caudal region	8–9	4–5

SL, standard length; HL, head length; MDB, maximum depth of the body; DCP, depth of caudal peduncle; PD1, predorsal length of anterior dorsal fin; PD2, predorsal length of posterior dorsal fin; PA, position of anal fin; PV, position of pelvic fin; PCFR, pectoral fin rays; D1R, rays in the anterior dorsal fin; D2R, rays in the posterior dorsal fin; PVRF, pelvic fin rays; AFR, anal fin rays; CFR, caudal fin rays.

Relationships of Placidichthys *within the family* Ophiopsidae

Following a review of *Ophiopsis*, Bartram (1975) erected the Family Ophiopsidae, including *Macrepistius* Cope, 1894 based on the lateral line extending onto the caudal fin. Later, Applegate (1988) described *Teoichthys* as part of Ophiopsidae and regarded *Heterolepidotus* [synonymous with *Brachyichthys* according to Gardiner 1960], as an ophiopsid. The first phylogenetic study including *Ophiopsis* and its suspected relatives (cf., *Brachyichthys*, *Heterolepidotus*, *Oshunia* and *Ionoscopus*) was by Gardiner *et al.* (1996), who suggested that *Ophiopsis* and *Macrepistius* are sister crown taxa. Grande & Bemis (1998) proposed the Order Ionoscopiformes in which the Ophiopsidae was included and restricted to *Ophiopsis* and *Macrepistius* (Fig. 7)

Brito (2000) described *Placidichthys bidorsalis* as a member of an uncertain family within the Order Ionoscopiformes. Alvarado-Ortega & Espinosa-Arrubarrena (2008) review the interrelationships within this order, recognizing *Ophiopsis*, *Macrepistius* and *Teoichthys* as belonging to Ophiopsidae (Fig. 7). The same authors also suggested the possible inclusion of *Placidichthys* within this family, a taxonomical position also accepted by Brito (2006).

Although it is beyond the scope of the present paper, a comprehensive study of the Family Ophiopsidae is in progress (Alvarado-Ortega & Brito, in prep.). Nevertheless, our analyses show (see Fig. 7) that *Placidichthys* is a well established member of the Ophiopsidae *sensu* Alvarado-Ortega and Espinosa-Arrubarrena (2008) and is probably the sister taxon of the clade *Teoichthys* + *Macrepistius* (Fig. 8).

The phylogenetic position of *Placidichthys* within the Ophiopsidae is difficult to establish, because the monophyly of the genus *Ophiopsis* has been questioned; it shows polymorphic conditions in those characters analyzed by Grande and Bemis (1998) and Alvarado-Ortega and Espinosa-Arrubarrena (2008), and additionally, *Placidichthys* seems not to share synapomorphies with its sister clade *Macrepistius* + *Teoichthys* (Fig. 8). Nevertheless, in the latter three genera there are features that suggest a possible evolutionary trend, including a reduction in the number of scale rows in the flank of the caudal region (Fig. 8, node B). In the caudal peduncle of *Ophiopsis proceras* there are about 14 scale rows (see Grande & Bemis 1998, Fig. 407), whereas there are 11 in *Macrepistius* and *Teoichthys* (see Schaeffer 1960, Fig. 4; Applegate 1988, Fig. 2), 8–9 in *Placidichthys bidorsalis* and just 5 in *P. tucanensis* (Figs 2, 3, 5, 6).

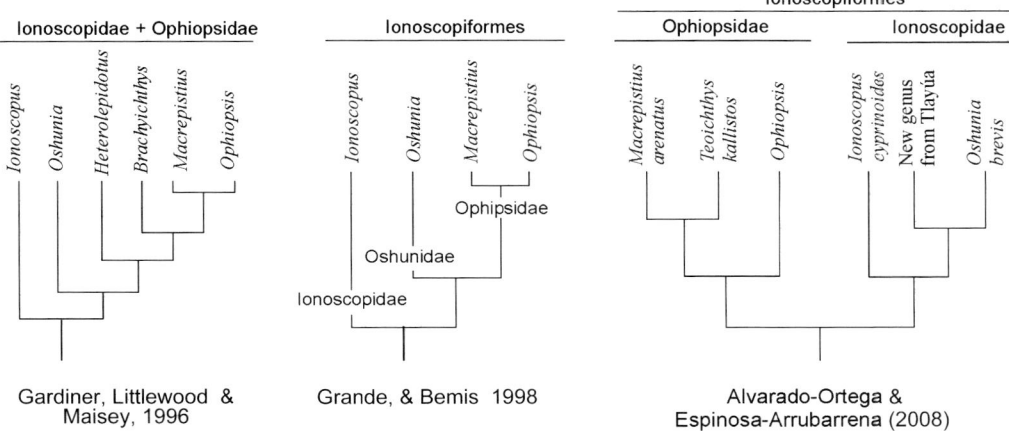

Fig. 7. Phylogenetic interrelationships of the ophiopsid fishes.

The genus Placidichthys, and its significance for a palaeobiogeographical distribution of the family Ophiopsidae

Placidichthys tucanensis sp. nov. From the Marizal Formation represents the earliest known occurrence of this genus, whose type species, *P. bidorsalis*, occurs in the Crato and Santana formations, both within the nearby Araripe Basin. The age of the Santana Formation is considered as Albian, while the age of the Crato Formation is probably Late Aptian (Pons *et al.* 1990). The precise age of the Marizal Formation is still in debate but is probably Aptian (Santos 1985).

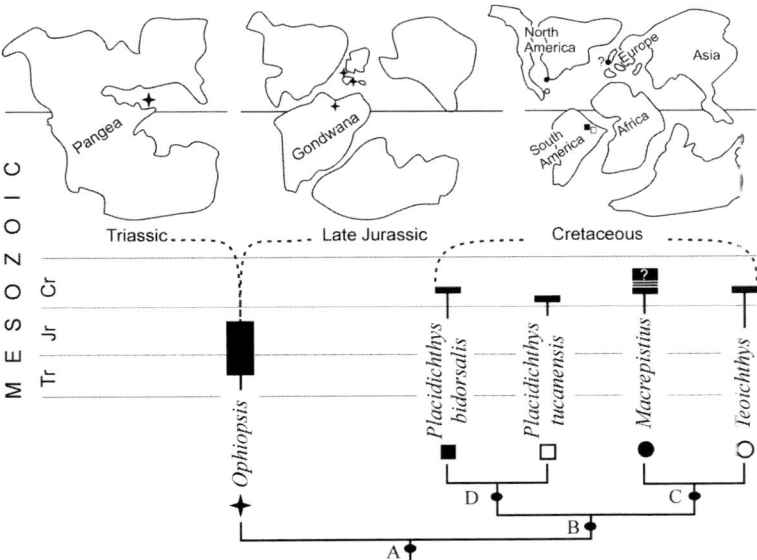

Fig. 8. Hypothesis of the relationships (based on Alvarado-Ortega & Espinosa-Arrubarrena 2008), stratigraphical ranges, and geographical distribution of the members of the Family Ophiopsidae. **Node A**: Short maxilla (which posteriorly is not extended beyond the posterior orbital margin); presence of lateral line ossicles between caudal fin rays; relative short lateral horns of rostral bone; heavy rhomboidal scales. **Node B**: Low number of scales rows in the caudal region (11 or less). **Node C**: Strong ornamentation of dermal skull bones. **Node D**: Presence of two dorsal fins, relatively longer head.

During the Aptian and Albian, South America was under the influence of transgressive events, when epicontinental sea ways apparently extended from the Caribbean Tethys area to the south, reaching several NE basins of Brazil (e.g. Parnaíba, Araripe, Tucano, and Sergipe–Alagoas Basins) (Brito 1997; Maisey 2000). Both, the Marizal and the Crato formations seem therefore to be part of this sequence of marine-influenced deposits. Nevertheless, the Marizal Formation represents a unique lagoonal deposit formed under marine influence over the entire Tucano Basin, whereas the Crato Formation was deposited during only one of several marine transgressions recorded in the Araripe Basin (Martill 1993).

Comparing the ichthyofaunas of the Tucano and Araripe basins, it is remarkable that only one species, *Vinctifer longirostris*, is common to both. The rest of the fauna including *Placidichthys* and the ichthyodectiforms differs at generic level. *Clupavos brasiliensis* and *Britoichthys marizalensis* are unknown outside the Marizal Formation.

On the other hand, a comparison between the fish faunas from the Crato and the Santana formations, both within Araripe Basin, shows several common species, including *Araripelepidotes temnurus*, *Cladocyclus gardneri*, *Santanichthys diasii* and *?Axelrodichthys araripensis* (Brito *et al.* 2005). In contrast, there are no common taxa between the Marizal and the Santana formations. This indicates that the potentially major differences between these faunas are probably related to differences in time of the depositions. Here we regard the Marizal Formation as lower Aptian.

Taking into account the temporal distribution of all the members of the Ophiopsidae, their relationships, as well as the presumed extent of the Tethys Sea including its epicontinental extensions, a plausible palaeobiogeographic scenario can be suggested (Fig. 8).

The development of the Tethys during the Mesozoic, began in the Triassic expanding from the East (Europe and N Africa) to the West (Caribbean and northern South America). Part of the Mediterranean Sea was formed during the Triassic; the Atlantic Ocean between South America and Africa opened during the Early Cretaceous (Aptian–Albian) (Matos 1992); whereas the opening of a Late Jurassic–Early Cretaceous Caribbean marine route was proposed by Gasparini (1985).

The basal genus of the Family Ophiopsidae, *Ophiopsis*, is restricted to the Triassic and Jurassic of the eastern part of Tethys and has been recorded from European and African localities. The oldest species are from the Middle Triassic: *O. lariensis* from Carinthia, Austria (Sieber 1955), and *O.*

lepterus from Perledo, Como, Italy (Belloti 1857). During the Late Jurassic, *Ophiopsis* underwent its highest diversification, resulting in at least seven species: *O. proceras* from Bavaria; *O. penicillatta*, *O. breviceps* and *O. dorsalis* from the Purbeck Beds, England; *O. attenuata* from Cerin and Bavaria; *O. montsechensis* from Montsech, Lerida, Spain; and *O. lepersonnei* from marine strata in Zaire (Bartram 1975).

During the Early Cretaceous the western part of the Tethys was inhabited by at least three ophiopsid genera, namely *Placidichthys*, *Teoichthys* and *Macrepistius*. The fact that they are high specialized fish suggests that they may have originated earlier. *Placidichthys* appears to be confined to the epicontinental seas of Gondwana having evolved into two species, *P. bidorsalis* and *P. tucanensis*. In contrast, the latter two genera have only been recorded from the northwestern region of the Aptian Tethys (Applegate 1988; Schaeffer 1960, 1971). Nevertheless, if we consider *Neorhombolepis* Woodward, 1888 from the Late Cretaceous, English Chalk (which has been regarded as possibly synonymous with, or a close relative of, *Macrepistius*) the range of this group can be extended into the Turonian (Fig. 8).

Conclusion

The presence of a divided dorsal fin is a synapomorphy shared by *Placidichthys tucanensis* sp. nov. and *P. bidorsalis*, the type species of this genus.

Although superficially similar to the type species, *P. tucanensis* sp. nov., is clearly distinguishable on at least four grounds: the absence of an anal fin; the lower number of flank scales in the caudal region; the much slenderer body shape; and the proportions of the body. Additional differences between these species are summarized in Table 1.

Although the monophyly of the Ophiopsidae requires further investigation and much of the phylogenetic interrelationships between its species awaits clarification, the distribution of characters found in the two species of *Placidichthys* suggest that this genus forms a subfamily within the Ophiopsidae.

The species of *Placidichthys* form a sister-taxon of the exclusively Cretaceous taxa *Teoichthys* + *Macrepistius* from the western Tethys.

Both Cretaceous and Western Tethyan ophiopsid groups show a discernible geographical distribution pattern. *Placidichthys* is known only from the Southern margin of the Tethys region (South America), whilst *Teoichthys* and *Macrepistius* are known only from N America and possibly Europe.

This paper is dedicated to Peter L. Forey for his important contributions on palaeoichthyology and systematics during his productive career. We would like to thank M. Richter, L. Cavin, and J. Kriwet for improving the manuscript as well as D. Martill for improving the English style. L. P. Machado, D. Mayrinck and C. R. Amaral helped during fieldwork. D. Serrette and L. P. Machado produced the photographs. This research was supported by a CNPq grant and by UERJ/ FAPERJ's 'Prociência' fellowship awarded to P. M. B. and a Postdoctoral fellowships from CNPq, (processo 151115/2005-2;) awarded to J.A.O.

References

ALVARADO-ORTEGA, J. & ESPINOSA-ARRUBARRENA, L. 2008. A new genus of ionoscopiform fish (Halecomorphi) from the Lower Cretaceous (Albian) lithographic limestones of the Tlayúa Quarry, Puebla, Mexico. *Journal of Paleontology* (in press).

APPLEGATE, S. P. 1988. A new genus and species of a holostean belonging to the Family Ophiopsidae, *Teoichthys kallistos*, from the Cretaceous near Tepexi de Rodríguez, Puebla. *Universidad Nacional Autónoma de México, Instituto de Geología, Revista*, **7**, 200–205.

BARTRAM, A. W. H. 1975. The holotype fish genus *Ophiopsis* Agassiz. *Zoological Journal of Linnean Society*, London, **56**, 183–205.

BARTRAM, A. W. H. 1977. A problematical Upper Cretaceous holostean fish genus *Aphanepygus*. *Journal of Natural History, London*, **11**, 361–370.

BASSANI, F. 1879. Vorläufge Mittheilungen über die Fischfauna der Insel Lesina. *Verhandlungen der Geologischen Reichsanstalt (Staatanstalt–Landesanstalt), Wien*, **1879**, 162–170.

BELLOTI, C. 1857. Descrizione di alcuna nuove specie di pesci fossili di Perledo e di altre localita lombarde. *In*: STOPPANI, A. (ed.) *Studii Geologici e Paleontologici sulla Lombardia*. Milano, Italia, 419–438.

BEURLEN, K. 1950. Alguns restos de crustáceos decápodas d'água doce fósseis do Brasil. *Anais da Academia Brasileira de Ciências, Rio de Janeiro*, **22**, 453–459.

BRITO, I. M. 1979. Bacias sedimentares e formações póspaleozóicas do Brasil. *Editora Interciência*, Rio de Janeiro.

BRITO, P. M. 1997. Révision des Aspidorhynchidae (Pisces-Actinopterygii) du Mésozoïque: ostéologie et relations phylogénétiques. *Geodiversitas, Paris*, **19**, 681–772.

BRITO, P. M. 2000. A new halecomorph with two dorsal fins, *Placidichthys bidorsalis* n. g., n. sp. (Actinopterygii: Halecomorphi) from the Lower Cretaceous of the Araripe Basin, northeast Brazil. *Comptes Rendus, Académie des sciences, Paris, Sciences de la Terre et des planètes*, **331**, 749–754.

BRITO, P. M. 2006. Considerações sobre os "holósteos" do Cretáceo da parte ocidental do Continente Gondwana. *In*: GALLO, V., BRITO, P. M., SILVA, H. A. & FIGUEIREDO, F. J. (eds) *Paleontologia de Vertebrádos: Artigos e Trabalhos Temáticos*. Interciência, Rio de Janeiro, 51–68.

BRITO, P. M., MAYRINCK, D., LEAL, M. E. C. & MARTILL, D. M. 2005. An overview of the Crato Formation ichthyofauna. *In*: POYATO-ARIZA, F. J. (ed.) *Fourth International Meeting on Mesozoic Fishes - Systematics, Homology and Nomenclature*. Ediciones Universidad Autónoma de Madrid, Spain, 47–49.

COPE, E. D. 1872. Observations on the systematic relations of the fishes. *Proceedings of the American Association for the Advancement of Sciences*, **20**, 317–343.

COPE, E. D. 1894. New and little known Paleozoic and Mesozoic fishes. *Journal of the Acaaemy of Natural Sciences, Philadelphia*, **9**, 427–448.

FIGUEIREDO, F. J. 2004. A new Euteleostean fish from the Lower Cretaceous of Tucano Basin, North-Eastern Brazil. *Arquivos do Museu Nacional, Rio de Janeiro*, **62**, 293–307.

GARDINER, B. G. 1960. A revision of certain actinopterygian and coelacanth fishes, chiefly from the Lower Lias. *Bulletin of the British Museum (Natural History), Geology*, **37**, 173–428.

GARDINER, B. G., LITTLEWOOD, D. T. J. & MAISEY, J. G. 1996. Interrelationships of basal neopterygians. *In*: STIASSNY, M. L. J., PARENTI, L. R. & JOHNSON, G. D. (eds) *Interrelationships of Fishes*. Academic Press. San Diego, California, 117–146.

GASPARINI, Z. B. 1985. Los reptiles marinos jurásicos de América del Sur. *Ameghiniana, Buenos Aires*, **22**, 23–34.

GRANDE, L. & BEMIS, W. E. 1998. A comprehensive phylogenetic study of amiid fishes (Amiidae) based on comparative skeletal anatomy. An empirical search for interconnected patterns of natural history. *Journal of Vertebrate Paleontology*, **18**, 1–690.

HUXLEY, T. H. 1861. Preliminary essay upon the systematic arrangement of the fishes of the Devonian epoch. *Memoirs of the Geological Survey of the United Kingdom, Decade*, **10**, 1–40.

MAISEY, J. G. 1991. *Ophiopsis*. *In*: MAISEY, J. G. (ed.) *Santana Fossils*. Tropical Fish Hobbyist, New York.

MAISEY, J. G. 2000. Continental break up and the distribution of fishes of Western Gondwana during the Early Cretaceous. *Cretaceous Research*, **21**, 281–314.

MARTILL, D. M. 1993. *Fossils of the Santana and Crato Formations, Brazil*. The Palaeontological Association, London.

MATOS, R. M. D. 1992. The north-east Brazilian rift system. *Tectonics*, **11**, 766–791.

PONS, D., BERTHOU, P. Y. & CAMPOS, D. A. 1990. Quelques observations sur la palynologie de l'Aptien supérieur et de l'Albien du Bassin d'Araripe (N.E. du Brésil). *In*: CAMPOS, D. A., BRITO, P. M., VIANA, M. S. & BEURLEN, K. (eds) *I Sinpósio sobre a Bacia do Araripe e Bacias interiors do Nordeste*. Departamento Nacional de Produção Mineral, Crato, 241–252.

ROXO, M. G. O. 1940. Preliminary note on fossil crustacea from Bahia, Brazil. *Anais da Academia Brasileira de Ciências, Rio de Janeiro*, **7**, 279–280.

SANTOS DA, R. S. & VALENÇA, J. G 1968. A Formação Santana e sua Paleoictiofauna. *Anais da Academia Brasileira de Ciências, Rio de Janeiro*, **40**, 339–360.

SANTOS DA, R. S. 1985. *Clupavus brasiliensis* n. sp. (Teleostei, Clupeiformes) do Cretáceo inferior-Formação Marizal, Estado da Bahia. *In*: CAMPOS, D. A., FERREIRA, C. S., BRITO, I. M. & VIANA, C. F. (eds) *Coletânia de Trabalhos Paleontológicos*. Departamento Nacional de Produção Mineral, Brasilia, 155–159.

SANTOS DA, R. S. 1990. *Vinctifer longirostris*, do Cretáceo inferior da Formação Marizal, Estado da Bahia, Brasil. *Anais da Academia Brasileira de Ciências, Rio de Janeiro*, **62**, 251–260.

SCHAEFFER, B. 1960. The Cretaceous holostean fish *Macrepistius*. *American Museum Novitates*, 2011, 1–18.

SCHAEFFER, B. 1971. The braincase of the holostean fish *Macrepistius*, with comments on neurocranial ossification in the Actiopterygii. *American Museum Novitates*, **2796**, 1–24.

SIEBER, R. 1955. Ein bemerkenswerter Fischfund aus der Mitteltrias Kärtens. *Carinthia*, **2**, 91–96.

WOODWARD, A. S. 1888. A synopsis of the vertebrate fossils of the English Chalk. *Proceedings of the Geological Association of London*, **10**, 273–338.

Cretaceous characiform fishes (Teleostei: Ostariophysi) from Northern Tethys: description of new material from the Maastrichtian of Provence (Southern France) and palaeobiogeographical implications

O. OTERO, X. VALENTIN & G. GARCIA

Laboratoire de Géobiologie, Biochronologie et Paléontologie humaine, CNRS UMR 6046, Faculté des Sciences Fondamentales et Appliquées, Université de Poitiers, 40 av. du Recteur Pineau, F-86 022 Poitiers Cedex, France (e-mail: olga.otero@univ-poitiers.fr)

Abstract: The order Characiformes (Teleostei: Otophysi) is one of the most diverse freshwater fish groups. It contains around 1400 living species in South and Central America and Africa. Their fossil record starts in the Cretaceous on both continents and also in Europe. Here, we describe and discuss the occurrences of new characiform fish teeth from Provence (Maastrichtian, S. France). Five morphological types are recognized. They belong to possibly three different taxa, and they are regarded as Characiformes indet. However, two of them have resemblances to alestin fishes and could be related to the African family Alestidae. The characiform fishes from Provence are among the oldest known in Europe, together with a freshwater characiform fish occurring in Romania, and the recently described marine fish *Sorbinicharax* from Italy. The biogeographical history of characiform fishes has been intensively discussed during the last three decades. The group is generally accepted to be Gondwanan and its diversification linked with the break-up of this continent, with two main scenarios depending on whether the group is archaeo- or telolimnic. Some authors also propose a Pangaean origin. The recent discoveries of *Sorbinicharax* and of the fossils from Provence change our view on the Cretaceous characiform diversity and their early ecology, and they also enable us to re-evaluate the proposed biogeographical scenarios, reinforcing the hypothesis of the telolimny of the group.

The order Characiformes (Teleostei: Otophysi) includes the well-known tetras and piranhas. It contains around 1400 living species. About 1200 are South and Central American, the rest are African. Research over the last decade has hardly improved our knowledge of their intrarelationships; but many nodes of their phylogenetic tree are still debated and the monophyly of the order Characiformes itself is contested by some authors. For example, Peng *et al.* (2006) suggest that the order Gymnotiformes nests within the order Characiformes on the basis of molecular data. However, most specialists now agree about the monophyly of several taxa within the order, notably the four African families, i.e. Distichodontidae and Citharinidae which are also considered to be sister-groups (Vari 1979; Fink & Fink 1981; Ortí & Meyer 1997), Hepsetidae (monogeneric with *Hepsetus*), and Alestidae (Paugy 1986, 1990; Murray & Stewart 2002; Zanata & Vari 2005). The family Alestidae corresponds to the African members of the non-monophyletic Characidae *sensu* Greenwood *et al.* (1966), the polyphyly of which is now widely accepted (e.g. Buckup 1998; Lucena & Menezes 1998; Tolédo-Piza 2000; Zanata & Vari 2005). The family Characidae as currently defined includes only American fishes. Whether they are based on morphological (Vari 1979, 1995; Buckup 1998) or DNA studies (Ortí & Meyer 1997; Calcagnotto *et al.* 2005), the various phylogenetic analyses agree about the sister relationship of African and South American taxa in three cases and also about the fact that, of the transatlantic groups they form, one sits at the stem of the tree of the order and the two others at its crown.

(1) Distichodontidae + Citharinidae (African) is the sister group of all the other characiform fishes (with basal South American members), except for Uj (1990) who proposed a sister relation with the family Alestidae, thus forming with Erythrinidae, Hepsetidae and Ctenoluciidae the sister group of all the other characiform fishes.

(2) The families Hepsetidae (African) and Erythrinidae (South American) form a monophyletic group either alone (Uj 1990; Ortí & Meyer 1997), or including other families, i.e. Ctenoluciidae (Vari 1979; Buckup 1998), Ctenoluciidae and Lebiasinidae (Calcagnotto *et al.* 2005). Roberts (1972) remarks that among characiforms, only hepsetids and erythrinids

From: CAVIN, L., LONGBOTTOM, A. & RICHTER, M. (eds) *Fishes and the Break-up of Pangaea*.
Geological Society, London, Special Publications, **295**, 155–164.
DOI: 10.1144/SP295.10   0305-8719/08/$15.00 © The Geological Society of London 2008.

are ambush predators with the particular behaviour of nest building and parental care.

(3) The family Alestidae (African) is the sister-group of *Acestrorhynchus* and forms a monophyletic group with Ctenoluciidae and *Brycon* + *Salminus* according to Ortí & Meyer (1997) and to Calcagnotto *et al.* (2005), whereas it is the sister group of *Brycon* + *Chalceus* according to Lucena (1993), and of *Brycon* and many others including *Acestrorhynchus*, Hepsetidae and Erythrinidae according to Buckup (1998). Uj (1990) only proposed a sister relation with the African monophyletic group Distichodontidae + Citharinidae.

Because of the Afro-South American distribution of living characiform fishes and the age of the fossils, a Gondwanan origin of the order is usually accepted (see also discussion). Depending on the ability of early members to stand salty waters, two different palaeobiogeographical scenarios have been proposed.

That living characiform fishes are strictly freshwater fishes can be interpreted as reflecting the archaeolimny of the group (the archaeo- and telolimny were defined by Patterson in 1975, according to primarily or secondarily fresh water habitat). This implies a vicariant scenario for the characiform fish historical biogeography. This hypothesis was first proposed by Lundberg (1993), who stressed two main points: (1) the diversification of the main taxa in the order Characiformes might have taken place on Gondwana before its break-up; and (2) early African characiform fishes would have to have suffered great extinctions in order to explain the lack of the many sister-groups of the South American families on this continent. A vicariant interpretation could also involve a primary break-up of Gondwana with possible temporary secondary connections between the lands formed, rather than just a unique break-up event. This would allow a better explanation of the differences between the American and African diversity and also the existence of three trans-Atlantic groups, due to three vicariant events (Patterson 1984; Fink *et al.* 1984; Maisey 1993, 2000; Lundberg *et al.* 1998).

However, a second interpretative scenario takes shape if the order is telolimnic. The hypothesis of the telolimny of the group is supported by the brackish or marine habitat of several basal otophysan fishes and a few extinct characiform fishes: *Lusitanichthys* and *Salminops* (Cenomanian, Portugal), which are considered to be basal characiform fishes (Gayet 1981, 1985) or basal ostariophysan fishes possibly at the stem of the Otophysi (e.g. Fink & Fink 1981; Fink *et al.* 1984; Patterson

1993); *Chanoides* (Campano-Maastrichtian and Eocene, Italy), which is a primitive otophysan fish (Patterson 1984; Taverne 2005); *Santanichthys* (Aptian, Brazil), which is the earliest otophysan fish known yet, and should possibly be placed at the stem of the order Characiformes (Filleul & Maisey 2004); *Sorbinicharax* (Campano-Maastrichtian, Italy), which is a characiform fish recently described from marine Tethyan waters (Taverne 2003); and some Eocene and Oligocene characiform fossils from France that are described from brackish environments (Cappetta *et al.* 1972; Gaudant 1980). Moreover, many gonorynchiform fishes and the representatives of two siluriform families inhabit coastal marine waters or brackish waters: the Plotosidae and the Ariidae to which are related some of the oldest catfish fossils. In the opinion of some authors (e.g. Chardon 1967; Gayet 1982, 1986), this reflects the telolimny of the order Characiformes (among others), and supports the hypothesis of marine dispersal between the newly separated continents of the fragmented Gondwana. Based on the same evidence, Calcagnotto *et al.* (2005) also call on a probable early ability of characiform fishes to withstand salty waters, to build an alternate palaeobiogeographical scenario to the vicariance with possible migration from one plate to another. They note that this scenario could appear to be relatively more parsimonious, *contra* Patterson (1984), Fink *et al.* (1984), and Filleul & Maisey (2004), among others.

Here, we describe and discuss the attribution of new characiform fishes from Provence (Maastrichtian, Southern France). They are among the oldest known, notably in Europe, together with the Campano-Maastrichtian marine fish *Sorbinicharax* from Italy (Taverne 2003), and a freshwater Maastrichtian characiform fish reported from Romania (Grigorescu *et al.* 1985). For a long time, the Romanian occurrence was the only one known north of the Tethys Sea for the Cretaceous, and it was logically interpreted as resulting from the trans-Tethyan dispersal(s) that affected vertebrate continental faunas during the Late Cretaceous (e.g. Gheerbrant & Rage 2006).

Geological context and age

The characiform teeth were collected by one of us (X.V.) from two new localities of the Provence Basin: Vérane and Les Pennes-Mirabeau (Fig. 1). The fossiliferous deposits are composed of marly horizons with carbonate rich palaeosols (nodules and root traces). They are located just above the Rognac Limestone (dated as Maastrichtian by Garcia & Vianey-Liaud 2001). The material has been obtained by screen-washing the deposits.

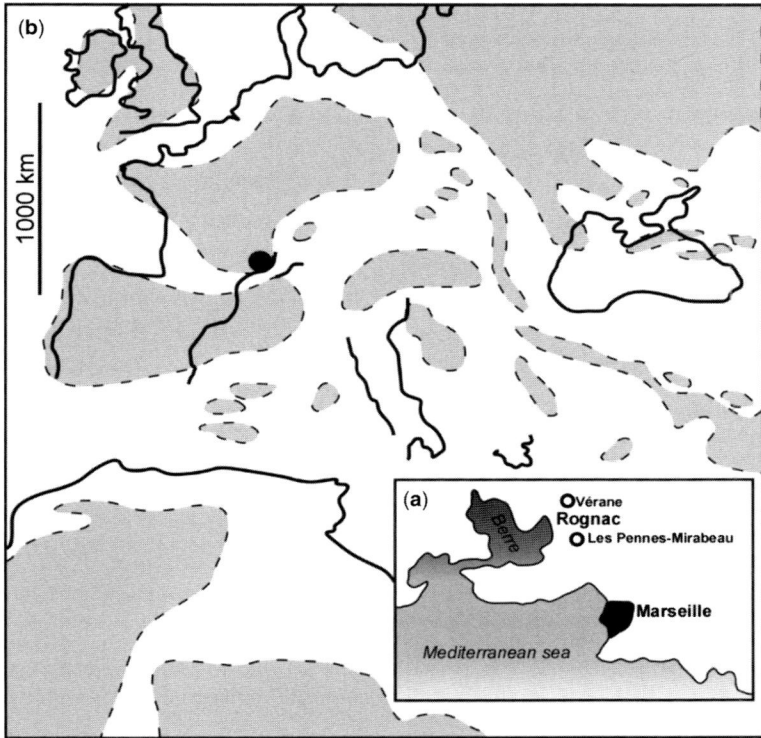

Fig. 1. Location of the Cretaceous sites with characiform fishes in the Bouches-du-Rhône, Southern France (**a**), and location on a schematic paleogeographic map of the European archipelago in the Maastrichtian (**b**), after Odin & Lamaurelle (2001).

The ichthyofossils are found in association with numerous small fossil remains including fragments of bones and teeth of dinosaurs, crocodilians, and squamates, turtle shells, eggshells, charophytes and gastropods. Together with the isolated teeth, which are attributed to characiform fishes, pharyngeal teeth, ganoid scales and bone fragments indicate a diverse ichthyofauna. The fauna is clearly continental and its aquatic component is probably fresh water. However, the palaeo-coastline is very close (Fig. 1) and we cannot yet exclude total or partial presence of brackish-water components until the faunal study is completed.

The specimens described and figured in this paper are housed in the collection of the University of Poitiers (France) with the abbreviations VRN (Vérane) and LMI (Les Pennes–Mirabeau).

Comparative material examined are specimens of living African species, with multicuspidate teeth, belonging to the family Alestidae (*Alestes baremoze*, *Alestes dentex*, *Brycinus macrolepidatus*, *Brycinus nurse*), and fossil specimens from the Oligocene of Oman and from the Miocene of Chad.

Description and comparison of the teeth

There are six teeth from Vérane (VER-03-001). They are multicuspidate and molariform, but they are too worn and fragmented to be described properly. Les Pennes–Mirabeau yielded around fifty multicuspidate teeth. Half of these are also too worn or fragmented to be described (LMI-003-11). However the rest are better-preserved and can be referred to five different morphological types. Most of them have an elongated crown in occlusal view. The triangular cusps are aligned on one row forming a crest along the main axis of the tooth, the cusps decreasing in size from the middle. A vertical section in the crown, perpendicular to the crest (and crown) main axis shows a concave face and a straight one. By analogy with the living alestin fishes, which they globally resemble, the concave face would be internal on the jaw bone (in those fishes, the teeth are organised in two rows on each bone). Among these elongated teeth, with cusps organized in a cutting crest, we distinguish three morphological types based on the number of cusps, on their shape and on the size and shape of the whole tooth (morphological types 1 to 3). The few other well-preserved teeth from les Pennes–Mirabeau belong to two other morphological types.

Morphological type 1 (Fig. 2a, b)

Nine teeth belong to the morphological type 1: LMI–03–001 (1 tooth, Fig. 2a), 002 (1 tooth, Fig. 2b), 003 (7 teeth).

These are teeth with the crown elongated in occlusal view and with five cusps forming a sharp triangular cutting crest, the main central cusp being much bigger than the others. The cusps are not conical but flattened along the axis of the cutting edge. They decrease in size, symmetrically (Fig. 2a) or not (Fig. 2b) on both sides of the main cusp. When the tooth is asymmetrical, one of the lateral cusps is very reduced (Fig. 2b), possibly due to chewing wear. The teeth of the morphological type 1 are between 1 and 2 mm high. They look like an oral tooth from the Middle Miocene of San-San (Gaudant 1996, fig. 6) and also to a tooth from the Oligocene fish *Eurocharax tourainei* (Gaudant 1979, pl.1.6), but the cusps are conical in the latter species. Such multicuspidate teeth exist in some *Alestes* fishes. They also resemble to some fossil tetragonopterid-related teeth, particularly those from the Miocene of Ecuador figured by Roberts (1974), rather than those from the Palaeocene of Bolivia figured by Gayet (1991), in which the main cusp is even bigger than in our material.

Morphological type 2 (Fig. 2c)

Five teeth belong to the morphological type 2: LMI–03–004 (1 tooth, Fig. 2c), 005 (4 teeth).

This morphological type is characterized by a crown with the presence of five or six cusps, nearly equal in size, forming the cutting edge. However, one main cusp can be distinguished in the middle of the crest. The cusps are slightly flattened along the crest axis. They give to the crown a smoothly bent overall shape (Fig. 2c). The teeth are more than 2 mm in height. They resemble some multicuspidate teeth from the Oligocene of Oman (Otero & Gayet 2001). They also resemble the rhoadsin-related Bolivian fossil teeth, which also have a flat and concave vertical section and several cusps nearly equal in size along a crest (Gayet 1991). However, the latter are much smaller and with no distinguishable main cusp.

Morphological type 3 (Fig. 2d)

Ten teeth belong to the morphological type 3: LMI–03–006 (1 tooth, Fig. 2d), 007 (9 teeth).

These are symmetrical, tricuspidate teeth with a central much bigger main cusp. The lateral cusps project on both sides of the crown. These teeth are smaller than 1 mm in height. Tricuspidate small teeth are frequently observed in alestid fishes notably at the external row of the upper jaw of adult alestins. In *Hydrocynus*, the adults show unicuspidate teeth but the juveniles have tricuspidate teeth (Roberts 1967; Brewster 1986). Teeth with such a shape have also been observed in Tertiary French and Omanese fossils (Capetta *et al.* 1972, fig. 8; Otero & Gayet 2001, fig. 4c, d). On the contrary, the tricuspidate teeth that exist in the fossil *Sindacharax* have a median cusp that is dramatically dominant (Stewart 2003), and the tooth general shape is molariform.

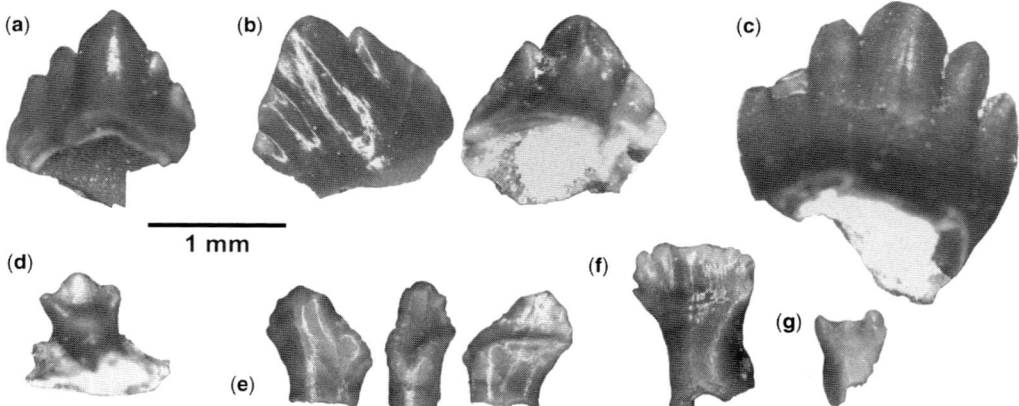

Fig. 2. Characiform teeth from the Maastrichtian deposits of Les Pennes-Mirabeau (Southern France): (**a**) LMI–03–001; (**b**) LMI–03–002, morphological type 1; (**c**) LMI–03–004, morphological type 2; (**d**) LMI–03–006, morphological type 3; (**e**) LMI–03–008, morphological type 4; (**f**) LMI–03–09; (**g**) LMI–03–010, morphological type 5. (**a, c, d, f, g**) in internal views only, (**b**) in external and internal views, (**e**) in external, lateral and internal views.

Morphological type 4 (Fig. 2e)

One tooth belongs to the morphological type 4: LMI–03–008 (Fig. 2e).

In occlusal view, the tooth has an oval, elongated crown with rounded cusps that border both margins of a central depression. The cusps are not at the same height on both margins, but form a triangular wall on one margin and a smooth low pad along the opposite side (Fig. 2e). The tooth is about 1mm in height. Some similar teeth from the Eocene of S France (Cappetta *et al.* 1972, fig. 15) and from the Oligocene of Oman (Otero & Gayet 2001) show a similar overall organization of the cusps in two rows. It also resembles one tooth of *Sindacharax mutetii* figured in occusal view by Stewart (2003, fig. 3.13). However, in all these latter cases the whole tooth is low with the two cusp rows being the same height.

Morphological type 5 (Fig. 2f, g)

Two teeth belong to the morphological type 5: LMI–03–09 (1 tooth, Fig. 2f), 010 (1 tooth, Fig. 2g).

These multicuspidate teeth have a high crown which is narrow at its base and distally enlarged in a cutting edge. One shows three, the other a dozen very small, smooth cusps roughly equal in size and aligned along the cutting edge (Fig. 2f, g). They do not resemble those usually found in the characiform fossil record from Europe. They resemble the *Parodon* teeth drawn by Roberts (1974, fig. 6), and also in their general shape the South American *Leporinus* (Roberts 1974, figs 4, 5).

Each morphological type shows affinities with several different taxa, but no tooth provides clear character that enables us to unequivocally refer it to any extinct or extant known taxa. So, we prefer to regard the teeth Characiformes indet., and suggest that morphological types 1–3, type 4 and type 5 respectively probably belong to three different taxa. We note that morphological types 1–3 and type 4 resemble alestid-like and alestid fishes, notably certain fossils from Europe and extant fishes from Africa. However, types 1–3 also resemble some South American taxa, and type 5 resembles only South American fishes.

Discussion and conclusion

For a long time, the Cretaceous characiform fossil record in Europe was limited to a freshwater characiform fish reported in Romania (Grigorescu *et al.* 1985). This poor fossil record is highly improved with the discovery of at least the three probable fossil characiform fishes from the Maastrichtian of Provence described here, together with that of *Sorbinicharax* in the Campano-Maastrichtian of Nardo, Italy (Taverne 2003). To assess whether these recent findings support one or other of the biogeographical scenarios proposed for the order Characiformes, we first review the fossil record according to two main aspects: (1) how confident are the taxonomic inferences for fossil isolated teeth; and (2) what is the succession through time of characiform fishes in South America, Africa, and more particularly in Europe, including their known habitat.

Characiform fossils and the knowledge of their past diversity

Multicuspidate fish teeth occur on the jaw of some characiform taxa, so fossil multicuspidate teeth are either referred to Characiformes indet., or to certain extant families, or even to fossil taxa. Most of the time, fossil teeth are found isolated. However, they are sometimes found *in situ* on the jaw bone and, in a few cases, in association with the skeleton. In the latter case, the attribution to the order is ascertained by the presence of a Weberian apparatus of characiform-type. But, because the bones of the characiform fishes are fragile and rarely preserved, the fossil record is mostly composed of isolated teeth. We know very little about the odontogenesis of the multicuspidate teeth and about the possible homologies and potential phylogenetical signification of their patterns and structures. Recent studies (Murray 2004; Trapani *et al.* 2005) indicate that in some characiform fishes at least, the multicuspidate teeth do not result from unicuspidate tooth fusion, as it was considered for a long time (Roberts 1967). They are more similar in structure and development to mammalian molars (Trapani *et al.* 2005). From their own observations and the data they found in literature, these authors note a relatively high polymorphism within living species and also during a single individual life time. These also question the balance between the morphological constraints (jaw growth), the impact of dietary changes during ontogeny and the developmental scheme of the dentition itself. The taxonomic inferences based on teeth resemblance are therefore weakly supported, notably for fossils found in provinces where the fossil record is discontinuous and where no extant members are present. That is exemplified by the difficulty to assign, or to refer with confidence, the teeth from the Maastrichtian of Provence to any fossil or living taxa. In contrast, certain extremely fragmentary fossils consisting of isolated teeth and jaw elements from Africa and South America can be confidently identified, sometimes at a generic or even at a specific level within extant or extinct families (e.g. Stewart 2003; Gayet *et al.* 2003).

Finally, whatever the number of taxa present in the Maastrichtian of Provence, and despite their resemblance to various extant and fossil alestid teeth, their accurate taxonomic attribution is not yet possible. We only can suspect affinities with the Alestidae. This is also the case for the other isolated fossil alestid-like multicuspidate teeth from the Tertiary of Europe (see below). Their relationships with each other also remain unknown.

Fossil record and ecology of early characiform fishes

The exceptionally well-preserved *Santanichthys* from the Aptian of Brazil is the earliest otophysan fish known and it was probably a marine or brackish fish. According to Filleul & Maisey (2004), it possibly should be placed at the stem of the order Characiformes, but they acknowledge that this attribution is controversial. If this assertion is accepted, it would represent a significant temporal extension for the characiform fossil record, since positively identified characiform fossil fishes are found up to now in Africa, South America and also in Europe only since the Late Cretaceous.

The oldest characiform known up to now is from Africa. Werner (1994) describes and figures one characiform-like tooth in the Cenomanian of the Wadi Milk Formation (Northern Sudan). The tooth is broken, but it is molariform in shape. Dutheil (1999) reports the presence of a probable characiform fish (fam. & gen. indet.) in the continental Cenomanian deposits of Kem Kem (SE Morocco), based on some isolated vertebrae and two small loose teeth that exhibit morphological similarities with characiform fishes, i.e. a molariform shape with a couple of acuminate tubercles. In the Paleogene, African data are rare, particularly when considering the living diversity and distribution in the African fresh waters. Multicuspidate alestid-like teeth are reported from the Paleocene in Morocco (Cappetta *et al.* 1978), Eocene in Algeria (Mahboudi *et al.* 1984), Oligocene in Somalia (van Couvering 1977) and in the Arabian Peninsula (Micklich & Roscher 1990; Otero & Gayet 2001). Murray (2003) described *Mahengecharax carrolli* from the Middle Eocene of Tanzania on the basis of an articulated skeleton (the only known in Africa), but no tooth is preserved. The attribution of *Mahengecharax* to the order Characiformes is contradicted by Zanata & Vari (2005). The four living families (Hepsetidae, Citharinidae, Distichodontidae and Alestidae) are present in the African Neogene deposits. This Neogene record is detailed in Stewart (2001),

to which should be added the data of Brunet *et al.* (2000) and Vignaud *et al.* (2002). All the fossil African characiform fishes are from freshwater environments.

In South America, the oldest characiform fishes come from the Maastrichto-Danian Formation el Molino. They are known by their incomplete skulls, Weberian apparatus, isolated dentaries, premaxillae and other bony elements, and by numerous loose teeth (Gayet & Meunier 1998). The conical teeth belong to erythrinids, whereas molariform and multicuspidate teeth are attributed to serrasalmins, tetragonopterinins, and rhoadsiinins (Gayet 1991; Gayet & Meunier 1998; Gayet *et al.* 2001, 2003). However, Patterson (1993) prefers to keep at least some of these in Characiformes *incertae sedis*. After the Cretaceous, the South American fossil record mostly consists of isolated teeth from the Miocene of Ecuador (Roberts 1974), Colombia (Lundberg *et al.* 1986), Argentina (Cione 1986), and Brazil (Monsch 1998; Gayet *et al.* 2003). All the fossil South American characiform fishes are freshwater fishes.

In Europe, *Sorbinicharax verraesi* is described from articulated skeletons collected in the Campano-Maastrichtian Italian site of Nardó, Italy (Taverne 2003). This marine characiform fish has unicuspidate teeth and, according to Taverne, belongs to its own family, which is supposed to be basal in the order (Taverne 2003). Cretaceous multicuspidate teeth from Europe were collected in the Maastrichtian deposits of Provence (S France) in Vérane and Les Pennes – Mirabeau (this paper). Grigorescu *et al.* (1985) referred teeth, found in the probably Maastrichtian deposits of the Hateg Basin (Romania), to Characidae indet. (should be considered Characiformes indet.). Multicuspidate alestid-like teeth are recorded in the Ypresian deposits from the London and Paris Basins (several localities), Languedoc (S France), Sardinia, and Spain (Cappetta *et al.* 1972; Cappetta & Thaler 1974; Patterson 1975; de la Peña 1993, 1995). Monod & Gaudant (1998) erect the genus *Alestoides* to which they relate part of this material. The Oligocene characiform record is limited to *Eurocharax tourainei* described by Gaudant (1979, 1980). This fossil species from Var (S France) is known by both its skeleton and multicuspidate teeth. The youngest characiform fish known in Europe comes from the Middle Miocene of Sansan (S France), from where Gaudant (1996) described six morphological types of tooth attributed to cf. *Alestes*, and from the Late Miocene of Portugal (Antunes *et al.* 1995). The early basal characiform *Sorbinicharax* (Taverne 2003) is a marine fish, and Eocene and Oligocene alestid-like fishes inhabited brackish environments

(Cappetta *et al.* 1972; Gaudant 1980), whereas others lived in fresh waters.

The Characiformes fossil record in Europe is discontinuous and their presence is only ascertained during short time periods in the Maastrichtian, Eocene, Oligocene and Miocene. However, whether their presence on the European continent was continuous, and not preserved in the fossil record, or truly discontinuous, cannot be inferred from any phylogenetical data.

Palaeobiogeography

The reconstruction of the paleobiogeographical history of a group should include what is known about its phylogeny, the available ecological data including that for extinct members, and the estimated dating of its origin and of the main diversifications within the group, all together with the palaeogeography of land masses. According to the estimated age of the order Characiformes, they have either a Pangaean or a Gondwanan origin.

A Pangaean origin means that the order diversifies on the supercontinent, before that Laurasia is clearly separated from Gondwana by an active margin which occurs around 160 Ma in the Callovian (Dercourt *et al.* 1993). This hypothesis is supported by few authors. Most recently, Peng *et al.* (2006) estimate through molecular study that, except for the Gymnotiformes, the otophysan orders originate before a mean estimated age of 170 Ma. It is not the aim of this paper to discuss the phylogeny and the estimated ages of divergence times they obtained. However, we underline the limits and also the interest of the proposal of a Pangaean origin by these authors: (1) this hypothesis implies that the order Characiformes (among others) originate much earlier than the first fossil occurrence: more than 40 Ma before *Santanichthys* which is the earliest known otophysan; (2) no Laurasian fossil evidence supports this hypothesis; (3) it does not explain the known fossil and living distribution and diversity of characiform fishes (see Introduction); (4) the early otophysan ecology is not taken into account. Nevertheless, their proposal has the advantage to call attention to the importance of new fossil discoveries, the necessity for a closer study of the fossil record itself and the progress due to reconsidering and clarifying systematic attributions. For instance, if *Santanichthys* is a characiform fish, this would imply a significant temporal extension for the order and not only for the Otophysi.

A West Gondwanan origin is most commonly accepted. It fits with both the living distribution of the fishes and the age and location in Africa and South America of most of the fossils. Depending on the early ecology of representatives of the order, two main scenarios explain the transatlantic distribution: the difference in the diversity of characiform fishes on each continent, and the presence of three extant trans-Atlantic groups. If characiform fishes are archeolimnic, the poly-phased fragmentation of Gondwana offers successive ways of dispersion between Africa and South America during the Early Cretaceous (e.g. Maisey 2000). If they are telolimnic, they had the ability to cross the young South Atlantic and did it at least twice (see the introduction).

In this frame of a Gondwanan origin, the presence of characiform fishes in the European continental waters implies the presence of trans-Tethyan way(s) of dispersal. From the Cretaceous until the earliest Miocene, there is no true land bridge (and sea coast) between Africa and Eurasia. However, during some time periods, in relation with sea-level falls, a series of temporary emersions of platforms made up discontinuous land routes (Dercourt *et al.* 2000; Gheerbrant & Rage 2006). This paleogeography also implies that some fishes inhabiting marine shallow (coastal) environment could have crossed the Tethys at the same time periods. During the Campano-Maastrichtian, such land routes allow the dispersion of freshwater vertebrates (Cavin *et al.* 1996, 2005) and also exchanges of various terrestrial vertebrates between Africa and Europe (Gheerbrant & Rage 2006). So, the dispersion of characiform fishes with alestid-like teeth from Africa would have then been possible and may explain the Maastrichtian records in Romania and France. Six dispersal phases are documented during the Palaeogene (Gheerbrant & Rage 2006). The highest known diversity in European characiform fishes (Ypresian) is correlated with the main dispersal phase from Africa to Laurasia (Gheerbrant & Rage 2006). A putative minor dispersal phase is located at the base of the Stampian (*ibid.*) and could be correlated with the Oligocene record of European characiform fishes. So, we cannot exclude that there is a single European lineage of characiform fish since the Maastrichtian, their past diversity, and that of other terrestrial vertebrates, on this continent can be explained by successive trans-Tethyan dispersals. That is true independent of the ecology of the migrants.

If the group is telolimnic, the non-freshwater characiform fishes that enable dispersal probably inhabited brackish and/or marine coastal waters and not open sea waters because the dispersal(s) appear correlated with continental faunal exchange(s). In the case of archaeolimny, the brackish and marine habitat of certain European characiform fishes would have been secondarily acquired at least twice, if they belong to a single lineage in Europe (once for *Sorbinicharax*, once for alestid-like fishes) or more if we accept several invasions of Europe.

Finally, the recent findings of Cretaceous characiform fishes in Europe support the hypothesis of the telolimny of the group, particularly the marine *Sorbinicharax* (Taverne 2003). So, we conclude that the existence of ancient characiform fishes with a certain ability to withstand salty waters and living in coastal environments would help to explain: (1) part of the Cretaceous fossil record of characiform fishes in Europe (at least *Sorbinicharax*); (2) possibly part of the living characifom trans-Atlantic distribution; and (3) probably at least part of the Tertiary European fossil record. Moreover, if characiform fishes are telolimnic the presence of new free marine proximal habitats, created in the marginal basins of the young South Atlantic, could have enhanced their diversification. So, the discovery of *Sorbinicharax* and of the fossils from Provence changes our view on the characiform Cretaceous diversity and early ecology, particularly in Europe and may enable a re-evaluation of their early history. The break-up of Gondwana appears to have greatly impacted the characiform evolutionary history and could have even enhanced their diversification.

We thank the local authorities (municipalities of Les Pennes Mirabeau and Velaux) and E. Turini who has taken part in the preparation of the material and for field assistance. We extend our gratitude to A. Longbottom, L. Cavin and an anonymous referee for their interesting comments and suggestions. This work was supported by funds from the Conseil Général des Bouches-du-Rhône and by the CNRS UMRS 6046 (University of Poitiers).

References

ANTUNES, M. T., BALBINO, A. & GAUDANT, J. 1995. Découverte du plus récent poisson Characiformes européen dans le Miocène terminal du Portugal. *Communications de l'Institut géologique des Mines*, **81**, 79–84.

BREWSTER, B. 1986. A review of the genus *Hydrocynus* Cuvier 1819 (Teleostei: Characiformes). *Bulletin of the British Museum (Natural History), Zoology Series*, **50**, 163–206.

BRUNET, M., BEAUVILAIN, A., BILLIOU, D. *ET AL.* 2000. Chad: Discovery of a vertebrate fauna close to the Mio-Pliocene boundary. *Journal of Vertebrate Paleontology*, **20**, 205–209.

BUCKUP, P. A. 1998. Relationships of the Characidiinae and phylogeny of characiform fishes (Teleostei: Ostariophysi). *In*: MALABARBA, L. R., REIS, R. E., VARI, R. P. *ET AL.* (eds) *Phylogeny and Classification of Neotropical Fishes*. Editora Pontificia Universidata Catolica do Rio Grande do Sul Porto Alegre, Brazil, 123–144.

CALCAGNOTTO, D., SCHAEFER, S. A. & DESALLE, R. 2005. Relationships among characiform fishes inferred from analysis of nuclear and mitochondrial gene sequences. *Molecular Phylogenetics and Evolution*, **36**, 135–153.

CAPPETTA, H. & THALER, L. 1974. Présence de poissons Characidae, caractéristiques de l'Eocène inférieur européen dans la formation lignifère de Sardaigne. *In*: Paleogeographia del Terziaro sardo nell'ambito del Meditteraneo occidentale. *Rendiconti del Seminario della Facultà di Scienze dell'Univiversita di Cagliari*, 69–71.

CAPPETTA, H., RUSSEL, D. E. & BRAILLON, J. 1972. Sur la découverte de Characidae dans l'Eocène inférieur français (Pisces, Cypriniformes). *Bulletin du Muséum national d'Histoire naturelle, Science Terre, 3è série*, **51**, 37–50.

CAPPETTA, H., JAEGER, J.-J., SABATIER, M. *ET AL.* 1978. Découverte dans le Paléocène du Maroc des plus anciens mammifères Euthériens d'Afrique. *Géobios*, **11**, 257–263.

CAVIN, L., VALENTIN, X. & MARTIN, M. 1996. Découverte d'*Atractosteus africanus* (Actinopterygii, Lepisosteidea) dans le Campanien inférieur de Ventabren (Bouches du Rhône, France). Implications paléobiogéographiques. *Revue de Paléobiologie*, **15**, 1–7.

CAVIN, L., FOREY, P. L., BUFFETAUT, E. *ET AL.* 2005. Latest European coelacanth shows Gondwanan affinities. *Biological Letters*, **2005**, 176–177.

CHARDON, M. 1967. Réflexions sur la dispersion des Ostariophysi à la lumière de recherches morphologiques nouvelles. *Annales de la Société royale zoologique de Belgique*, **97**, 35–58.

CIONE, A. L. 1986. Los peces continentales del Cenozoico de Argentina. Su significación paleoambiental y paleobiogeográfica. *Actas del III Congreso Argentino de Paleontología y Bioestratigrafía*, **2**, 101–106.

DE LA PEÑA, A. 1993. *Estudios de los Teleosteos de las cuencas continentales terciarias de la peninsula iberica*. PhD thesis, Universidad Complutense, Madrid.

DE LA PEÑA, A. 1995. Los Peces terciarios de las cuencas continentales ibéricas: Marco histórico y registro fósil conocido. *Coloquios de Paleontología*, Editorial Complutense, **47**, 26–46.

DERCOURT, J., RICOU, L.-E. & VRIELYNCK, B. (eds) 1993. *Atlas Tethys Palaeoenvironmental Maps*. 1–307.

DERCOURT, J., GAETANI, M., VRIELYNCK, B. *ET AL.* (eds) 2000. *Atlas Peri-Tethys, Palaeogeographical Maps*. CCGM/CGMW, Paris.

DUTHEIL, D. B. 1999. An overview of the freshwater fish fauna from the Kem Kem Beds (Late Cretaceous: Cenomanian) of Southeastern Morocco. *In*: ARRATIA, F. & SCHULTZE, H.-P. (eds) *Mesozoic Fishes 2 – Systematics and Fossil Record*. Proceedings of the International Meeting, Buckow, 1997, Dr F. Pfeil, Munich, 553–563.

FILLEUL, A. & MAISEY, J. G. 2004. Redescription of *Santanichthys diasii* (Otophysi, Characiformes) from the Albian of the Santana Formation and comments on its implications for otophysan relationships. *American Museum Novitates*, **3455**, 1–21.

FINK, S. V. & FINK, W. L. 1981. Interrelationships of the ostariophysan fishes (Teleostei). *Zoological Journal of the Linnean Society*, **72**, 297–353.

FINK, S. V., GREENWOOD, P. H. & FINK, W. L. 1984. A critic of recent work on fossil ostariophysan fishes. *Copeia*, **1984**, 1033–1041.

GARCIA, G. & VIANEY-LIAUD, M. 2001. Dinosaur eggshells as new biochronological markers in Late

Cretaceous continental deposits. *Palaeobiogeography, Palaeoclimatology, Palaeoecology*, **169**, 153–164.

GAUDANT, J. 1979. Sur la présence de dents de Characidae (Poisson, téléostéen, Ostariophysi), dans les "Calcaires à Bithynies" et les "Sables bleutés" du Var. *Géobios*, **12**, 451–457.

GAUDANT, J. 1980. *Eurocharax touraini* nov. gen., nov. sp. (poisson, téléostéen, Ostariophysi), nouveau Characidae fossile des "Calcaires à Bithynies" du Var. *Géobios*, **13**, 683–703.

GAUDANT, J. 1996. Signification paléobiogéographique de la découverte de dents de characiformes (Poissons Téléostéens) dans le Miocène moyen de Sansan (Gers). *Comptes rendus de l'Académie des Sciences, série IIa*, **322**, 683–703.

GAYET, M. 1981. Considérations relatives à la paléoécologie du gisement cénomanien de Laveiras (Portugal). *Bulletin du Muséum national d'Histoire naturelle de Paris, section C*, **4**, 21–41.

GAYET, M. 1982. Considérations sur la phylogénie et la paléobiogéographie des Ostariophysaires. *Géobios*, **6**, 39–52.

GAYET, M. 1985. Contribution à l'étude anatomique et systématique de l'ichthyofaune cénomanienne du Portugal. III. Complément à l'étude des Ostariophysaires. *Comunicações Serviços Geológicos do Portugal*, **71**, 91–117.

GAYET, M. 1986. About ostariophysan fishes: a reply to S. V. Fink, P. H. Greenwood, and W. L. Fink's criticism. *Bulletin du Muséum national d'Histoire naturelle, section C*, **8**, 393–409.

GAYET, M. 1991. "Holostean" and teleostean fish of Bolivia. *In*: SUAREZ-SORUCO, R. (ed.) *Fósiles y Facies de Bolivia, I (Vertebrados)*. Revista técnica de Yacimiento Petroleo Boliviano, **12**, 453–493.

GAYET, M. & MEUNIER, F. J. 1998. Maastrichtian to Early Late Paleocene Freshwater Osteichthyes of Bolivia: Additions and Comments. *In*: MALABARBA, L. R., REIS, R. E., VARI, R. P. *ET AL.* (eds) *Phylogeny and Classification of Neotropical Fishes*. Editora Pontificia Universidata Catolica do Rio Grande do Sul, Porto Alegre, Brazil, 85–110.

GAYET, M., MARSHALL, M. G., SEMPERE, T. *ET AL.* 2001. Middle Maastrichtian vertebrates (fishes, amphibians, dinosaurs and other reptiles, mammals) from Pajcha Pata (Bolivia). Biostratigraphic, palaeoecologic and palaeobiogeographic implications. *Palaeobiogeography, Palaeoclimatology, Palaeoecology*, **169**, 39–68.

GAYET, M., JÉGU, M., BOCQUETIN, J. *ET AL.* 2003. New characoids from the Upper Cretaceous and Paleocene of Bolivia and the Mio-Pliocene of Brazil: phylogenetic position and paleobiogeographic implications. *Journal of Vertebrate Paleontology*, **23**, 28–46.

GHEERBRANT, E. & RAGE, J.-C. 2006. Paleobiogeography of Africa: how distinct from Gondwana and Laurasia? *Palaeobiogeography, Palaeoclimatology, Palaeoecology*, **241**, 224–246.

GREENWOOD, P. H., ROSEN, D. E., WEITZMANN, S. H. *ET AL.* 1966. Phyletic studies of teleostean fishes, with a provisional classification of living forms. *Bulletin of the American Museum of Natural Sciences*, **131**, 339–456.

GRIGORESCU, D., HARTENBERGER, J.-L., RADULESCU, C. *ET AL.* 1985. Découverte de mammifères et dinosaures dans le Crétacé supérieur de Pui (Roumanie). *Comptes rendus de l'Académie des Sciences, Sciences de la Terre, série 2*, **301**, 1365–1368.

LUCENA, C. S. A. 1993. *Estudo filogenético da família Characidae com uma discussão dos grupos naturais propostos (Teleostei, Ostariophysi, Characiformes)*. PhD thesis, Universidade de São Paulo, Unpublished.

LUCENA, C. S. A. & MENEZES, N. A 1998. A phylogenetic analysis of *Roestes* Günther and *Gilbertolus* Eigenmann, with a hypothesis on the relationships of the Cynodontidae and Acestrorhynchidae (Teleostei: Ostariophysi: Characiformes). *In*: MALABARBA, L. R., REIS, R. E., VARI, R. P. *ET AL.* (eds) *Phylogeny and Classification of Neotropical Fishes*. Editora Pontificia Universidata Catolica do Rio Grande do Sul, Porto Alegre, Brazil, 261–278.

LUNDBERG, J. G. 1993. African-South American freshwater fish clades and continental drift: problems with a paradigm. *In*: GOLDBLATT, P. (ed.) *The Biotic Relationships between Africa and South America*. Yale University Press, New Haven, 156–199.

LUNDBERG, J. G., MACHADO-ALLISON, A. & KAY, R. 1986. Miocene characid fishes from Colombia: evolutionary stasis and extirpation. *Science*, **234**, 208–209.

LUNDBERG, J. G., MARSHALL, L. G., GUERRERO, J. *ET AL.* 1998. The stage for Neotropical fish diversification: A history of tropical South American Rivers. *In*: MALABARBA, L. R., REIS, R. E., VARI, R. P. *ET AL.* (eds) *Phylogeny and Classification of Neotropical Fishes*. Editora Pontificia Universicata Catolica do Rio Grande do Sul, Porto Alegre, Brazil, 13–48.

MAHBOUBI, M., AMEUR, R., CROCHET, J.-Y. & JAEGER, J.-J. 1984. Earliest known proboscidean from early Eocene of north-west Africa. *Nature*, **308**, 543–544.

MAISEY, J. G. 1993. A New Clupeomorph Fish from the Santana Formation (Albian) of NE Brazil. *American Museum Novitates*, **3076**, 1–15.

MAISEY, J. G. 2000. Continental break up and the distribution of Fishes of Western Gondwana during the early Cretaceous. *Cretaceous Research*, **21**, 281–314.

MICKLICH, N. & ROSCHER, B. 1990. Neue Fischfunde aus der Baid-Formation (Oligozän; Tihamat Asir, SW Saudi-Arabien). *Neues Jahrbuch für Geologie und Paläontologie*, **180**, 139–175.

MONOD, T. & GAUDANT, J. 1998. Un nom pour les poissons characiformes de l'Eocène inférieur et moyen du Bassin de Paris et du Sud de la France: *Alestoides eocaenicus* nov. gen., nov. sp. *Cybium*, **22**, 15–20.

MONSCH, K. A. 1998. Miocene fish faunas from the northwestern Amazonia basin (Colombia, Peru, Brazil) with evidence of marine incursions. *Palaeogeography, Palaeoclimatology, Palaeoecology*, **143**, 31–50.

MURRAY, A. M. 2003. A new characiform fish (Teleostei: Ostariophysi) from the Eocene of Tanzania. *Canadian Journal of Earth Sciences*, **40**, 473–48_.

MURRAY, A. M. 2004. Osteology and morphology of the characiform fish: *Alestes stuhlmannii* Pfeffer, 1896 (Alestidae) from the Rufigi river basin, East Africa. *Journal of Fish Biology*, **65**, 1412–1430.

MURRAY, A. M. & STEWART, K. M. 2002. Phylogenetic relationships of the African genera *Alestes* and *Brycinus* (Teleostei, Characiformes, Alestidae). *Canadian Journal of Zoology*, **80**, 1887–1899.

ODIN, G. S. & LAMAURELLE, M. A. 2001. The global Campanian-Maastrichtian stage boundary. *Episodes*, **24**, 229–238.

ORTÍ, G. & MEYER, A. 1997. The radiation of characiform fishes and the limits of resolution of mitochondrial ribosomal DNA sequences. *Systematic Biology*, **46**, 75–100.

OTERO, O. & GAYET, M. 2001. Palaeoichthyofauna from the Oligocene and Miocene of the Arabic Plate. Palaeoecological and palaeobiogeographical implications. *Palaeobiogeography, Palaeoclimatology, Palaeoecology*, **165**, 141–169.

PATTERSON, C. 1975. The distribution of the Mesozoic freshwater fishes. *Mémoire du Muséum national d'Histoire naturelle, série A*, **88**, 156–174.

PATTERSON, C. 1984. *Chanoides*, a marine Eocene otophysan fish (Teleostei: Ostariophysi). *Journal of Vertebrate Paleontology*, **4**, 430–456.

PATTERSON, C. 1993. Osteichthyes: Teleostei. In: BENTON, M. J. (ed.) *The Fossil Record 2*, 622–656.

PAUGY, D. 1986. *Révision systématique des* Alestes *et* Brycinus *africains (Pisces, Characidae)*. Etudes et Thèses, ORSTOM, Paris.

PAUGY, D. 1990. Note à propos des Petersiini (Teleostei: Characidae) d'Afrique Occidentale. *Ichthyological Exploration of Freshwater*, **1**, 75–84.

PENG, Z., HE, S., WANG, J., WANG, W. & DIOGO, R. 2006. Mitochondrial molecular clocks and the origin of the major Otocephalan clades (Pisces: Teleostei): A new insight. *Gene*, **370**, 113–124.

ROBERTS, T. R. 1967. Tooth formation and replacement in characoid fishes. *Stanford Ichthyological Bulletin*, **8**, 231–247.

ROBERTS, T. R. 1972. Ecology of fishes in the Amazon and Congo basins. *Bulletin Museum of Comparative Zoology*, **173**, 117–147.

ROBERTS, T. R. 1974. Characoid fish teeth from the Miocene deposits in the Cuenca Basin, Ecuador. *Journal of Zoology*, **175**, 259–271.

STEWART, K. M. 2001. The freshwater fish of Neogene Africa (Miocene-Pleistocene): systematics and biogeography. *Fish and Fisheries*, **2001**, 177–230.

STEWART, K. M. 2003. Fossils Fish Remains from Mio-Pliocene Deposits at Lothagam, Kenya. In:

LEAKEY, M. G. & HARRIS, J. H. (eds) *Lothagam, the Dawn of Humanity in Eastern Africa*, **3**, 76–111.

TAVERNE, L. 2003. Les poissons crétacés de Nardò. 16° *Sorbinicharax verraesi* gen. sp. nov. (Teleostei, Ostariophysi, Otophysis, Characiformes). *Bollettino del Museo Civico di Storia Naturale di Verona*, **27**, 29–45.

TAVERNE, L. 2005. Les poissons crétacés de Nardò. 20° *Chanoides chardoni*. sp. nov. (Teleostei, Ostariophysi, Otophysis). *Bollettino del Museo Civico di Storia Naturale di Verona*, **29**, 39–54.

TOLEDO-PIZA, M. 2000. The Neotropical fish subfamily Cynodontinae (Teleostei: Ostariophysi: Characiformes): a phylogenetic study and a revision of *Cynodon* and *Rhaphiodon*. *American Museum Novitates*, **3286**, 1–88.

TRAPANI, J., YAMAMOTO, Y. & STOCK, D. W. 2005. Ontogenetic transition from unicuspid to multicuspid oral dentition in a teleost fish: *Astyanax mexicanus*, the Mexican tetras (Ostariophysi: Characidae). *Zoological Journal of the Linnean Society*, **145**, 523–538.

UJ, A. 1990. *Etude comparative de l'ostéologie crânienne des poissons de la famille des Characidae et son importance phylogénétique*. PhD thesis, Université de Genève.

VAN COUVERING, J. A. H. 1977. Early record of freshwater fishes in Africa. *Copeia*, **1**, 163–166.

VARI, R. P. 1979. Anatomy, Relationships and Classification of the families Citharinidae and Distichodontidae (Pisces, Characoidea). *Bulletin of the British Museum (Natural History), Zoology*, **36**, 261–344.

VARI, R. P. 1995. The neotropical fish family Ctenoluciidae (Teleostei: Ostariophysi: Characiformes): supra and intrafamilial phylogenetic relationships, with a revisionary study. *Smithsonian Contributions to Zoology*, **564**, 1–97.

VIGNAUD, P., DURINGER, P., MACKAYE, H. T. *ET AL.* 2002. Geology and Paleontology of the Upper Miocene Toros-Menalla fossiliferous area, Djurab Desert, Northern Chad. *Nature*, **418**, 152–155.

WERNER, C. 1994. Die kontinentale Wirbeltierfauna aus der unteren Oberkreide de Sudan (Wadi Milk Formation). *Berliner geowissenshaften Abhandlungen*, **13**, 221–249.

ZANATA, A. M. & VARI, R. P. 2005. The family Alestidae (Ostariophysi, Characiformes): a phylogenetic analysis of a trans-Atlantic clade. *Zoological Journal of the Linnean Society*, **145**, 1–144.

Palaeobiogeography of Cretaceous bony fishes (Actinistia, Dipnoi and Actinopterygii)

LIONEL CAVIN

Department of Geology and Palaeontology, Muséum d'Histoire Naturelle, CP 6434 1211, Genève 6, Switzerland (e-mail: lionel.cavin@ville-ge.ch)

Abstract: Dispersal and vicariant patterns have been used as opposite concepts to explain biogeographical histories of organisms. Vicariance has been preferred to dispersal: the former is said to be falsifiable while the latter is regarded as a contingent hypothesis. If included in a temporal framework, however, a sister-group relationship between two taxa could be more parsimoniously explained by a dispersal event if both taxa are not contemporaneous in time. Published phylogenies of various clades of bony fishes are compared with evolution of the palaeogeographical framework during the Cretaceous, and possible causes involved in the observed patterns, such as vicariant events, dispersal events or radiations are suggested. Most Cretaceous patterns concerns east–west events (vicariance and dispersal) rather than north–south events. This is probably because the separation of Laurasia and Gondwana is already underway in the Late Jurassic and affected Cretaceous faunas only weakly. Late Cretaceous dispersal patterns constitute a more common phenomenon than previously expected. It is suggested that the entire autoecology of the fishes is a more significant parameter affecting dispersal ability than only their allegedly capacity to tolerate salt waters.

Ideas about the main processes in action in historical biogeography have been described as a pendulum swinging between two extreme points (de Queiroz 2005). One point is represented by the Darwin–Wallace biogeographic paradigm (in which a species has a founder population that disperses from a centre of origin) and the other is vicariance (supported by the validation of plate tectonic and by the rise of cladism, in which a species is split into two by the fragmentation of the land mass where it lives).

The dispersal model has been criticized as a 'telling-stories science' because it does not rest on a repeatable method. The critic is partly correct when looking at examples resulting from analyses of Recent clades (especially all Recent analyses resting on molecular-based phylogenies) because vicariant models can be easily tested by searching for the most parsimonious pattern fitting a palaeogeographical reconstruction. Dispersals are more flexible patterns and can always fit a palaeogeographical reconstruction by adding new hypothetical dispersal routes. This assertion is not true, however, if we include fossil taxa in the phylogenies within a time framework, such as for instance in the biochronogeographical paradigm of Hunn & Upchurch (2001). In that case, fossil distribution in time and space may sometimes be better explained (i.e. more parsimoniously) by using dispersal events.

The bony fishes are a good proxy to assess the importance of vicariance versus dispersal events during their evolutionary history because: (1) they live, and lived in all aquatic environments making possible the comparison between freshwater and marine patterns; (2) their fossil record is proportionally good compared to other vertebrates; and (3) the phylogenetic framework is rather well-resolved. Comparison of bony fish diversity and environmental features through the Cretaceous indicates than diversity of marine actinopterygians as a whole is correlated to sea surface temperature (Cavin *et al.* 2007a). Moreover, the fossil record indicates freshwater radiations in restricted provinces. Both signals, co-evolution of fish diversity with sea temperature, and with radiation events, are pointed out in the descriptions of the evolutionary histories of fish clades.

The Cretaceous is a period characterized by high rate of oceanic spreading that caused a 'burst' in the break-up of Pangaea. Furthermore, in the mid-Cretaceous high sea stand and continental seas crossing continents made continental provincialism greater than today.

In this paper, published phylogenies of various clades of bony fishes are compared with the evolution of the palaeogeographical framework in the Cretaceous, and possible explanations for the observed patterns are given using criteria of spatial and temporal distribution.

Methods

Vicariance and dispersal events are regarded here as, essentially, a distinction between observable

From: CAVIN, L., LONGBOTTOM, A. & RICHTER, M. (eds) *Fishes and the Break-up of Pangaea.*
Geological Society, London, Special Publications, **295**, 165–183.
DOI: 10.1144/SP295.11   0305-8719/08/$15.00 © The Geological Society of London 2008.

patterns; but in both cases the processes involved in speciation events are likely to be similar at the species or population level. Discrimination between both patterns is made possible by confronting phylogenies with the evolution of the palaeogeographical framework through time.

Each pattern is regarded as the most parsimonious one depending of the observed spatial and temporal distributions. The distinction is defined as follows (Fig. 1):

- Vicariance is assumed when a cladogenetic event is contemporaneous with a split of the province occupied by the sister-taxa. Marine fish species separated by barriers, such as marine currents, surface gradients of temperature and salinity, great depths or freshwater and sediment outflows from rivers may show vicariant patterns (Heads 2005) that could be detected by vicariance biogeographical tools in the same way as for continental organisms. Practically, a vicariant event is mapped when two occurrences from two different contemporaneous formations are sister-taxa (Fig. 1a), or situated in a pectinated position in the tree (Fig. 1b). The latter situation is not a vicariant case *sensu stricto*, as the vicariance actually occurred between the basal-most taxon and the whole sister-clade. But the approximation made here is justified, as the phylogenies used cannot attempt to get the same resolution as modern phylogeny (Cavin *et al.* 2007a).
- Dispersal is assumed when a taxon shows: (1) a different geographic location and a younger age than the more basal and more derived clades in a pectinated pattern (Fig. 1c); and (2) a different geographic location than the reconstructed location of the common ancestor of the sister group and a younger age (Fig. 1d). Detection

of a dispersal event between two sister taxa does not imply that one of these taxa effectively disperses from one geographic province to the other, but that members of the lineage containing both taxa spread from one province to the other.

Both patterns, vicariance and dispersals, are falsifiable by integrating new data (new fossil occurrence and/or new phylogenetic hypothesis).

In addition to both patterns above, regarded as the main indicators of factors affecting historical biogeography, radiation events were mapped when several taxa with short ghost lineages within a clade occur in the same geographic area, even if the precise branching pattern among taxa is not resolved.

The systematic working unit used in this study is generally the genus, but species may constitute the working-unit if those are well-defined and well-resolved within a phylogenetic hypothesis.

Results

Latimeroidei

The phylogeny of the suborder is from Forey (1998) with an addition from Clement (2005) (Fig. 2). *Macropoma* is resolved here as the sister-group of *Wenzia* + *Latimeria*, which is the pattern found by Clement in four of the five most parsimonious trees. Obvious events recognised in this clade are the vicariance between African and South Africa between *Mawsonia* and *Axelrodichthys* during the opening of South Atlantic in the Early Cretaceous, and probable dispersals for terminal Cetaceous mawsoniids. The vicariant event may have occurred between the two genera, but it is more likely to have occurred between several species within each genus (as *Mawsonia* is recorded from Africa and South America, and *Axelrodichthys* may also have occurred in both landmasses; Cavin & Forey 2004). In the terminal Cretaceous, mawsoniids of uncertain affinities have been described from Southern France (Cavin *et al.* 2005a) and Madagascar (Gottfried *et al.* 2004). As these occurrences are much younger than the all other mawsoniids, and as they occurred in geographic areas different that the expected location of the ancestor of *Mawsonia* + *Axelrodichthys* (Western Gondwana), they possibly reach their location by dispersals from Africa.

Dipnoi

Phylogeny and historical biogeography of post-Palaeozoic lungfishes have been recently explored (Cavin *et al.* 2007b) (Fig. 3). According to these

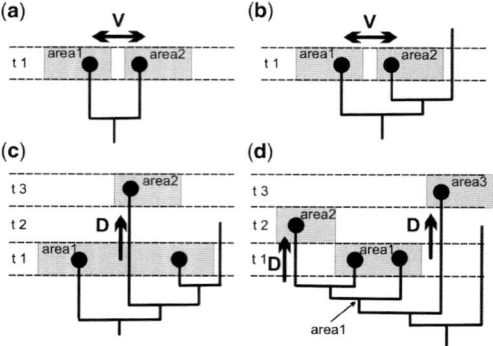

Fig. 1. Method used to detect vicariant events (**a** and **b**) and dispersal events (**c** and **d**). See text for explanation.

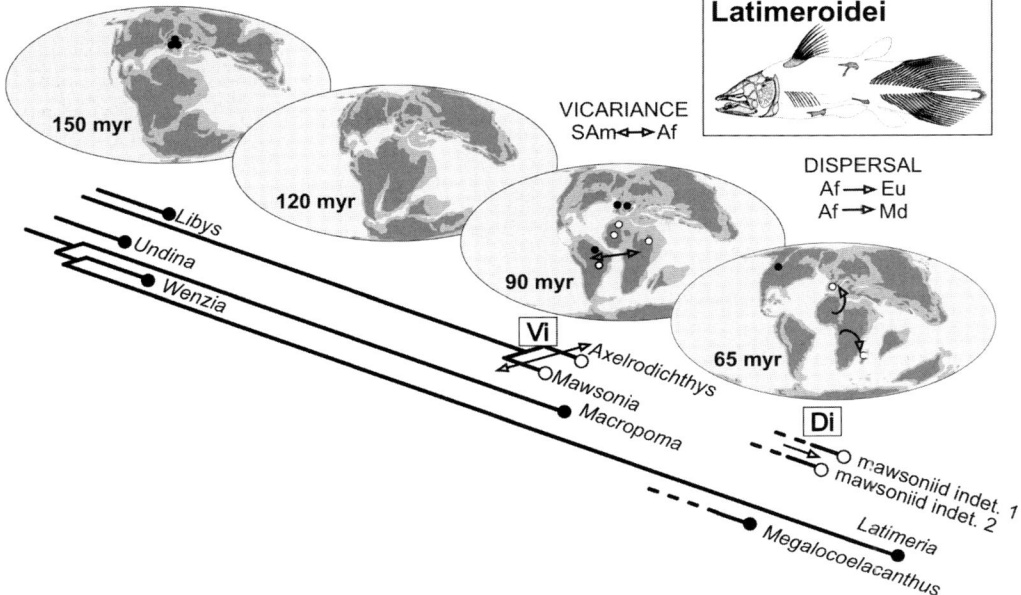

Fig. 2. Cretaceous historical biogeography of Latimeroidea. Abbreviations: Af, Africa; Di, dispersal event; Eu, Europe; Md, Madagascar; SAm, South America; Vi, vicariant event. Black spot, marine occurrence; white spot, freshwater occurrence.

results, the extant Australian *Neoceratodus* is a representative of an old, pre-Cretaceous lineage with a Gondwanan distribution (Australia, Africa, South America). A speciation event between two species of *Ferganoceratodus* (based on skull materials), regarded as a probable vicariant event since both species occurred within a short time interval, is recorded in Asia between *F. jurassicus*

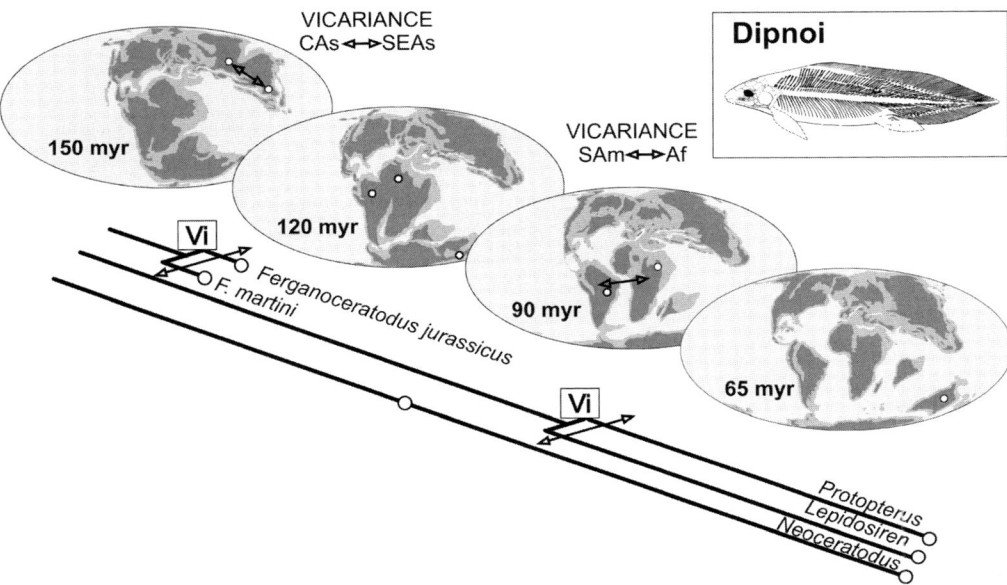

Fig. 3. Cretaceous historical biogeography of Dipnoi. Abbreviations as in Figure 1 plus: CAs, C Asia; SEAs, SE Asia.

from the Middle Jurassic of Kirghiztan (Nessov & Kaznyshkin 1985) and *F. martini* from the Late Jurassic–Early Cretaceous of Thailand (Cavin *et al.* 2007*b*). A well supported vicariant cladogenetic event is the separation of *Lepidosiren* and *Protopterus* during the fragmentation of Western Gondwana into South America and Africa during the Early Cretaceous.

Polypteridae

Polypterids are regarded as the basal most living actinopterygians, although Recent species show many autapomorphies. They are restricted today to the fresh waters of Africa. A handful of Tertiary polypterid fossils have been recorded in that continent (Greenwood 1984; Otero *et al.* 2006). Based on spiny ray morphology, Gayet *et al.* (2002) described a polypterid radiation in the early Late Cretaceous in Niger and Sudan. More complete articulated polypterids, but with the head missing, have been described from the Cenomanian of the Kem Kem beds in Morocco (Dutheil 1999). Isolated scales from the Late Cretaceous and Early Palaeogene of Bolivia have been referred to two genera of polypterids (Gayet & Meunier 1991, 1992, 1998) on the basis of histological apomorphies (Daget *et al.* 2001). This is the only occurrence of polypterids outside Africa. Because no phylogeny including fossils has been built up so far, no palaeogeographical pattern can be proposed for that group. The presence of polypterids on both side of S Atlantic in the Late Cretaceous suggests a vicariant event during the opening of the S Atlantic. However, if polypterids are correctly placed as the basal most clade of actinopterygians, the lineage should have individualised in the Late Palaeozoic, and the lineage may have remained unrecognized, possibly for not possessing autapomorphic features that characterized its later representatives. The early Late Cretaceous hypothesis of a polypterid radiation, based on fragmentary remains only, is pending a confirmation.

Chondrostei

The extinct family peipiaosteids shows a freshwater radiation in the basal Cretaceous of East Asia (Fig. 4). Palaeobiogeography of polyodontids in the Late Cretaceous is complex. According to a recent

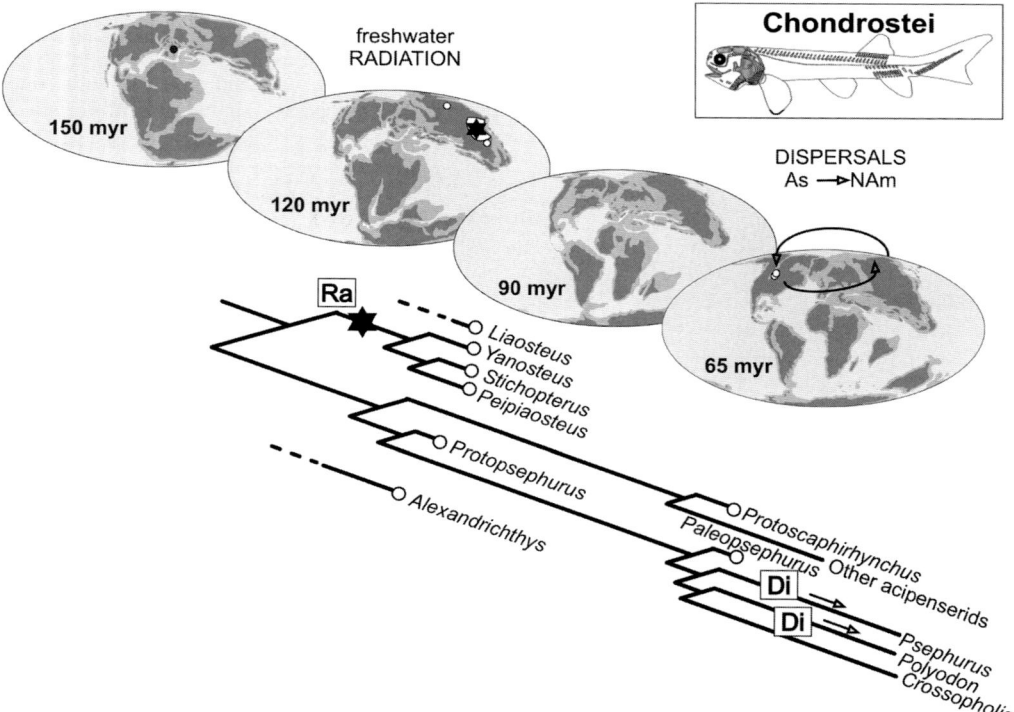

Fig. 4. Cretaceous historical biogeography of Chondrostei. Abbreviations as in Figure 1 plus: As, Asia; NAm, N America; Ra, radiation event.

phylogeny (Grande *et al.* 2002) one should either suppose: (1) a double vicariant events between *Palaeopsephurus* and other polyodontids, and between *Psephurus* and other polyodontids straddling NE Asia and NW America or; (2) a series of dispersals between NE Asia and NW America. The latter solution is favoured in Figure 4 because there are no contemporaneous fossil occurrences in the Late Cretaceous of both landmasses. The N Hemisphere distribution of acipenserids is regarded by Choudhury & Dick (1998) as the result of Late Cretaceous and Tertiary dispersals. As the oldest known acipenserid, *Protoscaphirhynchus*, occurs in North America, I assume that the dispersal spread from that land mass towards Asia.

Semionotiformes

Semionotiforms include the semionotids and the lepisosteids (Cavin & Suteethorn 2006), and probably the macrosemiids (Olsen & McCune 1991; Brito 1997). Recently, Grande (2005) grouped this order with the halecomorphs within a monophyletic clade, thus resuscitating the long regarded non-monophyletic Holostei. Lepisosteids are currently under study by Grande & Bemis (Grande, personal communication, 2005) and the important changes in the phylogeny and systematic of that order that will result from this study makes a search for biogeographical patterns premature at present. One may, however, mention the occurrence in the Late Cretaceous of Europe of a gar otherwise known in the early Late Cretaceous of Africa, ?*Atractosteus africanus*, indicative of a probable dispersal event between these two landmasses (Cavin *et al.* 1996). Non-gar and non-macrosemiids semionotiforms (i.e. the semionotids *sensu lato*) potentially possess a good biogeographical signal since most species from the Early Cretaceous occur in freshwater deposits from Europe, South America, Africa and Asia.

However, a revision of these fishes is needed to draw any biogeographical patterns. A phylogeny of Macrosemiids has been recently proposed by González-Rodríguez *et al.* (2004). According to this study, the Late Jurassic sister-genera *Propterus* and *Histionotus* occur in sympatry in Europe. Five species have been described in each genus, indicative of a little radiation. The Albian Mexican *Macrosemiocotzus* is resolved as a trichotomy with the Late Jurassic *Macrosemius* and the Triassic *Legnonotus*, making difficult the recognition of a biogeographical pattern. González-Rodríguez & Reynoso (2004) observed a radiation in *Notagogus* ranging from the Late Jurassic to the Albian. They suggest two dispersal events between Central and Western Tethys, each one corresponding to one of the two species recorded in Mexico. These results are in accordance with dispersals as defined here, since the Mexican species are younger than their European sister taxa.

Amioidea

Phylogeny and historical biogeography of that clade have been explored by Grande & Bemis (1998). These data were used to construct Figure 5. A freshwater radiation occurred in the basal Cretaceous of E Asia with the sinamiids Because the Late Jurassic (*Solnhofenamia*) and Early Cretaceous (amiopsins) amioids occurred in Europe, one may suggest a vicariant event between the Asian sinamiids and these amiids (the latter do not form a monophyletic group on the cladogram, but they did in the Early Cretaceous if the ghost lineage of other amiids are taken into account). The Early Cretaceous vidalamiins show evidence of a triple vicariant event between: (1) Laurasian vidalamiinis and Gondwanan calamopleurinis; (2) species of the mainly freshwater or euryhaline African and South American *Calamopleurus* (Forey & Grande 1998); and (3) marine species of Western and Eastern Tethyan *Pachyamia*. In the Late Cretaceous and in the Palaeogene, *Amia* and *Cyclurus* have both widespread distributions in the Northern Hemisphere. Because the intrarelationships of species within both genera are unresolved, it is unclear if the distribution pattern is the result of dispersal or vicariant events (Grande & Bemis 1998).

Pycnodontiformes

The phylogeny of this order is from Poyato-Ariza & Wenz (2002) (with additions from Kriwet (2004) for *Hensodon*, Poyato-Ariza & Wenz (2004) for *Turbomesodon* and Poyato-Ariza & Wenz (2005) for *Akromystax*) (Fig. 6). One cannot detect any link between the phylogenetic history of that clade and the changing geographical pattern. During the time interval under consideration, two localities show a rather high diversity of pycnodonts, the Late Jurassic localities of S Germany and the early Late Cretaceous localities in Lebanon. Four or the five genera present in the Cenomanian of Lebanon belong to an endemic clade, the Coccodontidae and may be regarded as the result of an ecological radiation. On the other hand, the six genera recorded in Germany are members of different clade with long ghost lineages. This pycnodont assemblage is probably the result of favourable environment conditions, the proximity of coral reefs, but not the result of a local radiation event.

Pachycormiformes

Lambers (1992) proposed a phylogeny for the pachycormiforms. As most of the genera occurred

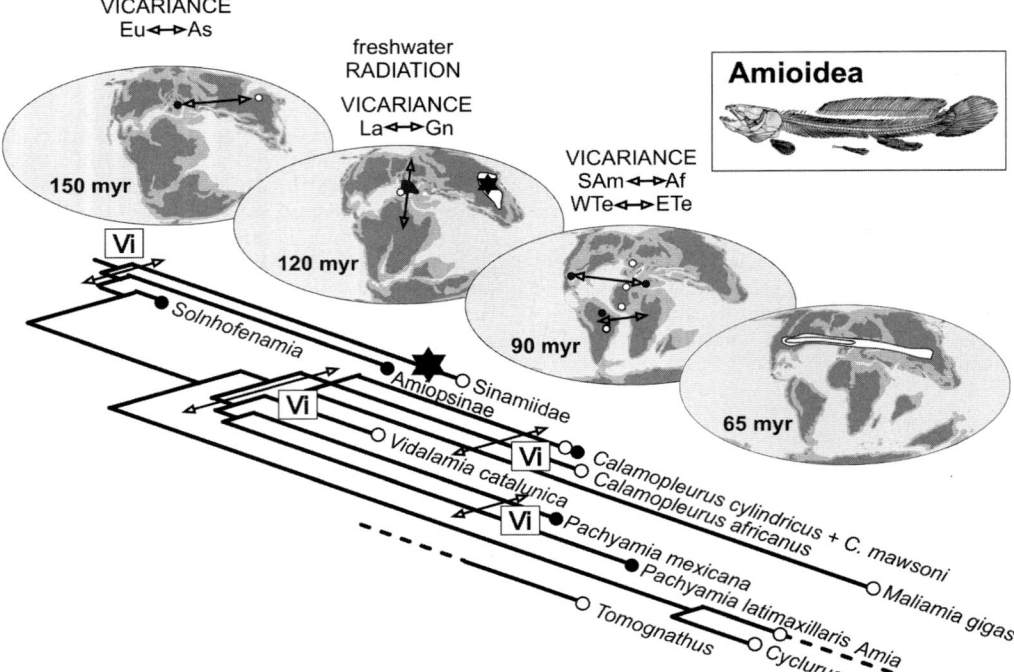

Fig. 5. Cretaceous historical biogeography of Amioidea. Abbreviations as in Figures 1–4 plus: ETe, Eastern Tethys; Eu, Europe; Gn, Gondwana; La, Laurasia; WTe, Western Tethys.

in the Late Jurassic of Germany, the palaeogeographical signal for the time interval under concern here is weak. *Protosphyraena*, regarded by Lambers as the sister-genus of *Orthocormus* from the Late Jurassic of Germany, is a widespread genus and its large fusiform body is typical of a fast swimmer pelagic fish.

Aspidorhynchiformes

The phylogeny and palaeobiogeography of this order has been discussed by Brito (1997). Although the relationships of the numerous species of the three genera included in that order are still unresolved, the general pattern is a Pangaean distribution for the Jurassic basal *Aspidorhynchus*, then a vicariance event in the Late Jurassic–Early Cretaceous between the mainly Laurasian *Belonostomus* and the Gondwanan *Vinctifer*.

Ichthyodectiformes

The phylogeny and historical biogeography have been addresses recently (Fig. 7; Cavin & Forey 2008), but the palaeogeographical signal is very weak. The only possible patterns are a

mid-Cretaceous vicariant event between the European *Gillicus serridens* and the Mexican '*Unamichthys*' *espinosai* and Late Cretaceous vicariant events between European and North American species within the genera *Prosaurodon*, *Saurodon*, *Ichthyodectes* and *Xiphactinus*.

Osteoglossomorpha

Although the position of osteoglossomorphs among teleosts is still debated, the intrarelationships within the clade show consistency between studies based on morphological (Hilton 2003) and molecular (Lavoué & Sullivan 2004) grounds. The phylogeny in Figure 8 is from Hilton (2003), with additional information from Li & Wilson (1999) for some fossil forms. In the Early Cretaceous, an important freshwater radiation event is recorded in E Asia affecting lycopterids, some basal hiodontids and some basal osteoglossoids. If the phylogenetic position of *Ostariosoma* found by Hilton is correct, it implies important consequences for the palaeobiogeographical history of the clade because this North American taxon is located in a more derived position than a series of Asian taxa, and is in a more basal position than a mainly Gondwanan

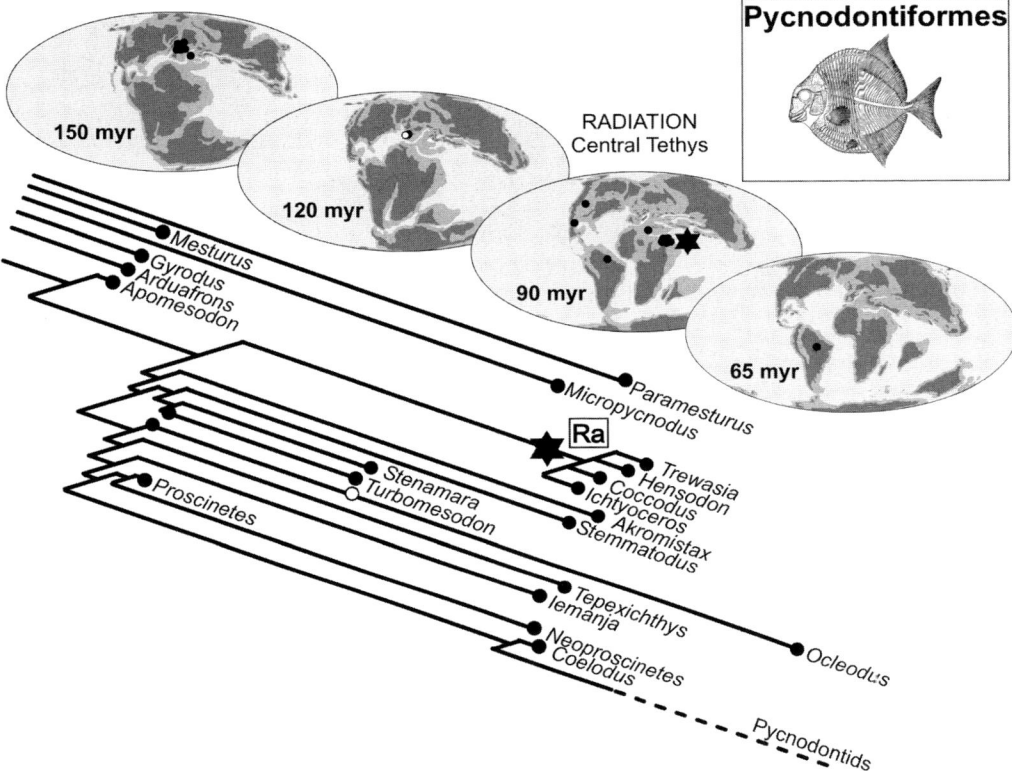

Fig. 6. Cretaceous historical biogeography of Pycnodontiformes. Abbreviations as in previous Figures.

clade. According to the Late Cretaceous–Paleocene age of *Ostariosoma*, and following the rules defined above, I favour a dispersal event from Asia to North America some time in the Late Cretaceous. The separation between the Laurasian lycopterids, hiodontids and other basal osteoglossomorphs with the mainly Gondwanan osteoglossiforms is possibly the result of a vicariant event between these two landmasses. *Cretophaerodus* from the Late Cretaceous and *Joffrichthys* from the Paleocene of North America are also regarded here as the result of dispersals from an unknown Gondwanan landmass towards North America. As a consequence, the relatively diverse North American osteoglossomorph assemblage from the Late Cretaceous and Paleocene may have been the results of four, nearly isochronous, dispersal events (hiodontids, *Ostariosoma*, *Joffrichthys*, osteoglossids), including two from Asia. Although the phylogenies of fossil and Recent heterotins are not resolved, the occurrence of representatives of that lineages on both side of the South Atlantic in the mid-Cretaceous (*Laelichthys* and *Paradercetis*)

indicates a likely vicariant event. Osteoglossid historical biogeography is discussed by Kumazawa & Nishida (2000).

Elopomorpha

The diversity of elopomorphs as a whole co-evolves with sea surface temperature (Cavin *et al.* 2007*a*). Belouze (2002) proposed a phylogenetic hypothesis of the Late Cretaceous anguilliforms. She found a pectinated pattern for *Enchelurus* (*Abisaadia* (*Luenchelys* (*Anguillavus* (*Hayenchelys, Urenchelys*)))) indicative of a Cenomanian radiation in C Tethys (*Abisaadia, Luenchelys, Anguillavus, Hayenchelys*), with a possible extension of the genus *Urenchelys* westwards with *U. anglicus* in the Cenomanian Chalk and *U. abditus* in the Coniacian–Santonian Niobrara Formation. The genus, however, is still present in the Santonian–Campanian of C Tethys with *U. avus* alongside the basal *Enchelurus*. There is no recent investigation of the phylogenetic relationships within other Cretaceous elopomorph clades (elopids, megalopids, osmeroidids, albulids,

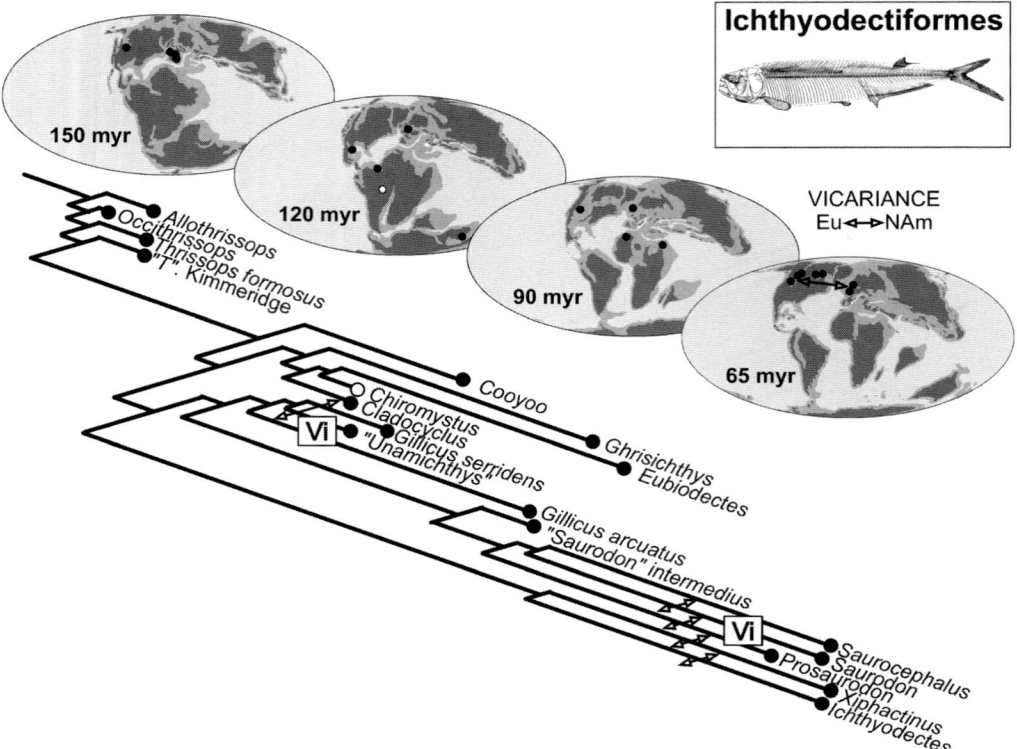

Fig. 7. Cretaceous historical biogeography of Ichthyodectiformes. Abbreviations as in previous Figures.

pterothrissids, ?phyllodontids), preventing the detection of palaeogeographical signal.

Tselfatiiformes

The phylogeny and biogeography of tselfatiiforms have been recently addressed by Taverne & Gayet (2005). Biogeographic patterns are difficult to detect because the group as a whole ranges in a short time interval (Albian–Campanian) and the phylogenetic hypothesis available is not strongly supported. Two patterns are however discernable in the historical biogeography of that clade: a widespread Tethyan distribution of the genus *Tselfatia* in the Cenomanian–Turonian and an important Late Cretaceous marine radiation of species in the Western Interior Sea.

Pachyrhizodontoidei

The phylogeny of this clade in Figure 9 is from Cavin (2001) with addition from Blanco & Cavin (2003). *Pachyrhizodus* has a long stratigraphic range, from the Albian to the Maastrichtian, and shows a radiation of species with a worldwide distribution. The only historical biogeographic event detected in that clade is a Turonian vicariant event between the Central Tethyan species *Goulmimichthys arambourgi* and the Western species *G. roberti*. However, a revision of the complex *Rhacolepis–Pachyrhizodus–Goulmimichthys* is pending and could lead to modifications of the historical biogeographical patterns proposed here. Although relatively common in the mid-Cretaceous fossil record, pachyrhizodontid fishes appear to be absent from the very rich Lebanese assemblages.

Protobramoidei

Protobramids, placed either as the basal most clade of tselfatiiforms (Taverne & Gayet 2005) or grouped with *Araripichthys* and *Acanthichthys* within the protobramoids (Cavin 2001, fig. 9), show a little radiation event in Eastern Tethys with three genera and four species. Species of the genus *Araripichthys* offer evidence of vicariance between S and C Atlantic in the mid-Cretaceous with two South American species (Maisey & Moody 2001), a Mexican one (Blanco & Cavin 2003) and an African one (Cavin 1997).

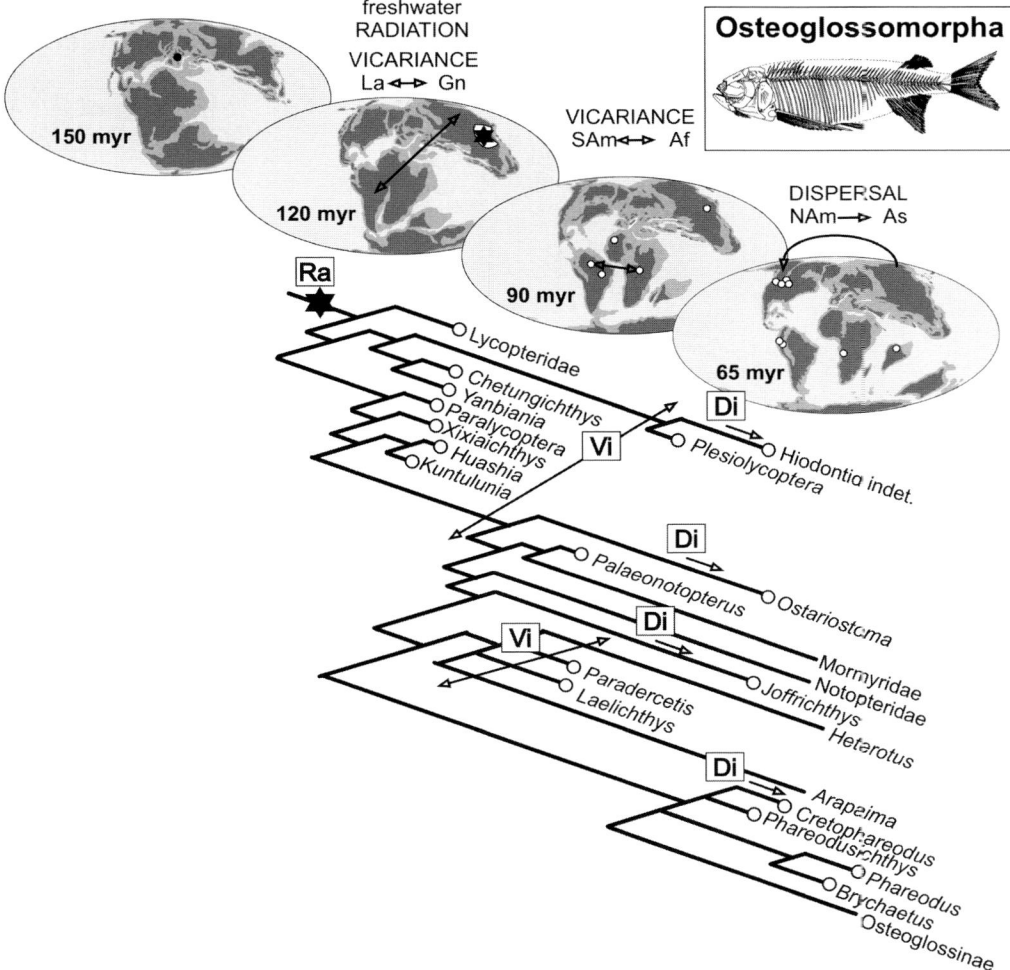

Fig. 8. Cretaceous historical biogeography of Osteoglossomorpha. Abbreviations as in previous Figures.

Clupeomorpha

Phylogeny and biogeography of basal clupeomorphs and Paraclupeidae have been recently addressed by Chang & Chen (2000), Maisey (2000), Chang & Maisey (2003), Zaragüeta Bagils (2004) and Forey (2004). The phylogenetic patterns from these studies differ from each other and here some recurrent patterns found in most of the studies are commented on, together with their palaeobiogeographical implications. The sister-species *Ellimmichthys longicostatus* and *E. goodi*, respectively in the Early Cretaceous of Brazil and Equatorial Guinea, are indicative of vicariance between both side of S Atlantic (Maisey 2000). The occurrence in the Early Cretaceous of China

of the sister-genus of *Ellimmichthys* and *Paraclupea*, is hard to explain from a palaeobiogeographical point of view, as well as the distribution of the species of the non-monophyletic *Diplomystus*: these patterns are discussed by Chang & Chen (2000). As for other freshwater clades, dispersals between NE Asia and NW North America are suspected in the Late Cretaceous.

Chanoidea

Phylogeny of the suborder has been computed from data from Grande & Poyato-Ariza (1999) with the addition of a new taxon from the mid-Cretaceous of Morocco currently under description (Fig. 10). Two main events are detected in that clade: the

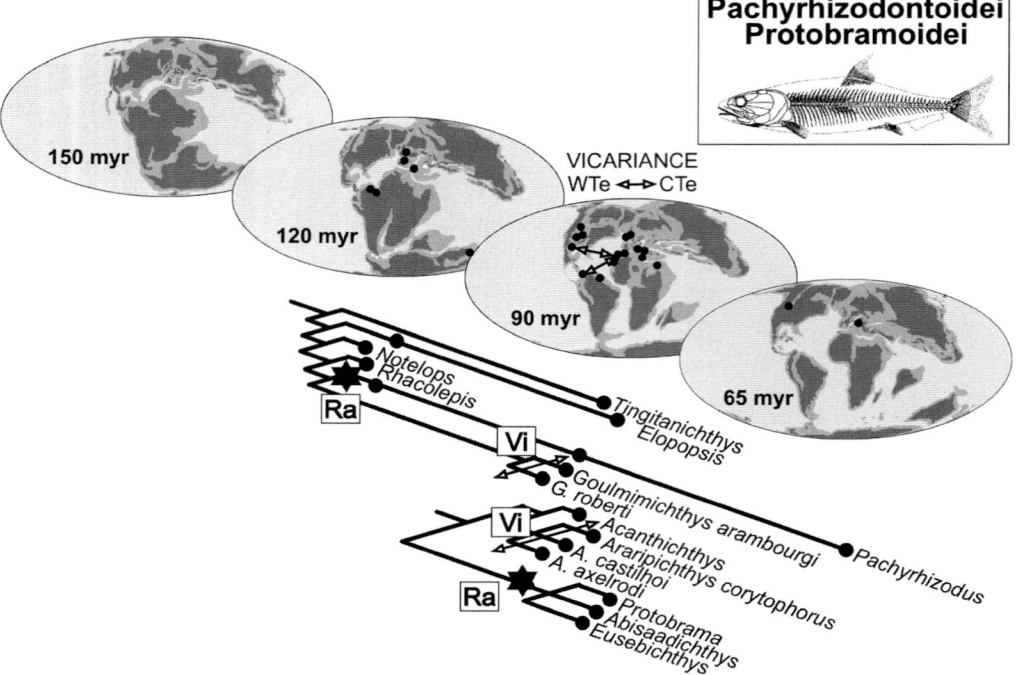

Fig. 9. Cretaceous historical biogeography of Pachyrhizodontoidei and Protobramoidei. Abbreviations as in previous Figures.

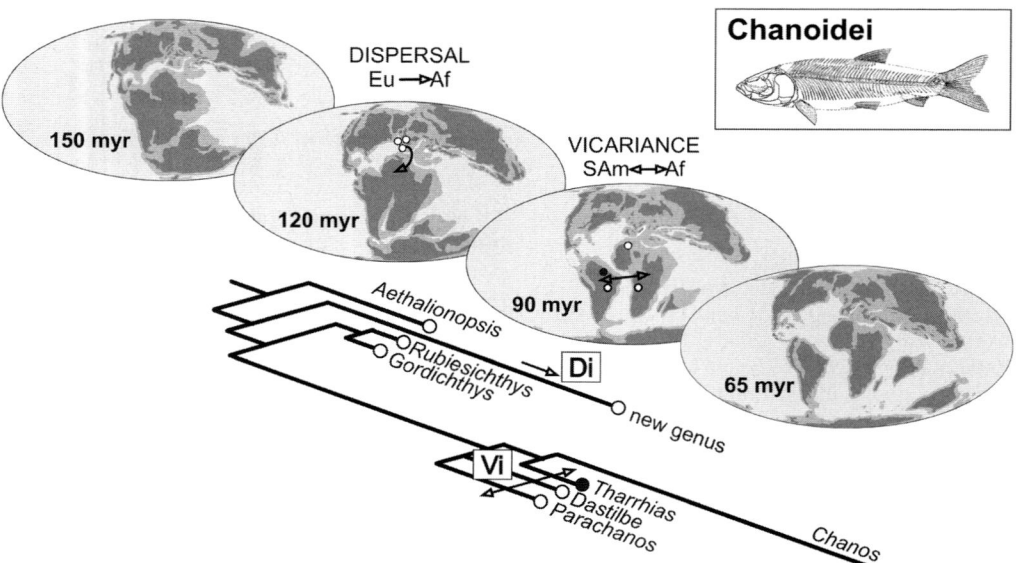

Fig. 10. Cretaceous historical biogeography of Chanoidei. Abbreviations as in previous Figures.

basal most chanoids are all from Early Cretaceous freshwater or brackish deposits of Europe, with the exception of the mid-Cretaceous new Moroccan genus occurrence, indicative of a dispersal from Europe to Africa; The second event is a vicariance between South American (*Tharrhias*, *Dastilbe*) and African (*Parachanos*) chanids in the mid-Cretaceous.

Otophysi

Otophysan fishes are expected to provide a good palaeogeographical signal because they are primary freshwater fishes. Recent biogeographic studies of otophysans as a whole (Saitoh *et al.* 2003; Briggs 2005) or of otophysan subgroups (Diogo 2004 for catfishes; Orti & Meyer 1997 for characiforms for instance), based on phylogenies and geographic distributions of Recent taxa only, suggest an old, pre-Cretaceous Pangaean diversification of modern lineages.

On the basis of the complex geographic distribution of catfish families, (their phylogenetic relationships showing no obvious vicariant events, and the presence of basal characiforms and chanids in the early Cretaceous) Diogo (2004) argued that catfishes should have an old,

pre-Cretaceous, Pangaean origin that was followed by a complex series of Early Cretaceous dispersal events. Referring to the same evidence, a younger radiation and dispersals are suggested here for Recent catfish families, as well as for Recent characiform families (Fig. 11), although the structure of the phylogenetic reconstruction implies a common ancestor of otophysans, and of otophysans plus anatophysans (ostariophysans), in the Late Jurassic (Arratia [1997] described a possible basal ostariophysan in the Late Jurassic locality of Solnhofen, Germany). The hypothesis proposed here rests on four points: (1) the catfish phylogenetic hypothesis of Diogo shows the three basal-most pectinated clades represented by South American families only, the diplomystids, the loricaroids and the cetopsids (loricaroids represented by six South American families). This pattern implies on the one hand that the first stage of the evolution of siluriforms occurred in South America, and on the other hand that South America was already partly or completely isolated from other continental blocks preventing vicariant events among representative of this first radiation. A South American origin for catfishes is also supported by the fact that more than half the catfish species occur today on that continent; (2) although rare, the Cretaceous

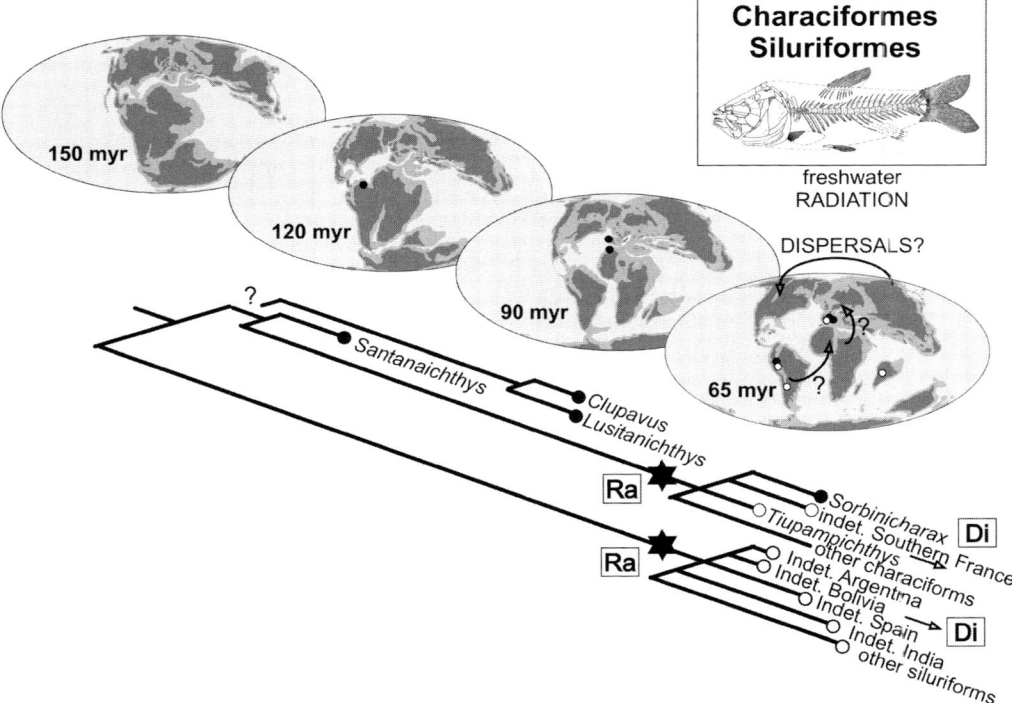

Fig. 11. Cretaceous historical biogeography of Characiformes and Siluriformes. Abbreviations as in previous Figures.

fossil record of otophysi is not lacking, but consists of stem taxa with no obvious relationships to Recent families. These stem groups are the clupavids, basal ostariophysean from the Central Tethyan (Gayet 1982a), and *Santanichthys*, the basal most characiforms according to Filleul & Maisey (2005). Clupavids and *Santanichthys* have been found in marine deposits and represent stem groups rather than members of Recent clades, indicating that extant families were likely not individualized at that time (for characiforms at least); (3) fossil catfishes are known in the Late Cretaceous of South America (Cione 1987; Gayet & Meunier 2003), Europe (de la Peña & Soler-Gijón 1995) and India (Cione & Prasad 2002). This widespread distribution may correspond to the first dispersal event of catfishes via unknown routes (a more exact scenario could be made clear once affinities of these taxa will be sorted out. However, affinities between South American and European faunas have already be pointed out in the Late Cretaceous, as well as dispersal events between India and mainland Asia [Rage & Jaeger 1995]). Based on other evidence, Hardman (2005) suggests a dispersal event for the ictalurids from NE Asia to NW North America in the Late Cretaceous; and (4) eventually, although I agree with the statement that 'absence of evidence is not evidence of absence', this assertion should not be used as justification to refute all data provided by the distribution of taxa extracted from the fossil record. Late Jurassic and Early Cretaceous freshwater fish assemblages are known from China (Jehol biota), SE Asia, Africa, South America and Europe. These assemblages systematically show the same range of taxa, mainly chondrostei, freshwater semionotiforms, amiiforms, basal osteoglossomorphs and some rarer clades, e.g. siyuichthyids and ichthyodectiforms. Considering an early phylogenetic and geographic radiation of ostariophysans implies that representatives of most Recent lineages are present, but are still undiscovered, in all these fossil assemblages. Although possible, this hypothesis looks unparsimonious.

Ability of dispersal in catfishes has generally been attributed to the heuryaline mode of life of the representatives of some families. Diogo (2004) however, refuted this hypothesis by showing that the marine taxa are well nested in the catfish phylogeny and that marine taxa are not able to cross ocean basins. Good dispersal capacities of catfishes may be related to the ability of several representatives of the group to live in oxygen poor waters and even, in some cases, to travel overland and disperse from one basin to another. This physiological capacity of several siluriform fishes allows them to easily disperse within continental areas.

Ability for fishes to disperse between freshwater basins within a continent is probably a more significant advantage than the ability to cross short marine barriers. It has been shown that ecology may be far more important than distance in determining large-scale biogeographic patterns, e.g. hylid frogs disperse remarkable distances within a similar climatic regime, but are unable to disperse even short distances if major transitions in climatic regimes are involved (Smith *et al.* 2005).

The pattern of characiform biogeographic history is problematic to explain too. It has been suggested that several vicariant events occurred between Africa and South America, with African faunas experiencing more extinctions than South America afterwards (Orti & Meyer 1997). Characiforms have been reported in the Late Cretaceous (Taverne 2003) and in the Palaeogene of Europe (Cappetta *et al.* 1972). European occurrences are probably the result of dispersals from southern continents (Gaudant 1980; Gayet *et al.* 2003) because all the Cretaceous forms, and some of the Tertiary ones, are marine or euryhaline. For the same reasons as discussed above for siluriforms, and because the Cretaceous fossil record of characiforms is mainly restricted to terminal Cretaceous with marine or euryhaline forms, the radiation of Recent families is suggested to have occurred in the terminal Cretaceous and was rapidly followed by dispersal events (Fig. 11).

The historical biogeography of cypriniforms is more puzzling. According to modern distribution and diversity, cypriniforms have been thought to originate in Asia, where the Tertiary fossil record is rather good. Based on the currently recognized phylogenetic position of the order, however, Briggs (2005) suggested that ancestral forms once occupied South America and Africa, where they became extinct possibly due to competition with characiforms.

Gymnotiforms, regarded as the sister-group of siluriforms (Fink & Fink 1996) or of characiforms (Saitoh *et al.* 2003), have no fossil record in the Mesozoic. That their distribution is restricted to South America (and Central America for some families) strengthens the assumption that otophysans originated on this continent.

To summarize, the phylogenetic positions of the major clades of otophysans imply their ancient origin, no later than the Late Jurassic and possibly in South America (Briggs 2005). However, I hypothesize that these lineages remained cryptic and weakly diversified and were represented mainly by stem groups confined in restricted geographical areas until the Late Cretaceous. These geographic provinces could be South America for catfishes and characiforms, and an unknown location for cypriniforms. This ecologically and geographically limited extension may have been caused by competition with dominant freshwater clades of that time. The radiation and individualization of modern families occurred in the Late Cretaceous and in the Tertiary, and was rapidly followed by geographical spreading, mainly through dispersals. Although these dispersal events imply the crossing of some marine barriers, these were relatively rare and short in distance. The ability to colonize new environments and/or ecological niches, which were rather common in the basalmost Tertiary, is regarded as a more important parameter for dispersal than the ability to cross a marine barrier.

If this scenario is right, so it is relatively well-documented by the fossil record: the fossil record of freshwater non-ostariophysean taxa in the Cretaceous, as well as the freshwater fossil record of ostariophysans in the Tertiary, is both diversified and abundant, as expected due to a Late Cretaceous and Tertiary ostariophysan worldwide radiation.

Aulopiformes

Phylogenies of aulopiformes in Figure 12 are from Fielitz (2004) for the enchodontids at the species level and Gallo *et al.* (2005) for the dercetids, with the additions from Taverne (2005*a* and *b*). According to the definitions of the biogeographical events above, there is one vicariant event between both sides of the South Atlantic in the mid-Cretaceous (*Cyranichthys* and a new Brazilian genus) and one between North Africa and North America at the same time (*Enchodus venator* and *E. shumardi*). In the Late Cretaceous, there are two vicariant events between Europe and North America (*Enchodus gracilis* and the more derived *Enchodus* on one hand, *Cimolichthys levisiensis* and *C. nepaholica* on the other). A mid-Cretaceous radiation of *Rhynchodercetis* is observed in the Tethys, with several species (5 at least) widely distributed in Tethys, as well as a Late Cretaceous

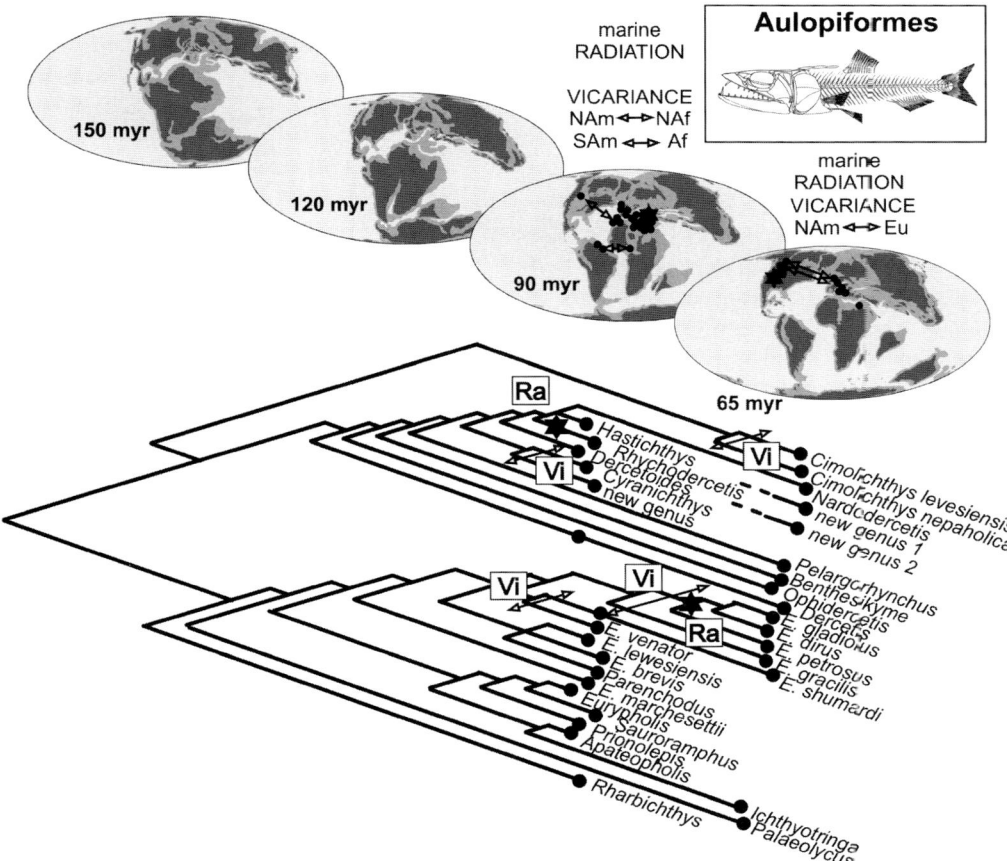

Fig. 12. Cretaceous historical biogeography of Aulopiformes. Abbreviations as in previous Figures.

178 L. CAVIN

radiation of *Enchodus* in North America. To these events may be added a possible vicariant event between Eastern and Central Tethys in the mid-Cretaceous (*E. lewesiensis/E. brevis + Parenchodus*). Taverne (2005*a* and *b*) reported the presence of four species representing four genera in the Campanian–Maastrichtian of Nardo, Italy. Because the two species described, up to now, are not closely-related, they are not evidence of a radiation event in that area. Taken as a whole, the diversity of aulopiforms correlated with sea temperature (Cavin *et al.* 2007*a*) and the various events described above form part of a major teleost radiation starting in the mid-Cretaceous.

Basal acanthomorphs

This non-monophyletic group comprises myctophiiforms, ctenosquamata *incertae sedis*, polymixiiforms and sphenocephaliforms. The intrarelationships within these groups and the interrelationships between them are poorly resolved and their palaeogeographical signal cannot be assessed. As a whole, this grade shows a radiation in the

mid-Cretaceous follows by a slight regular decrease that correlates well with variation of sea temperature (Cavin *et al.* 2007*a*).

Beryciformes

Gayet (1982*b*) provided a hand-drawn cladogram for the Cretaceous beryciforms. In Figure 13 these data have been used, with the addition of the trachichthyoid *Antarctiberyx* (without phylogenetic placement) (Grande & Chatterjee 1987), of the lissoberycinae *Hgulichthys* (Otero *et al.* 1995), of the holocentroids *Paracentrus* and *Pelotius* (without phylogenetic placement) (Forey *et al.* 2003; Gallo-da-Silva & de Figueiredo 1999 respectively) (Fig. 13). Few palaeogeographical patterns are detected. A vicariant event possibly occurred between Northern and Southern Tethys in the mid-Cretaceous (*Caproberyx* and *Stichoberyx*) and two radiation events: the alloberycins (with three genera and five species in the locality of Sahel Alma) and the genus *Hoplopteryx* with eight species.

It is surprising that the diversity of this exclusively marine family, with an important

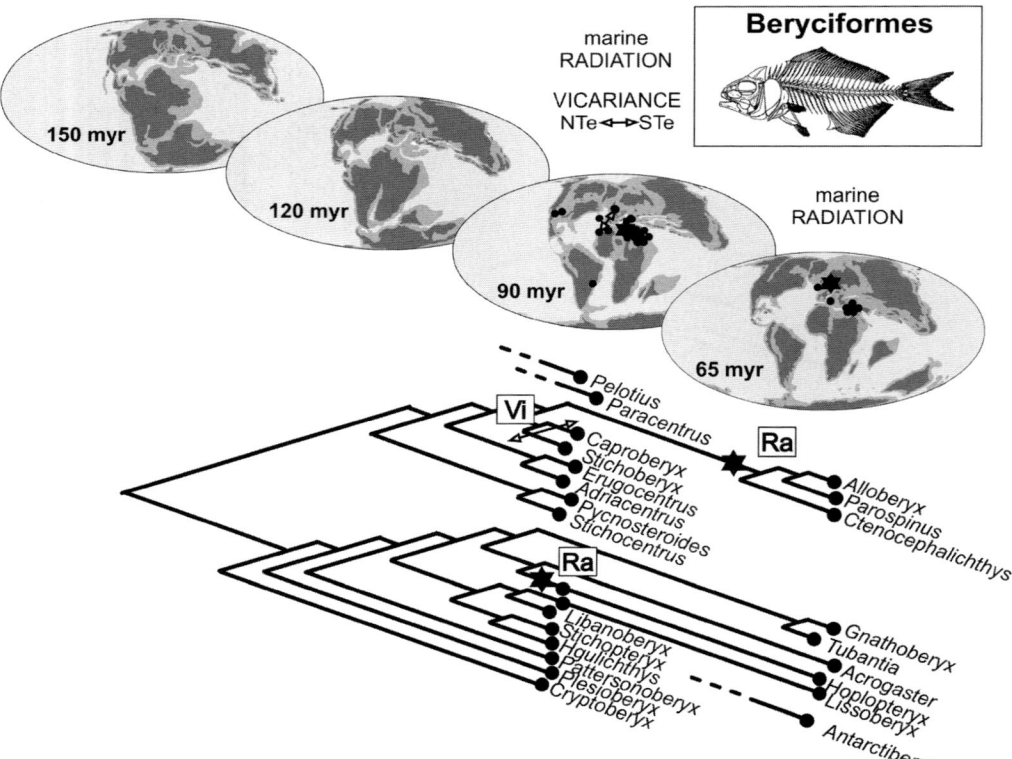

Fig. 13. Cretaceous historical biogeography of Beryciformes. Abbreviations as in previous Figures.

diversification in the mid-Cretaceous, is not correlated with sea temperature (Cavin *et al.* 2007*a*).

Other

Actinopterygians belonging to other clades are known in the Cretaceous (crossognathids, gonorynchids, salmoniforms, stomiiforms, perciforms, amongst others), but their phylogenetic relationships are too uncertain so far to provide palaeogeographic signals.

Conclusion

Figure 14 synthesizes all the patterns detected in the various bony fish clades from the Late Jurassic to the Late Cretaceous. As a preliminary comment, the global pattern shown here suffers from various biases dependent on the quality of the fossil record and of the resolution of the available phylogenies. However, because the results are based on testable data, they constitute a preliminary hypothesis that may be tested by further fossil discoveries and/or phylogenies. The amount of events detected increases through time, with only 2 detectable events in the Late Jurassic and 15 at least in the Late Cretaceous. This rise is related to the richer Late Cretaceous fossil record and to the better resolved phylogenetic relationships of these taxa, but not to a genuine rise of geographically-assignable cladogenetic events. Most of the observed patterns concerned east-west events (both vicariance and dispersal) rather than north-south events. This is probably because the separation between Laurasia and Gondwana is already underway in the Late Jurassic and affects only weakly the Cretaceous faunas. The east-west pattern concerns mainly taxa from Africa versus South America and Central versus Western Tethys in the mid-Cretaceous, and Europe versus North America in the Late Cretaceous. These results are in accordance with the time of the opening of the Atlantic Ocean starting in the South then extending northwards. Dispersals appear to be abundant between NE Asia and NW North America in the Late Cretaceous, as exemplified by other vertebrates such as dinosaurs. Dominant direction of dispersals is from Asia to North America. Although the richest Mesozoic fish assemblages occur in the mid-Cretaceous of Lebanon, the taxa from these localities show few biogeographical patterns. I suggest that this fact reflects a genuine phenomenon indicative of a genuine diversification of mid-Cretaceous marine fishes in that area that are mainly affected by physical parameters, such as sea temperature, and not by palaeogeographic events, such as land mass separation or connections. If true, this region may correspond to a centre of

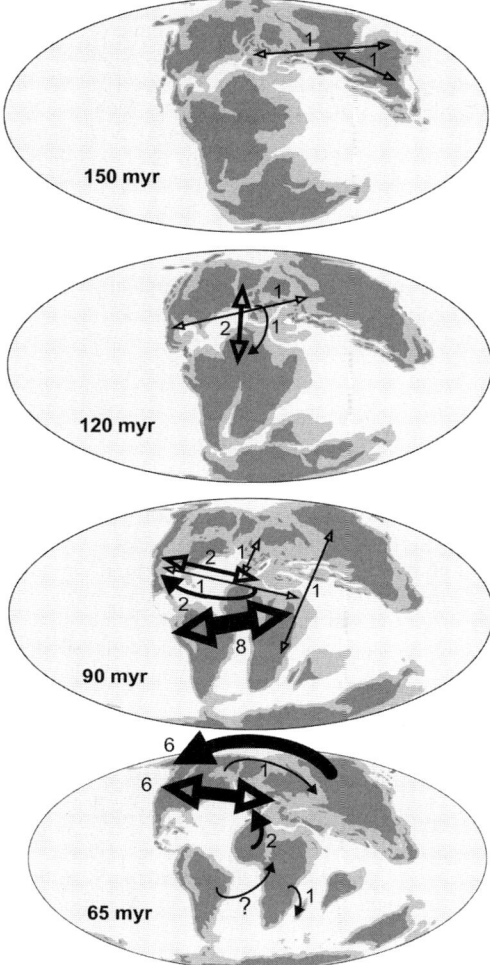

Fig. 14. Schematic representation of bony fish vicariant (double-headed arrows) and dispersal (single-headed arrow) events from the Late Jurassic to the Late Cretaceous. Width of the arrows is in proportion to the amount of events.

origination as existing today (Briggs 2003; Briggs 2006; Cavin *et al.* 2005*b*).

Vicariance is often preferred to dispersal in biogeographic reconstructions because the former is said to be falsifiable while the latter is regarded as a contingent hypothesis. If included in a temporal framework, however, a sister-group relationship between two taxa may be more parsimoniously explained by a dispersal event if both taxa are not contemporaneous in time. The direction of the dispersal is indicated by age succession, from the geographic area of the older taxon to the geographic area of the younger one. As for vicariance hypothesis, this dispersal hypothesis is falsifiable by the discovery of new fossils that could: (1) modify the phylogenetic hypothesis and subsequently the resulting biogeographical pattern; or (2) modify the temporal succession, and consequently either alters the direction of the dispersal or favours a vicariant event over a dispersal one if both taxa appear to be contemporaneous in time.

Dispersals of freshwater fishes in the Late Cretaceous are probably a more common phenomenon than previously expected, because most of the marine barriers were still relatively narrow and likely susceptible to width variations in relation to sea level fluctuations at that time. Moreover, it is suggested that the fish autoecology as a whole is a more significant parameter allowing an assessment of dispersal ability rather than simply their capacity to tolerate salt waters. Reproductive strategy (K versus r modes), physiological machinery (air breathing ability) and thermal flexibility are fundamental factors that allow dispersal within, and in between, continental landmasses.

Another trend that is detectable in this survey is a tendency in several clades to start their evolutionary history in marine environments, then to confine it to freshwater environments. This trend is obvious for the dipnoi (although the marine phase is much more ancient in the Devonian), chondrosteids, semionotids, aminoids and aspidorhynchids and it is suspected to be present in characids and possibly polypterids. Searching for the cause of such a trend is risky. One hypothesis is that: if exhaustion of morphological characters (Wagner 2000) is confirmed for bony fish clades, the consequence is a decrease in morphological diversification through time and then there is a decrease of competitive ability, especially in the marine environment where the rate of origination is high. The rapid marine species turnover may lead most ancient clades to become extinct, while they endure in freshwater environments.

I want to express my deepest gratitude to Peter L. Forey, for his supervision and collaboration at the start of my career, and for his friendship. I thank P. and J. C. Briggs (Philomath) for their comments on this manuscript.

References

ARRATIA, G. 1997. Basal Teleosts and teleostean phylogeny. *Palaeo Ichthyologica*, **7**, 5–168.

BELOUZE, A. 2002. Compréhension morphologique phylogénétique des taxons actuels et fossiles rapportés aux anguilliformes ("poissons", téléostéens). *Documents des laboratoires de géologie Lyon*, **158**, 1–401.

BLANCO, A. & CAVIN, L. 2003. New teleostei from the Agua Nueava Formation (Turonian), Vallecillo, NE Mexico. *Comptes Rendus Palevol*, **2**, 299–306.

BRIGGS, J. C. 2003. Marine centres of origin as evolutionary engines. *Journal of Biogeography*, **30**, 1–18.

BRIGGS, J. C. 2005. The biogeography of otophysan fishes (Ostariophysi: Otophysi): a new appraisal. *Journal of biogeography*, **32**, 287–294.

BRIGGS, J. C. 2006. Proximate sources of marine biodiversity. *Journal of biogeography*, **33**, 1–10.

BRITO, P. M. 1997. Révision des Aspidorhynchidae (Pisces, Actinopterygii) du Mésozoïque: ostéologie, relations phylogénétiques, données environnementales et biogéographiques. *Geodiversitas*, **19**, 681–772.

CAPPETTA, H., BRAILLON, J. & RUSSELL, D. E. 1972. Sur la découverte de Characidae (Pisces, Cypriniformes) dans l'Eocène inférieur français. *Bulletin du Muséum National d'Histoire Naturelle, Section C: Sciences de la Terre, 3ème série*, **51**, 37–50.

CAVIN, L. 1997. Nouveaux teleostei du gisement du Turonien inférieur de Goulmima (Maroc). *Comptes Rendus de l'Académie des Sciences, Sciences de la Terre et des Planètes*, **325**, 719–724.

CAVIN, L. 2001. Osteology and phylogenetic relationships of the teleost *Goulmimichthys arambourgi* Cavin, 1995, from the Upper Cretaceous of Goulmima, Morocco. *Ecolgae geologicae Helvetiae*, **94**, 509–535.

CAVIN, L. & FOREY, P. L. 2004. New mawsoniid coelacanth (Sarcopterygii: Actinistia) remains from the Cretaceous of the Kem Kem beds SE Morocco. *In:* TINTORI, A. & ARRATIA, G. (eds) *Mesozoic Fishes 3 – Systematics, Paleoenvironments and Biodiversity*, Dr F. Pfeil, Munich, 493–506.

CAVIN, L. & SUTEETHORN, V. 2006. A new Semionotiformes (Actinopterygii, Neopterygii) from Late Jurassic – Early Cretaceous of Northeastern Thailand with comments on the semionotiformes relationships. *Paleontology*, **49**, 339–353.

CAVIN, L., MARTIN, M. & VALENTIN, X. 1996. Découverte d'*Atractosteus africanus* (Actinopterygii, Lepisosteidae) dans le Campanien inférieur de Ventabren (Bouches-du-Rhône, France). Implications paléobiogéographiques. *Revue de Paléobiologie*, **15**, 1–7.

CAVIN, L., FOREY, P. L., BUFFETAUT, E. & TONG, H. 2005a. Latest European coelacanth shows Gondwanan affinities. *Biology Letters*, **2005**, 176–177.

CAVIN, L., JURKOVŠEK, B. & KOLAR-JURKOVŠEK, T. 2005b. The mid-Cretaceous fish assemblages from the Komen-Trieste plateau in Slovenia: its palaeogeographic and palaeoenvironmental significance. *In:* POYATO-ARIZA, F. J. (ed.) *Fourth International Meeting on Mesozoic Fishes – Systematics, homology and Nomenclature – Extended Abstracts*, Miraflores de la Sierra, Madrid, Spain, UAM, 67–68.

CAVIN, L. & FOREY, P. L. 2008. Osteology of *Eubiodectes libanicus* (Pictet & Humbert, 1866) and some other ichthyodectiformes (Teleostei): phylogenetic implications. *Journal of Systematic Palaeontology* (in press).

CAVIN, L., FOREY, P. L. & LÉCUYER, C. 2007a. Correlation between environment and Late Mesozoic ray-finned fish evolution. *Palaeogeography, Palaeoclimatology, Palaeoecology*, **245**, 353–367.

CAVIN, L., SUTEETHORN, V., BUFFETAUT, E. & TONG, H. 2007b. A new Thai Mesozoic lungfish (Sarcopterygii, Dipnoi) with an insight into post-Palaeozoic dipnoan evolution. *Zoological Journal of the Linnean Society*, **149**, 141–177.

CHANG, M.-M. & CHEN, Y.-Y. 2000. Late Mesozoic and Tertiary ichthyofaunas from China and some puzzling patterns of distribution. *Vertebrata PalAsiatica*, **38**, 161–175.

CHANG, M. M. & MAISEY, J. G. 2003. Redescription of *Ellimma branneri* and *Diplomystus shengliensis*, and relationships of some basal clupeomorphs. *American Museum Novitates*, **3404**, 1–35.

CHOUDHURY, A. & DICK, T. A. 1998. The historical biogeography of sturgeons (Osteichthyes: Acipenseridae): a synthesis of phylogenetics, palaeontology and palaeogeography. *Journal of Biogeography*, **25**, 623–640.

CIONE, A. L. 1987. The Late Cretaceous fauna of Los Alamitos, Patagonia, Argentina. Part II-The Fishes. *Revista del Museo argentino de Ciencias Naturales "Bernardino Rivadavia" e Instituto nacional de Investigacion de Las Ciencias Naturales*, **3**, 111–120.

CIONE, A. L. & PRASAD, G. V. R. 2002. The oldest known catfish (Teleostei: Siluriformes) from Asia (India, Late Cretaceous). *Journal of Paleontology*, **76**, 190–193.

CLEMENT, G. 2005. A new coelacanth (Actinistia, Sarcopterygii) from the Jurassic of France, and the question of the closest relative fossil to *Latimeria*. *Journal of Vertebrate Paleontology*, **25**, 481–491.

DE QUEIROZ, A. 2005. The resurrection of oceanic dispersal in historical biogeography. *Trends in Ecology and Evolution*, **20**, 68–73.

DAGET, J., GAYET, M., MEUNIER, F. & SIRE, J.-Y. 2001. Major discoveries on the dermal skeleton of fossil and Recent polypteriforms: a review. *Fish and Fisheries*, **2001**, 113–124.

DIOGO, R. 2004. Phylogeny, origin and biogeography of catfishes: support for a Pangean origin of "modern teleosts" and reexamination of some Mesozoic Pangean connections between Gondwanan and Laurasian supercontinents. *Animal Biology*, **54**, 331–351.

DUTHEIL, B. D. 1999. The first articulated fossil cladistian: *Serenoichthys kemkemensis*, gen. et sp. nov., from the Cretaceous of Morocco. *Journal of Vertebrate Paleontology*, **19**, 243–246.

FIELITZ, C. 2004. The phylogenetic relationships of the Enchodontidae (Teleostei: Aulopiformess). *In*: ARRATIA, G., WILSON, M. V. H. & CLOUTIER, R. (eds) *Recent advances in the origin and early radiation of vertebrates*. Dr F. Pfeil, Munich, 619–634.

FILLEUL, A. & MAISEY, J. G. 2005. Redescription of *Santanaichthys diasii* (Otophysi, Characiformes) from the Albian of the Santana Formation and comments on its implications for Otophysan relationships. *American Museum Novitates*, **3455**, 1–21.

FINK, S. V. & FINK, W. L. 1996. Chapter 11. Interrelationships of Ostariophysan Fishes (Teleostei). *In*: STIASSNY, M. L. J., PARENTI, L. R. & JOHNSON, G. D. (eds) *Interrelationships of Fishes*, Academic Press, 209–249.

FOREY, P. L. 1998. *History of the colacanth fishes*. Chapman & Hall.

FOREY, P. L. 2004. A three-dimensional skull of a primitive clupeomorph from the Cenomanian English Chalk, and implications for the evolution of the clupeomorph

acusticolateralis system. *In*: TINTORI, A. & ARRATIA, G. (eds) *Mesozoic Fishes 3 – Systematics, Paleoenvironments and Biodiversity*. Dr F. Pfeil, Munich, 405–427.

FOREY, P. L. & GRANDE, L. 1998. An African twin to the Brazilian *Calamopleurus* (Actinopterygii: Amiidae). *Zoological Journal of the Linnean Society*, **123**, 179–195.

FOREY, P. L., YI, L., PATTERSON, C. & DAVIES, C. E. 2003. Fossil fishes from the Cenomarian (Upper Cretaceous) of Namoura, Lebanon. *Journal of Systematic Palaeontology*, **1**, 227–330.

GALLO-DA-SILVA, V. & DE FIGUEIREDO, F. J. 1999. *Pelotius hesselae*, gen. et sp. nov. (Teleostei: Holocentridae) from the Cretaceous (Turonian) of Pelotas basin, Brazil. *Journal of Vertebrate Paleontology*, **19**, 263–270.

GALLO, V., SILVA DA, H. M. A. & DE FIGUEIREDO, F. J. 2005. The interrelationships of Dercetidae (Neoteleostei, Aulopiformes). *In*: POYATO-ARIZA, F. J. (ed.) *Fourth International Meeting on Mesozoic Fishes - Systematics, homology and Nomenclature - Extended Abstracts*, Miraflores de la Sierra, Madrid, Spain, UAM, 101–104.

GAUDANT, J. 1980. *Eurocharax tourainei* nov. gen., nov. sp. (Poisson Téléostéen, Ostariophysi): nouveau characidae fossile des "calcaires à Bythinies" du Var. *Geobios*, **13**, 683–703.

GAYET, M. 1982a. Considération sur la Phylogénie et la Paléobiogéographie des Ostariophysaires. *Geobios*, **MS 6**, 39–52.

GAYET, M. 1982b. Essai de définition des relations phylogénétiques des Holocentridea nov. et des Trachchthyoidea nov. (Pisces, Acanthoptreygii, Béryciformes). *Bulletin du Muséum national d'Histoire naturelle, Paris, 4e série, C*, **4**, 21–41.

GAYET, M. & MEUNIER, F. J. 1991. First discovery of Polypteridae (Pisces, Cladistia, Polypteriformes) outside of Africa. *Geobios*, **24**, 463–466.

GAYET, M. & MEUNIER, F. J. 1992. Polyptériformes (Pisces, Cladistia) du Maastrichtien et du Paléocène de Bolivie. *Geobios*, **MS 14**, 159–168.

GAYET, M., MEUNIER, F. J. 1998. Maastrichtian to Early Paleocene Freshwater Osteichthyes of Bolivia: Additions and Comments. *In*: MALABARA, L. R., REIS, R. E., VARI, R. P., LUCENA, Z. M. S., LUCENA, C. A. S. (eds) *Phylogeny and classification of neotropical fishes*. Porto Alegre, Editora Pontificia Universidate Catolica do Rio Grande do Sul, 85–110.

GAYET, M. & MEUNIER, F. J. 2003. Palaeontology and Palaeobiogeography of catfishes. *In*: ARRATIA, G., KAPOOR, B. G., CHARDON, M. & DIOGO, R. (eds) *Catfishes*. Science Publishers, Enfield, NH, **2**, 491–522.

GAYET, M., MEUNIER, F. J. & WERNER, C. 2002. Diversification in Polypteriformes and special comparison with the Lepisosteiformes. *Palaeontology*, **45**, 361–376.

GAYET, M., JEGU, M., BOCQUENTIN, J. & NEGRI, F.R. 2003. New Characoids from the upper Cretaceous and Paleocene of Bolivia and the Mio-Pliocene of Brazil: Phylogenetic position and palaeobiogeographic implications. *Journal of Vertebrate Paleontology*, **23**, 28–46.

GONZÁLEZ-RODRÍGUEZ, K. & REYNOSO, V.-H. 2004. A new *Notagogus* (Macrosemiidae, Halecostomi) species from the Albian Tlayua Quarry, Central Mexico. *In*: TINTORI, A. & ARRATIA, G. (eds) *Mesozoic Fishes 3 – Systematics, Paleoenvironments and Biodiversity*. Dr F. Pfeil, Munich, 265–278.

GONZÁLEZ-RODRÍGUEZ, K., APPLEGATE, S. P. & ESPINOSA-ARRUBARRENA, L. 2004. A new world macrosemiid (Pisces: Neopterygii-Halecostomi) from the Albian of Mexico. *Journal of Vertebrate Paleontology*, **24**, 281–289.

GOTTFRIED, M. D., ROGERS, R. R. & CURRY ROGERS, K. 2004. First record of Late Cretaceous coelacanths from Madagascar. *In*: ARRATIA, G., WILSON, M. V. H. & CLOUTIER, R. (eds) *Recent advances in the origin and early radiation of vertebrates*. Dr F. Pfeil, Munich, 687–691.

GRANDE, L. 2005. Phylogenetic study of gars and closely related species, based mostly on skeletal morphology. The resurrection of Holostei. *In*: POYATO-ARIZA, F. J. (ed.) *Fourth International Meeting on Mesozoic Fishes – Systematics, homology and Nomenclature – Extended Abstracts*, Miraflores de la Sierra, Madrid, Spain, UAM, 119–121.

GRANDE, L. & BEMIS, W. E. 1998. A Comprehensive Phylogenetic Study of Amiid Fishes (Amiidae) Based On Comparative Skeletal Anatomy. An Empirical Search for Interconnected Patterns of Natural History. *Supplement Journal of Vertebrate Palaeontology, Memoir 4*, **18**, 1–690.

GRANDE, L., JIN, F., YABUMOTO, Y. & BEMIS, W. E. 2002. *Protopsephurus liui*, a well-preserved primitive paddlefish (Acipenseriformes: Polyodontidae) from the Lower Cretaceous of China. *Journal of Vertebrate Paleontology*, **22**, 209–237.

GRANDE, L. & CHATTERJEE, S. 1987. New Cretaceous fish fossils from Seymour Island, Antarctic Peninsula. *Palaeontology*, **30**, 829–837.

GRANDE, T. & POYATO-ARIZA, F. J. 1999. Phylogenetic relationships of fossil and Recent gonorynchiform fishes (Teleostei: Ostariophysi). *Zoological Journal of the Linnean Society*, **125**, 197–238.

GREENWOOD, P. H. 1984. *Polypterus* and *Erpetoichthys*: Anachronistic Osteichthyans. *In*: ELDREDGE, N. S. (ed.) *Living Fossils*. 143–147.

HARDMAN, M. 2005. The phylogenetic relationships among non-diplomystid catfishes as inferred from mitochondrial cytochrome b sequences; the search for the ictalurid sister taxon (Otophysi: Siluriformes). *Molecular Phylogenetics and Evolution*, **37**, 700–720.

HEADS, M. 2005. Towards a panbiogeography of the seas. *Biological Journal of the Linnean Society*, **84**, 675–723.

HILTON, E. J. 2003. Comparative osteology and phylogenetic systematics of fossil and living bony-tongue fishes (Actinopterygii, Teleostei, Osteoglossomorpha). *Zoological Journal of the Linnean Society*, **137**, 1–100.

HUNN, C. G. & UPCHURCH, P. 2001. The importance of time/space in dignosing the causality of phylogenetic events: towards a "chronobiogeographical" paradigm. *Systematic biology*, **50**, 391–407.

KRIWET, J. 2004. A new pycnodont fish genus (Neopterygii: Pycnodontiformes) from the Cenomanian (Upper Cretaceous) of Mount Lebanon. *Journal of Vertebrate Paleontology*, **24**, 525–532.

KUMAZAWA, Y. & NISHIDA, M. 2000. Molecular phylogeny of Osteoglossoids: a new model for Gondwanian origin and plate tectonic transportation of the Asian Arowana. *Molecular Biology and Evolution*, **17**, 1869–1878.

LAMBERS, P. 1992. *On the Ichthyofauna of the Solnhofen Lithographic Limestone (Upper Jurassic, Germany)*. Unpublished PhD thesis, University of Groningen, 1–336.

LAVOUÉ, S. & SULLIVAN, J. P. 2004. Simultaneous analysis of five molecular markers provides a well-supported phylogenetic hypothesis for the living bony-tongue fishes (Osteoglossomorpha: Teleostei). *Molecular phylogenetics and evolution*, **33**, 171–185.

LI, G. Q. & WILSON, M. V. H. 1999. Early divergence of Hiodontiformes *sensu stricto* in East Asia and phylogeny of some Late Mesozoic teleosts from China. *In*: ARRATIA, G. & SCHULTZE, H.-P. (eds) *Mesozoic Fishes 2 – Systematics and Fossil Record*, Dr F. Pfeil, Munich, 369–384.

MAISEY, J. G. 2000. Continental break up and the distribution of fishes of Western Gondwana during the Early Cretaceous. *Cretaceous Research*, **2000**, 281–314.

MAISEY, J. G. & MOODY, J. M. 2001. A review of the problematic teleost fish *Araripichthys*, with a description of a new species from the Lower Cretaceous of Venezuela. *American Museum Novitates*, **3324**, 1–27.

NESSOV, L. A. & KAZNYSHKIN, M. N. 1985. A lungfish and turtles from Upper Jurassic of Nothern Fergana, Kirghiz SSR. *Vestnik Zoologii*, **1**, 33–39.

ORTI, G. & MEYER, A. 1997. The radiation of characiform fishes and the limits of resolution of mitochondrial ribosomal DNA sequences. *Systematic Biology*, **46**, 75–100.

OLSEN, P. E. & MCCUNE, A. R. 1991. Morphology of the *Semionotus elegans* group from the Early Jurassic part of the Newark Supergroup of Eastern North America with comments on the family Semionotidae (Neopterygii). *Journal of Vertebrate Paleontology*, **11**, 269–292.

OTERO, O., DUTOUR, Y. & GAYET, M. 1995. *Hgulichthys*, nouveau genre de Lissoberycidae (Trachichthyiformes, Trachichtyoidea) du Cénomanien inférieur marin de Hgula (Liban). Implications phylogénétiques. *Geobios*, **28**, 711–717.

OTERO, O., LIKIUS, A., VIGNAUD, P. & BRUNET, M. 2006. A new polypterid fish: *Polypterus faraou* sp. nov. (Cladistia, Polypteridae) from the Late Miocene, Toros-Menalla, Chad. *Zoological Journal of the Linnean Society*, **146**, 227–237.

PEÑA, DE LA, A. & SOLER-GIJON, R. 1995. The first siluriform fish from the Cretaceous-Tertiary boundary interval of Eurasia. *Lethaia*, **29**, 85–86.

POYATO-ARIZA, F. J. & WENZ, S. 2002. A new insight into pycnodontiform fishes. *Geodiversitas*, **24**, 139–248.

POYATO-ARIZA, F. J. & WENZ, S. 2004. The new pycnodontid fish genus *Turbomesodon*, and a revision of

Macromesodon based on new material from the Lower Cretaceous of Las Hoyas, Cuenca, Spain. *In*: TINTORI, A. & ARRATIA, G. (eds) *Mesozoic Fishes 3 – Systematics, Paleoenvironments and Biodiversity.* Dr F. Pfeil, Munich, 341–378.

POYATO-ARIZA, F. J. & WENZ, S. 2005. *Akromystax tilmachiton* gen. et sp. nov. a new pycnodontid fish from the Lebanese Late Cretaceous of Haqel and En Nammoura. *Journal of Vertebrate Paleontology*, **25**, 27–45.

RAGE, J.-C. & JAEGER, J.-J. 1995. The sinking Indian raft: a response to Thewissen and McKenna. *Systematic Biology*, **44**, 260–264.

SAITOH, K., MIYA, M., INOUE, J. G., ISHIGURO, N. B. & NISHIDA, M. 2003. Mitochondrial genomics of Ostariophysan fishes: perspectives on phylogeny and biogeography. *Journal of Molecular Evolution*, **56**, 464–472.

SMITH, S. A., STEPHENS, P. R. & WIENS, J. J. 2005. Replicate pattern of species richness, historical biogeography, and phylogeny in holarctic treesfrogs. *Evolution*, **59**, 2433–2450.

TAVERNE, L. 2003. Les poissons crétacés de Nardo. 16°. *Sorbinicharax verraesi* gen. et sp. nov. (Teleostei, Ostariophysi, Otophysi, Characiformes). *Bollettino*

del Museo Civico di Storia Naturale di Verona, **27**, 29–45.

TAVERNE, L. 2005a. Les poissons crétacés de Nardo. 21°. *Ophidercetis italiensis* gen. et sp. nov. (Teleostei, Aulopiformes, Dercetidae). Une solution ostéologique au problème des genres *Dercetis* et *Benthesikyme* (=*Leptotrachelus*). *Bollettino del Museo Civico di Storia Naturale di Verona*, **29**, 55–79.

TAVERNE, L. 2005b. Les poissons crétacés de Nardo. 22°. *Nardodercetis vandewallei* gen. et sp. nov. (Teleostei, Aulopiformes, Dercetidae). *Bollettino del Museo Civico di Storia Naturale di Verona*, **29**, 81–93.

TAVERNE, L. & GAYET, M. 2005. Phylogenetical relationships and paleozoogeography of the marine Cretaceous Tselfatiiformes (Teleostei, Clupeocephala). *Cybium*, **29**, 65–87.

WAGNER, P. J. 2000. Exhaustion of morphologic character states among fossil taxa. *Evolution*, **54**, 365–386.

ZARAGÜETA BAGILS, R. 2004. Basal clupeomorphs and ellimmichthyiform phylogeny. *In*: TINTORI, A. & ARRATIA, G. (eds) *Mesozoic Fishes 3 – Systematics, Paleoenvironments and Biodiversity.* Dr F. Pfeil, Munich, 391–404.

Osteoglossomorpha: phylogeny, biogeography, and fossil record and the significance of key African and Chinese fossil taxa

M. V. H. WILSON[1] & A. M. MURRAY[1,2]

[1]Department of Biological Sciences and Laboratory for Vertebrate Paleontology, University of Alberta, Edmonton, Alberta T6G 2E9, Canada (e-mail: mark.wilson@ualberta.ca)

[2]Research Division, Canadian Museum of Nature, P.O. Box 3443, Station D, Ottawa, ON K1P 6P4, Canada

Abstract: The Osteoglossomorpha are a clade of primitive teleostean fishes with modern representatives in five biogeogeographic regions and fossil representatives on six continents. The centre of modern diversity is in Africa but the centre of fossil diversity is in E Asia. Key fossil taxa include: †*Phareodus*, †*Joffrichthys*, and †*Ostariostoma* in N America; †*Lycoptera*, †*Paralycoptera*, and †*Huashia* among others in E Asia; †*Brychaetus* and possibly †*Thaumaturus* in Europe; †*Palaeonotopterus*, †*Singida*, and †*Chauliopareion* in Africa; †*Tavernichthys* in India; and †*Musperia* in SE Asia.

Morphological phylogenies to date have disagreed on three main points: the relationships of †*Lycoptera*, of *Pantodon*, and of Notopterids and Mormyrids. Molecular phylogenies have similarly differed on the last two points. In this study a combined set of morphological data was generated from previous studies, including data from three recently described or redescribed taxa (the African †*Singida* and †*Chauliopareion* and the Chinese †*Xixiaichthys*) and maximum parsimony was used to generate a revised hypothesis of relationships. Our analysis recovered †*Lycoptera*, †*Paralycoptera* + †*Tanolepis*, and †*Xixiaichthys* as stem-group osteoglossomorphs, †*Singida* as sister to *Pantodon* within Osteoglossidae, †*Chauliopareion* as a stem osteoglossid, †*Ostariostoma* as a stem osteoglossiform, and Notopteridae as sister to Mormyroidea and †*Palaeonotopterus*.

These results do not lend themselves to easy explanations of osteoglossomorph biogeography involving either dispersal from a centre of origin or vicariant division of a widely distributed ancestor. Recent suggestions of an ancient (Palaeozoic) origin for osteoglossomorphs are flawed. The evidence, instead, is consistent with an origin within the Mesozoic and the biogeographic explanation involves extensive extinction of clades from continents where they occurred in the past.

The Osteoglossomorpha are a clade of relatively primitive teleostean fishes with a significance for evolutionary biology that far outweighs their relatively modest diversity. They have been of early morphological and behavioural interest because of their unique anatomy and the ability of some members to generate electric fields and communicate with them. They have an extensive fossil record on six continents. They are the subject of a number of phylogenetic debates concerning their place among the teleosts, the relationships of key fossil and living members, and the role of morphological and molecular evidence. In addition, their geographic distribution in the fresh waters of five biogeographic regions has been cited as evidence for dispersal from a centre of origin and, contrarily, for vicariance stemming from Pangaean or Gondwanan continental divisions.

Recent discoveries of new fossil osteoglossomorphs, especially in China and in Africa, have added significant diversity to the group. Despite Africa's role as the centre of living osteoglossomorph biodiversity, the fossil record of the group on that continent is not extensive. From the Eocene of Tanzania, additional material of the osteoglossoid †*Singida* Greenwood & Patterson, 1967, and the new genus †*Chauliopareion* Murray & Wilson, 2005, along with the discovery of the Early Cretaceous notopterid †*Palaeonotopterus* in Morocco (Forey 1997), have improved the African record, but the systematic position of the two African fossil osteoglossoids remains uncertain. The situation in E Asia is the reverse with respect to fossil and Recent diversity. China has an extremely diverse fossil record (e.g. Zhang 1998, 2004), but no living representatives.

The purpose of the present paper is to review the distribution and fossil record of osteoglossomorphs, to place certain well-preserved fossils in their phylogenetic context with emphasis on the most recently described genera from Africa and China, and to evaluate recent ideas about the age of the clade and its biogeographic history.

From: CAVIN, L., LONGBOTTOM, A. & RICHTER, M. (eds) *Fishes and the Break-up of Pangaea*.
Geological Society, London, Special Publications, **295**, 185–219.
DOI: 10.1144/SP295.12   0305-8719/08/$15.00 © The Geological Society of London 2008.

Diversity and distribution of extant osteoglossomorphs

Extant osteoglossomorphs are found in the fresh waters of the Nearctic (North American), Neotropical (South American), Ethiopian (African), Oriental (SE Asian) and Australian biogeographic regions. The centre of diversity at the level of species and higher taxa is in Africa (Fig. 1), which has representatives of five of the six families.

The main groups of living osteoglossomorphs are the Hiodontidae, Osteoglossidae, Pantodontidae (included here in Osteoglossidae), Notopteridae and Mormyroidea. The Hiodontidae, or mooneyes, classified in the order Hiodontiformes, are usually considered to be the living sister-group of the remaining osteoglossomorphs. There is only one genus of hiodontid with two extant species, *Hiodon tergisus* (the mooneye) and *Hiodon alosoides* (the goldeye), both distributed in the interior of North America. Fossil hiodontids, discussed in detail below, are illustrated in Figure 2.

The Osteoglossiformes according to most modern authorities (Li & Wilson 1996*a*; Lavoué & Sullivan 2004; Zhang 2006) can be divided into two suborders, the Osteoglossoidei and the Notopteroidei. Fossil osteoglossiforms are discussed below and illustrated in Figures 3–5. The position of the Pantodontidae, a monotypic family consisting only of the African species *Pantodon buccholzi*, the butterflyfish (Fig. 6c), is controversial. Kumazawa & Nishida (2000) group it with Notopteridae, Lavoué & Sullivan (2004) place it as sister to all other Osteoglossoidei on molecular evidence, while Li *et al.* (1997*b*), Hilton (2003), and Zhang (2006) have it more closely related to Osteoglossidae or Osteoglossinae on morphological grounds.

The Osteoglossidae, apart from *Pantodon*, comprise two extant subfamilies, Osteoglossinae and Heterotidinae. Osteoglossinae contain two living genera. *Osteoglossum* is confined to the Amazon region of South America (Fig. 1), where it is represented by *O. ferreirai* (the black aruana) and *O. bicirrhosum* (the silver aruana; Fig. 6b). *Scleropages* is distributed in SE Asia (*S. formosus* and possibly other species) and in northern Australia and New Guinea (*S. leichardti*).

The subfamily Heterotidinae contains two living monotypic genera, each on its own continent (Fig. 1). *Heterotis niloticus* inhabits Africa, while *Arapaima gigas* (Fig. 6a) inhabits South America but is raised commercially in other areas.

The Notopteridae at one time were thought to be related to the Hiodontidae (Greenwood 1973) but are now considered to be the sister group of the Mormyroidea (Li & Wilson 1996*a*; Lavoué & Sullivan 2004; Zhang 2006) as suggested by Greenwood (1971), or else of the Osteoglossidae (Hilton 2003). Notopteridae (featherbacks or

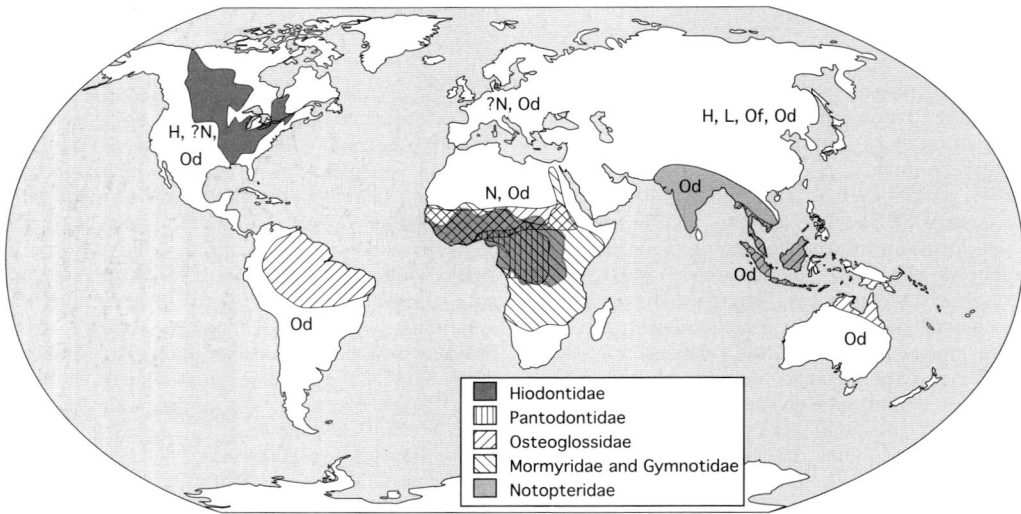

Fig. 1. Map of the modern world showing the approximate areas of native distribution of higher taxa of osteoglossomorphs, and taxa occurring as fossils in major geographic regions. Recent distribution data for Hiodontidae are from Hilton (2002) and for other taxa from Berra (1981). Abbreviations: H, Hiodontiformes; L, Lycopteridae and other potentially basal Osteoglossomorpha; N, Notopteroidea and possible fossil relatives (†*Ostariostoma* in North America and †*Thaumaturus* in Europe); Od, Osteoglossidae; Of, potential stem-group Osteoglossiformes.

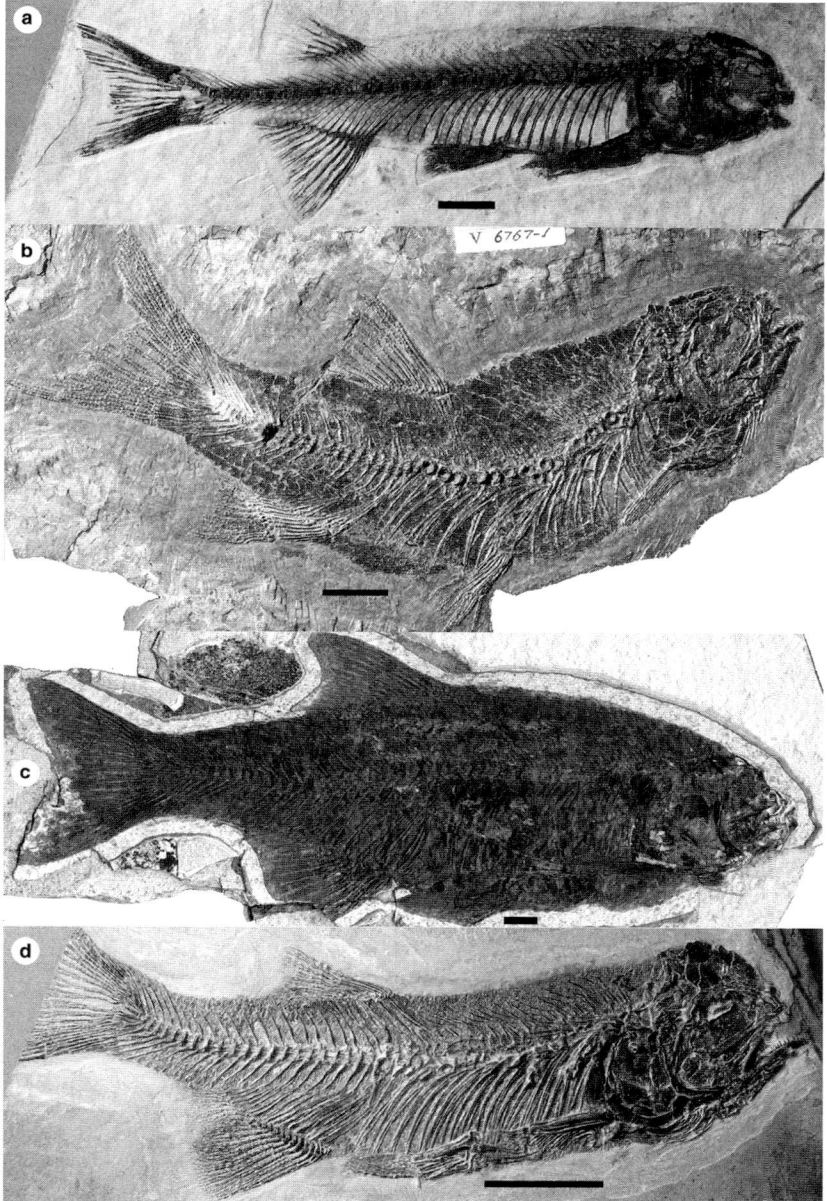

Fig. 2. Fossil osteoglossomorphs from Asia and North America. (**a**), †*Lycoptera davidi* (Sauvage, 1880) from Liaoning, China, Early Cretaceous, uncatalogued IVPP specimen; †*Lycoptera* was classified in the Hiodontiformes (then including Notopteroidei) by Greenwood (1970), but as a stem-group osteoglossomorph by Li & Wilson (1996a, 1999), by Zhang (2006), and the present study; its position was basal but unresolved in Hilton (2003). (**b**), †*Yanbiania wangqingica* Li, 1987, China, Early Cretaceous, holotype IVPP V6767-1; Chang (1999), Chang and Miao (2004), and Zhang (2006) have suggested that †*Yanbiania* is a junior synonym of †*Jiaohichthys* Ma, 1983; Zhang (2006) places it as a stem-group hiodontiform as suggested by Li & Wilson (1999). (**c**), †*Eohiodon woodruffi* Wilson, 1978, from British Columbia, Canada, Eocene, UALVP specimen; Hilton & Grande (2008) present evidence for synonymy of †*Eohiodon* Cavender, 1966, with *Hiodon* Lesueur, 1818. (**d**), *Hiodon consteniorum* Li and Wilson, 1994, from Montana, USA, Eocene, holotype UALVP 38875. Scale bars = 1 cm.

Fig. 3. Some of the fossil taxa from the Early Cretacous of China that have been suggested to be stem-group osteoglossiforms or stem-group osteoglossomorphs. (**a**), †*Tongxinichthys microdus* Ma, 1980, holotype IVPP 2332.1; a stem osteoglossomorph according to Zhang (2006). (**b**), †*Jinanichthys longicephalus* Ma & Sun, 1988, holotype IVPP V10149-51; a stem osteoglossomorph according to Zhang (2006). (**c**), †*Huashia gracilis* Chang & Chou, 1977, holotype IVPP V2996.1; grouped with †*Kuntulunia* as a stem heterotidine (Li and Wilson 1999), stem osteoglossiform (Zhang 1998, 2004) or osteoglossomorph *incertae sedis* (Zhang 2006). (**d**), †*Kuntulunia longipterus* Liu *et al.*, 1982, IVPP 8556.27; relationships as for †*Huashia*. Scale bars = 1 cm.

Fig. 4. Selected fossil representatives of the Osteoglossidae from North America. (**a**), †*Phareodus testis* (Cope, 1877), from Wyoming, USA, Eocene, UALVP 17659; a member of the Osteoglossinae according to Li *et al*. (1997), Hilton (2003), and Zhang (2006), but a stem-group member of the Heterotidinae in the present study. (**b**), †*Joffrichthys symmetropterus* Li and Wilson, 1996*b*, from Alberta, Canada, Paleocene, holotype UALVP 23705; a stem-group member of the Heterotidinae according to Li and Wilson (1996*b*) and the present study, but a stem osteoglossid (the latter included *Pantodon*) according to Hilton (2003). Scale bars = 1 cm.

knifefishes) include *Notopterus notopterus* (Fig. 7b) of southern and SE Asia, and three other genera (*Chitala* with four species, *Papyrocranus* with two and *Xenomystus* with one) in Africa, India, and SE Asia (Nelson 2006; fig. 1).

The Mormyroidea include two families both confined to Africa. The Mormyridae (elephantfishes) are the most diverse group of osteoglossomorphs with 18 genera and about 200 species in tropical Africa and the Nile drainage (Nelson 2006; fig. 1). Representative genera include *Hippopotamyrus*,

Marcusenius, and *Mormyrus* (Fig. 7c–e). Sister to the Mormyridae is the monotypic family Gymnarchidae, represented by *Gymnarchus niloticus* (the aba) in tropical Africa and the Nile drainage (Nelson 2006).

Osteoglossomorphs have traditionally been considered to be 'primary-division' freshwater fishes (Darlington 1957), restricted to fresh water throughout life and thus potentially key indicators of the biogeographic history of their continental regions. Certainly extant species seem to be largely

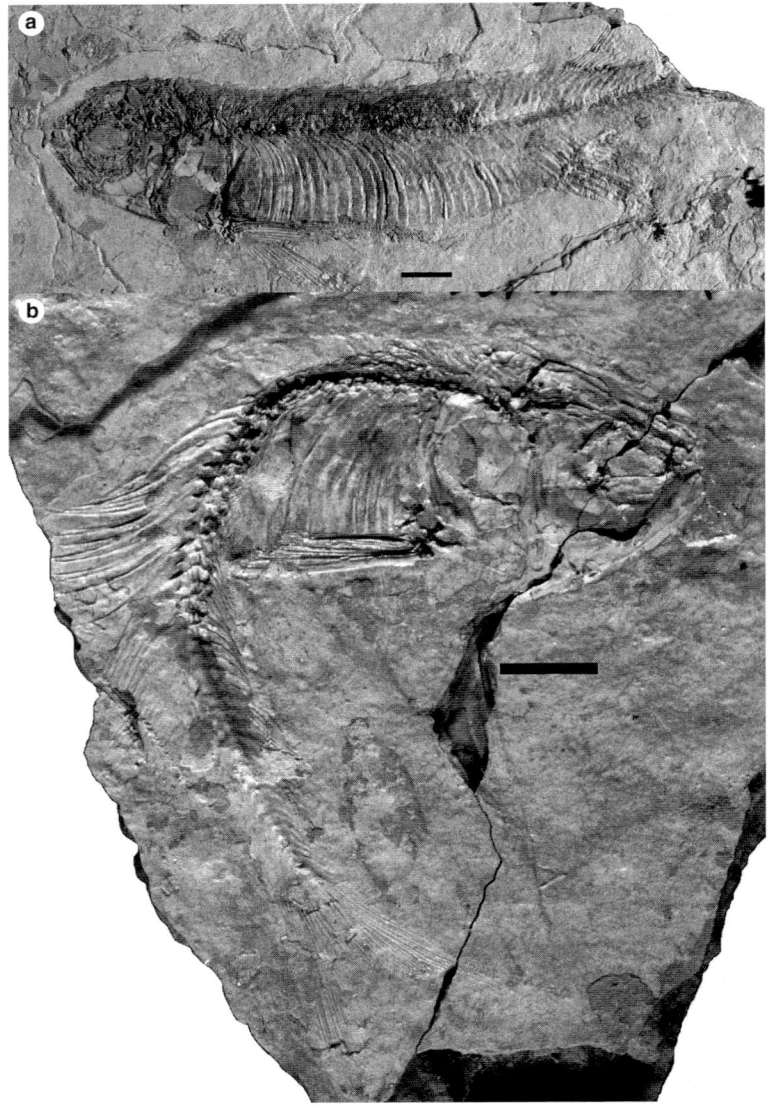

Fig. 5. Eocene African osteoglossomorphs from Mahenge, Tanzania. (**a**), †*Chauliopareion mahengeense* Murray and Wilson, 2005, paratype NMT WM 311/96, a stem-group osteoglossid according to the present study. (**b**), †*Singida jacksonoides* Greenwood & Patterson, 1967, NMT WM 241/96, an osteoglossine according to Li and Wilson (1999), Hilton (2003), and Zhang (2006), but sister to *Pantodon* within Pantodontinae, Osteoglossidae, in the present study. Scale bars = 1 cm.

restricted to fresh waters. However, Darlington advocated caution with respect to osteoglossids because of reports that †*Brychaetus* inhabited marine environments and because the distribution of *Scleropages*, on either side of Wallace's Line in the Indonesian Archipelago, suggested past marine dispersal.

The African-centred distribution of modern osteoglossomorphs could be interpreted, from a dispersalist standpoint, to suggest that the group originated in Africa and spread from there to other parts of the world, as Darlington (1957) thought for the South American and SE Asian osteoglossids, although he saw SE Asia as the centre of origin for many other freshwater fishes.

There are no extant species in Europe or in most of Asia (Fig. 1), yet the fossil record in China (see below) exhibits the greatest diversity. The

Fig. 6. Selected extant representatives of the Osteoglossidae and the only known species of *Pantodon* (Pantodontinae here; Pantodontidae of some authors). (**a**), *Arapaima gigas*, the giant arapaima or pirarucu, native distribution in the Amazon Basin; large dried specimen photographed in oblique view in Taiwan by Katja Rodriguez of CMN; *Arapaima gigas* is raised commercially in South America and Southeast Asia for sale to world markets including Japan and Europe; *Arapaima* and the African *Heterotis niloticus* are the two extant members of the Heterotidinae. (**b**), *Osteoglossum bicirrhosum*, the silver aruana, CMN uncatalogued, from the Amazon region of South America; the two extant genera in the subfamily Osteoglossinae are the South American *Osteoglossum* and the Southeast Asian and Australian *Scleropages*. (**c**), *Pantodon buchholzi*, the butterfly fish, CMN uncatalogued, from Africa, is traditionally treated as the only member of the Pantodontidae; *Pantodon* was classified within the Osteoglossoidei by Li and Wilson (1996a), Hilton (2003), and Zhang (2006) on morphological evidence, but as the sister of all other living Osteoglossiformes (Osteoglossoidei + Notopteroidei) by Lavoué *et al.* (2004) on molecular evidence. The present morphological study finds it as sister to †*Singida* within Pantodontinae, one of three subfamilies of Osteoglossidae. Scale bars = 1 cm.

sister-group of all other osteoglossomorphs, the so-called most basal group, is the Hiodontidae, restricted to North America in the modern fauna, casting doubt on African origins. Shen (1989, 1990, 1996) suggested dispersalist scenarios with an East Asian origin, based on the finding of numerous primitive fossil osteoglossomorphs and hiodontiforms in that region.

The overall distribution might, on the other hand, be suggested to indicate Pangaean origins if the group were ancient enough. Kumazawa & Nishida (2000) have argued this using molecular clock methods to arrive at a Palaeozoic time of

origin (but see discussion below), while the extant Osteoglossiformes have been considered to be a classic example of a Gondwanan distribution, occurring as they do on most of the parts of the former Gondwana (South America, Africa, India, Australia, but not Antarctica) as well as in SE Asia. Wilson & Williams (1992), Li (1997), and Li & Wilson (1999) argued that the present distribution is not a reliable guide to biogeographic history because it is partly an artifact of the extinction of member clades in North America, Europe, Central Asia, China and India since the Eocene (see also Kumar *et al.* 2005).

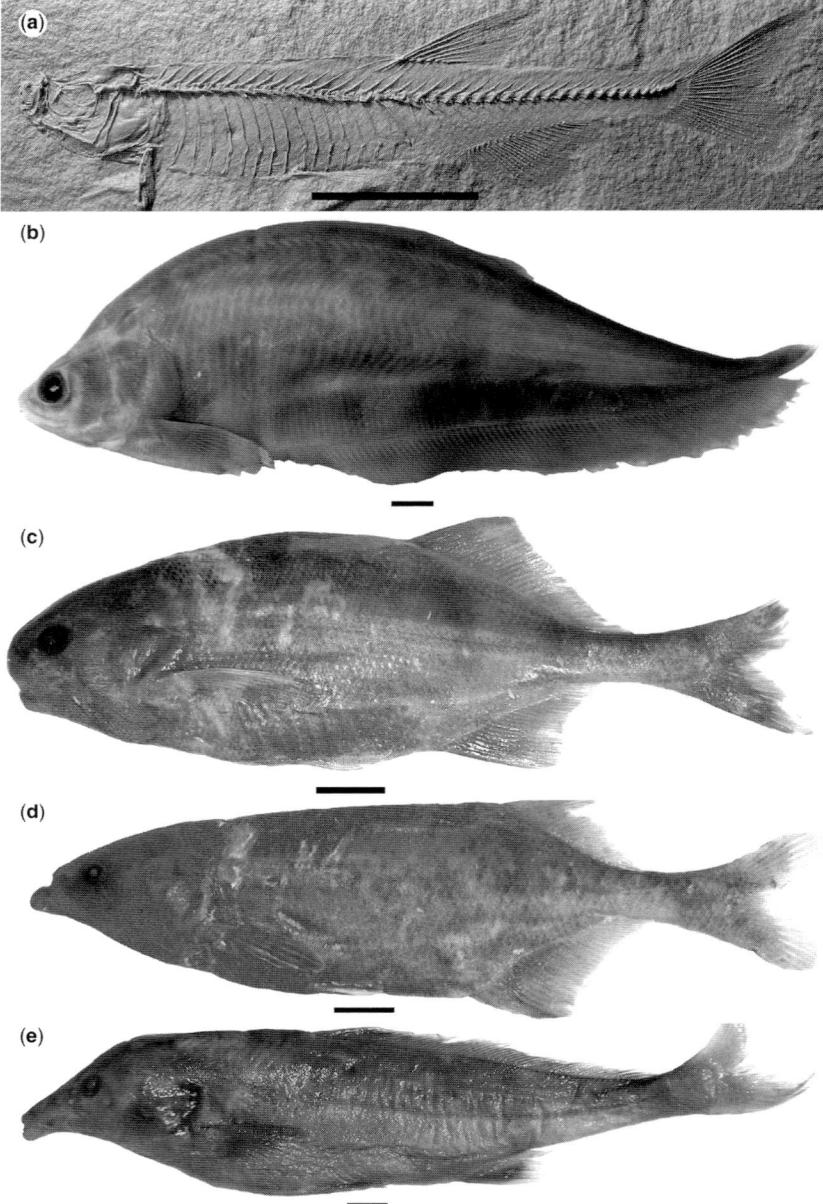

Fig. 7. Representatives of extant Notopteridae and Mormyridae, and the fossil †*Ostariostoma*. (**a**), †*Ostariostoma wilseyi* Schaeffer, 1949, from Montana, USA, latest Cretaceous or early Paleocene, cast of FMNH PU14728; †*Ostariostoma* was classified with doubt in the Hiodontoidea (then including †Lycopteridae) by Grande & Cavender (1991) but as a stem-group member of the Notopteroidei by Li and Wilson (1999), as the sister of Notopteridae by Zhang (2006), and as a stem-group member of the Osteoglossiformes by Hilton (2003) and the present study. (**b**), *Notopterus notopterus*, Asian knifefish or featherback, CMN 63-0122, from Thailand, family Notopteridae. Notopterids are classified variously as sister to Osteoglossidae (Hilton 2003), to *Pantodon* (Kumazawa and Nishida 2000), or to Mormyroidea (Li and Wilson 1999, Lavoué and Sullivan 2004, this study). (**c**), *Hippopotamyrus grahami* (formerly in the genus *Marcusenius*), Graham's stonebasher, CMN 81-0254, from Lake Victoria, Tanzania, family Mormyridae. (**d**), *Marcusenius victoriae*, Victoria stonebasher, Africa, family Mormyridae. (**e**), *Mormyrus kannume*, elephant-snout fish, CMN 63-0122, from Lake Victoria, Tanzania, family Mormyridae. Scale bars = 1 cm.

Morphological studies

The Osteoglossomorpha have been the subject of numerous morphological studies over more than a century. Indeed the modern concept of the group's membership has not changed significantly since the work of Ridewood (1904, 1905) and, later, Gregory (1933) on cranial osteology, except for a period during the last century when some stem-group fossil teleosts such as ichthyodectiforms were mistakenly included with osteoglossiforms in a single group, a practice rectified by Patterson & Rosen (1977).

Other notable studies include those of: Roellig (1967, 1974) on fossil and extant osteoglossids; Greenwood (1963, 1966, 1971) on the swimbladder of notopterids, caudal skeleton of osteoglossoids, and gill arch musculature of osteoglossomorphs; Nelson (1968, 1969, 1972) on gill arches, infraorbital bones, and the gut of osteoglossomorphs; and a series of papers by Taverne (1968, 1972, 1974*a*–*c*, *e*, 1975*a*, *b*, 1976*a*, *b*, 1977, 1978, 1979) on skeletal anatomy of most of the living genera.

More recently, Schultze & Arratia (1988) clarified homologies in the caudal skeleton, Sanford & Lauder (1989) and Hilton (2001) evaluated the 'tongue bite' mechanism that characterizes most of the members of the group, Hilton (2002) redescribed the osteology of *Hiodon* and Moritz & Britz (2005) discussed the homology of the basipterygoid articulation in *Pantodon*.

Fossil record

The fossil record of the Osteoglossomorpha is among the most extensive of any living clade of fishes of comparable diversity, with representatives on six continents plus India and SE Asia (Fig. 1).

North America

In North America, fossil osteoglossids were recognized as long ago as 1871, when Cope named *Osteoglossum encaustum* (now †*Phareodus encaustus*) from the Eocene of Wyoming, USA. The genus †*Phareodus* was coined by Leidy (1873), and Cope (1877) soon afterward named †*Dapedoglossus testis* (now †*Phareodus testis*; see Fig. 4a). Further studies on †*Phareodus* were completed by Grande (1980, 1984) and by Li *et al.* (1997*a*). A possible osteoglossid, †*Chandlerichthys*, was named from a poorly-preserved specimen of Late Cretaceous age from Alaska by Grande (1986), and an undoubted osteoglossid (†*Cretophareodus*) from the Cretaceous of Alberta, Canada, by Li (1996). The probable occurrence of the osteoglossid genus †*Brychaetus* was reported by Weems & Horman (1983) from the Eocene of Maryland.

Osteoglossids in the subfamily Heterotidinae were recognized from the Paleocene of North America as †*Joffrichthys symmetropterus* Li & Wilson, 1996*b* (Fig. 4b), and a second species, †*J. triangulpterus* Newbrey & Bozek, 2000, was added from the Paleocene of North Dakota (see also Newbrey & Bozek 2003).

An enigmatic latest Cretaceous or earliest Paleocene fish from Montana is †*Ostariostoma wilseyi* Schaeffer, 1949 (Fig. 7a), originally assigned to Clupeoidei or Ostariophysi. Redescribed by Grande & Cavender (1991) and placed close to Hiodontidae, which at the time was classified with Notopteridae in the Notopteroidei, †*Ostariostoma* was suggested by Li & Wilson (1996*a*) to belong in their revised Notopteroidei, now excluding Hiodontidae but including Mormyridae and Gymnarchidae. Later authors who have considered †*Ostariostoma* have agreed with this (Zhang 2006), or alternatively, placed it as sister to all osteoglossiforms (Hilton 2003). Li & Wilson (1999) further suggested a relationship between †*Ostariostoma* and the problematic European Eocene genus †*Thaumaturus*.

The native North American family Hiodontidae was not recognized in the fossil record until Cavender (1966) redescribed an Eocene fish that had been originally described in the cyprinid genus *Leuciscus*. Renamed †*Eohiodon rosei* (Hussakof 1916) by Cavender (1966), the species was subsequently found to be widely distributed in British Columbia, Canada (Wilson 1977). Cavender (1968) also reported scales of hiodontids, identified as "cf. *Hiodon*" also from Oregon. A second species, †*E. woodruffi* Wilson, 1978, was found in both British Columbia and Washington State, USA, and a third species, †*E. falcatus* Grande, 1979, from Wyoming. Li & Wilson (1994) named †*Hiodon consteniorum* from the Eocene of Montana, and Li *et al.* (1997*b*) reviewed the records of †*Eohiodon* then known. Aspects of the biology of †*Eohiodon* were addressed by Wilson & Williams (1992), and by Wilson (1996*a*, *b*). Hilton (2002) listed other named fossils, considered by him to be *nomina dubia*, of *Hiodon* from North America.

Late Cretaceous hiodontids were first identified from North America by Brinkman & Neuman (2002) on the basis of vertebral centra from fluvial formations. Studies on the growth rate and small body size of Cretaceous hiodontids are reported by Newbrey & Wilson (2005) and Newbrey *et al.* (2007).

Northeastern Asia

Despite having no living representatives of the Osteoglossomorpha, Siberia and China are the centre of diversity of fossil osteoglossomorphs

(Figs 1, 2a–b, 3), due to an abundance of freshwater formations of appropriate ages, especially Early Cretaceous (formerly many of these formations were thought to be Late Jurassic in age) and Eocene (Chang & Chow 1986; Bannikov 1993; Chang 1999).

The Cretaceous genus †*Lycoptera* Müller, 1847, occupies a special place in osteoglossomorph history and phylogeny, although its full significance was not recognized for more than a hundred years after its first description. †*Lycoptera middendorffi* Müller, 1847, from the Transbaikal area of Siberia, was not recognized as an osteoglossomorph until Greenwood (1970) noted the special similarity of †*Lycoptera* to living Hiodontidae, including features of the otoliths, parasphenoid, temporal fenestra and caudal skeleton. Cockerell (1925) had studied †*L. middendorffi*, focusing on its scales. He recognized that †*Prolebias davidi* Sauvage, 1880, from China, was another species of †*Lycoptera*, but had thought them to belong to the Ostariophysi. Takai (1943) and Gaudant (1968) had also studied †*Lycoptera* in detail without making the connection with osteoglossomorphs.

Recent authors have treated †*Lycoptera* either essentially as Greenwood had it, closely related to Hiodontidae (Taverne 1998), as a stem-group member of Osteoglossomorpha as a whole (Li & Wilson 1996a, 1999; Zhang 2006), or in an unresolved but still basal position (Hilton 2003). An exception is Shen's (1996) conclusion, not followed by others, that †*Lycoptera* and certain other taxa discussed below are not osteoglossomorphs at all. The possibility (Li & Wilson 1996a) that †*Lycoptera* and some other Early Cretaceous genera from China might in fact be stem-group osteoglossomorphs and/or stem-group osteoglossiforms, rather than hiodontiforms (Taverne 1998), has greatly changed perceptions about the early history of the Osteoglossomorpha.

The Early Cretaceous genus †*Aokiichthys* Yabumoto, 1994, from Japan, was assigned to the †Lycopteridae by its author. Another apparently more derived Early Cretaceous osteoglossomorph from Japan is currently under study by the same author (Yabumoto 2005). The Palaeogene subgenus †*Gobihiodon* Sytchevaskaya, 1986, a putative hiodontid, is from Mongolia. Li (1997) speculated that it might be a junior synonym of †*Plesiolycoptera*. †*Opsithrissops* Danil'chenko, 1968, is a marine putative osteoglossomorph from Turkmenistan. The relationships of †*Aokiichthys*, †*Gobioihiodon*, and †*Opsithrissops* require further study.

The Early Cretaceous of China has, in recent decades, given us a tremendous diversity of osteoglossomorph fossil taxa (see list *in* Zhang 1998). For more details about most of these Chinese taxa see especially Chang (1999) and Zhang (2006).

Chinese Cretaceous genera include †*Yanbiania* Li, 1987 (Fig. 2b), considered now by Chang (1999) to be a possible junior synonym of †*Jiaohichthys* Ma, 1983. According to Li & Wilson (1996a, 1999), †*Yanbiania* is a stem-group hiodontiform, while Zhang (2006) similarly finds †*Jiaohichthys* to be sister-taxon to †*Eohiodon* within Hiodontidae.

†*Huashia* Chang & Chou, 1977 (Fig. 3c), was thought to be related to *Chanos* by its describers, then to †*Thaumaturus* (from Europe) by Ma (1986), but was later united with †*Kuntulunia* in Huashiidae by Shen & Zhang (1991). †*Kuntulunia* Liu et al., 1982 (see also Liu et al. 1985; Fig. 3c), which was classified with †*Huashia* in Huashiidae (Shen et al. 1991; Zhang 1998), is a relative of Osteoglossidae according to Li & Wilson (1996b, 1999), or of uncertain position in Osteoglossomorpha according to Zhang (2006).

†*Plesiolycoptera* Chang & Chou, 1976, found in a drill core of Late Cretacous age, was classifed as a basal hiodontiform by Li & Wilson (1996a, 1999), but Chang (1999) cautioned that the specimens are too incomplete to code certain characters properly and the genus was not included in the analyses of Zhang (1998, 2006).

†*Tanolepis* Jin, 1994 (a replacement name for the preoccupied †*Tanichthys* Jin, 1991), was originally described in Hiodontidae. Jin et al. (1995) suggested that it might be a junior synonym of †*Paralycoptera*, while Li & Wilson (1996a, 1999) and Li et al. (1997b) continued to treat it separately as a basal osteoglossiform closely related to †*Paralycoptera*.

†*Tongxinichthys* Ma, 1980 (Fig. 3a), was described in Lycopteridae. Revised by Zhang & Jin (1999), it was resolved as a stem-group osteoglossomorph by Shen (1996); as sister-taxon to †*Jiuquanichthys*, the two genera in an unresolved basal osteoglossomorph position by Zhang & Jin (1999); as more primitive than †*Lycoptera* by Li & Wilson (1999); and as more derived than †*Lycoptera* and unrelated to †*Jiuquanichthys* by Zhang (2006).

†*Xixiaichthys* Zhang, 2004, was originally classified as a primitive member of the Osteoglossiformes but as an unresolved primitive osteoglossomorph by Zhang (2006).

†*Jinanichthys* Ma & Sun, 1988 (Fig. 3b) has a complex taxonomic history (a junior synonym is †*Liaoxiichthys* Su, 1992, according to Zhang et al. 1994; see summary *in* Zhang, 2006). It is a stem osteoglossomorph according to Zhang (2006).

Cenozoic osteoglossomorphs have also been found in China, though some of them remain undescribed. Among those that have been described is †*Eohiodon shuyangensis* Shen, 1989, assigned by its author to a genus otherwise only known from

North America. Su (1986) described the Eocene osteoglossid †*Sinoglossus lushanensis*, which is usually classified now in the Heterotidinae (Li & Wilson 1996a; Zhang 2006).

Europe and Western Asia

The osteoglossomorph fossil record from Europe is relatively meager. Woodward (1901) named †*Brychaetus muelleri* based on fossils from the Eocene of Isle of Sheppey, England. †*Brychaetus* was further studied by Roellig (1974) and by Taverne (1974d). †*Brychaetus* is a rarity among osteoglossomorphs, fossil and Recent, because it inhabited marine environments (Patterson 1975). Li *et al.* (1997a) argued that †*Brychaetus* was a junior synonym of †*Phareodus*, and Zhang's (2006) results supported this placement, but Taverne (1998, p. 157) disagreed, and Kumar *et al.* (2005) continued to recognize †*Brychaetus* as distinct from †*Phareodus*.

Taverne (1998) added to the list of putative osteoglossomorphs from Europe when he described or redescribed three forms from the Eocene (marine) of Monte Bolca, Italy. He placed †*Monopteros* Volta, 1796, in Osteoglossiformes, †*Thrissopterus* Heckel, 1856, in the Arapaimidae (Arapaiminae of other authors), and the new genus †*Foreyichthys* in a basal position within Osteoglossomorpha. To date other authors have not attempted to include these taxa in phylogenetic analyses.

One of the most problematic fossil fishes in Europe is †*Thaumaturus*, which had been known from Eocene deposits for more than a century when Gaudant (1981) suggested it might have osteoglossomorph affinities. Ma (1986) suggested an affinity with the Chinese genus †*Huashia*, while Li & Wilson (1996a, 1999) suggested that, like †*Ostariostoma*, it might be a stem-group member of the Notopteroidei (including Mormyroidea).

India, Southeast Asia and Australia

These regions have in common that only osteoglossid fossils have been found to date. From India, several localities have yielded fragmentary dentigerous bones along with squamules, which are the polygonal fragments of reticulated scales known from certain osteoglossid genera. Jolly & Bajpal (1988), for example, describe middle Eocene examples. Squamules are relatively common in rocks of Late Cretaceous through Eocene age in India (Kumar *et al.* 2005).

Recently, Kumar *et al.* (2005) became the first to describe an osteoglossid from the Indian subcontinent based on an articulated fossil skull from Paleocene or Eocene rocks. They named it †*Tavernichthys bikeranericus* and assigned it to Osteoglossinae.

Osteoglossid remains from SE Asia consist of similar fragmentary material of †*Musperia radiata* from the Eocene of Sumatra (Sanders 1934; Taverne 1978). Li *et al.* (1997a) suggested that it might prove to be a synonym of †*Phareodus*.

In Australia, Hills reported osteoglossid remains based on partial skeletons, establishing †*Phareodus queenslandicus* Hills, 1934. Hills (1936) later identified an opercle as *Scleropages* aff. *leichardti*. Taverne (1973) erected the new genus †*Phareoides* for †*Phareodus queenslandicus*, but Li (1994) argued that †*Phareoides* is a junior synonym of †*Phareodus*. Phylogenetic results of Li *et al.* (1997a) placed †*P. queenslandicus* as closer to †*Phareodus encaustus* than to †*Phareodus testis*.

South America

Few osteoglossomorph fossils have been found so far in South America. Santos (1988) described †*Laeliichthys ancestralis* based on fossils of Aptian (late Early Cretaceous) age from Brazil, and allocated it to the Arapaimidae, erecting the monotypic subfamily †Laeliichthyinae. Li & Wilson (1997a, 1999) placed it as a basal stem-group member of the Heterotidinae, which includes *Arapaima*.

Fragmentary osteoglossid remains from the Maastrichtian to Paleocene of Bolivia were identified by Gayet & Meunier (1983) as belonging to Osteoglossidae, based on squamules. Fragmentary skull elements led to the erection of the new genus and species †*Phareodusichthys taverni* Gayet, 1991, along with other osteoglossomorphs in open nomenclature. Gayet & Meunier (1998) reviewed the Bolivian osteoglossids, identifying premaxillae, dentaries, and a basioccipital as belonging to the Heterotidinae close to *Arapaima*, and premaxillae and dentaries as pertaining to the Phareodontinae, as †*Phareodusichthys taverni*. Lundberg & Chernoff (1992) assigned a basioccipital from the Miocene of Colombia to the extant genus *Arapaima*.

Africa

The osteoglossomorph fossil record of Africa is not extensive despite its role as the centre of modern biodiversity for the group, though discoveries of Eocene osteoglossoid fossils in Tanzania and of Early Cretaceous Notopteridae from Morocco have improved the African record recently. Murray (2000) reviewed the record of fossil fishes from Africa up to the early Cenozoic.

Among the earliest finds were remains assigned to †*Brychaetus* from Morocco (Arambourg 1935, 1952) and from the Paleocene of the Congo Basin (Darteville & Casier 1949). Taverne (1969, 1974*d*, 1975*c*) reported on remains assigned to †*Brychaetus* from the Paleocene and Eocene and of a Cretaceous (Cenomanian) species from Zaire, †*Paradercetis kipalaensis* Casier, 1965, which he felt was related to *Heterotis*, a point accepted by Lundberg & Chernoff (1992). Bonde (1996) considered the Early Cretaceous †*Chanopsis lombardi* from western Africa to belong to the Osteoglossidae and Taverne (1984) also considered that it may be an osteoglossid. Other fossil osteoglossiforms from Africa (see Maisey 2000; Murray 2000) have been placed in other families or are of uncertain position, or are based only on squamules.

Recent important discoveries in Africa include that of †*Palaeonotopterus greenwoodi* Forey, 1997, based on a braincase from the mid-Cretaceous Kem Kem Beds of Morocco. Forey felt that †*Palaeonotopterus* was sister to extant notopterids, and Cavin & Forey (2001) provided additional details. Taverne & Maisey (1999) described another notopterid skull of Early Cretaceous age from Morocco, and Taverne (2000, 2004) offered new observations on †*Palaeonotopterus*, suggesting new autapomorphies for the genus.

Fossil osteoglossomorphs from Tanzania were first reported by Greenwood & Patterson (1967), who named †*Singida jacksonoides* based on peculiar fishes from the Eocene of that country. †*Singida* lacks teeth on its maxilla, premaxilla, and dentary.

Harrison *et al.* (2001) reported the recovery of additional osteoglossid remains from Mahenge, Tanzania. These were formally described by Murray & Wilson (2005), who described new features of †*Singida jacksonoides* and named a new genus and species, †*Chauliopareion mahengeense*. The two species from Mahenge are superficially similar but differ in the shapes and proportions of skull bones and in the fact that †*Chauliopareion* bears teeth on its dermal jaw bones. The phylogenetic position of these two fishes was considered to be within Osteoglossiformes (including *Pantodon*), either as successive stem taxa to Osteoglossoidei using data from Li & Wilson (1997*b*) or as close relatives of *Pantodon* using data from Hilton (2003). The relationships of these important African forms are further explored below.

Phylogenetic controversies

It is beyond the scope of the present paper to offer a full review of the phylogenetic history of the Osteoglossomorpha. Consult the recent papers by Hilton (2003) and Zhang (2006) for a more complete history. Here we will briefly mention some past and current controversies. Some of these debates involve different sets of terminal taxa and of characters and states in morphological analyses, and others involve agreement and differences between morphological (including palaeontological) and molecular analyses.

The position of osteoglossomorphs within Teleostei has been the subject of recent debates, with Patterson & Rosen (1977), Patterson (1998), and others arguing that osteoglossomorphs are the sister group of all other living teleosts, and Arratia (1997, 1998) arguing that elopomorphs have that distinction. The present study is not designed to answer this question and our results should not be interpreted as supporting one conclusion over the other.

Relationships within Osteoglossomorpha that remain in dispute include the systematic position of mormyrids, notopterids, and most especially of the lone pantodontid *Pantodon buchholzi*. While notopterids were, at one time, thought to be closely related to hiodontids (see discussion above), recently authors have placed them as sister-group to Mormyroidea (Li & Wilson 1996*a*; Lavoué & Sullivan 2004; Zhang 2006) in a revised Notopteroidei, or as sister-group to mormyrids and osteoglossids (Kumazawa & Nishida 2000), or else as sister-group to osteoglossids alone (Hilton 2003).

Another area of debate involves the relationships of key fossil taxa such as †*Lycoptera* and †*Jiaohichthys* (=†*Yanbiania*) from Asia, †*Singida* and †*Chauliopareion* from Africa, and †*Ostariostoma* and †*Joffrichthys* from North America, as discussed above.

Materials and methods

The phylogenetic analysis, including the new information about †*Singida* and †*Chauliopareion* from Africa and †*Xixiaichthys* from China, was conducted using the computer program PAUP 4.b1 (PPC/Altivec) (Swofford 2002). Both heuristic and branch-and-bound searches were used and gave the same results. We used a 'furthest' addition sequence, with no topological constraints enforced, no ancestral taxa identified, and 'parsimony' as the optimality criterion.

All characters were run as unordered and unweighted. Character changes were optimized onto the resulting tree using MacClade 4.08 OSX (Maddison & Maddison 2005) showing unambiguous changes only.

Information on some taxa was taken from the literature (Taverne 1972, 1974*e*, 1977, 1978, 1979, 1980, 2000, 2004; Li 1994, 1996; Li & Wilson

1996*a*, 1996*b*; Li *et al.* 1997*a*, 1997*b*; Forey 1997; Taverne & Maisey 1999; Cavin & Forey 2001; Hilton 2002, 2003; Zhang 2004). Additional material examined is listed in Appendix 1.

Phylogenetic analysis

Murray & Wilson (2005) assessed character states for †*Singida jacksonoides* and †*Chauliopareion mahangeense*, from the Eocene of Africa, using two separate character matrices from Hilton (2003) and Li *et al.* (1997*b*), in order to determine the relationships of the two African genera. Here we use a combined data set, derived from those same two data matrices. Although Li & colleagues have produced a number of data matrices, we use the matrix from Li *et al.* (1997*b*) as it is the most recent of those data sets, despite publication dates. We determined whether or not there was overlap in the two matrices by combining the two data sets.

Taxa. Hilton (2003) and Li *et al.* (1997*b*) included many of the same taxa in their analyses, but a few differed. Li *et al.* (1997*b*) included more fossil taxa than Hilton (2003), and used both †*Cladocyclus* and the Clupeoidei as outgroups. Hilton (2003) used only *Elops* as his outgroup. We have kept all three as outgroups, reasoning that a single outgroup or inappropriate outgroups can contribute to erroneous results, although this decision causes some missing data for each. Hilton (2003) used three notopterids, only one genus of which was the same as one of the two notopterids included in Li *et al.* (1997*b*). Hilton further used three genera of mormyroids, but Li *et al.* (1997*b*) did not list the mormyroids examined by them. Because we are more interested in the relationships of the Osteoglossidae, we have included the notopterids and mormyroids as single taxa in the analysis, as in Li *et al.* (1997*b*), coding them as polymorphic where Hilton (2003) noted differences among genera, although we also show the data (Appendix 2) for the individual taxa coded by Hilton (2003).

We have also added data for two recently described species, the osteoglossid †*Chauliopareion mahangeense* Murray & Wilson, 2005, of Tanzania, and the osteoglossiform †*Xixiaichthys tongxinensis* Zhang, 2004, of China based on the text and photographs of the original description, and an examination of the type specimen by one of us (MW). We have also added the additional data for †*Singida jacksonoides* noted in Murray & Wilson (2005), and examined additional material of taxa available to us (Appendix 1) in order to confirm character states.

Characters. Li *et al.* (1997*b*) considered 60 characters (denoted as L1–L60 below). Hilton (2003)

listed 72 characters in his matrix (denoted as H1–H72 below). Although Hilton did not directly compare his characters to those of Li *et al.* (1997*b*) he did use characters from other papers by Li & colleagues, which are also characters used by Li *et al.* (1997*b*). Forty characters of Hilton (2003) overlap with 39 characters of Li *et al.* (1997*b*) [two of Hilton's characters (3 and 4) are equivalent to one character of Li *et al.* (character 38)]. Of these characters, 26 are essentially the same characters with the same states, although some have slightly different descriptions. Only seven of these are coded the same way for the overlapping taxa by both Hilton (2003) and Li *et al.* (1997*b*). The seven characters in agreement between the two studies, H11/L7, H12/L56, H24/L43, H25/L25, H41/L58, H55/L60 and H61/L36, were coded the same way for each taxon in common to the two studies. For these seven characters in our data matrix, we deleted the duplicate set.

The remainder of the 26 characters that were essentially the same between the two studies (19 characters in total) display some variation between the two studies in coding for overlapping taxa. For these 19 characters, Hilton (2003) explained some of the reasons for the differences in coding (e.g. Li *et al.* (1997*b*) might have coded an unknown state as a '0' instead of '?'). The following is our comparison of the characters in the two matrices and an explanation of the coding we have used in the combined matrix.

The following characters have essentially the same states but the coding disagrees between the two matrices:

1. H6/L4 – position of the nasal bones relative to the mesethmoid and frontal bones. Although similar states were defined in the two data matrices, different states were coded for †*Phareodus*, †*Ostariostoma* and mormyroids. For †*Ostariostoma* the difference in coding is a difference of opinion as to the identity of the bones, and we have coded it as unknown. For †*Phareodus* we have coded it as Li *et al.* (1997*b*) did, based on figures in Li (1994, 1996), and for the mormyroids we have followed Hilton (2003) based on his arguments.

2. H9/L5 – presence or absence of the basipterygoid process. The two matrices have the same states but different codings for †*Ostariostoma* and mormyroids. Li *et al.* (1997*b*) coded the basipterygoid process as absent, whereas Hilton (2003) coded it is unknown. Reexamination of a cast of the only known specimen of †*Ostariostoma* shows that the relevant portion of the

parasphenoid is visible and there is apparently no basipterygoid process, so we have followed the coding of Li *et al.* (1997*b*). We have coded the mormyroids as polymorphic because of the different representative genera examined by Hilton (2003) and Li *et al.* (1997*b*).

3. H10/L57 – supratemporal commissure passing through the parietals. The two matrices have the same states but different codings for †*Lycoptera, Heterotis, Arapaima, Scleropages, Osteoglossum*, and mormyroids. We have followed Hilton (2003) who cited Cavin & Forey (2001) as having noted that Li *et al.* (1997*b*) made a coding error.

4. H20/L10 – supraorbital bone present or absent. The matrices have the same states but different coding for †*Lycoptera*. According to Hilton (2003), †*Lycoptera* was originally described as having one and then redescribed as not having one. Because of this discrepancy, we have followed Hilton (2003) and coded †*Lycoptera* as unknown for this character.

5. H22/L14 – arrangement of infraorbital bones. The two matrices have slightly different descriptions and character states. Hilton (2003) used the number of infraorbital bones excluding the antorbital and dermosphenotic, whereas Li *et al.* (1997*b*) described it as infraorbitals four and five separate or fused together. Despite these different descriptions, the character is essentially the same. The two matrices have different codings for †*Lycoptera, Pantodon*, and †*Ostariostoma*. Hilton (2003) coded †*Lycoptera* as unknown, as he could not determine the number. However, the original description agrees with Li *et al.* (1997*b*) and we use their coding. †*Ostariostoma* was coded as unknown by Hilton (2003) and we agree, as the number of posterior infraorbitals is uncertain. Hilton (2003) noted that *Pantodon* is unique among living osteoglossomorphs in having five infraorbital bones, the first two elements homologous to the single first infraorbital of other osteoglossomorphs based on correlation with the number of neuromasts (Nelson 1969); we therefore follow his coding for *Pantodon*. Additionally, we re-examined several specimens of †*Joffrichthys* (not included in the matrix of Li *et al.* 1997*b*) that demonstrate the infraorbitals well, and we code this genus as having four infraorbitals, unlike Hilton (2003) who coded this character as unknown for that genus.

6. H23/L53 – first infraorbital. Although Li *et al.* (1997*b*) used the character of whether

the antorbital and first infraorbital were separate or fused, and Hilton (2003) described the position of the first infraorbital, these are essentially the same character. The two matrices differ in coding for †*Lycoptera* and †*Ostariostoma*. Hilton (2003) codes both as unknown, †*Lycoptera* because of poor preservation of the material, and †*Ostariostoma* because of difficulty identifying the bones. Li *et al.* (1997*b*) coded both genera as having the antorbital and first infraorbital separate from each other. The description of †*Lycoptera davidi* by Gaudant (1968), the redescription of †*L. middendorffi* by Greenwood (1970), the redescription of †*Ostariostoma* by Grande & Cavender (1991), and our own examination of a cast of the holotype of the latter all agree with Li *et al.* (1997*b*), and so we have used their coding.

7. H28/L28 – the morphology of the hyomandibular head. Although the character states described by Hilton (2003: neurocranial head one or two continuous, two separate, or two bridged) and Li *et al.* (1997*b*: head single, double, double bridged) differ slightly, they are essentially the same. The two matrices had different codings for †*Eohiodon*, †*Phareodus*, *Heterotis*, *Arapaima* and †*Ostariostoma*. Hilton (2003) listed †*Eohiodon* as bridged, *Heterotis* and *Arapaima* as having two separate heads, and †*Phareodus* and †*Ostariostoma* as unknown. Li *et al.* (1997*b*) listed †*Eohiodon* as double, and *Heterotis*, *Arapaima* and †*Phareodus* as single. Hilton (2003) referred to a new study of †*Eohiodon* and we accept his coding for that genus, as well as that for *Heterotis* (see Taverne 1977), and †*Ostariostoma* (pers. obs.). †*Phareodus* clearly has one continuous hyomandibular head (pers. obs., UALVP 12712). Additionally, †*Joffrichthys*, which Hilton (2003) coded as unknown, has a single head (pers. obs., UALVP 31544).

8. H33/L39 – the depth-to-width ratio of the opercle. Li *et al.* (1997*b*) had two states: less than two and greater than two. Hilton modified the second state to be approximately two or greater. The two matrices have different codings for *Pantodon, Scleropages*, and *Osteoglossum*, all of which Li *et al.* (1997*b*) coded as having an opercle depth-to-width ratio less than two, but Hilton (2003) coded as having a ratio of two or greater. This may have been an error in the matrix of Li *et al.* (1997*b*), as our examination of material shows that the ratio is clearly two or greater in these genera.

9. H34/L48 – a posterodorsal process on the opercle. The two matrices have the same states, but different coding for †*Eohiodon* and †*Ostariostoma*. We follow Hilton (2003) for †*Eohiodon* based on his study of all three species that showed the posterodorsal process of the opercle to be present (the specimens examined by Li *et al.* (1997*b*) did not have this area preserved). Examination of †*Ostariostoma* shows the process to be absent, and thus we agree with Li *et al.* (1997*b*) rather than Hilton (2003) who coded it as unknown.

10. H39/L52 – posterior end of maxilla lies on angular or on dentary. The same states are used in both data sets, but there are different codings for †*Lycoptera*, †*Ostariostoma*, and mormyroids. Li *et al.* (1997*b*) coded all as lying on the angular, whereas Hilton (2003) coded †*Lycoptera* and †*Ostariostoma* as unknown, and mormyroids as having the maxilla lying on the dentary. Hilton (2003) stated that the mormyroid condition is likely not homologous, but the maxilla is definitely on the dentary, so he coded it that way and we have followed that. Although Hilton (2003) considered that the maxilla in †*Ostariostoma* was displaced and therefore the state could not be determined, we find it clear that the maxilla lies on the angular, and we also follow Li *et al.* (1997*b*) regarding †*Lycoptera*. Hilton (2003) also coded the state as unknown in †*Joffrichthys*, but the maxilla clearly lies on the angular (pers. obs., UALVP 31564 and the holotype).

11. H40/L13 – supramaxilla present or absent. The two matrices have the same states, but differ in coding for †*Lycoptera*. We follow Li *et al.* (1997*b*) in coding the supramaxilla as present; although Hilton (2003) coded it as unknown, he did note that one may be present in one of his specimens.

12. H47/L54 – toothplate on basihyal. The two matrices have the same states with different coding for †*Lycoptera*, †*Phareodus*, and mormyroids. Li *et al.* (1997*b*) coded †*Lycoptera* and †*Phareodus* as primitive (present), but Hilton (2003) coded them as unknown (although he noted it was recorded as present in the original description of †*Lycoptera* and it might be present in the material he examined). Such a toothplate is clearly illustrated by Gaudant (1968, fig. 11) for †*Lycoptera davidi*. We therefore code it as present. The discrepancy in the mormyroids was based on the genera examined, and therefore we code them as polymorphic. We also

follow Li *et al.* (1997*b*) in coding †*Phareodus* as present for this character.

13. H49/L34 – basihyal tooth plate and basibranchial tooth plate separate or fused together. Although the character states agree, the matrices differ in coding for †*Lycoptera*, *Heterotis*, *Arapaima*, †*Phareodus*, and mormyroids. Hilton (2003) coded all except mormyroids as unknown, and mormyroids as either primitive or unknown. Li *et al.* (1997*b*) coded †*Lycoptera*, *Heterotis*, and *Arapaima* as plesiomorphic (separate), and †*Phareodus* and mormyroids as derived (fused). Although Hilton (2003) could not determine the condition in †*Phareodus*, Li *et al.* (1997*b*) clearly could and described it, so we follow their coding. Hilton (2003) noted that *Arapaima*, *Heterotis*, and some mormyroids lack a basihyal toothplate, so he coded this as unknown, and he also coded †*Lycoptera* as unknown because of uncertain homology. We have coded *Arapaima* and *Heterotis* as 'inapplicable' and mormyroids as polymorphic (primitive and inapplicable).

14. H57/L27 – length of dorsal arm of posttemporal. The same states are used in both matrices (less than 1.5 times as long as ventral arm, more than twice as long as ventral) but the coding differs for †*Lycoptera*, *Pantodon*, †*Ostariostoma*, and mormyroids. Li *et al.* (1997*b*) coded all as less than 1.5 times, but Hilton (2003) coded †*Lycoptera*, *Pantodon* and †*Ostariostoma* as greater than twice, and mormyroids as unknown. Hilton (2003) said that one of his specimens of †*Lycoptera* showed the longer limb, but noted that this should be confirmed in other specimens. The specimens we examined do not show a longer limb, so we have followed Li *et al.* (1997*b*) instead. Hilton (2003) noted that †*Ostariostoma* and *Pantodon* were probably mis-coded by Li *et al.* (1997*b*) so we follow Hilton (2003) for those genera. Hilton (2003) noted that mormyroid genera he included do not have a distinct ventral arm; however, other mormyroids do. We have therefore coded them as unknown, which will give the same result as coding them as polymorphic for the two states, or coding them as inapplicable.

15. H65/L12 – number of principal branched caudal fin rays. The two matrices have the same states (17+, 16, 15 or fewer); however, the coding is different for †*Ostariostoma*. Li *et al.* (1997*b*) coded †*Ostariostoma* as having 15 or fewer, whereas Hilton coded the same specimen as having 16. The conflict

is because the only known specimen has 18 principal rays, but only 15 branched rays because there are two lower unbranched rays (pers. obs.), probably as an individual abnormality. We have changed this character to be the number of principal rays (being 19+, 18, 17 or fewer), which resolves the conflict.

16. H67/L21 – neural spine on first ural centrum. Although the two matrices have the same states, the coding for †*Lycoptera* is different, with Li *et al.* (1997*b*) giving the state as absent or rudimentary and Hilton (2003) coding it as unknown because different specimens examined or in the literature have shown the genus to have all three character states. According to Zhang (pers. comm.), specimens of †*Lycoptera* can have no ural spines, a rudimentary spine, one fully developed neural spine, or a rudimentary spine and a fully developed one, but presence of two full neural spines on the first ural centrum is extremely rare. We have therefore coded the character state as polymorphic (0 or 1) in †*Lycoptera*.

17. H68/L9 – number of epurals. The states are the same in the two data sets, but there is a different coding for *Heterotis, Arapaima,* †*Phareodus, Pantodon, Scleropages, Osteoglossum* and mormyroids. Li *et al.* (1997*b*) coded all of these as having one epural, but Hilton (2003) coded all as having no epurals, except for †*Phareodus*, which he coded as unknown. This difference is because Hilton (2003) identified the epural of Li *et al.* (1997*b*) as a uroneural. We have followed Hilton (2003) for the character state coding, and have also coded †*Tanolepis* as unknown.

18. H69/L50 – development of the neural spine on the first preural centrum. The two matrices agree except that Li *et al.* (1997*b*) coded *Hiodon* and †*Eohiodon* as having a full neural spine and Hilton (2003), after examining many specimens, found the two genera are actually polymorphic. We have followed his coding for those two genera. Although Hilton (2003) coded †*Ostariostoma* as unknown, we agree with Li *et al.* (1997*b*) that †*Ostariostoma* has the primitive state.

19. H70/L51 – number of neural spines on the second preural centrum. The states defined in the two studies differ slightly. Li *et al.* (1997*b*) gave the states as single (0), and double or potentially double (1), whereas Hilton (2003) changed the derived state to two spines present. Nevertheless, for *Hiodon*

and †*Phareodus*, codings disagreed. Li *et al.* (1997*b*) coded *Hiodon* as double or potentially double, and †*Phareodus* as single, but Hilton (2003) coded both as polymorphic. We have coded both as polymorphic, as the authors of both papers noted polymorphisms in these genera. Hilton (2003) also noted that *Papyrocranus* was polymorphic based on his single specimen compared with Taverne (1978), but described that specimen as a possible teratological variation. As it is a single specimen, we coded the family Notopteridae as having the primitive state, not polymorphic.

The remaining 13 characters, of the 39 that were used by Li *et al.* (1997*b*) and earlier studies and were also used by Hilton (2003), were modified by Hilton (2003) by including fewer or more character states or by redefining character states, as follows:

(1) H1/L6 – the temporal fossa (Hilton 2003; also described as the pre-epiotic fossa or temporal fenestra by Li *et al.* 1997*b*). Li *et al.* (1997*b*) had two states, absent or present; however, Hilton (2003) split the 'present' state into five states based on the bones that surround it. We find the number of character states to be problematic given the relatively few taxa studied, and therefore have reduced the number of states. In Hilton's (2003) data matrix, state 1 is found in the mormyroids, one of the three notopterids and †*Palaeonotopterus*, and state 4 is found only in the two other notopterids. As we are more interested in osteoglossid relationships, we have combined character state 4 (fossa bordered by exoccipital and pterotic) with character state 1 (fossa bordered by epioccipital, exoccipital and pterotic) into a single state (exoccipital contributes to border of fossa). A third character state (state 5) was autapomorphic for *Heterotis* in Hilton's (2003) data matrix. Hilton (2003) coded this genus as having the fossa bordered by the parietal and pterotic. However, Taverne (1977) noted that in juvenile *Heterotis* the fossa is bordered by the pterotic, parietal, epioccipital, and exoccipital. In the adult, although the exoccipital is excluded, the epioccipital maintains a contribution. We have therefore coded *Heterotis* as having character state 2 (fossa bordered by the epioccipital, pterotic and parietal) based on the adult condition. Because of this, state 5 is no longer a condition of any taxon and can be deleted. Although Hilton's (2003) states differed from those

of Li *et al.* (1997*b*), most of the coding agreed except for †*Phareodus, Scleropages, Osteoglossum*, †*Ostariostoma*, Mormyroidea and Notopteridae, which Li *et al.* (1997*b*) coded as 'absent' and Hilton (2003) coded as unknown in †*Phareodus*, but as one of the several states of 'present' in the others. This difference likely centres on determining the homologies of various fossae in the skull. We have followed Hilton's (2003) coding (with the above changes in character states) for these taxa.

(2) H2/L40 – shape of extrascapular. Hilton (2003) used more character states than Li *et al.* (1997*b*), and a comparison among them is difficult. We have arbitrarily chosen to use Hilton's (2003) states and codings.

(3) H3 and H4/L38 – shape of frontal bones anteriorly and absence/presence of a supraorbital shelf. Hilton (2003) essentially split the equivalent character of Li *et al.* (1997*b*) into two characters, with additional states. We have used the two separate characters and codings of Hilton (2003).

(4) H7/L18 – shape of nasal bones. Hilton (2003) had an extra state, which essentially split one of Li *et al.*'s (1997*b*) states in two. Despite this, the only disagreement in coding between the two matrices is for †*Eohiodon*, which Hilton (2003) noted was based on new observations; we have followed Hilton's (2003) coding for this genus.

(5) H26/L29 – shape of dermosphenotic. Hilton (2003) has an additional state, which only relates to mormyroids and notopterids, and we have included this. The only disagreement in coding is for †*Lycoptera*, which Hilton (2003) coded as unknown, but we follow Li *et al.* (1997*b*) in coding it as triangular, based on the original description.

(6) H30/L26 – bones of palatoquadrate. Hilton (2003) used different character states and descriptions than did Li *et al.* (1997*b*), and we have followed Hilton (2003).

(7) H32/L20 – preopercular sensory canals. Hilton (2003) modified this character and added two extra states but the character incorporated Li *et al.*'s (1997*b*) character and states. We have used Hilton's (2003) modifications.

(8) H35/L59 – subopercle. Li *et al.* (1997*b*) used presence or absence as character states, whereas Hilton (2003) modified the 'present' state into two based on position and shape. We have used the character states of Hilton (2003).

(9) H37/L47 – ascending process of premaxilla. Hilton (2003) combined states 1 and 2 that were used by Li *et al.* (1997*b*) and we have followed that. However, there is a conflict in the coding for †*Eohiodon, Heterotis* and mormyroids. We have followed the coding used by Hilton based on figures in the literature and examination of material.

(10) H45/L15 – bony elements associated with second ventral gill arch. Although Hilton (2003) used an additional state, which we have also used, the only conflict between the two data matrices is for *Hiodon*. Li *et al.* (1997*b*) considered this genus to have associated bony elements whereas Hilton (2003) considered these to be absent. This disagreement is caused by interpretation of homology of elements. Hilton (2003) suggested that, although *Hiodon* has tendons in a similar position, the homology of these with the bones of other osteoglossomorphs has not been determined; therefore, *Hiodon* cannot be said to possess them. We follow Hilton (2003) here.

(11) H66/L1 – number of uroneurals. Hilton combined two of the states used by Li *et al.* (1997*b*). Several coding conflicts occur between the two matrices, for *Heterotis, Arapaima, Pantodon, Scleropages, Osteoglossum* and mormyroids, all coded as having none by Li *et al.* (1997*b*) and as having one or two by Hilton (2003), and for †*Phareodus*, coded as having none by Li *et al.* (1997*b*) and coded as unknown by Hilton (2003). The conflict results from Hilton's identifying a bone as an uroneural that Li *et al.* (1997*b*) interpreted as an epural (see also character H68/L9). †*Phareodus* was coded as unknown because the bone may be an epural or it may be an uroneural. We have adopted the coding and interpretation of Hilton (2003) for this character.

(12) H71/L2 – number of hypurals. Hilton (2003) combined states used by Li *et al.* (1997*b*) so that states: (0) more than seven; (1) seven; (2) six; and (3) five or fewer, became states: (0) seven, (1) six or fewer; however, the coding agrees between the two matrices. We have used the reduced number of states, but modified state zero to 'seven or more,' as some of the taxa in Li *et al.* (1997*b*) and our matrix have more than seven hypurals.

(13) H72/L31 – scales. Hilton (2003) has an additional state, having divided the derived state used by Li *et al.* (1997*b*; reticulate) into two (radial and reticulate furrows

present; furrows only over entire scale). We have used the additional state. The coding of states differs only for *Pantodon*, which was coded as 'not reticulate' by Li *et al.* (1997*b*) and as 'having furrows over the entire scale' by Hilton (2003), and for †*Ostariostoma*, which was coded as 'not reticulate' by Li *et al.* (1997*b*) and coded as 'unknown' by Hilton (2003). We agree with Hilton (2003) for *Pantodon*. The scales of †*Ostariostoma* are scarcely visible (pers. obs.), so we have coded it as 'unknown'; however, it is not reasonable that the scales would be reticulate or furrowed when they are so thin as to be scarcely visible.

Most of the 13 characters listed above were coded as having the primitive state in the taxa included by Li *et al.* (1997*b*) that were not included by Hilton (2003), so the coding used by Li *et al.* (1997*b*) was retained. The exception is character H35/L59, where Hilton divided the primitive state into two. The character states for the additional taxa were determined from the literature or specimens.

Hilton (2003) did not use 21 of the characters that were used by Li *et al.* (1997*b*). Some of these characters were removed by Hilton (2003) because they referred to taxa that were not included in his analysis, and others were removed based on justifications given by him. Of these 21 characters, we deleted six (characters 11, 32, 41, 42, 45 and 49) based on the reasoning of Hilton (2003), but retained the other 15 for the following reasons:

(1)   L3: number of pelvic fin rays. Although Hilton (2003) said that it is difficult to get ray counts in fossils, we find that many fossils provide a clear count and we have retained this character and added the information for a number of taxa.

(2)   L8: swimbladder–ear connection. Hilton (2003) did not comment on this character and we have retained it, despite a lack of information on the state in fossil specimens.

(3)   L16: intestine coiling to side of esophagus and stomach. Hilton (2003) removed this character as it cannot be determined in fossils. However, it can be coded for living taxa and we have retained it.

(4)   L17: opercle shape; and L55: shape of the postero-ventral margin of opercle. Hilton (2003) excluded both of these characters, stating that the descriptions of the character states were not clear and are dependent on the specimen and observer. However, the opercular bones of osteoglossomorphs do

appear to have a variety of characters that might be phylogenetically significant, as even Hilton (2003) noted. We have replaced the two characters of Li *et al.* (1997*b*) with two new characters that we believe are less subjective but retain the sense of the differences in opercular bones that Li *et al.* (1997*b*) were describing. The relative height compared to width of the opercle was used by both Li *et al.* (1997*b*) and Hilton (2003), and this already incorporates part of the differences among opercular bones. A second difference is the shape of the opercle dorsal to the hyomandibular facet, where the opercle is rounded in many genera but flattened or truncated in others, and has a posterior recurved process in *Hiodon* and †*Eohiodon*. The second replacement character that we suggest is the ventral portion of the opercle being rounded or pointed but distinctly tapered compared to the mid-point of the opercle (e.g. †*Singida*), distinctly curved but of similar width to the midpoint of the bone (e.g. †*Chauliopareion*), or flattened or only broadly rounded (e.g. *Hiodon*).

(5)   L19: fusion of upper hypurals and second ural. Hilton (2003) did not discuss this character, and we have retained it.

(6)   L22: second infraorbital shape and size. Hilton (2003) suggested that the shapes are difficult to interpret in some species and some that were coded the same by Li *et al.* (1997*b*) actually seem very different. We have retained this character but modified the descriptions of the character states and recoded the specimens based on the literature and material available to us.

(7)   L23: shape of dorsal fin. Although Hilton (2003) suggested that the advanced state 'rounded' is not necessarily homologous among groups, and that variation occurs in notopterid species, we chose to retain it because the character states are simply hypotheses of homology and convergences among taxa should become evident in the resulting cladogram. We have, however, re-evaluated the character states and codings for the taxa in this analysis. The new states are: (1) triangular or falcate; (2) rounded; (3) elongate with first few rays shorter than posterior ones. This last character state is new and distinguishes the short-based rounded fins (state 2) of some forms from the greatly elongated fins of some other taxa.

(8) L 24: relative length of the posterior rays of dorsal and anal fins. Hilton (2003) suggested that this character and the preceding character are related to each other, and therefore cause unnecessary duplication in the data set. However, not all taxa in Li *et al.*'s (1997*b*) data set were coded the same for each character, indicating that the characters are not dependent upon each other. Therefore we have retained both.

(9) L30: enlargement of first through third infraorbitals. Hilton (2003) did not comment on this character and we have retained it.

(10) L33: anterior extent of preopercle. We have modified the description of this character slightly: instead of describing it as the anterior extent of the horizontal arm, we have used the anterior extent of the ventral portion, in acknowledgement that the preopercle in some taxa does not have a defined horizontal arm, as noted by Hilton (2003).

(11) L35: shape of the posterior edge of the nasal in taxa with a gutterlike or irregularly subrectangular nasal bone. Hilton (2003) noted that many taxa in which this state should have been coded as inapplicable were coded as 'zero' in some of the papers of Li and colleagues. We have recoded some taxa as inapplicable as suggested.

(12) L37: angle of jaws. Hilton (2003) removed this character because he suggested that the angle of the jaws is related to lengths of the maxilla and mandible, and the angle of the hyomandibula, such that it is partially included in other characters. However, the lengths of the maxilla and dentary are only included in one of Hilton's (2003) characters (# 39) and that character is actually a measure of the length of the maxilla relative to the length of the dentary, not in relation to any other features. We have retained this character.

(13) L44: utriculus connection with the sacculus and lagena. Hilton (2003) did not use this character as he could not confirm the condition in his specimens. However, it has been cited as a character to unite the Mormyroidei and Notopteridae, not recovered as a clade by Hilton (2003), and therefore we retain it so as not to be biased against that grouping.

(14) L46: sexually dimorphic anal fin. Hilton (2003) noted that this character was coded as present only in species of *Hiodon* and †*Eohiodon*, and that it is difficult to determine for fossils. However, the anal fin is also sexually dimorphic in the fossil †*Chauliopareion*. We have retained the character, but unlike Li *et al.* (1997*b*), we have coded it as unknown in fossil genera where only a single or few specimens are known (e.g. †*Ostariostoma*). For fossil taxa represented by many specimens, we feel that a lack of dimorphism can be coded as such, rather than as unknown, as it is unlikely that only a single gender would have been preserved. Additionally, we have coded mormyroids as polymorphic, as some mormyroids exhibit sexual dimorphism in the anal fin (Hilton 2003), even though the mormyrid dimorphism differs significantly from that seen in hiodontids.

Based on the assessments above, our data matrix resulting from the combined matrices of Hilton (2003) and Li *et al.* (1997*b*) has 87 characters (Appendix 3). The three mormyroid and three notopterid genera used by Hilton (2003) were each combined into a single taxon. The resulting matrix included 23 taxa and 76 parsimony-informative characters, some with multiple states (the uninformative characters are retained in the matrix because they will be useful in other studies with inclusion of different terminal taxa).

Results of phylogenetic analysis

The heuristic and the branch-and-bound searches both found three equally short trees of 225 steps. Tree statistics are: Consistency Index 0.53; Retention Index 0.67; and Re-scaled Consistency Index 0.35. The three trees differ only in the sister-group relationships among three taxa, †*Sinoglossus, Heterotis,* and *Arapaima*, with all three possible arrangements being found. The strict consensus tree is identical to the majority-rule tree and is shown in Figure 8. All clades shown are supported by all three shortest trees. Bootstrap analysis using heuristic searches found relatively few nodes with good support, meaning that most of the clades depend on relatively few synapomorphies. Decay analysis gave a similar result, with most of the clades having a decay value of 1. The exceptions are the crown Osteoglossomorpha (decay of 3 steps), the Hiodontiformes, of which only †*Eohiodon* and *Hiodon* were included in the present study (decay of 5 steps), *Scleropages* + *Osteoglossum* (decay of 4 steps), and †*Paralycoptera* + †*Tanolepis* (decay of 2 steps).

Although some aspects of the phylogeny agree with results of other workers, other aspects differ among investigators. Notable findings from the current study include recovery of †*Lycoptera* as

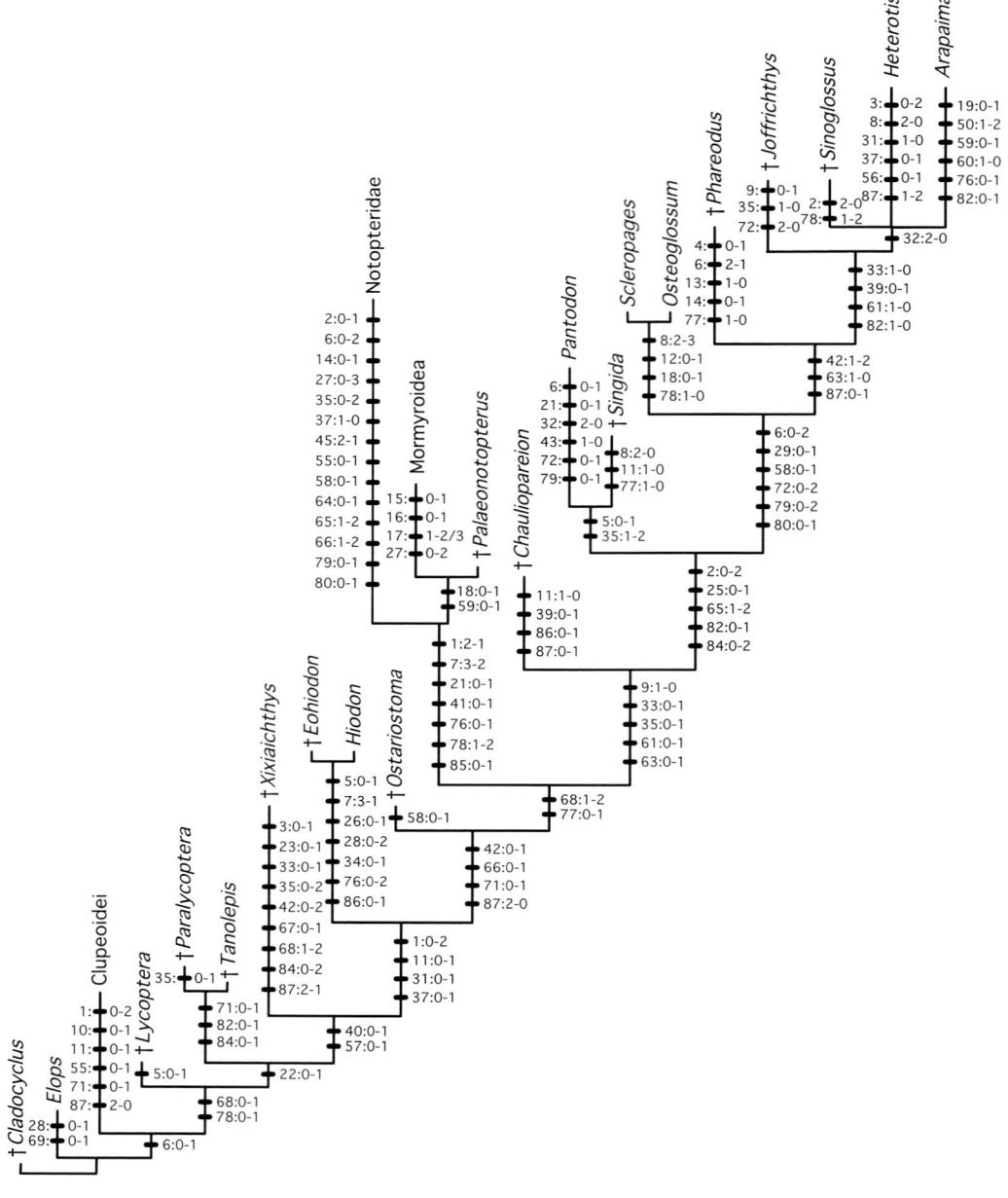

Fig. 8. Phylogeny of osteoglossomorphs resulting from the maximum-parsimony analysis in this paper. The illustrated tree is the strict consensus (identical to the majority-rule consensus) of three shortest trees of length 225. See text for explanation. Branch lengths are proportional to the number of character-state changes. For each change, the character number (X) and the states before (Y) and after (Z) are shown in the form X:Y-Z.

the sister of all other osteoglossomorphs among the studied taxa, with †*Paralycoptera* + †*Tanolepis*, followed by †*Xixiaichthys*, as more crownward stem osteoglossomorphs (Fig. 8). †*Lycoptera* was

a stem osteoglossomorph in the results of Li *et al.* (1997*b*) and Zhang (2006) but was of uncertain position in the phylogeny of Hilton (2003). Notopteridae are here united with the Mormyroidei +

†*Palaeonotopterus* in Notopteroidei, in agreement with Li & Wilson (1996*a*), Lavoué & Sullivan (2004) and Zhang (2006), but contrary to the conclusions of Kumazawa & Nishida (2000) and Hilton (2003).

Osteoglossidae remain monophyletic with the inclusion of both *Pantodon* and †*Singida*. *Pantodon* is recovered as extant sister to all other Osteoglossidae, and †*Singida* as extinct sister to *Pantodon*. This relationship for *Pantodon* is a novel result, and is unlike the conclusions of Li *et al.* (1997*b*) and Hilton (2003), who placed both genera within the Osteoglossinae, Kumazawa & Nishida (2000), who grouped *Pantodon* with Notopteridae, Lavoué & Sullivan (2004), who recovered *Pantodon* as sister to all extant Osteoglossiformes (i.e. including notopteroids) and Zhang (2006), who united *Pantodon* but not †*Singida* with Osteoglossinae. These new results are consistent with dividing Osteoglossidae into three subfamilies, listing Pantodontinae before Heterotidinae and Osteoglossinae to convey the phylogenetic information.

†*Chauliopareion* (Fig. 5a) is recovered here as a stem osteoglossid (Fig. 8), in contrast to the conclusion of Murray & Wilson (2005), who grouped it within Osteoglossidae along with *Pantodon*, †*Singida*, and other osteoglossids. The superficial similarity in appearance between †*Singida* and †*Chauliopareion* is thus not reflected as a close relationship in the new phylogeny, but might still be indicative of a primitive morphology for the family.

Notwithstanding the above clarifications, there remains much work to be done, especially the inclusion of the many additional osteoglossomorph and putative osteoglossomorph genera that have been named in the literature, before we arrive at a robust phylogeny including both fossil and extant taxa for this group of fishes.

Biogeography

The biogeographic relationships of osteoglossomorph species have been the subject of numerous papers, some dealing with populations of a single nominal species (e.g. *Scleropages formosus*; Tang *et al.* 2004), and others dealing with more inclusive groups (e.g. Osteoglossoidei, Kumazawa & Nishida 2000). In order to understand the biogeography of a group, the patterns and methods by which it gained its past and modern distributions, it is necessary to have a good knowledge of the phylogenetic relationships among taxa, and also an idea of the age of the lineages within the group. Without an understanding of how the taxa under study are related to one another, biogeographic hypotheses cannot be meaningful

because they are based only on assumptions of relationship, and furthermore they are untestable (Greenwood 1983). Similarly, although a pattern of distribution may indicate the biogeographic history of a group (for example, the current disjunct distribution of a group in Africa and South America might suggest an original continuous distribution across Gondwana), in the absence of information about the ages of the lineages, such a pattern is based only on an assumption and cannot be tested.

The age of the Osteoglossomorpha

Two methods are commonly used for determining the ages of lineages: the fossil record and molecular-clocks. As emphasized by Smith & Peterson (2002), fossils date a specific lineage, and also indirectly the sister-group lineage even if there are no fossil data for the sister group. An age based on fossil information will, by necessity, be a minimum age for the lineage, as the lineage must have predated the first appearance of the fossil. Molecular clock data can also be used to date a divergence between two lineages, although many published molecular clocks tend to give ages that are anomalously older than those that can be confirmed by fossil data.

Fossil data are the only concrete evidence that a given taxon was present in a given place at a given time. Although there can be problems with fossil taxa (see Smith & Peterson 2002), including a difficulty in determining their relationships and inadequate dating of the rocks in which they are found, these difficulties are not insurmountable. Many fossils have been placed reliably in phylogenetic schemes, and fossils can often be reliably, if not always precisely, dated.

Molecular-clock dating of lineages is also somewhat problematic. The premise is that genetic changes within a taxon or in certain classes of mutations occur at a steady or predictable rate, and that the amount of divergence can be used to date the divergence between two lineages. Although, in theory, dating by molecular-clocks can be independent of the fossil record (Smith & Peterson 2002), many molecular biologists use key fossil occurrences to calibrate the molecular-clock, and therefore it is not completely independent of the fossil data. In some cases in which fossils are not used to calibrate the molecular clock, major geological (i.e. assumed vicariant) events might be used to date divergence of lineages. Although this can, in theory, be a useful way to date divergences, there is danger of circularity in drawing biogeographic conclusions from such results. If an assumed vicariant event has been used to date a divergence, that same divergence cannot then be used as evidence for a vicariant biogeographic pattern.

The calibration of a molecular-clock that is independent of fossil and geological data is based on the surmise that point mutations in a gene sequence accumulate randomly, and the amount of sequence differentiation between homologous genes of two taxa indicates how long the two have been separated (Smith & Peterson 2002). However, rates of mutation or 'molecular evolution' may vary greatly among different taxa (Bromham & Penny 2003), and may also vary over time within a lineage (e.g. Ruber & Zardoya 2005). Whether using lineages dated by fossils or divergence dates based on molecular-clocks to interpret the biogeography of a group, it is important to understand the limitations of the method used.

Kumazawa & Nishida (2000) reconstructed the biogeography of the Osteoglossiformes based on a molecular phylogeny and molecular-clock. Their scheme of relationships (2000, fig. 1) is broadly similar to that of Hilton (2003) and other recent authors for the family Osteoglossidae, with the exception of the placement of *Pantodon*. The two phylogenies also differ in the placement of Mormyroidei and Notopteridae, with Hilton (2003, fig. 7) showing the notopterids as the sister group to the osteoglossids, and Kumazawa & Nishida (2000) placing the mormyroids as the sister group to the osteoglossids. Meanwhile, Zhang agreed with Li *et al.* (1997b) that mormyroids are sister to notopterids. Unfortunately, Kumazawa & Nishida (2000) failed to include the genus *Hiodon* in their analysis; *Hiodon* is commonly considered to be the living sister-group of the Osteoglossiformes (e.g. Li *et al.* 1997b; Hilton 2003; Zhang 2006). Omission of the sister group of a study group is a major procedural flaw.

The age of origin for the Osteoglossiformes (i.e. the divergence between that lineage and other teleosts) was calculated by Kumazawa & Nishida (2000) to be 341 Million years ago (Ma), or 335 +/− 28 Ma. Such an age for the group is anomalously old, and is not supported by the fossil record. If true, it would mean that osteoglossiforms arose during the Early Carboniferous and that there is a gap of roughly 200 Ma before their first fossil appearance in the Early Cretaceous, during a time when there are abundant and diverse fossils of non-teleostean fishes. In fact, this Early Carboniferous age of divergence for the Osteoglossiformes predates by more than 100 Ma the first appearance of the earliest Teleostei *sensu lato* represented by pholidophoriforms in the Late Triassic (Arratia 1997), and the oldest fossil record of crown-group teleosts represented by the elopomorph †*Anaethalion zapporum* in the Kimmeridgian (Late Jurassic) of Germany (Arattia 2000).

The molecular-clock of Kumazawa & Nishida (2000) was based on a previous clock for bony fishes (Kumazawa *et al.* 1999), which in turn was calibrated using three points: (1) the breakup of Africa/South America to date the divergence of African and neotropical cichlids at 100 Ma (80–120 Ma); (2) the divergence of sarcopterygian and actinopterygian fishes at 450 Ma (based on a previous study [Kumar and Hedges 1998], which used 44 genes to date the actinopterygian/tetrapod divergence at 450 +/− 35.5 Ma); and (3) the divergence between bony fishes and sharks (Osteichthyes and Chondrichthyes; 528 Ma) also following Kumar & Hedges (1998), who dated this divergence at 528 +/− 56.4 Ma using 15 genes. Kumazawa & Nishida (2000) then calculated their molecular clock from gamma-corrected maximum-likelihood and Poisson distances for the ND2/cytb gene amino acid sequences. The divergence dates of Kumar & Hedges (1998) for Actinopterygii/Tetrapoda (or Sarcopterygii following Benton's (1997) classification) and Osteichthyes/Chondrichthyes were in turn based on an analysis of nuclear genes, calibrated using a single calibration point: the divergence time between mammals and birds, which was assigned a date of 310 Ma. This date was based on the fossil record of synapsids and diapsids, which first appear in the Carboniferous, and was considered a good date because other fossils record a transition between sarcopterygian fishes and tetrapods at 370–360 Ma and the appearance of early amphibians at 338 Ma; therefore, the fossil record of the synapsids and diapsids likely does not underestimate the actual divergence time by very much. Even if the detailed criticisms of the 310 Ma date for bird/mammal divergence (Graur & Martin 2004) are ignored, there are still problems with the calibration points used by Kumazawa & Nishida (2000).

Two of the calibration points (numbers 2 and 3 above) for the molecular clock of Kumazawa & Nishida (2000) are not independent of each other as both are calculated ages provided by Kumar & Hedges (1998) based on a molecular clock calibrated by mammals and birds. The third calibration point of Kumazawa & Nishida (2000) is based on a lineage split presumed to have been caused by a vicariance event − this age for the split between Neotropical and African lineages of cichlids is not accepted by some authors and has not been supported either by more recent molecular dating (Vences *et al.* 2001) or by the fossil record of cichlids (Murray 2001). Further, Smith & Peterson (2002) highlight the problems caused by using calibration points too remote from the study group, as in the split between chondrichthyans and osteichthyans used by Kumazawa & Nishida (2000). Therefore, none of the dates used by Kumazawa & Nishida (2000) can be considered appropriate for calibrating a molecular clock for osteoglossiforms.

At present, the only reliable evidence available for the age of the osteoglossomorphs is found in the fossil record. What we can say up to now is that basal members of the group (†*Lycoptera* and other Chinese taxa) are in evidence by the Early Cretaceous (the age of the deposits where many of these fishes are found has been corrected [Swisher *et al.* 1999; Chang & Miao 2004] from the previously suggested Late Jurassic age). Some other Early Cretaceous osteoglossiforms have been placed in Recent families (see Maisey 2000), which would indicate that the order must by necessity be significantly older than these records. However, with the oldest stem-group teleostean fishes being at most of Late Triassic age, and with the oldest known crown-group teleosts being of Late Jurassic age (Arratia 1997), we do not think it likely that the Osteoglossomorpha will be found to have originated any earlier than the Jurassic Period.

Fossil osteoglossomorphs and biogeography

Because various hypotheses of relationships for the osteoglossomorph lineages have resulted from different analyses (e.g. Kumazawa & Nishida 2000; Hilton 2003; Lavoué & Sullivan 2004; this paper) it is premature to attempt a biogeographic reconstruction for the whole group. However, some suggestions can be made based on the taxa that are relatively stable in placement in this and other analyses.

The basal-most lineages, in studies that include fossils, are fossil taxa from Asia (e.g. Li *et al.* 1997*b*; Hilton 2003; Zhang 2006). In the present study, †*Lycoptera* is recovered as the most basal osteoglossomorph, as Li & Wilson (1996*a*, 1999) had suggested. †*Paralycoptera* and †*Tanolepis*, which are basal osteoglossiforms according to Li & Wilson (1999) and Zhang (2006), form a clade that is in the osteoglossomorph stem group in the present analysis (Fig. 8). †*Xixiaichthys* is recovered as another stem osteoglossomorph (Fig. 8). The most basal lineage with living members is the Hiodontiformes (e.g. Li *et al.* 1997*b*; Hilton 2003; Lavoué & Sullivan 2004), found only in North America today but with fossil representatives in both North America and China (Li *et al.* 1997*b*; Li & Wilson 1999; Zhang 2006). Li & Wilson (1999) and Zhang (2006), who included more Chinese fossil genera in their analyses than we have included, also found stem members of the Osteoglossidae or its subfamilies in the fossil record of China, such as †*Huashia* (Fig. 3c) and †*Kuntulunia* (Fig. 3d).

This pattern, which has only been revealed by the fossil record, may indicate an origin for the group in Asia with subsequent dispersal to North America (Nelson 1969; Chang & Chou 1976; reviewed *in* Patterson 1981); however, following Patterson (1975, 1981) and Nelson & Ladiges (2001), it could also be interpreted as a widespread ancestral lineage that was isolated after the separation of the two landmasses, as Wilson & Williams (1992) and Li *et al.* (1997*b*) have suggested. Eastern Asia and NW North America were connected at various times in the past, including during the middle of the Cretaceous (see maps in Smith *et al.* 1994), at a time when the hiodontiform clade had begun to diversify.

Both molecular (Lavoué & Sullivan 2004) and morphological (Li *et al.* 1997*b*; Hilton 2003) analyses have recovered the sister-group relationship between Heterotidinae (*Arapaima* + *Heterotis*) and Osteoglossinae (*Scleropages* + *Osteoglossum*). If these pairs are distributed as a result of the fragmentation of Gondwana, the ancestral lineage of Osteoglossidae must extend back to the Late Cretaceous. On the other hand, as mentioned above, closely related forms of *Scleropages* occurs on both sides of Wallace's Line, pointing to some past marine dispersal event. Moreover, the existence of marine fossil osteoglossids such as †*Brychaetus* (in coastal deposits of Europe and North America) and of †*Phareodus* and close relatives on widely separated land masses (†*Phareodus* and †*Cretophareodus* in North America, †*Phareodusichthys* in South America, †*Musperia* in SE Asia, †*Phareodus* = † *Phareoides* in Australia) renders this group nearly cosmopolitan and suggests that marine dispersal for early osteoglossids cannot be discounted (Patterson 1975; Maisey 2000).

The placement of the remaining taxa differs among analyses. Li *et al.* (1997*b*) and Hilton (2003) both placed *Pantodon* within the Osteoglossidae, closer to Osteoglossinae than to Heterotidinae, whereas Lavoué & Sullivan (2004) recovered *Pantodon* as the sister-group to all other osteoglossiforms (including mormyroids and notopterids). Their novel molecular result should prompt careful consideration of the synapomorphies that have been used to support an osteoglossid relationship in the morphological studies, as well as a search for possible synapomorphies to support its more basal position. In our analysis above, if the fossil taxa are ignored, *Pantodon* is the sister group to the clade containing both the Osteoglossinae and Heterotidinae. However, Lavoué & Sullivan (2004) and other molecular studies are limited by their inability to use data from fossil taxa, including †*Singida*, recovered in our analysis as the sister to *Pantodon* (Fig. 8), and more basal taxa, such as †*Chauliopareion*, that could also influence the systematic position of extant species.

The analyses by Li *et al.* (1997*b*), Lavoué & Sullivan (2004) and Zhang (2006) resulted in the Notopteridae and Mormyroidei being united in a group (together with †*Ostariostoma* in the case of the morphological analyses), whereas Hilton (2003) recovered †*Ostariostoma* as sister to all other osteoglossiforms, and notopterids as closer to osteoglossids than are mormyroids. Our results for †*Ostariostoma* agree with those of Hilton (2003), but the notopterids are found to be the sister group to the mormyroids plus †*Palaeonotopterus*, a conclusion more in agreement with that of Li *et al.* (1997*b*), Lavoué & Sullivan (2004) and Zhang (2006). The Notopteroidei (notopterids and mormyroids) taken together are found in Africa, India, and SE Asia (Fig. 1). As indicated by the mid-Cretaceous age of †*Palaeonotopterus* from Morocco, their origin could well predate the initial breakup of Gondwana, making their absence from Australia and South America anomalous. A vicariance explanation of their distribution fits better with an origin after the separation of South America and Australia from the other Gondwanan landmasses, but before the separation of India from Africa. However, the caveats expressed above suggest that simple explanations should be treated with caution.

African Osteoglossidae

The Osteoglossidae (in which we include *Pantodon*) in Africa are represented by two monotypic extant genera, *Heterotis niloticus* and *Pantodon buchholzi*, and three fossil taxa, †*Singida*, †*Brychaetus*, and †*Paradercetis*, the latter based on a skull roof only. †*Brychaetus*, arguably the only marine member of the Osteoglossiformes (Taverne 1974*d*; Patterson 1975), is a widely distributed genus. In Africa it is known by fragments from the Eocene of Morocco and the Paleocene of West Africa and Niger. Although †*Brychaetus* was not included in our analysis, it is closely related to or a synonym of †*Phareodus* (Li *et al.* 1997*a*; Zhang 2006).

The African osteoglossids thus do not form a monophyletic group to the exclusion of non-African representatives of the family. Neither the family nor its subfamilies, except for the monotypic Pantodontinae, is endemic. If African osteoglossids were restricted to fresh waters in the past (this is, by no means, certain as †*Brychaetus* is known from marine deposits), then the family as a whole, including †*Chauliopareion*, Pantodontinae, Heterotidinae, and Osteoglossinae, suggests the existence of past connections across or around the present-day Atlantic (*Arapaima* and fossil relatives in South America,

†*Joffrichthys* in North America) and Indian oceans (†*Phareodus*/†*Musperia*, †*Tavernichthys* and *Scleropages* in India, SE Asia, Indonesia, and Australia).

Conclusion

There is much work still to do on the relationships and biogeographic history of osteoglossomorph fishes. Problematic taxa such as *Pantodon* in the modern fauna and †*Thaumaturus* and †*Paralycoptera* among the fossils remain to be placed with confidence into a phylogenetic scheme. Many fossil taxa, especially in the diverse Early Cretaceous assemblages of China, will yield important data, resulting in more complete data matrices for morphological characters. We can also look forward to more complete taxon sampling of living taxa in future morphological and molecular studies. A comprehensive phylogenetic analysis of fossil and extant genera of Osteoglossomorpha is now probably beyond the scope even of the most ambitious doctoral thesis, but international cooperation that has already begun should allow collaborative progress toward that goal.

The biogeographic history of the Osteoglossomorpha was undoubtedly complex. The remarkable diversity of basal osteoglossomorphs and primitive osteoglossiforms in SE Asia and the centre of modern biodiversity in Africa are two phenomena that, on present knowledge, seem inexplicable by simple hypotheses of centres of origin, or of Pangaean or Gondwanan continental breakup. Future work will undoubtedly lead to more discoveries of fossil osteoglossomorphs in areas where they are now rare, especially Europe, South America, SE Asia, and Africa. One of the most intriguing groups of fishes will continue to reward our interest.

We sincerely thank the organizers of this volume for the opportunity to contribute a paper in honour of our respected colleague and friend Dr. P. L. Forey. Dr. Forey's pioneering work has been an example of excellence in the field of palaeoichthyology, and he continues to lead the way into interesting research subjects. On a personal note, the first author is indebted to Peter for establishing palaeoichthyology at the University of Alberta and then for vacating the position to return to the U.K. in 1975, allowing MVHW to succeed him at the university; the second author has just recently accepted a position at the University of Alberta, and thus is also following in Peter's footsteps. We thank J. Bruner for bibliographic assistance, and K. Seymour, G. Gunnell and T. Harrison for lending material. We also thank G. Arratia, E. Hilton, Mee-mann Chang, and Jiang-Yong Zhang for discussion and the latter two for hosting a recent visit by MVHW to IVPP, Beijing, China. Reviewers E. Hilton and Jiang-Yong Zhang provided helpful comments. Funding was received from the

National Sciences and Engineering Research Council of Canada Discovery Grant A9180 to MVHW.

Appendix 1. List of material examined

Fossil material

†*Chauliopareion mahengeense* Murray & Wilson, 2005: WM 490/96 (holotype), WM 311/96 (paratype), WM 244/96, WM 272/96, WM 378/96, WM 351/96, WM 492/96, WM 497/96, WM 524/96, WM 531/96; †*Cretophareodus alberticus* Li, 1996; ROM 1323; †*Eohiodon rosei* Cavender, 1966: CMN 2100, CMN 2101, UALVP 12436, †*E. woodruffi* Wilson, 1978, CMN 9891, UALVP 12436; †*Joffrichthys symmetropterus* Li & Wilson, 1996*b*: UALVP 23705, 31545; †*Lycoptera muroii* (Takai, 1943): CMN 41640 (a slab with more than ten specimens); †*Ostariostoma wilseyi* Schaeffer, 1949: cast of FMNH PF10279; †*Phareodus encaustus* (Cope, 1871): CMN 51984; †*P. testis* (Cope, 1877): UALVP 17657, 17658, 17659; †*Singida jacksonoides* Greenwood & Patterson, 1967: MP 80, WM 109/96, WM 197/96, WM 241/96, WM 265/96, WM 298/96, WM 314/96, WM 315/96, WM 389/96, WM 480/96, WM 536/96.

Recent material

†*Osteoglossum bichirrosum* (Cuvier, 1829): ROM R6621 (skeleton); †*Scleropages formosus* (Müller & Schlegel, 1844): ROM R6617 (skeleton).

Institutional Abbreviations:

CMN, Canadian Museum of Nature, Ottawa, Ontario, Canada; FMNH, Field Museum of Natural History, Chicago, Illinois, USA; IVPP, Institute of Vertebrate Paleontology and Paleoanthropology, Beijing, China; NMT WM, specimens in the National Museum of Tanzania collected in 1996; ROM, Royal Ontario Museum, Toronto, Ontario, Canada; UALVP, Laboratory for Vertebrate Paleontology, University of Alberta, Edmonton, Alberta, Canada.

Appendix 2

Characters and character states used in analysis. In the following character and character-state list, the notations in brackets after the character description (H#, L#) refer to the characters of Hilton (2003) and Li *et al.* (1997*b*), respectively, that correspond to the character we have used, and subject to the modifications explained above.

(1) Temporal fossa (H1, L6):
    (0) absent
    (1) present, with the exoccipital making a contribution to the border
    (2) present, bordered by epioccipital, pterotic and parietal
    (3) present, bordered by epioccipital, and pterotic

(2) Shape of extrascapular (H2, L40):
    (0) expanded
    (1) reduced and irregularly shaped
    (2) reduced and tubular

(3) Shape of frontal bones (H3, L38):
    (0) anterior margin narrower than posterior margin
    (1) anterior margin about equal in width to posterior margin
    (2) anterior margin wider than posterior margin

(4) Supraorbital shelf of frontal bone (H4, L38):
    (0) absent
    (1) present

(5) Length of frontal bone (H5):
    (0) over twice as long as parietal
    (1) less than twice as long as parietal

(6) Relationship of nasal bones (H6, L4):
    (0) some part separated by anterior portion of frontals
    (1) separated only by ethmoid bones
    (2) meeting each other in midline

(7) Nasal bones (H7, L18):
    (0) tubular but not curved
    (1) tubular and strongly curved
    (2) gutter-like
    (3) flat and broad

(8) Parasphenoid teeth (H8):
    (0) absent
    (1) small
    (2) large and found along the length of the parasphenoid
    (3) large and restricted to the basal portion of the parasphenoid

(9) Basipterygoid process (H9, L5):
    (0) present
    (1) absent

(10) Supratemportal commissure passing through the parietals (H10, L57):
    (0) absent
    (1) present

(11) Supraorbital sensory canal (H11, L7):
    (0) ending in parietal
    (1) ending in frontal

(12) Orbitosphenoid (H12, L56):
    (0) present
    (1) absent

(13) Basisphenoid (H13):
    (0) present
    (1) absent

(14) Basioccipital process of the parasphenoid (H14):
    (0) divided
    (1) median

(15) Ventral occipital groove (H15):
    (0) present
    (1) absent

(16) Intercalar (H16):
    (0) present
    (1) absent

(17)   Cranial nerve foramen/foramina (H17):
        (0)   in the prootic
        (1)   straddling the suture between the prootic and pterosphenoid
        (2)   straddling the suture between the sphenotic and pterosphenoid
        (3)   foramina separate from each other, straddling the suture between the prootic, sphenotic and the pterosphenoid (dorsally) and one straddling the suture between the prootic, pterosphenoid and parasphenoid (ventrally)

(18)   Suture between the parasphenoid and sphenotic (H18):
        (0)   absent
        (1)   present

(19)   Foramen for cranial nerve VI (H19):
        (0)   opens within the prootic bridge
        (1)   opens anterior to the prootic bridge

(20)   Supraorbital bone (H20, L10):
        (0)   present
        (1)   absent

(21)   Otic and supraorbital sensory canal (H21):
        (0)   in bony canals
        (1)   partially or completely in grooves

(22)   Number of bones in the infraorbital series, not including the dermosphenotic or the antorbital if present (H22, L14):
        (0)   five
        (1)   four

(23)   first infraorbital (H23, L53):
        (0)   ventral to orbit
        (1)   anterior and ventral to orbit

(24)   Condition of the infraorbital sensory canal in at least some infraorbitals (H24, L43):
        (0)   enclosed in a bony canal
        (1)   open in a gutter

(25)   Palatoquadrate area behind and below the orbit (H25, L25):
        (0)   not completely covered by the infraorbitals
        (1)   completely covered by infraorbitals

(26)   Dermosphenotic (H26, L29):
        (0)   triangular
        (1)   triradiate
        (2)   tubular

(27)   Posterior extent of the fossa on the neurocranium for the hyomandibula (H27):
        (0)   formed of the pterotic
        (1)   formed of the pterotic and intercalar
        (2)   formed of pterotic and exoccipital
        (3)   formed of exoccipital and intercalar

(28)   Neurocranial heads of the hyomandibula (H28, L28):
        (0)   one head or two heads but continuous
        (1)   two heads, separate
        (2)   two heads, bridged

(29)   Anterior process (wing) of the hyomandibula that contacts the entopterygoid (H29):
        (0)   absent
        (1)   present

(30)   Bones of palatoquadrate (H30, L26):
        (0)   two lateral elements
        (1)   one lateral element
        (2)   one element, laterally and medially

(31)   Autopalatine bone (H31):
        (0)   present
        (1)   absent

(32)   Preopercular sensory canal (H32, L20):
        (0)   opens by pores the entire length of the canal
        (1)   opens by pores ventrally and a groove dorsally
        (2)   opens by pores dorsally and a groove ventrally
        (3)   opens by a groove the entire length of the canal

(33)   Opercle depth to width ratio (H33, L39):
        (0)   less than two
        (1)   about two or greater than two

(34)   Posterodorsal spine on the opercle (H34, L48):
        (0)   absent
        (1)   present

(35)   Subopercle bone (H35, L59):
        (0)   large and ventral to the opercle
        (1)   small and anterior to the opercle
        (2)   absent

(36)   Gular bone (H36):
        (0)   present
        (1)   absent

(37)   Ascending process of the premaxilla (H37, L47):
        (0)   well developed
        (1)   only slightly developed if at all

(38)   Premaxillae (H38):
        (0)   paired
        (1)   median

(39)   Posterior portion of maxilla (H39, L52):
        (0)   lies on angular
        (1)   lies on dentary

(40)   Supramaxillae (H40, L13):
        (0)   present
        (1)   absent

(41)   Mandibular canal (H41, L58):
        (0)   enclosed in a bony tube
        (1)   open in a groove

(42)   Posterior bones of the lower jaw (H42):
        (0)   angular and retroarticular bones fused
        (1)   angular and articular bones fused
        (2)   all separate
        (3)   all fused

(43)   Retroarticular bone (H43):
        (0)   included in the articulation with the quadrate
        (1)   excluded from the articulation with the quadrate

(44) Medial wall of the Meckelian fossa of the lower jaw (H44):
    (0) present
    (1) absent

(45) Bony elements associated with the second ventral gill arch (H45, L15):
    (0) absent
    (1) present as autogenous elements
    (2) present as a bony process on the second hypobranchial

(46) Toothplates associated with basibranchial 4 (H46):
    (0) present
    (1) absent

(47) Basihyal toothplate (H47, L54):
    (0) present
    (1) absent

(48) Basihyal toothplate (H48):
    (0) flat
    (1) with ventrally directed processes

(49) Basibranchial toothplate and basihyal toothplate (H49, L34):
    (0) separate
    (1) continuous

(50) Basihyal (H50):
    (0) present and ossified
    (1) present and cartilaginous
    (2) absent

(51) Hypohyals (H51):
    (0) two ossified pairs present
    (1) one ossified pair present
    (2) one ossified pair present but greatly reduced in size

(52) Infrapharyngobranchial 3 (H52):
    (0) undivided
    (1) divided into two elements

(53) Infrapharyngobranchial 1 (H53):
    (0) present
    (1) absent

(54) Orientation of infrapharyngobranchial 1 (H54):
    (0) proximal tip anteriorly directed
    (1) proximal tip posteriorly directed

(55) Abdominal scutes (H55, L60):
    (0) absent
    (1) present as paired structures

(56) Epipleural bone (H56):
    (0) absent
    (1) only a few bones in anterior caudal region
    (2) present throughout abdominal and caudal region

(57) Dorsal arm of the posttemporal bone (H57, L27):
    (0) less than 1.5 times as long as the ventral arm
    (1) more than twice as long as the ventral arm

(58) Lateral line that pierces the supracleithrum (H58):
    (0) present
    (1) absent

(59) Cleithrum (H59):
    (0) with no or only a slight medial lamina
    (1) with a broad medial lamina

(60) Coracoid fenestra (H60):
    (0) absent
    (1) present

(61) First pectoral fin ray (H61, L36):
    (0) normal
    (1) greatly expanded

(62) Post-pelvic bone (H62):
    (0) absent
    (1) present

(63) Pelvic bone (H63):
    (0) slender
    (1) possesses a thin deep lamella in dorsoventral plane

(64) Posterior end of anal fin (H64):
    (0) separate from caudal fin
    (1) continuous with caudal fin

(65) Number of principal caudal fin rays (H65, L12):
    (0) 19 or more
    (1) 18
    (2) 17 or fewer

(66) Uroneurals (H66, L1):
    (0) three or more
    (1) two or one
    (2) absent

(67) Neural spine on ural centrum 1 (H67, L21):
    (0) absent or rudimentary
    (1) one or more

(68) Epurals (H68, L9):
    (0) two or three
    (1) one
    (2) absent

(69) Neural spine on the first preural centrum (H69, L50):
    (0) complete
    (1) rudimentary
    (2) absent

(70) Number of neural spines on the second preural centrum (H70, L51):
    (0) one
    (1) two

(71) Number of hypurals (H71, L2):
    (0) seven
    (1) six or fewer

(72) Scales (H72, L31):
    (0) no reticulate furrows
    (1) both radial and reticulate furrows present
    (2) reticulate furrows only present over entire scale

(73) Pelvic fin ray number (L3):
    (0) more than seven
    (1) seven
    (2) six or fewer

(74) Swimbladder–ear direct connection (L3):
    (0) absent
    (1) present

(75) Intestine (L16):
    (0) coils to right of oesophagus and stomach
    (1) coils to left of oesophagus and stomach

(76) Opercle shape dorsal to facet for articulation with hyomandibula (L17):
    (0) rounded
    (1) flattened or truncated
    (2) flattened with posterior recurved process

(77) Upper hypurals and second ural (L19):
    (0) not fused
    (1) fused

(78) Second infraorbital shape and size (L22):
    (0) more or less slender or tubular and small in size
    (1) triangular or rectangular and smaller than third infraorbital
    (2) expanded and equivalent in size to or larger than third infraorbital

(79) Dorsal fin shape (L23):
    (0) base moderately long, fin triangular or falcate
    (1) base very short, much shorter than fin height, or fin absent
    (2) base moderately long to very long, fin with rounded outline anteriorly and posteriorly

(80) Posterior rays of dorsal and anal fin (L24):
    (0) shorter than anterior ones
    (1) longer than or as long as anterior ones

(81) 'Cheek wall' formed by enlargement of first to third infraorbitals (L30):
    (0) absent
    (1) present

(82) Ventral part of preopercle (L33):
    (0) extending anteriorly to beneath orbit or to level of posterior edge of orbit
    (1) anteriorly does not reach level of orbit

(83) Posterior edge of nasal when it is gutter-like or irregularly subrectangular (L35):
    (0) straight or slightly curved
    (1) strongly curved and extending backward

(84) Angle of jaws (L37):
    (0) anterior to middle vertical line of orbit
    (1) between middle vertical line and posterior edge of orbit
    (2) behind orbit

(85) Utriculus (L44):
    (0) connected with sacculus and lagena
    (1) completely separated from sacculus and lagena

(86) Anal fin sexual dimorphism (L46):
    (0) absent
    (1) present

(87) Ventral margin of opercle (L55):
    (0) rounded or pointed and narrower than mid-point of opercle
    (1) curved but not greatly narrowed compared to midpoint of opercle
    (2) flattened or only very slightly rounded

Appendix 3. Character–taxon matrix

Taxon	1–5	6–10	11–15	16–20	21–25	26–30	31–35	36–40	41–45	46–50	51–55	56–60	61–65	66–70	71–75	76–80	81–85	86–87
†Cladocyclus	0?00?	00?00	00???	????0	?0000	0?0?0	?000?	?0?00	0????	?0?0?	?????	?0???	????0	00001	000??	?0000	00-0?	0?
Clupeoidei	2?00?	10?11	10???	????0	?0000	0?0?0	?000?	?0?00	0????	?0?0?	????1	?0???	????0	00000	10210	00000	00-00	00
Elops	00000	00110	00000	00000	00000	00100	00000	00000	00000	00000	00000	20000	00000	00010	00???	00100	??-??	22
†Lycoptera	??001	10210	00???	?????	00000	0?0?0	00001	?0?00	0?21?	?000?	?????	?0???	0?001	0B100	002??	00100	00-0?	02
†Paralycoptera	0?00?	?????	0????	?????	?0000	0?0??	?0000	?0?00	0????	?0???	?????	?0???	?????	00?00	10???	?0?00	00-0?	??
†Tanolepis	0?00?	?????	0????	?????	?107?	0???0	?000?	?0?00	0????	?0???	?????	?0???	?????	00?00	?0?00	?0200	01-1?	??
†Sinoglossus	?000?	2????	10???	?????	?112?	0????	?000?	?0211	0????	?0102	?????	?0???	????2	???0	?2?2?	0?221	1000?	?1
†Eohiodon	20001	11210	0????	????1	01000	1?200	?0010	11001	00012	?0102	????0	01000	0-001	001B0	0011?	20100	00-0?	12
Hiodon	20001	11210	00001	00001	01000	11200	10010	11001	00010	00100	00000	01000	01001	001BB	00111	20100	00-00	12
†Joffrichthys	?2001	?????	10???	?????	01?01	0?0??	0011	?1?01	0??1?	?????	?????	0-???	0?02	?1?00	00111	?01E?	?02??	?1
Heterotis	22201	23001	10101	00001	01201	00111	11011	1011	02002	11-1	11000	10101	00002	11200	12201	01121	10000	02
Arapaima	32001	23001	10101	01011	01101	00111	10011	10011	02002	01-2	11000	00110	00002	11200	12201	11121	11000	01
†Phareodus	?2210	13?00	10010	?????	01001	0001?	10001	10001	0210?	2001?	????0	00?21	1?002	?1?00	122??	00121	0112?	01
Pantodon	22101	13200	10111	01001	11001	00001	10101	10101	01002	00011	101-0	01001	10102	11200	11201	01110	01120	00
†Singida	22101	03000	00???	?????	01001	000??	10102	2-01	01?1?	?????	?????	0002?	10102	11200	00100	00100	01022	00
Scleropages	32100	23301	11100	00101	01001	00011	B2101	11001	01102	10011	10000	00101	10102	11200	12201	01021	01120	00
Osteoglossum	32100	23301	11100	00101	01001	00011	12101	11001	01102	10011	10000	00101	10102	11200	12201	01021	01120	00
†Ostariostoma	2?000	??210	10???	0?010	0?010	0????	?3000	?1?01	019??	?????	?????	0112?	0?001	10100	1?2??	00100	00-0?	?0
Mormyroidea	1000B	022B0	1D111	11010	22002	22002	10000	11111	13?B2	1B???	C0010	07011	00001	10200	11211	11200	00001	B2
Petrocephalus	10000	02200	12111	11010	22002	22002	10000	11111	13?02	10002	10010	07011	00001	10200	11???	?220?	?????	??
Gnathonemus	10001	02200	13111	11010	22002	22002	10000	11111	13712	11--2	20010	07011	00001	10200	11???	?220?	?????	??
Campylomormyrus	10000	02200	12111	11010	22002	22002	10000	11111	13?12	11--2	20010	07011	00001	10200	11???	?220?	?????	??
Notopteridae	11C00	22C11	01011	01011	E3001	E3001	10001	10001	11101	10101	10B?1	00101	00712	21200	10211	11211	00001	00
Chitala	11200	22111	10010	01011	11010	03001	12002	10001	11101	10101	101-1	00101	00012	21200	10???	1?21?	21???	?0
Xenomystus	11100	22211	10010	01011	11010	23001	12002	10001	11101	10101	101-1	00101	00012	21200	1?21?	1?21?	?0???	?0
Papyrocranus	11100	22211	10110	01011	11010	23001	12002	10001	11101	10101	10001	00101	00-12	2120B	10???	1?21?	?0???	?0
†Palaeonotopterus	1000?	??210	1000?	0110?	?0000	?000?	?????	?????	?????	?????	?????	2-21?	?????	?????	?????	?????	?0-??	??
†Chauliopareion	20100	03-01	00???	?????	01000	000??	?1011	?1011	021??	?????	????0	01021	10101	?-?0	102??	0?1?0	0000?	11
†Xixiaichthys	0?100	1322?	000??	????1	?1100	??00?	10001	10001	02???	?0???	0??20	01?0?	0?000	01200	0012?	00100	0002?	?1

Notes: The data matrix was analysed with multistate characters entered in the format required by PAUP; however, for ease of aligning the matrix, we have replaced these codes with the following letters:
A = states 0, 1, and 2 present; B = states 0 and 1 present; C = states 1 and 2 present; D = states 2 and 3 present; E = states 0 and 2 present;
The following standard symbols are also used:
? = state unknown
- = character inapplicable.

References

ARAMBOURG, C. 1935. Note préliminaire sur les vertébrés fossiles des phosphates du Maroc. *Bulletin de la Société Géologique de France*, **5**, 413–439.

ARAMBOURG, C. 1952. Les vertébrés fossiles des gisements de phosphates (Maroc-Algérie-Tunisie). *Service Géologique du Maroc, Notes et Mémoires*, **92**, 1–372.

ARRATIA, G. 1997. Basal teleosts and teleostean phylogeny. *Palaeo Ichthyologica*, **7**, 5–168.

ARRATIA, G. 1998. Basal teleosts and teleostean phylogeny: response to C. Patterson. *Copeia*, **1998**, 1109–1113.

ARRATIA, G. 2000. Remarkable teleostean fishes from the Late Jurassic of southern Germany and their phylogenetic relationships. *Mitteilungen aus dem Museum für Naturkunde in Berlin, Geowissenschaftliche Reihe*, **3**, 137–179.

BANNIKOV, A. F. 1993. The succession of the Tethys fish assemblages exemplified by the Eocene localities of the southern part of the former USSR. *Kaupia, Darmstädter Beiträge zur Naturgeschichte*, **2**, 241–246.

BENTON, M. J. 1997. *Vertebrate Palaeontology*. Second edn. Reprinted 2000, Blackwell Science, Oxford.

BERRA, T. M. 1981. *An Atlas of Distribution of the Freshwater Fish Families of the World*. University of Nebraska Press, Lincoln, Nebraska.

BONDE, N. 1996. Osteoglossids (Teleostei: Osteoglossomorpha) of the Mesozoic. Comments on their interrelationships. *In*: ARRATIA, G. & VIOHL, G. (eds) *Mesozoic Fishes – Systematics and Paleoecology*. Dr F. Pfeil, Munich, Germany, 273–284.

BRINKMAN, D. B. & NEUMAN, A. G. 2002. Teleost centra from uppermost Judith River Group (Dinosaur Park Formation, Campanian) of Alberta, Canada. *Journal of Paleontology*, **76**, 138–155.

BROMHAM, L. & PENNY, D. 2003. The modern molecular clock. *Nature Reviews Genetics*, **4**, 216–224.

CASIER, E. 1965. Poissons fossiles de la série du Kwango (Congo). *Annales Musée Royal de l'Afrique Centrale, Série in 8°, Sciences Géologiques*, **50**, 1–64.

CAVENDER, T. M. 1966. Systematic position of the North American Eocene fish, 'Leuciscus' rosei Hussakof. *Copeia*, **1966**, 311–320.

CAVENDER, T. M. 1968. Freshwater fish remains from the Clarno Formation, Ochoco Mountains of north-central Oregon. *The Ore Bin*, **30**, 125–141.

CAVIN, L. & FOREY, P. L. 2001. Osteology and systematic affinities of *Palaeonotopterus greenwoodi* Forey 1997 (Teleostei: Osteoglossomorpha). *Zoological Journal of the Linnean Society*, **133**, 25–52.

CHANG, M.-M. 1999. 'Mid'-Cretaceous fish faunas from northeast China. *In*: ARRATIA, G. & SCHULTZE, H.-P. (eds) *Mesozoic Fishes 2 – Systematics and Fossil Record*. Dr F. Pfeil, Munich, 469–480.

CHANG, M.-M. & CHOU, J.-J. 1976. Cretaceous fishes from northeast China. 1. Discovery of *Plesiolycoptera* from Songhuajiang-Liaohe Basin and origin of Osteoglossomorpha. *Vertebrata PalAsiatica*, **14**, 146–153.

CHANG, M.-M. & CHOU, C.-C. 1977. On Late Mesozoic fossil fishes from Zhejiang Province, China. *Memoirs of the Institute of Vertebrate Paleontology and Paleoanthropology, Academia Sinica*, **12**, 1–59.

CHANG, M.-M. & CHOW, C.-C. 1986. Stratigraphic and geographic distributions of the Late Mesozoic and Cenozoic fishes of China. *In*: UYENO, T., ARAI, R., TANIUCHI, T. & MATUSUURA, K. (eds) *Indo-Pacific Fish Biology: Proceedings of the Second International Conference on Indo-Pacific Fishes*. Ichthyological Society of Japan, Tokyo, 529–539.

CHANG, M.-M. & MIAO, D. 2004. An overview of Mesozoic fishes in Asia. *In*: ARRATIA, G. & TINTORI, A.(eds) *Mesozoic Fishes 3 – Systematics, Paleoenvironments and Biodiversity*. Dr F. Pfeil, Munich, Germany, 535–563.

COCKERELL, T. D. A. 1925. The affinities of the fish *Lycoptera middendorffi*. *Bulletin of the American Museum of Natural History*, **11**, 313–317.

COPE, E. D. 1871. On the fishes of the Tertiary shales of Green River, Wyoming Territory. *United States Geological and Geographical Survey of the Territories. Annual Report, 1871*, 425–431.

COPE, E. D. 1877. On the classification of the extinct fishes of the lower types. *American Association for the Advancement of Science, Proceedings*, **26**, 292–300.

CUVIER, G. 1829. Le Règne Animal, distribué d'après son organization, pour servir de base à l'histoire naturelle des animaux et d'introduction à l'anatomie comparée. *Règne Animal Edition 2*, **2**, 1–406.

DANIL'CHENKO, P. G. 1968. Fishes of the upper Paleocene of Turkmenia. *In*: OBRUCHEV, D. V. (ed.) *Essays on the Phylogeny and Systematics of Fossil Fishes and Agnathans*. Nauka Press, Moscow, 113–156.

DARLINGTON, P. J. JR. 1957. *Zoogeography: the Geographical Distribution of Animals*. John Wiley & Sons, Inc., New York.

DARTEVILLE, D. E. & CASIER, E. 1949. Les poissons fossiles du Bas-Congo et des régions voisines. III. Neopterygii. *Annales du Musée du Congo Belge*, **3**, 205–255.

FOREY, P. L. 1997. A Cretaceous notopterid (Pisces: Osteoglossomorpha) from Morocco. *South African Journal of Science*, **93**, 564–569.

GAUDANT, J. 1968. Recherches sur l'anatomie et la position systématique du genre *Lycoptera* (poisson téléostéen). *Mémoires de la Société Géologique de France (Nouvelle Série)*, **109**, 1–40.

GAUDANT, J. 1981. Sur *Thaumaturus* Reuss (Poisson téléostéen), osteoglossomorphe fossile du Cénozoic européen. *Comptes Rendus de l'Académie des Sciences, Paris*, **293**, 787–790.

GAYET, M. 1991. 'Holostean' and teleostean fishes of Bolivia. *In*: SUROCO, R. S. (ed.) *Fosiles y Facies de Bolivia. Revista Técnica de YPFB*, **12**, 453–494.

GAYET, M. & MEUNIER, F. J. 1983. Écailles actuelles et fossiles d'Ostéoglossiformes (Pisces, Teleostei). *Comptes Rendus de l'Académie des Sciences, Paris*, **287**, 867–870.

GAYET, M. & MEUNIER, F. J. 1998. Maastrichtian to early late Paleocene freshwater Osteichthyes of Bolivia: additions and comments. *In*: MALABARBA, L. R., REIS, R. E., VARI, R. P. ET AL. (eds) *Phylogeny and Classification of Neotropical Fishes*. EDIPUCRS, Porto Alegre, 87–110.

GRANDE, L. 1979. *Eohiodon falcatus*, a new species of hiodontid (Pisces) from the late Early Eocene Green River Formation of Wyoming. *Journal of Paleontology*, **53**, 103–111.

GRANDE, L. 1980. Paleontology of the Green River Formation, with a review of the fish fauna. *Geological Survey of Wyoming Bulletin*, **63**, 1–333.

GRANDE, L. 1984. Paleontology of the Green River Formation, with a review of the fish fauna. (2nd edn). *Bulletin of the Geological Survey of Wyoming*, **63**, 1–333.

GRANDE, L. 1986. The first articulated freshwater teleost fish from the Cretaceous of North America. *Palaeontology*, **29**, 365–371.

GRANDE, L. & CAVENDER, T. M. 1991. Description and phylogenetic reassessment of the monotypic †Ostariostomidae (Teleostei). *Journal of Vertebrate Paleontology*, **11**, 405–416.

GRAUR, D. & MARTIN, W. 2004. Reading the entrails of chickens: molecular timescales of evolution and the illusion of precision. *Trends in Genetics*, **20**, 80–86.

GREENWOOD, P. H. 1963. The swimbladder in African Notopteridae (Pisces) and its bearing on the taxonomy of the family. *British Museum (Natural History) Zoology, Bulletin*, **11**, 379–412.

GREENWOOD, P. H. 1966. The caudal fin skeleton in osteoglossoid fishes. *Annals and Magazine of Natural History, Series 13*, **9**, 581–597.

GREENWOOD, P. H. 1970. On the genus *Lycoptera* and its relationship with the family Hiodontidae (Pisces, Osteoglossomorpha). *British Museum (Natural History) Zoology, Bulletin*, **19**, 257–285.

GREENWOOD, P. H. 1971. Hyoid and ventral gill arch musculature in osteoglossomorph fishes. *British Museum (Natural History) Zoology, Bulletin*, **22**, 1–55.

GREENWOOD, P. H. 1973. Interrelationships of osteoglossomorphs. *In*: GREENWOOD, P. H. MILES, R. S. & PATTERSON, C. (eds) *Interrelationships of Fishes*. Academic Press, London, 307–332.

GREENWOOD, P. H. 1983. The zoogeography of African freshwater fishes: Bioaccountancy or biogeography? *In*: SIMS, R. W., PRICE, J. H. & WHALLEY, P. E. S. (eds) *Evolution, Time and Space: The Emergence of the Biosphere*. Systematics Association Special Volume no. 23, Academic Press, London and New York, 179–199.

GREENWOOD, P. H. & PATTERSON, C. 1967. A fossil osteoglossoid fish from Tanzania (E. Africa). *Zoological Journal of the Linnean Society*, **47**, 211–233.

GREGORY, W. K. 1933. Fish Skulls: A study of the evolution of natural mechanisms. *Transactions of the American Philosophical Society, New Series*, **23**, 75–481.

HARRISON, T., MSUYA, C. P., MURRAY, A. M., JACOBS, B. F., BÁEZ, A. M., MUNDIL, R. & LUDWIG, K. R. 2001. Paleontological investigations at the Eocene locality of Mahenge in north-central Tanzania, East Africa. *In*: GUNNEL, G. F. (ed.) *Eocene Biodiversity: Unusual Occurrences and Rarely Sampled Habitats*. Kluwer Academic, New York, 39–74.

HECKEL, J. 1856. Beiträge zur Kenntniss der fossilen Fische Österreichs. *Denkschriften des kaiserlichen Akademie der Wissenschaften, Mathematisch-Naturwissenschaftliche Klasse*, **11**, 187–214.

HILLS, E. S. 1934. Tertiary fresh water fishes from southern Queensland. *Memoirs of the Queensland Museum*, **10**, 157–174.

HILLS, E. S. 1936. Tertiary fresh-water fishes and crocodilian remains from Gladstone and Duaringa, Queensland. *Memoirs of the Queensland Museum*, **12**, 96–100.

HILTON, E. J. 2001. Tongue bite apparatus of osteoglossomorph fishes: variation of a character complex. *Copeia*, **2001**, 372–381.

HILTON, E. J. 2002. Osteology of the extant North American fishes of the genus *Hiodon* Lesueur, 1818 (Teleostei: Osteoglossomorpha: Hiodontiformes). *Fieldiana*, **100**, 1–142.

HILTON, E. J. 2003. Comparative osteology and phylogenetic systematics of fossil and living bony-tongue fishes (Actinopterygii, Teleostei, Osteoglossomorpha). *Zoological Journal of the Linnean Society*, **137**, 1–100.

HILTON, E. J. & GRANDE, L. 2008. Fossil Mooneyes (Teleostei: Hiodontiformes, Hiodontidae) from the Eocene of western North America, with a reassessment of their taxonomy. *In*: CAVIN, L., LONGBOTTOM, A. & RICHTER, M. (eds) *Fishes and the Break-up of Pangaea*. Geological Society, London, Special Publications, **295**, 221–251.

HUSSAKOF, L. 1916. A new cyprinid fish, *Leuciscus rosei*, from the Miocene of British Columbia. *American Journal of Science, series 4*, **42**, 18–20.

JIN, F. 1991. A new genus and species of Hiodontidae from Xintai, Shandong. *Vertebrata PalAsiatica*, **29**, 46–54.

JIN, F. 1994. A nomen novum for *Tanichthys*. *Vertebrata PalAsiatica*, **32**, 70.

JIN, F., ZHANG, J.-Y. & ZHOU, Z.-H. 1995. Late Mesozoic fish fauna from western Liaoning, China. *Vertebrata PalAsiatica*, **33**, 169–193.

JOLLY, A. & BAJPAL, S. 1988. Fossil Osteoglossidae from the Kalakot Zone (middle Eocene): implications for paleontology, plaeobiogeography and correlation. *Bulletin of the Indian Geologists Association*, **21**, 71–79.

KUMAR, S. & HEDGES, S. B. 1998. A molecular timescale for vertebrate evolution. *Nature*, **392**, 917–920.

KUMAR, K., RANA, R. S. & PALIWAL, B. S. 2005. Osteoglossid and lepisosteid fish remains from the Paleocene Palana Formation, Rajasthan, India. *Palaeontology*, **48**, 1187–1209.

KUMAZAWA, Y. & NISHIDA, M. 2000. Molecular phylogeny of osteoglossoids: a new model for Gondwanian origin and plate tectonic transportation of the Asian arowana. *Molecular Biology and Evolution*, **17**, 1869–1878.

KUMAZAWA, Y., YAMAGUCHI, M. & NISHIDA, M. 1999. Mitochondrial molecular clocks and the origin of euteleostean biodiversity: familial radiation of perciformes may have predated the Cretaceous/Tertiary boundary. *In*: KATO, M. (ed.) *The Biology of Biodiversity*. Springer, Tokyo, 35–52.

LAVOUÉ, S. & SULLIVAN, J. P. 2004. Simultaneous analysis of five molecular markers provides a well-supported phylogenetic hypothesis for the living bony-tongue fishes (Osteoglossomorpha: Teleostei). *Molecular Phylogenetics and Evolution*, **33**, 171–185.

LEIDY, J. 1873. Notice of remains of fishes in the Bridger Tertiary Formation of Wyoming. *Proceedings of the Academy of Natural Sciences of Philadelphia*, **25**, 97–99.

LESUEUR, C. A. 1818. Descriptions of several new species of North American fishes. *Journal of the Academy of Natural Sciences of Philadelphia*, **1**, 359–368.

LI, G.-Q. 1987. A new genus of Hiodontidae from Luozigou Basin, East Jilin. *Vertebrata PalAsiatica*, **25**, 91–107.

LI, G.-Q. 1994. Systematic position of the Australian fossil osteoglossid fish †*Phareodus* (=*Pharoides*) *queenslandicus* Hills. *Memoirs of the Queensland Museum*, **37**, 287–300.

LI, G.-Q. 1996. A new species of Late Cretaceous osteoglossid (Teleostei) from the Oldman Formation of Alberta, Canada, and its phylogenetic relationships. *In*: ARRATIA, G. & VIOHL, G. (eds) *Mesozoic Fishes – Systematics and Paleoecology*. Dr F. Pfeil, Munich, Germany, 285–298.

LI, G.-Q. 1997. Notes on the historical biogeography of the Osteoglossomorpha (Teleostei). *Proceedings of the 30th International Geological Congress*, **12**, 54–66.

LI, G.-Q. & WILSON, M. V. H. 1994. A new species of *Hiodon* from the Eocene of Montana, with notes on the evolution of the postcranial skeleton in Hiodontidae (Teleostei). *Journal of Vertebrate Paleontology*, **14**, 153–167.

LI, G.-Q. & WILSON, M. V. H. 1996a. Phylogeny of Osteoglossomorpha. *In*: STIASSNY, M. L. J., PARENTI, L. R. & JOHNSON, G. D. (eds) *Interrelationships of Fishes*. Academic Press, New York, 163–174.

LI, G.-Q. & WILSON, M. V. H. 1996b. The discovery of Heterotidinae (Teleostei: Osteoglossidae) from the Paleocene Paskapoo Formation of Alberta, Canada. *Journal of Vertebrate Paleontology*, **16**, 198–209.

LI, G.-Q. & WILSON, M. V. H. 1999. Early divergence of Hiodontiformes *sensu stricto* in East Asia and phylogeny of some Late Mesozoic teleosts from China. *In*: ARRATIA, G. & SCHULTZE, H.-P. (eds) *Mesozoic Fishes 2 – Systematics and Fossil Record*. Dr F. Pfiel, Munich, 369–384.

LI, G.-Q., GRANDE, L. & WILSON, M. V. H. 1997a. The species of †*Phareodus* (Teleostei: Osteoglossidae) from the Eocene of North America and their phylogenetic relationships. *Journal of Vertebrate Paleontology*, **17**, 487–505.

LI, G.-Q., WILSON, M. V. H. & GRANDE, L. 1997b. Review of *Eohiodon* (Teleostei: Osteoglossomorpha) from western North America, with a phylogenetic reassessment of Hiodontidae. *Journal of Paleontology*, **71**, 1109–1124.

LIU, X.-T., MA, F.-Z. & LIU, Z.-C. 1982. Pisces. *In*: Geological Bureau of New Mongol Autonomous Region (eds) *The Mesozoic Stratigraphy and Paleontology of Guyang Coalbearing Basin, Nei Mongol, China*. Geological Publishing House, Beijing, 101–122.

LIU, X.-T., MA, F.-Z. & LIU, Z.-C. 1985. Discovery of *Kuntulunia* from the Shanganning Basin of North

China and its stratigraphic significance. *Vertebrata PalAsiatica*, **23**, 255–263.

LUNDBERG, J. G. & CHERNOFF, B. 1992. A Miocene fossil of the Amazonian fish *Arapaima* (Teleostei, Arapaimidae) from the Magdalena River region of Colombia – biogeographic and evolutionary implications. *Biotropica*, **24**, 2–14.

MA, F.-Z. 1980. A new genus of Lycopteridae from Ningxia, China. *Vertebrata PalAsiatica*, **18**, 286–295.

MA, F.-Z. 1983. Early Cretaceous primitive teleosts from the Jiaohe Basin of Jilin Province, China. *Vertebrata PalAsiatica*, **21**, 17–31.

MA, F.-Z. 1986. On the generic status of *Lycoptera tungi*. *Vertebrata PalAsiatica*, **24**, 260–268.

MA, F.-Z. & SUN, J. R. 1988. Jura-Cretaceous ichthyofaunas from Sankeyushu section of Tonghua, Jilin. *Acta Palaeontologica Sinica*, **27**, 694–711.

MADDISON, D. L. & MADDISON, W. P. 2005. *MacClade 4, Release Version 4.08*. Sinauer Associates, Sunderland, Massachusetts.

MAISEY, J. G. 2000. Continental break up and the distribution of fishes of Western Gondwana during the Early Cretaceous. *Cretaceous Research*, **21**, 281–314.

MORITZ, T. & BRITZ, R. 2005. Ontogeny and homology of the basipterygoid articulation in *Pantodon buchholzi* (Teleostei: Osteoglossomorpha). *Zoological Journal of the Linnean Society*, **144**, 1–13.

MÜLLER, J. 1847 [published in 1848]. Fossile Fische. *In*: VON MIDDENDORFF, A. T. (ed.) Reise in Den Aussersten Norder und Osten Sibiriens Wahrend der Jahre 1843 und 1844. *St. Petersburg, Kaiserlichen Akademie der Wissenschaften*, **1**, 260–264.

MÜLLER, S. & SCHLEGEL, H. 1844. Beschrijving van een' nieuwen Zoetwater-visch van Borneo, *Osteoglossum formosum*. *Verhandlingen over de Natuurlijke Geschiedenis der Nederlandsche Overzeesche Bezittingen Leiden*, **2**, 1–7.

MURRAY, A. M. 2000. Review of the Palaeozoic, Mesozoic and Early Cenozoic fishes of Africa. *Fish and Fisheries*, **1**, 111–145.

MURRAY, A. M. 2001. Oldest fossil cichlids (Teleostei, Perciformes): Indication of a forty-five million year old species flock. *Proceedings of the Royal Society, London, series B, Biological Sciences*, **268**, 679–684.

MURRAY, A. M. & WILSON, M. V. H. 2005. Description of a new Eocene osteoglossid fish and additional information on †*Sindiga jacksonoides* Greenwood and Patterson, 1967 (Osteoglossomorpha), with an assessment of their phylogenetic relationships. *Zoological Journal of the Linnean Society*, **144**, 213–228.

NELSON, G. J. 1968. Gill arches of some teleostean fishes of the division Osteoglossomorpha. *Zoological Journal of the Linnean Society*, **47**, 261–277.

NELSON, G. J. 1969. Infraorbital bones and their bearing on the phylogeny and geography of Osteoglossomorph fishes. *American Museum Novitates*, **2394**, 1–37.

NELSON, G. J. 1972. Observations on the gut of Osteoglossomorpha. *Copeia*, **1972**, 325–329.

NELSON, J. S. 2006. *Fishes of the World. Fourth Edition*. John Wiley & Sons, Inc., Hoboken, New Jersey.

NELSON, G. & LADIGES, P. Y. 2001. Gondwana, vicariance biogeography and the New York School revisited. *Australian Journal of Botany*, **49**, 389–409.

NEWBREY, M. G. & BOZEK, M. A. 2000. A new species of *Joffrichthys* (Teleostei: Osteoglossidae) from the Sentinel Butte Formation, (Paleocene) of North Dakota, USA. *Journal of Vertebrate Paleontology*, **20**, 12–20.

NEWBREY, M. G. & BOZEK, M. A. 2003. Age, growth, and mortality of *Joffrichthys triangulpterus* (Teleostei: Osteoglossidae) from the Paleocene Sentinel Butte Formation, North Dakota, U.S.A. *Journal of Vertebrate Paleontology*, **23**, 494–500.

NEWBREY, M. G. & WILSON, M. V. H. 2005. Recognition of annular growth on centra of Teleostei with application to Hiodontidae of the Cretaceous Dinosaur Park Formation. *In*: BRAMAN, D. R., THERRIEN, F., KOPPELHUS, E. B. *ET AL*. (eds) *Dinosaur Park Symposium*. Special Publication of the Royal Tyrrell Museum, Drumheller, Alberta, 61–68.

NEWBREY, M. G., WILSON, M. V. H. & ASHWORTH, A. C. 2007. Centrum growth patterns provide evidence for two small taxa of Hiodontidae in the Cretaceous Dinosaur Park Formation. *Canadian Journal of Earth Sciences*, **44**, 721–732.

PATTERSON, C. 1975. The distribution of Mesozoic freshwater fishes. *Muséum National d'Histoire Naturelle, Mémoires, Série A, Zoologie*, **88**, 156–174.

PATTERSON, C. 1981. The development of the North American fish fauna – a problem of historical biogeography. *In*: FOREY, P. L. (ed.) *The Evolving Biosphere*. Cambridge University Press, Cambridge, England, 265–281.

PATTERSON, C. 1998. Comments on basal teleosts and teleostean phylogeny, by Gloria Arratia. *Copeia*, **1998**, 1107–1109.

PATTERSON, C. & ROSEN, D. E. 1977. Review of ichthyodectiform and other Mesozoic teleost fishes and the theory and practice of classifying fossils. *Bulletin of the American Museum of Natural History*, **158**, 81–172.

RIDEWOOD, W. G. 1904. On the cranial osteology of the fishes of the families Mormyridae, Notopteridae, and Hyodontidae. *Zoological Journal of the Linnean Society*, **29**, 188–217.

RIDEWOOD, W. G. 1905. On the cranial osteology of the fishes of the families Osteoglossidae, Pantodontidae, and Phractolaemidae. *Zoological Journal of the Linnean Society*, **29**, 252–282.

ROELLIG, H. F. 1967. The Osteoglossidae, fossil and Recent. Ph.D. thesis, Columbia University, New York.

ROELLIG, H. F. 1974. The cranial osteology of *Brychaetus muelleri* (Pisces Osteoglossidae), Eocene, Isle of Sheppey. *Journal of Paleontology*, **48**, 947–951.

RUBER, L. & ZARDOYA, R. 2005. Rapid cladogenesis in marine fishes revisited. *Evolution*, **59**, 1119–1127.

SANDERS, M. 1934. Die fossilen Fische der alttertiären Süsswasserablagerungen aus Mittel-Sumatra. *Verhandelingen van het Geologisch-Mijnbouwkundig Genootschap voor Nederland en Koloniën, Geologische Series*, **11**, 1–144.

SANFORD, C. P. & LAUDER, G. V. 1989. Functional morphology of the 'tongue-bite' in the Osteoglossomorph fish *Notopterus*. *Journal of Morphology*, **202**, 379–408.

SANTOS, R. D. S. 1988. *Laeliichthys ancestralis*, novo gênero e espécie de Osteoglossiformes do Aptiano da Formaçao Areado, estado de Minas Gerais, Brasil.

MME–DNPM, Geologia 27, Paleontologia e estratigrafia, **2**, 161–167.

SAUVAGE, H.-É. 1880. Notes sur les poissons fossiles (suite). *Bulletin de la Société Géologique de France*, **8**, 451–462.

SCHAEFFER, B. 1949. A teleost from the Livingston Formation of Montana. *American Museum Novitates*, **1427**, 1–16.

SCHULTZE, H.-P. & ARRATIA, G. 1988. Reevaluation of the caudal skeleton of some actinopterygian fishes: II. *Hiodon, Elops*, and *Albula*. *Journal of Morphology*, **195**, 257–303.

SHEN, M. 1989. *Eohiodon* from China and the distribution of osteoglossomorphs. *Vertebrata PalAsiatica*, **27**, 237–247.

SHEN, M. 1990. Fossil osteoglossomorphs (teleost fish) in China and their zoogeographical implication. *In*: WILEY, T. J., HOWELL, D. G. & WONG, F. L. (eds) *Terrane Analysis of China and the Pacific Rim*. Circum-Pacific Council for Energy & Mineral Resources, Earth Sciences Series, Houston, 223–226.

SHEN, M. 1996. Fossil 'osteoglossomorphs' from East Asia and their implications for teleostean phylogeny. *In*: ARRATIA, G. & VIOHL, G. (eds) *Mesozoic Fishes–Systematics and Paleoecology*. Dr F. Pfeil, Munich, 261–272.

SHEN, M., JIN, F. & ZHANG, J.-Y. 1991. The interrelationships of Huashiidae (Teleostei) and its implication on systematics. *Vertebrata PalAsiatica* **29**, 245–263.

SMITH, A. B. & PETERSON, K. J. 2002. Dating the time of origin of major clades: molecular clocks and the fossil record. *Annual Reviews in Earth and Planetary Sciences*, **30**, 65–88.

SMITH, A. G., SMITH, D. G. & FUNNELL, B. M. 1994. *Atlas of Mesozoic and Cenozoic Coastlines*. Cambridge University Press, Cambridge, 1–99.

SU, D.-Z. 1986. The discovery of a fossil osteoglossid fish in China. *Vertebrata PalAsiatica*, **24**, 10–19.

SU, D.-Z. 1992. On teleostean fossils from Nieerku Formation of eastern Liaoning and the generic status of *Lycoptera longicephalus*. *Vertebrata PalAsiatica*, **30**, 54–70.

SWISCHER, I. C. C., WANG, Y.-Q., WANG, X.-L., XU, X. & WANG, Y. 1999. Cretaceous age for the feathered dinosaurs of Liaoning, China. *Nature*, **400**, 58–61.

SWOFFORD, D. L. 2002. *PAUP*. Phylogenetic Analysis Using Parsimony (*and Other Methods). Version 4*. Sinauer Associates, Sunderland, Massachusetts.

SYTCHEVSKAYA, E. C. 1986. Palaeogene freshwater fish fauna of the USSR and Mongolia. *Trudy Sovmestnaya Sovetsko-Mongol'skaya Paleontologicheskaya Ekspeditsiya*, **29**, 1–157.

TAKAI, F. 1943. A monograph on the lycopterid fishes from the Mesozoic of eastern Asia. *Journal of the Faculty of Science, Tokyo University, Series 2*, **6**, 207–270.

TANG, P. Y., SIVANANTHAN, J., PILLAY, S. O. & MUNIANDY, S. 2004. Genetic structure and biogeography of Asian Arowana (*Scleropages formosus*) determined by microsatellite and mitochondrial DNA analysis. *Asian Fisheries Science*, **17**, 81–92.

TAVERNE, L. 1968. Ostéologie du genre *Gnathonemus* Gill *sensu stricto* [*Gnathonemus petersii* (Gthr) et espèces voisines] (Pisces Mormyriformes). *Annales du Musée Royal de l'Afrique Centrale, Série 8, Sciences Zoologiques,* **170,** 1–91.

TAVERNE, L. 1969. Sur un squelette caudal d'Ostéoglossomorphe (*Brychaetus*?) dans le Paléocène (Montien) de Landana (Enclave de Cabinda). Établissement d'une nouvelle espèce pour les restes de *Brychaetus* de Landana: *Brychaetus caheni* sp. nov. *Revue de Zoologie et de Botanique Africaines,* **79,** 125–131.

TAVERNE, L. 1972. Ostéologie des genres *Mormyrus* Linné, *Mormyrops* Müller, *Hyperopisus* Gill, *Isichthys* Gill, *Myomyrus* Boulenger, *Stomatorhinus* Boulenger et *Gymnarchus* Cuvier, considérations générales sur la systématique des poissons de l'ordre des Mormyriformes. *Annales du Musée Royal de l'Afrique Centrale, Série 8, Sciences Zoologiques,* **200,** 1–194.

TAVERNE, L. 1973. Établissement d'un genre nouveau, *Phareoides,* pour *Phareodus queenslandicus* Hills, E. S., 1934 (Pisces Osteoglossiformes) du tertiaire d'Australie. *Bulletin de la Société Belge de Géologie, de Paléontologie, et d'Hydrologie,* **82,** 497–499.

TAVERNE, L. 1974a. Sur une adaptation au vol des lépidotriches pectoraux *de Pantodon* Peters (Pisces Osteoglossiformes). *Revue Zoologique africaine,* **88,** 221–223.

TAVERNE, L. 1974b. Sur la sagitta des Mormyridae (Pisces Osteoglossomorphes). *Revue Zoologique africaine,* **88,** 281–285.

TAVERNE, L. 1974c. Sur l'origine des processus intracraniens vésicaux du basioccipital des Mormyridae (Téléostéens Ostéoglossomorphes). *Revue Zoologique africaine,* **88,** 374–376.

TAVERNE, L. 1974d. À propos de *Brychaetus* Woodward, A. S., 1901 (Eocène d'Afrique et d'Europe) et de ses rapports avec les Osteoglossidae actuels et fossiles (Pisces Osteoglossomorphes). *Revue Zoologique africaine,* **88,** 724–734.

TAVERNE, L. 1974e. Sur le 'vomer' des Mormyridae et l'ethmoïde latéro-basal des Ichthyodectiformes (Pisces Osteoglossomorpha). *Revue Zoologique Africaine,* **88,** 837–842.

TAVERNE, L. 1975a. Sur la présence d'une structure archaïque, la portion supraoculaire du canal sensoriel circumorbitaire, chez les Notopteridae (Pisces Osteoglossiformes). *Revue Zoologique africaine,* **89,** 92–95.

TAVERNE, L. 1975b. Deuxième note sur l'ethmoïde latéro-basal des Poissons Ostéoglossomorphes et son homologie avec le rhinal des Holostéens à la lumière du cas des Notopteridae. *Revue Zoologique africaine,* **89,** 629–634.

TAVERNE, L. 1975c. Sur l'existence d'un Poisson Osteoglossoïde fossile proche parent de l'actuel genre *Heterotis* dans le Crétacé moyen du Kwango (Zaïre). *Revue Zoologique africaine,* **89,** 965–968.

TAVERNE, L. 1976a. Le rhinal (ethmoïde latéro-basal) chez l'Ostéoglossomorphe africain *Gymnarchus niloticus* (Pisces, Mormyriformes). *Revue Zoologique africaine,* **90,** 14–16.

TAVERNE, L. 1976b. Sur l'existence d'une chambre osseuse prootico-basioccipitale pour le sac vasculaire posthypophysaire chez les Notopteridae adultes (Pisces Osteoglossomorpha). *Revue Zoologique africaine,* **90,** 463–469.

TAVERNE, L. 1977. Ostéologie, phylogénèse et systématique des Téléostéens fossiles et actuels du super-ordre des Ostéoglossomorphes. Première partie. Ostéologie des genres *Hiodon, Eohiodon, Lycoptera, Osteoglossum, Scleropages, Heterotis* et *Arapaima. Académie Royale de Belgique, Mémoires de la Classe des Sciences, Collection in-8°-2ième série,* **42.**

TAVERNE, L. 1978. Ostéologie, phylogénèse et systématique des Téléostéens fossiles et actuels du super-ordre des Ostéoglossomorphes. Deuxième partie. Ostéologie des genres *Phareodus, Phareoides, Brychaetus, Musperia, Pantodon, Singida, Notopterus, Xenomystus* et *Papyrocranus. Académie Royale de Belgique, Mémoires de la Classe des Sciences, Collection in-8°-2ième série,* **42,** 1–213.

TAVERNE, L. 1979. Ostéologie, phylogénèse et systématique des Téléostéens fossiles et actuels du super-ordre des Ostéoglossomorphes. Troisième partie. Evolution des structures ostéologiques et conclusions générales relatives à la phylogénèse et à la systématique du super-ordre. *Académie Royale de Belgique, Mémoires de la Classe des Sciences, Collection in-8°-2ième série,* **43,** 1–168.

TAVERNE, L. 1980. Sur quelques particularites ostéologiques du crâne d'*Arapaima* Müller, J., 1843 (Téléostéens Osteoglossomorphes). *Bulletin de l'Institut Royal des Sciences Naturelle Belgique,* **52,** 1–5.

TAVERNE, L. 1984. À propos de *Chanopsis lombardi* du Crétacé inférieur du Zaïre (Teleostei, Osteoglossiformes). *Revue Zoologique africaine,* **98,** 578–590.

TAVERNE, L. 1998. Les ostéoglossomorphes marins de l'Éocène du Monte Bolca (Italie): *Monopteros* Volta 1796, *Thrissopterus* Heckel, 1856 et *Foreyichthys* Taverne, 1979. Considérations sur la phylogénie des téléostéens ostéoglossomorphes. *Studi e Richerch sui Giacimenti Terziari di Bolca.* Museo di Historia Naturale, Verona, **7,** 67–158.

TAVERNE, L. 2000. Nouvelles données ostéologiques et phylogénétiques *sur Palaeonotopterus greenwoodi,* notoptéridé (Teleostei, Osteoglossomorpha) du Cénomanien inférieur continental (Crétacé) du Maroc. *Stuttgarter Beiträge zur Naturkunde Serie B (Geologie und Paläontologie),* **293,** 1–24.

TAVERNE, L. 2004. On a complete hyomandibular of the Cretaceous Moroccan notopterid *Palaeonotopterus greenwoodi* (Teleostei, Osteoglossomorpha). *Stuttgarter Beiträge zur Naturkunde Serie B (Geologie und Paläontologie),* **348,** 1–7.

TAVERNE, L. & MAISEY, J. G. 1999. A notopterid skull (Teleostei, Osteoglossomorpha) from the continental Early Cretaceous of southern Morocco. *American Museum Novitates,* **3260,** 1–12.

VENCES, M., FREYHOF, J., SONNENBERG, R., KOSUCH, J. & VEITH, M. 2001. Reconciling fossils and molecules: Cenozoic divergence of cichlid fishes and the biogeography of Madagascar. *Journal of Biogeography,* **28,** 1091–1099

VOLTA, G. S. 1796. *Ittiolitologia Veronese del Museo Bozziano ora annesso a quello del Conte Giovambattista Gazola e di altri Gabinetti di Fossili Veronesi.* Dalla Stampa Giulari, **2** vol.

WEEMS, R. E. & HORMAN, S. R. 1983. Teleost fish remains (Osteoglossidae, Blochiidae, Scombridae, Triodontidae, Diodontidae) from the lower Eocene

Nanjemoy Formation of Maryland. *Proceedings of the Biological Society of Washington*, **96**, 38–49.

WILSON, M. V. H. 1977. Middle Eocene freshwater fishes from British Columbia. *Life Sciences Contributions, Royal Ontario Museum*, **113**, 1–61.

WILSON, M. V. H. 1978. *Eohiodon woodruffi* n. sp. (Teleostei, Hiodontidae), from the middle Eocene Klondike Mountain Formation near Republic, Washington. *Canadian Journal of Earth Sciences*, **15**, 679–686.

WILSON, M. V. H. 1996a. Fishes from Eocene lakes of the Interior. *In*: LUDVIGSEN, R. (ed.) *Life in Stone: A Natural History of British Columbia's Fossils*. University of British Columbia Press, Vancouver, 212–224.

WILSON, M. V. H. 1996b. The Eocene fishes of Republic, Washington. *Washington Geology*, **24**, 30–31.

WILSON, M. V. H. & WILLIAMS, R. R. G. 1992. Phylogenetic, biogeographic, and ecological significance of early fossil records of North American freshwater teleostean fishes. *In*: MAYDEN, R. L. (ed.) *Systematics, Historical Ecology, and North American Freshwater Fishes*. Stanford University Press, Stanford, California, 224–244.

WOODWARD, A. S. 1901. *Catalogue of the fossil fishes in the British Museum (Natural History), Part 4*. British Museum (Natural History), London.

YABUMOTO, Y. 1994. Early Cretaceous freshwater fish fauna in Kyushu, Japan. *Bulletin of the Kitakyushu Museum of Natural History*, **13**, 107–254.

YABUMOTO, Y. 2005. Early Cretaceous osteoglossiform fishes from central Japan, with notes on the origin of the Osteoglossidae. *In*: POYATO-ARIZA, F. J. (ed.) *Fourth International Meeting on Mesozoic Fishes - Systematics, Homology, and Nomenclature, Miraflores de la Sierra, Extended Abstracts*. Ediciones Universidad Autónoma de Madrid, Madrid, Spain, 275–276.

ZHANG, J.-Y. 1998. Morphology and phylogenetic relationships of †*Kuntulunia* (Teleostei: Osteoglossomorpha). *Journal of Vertebrate Paleontology*, **18**, 280–300.

ZHANG, J.-Y. 2004. New fossil osteoglossomorph from Nigxia, China. *Journal of Vertebrate Paleontology*, **24**, 515–524.

ZHANG, J.-Y. 2006. Phylogeny of Osteoglossomorpha. *Vertebrata PalAsiatica*, **44**, 43–59.

ZHANG, J.-Y. & JIN, F. 1999. A revision of †*Tongxinichthys* Ma 1980 (Teleostei: Osteoglossomorpha) from the Lower Cretaceous of northern China. *In*: ARRATIA, G. & SCHULTZE, H.-P. (eds) *Mesozoic Fishes – Systematics and Fossil Record*. Dr F. Pfeil, Munich, 385–396.

ZHANG, J.-Y., JIN, F. & ZHOU, Z.-H. 1994. A review of the Mesozoic osteoglossomorph fish *Lycoptera longicephalus*. *Vertebrata PalAsiatica*, **32**, 41–59.

Fossil Mooneyes (Teleostei: Hiodontiformes, Hiodontidae) from the Eocene of western North America, with a reassessment of their taxonomy

ERIC J. HILTON[1] & LANCE GRANDE[2]

[1]*Department of Fisheries Science, Virginia Institute of Marine Science, Gloucester Point, VA 23062, USA (e-mail: ehilton@vims.edu)*

[2]*Field Museum of Natural History, 1400 South Lake Shore Drive, Chicago IL 50605, USA (e-mail: lgrande@fieldmuseum.org)*

Abstract: The skeletal anatomy of fossil hiodontids from western North America is examined based on newly-prepared specimens, including several specimens that were prepared using the acid transfer method and some using the 'lost fossil' technique. This study resulted in many new interpretations and clarifications, such as the presence of a curved tubular nasal bone and a posterodorsal spine on the opercle of '†*Eohiodon*', as found in extant *Hiodon*. We also further describe the variation of the caudal skeleton that has been known in both fossil and extant *Hiodon*. For instance, the neural spine of preural one is most often fully developed (as it is in a minority of extant *Hiodon* specimens), although in some specimens it is rudimentary, as it is in most specimens of living taxa. We review the characters that have been used in recent analyses of relationships of osteoglossomorph fishes. After correcting the descriptions of the fossil taxa, we could find no valid synapomorphies to separate the genus †*Eohiodon* from the genus *Hiodon*. Therefore, we conclude that †*Eohiodon* should be regarded as a synonym of *Hiodon*.

The family Hiodontidae (Osteoglossomorpha) has been interpreted as the extant sister-group of the group containing all other living osteoglossomorph fishes (e.g. Taverne 1979, 1998; Li & Wilson 1996*a*; Hilton 2003; Lavoué & Sullivan 2004). The family Hiodontidae *sensu* Li & Wilson (1999), which is coextensive with their order Hiodontiformes, contains four genera: †*Plesiolycoptera* Chang & Chou (1976) (late Early Cretaceous, China), †*Yanbiania* Li (1987) (late Early Cretaceous, China), †*Eohiodon* Cavender (1966) (Eocene, western North America and potentially China; see below) and *Hiodon* Lesueur (1818) (Eocene to Recent: North America). Other fossil taxa have been included in this family as well [e.g. †*Jiaohichthys* Ma (1983), which probably is a senior synonym of †*Yanbiania*; see Chang (1999); table 3; Chang & Miao (2004)], although further study of many of these taxa is needed to validate their correct generic placement.

Specimens assigned to †*Eohiodon* have been described from several localities in western North America (Fig. 1). †*Eohiodon rosei* (Hussakoff 1916) was first described as belonging to the cyprinid genus *Leuciscus* Cuvier (*ex* Klein), 1816. Cavender (1966) restudied Hussakoff's specimens of †'*Leuciscus*' *rosei* and recognized its similarity to *Hiodon*, an extant genus of the basal teleostean group Osteoglossomorpha from central and northern North America. Cavender (1966) established the genus †*Eohiodon* for this species and regarded it as closely-related to the extant *Hiodon*. †*Eohiodon rosei* (Fig. 2a), is known from the Tranquille beds (containing the type locality), the Allenby Formation and the Horsefly Beds, all from British Columbia (Wilson 1977, 1978). Since Cavender's (1966) naming of the genus, four additional species have been described. †*Eohiodon woodruffi* Wilson (1978) (Fig. 2b), from the Eocene Klondike Mountain Formation (Washington), Tunnel Creek (Montana), and the Horsefly Beds (British Columbia), was found to differ from †*E. rosei* by having more anal fin rays and a slightly deeper body (although body depth was not statistically significantly different; Wilson 1978, p. 648). The following year, †*E. falcatus* Grande, 1979 (Fig. 2c), from the Fossil Butte Member of the Green River Formation of SW Wyoming, was described as differing from †*E. rosei* by having a greater number of dorsal and anal fin rays and pterygiophores, a more strongly falcate dorsal fin, by the proportions of the head and in the placement of the paired fins. Of any fossil hiodontid, this species is known from the greatest number of well-preserved specimens by far. Interestingly, Grande & Buchheim (1994) noted that over 100 specimens are known from a near shore deposit of the Fossil Butte Member

From: CAVIN, L., LONGBOTTOM, A. & RICHTER, M. (eds) *Fishes and the Break-up of Pangaea.*
Geological Society, London, Special Publications, **295**, 221–251.
DOI: 10.1144/SP295.13   0305-8719/08/$15.00 © The Geological Society of London 2008.

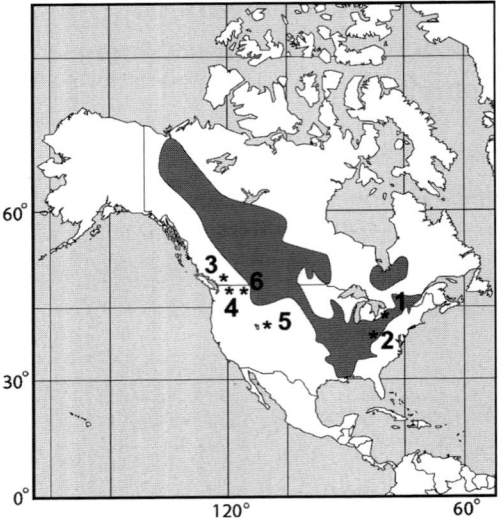

Fig. 1. Type localities of the species of *Hiodon* Lesueur, 1818, listed in order of description. **1**, *H. tergisus* Lesueur (1818); Lake Erie at Buffalo, New York, USA; **2**, *H. alosoides* (Rafinesque 1819); Ohio River at Cincinnati, Ohio, USA; **3**, †*H. rosei* (Hussakof 1916); Tranquille Beds, Red Point on Kamloops Lake, British Columbia, Canada; **4**, †*H. woodruffi* (Wilson 1978); Klondike Mountain Formation, Washington, USA; **5**, †*H. falcatus* (Grande 1979); Green River Formation, Wyoming, USA; **6**, †*H. consteniorum* Li & Wilson (1994); Kishenehn Formation, Montana, USA. Grey indicates range of extant species.

(their F–2 deposits, locality H), whereas only one specimen had been recorded from any of the several mid-lake localities of this formation (see also Grande 2001).

The remaining two nominal species of †*Eohiodon* are from formations in Asia. †*Eohiodon parvus* Sytchevskaya (1986) was described from freshwater deposits of Mongolia (Paleocene and Eocene) and Kazakhstan (Eocene and Oligocene) and was placed in the subgenus, †*Gobiohiodon* Sytchevskaya (1986). Li (1994, fig. 7.11) included this species in the genus †*Plesiolycoptera*, but gave no explanation for this synonymy (see also Li & Wilson 1999). †*Eohiodon shuyangensis* Shen (1989) was described based on a single poorly-preserved specimen from the Eocene freshwater deposits of Jiangsu Province, China. Li (1994) considered this specimen to possibly be a juvenile specimen of †*Phareodus* Leidy (1873). The published descriptions of these two Asian species of †*Eohiodon* do not allow us to comment further on their taxonomic assignments, but we suggest that further study is warranted.

The anatomy and systematics of the North American representatives of the genus †*Eohiodon*

were reviewed by Li *et al.* (1997). In addition to providing the most extensive review to date of the morphology of †*Eohiodon*, these authors synonymized †*E. falcatus* with †*E. woodruffi* (i.e. they considered the only two valid North American species to be †*E. rosei* and †*E. woodruffi*; see also Bruner 1992). Li *et al.* (1997) further suggested that †*E. woodruffi* differed from †*E. rosei* by having also an 'anteriorly slender maxilla, and a dorsally and posteriorly slightly excavated opercle.'

This paper has three main goals. First, to provide a review of the osteology of taxa assigned to †*Eohiodon*, based on a study of newly collected and prepared specimens. Second, to use the new data generated by the first part of our study in combination with the results of Hilton's (2002) osteological study of the extant *Hiodon* (Fig. 3), to critically examine the characters used by Li *et al.* (1997) at various taxonomic levels within Hiodontidae. Third, to comment on the taxonomy of hiodontid fishes.

Methods and materials

Specimen preparation

Subsequent to their original descriptions, newly found and better-preserved specimens attributable to each of the three nominal species have been discovered, and these form the basis of much of our study. New specimens were prepared both mechanically and chemically. Mechanically prepared specimens were exposed using a pin-vise, air-scribe or air-abrasive tools. Six specimens from the Green River formation were prepared using the acid-transfer technique of Toombs & Rixon (1959; see also Grande & Bemis 1998). Prior to each acid-immersion, loose matrix was carefully scraped from the specimen using a dental pick so as to quicken the process of acid preparation. Three specimens preserved mainly as impressions (AMNH 8059; AMNH 8059a; AMNH 8060;) were prepared using the 'lost fossil' method, in which acid was used to etch remaining bone from the impressions (e.g. see Grande 1987). Black latex peels (see Grande & Bemis 1998) were made and studied for these and two other specimens that were preserved as impressions (UALVP 21314; TMP 86.48.3). All specimens were coated with ammonium chloride sublimate prior to photography.

Materials examined

Comparative specimens of extant *Hiodon* consisted of both dry skeletons prepared using a dermestid beetle colony and cleared and stained specimens prepared following a protocol modified from

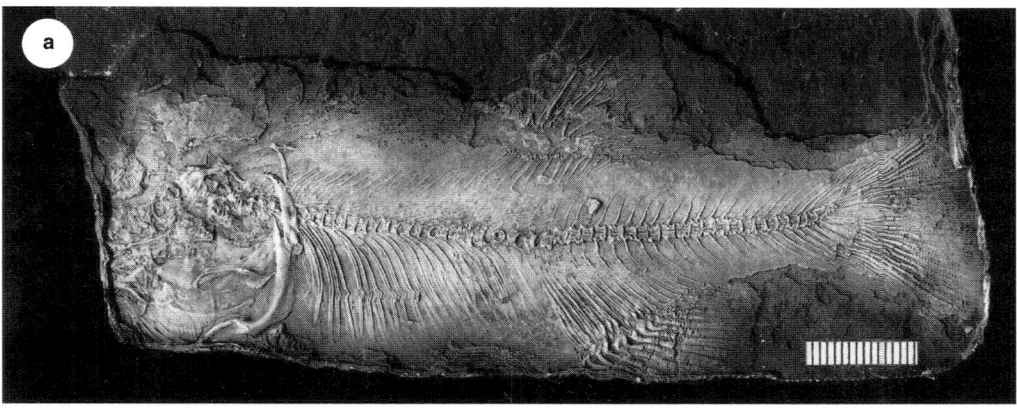

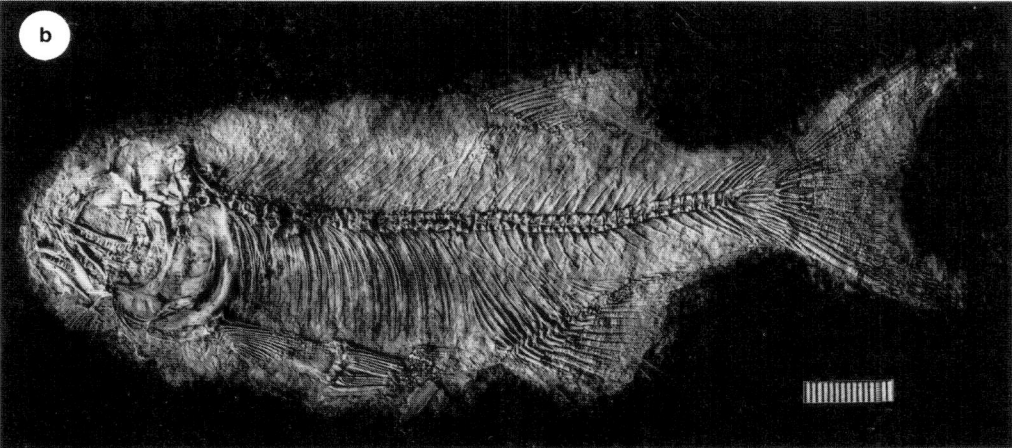

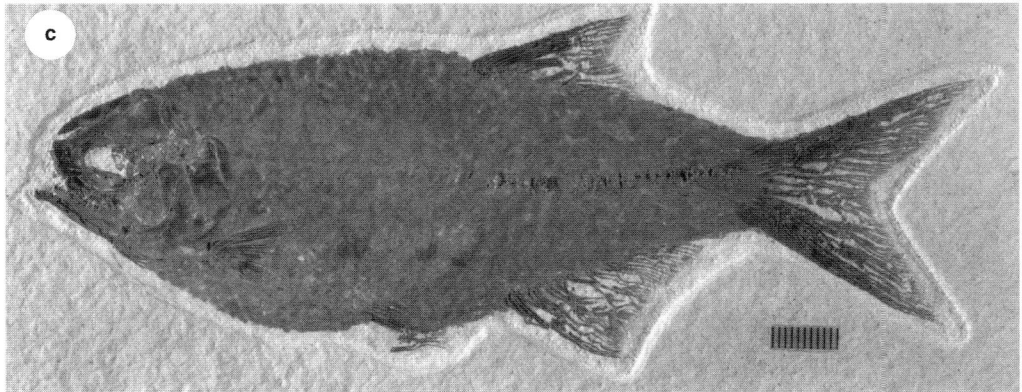

Fig. 2. Whole skeletons of nominal North American species of fossil *Hiodon*. **a**, †*H. rosei* (Hussakof 1916) (AMNH 8059); **b**, †*H. woodruffi* (Wilson 1978) (UALVP 41213); **c**, †*H. falcatus* (Grande 1979) (FMNH PF15337). Specimens of †*H. rosei* and †*H. woodruffi* are black latex peels of impressions coated with ammonium chloride prior to photography; anterior facing left (a, b, images are reversed). Scale bar in millimetres.

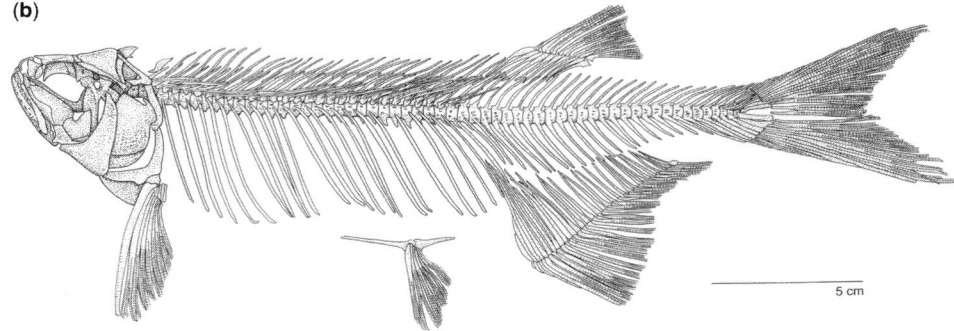

Fig. 3. Whole skeleton of a female *Hiodon alosoides* (Rafinesque 1819) (UMA F10150, 293 mm SL). Anterior facing left.

Dingerkus & Uhler (1977). Specimens examined are listed in Hilton (2002). A dagger (†) is used to indicate taxa known exclusively as fossils.

†*Hiodon consteniorum.* UALVP 38875 (holotype, whole skeleton); UALVP 24200 (paratype, whole skeleton). Both specimens from the late Eocene Coal Creek Member of the Kishenehn Formation, Montana.

†*Eohiodon rosei.* AMNH 8059a (head only; unknown SL; from the Eocene Tranquille Beds, Kamloops Group, of British Columbia); AMNH 8059 (paratype, whole skeleton except head disarticulated and incomplete; *c.* 105 mm SL; from the Eocene Tranquille Beds, Kamloops Group, of British Columbia); AMNH 8060 (whole skeleton except anterior portion of head missing; *c.* 115 mm SL; from the Eocene Tranquille Beds, Kamloops Group, of British Columbia); TMP 2005.01.27 (latex peel of TMP 86.48.03; whole skeleton except orbital and ethmoid regions of skull missing; *c.* 100 mm SL; from the Eocene of British Columbia, formation unknown but locality

is probably part of the McAbee locality of the Kamloops Group); UALVP 12436 (head and body, anterior to dorsal fin, unknown SL; from the Eocene Tranquille Beds, Kamloops Group, of British Columbia); UALVP 13405 (cast of holotype in part and counter part; whole skeleton, *c.* 100 mm SL; from the Eocene Tranquille Beds, Kamloops Group, of British Columbia).

†*Eohiodon woodruffi.* FMNH PF12345 (latex peel of UALVP 13227, holotype; whole skeleton, 108 mm SL; from the middle Eocene Klondike Mountain Formation of Washington); UALVP 41213 (whole skeleton, 130 mm SL; from the Eocene, Horsefly Beds of British Columbia); UALVP 22905 a, b (whole skeleton, 125 mm SL; from the Eocene Horsefly Beds of British Columbia); UALVP 13265 a, b (paratype; whole skeleton, *c.* 45 mm SL; from the middle Eocene Klondike Mountain Formation of Washington); UALVP 37129 a, b (*c.* 75 mm SL; from the Eocene–Oligocene Kishenehn Formation of Montana); UALVP 24135 (whole skeleton,

c. 85 mm SL; from the Eocene–Oligocene Kishenehn Formation of Montana).

†*Eohiodon falcatus*. FMNH PF9878 (whole skeleton, 80 mm SL); FMNH PF15176 (whole skeleton, 80 mm SL); FMNH PF9881 (whole skeleton, acid prepared, *c*. 130 mm SL); FMNH PF10424 (whole skeleton, 138 mm SL); FMNH PF10637 (whole skeleton, head partially disarticulated, *c*. 115 mm SL); FMNH PF10638 (whole skeleton except missing caudal skeleton, acid prepared, *c*. 160 mm SL); FMNH PF15167 (whole skeleton, acid prepared, 185 mm SL); FMNH PF15174 (whole skeleton, acid prepared, 105 mm SL); FMNH PF15175 (whole skeleton, acid prepared, *c*. 120 mm SL); FMNH PF16177 (whole skeleton, 162 mm SL); FMNH PF13065 a, b (whole skeleton, acid prepared, 105 mm SL); FMNH PF12516 (whole skeleton, 157 mm SL); UMA F10651 (whole skeleton, 124 mm SL); UMA F10614 (whole skeleton, 70 mm SL). All from the late early Eocene freshwater deposits of the Fossil Butte Member of the Green River Formation (F–2 deposits, Locality H of Grande & Buchheim 1994).

†*Eohiodon* sp. FMNH PF12991 (partial head only; unknown SL; from the middle Eocene Allenby Formation of British Columbia); UALVP 41165 (two fishes preserved in part and counterpart, one nearly complete, one head only; from the Eocene Horsefly Beds of British Columbia).

Abbreviations

Anatomical. **ang-rar**, anguloretroarticular; **ar**, articular; **bbtp**, basibranchial toothplate (= anterior basibranchial toothplate of Hilton 2002); **bhtp**, basihyal toothplate; **boc**, basioccipital; **br**, branchiostegal; **c**, centrum; **cha**, anterior ceratohyal; **cl**, cleithrum; **co**, coracoid; **d**, dentary; **dsp**, dermosphenotic; **ecp**, ectopterygoid; **enp**, endopterygoid; **ep**, epural; **es**, extrascapular; **fr**, frontal; **ga**, gill arch element (no further identification possible); **h**, hyomandibula; **hbr**, bony bridge between anterior and posterior cranial articulatory heads of the hyomandibula; **hy**, hypural; **hhv**, ventral hypohyal; **io**, infraorbital; **iop**, interopercle; **lem**, lateral ethmoid; **m**, maxilla; **met**, mesethmoid; **mpt**, metapterygoid; **n**, nasal; **nspu**, neural spine of a preural centrum; **nsu**, neural spine of a ural centrum; **op**, opercle; **ors**, orbitosphenoid; **pas**, parasphenoid; **pcf**, pectoral fin; **phy**, parhypural; **pmx**, premaxilla; **pop**, preopercle; **pro**, prootic; **pt**, posttemporal; **pto**, pterotic; **pts**, pterosphenoid; **pu**, preural centrum; **q**, quadrate; **r**, rib; **ra**, radial; **sc**, scapula; **scl**, supracleithrum; **soc**, supraoccipital; **sop**, subopercle; **spo**, sphenotic; **sr**, sclerotic ring; **stcn**, supratemporal sensory canal; **sym**, symplectic; **un**, uroneural.

Institutional. **AMNH**, American Museum of Natural History, New York; **FMNH**, Field Museum of Natural History, Chicago; **TMP**, Royal Tyrrell Museum of Palaeontology, Drumheller; **UALVP**, University of Alberta Laboratory for Vertebrate Palaeontology, Edmonton; **UMA**, University of Massachusetts Museum of Natural History, Amherst.

Systematic description

Division Teleostei Müller
Superorder Osteoglossomorpha Greenwood *et al.*
Order Hiodontiformes Taverne
Family Hiodontidae Cuvier & Valenciennes
Genus *Hiodon* Lesueur, 1818

Rejected synonyms. *Glossodon* (Rafinesque 1818), *Amphiodon* (Rafinesque 1819), *Clodalus* (Rafinesque 1820), *Elattonistius* (Gill & Jordan, *in* Jordan & Bean 1877), †*Eohiodon* (Cavender 1966).

Type species. *Hiodon tergisus* (Lesueur, 1818).

Species included as valid. *Hiodon tergisus* (Lesueur 1818), *Hiodon alosoides* (Rafinesque 1819), †*Hiodon rosei* (Hussakof 1916), †*Hiodon woodruffi* (Wilson 1978), †*Hiodon falcatus* (Grande 1979), †*Hiodon consteniorum* (Li & Wilson 1994). See *Remarks*.

Emended generic diagnosis. Differing from other hiodontid genera in possessing a posterodorsal spine on the opercle and a thin tubular nasal bone that is curved at *c*. 90°; postpelvic bone present (known only for extant taxa).

Remarks. We have been unsuccessful in finding any discrete (e.g. osteological) character that is uniquely derived for †*Eohiodon* to distinguish it as a monophyletic group relative to extant species of *Hiodon* (i.e. the relationships among the nominal fossil species and the extant *Hiodon* are unresolved). Many previous diagnoses for the genera *Hiodon* (e.g. Li & Wilson 1994) and †*Eohiodon* (e.g. Cavender 1966, Li *et al.* 1997) present several meristic data as diagnostic for their respective genera. However, when all taxa are included in *Hiodon* as conceived here (i.e. taxa historically included in both *Hiodon* and †*Eohiodon*), the ranges for these data become continuous, or nearly so. We therefore recognize an expanded genus *Hiodon*. Characters presented as synapomorphies by Li *et al.* (1997) for †*Eohiodon* and *Hiodon*, and our interpretations concerning these characters are detailed in the Discussion section.

Fig. 4. †*Hiodon consteniorum* Li & Wilson (1994). Paratype (UALVP 24200). Anterior facing left (image reversed). Scale bar in millimetres.

The inclusion of taxa described as †*Eohiodon* in *Hiodon* extends the temporal range of the genus as far back as late Early Eocene (Green River Formation; Grande 1979, 1984). †*Hiodon consteniorum* (Fig. 4) is from the late Eocene Coal Creek Member of the Kishenehn Formation (Montana). If '†*Eohiodon*' *parvus* from the Paleocene of Mongolia proves to belong in *Hiodon* as other species of '†*Eohiodon*' (we require more compelling evidence before this can be accepted), this would extend the temporal range of the genus even further. Isolated vertebral centra from the Late Cretaceous (Campanian) Dinosaur Park Formation of southern Alberta and Saskatchewan (Brinkman & Neuman 2002; Newbrey & Wilson 2005) cannot be more precisely identified except to the family Hiodontidae.

Relatively basal fossil hiodontiform taxa are known from the Early Cretaceous of Asia (e.g. †*Jiaohichthys*), as are taxa that are potentially related to Hiodontidae but of uncertain affinity (e.g. †*Lycoptera* Müller, 1848; see Hilton 2003). This suggests that the origin of Hiodontidae occurred in Asia by the Early Cretaceous, as was noted by Li & Wilson (1999). The presence of hiodontid vertebrae in the Late Cretaceous of North America indicates that the family was more widespread in the Cretaceous than in more recent times, and that there was extinction in Asia that restricted the range of Hiodontidae to North America (e.g. Li *et al.* 1997).

Our recognition of six valid species within the genus *Hiodon* (i.e. the two extant species, †*H. consteniorum*, and the three species of '†*Eohiodon*') differs from that of Li *et al.* (1997) in that we continue to recognize †*H. falcatus*. Given the continuity in meristic data between the taxa (e.g. Table 1; see discussion below), we suggest that the alpha-level taxonomy of *Hiodon*

needs to be further studied so that the variation (meristic and otherwise) within species is better understood. We do note, also, that Newbrey *et al.* (2005) found that †*H. falcatus* differed significantly from †*H. woodruffi* in growth patterns (e.g. growth rate and life span) whereas †*H. woodruffi* and †*H. rosei* were overlapping in their growth patterns. Newbrey *et al.* (2007) recently presented evidence for two hiodontid taxa represented by isolated centra in the Cretaceous Dinosaur Park Formation. The phylogenetic relationships among the six described species of *Hiodon* remain unclear.

Anatomical descriptions

A note on the preservation and preparation of specimens

Fossil hiodontids are typically preserved in lateral view due to the laterally compressed body form typical of these fishes (e.g. Cavender 1966). All specimens of †*Hiodon falcatus* examined here were preserved primarily as bone (in some cases, the bone was broken away during collection, leaving a detailed impression; see below). †*Hiodon rosei* and †*H. woodruffi* are typically preserved as either flattened specimens or as impressions. The TMP and AMNH specimens of †*H. rosei* (including Hussakof's paratypes) are preserved as impressions in a hard, fine-grained matrix that allows for highly detailed latex peels to be made, as was noted by Cavender (1966); these specimens served as the basis for much of our study of this taxon. One specimen of †*H. woodruffi* that we examined (UALVP 41213) was preserved as an impression in a coarser matrix, although a highly detailed latex peel could still be made. Most of the remaining specimens of †*H. rosei* and

Table 1. *Published ranges for some meristic data of specimens assigned to the three described taxa in the genus* †*Eohiodon and those of the genus Hiodon*

Study	Dorsal fin rays	Dorsal fin pterygiophores	Anal fin rays	Anal fin pterygiophores	Abdominal vertebrae	Caudal vertebrae	Total vertebrae
†*Hiodon rosei*							
Cavender 1966	12–13	14–15	15–16?	17–18	—	25?	47–49
Wilson 1978	10–12	13–16	13–17	17–18	22	24	44–49
Li *et al.* 1997	11–13	13–14	15–18	16–18	22–23	23–25	46–47
Total range for †*H. rosei*	**10–13**	**13–16**	**13–18**	**16–18**	**22–23**	**23–25**	**46–49**
†*Hiodon woodruffi*							
Wilson 1978	12–15	—	18–19	—	22–24	24–25	47–49
Li *et al.* 1997	13–15	14–17	17–23	17–22	23–24	23–25	46–49
Total range for †*H. woodruffi*	**12–15**	**14–17**	**17–23**	**17–22**	**22–24**	**23–25**	**46–49**
Total range if †*H. woodruffi* and †*H. falcatus* are synonymized	**12–15**	**14–17**	**17–24**	**17–25**	**22–24**	**23–26**	**46–50**
†*Hiodon falcatus*							
Grande 1979	15	16	22	23	24	25	49
Li *et al.* 1997	12–14	15–17	21–24	21–25	24	25–26	49–50
Total range for †*H. falcatus*	**12–15**	**15–17**	**21–24**	**21–25**	**24**	**25–26**	**49–50**
†*Hiodon consteniorum*							
Li & Wilson 1994	13	14	20+	18	27–28	25	52–53
Hiodon tergisus							
Hilton 2002	12–13	13–15	25–28	28–30	30–31	26–27	54–57
Hiodon alosoides							
Hilton 2002	10–11	11–13	31–32	32–36	31–33	26–29	58–60

Dashes (—) indicate values not reported in the cited study. Fin ray counts of extant *Hiodon* are reported as Hilton's 'branched fin rays plus one' to be equivalent to the principle fin ray counts of the other studies.

†*H. woodruffi* examined are very poorly-preserved. The bones of these fossils are soft and were fused during or after fossilization so that few details of individual skeletal elements could be studied. Some of the meristic data (i.e. vertebral and fin ray counts) were also difficult to record accurately. In some specimens of †*H. woodruffi* that we studied, however, the bone is well-preserved (e.g. UALVP 22905), and great detail can be seen. Specimens of †*H. falcatus*, from the Green River Formation, have a combination of traits ideal for acid-transfer preparation (i.e. hard bone preserved in a soft limestone matrix that reacts well with the acid). The matrix of these specimens is fine grained so that the impressions of bones that have broken away are remarkably crisp and the polyester resin used in the transfer preparation process fills in the missing bone and a 'complete' skeleton can be studied. †*Hiodon falcatus* is also known from a far greater number of better-preserved specimens than other taxa, including a broad range of sizes representing a growth series of specimens (Fig. 5).

Morphometric and meristic data

Much meristic data has been published for the fossil species of *Hiodon* in their original descriptions (Cavender 1966; Wilson 1978; Grande 1979) and more recently by Li *et al.* (1997), and thus these data were not emphasized in our study. However, it is useful here to reiterate the similarity of counts among the fossil species of *Hiodon* (e.g. Table 1). Wilson (1978) noted the large degree of overlap between †*H. rosei* and †*H. woodruffi* and Grande (1979) found that †*H. falcatus* was similar to †*H. rosei* in many counts, although the two taxa also, differed in some (e.g. dorsal and anal fin rays and pterygiophores). Li *et al.* (1997, tables 2, 3) presented revised ranges of many meristic values for the three species (note that specimens of †*H. falcatus* were included in †*H. woodruffi* in their study). These authors concluded that there are only two valid species (†*H. rosei* and †*H. woodruffi*) based in part on the similarity of meristic data (i.e. †*H. falcatus* = †*H. woodruffi*). However, all fossil species show overlap in their ranges and, as shown in Table 1, there is no single meristic that allows for distinction between the three species. Although we acknowledge that overlap of ranges of meristic data, by itself, is not a sound basis for taxonomic decisions and until the variation is better understood among the species, we continue to recognize all three nominal species of '†*Eohiodon*' as members of the genus *Hiodon*.

The variation observed in fossil and extant *Hiodon* may have been produced through both taxonomic and environmental influences. In particular, trends in characteristics such as numbers of fin rays and number of vertebrae may reflect environmental or ecological differences, as was suggested by Cavender (1966). For example, †*H. falcatus* probably inhabited a subtropical environment (Grande 1994), while living *Hiodon* live in temperate waters (e.g. Scott & Crossman 1973). Significant differences in body size (reflected by centrum morphology) and longevity have been found to occur between Cretaceous and extant hiodontids (Newbrey & Wilson 2005), and Eocene hiodontids fall out between the two (e.g. Newbrey *et al.* 2005). Ongoing study of the growth characteristics of fossil and living hiodontids (M. Newbrey, pers. comm., 2006; see also Newbrey *et al.* 2007) will help to clarify species-specific life-history patterns and the relationship between morphology and environment across evolutionary time for hiodontid fishes.

Dermal skull roof

The skull roof is typically damaged in fossil *Hiodon*, particularly in its posterior region. As in the extant species of *Hiodon* (e.g. Hilton 2002) the paired extrascapulars are large, superficial dermal elements that cover most of the skull roof and braincase posterior to the frontals, including the parietals, supraoccipital, pterotics, and epioccipitals. In a specimen of †*Hiodon* sp. (FMNH PF12991, †*H. rosei*) that consists of a few disarticulated skull elements, the parietal from the right side is clearly seen in ventral view and closely matches the shape of the parietal in extant *Hiodon*. The main portion of the parietal is a somewhat rectangular element that slightly overlaps the posterior margin of the frontal. There is a distinct posterior extension, which in extant taxa forms the dorsal border of the temporal fossa (Hilton 2002). The frontal, which is exposed in most specimens, is also similar in shape to that of extant *Hiodon*. The left and right frontals clearly meet one another in the midline of the skull, and the lateral edge tapers slightly so that the anterior portion is narrower than the posterior part of the bone (Figs 6–11). In several of our specimens (e.g. FMNH PF15167, †*H. falcatus*; UALVP 22905a, †*H. woodruffi*; AMNH 8059a, †*H. rosei*) the slender nasal is completely preserved and is strongly curved, as found in extant *Hiodon* (Hilton 2002, fig. 28; e.g. see Figs 6–11).

Neurocranium, ethmoid region, and ventral dermal bones

Most of the occipital region of the neurocranium (and its presumed constituent elements, e.g.

Fig. 5. Growth series of †*Hiodon falcatus* from the Green River Formation. **a**, FMNH PF10955, 30 mm SL; **b**, FMNH PF9878, 80 mm SL; **c**, FMNH PF12516, 157 mm SL. Scale bars in millimetres.

Fig. 6. Skull of †*Hiodon rosei* (AMNH 8059a). Anterior facing left (image reversed). Specimen is a black latex peel of impression coated with ammonium chloride prior to photography. Scale bar in millimetres.

epioccipitals, exoccipitals, intercalars) cannot be studied due to being crushed or covered by overlying dermal bones (e.g. the extrascapulars). In one specimen of †*Hiodon* sp. from the Horsefly Beds (UALVP 41165), the supraoccipital is well-preserved in part and counterpart and is concave ventrally and bears a posterior median crest, as in extant *Hiodon*; the supraoccipital crest also can be seen through the extrascapulars in a specimen of †*H. rosei* (e.g. Figs 6–7). The basioccipital is preserved in posterior view on specimen

FMNH PF10638 (†*H. falcatus*). As in extant *Hiodon*, there is a deep aortal groove that runs the length of its ventral surface. There is a depression in the posterior face of the basioccipital that is interpreted as the notochordal pit, which marks the anterior extent of the notochord in extant *Hiodon* (Hilton 2002). In FMNH PF10638 (Figs 12–13), the dorsal surface of the basioccipital is exposed and shows a pair of chambers for the lagenar otoliths, similar to extant *Hiodon* (Hilton 2002, fig. 30).

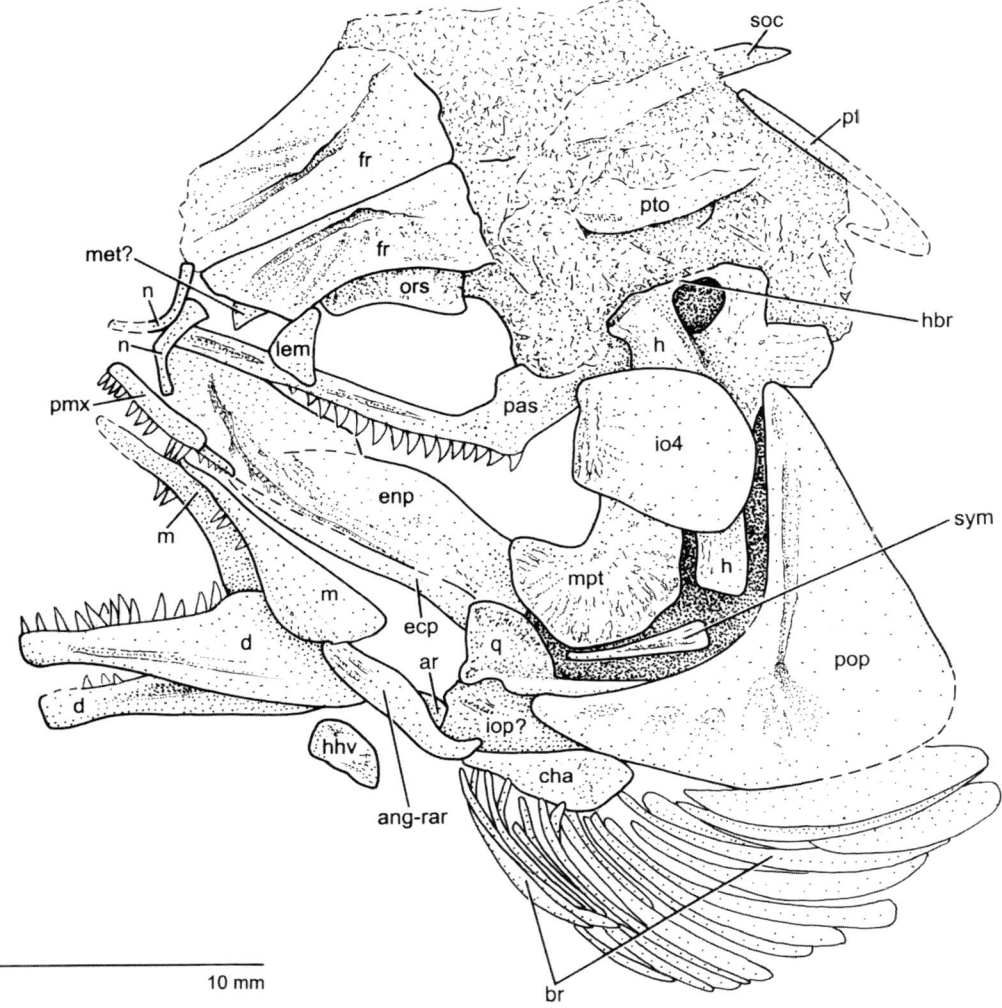

Fig. 7. Skull of †*Hiodon rosei* (AMNH 8059a). Line drawing of Figure 6.

As for the occipital region, the details of most of the otic region cannot be determined. The sphenotic appears to have a slight lateral wing and contribute to the anterior articulatory facet for the hyomandibula (e.g. Figs 8–9). Although mostly obscured by the overlying hyomandibula, the prootic appears to form a continuous wall with the parasphenoid, which is the lateral wall of the posterior myodome in extant *Hiodon* (e.g. Hilton 2002, figs 20–21, 34). In FMNH PF9881 the left pterotic (along with other parts of the skull roof) is disarticulated and exposed in an oblique ventrolateral view. This bone comprises dermal (= dermopterotic) and chondral (= autopterotic) portions that are fused together, and are identical to this element in

extant *Hiodon* (Hilton 2002, fig. 29). There is an anteroventral lamella of bone on the chondral portion that corresponds to the lamella that forms the medial wall of a fossa for the *dilatator operculi* muscle (Hilton 2002). The dermal portion of the pterotic carries the otic sensory canal along the lateral edge of the posterior skull roof, and is slightly concave dorsally, forming the lateral margin of the temporal fossa, as in extant taxa (this fossa can often be seen as a depression through the overlying extrascapulars; e.g. Figs 6–7).

The orbitosphenoid appears to be the largest bone of the sphenotic region of the neurocranium. In those specimens in which it is preserved, the ventral margin is slightly curved. In an acid

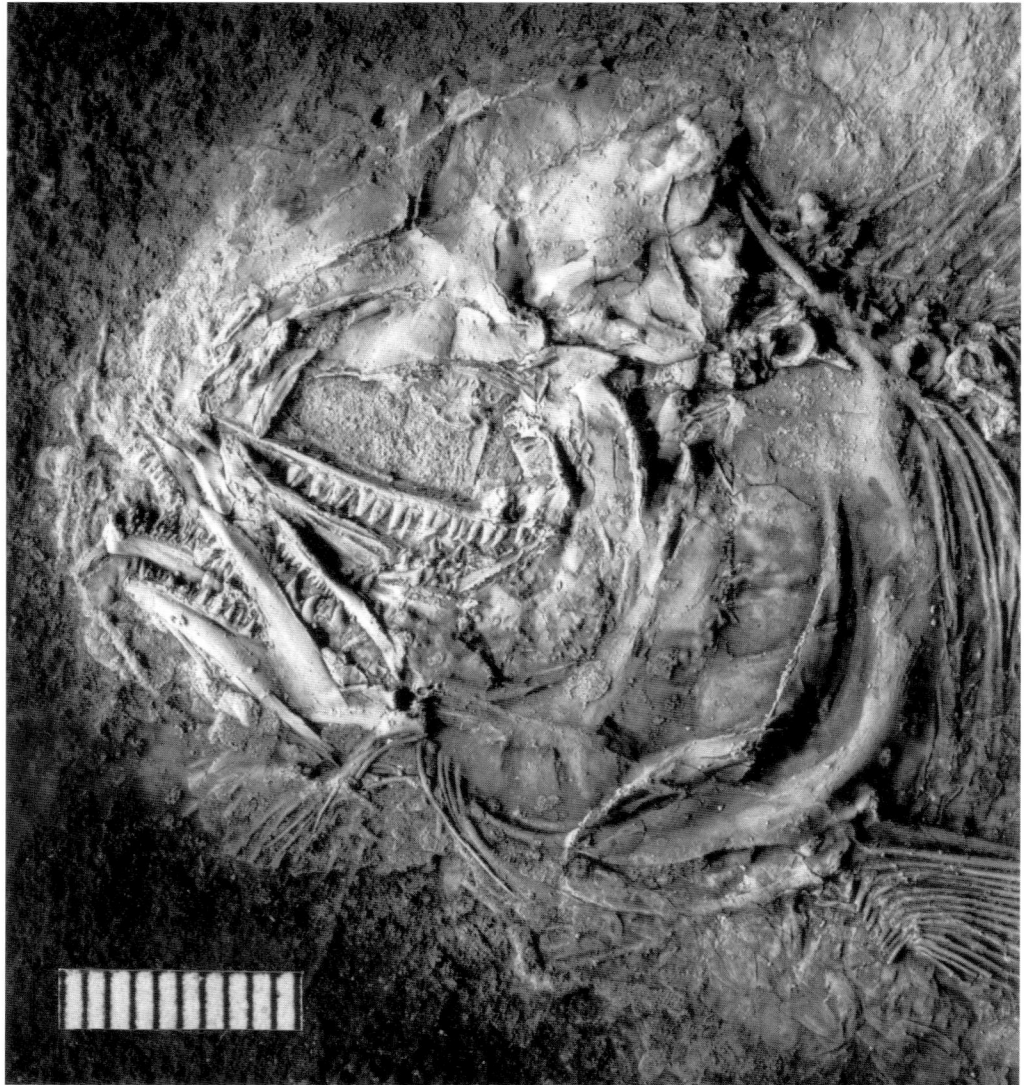

Fig. 8. Skull of †*H. woodruffi* (UALVP 41213). Anterior facing left (image reversed). Specimen is a black latex peel of impression coated with ammonium chloride prior to photography. Scale bar in millimetres.

prepared specimen of †*H. falcatus* (FMNH PF10638), the dorsal surface of the orbitosphenoid is exposed and is strongly concave, as it is in extant *Hiodon*. The pterosphenoid is preserved in a specimen of †*H. woodruffi* (UALVP 41213; Figs 8–9), but no details can be determined. Nothing is known of the basisphenoid.

Very little is known of the ethmoid region of the neurocranium in fossil *Hiodon*. Cavender (1966, fig. 2) identified the mesethmoid at the very anterior tip of the neurocranium. In our study of this specimen (Figs 6–7), we reinterpreted his mesethmoid as a combination of the left and right nasals, which have been broken (i.e. they are no longer tubular). An element that is mostly covered by the frontals is possibly the mesethmoid that has been displaced posteriorly. The lateral ethmoid can be identified in specimens of all three species (e.g. Figs 6–11) and has a triangular dermal flange that is prominent in lateral view, as in extant *Hiodon* (Hilton 2002, fig. 13).

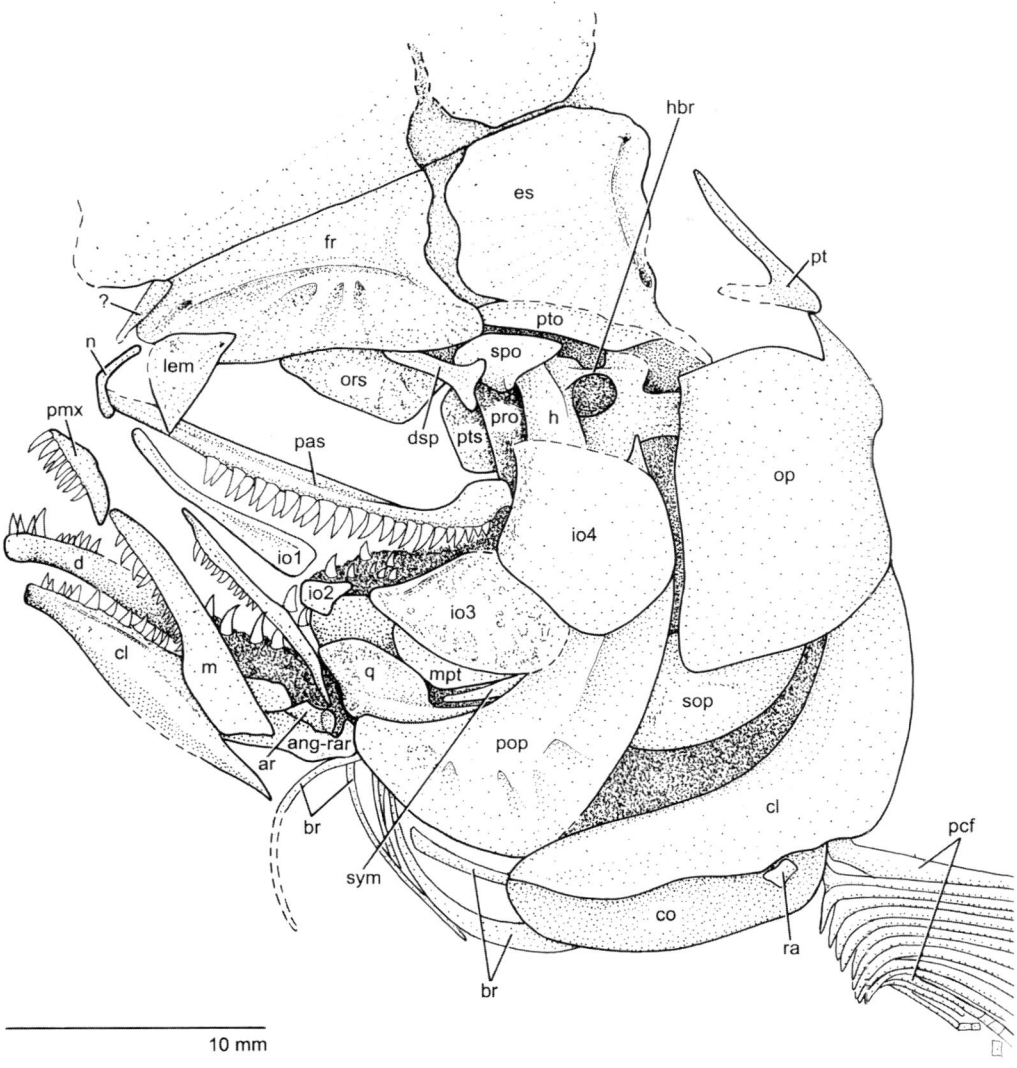

Fig. 9. Skull of †*H. woodruffi* (UALVP 41213). Line drawing of Figure 8.

The parasphenoid of hiodontids generally is very striking because of its greatly enlarged, conical dentition. The parasphenoid teeth of fossil *Hiodon* appear to be more robust than those of extant *Hiodon*, as noted also by Cavender (1966) and Grande (1979), although we did not quantify this. The parasphenoid has a prominent median crest along most of its length, and tapers anteriorly to a point. Nothing is known of the vomer in fossil *Hiodon*. In extant species, the vomer is small, edentulous, and is easily displaced in preparation of skeletons.

Opercular bones and ventral hyoid arch

The opercular series consists of paired preopercle, opercle, subopercle, and branchiostegal rays; paired interopercles are not preserved in our specimens except possibly in AMNH 8059a (†*H. rosei*; Fig. 7); in extant *Hiodon* these elements lie medial to the preopercles, which almost completely obscure them in lateral view. There are 8–10 branchiostegals (e.g. Cavender 1966; Wilson 1978; Grande 1979; Li *et al.* 1997), although the left and right series are often superimposed

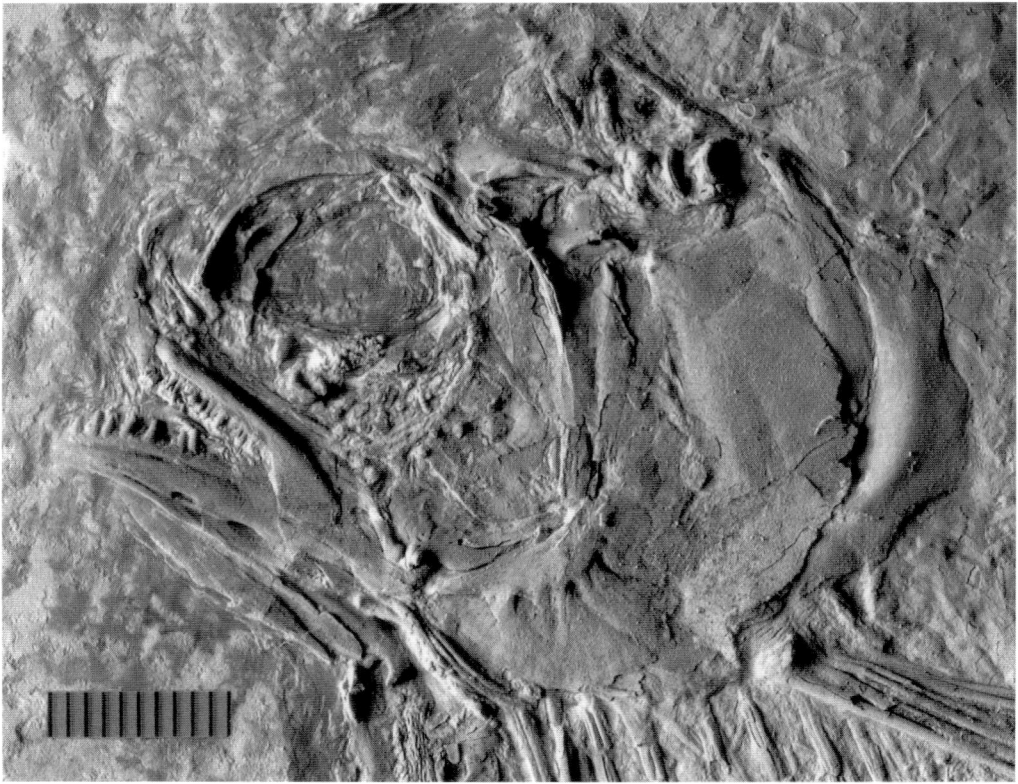

Fig. 10. Skull of †*Hiodon falcatus* (FMNH PF15167; acid prepared specimen). Specimen coated with ammonium chloride prior to photography. Anterior facing left (image reversed). Scale bar in millimetres.

and jumbled (e.g. Figs 6–7), making precise counts difficult.

The opercle is somewhat rectangular in shape and bears a posterior extension and a pointed process on the posterodorsal margin, as described by Cavender (1966; contrary to Li *et al.* 1997; see Discussion). The posterior border of the opercle is broken in most specimens but we observed a posterodoral spine similar to that of extant *Hiodon* in specimens of all three species formerly classified as †*Eohiodon* (e.g. †*H. rosei*, AMNH 8059a, TMP 2005.01.27; †*H. woodruffi*, UALVP 41213; †*H. falcatus*, FMNH PF15167; this last specimen is the same that Hilton 2002 refers to as possessing a posterodorsal spine, but his observation was made prior to acid-preparation of the specimen).

The ventral portion of the hyoid arch is poorly known in fossil *Hiodon* because more superficial bones (e.g. those of the suspensorium) typically cover the constituent elements, although some are visible in our partially disarticulated specimens. For example, the hourglass-shaped anterior

ceratohyal is visible on AMNH 8059a (†*H. rosei*) and FMNH PF10637 (†*H. falcatus*). The ventral hypohyal is preserved on AMHH 8059a (Figs. 6–7; †*H. rosei*) and FMNH PF10637 (†*H. falcatus*) and is essentially the same as that of extant *Hiodon* (Hilton 2002, fig. 55).

The basihyal toothplate bears enlarged caniniform teeth that appear to be more stout than those of extant *Hiodon* as do the parasphenoid teeth, as was noted also by Cavender (1966). The toothplate itself is ventrally deeply concave (†*H. falcatus*, FMNH PF10637), suggesting that, as in extant *Hiodon*, it grows ventrally and laterally to surround the anterior cartilage of the basihyal (Nelson 1968; Hilton 2002). Hilton (2002, fig. 58, table 8) noted variation in the length of the basihyal toothplate among hiodontids, and that taxa formerly assigned to †*Eohiodon* (represented in his study by †*H. falcatus*) had a shorter basihyal toothplate than other hiodontids (i.e. 49% lower jaw length compared to 53% in *H. alosoides*, 60% in †*H. consteniorum*, and 70% in *H. tergisus*).

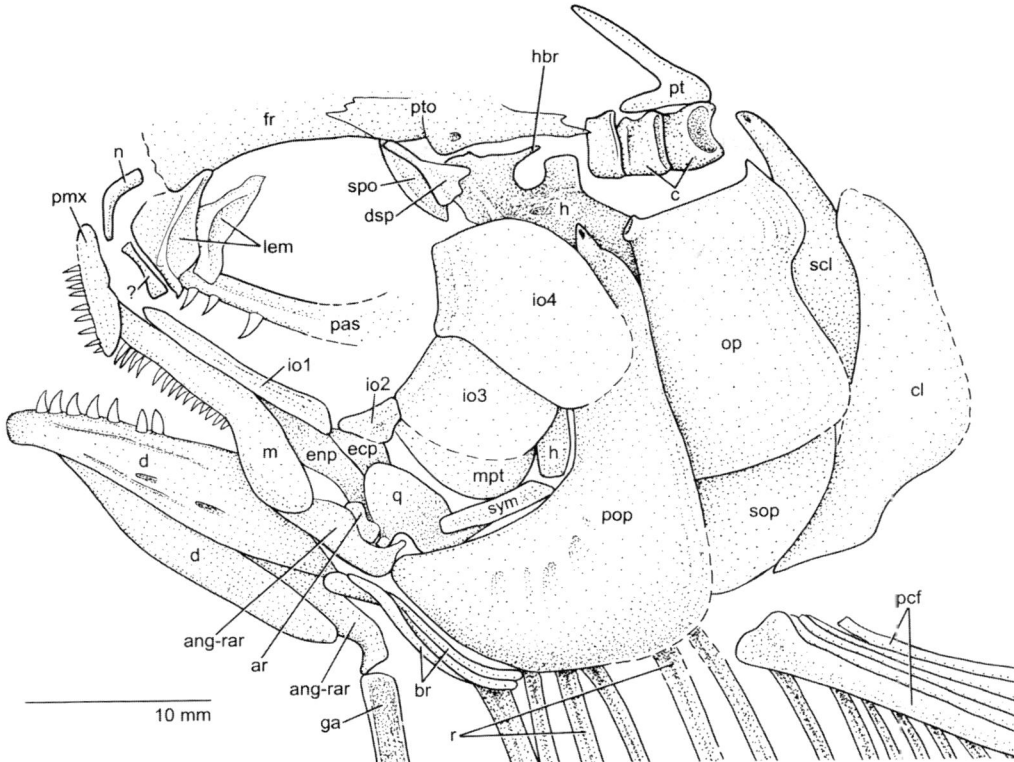

Fig. 11. Skull of †*Hiodon falcatus* (FMNH PF15167; acid prepared specimen). Line drawing of Figure 10.

Infraorbital bones

The infraorbital bones of hiodontids generally are very thin elements (e.g. Nelson 1969) and are poorly-preserved in fossil taxa. Individual elements of the infraorbital series can be made out on several specimens of fossil taxa (e.g. see Figs 6–9). The outline of the infraorbital series however is clearly seen in FMNH PF15167 (†*H. falcatus*, Figs 10–11), and it closely resembles that of extant *Hiodon* in the shape and arrangement of individual elements. This series of bones consists of an elongate anterior element (io1) that lies beneath most of the orbit (Figs 10–11). The second infraorbital (io2) is the smallest of the series. The third and fourth (io3, io4) are larger, with io4 being the largest of the series. A small triradiate dermosphenotic is well preserved in UALVP 41213 (†*H. woodruffi*, Figs 8–9) and is similar to the same element in extant *Hiodon*. See Hilton (2002) for further discussion of hiodontid infraorbitals.

No elements could be positively identified as sclerotic bones. In extant *Hiodon* these are very delicate ossifications that form relatively late during ontogeny (Hilton 2002, fig. 37).

Oral jaws

The upper jaw of fossil *Hiodon* consists of paired premaxillae and maxillae; as in most osteoglosso-morphs, there are no supramaxillae. The premaxilla was rarely well-preserved in the studied specimens. However, in those few specimens where the element was nearly complete, it seems that there are generally fewer teeth (about 11 or 12 in †*H. falcatus*) than in extant *Hiodon* (taxonomically variable, 13–25, with a few individuals having 10–11; Hilton 2002, tables 6, 7). The premaxilla, in lateral view, tapers both anteriorly and poster-iorly, and lacks the anterior ascending process of other osteoglossomorphs (e.g. †*Lycoptera*, Hilton 2003, fig. 17). Its exact shape is difficult to evaluate due to different orientations in different specimens. For example, in †*H. falcatus*, in some specimens, there does appear to be a concavity in the central portion of its dorsal margin, as in extant *Hiodon* (Hilton 2002, fig. 38; Li *et al.* 1997, character 49), whereas

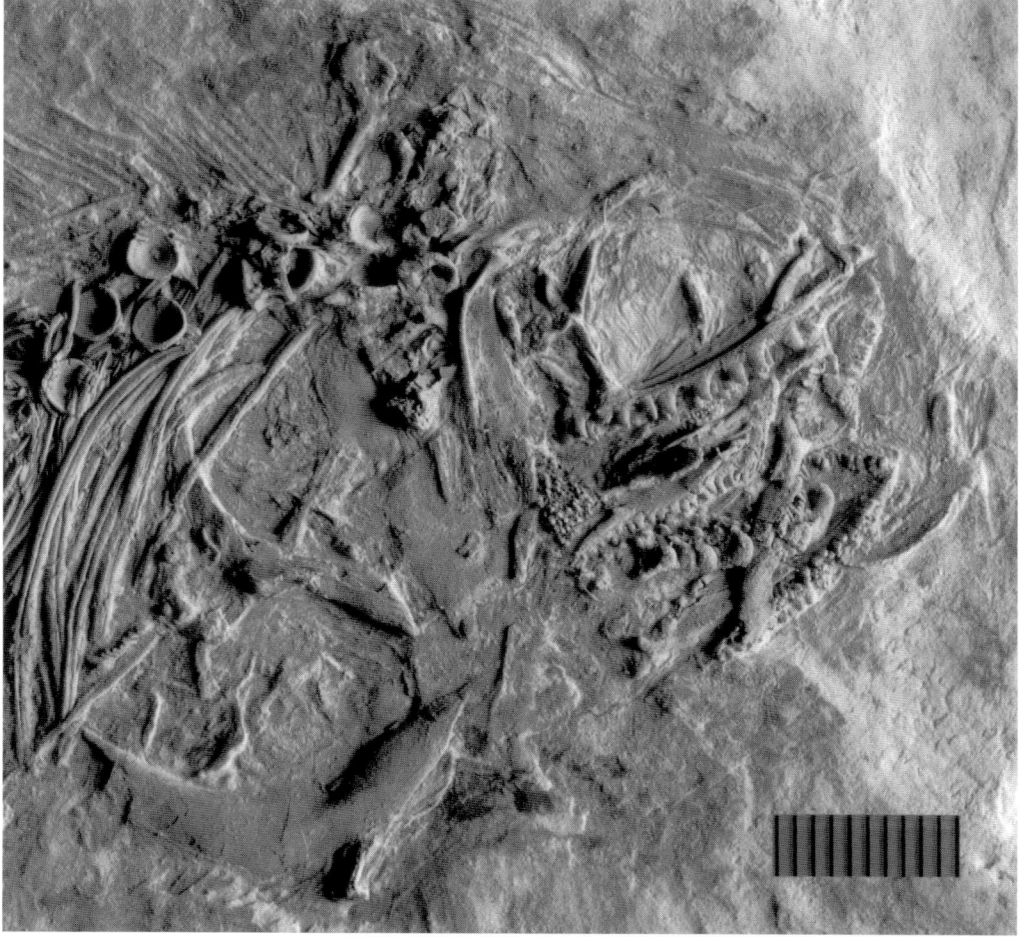

Fig. 12. Skull of †*Hiodon falcatus* (FMNH PF10638). Specimen was acid prepared and coated with ammonium chloride prior to photography. Anterior facing right. Scale bar in millimetres.

in others the dorsal margin is relatively flat or slightly convex (e.g. †*H. falcatus*, FMNH PF13065a). See Discussion and Hilton (2003, 84–85, fig. 40) for further discussion of hiodontid premaxillae.

The maxilla bears about 13 teeth in †*H. falcatus*, compared to 11–17 in *H. tergisus* and 14–30 in *H. alosoides* (see Hilton 2002, tables 6, 7; fig. 40). The maxilla is similar in shape to that of extant *Hiodon*. The posterior portion of this element is edentulous and much deeper than it is anteriorly. Anterior to the toothed portion, there is a short, medially directed edentulous process.

The lower jaw comprises three distinct elements visible in lateral view (dentary, anguloretroarticular and articular); a coronomeckelian bone was not found but this is likely due to lack of preservation. The dentary is the only toothed element of the lower jaw. In FMNH PF15174 (†*H. falcatus*) there are 26 teeth along its dorsal margin (as in extant taxa, these may be intraspecifically variable; see Hilton 2002, tables 6, 7, fig. 43). A series of large lateral teeth is present, with smaller more medial teeth distributed along the length of the dentary. The retroarticular portion of the anguloretroarticular possesses a well-developed post-articular process (Figs 6–11), as in extant *Hiodon* (Hilton 2002, fig. 38). The medial surface of the lower jaw also is similar in all respects to that of extant *Hiodon*, including the absence of a medial bony covering to the meckelian fossa on the dentary (Hilton 2002, 2003). The dentary is deeply notched posteriorly, with the dermal angular portion of the anguloretroarticular filling in this notch. The articular is mostly hidden

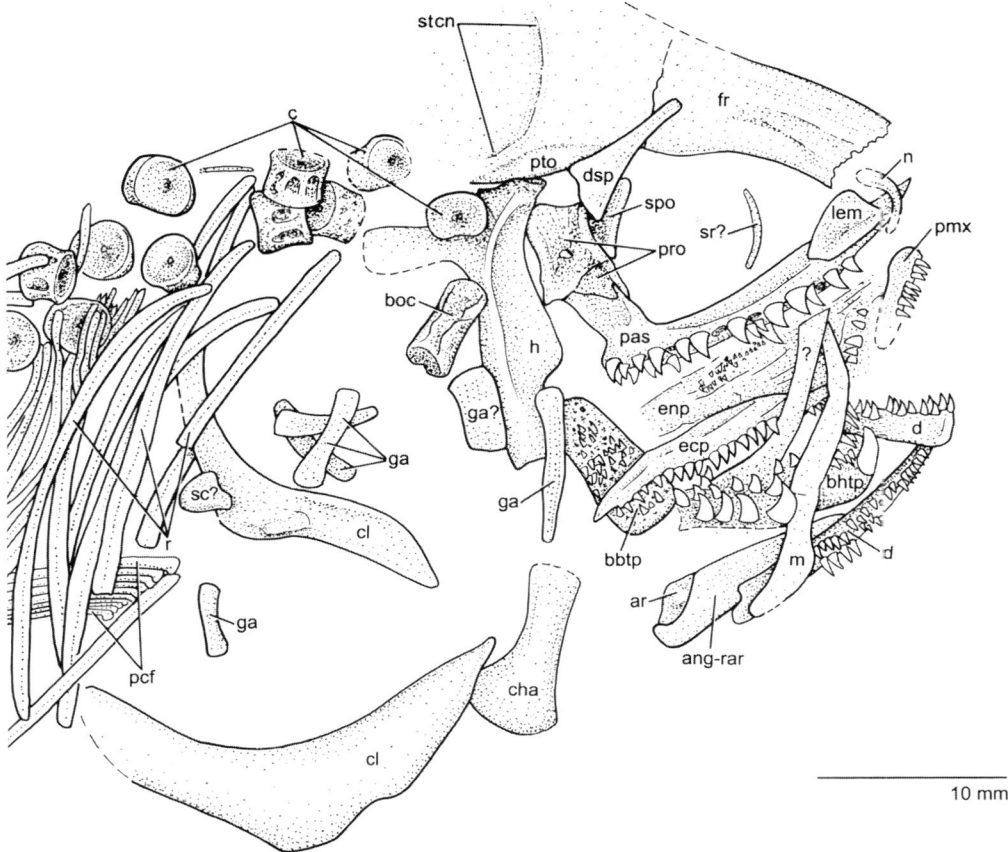

Fig. 13. Skull of †*Hiodon falcatus* (FMNH PF10638). Line drawing of Figure 12.

in lateral view, although in UALVP 41213 (†*H. woodruffi*; Figs 8–9) and FMNH PF15167 (†*H. falcatus*; Figs 10–11), the jaw joint is clearly formed by the articular anteriorly and the anguloretroarticular posteriorly.

Suspensorium

The suspensorium of fossil hiodontids is generally covered by overlying elements, including the thin infraorbitals and, more substantially, the opercular and jaw bones. However, from what can be observed, the suspensorium of fossil *Hiodon* is very similar to that of extant species (e.g. Hilton 2002, figs 45–48), and consists of the hyomandibula, symplectic, quadrate, metapterygoid, dermopalatine, endopterygoid and ectopterygoid.

As in *Hiodon*, the hyomandibula bears three dorsal articulatory heads (two cranial and an opercular head). In most specimens, the dorsal end of

the hyomandibula is damaged or hidden by the skull roof. In one of our specimens of †*H. falcatus* (FMNH PF15177; Fig. 14), the dorsal end of the hyomandibula is exposed, and a complete bony bridge between the two, similar to that of extant *Hiodon*, is clearly seen. This bridge is often broken in specimens in which it is exposed (e.g. Figs 10–11). We also discovered this bridged hyomandibula in specimens of †*H. rosei* (e.g. Figs 6–7; AMNH 8059a) and †*H. woodruffi* (e.g. UALVP 13265a; UALVP 41213; Figs 8–9). The symplectic is a slender wedge-shaped bone positioned between the main body of the quadrate and its pre-opercular process.

The quadrate is exposed in many of our specimens and is nearly identical to that of extant *Hiodon*. There is a well-developed knob-like articulatory condyle for the lower jaw joint on the quadrate. The main portion of the quadrate is flat and bears a somewhat rounded dorsal margin that

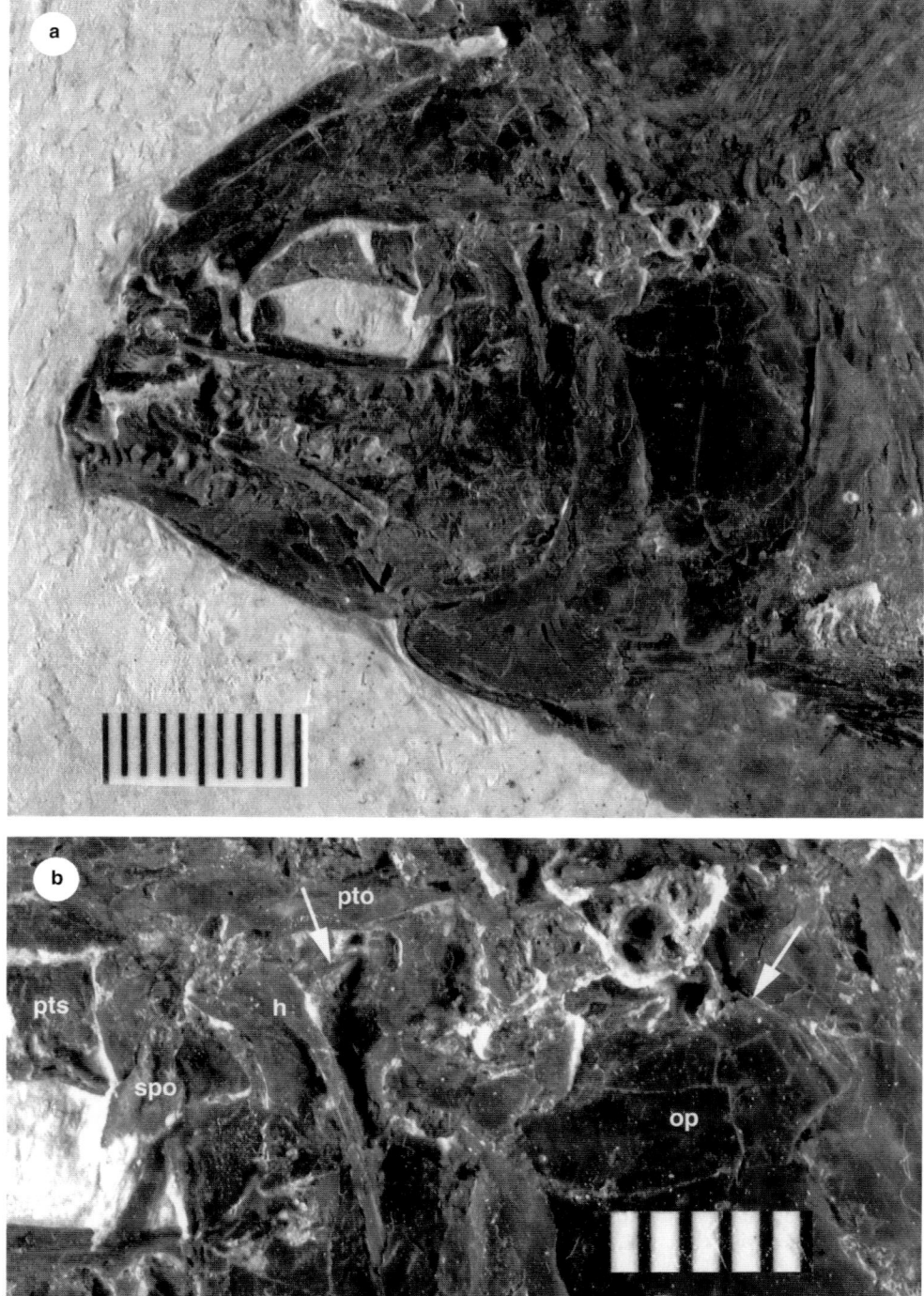

Fig. 14. Skull of †*Hiodon falcatus* (FMNH PF15177). **a**, head preserved in left lateral view; **b**, close up of posterior portion of skull showing detail of hyomandibula and opercle. Left-hand arrow points to hyomandibular bridge and right-hand arrow points to opercular spine. Anterior facing left. Scale bars in millimetres.

contacts the metapterygoid, endopterygoid and ectopterygoid. The preopercular process is well developed and is tightly associated with the horizontal limb of the preopercle, with which it overlaps slightly in lateral view. The preopercular process of †*H. rosei* (e.g. AMNH 8059a) appears to be longer and much more slender than in the other species, but it is difficult to interpret this because most available specimens of †*H. rosei* do not clearly show the quadrate.

In the specimens in which it can be seen, typically through the thin overlying infraorbitals (e.g. Figs 6–11), the shape of the metapterygoid of fossil *Hiodon* species closely resembles that of extant *Hiodon*. The posterior and ventral borders of the metapterygoid are rounded, and the antero-dorsal border bears a deep concavity.

As in extant *Hiodon*, the dermopalatine and ectopterygoid are independent of one another (fused in certain other osteoglossomorphs; Hilton 2003). Both elements are robust and toothed along their lateral margins. The endopterygoid, by contrast, is a thin broad element, although its exact shape cannot be determined; it is unclear if it bore teeth due to lack of preservation. There is no trace of an autopalatine, which remains cartilaginous in extant *Hiodon* (e.g. Hilton 2002).

Gill arches

In some of our acid-prepared specimens of †*Hiodon falcatus*, disarticulated gill arch elements are scattered in the area posterior and ventral to the skull and pectoral girdle (Figs 10–13). These elements are simple slats of bone that are slightly concave, which presumably is the side that supported the gill filaments. Because they are simple (i.e. they lack uncinate processes) elongate elements, these bones are likely either epibranchials or ceratobranchials (e.g. see Hilton 2002, figs 51–56), although their exact identification is impossible.

The basibranchial toothplate is preserved in several of our acid-prepared specimens of †*Hiodon falcatus* (e.g. Figs 12–13) and matches that of extant *Hiodon*, with a dense array of small teeth and a straight anterior margin that, in the extant species, abuts the posterior margin of the basihyal toothplate (see Hilton 2002, fig. 53).

Vertebral column

Few details of the vertebral centra of fossil *Hiodon*, beyond meristic data, are available in the literature. The amphicoelous, spool-shaped centra are very much like those of extant *Hiodon*, with longitudinal, bridging struts. The first centrum of extant *Hiodon* articulates with the basioccipital and the paired exoccipitals through a tripartite surface; such an arrangement could not be verified for the fossil species because this region is covered by overlying bones. The notochord is interpreted here as persistent though greatly constricted, because a small notochordal foramen in the centre of the centra was discovered in some of our specimens (e.g. †*H. falcatus*, FMNH PF10638), as is found in extant *Hiodon* (Hilton 2002, fig. 68). The parapophyses are fused to the centra, are leaf-shaped and become progressively elongate and ventrally directed posteriorly in the abdominal region, as in extant *Hiodon* (Hilton 2002, fig. 61). The slender, curved ribs loosely articulate with the centra in sockets posterior to the parapophyses. Each rib bears a slight sulcus along its length, similar to the ribs of extant *Hiodon*.

A series of epineural bones is attached to the neural arches of the abdominal region. The neural arches of the abdominal region remain autogenous from the centra, and the left and right portions do not fuse to form a median neural spine. In the caudal region, however, both the neural and haemal arches are fused to the centra. In †*H. falcatus* and †*H. woodruffi* the neural and haemal arches are median structures, as in extant *Hiodon* (Hilton 2002, figs 68–69). In a specimen of †*H. rosei* (TMP 2005.01.27), the left and right portions of the neural and haemal spines (anterior to those that support the caudal fin) appear to remain separate from one another. Other similar-sized specimens (e.g. AMNH 8059a) do not show this, so it is difficult to interpret.

A series of slender, gently curved supraneurals is positioned in the interneural spaces anterior to the dorsal fin. As in extant *Hiodon* (Hilton 2002, figs 61–62), the anteriormost supraneural is an enlarged, broadly flattened element (particularly visible in TMP 2005.01.27).

Caudal fin and skeleton

The caudal skeletons of fossil species of *Hiodon* have been described and/or illustrated frequently (e.g. Cavender 1966, fig. 5; Taverne 1977, fig. 35; Wilson 1977, 1978; Grande 1979; and Li *et al.* 1997, fig. 5), and their similarity to those of extant *Hiodon* has been noted an equal number of times. The caudal fin itself comprises 18 principle fin rays (1:8:8:1) and a variable number of segmented and unsegmented procurrent fin rays on both the dorsal and ventral margins.

There are, as in extant *Hiodon*, seven hypurals in the fossil species that are supported by two ural centra. Li *et al.* (1997) reported finding eight hypurals in two specimens of †*H. falcatus* (FMNH PF9878, FMNH PF9880); our interpretation of these specimens differs. In these specimens, the bases of the fin rays that embrace the posterior hypurals are partially broken away, so that the element identified by these authors as the eighth hypural is in fact the hemitrichium of a fin ray from the 'down side' of the specimen. Only seven hypurals are present in extant *Hiodon*. Schultze & Arratia (1988) reported eight hypurals in small specimens of *Hiodon* and they hypothesized that the eighth was resorbed during ontogeny. Hilton (2002), however, found only seven hypurals at all stages of ontogeny in his study of *Hiodon*. In any case, the normal number of hypurals in *Hiodon* and those species assigned to '†*Eohiodon*' appears to be seven.

The neural spine of preural centrum one is variable in its form in fossil *Hiodon*. In most specimens (and all specimens of †*H. rosei* and †*H. woodruffi* with an interpretable caudal skeleton that were examined here), the neural spine is fully formed and equal in length to the preceding spines (e.g. Figs 15–17). This is the condition in a small percentage of specimens of extant *Hiodon* (Hilton 2002). In some specimens of †*H. falcatus* (e.g. FMNH PF15175; FMNH PF9878), the neural spine of preural centrum one is reduced (Fig. 18), as is the typical condition of extant *Hiodon* (e.g. Hilton 2002). Wilson (1977, p. 12) also described a short neural spine on preural centrum 1 for specimens of †*H. rosei*.

We also want to point out our reinterpretation of the caudal skeleton of †*Hiodon rosei* from that which has been described and illustrated previously (Cavender 1966, fig. 5B; Taverne 1977, fig. 35), and in particular of specimen AMNH 8059 (Fig. 15). The element we consider to be the fully developed neural spine of preural centrum one has, in the past, been interpreted to be the epural. The reason for our reinterpretation is the evidence for a thin connection to the first preural centrum near the base of this element. The continuity between the neural spine and the centrum is often exceptionally thin and fragile in the immediately preural vertebrae in extant *Hiodon* (e.g. Hilton 2002, figs 75–76). Also, the single epural of hiodontids is often much more closely associated with the uroneurals in the other fossil species and in extant *Hiodon* (Hilton 2002), and may be partially covered by them laterally. Wilson (1977, p. 12) also commented on the variation in the position of the epural in †*H. rosei*, noting that it varies 'from close and parallel to the neural spine of preural centrum 2, where it resembles a continuation of the neural spine of preural centrum 1; to close to the upward curving uroneurals, where it resembles an additional uroneural.'

Dorsal/anal fins and supports

The skeletons of the dorsal and anal fins of fossil *Hiodon* species are similar to those found in extant members of the genus. A series of elongate proximal radials strongly interdigitate with the neural and haemal spines (dorsal and anal fin radials, respectively). All species of fossil *Hiodon* have the dorsal fin origin anterior to that of the anal fin (i.e. *H. alosoides*, Fig. 3, is the only species, fossil or extant, in which the dorsal fin originates opposite or, more commonly, posterior to the anal fin insertion). In those specimens thought to be males (e.g. FMNH PF10639) based on the shape of the anal fin (see Discussion), the lateral ridges on the proximal radials of the anal fin, particularly on the anterior part of the fin, are more pronounced than in the presumed females (e.g. FMNH PF10637) and the bases of the fin rays are much more robust (e.g. see Hilton 2002, figs 80–81; also, compare the specimens of †*H. rosei* and †*H. woodruffi*, considered to be males, with that of †*H. falcatus*, a female, shown in Fig. 2).

There is a broad difference among species in the number of elements in the fins of fossil *Hiodon*, as has been already reported in the literature (see Table 1). Although no new meristic data was collected in this study, we will reiterate that specimens of †*H. rosei* have a much shorter fin than †*H. falcatus* (e.g. in TMP 2005.01.27 there are 13 dorsal fin and 15 anal fin proximal radials, compared with 17 dorsal fin and 21 anal fin proximal radials in FMNH PF15174).

Pectoral girdle and fin

The pectoral girdle of fossil *Hiodon* closely resembles that of the extant species. The dorsalmost element is the posttemporal, which has an elongate dorsal limb and a relatively short ventral limb. Its exact relation to the skull cannot be determined because it is typically displaced. The supracleithrum is slightly curved, and is flattened on its dorsolateral surface at the point at which it articulates with the posttemporal. This is also the portion that is pierced by the lateral line sensory canal, seen clearly in FMNH PF10638 and FMNH PF10637 (†*H. falcatus*). The cleithrum is the largest element of the pectoral girdle and is the exact same shape as in extant *Hiodon* (e.g. cf. Figs 8–12 with Hilton 2002, figs 82–85). Although portions of the coracoid are preserved (e.g. Figs 8–9), the details of its shape and the relationship between the cleithrum and coracoid cannot be determined from our material (e.g. it cannot be determined if the two elements form a fenestra; see Hilton 2002, fig. 84).

The medial, fin supporting elements of the pectoral girdle (e.g. scapula, mesocoracoid, portions of the coracoid) are predominantly hidden by the cleithrum, and only pieces of them are exposed on most of our specimens (e.g. †*H. falcatus*, FMNH

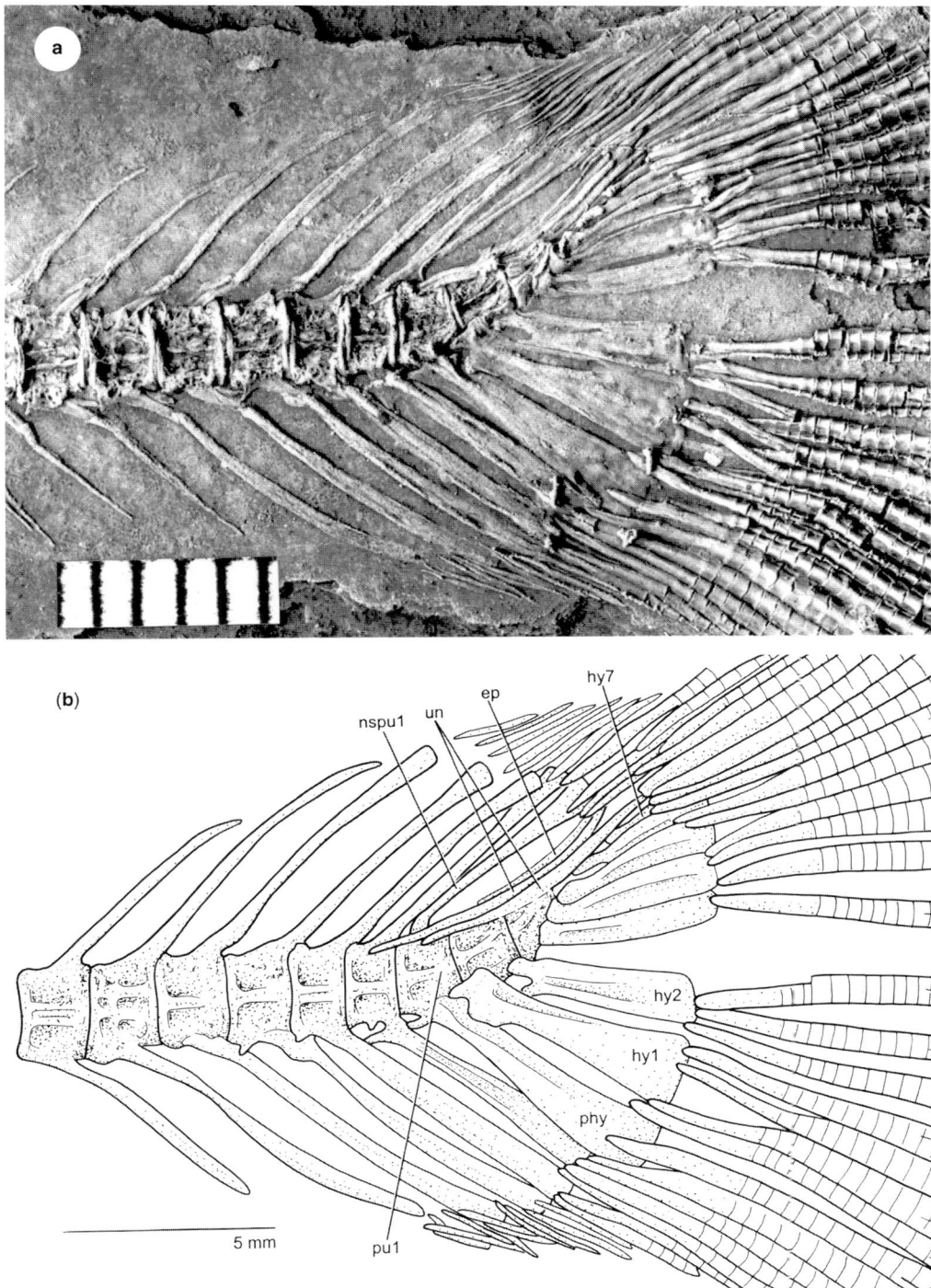

Fig. 15. a, photograph; **b**, line drawing of the caudal skeleton of †*Hiodon rosei* (AMNH 8059). Specimen is a black latex peel of impressions coated with ammonium chloride prior to photography. Anterior facing left. Scale bar in millimetres.

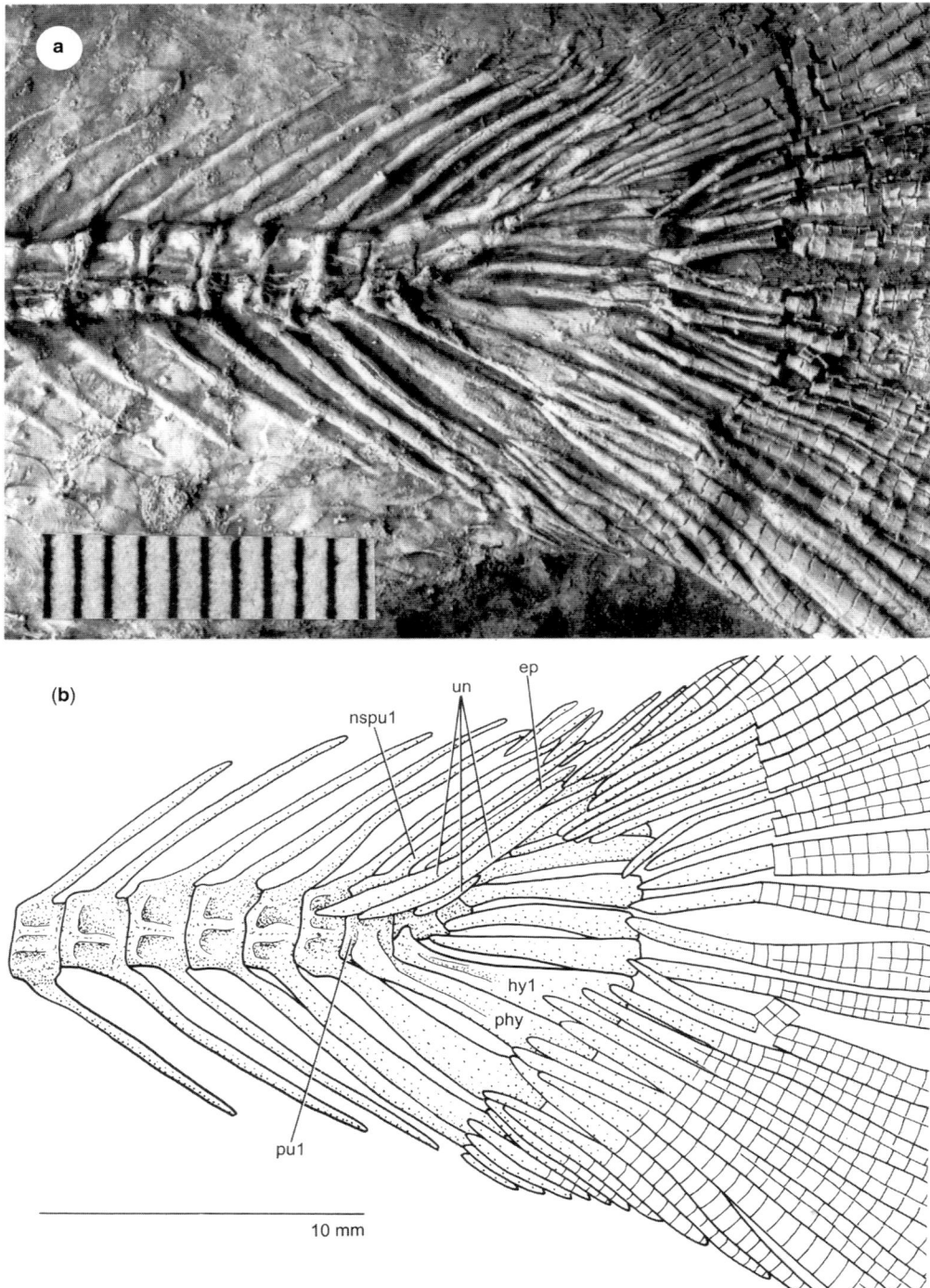

Fig. 16. **a**, photograph; **b**, line drawing of the caudal skeleton of †*Hiodon woodruffi* (UALVP 41213). Specimen is a black latex peel of impressions coated with ammonium chloride prior to photography. Anterior facing left (image reversed). Scale bar in millimetres.

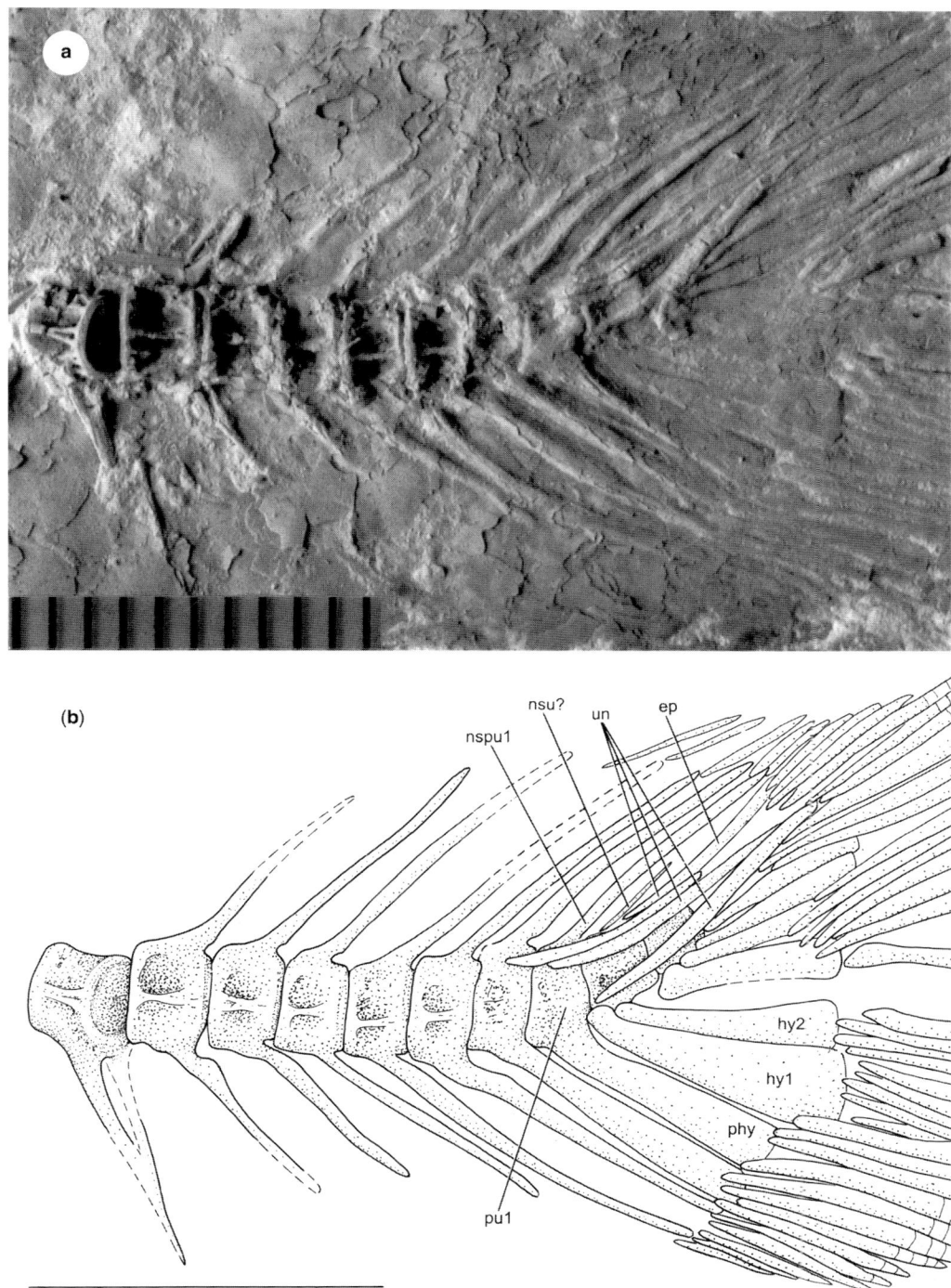

Fig. 17. a, photograph; **b**, line drawing of the caudal skeleton of †*Hiodon falcatus* (FMNH PF9881; acid prepared specimen) showing full neural spine on pu1. Specimen coated with ammonium chloride prior to photography. Anterior facing left (image reversed). Scale bar in millimetres.

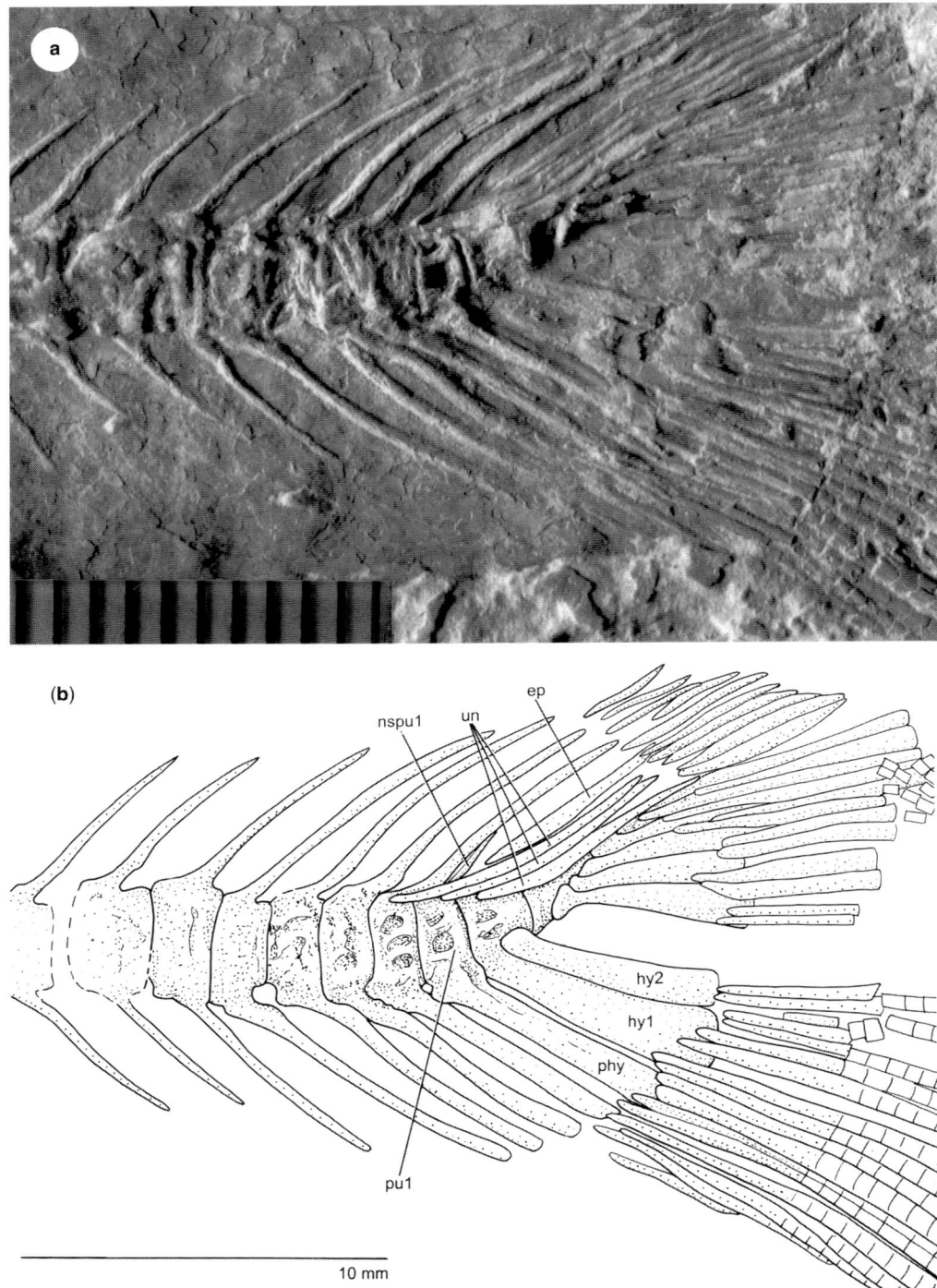

Fig. 18. a, photograph; **b**, line drawing of the caudal skeleton of †*Hiodon falcatus* (FMNH PF15175; acid prepared specimen) showing reduced neural spine on pu1. Specimen coated with ammonium chloride prior to photography. Anterior facing left (image reversed). Scale bar in millimetres.

PF10367, FMNH PF15174). In FMNH PF13065a (†*H. falcatus*), the mesocoracoid is exposed and resembles that of extant *Hiodon*, with a broad dorsolateral portion and a smoothly curved middle portion that corresponds to its contribution to the pectoral fin musculature canal (e.g. Hilton 2002). Nothing can be reported of the arrangement or form of the pectoral fin radials.

The first pectoral fin ray is the largest and has an expanded proximal base, and is the only unbranched ray of the fin, which comprises 12–13 fin rays (Li *et al.* 1997; personal observation).

Pelvic girdle and fin

The pelvic girdle of fossil *Hiodon*, as in extant species, is dominated by a pair of elongate pelvic bones that are expanded posteriorly and tapered anteriorly; the presence of ossified radials or the details of the pelvic bones themselves (e.g. the presence of a distinct ventral process; Hilton 2002, fig. 90) could not be determined. The post-pelvic bone found in extant *Hiodon*, which extends posteriorly from the pelvic girdle in the midline of the body (Hilton 2002, figs 89–90), was not found in any of our fossil specimens, although this is likely due to lack of preservation and its absence cannot be confidently determined. In most fossil specimens examined here, the fin rays of the left and right pelvic fins are preserved superimposed on one another, due to the typically lateral preservation of these fishes (because of the laterally compressed form of their bodies). This mode of preservation obscures the region in which the post-pelvic bone lies in *Hiodon*. Even in those specimens in which the pelvic girdle and fins are preserved more or less dorsoventrally, it is difficult to tell unambiguously whether or not a post-pelvic bone is present. *Hiodon* appears to be unique among teleosts in having this bone (Hilton 2002).

Also because of the way in which the pelvic fins are preserved, it is difficult to get reliable counts of fin rays from the fossils. Li *et al.* (1997) report seven fin rays for all hiodontids, and this is consistent with those fossil *Hiodon* for which we are confident in our counts (see Discussion). In FMNH PF13064 (†*H. falcatus*) we observed a detached pelvic splint similar in shape and proportions to that of extant *Hiodon* (Hilton 2002, fig. 89).

Scales

The species of *Hiodon*, both fossil and living, have thin cycloid scales with a rounded posterior border and fine radii on their anterior field (see Hilton 2002, figs 92–93). Grande (1984) reported 9–10 scale rows above and 8–10 scale rows below the

vertebral column for †*H. falcatus*. No meristic data were collected in this study, but we can confidently report that there appears to be fewer scales along the lateral line in †*H. falcatus* than in extant species (e.g. about 40–45 in FMNH PF15167, cf. 53–63 in extant species; Hilton 2002 tables 21–22).

Discussion

The following is a critique of the characters identified by Li *et al.* (1997) as synapomorphies at various hierarchical levels within Hiodontidae (*sensu* Li & Wilson 1994; co-extensive with their Hiodontiformes) in light of the new information now available for fossil hiodontids (this study), extant *Hiodon* (Hilton 2002), and the systematic analysis of Osteoglossomorpha published by Hilton (2003).

Hiodontidae

A seven-rayed pelvic fin was first identified as a synapomorphy of the family Hiodontidae by Li & Wilson (1994, character 8; see also Li & Wilson 1996a, 1999; Li *et al.* 1997). Hilton (2002) confirmed that the typical number of fin rays in the extant species of *Hiodon* was seven, although he discovered some specimens that have six rays on one or both pelvic fins. Hilton (2003, p. 88) found it difficult to make reliable counts for many fossil osteoglossomorph taxa, and therefore excluded this character from his analysis, although he noted that he was 'able to confirm seven pelvic fin rays in *Hiodon* (Hilton 2002) and less than seven in all other living osteoglossomorphs that were examined.' In most fossil specimens of *Hiodon* (including '†*Eohiodon*') examined in the present study, the pelvic fin rays could not be unambiguously counted. In general this is because the fishes are preserved in lateral view, and the left and right fins become superimposed and are difficult to differentiate. This difficulty is also apparent in the original species descriptions: Cavender (1966, p. 315) described the number of fin rays in †*H. rosei* as 'undeterminable', Wilson (1978, p. 684) described †*H. woodruffi* as having '*about* seven rays' (our emphasis); and Grande (1979: 108) considered †*H. falcatus* to have '8 or 9 rays.'

Li *et al.* (1997, p. 1113; character 17) recovered a distinctively shaped opercle as a synapomorphy of the family Hiodontidae. Although this character was not used in the analysis of Hilton (2003; see discussion by Hilton 2003, p. 86, fig. 41), the opercle of fossil hiodontids is similar in shape to the extant species of *Hiodon* and is not in question here (in fact we regard the opercle of taxa formerly assigned to †*Eohiodon* as more similar in shape; see below).

The condition of having the dorsal arm of the posttemporal more than twice as long as the ventral arm was found, among osteoglossomorphs, only in †*Yanbiania*, †*Eohiodon*, and *Hiodon* by Li *et al.* (1997, character 27) and was therefore considered a synapomorphy of Hiodontidae. As discussed by Hilton (2003), there are problems with this character as defined and coded for by these authors. Several osteoglossomorphs that were coded as lacking this condition have the dorsal arm twice as long as the ventral arm (e.g. †*Ostariostoma* Schaeffer 1949; see Grande & Cavender 1991, fig. 2). Additionally, mormyroids are difficult to code for this character, as many mormyrids, for example, lack a distinct ventral arm of the posttemporal (see discussion in Hilton 2003). Hilton (2003) interpreted this character supporting Osteoglossomorpha as a whole, with several reversals to the condition of having the dorsal arm of the posttemporal less than two times as long as the ventral arm.

Having the two neurocranial articulatory heads of the hyomandibula joined by a bridge of bone (e.g. illustrated in Hilton 2002, fig. 45) was only found in *Hiodon* and †*Yanbiania* by Li *et al.* (1997, character 28, state 2). However, as shown above, the dorsal heads of the hyomandibula in each of the three North American species previously included in †*Eohiodon* are joined by a thin strut of bone as well (Figs 7, 9, 11, 14). Two independent heads (their state 1) that articulate with the neurocranium was considered to be a synapomorphy of †*Eohiodon* (see below). We have not been able to examine specimens of †*Yanbiania* or †*Plesiolycoptera*, and therefore defer comment on the condition in these taxa. See also the discussion of this character by Hilton (2003, p. 48–49).

A triradiate dermosphenotic was found to be a synapomorphy of the family Hiodontidae by Li *et al.* (1997, character 29), and we confirm that it is present in all species of *Hiodon* as conceived here (i.e. including species of †*Eohiodon*). We regard the condition in †*Yanbiana* and †*Plesiolycoptera* to be ambiguous, as these taxa are known from very few specimens that have not been satisfactorily illustrated or studied (see comments by Chang 1999). This character was scored as unknown for †*Lycoptera* by Hilton (2003), and was therefore interpreted as support either of †*Eohiodon* + *Hiodon* (the only hiodontids included in his analysis) or of †*Lycoptera* + Hiodontidae (a group not supported in his strict consensus tree).

†Eohiodon + Hiodon

Li *et al.* (1997, character 7) found that the supraorbital sensory canal ending in the frontal (as opposed to ending in the parietal) supports the group †*Eohiodon* + *Hiodon*. The condition in extant *Hiodon* is, however, variable, with some individuals having the supraorbital sensory canal extending posteriorly into the parietal (Hilton 2002). Hilton (2003) found the supraorbital canal ending in the frontal (coded polymorphic for *Hiodon*) to support Osteoglossomorpha as a whole, with a further change in †*Lycoptera* (his tree 1) or all osteoglossomorphs to the exclusion of †*Lycoptera* (his tree 2). It is possible that this distribution is an artifact of taxon sampling in this analysis (only *Elops* Linnaeus, 1758 was used as the outgroup) and that the supraorbital canal ending in the frontal is a character at a broader level of phylogeny.

The only other character that Li *et al.* (1997, character 46, their fig. 7) found to support †*Eohiodon* + *Hiodon* is the presence of a sexually dimorphic anal fin (see also discussion by Li & Wilson 1999). The sexual dimorphism of the external shape of the anal fin of *Hiodon* has long been known (e.g. Kirtland 1847). Within osteoglossomorphs, some mormyrids also are known to have a sexually dimorphic anal fin shape (e.g. Iles 1960; Okedi 1969; Brown *et al.* 1996), although this is a clearly different manifestation of sexual dimorphism than that found in *Hiodon*. In extant *Hiodon*, there is dimorphism in both external and internal structure of the anal fin (see Hilton 2002, figs 80–81). In males, the proximal pterygiophores bear greatly exaggerated lateral flanges of bone (Hilton 2002). In mature males, the anterior margin of the anal fin is rounded, whereas in juvenile males and all females the margin of the anal fin is straight (e.g. Roberts 1989). Similarly shaped anal fins have been recognized also in fossil *Hiodon* (e.g. Cavender 1966; Wilson 1977; Li *et al.* 1997; personal observation), although the sizes of specimens that display these different shapes are much smaller than the size at which *Hiodon* matures. This led Wilson & Williams (1992, p. 239) to suggest that, 'notwithstanding the anatomical similarity, at least some [†]*Eohiodon* species must have differed substantially from *Hiodon* in terms of life history, maturing, or at least becoming sexually dimorphic at a much younger age and smaller size.' Although this character was excluded by Hilton (2003) from his analysis, two forms of the anal fin in fossil species of *Hiodon* do exist, and it is likely that this difference was correlated with sex, as in the extant forms (ultimately an untestable, although not unreasonable, hypothesis for fossil taxa). In some instances, when sufficient numbers of fossil specimens are known from a single locality and can be treated as a population, it may be possible to statistically test the hypothesis that these are sexual dimorphisms (e.g. see

Wilson 1977), particularly given a modern 'known' model for comparison. However, several osteoglossomorph taxa that Li *et al.* (1997) coded for this character are known from a single specimen (e.g. †*Ostariostoma*; Grande & Cavender 1991), only a few specimens (e.g. †*Yanbiania*; Li 1987), or incompletely- and poorly-preserved specimens (e.g. †*Plesiolycoptera*; Chang 1999) and thus cannot be scored anything but as unknown (i.e. a '?'), and we suggest caution in the use of this and similar characters in systematic analyses.

†Eohiodon

Li *et al.* (1997, fig. 7, character 28) indicated only a single character supporting the monophyly of the genus †*Eohiodon*: the presence of a hyomandibula with two distinct heads that articulate with the neurocranium. According to these authors, the two heads do not possess the thin strut of bone that forms a bridge between them, as found in extant *Hiodon* (e.g. Taverne 1977; Hilton 2002) and †*Yanbiania* (e.g. Li 1987; Li & Wilson 1999). Cavender (1966) also described the two heads of the hyomandibula as separate in his description of †*H. rosei* (although see Taverne's 1977; fig. 30 illustration of one of the paratypes, in which he indicates the presence of a bridged hyomandibula). However, as shown above, all three species formerly assigned to †*Eohiodon* have a hyomandibula similar to that in extant *Hiodon*. Its previously reported absence was an artifact of insufficient preservation and preparation, because we found it to be present in carefully prepared new specimens.

A second character concerning the shape of the premaxilla was reported by Li *et al.* (1997, character 47) to have changed within †*Eohiodon*. The premaxilla of †*H. rosei* was scored by Li *et al.* (1997, p. 1123, character 47) as possessing an ascending process ('anterior portion raised'), and this was interpreted as an autapomorphy of this taxon by these authors. These authors further differentiated between the condition in †*H. woodruffi* ('anterior portion not raised') and that of extant *Hiodon* ('anterior portion lower than posterior portion'). Hilton (2003, fig. 40) was not able to sort this character satisfactorily into distinct character states. There is variation in the shape of the premaxilla of fossil and living *Hiodon* that is perhaps of systematic value. However, we were unable to match our observations with those described and coded by Li *et al.* (1997). See further discussion of this and a related character below.

Here we note that Zhang (2006) found the absence of a neural arch on the first ural centrum to support †*Eohiodon* + †*Jiaohichthys*. Hilton (2003, character 67) used a similar character in his analysis, but, following Li *et al.* (1997),

grouped the states of 'absent' and 'rudimentary', which were separated by Zhang (2006, character 48). We view Zhang's coding of this character in specimens assigned to †*Eohiodon* to be problematic (we have not seen specimens of †*Jiaohichthys* so cannot comment on this taxon), as the rudimentary neural spine of the ural centrum in adult extant *Hiodon* is covered by the uroneurals (Hilton 2002, fig. 72) and can only be seen early in development or upon disarticulation (Hilton 2002, figs 74, 73, respectively); we have not seen specimens of fossil hiodontids sufficiently preserved to code a ural neural arch as absent or rudimentary with confidence.

Hiodon

Li *et al.* (1997, character 18) found the presence of a tubular and strongly curved nasal bone to be a synapomorphy of *Hiodon*. They described the nasal bone of taxa assigned to †*Eohiodon* as tubular and slightly curved. A tubular but straight nasal bone was found (homoplastically) to support the group †*Eohiodon* + †*Jiaohichthys* by Zhang (2006). However, Grande (1979, p. 105), in his description of †*H. falcatus*, noted that the nasal bone was similar in shape to *Hiodon*, and that it has 'approximately a 100° angle at the bend.' Indeed, as shown above, the nasals of fossil *Hiodon* are strongly bent, much as in extant *Hiodon* (Hilton 2002, figs 28–29). This character, therefore, is better interpreted as a synapomorphy of an expanded *Hiodon* (i.e. *Hiodon* = *Hiodon* + †'*Eohiodon*').

Two characters considered to be synapomorphies of *Hiodon* by Li *et al.* (1997) concern the morphology of the premaxillae. The first of these (their character 47) describes the 'anterior portion [of the premaxillae as being] lower than [the] posterior portion.' In extant *Hiodon*, the anterior portion of the premaxilla is low, rising slightly where it meets the anterior ethmoid cartilage. As far as we can tell, a similarly shaped premaxilla is found in at least some fossil *Hiodon* in that it appears to taper slightly anteriorly, although this is not without some reservation (see description above). In †*H. consteniorum*, we observed variation of shape of the premaxilla between the two known specimens. In the holotype, the anterior and posterior halves of the premaxilla are separated by a deep notch, whereas in the paratype, the anterior portion is much deeper than the posterior portion. Li *et al.* (1997, character 49) also considered the presence of a mid-dorsal concavity on the premaxilla to be a synapomorphy of extant *Hiodon*. As for other characters that these authors used regarding the shape of the premaxilla, we were unable to find consistent differences in our specimens that match the coding of Li *et al.* (1997); see discussion by Hilton (2002).

Another character that was considered by Li et al. (1997) to be uniquely derived in the genus *Hiodon* is the presence of a spine on the posterodorsal portion of the opercle. Cavender (1966, p. 315), however, identified this structure in his description of †*Hiodon rosei*, which he described as possessing an opercle 'like that of [extant] *Hiodon* with the distinctive notch present in the posterior border and the posterodorsal corner drawn out dorsally to a point.' In the figure presented by Li & Wilson (1994, fig. 6) demonstrating the absence of an opercular spine in non-*Hiodon* hiodontids, the region that would bear such a spine in their illustrated specimen of '†*Eohiodon*' is completed by a rounded border by a dashed line, indicating uncertainty of the exact morphology of this region. We also found this opercular spine in specimens of †*H. woodruffi* and †*H. falcatus* (see above), and therefore regard it as a synapomorphy of an expanded *Hiodon*.

Two characters of the caudal skeleton were also considered by Li et al. (1997) to be synapomorphies of the genus *Hiodon* (and to distinguish it from '†*Eohiodon*'). The first of these concerns the presence of a rudimentary neural spine on the first preural centrum (Li et al. 1997, character 50). Li & Wilson (1994) first noted this character as a synapomorphy of the genus *Hiodon*, although they recognized the condition in extant members is variable (see Schultze & Arratia 1988; Hilton 2002). As shown above, some fossil specimens of *Hiodon* (=†*Eohiodon*) do have a rudimentary neural spine on pu1, just as in extant *Hiodon* (see Hilton 2002). However, the frequency of this variation (i.e. the presence of a rudimentary neural spine) is relatively low, similar to the variant condition (i.e. the presence of a full neural spine) found in extant *Hiodon*. Hilton (2003) considered a full nspu1 to be a synapomorphy of Osteoglossomorpha, with †*Eohiodon* and *Hiodon* being polymorphic (the condition in †*Lycoptera* is unclear; see discussion in Hilton 2003).

The second character of the caudal skeleton that Li et al. (1997, character 51) cited as a synapomorphy of *Hiodon* concerns the number of neural spines on the second preural centrum. *Hiodon* was regarded as having, or potentially having, two neural spines on this centrum. Hilton (2002), while acknowledging that several specimens have been illustrated with two neural spines on pu2 (see Monod 1968; Schultze & Arratia 1988; Li & Wilson 1994), did not observe any specimens with this character state in his sample, nor did we in this study, suggesting that it is a polymorphic character state (although the exact frequency is unknown). In Hilton's (2003) analysis, this character state was coded as polymorphic for *Hiodon*, †*Phareodus* and *Papyrocranus*, and was therefore interpreted as an autapomorphy found in only

some specimens of these taxa. The only taxon for which Hilton (2003) coded this character as fixed for the derived state was †*Joffrichthys* Li & Wilson, 1996b, although this may be an artifact of sample size (there is only a single specimen with an interpretable caudal skeleton).

Conclusions

In his description of the genus †*Eohiodon*, Cavender (1966, p. 314) noted that it 'possesses characters ... which indicate a greater degree of separation than is found between the two species of *Hiodon*. For this reason, I have placed the fossil in a separate genus.' Cavender's (1966) characters include several body measurements (e.g. head length), for which the ranges became continuous with those of extant *Hiodon* with the description of later species (e.g. †*H. falcatus*, Grande 1979; †*H. consteniorum*, Li & Wilson 1994). Wilson (1977, p. 15) noted that 'The Eocene genus [†]*Eohiodon* is remarkably similar to *Hiodon* in the details of its osteology, and can only be distinguished by anal fin and trunk vertebral counts, a few related body proportions, and size at maturity.' The coding of the one previously proposed osteological synapomorphy of the genus †*Eohiodon* (two articulatory heads of the hyomandibula that are unbridged; Li et al. 1997) has been found to be incorrect based on newly prepared specimens. Additionally, all of the synapomorphies proposed by Li et al. (1997) for *Hiodon* that can be scored for fossils either have been found in these taxa as well, or are considered to be problematic. We have been unable to find any characters that distinguish †*Eohiodon* as a monophyletic group that is separate from *Hiodon* and we conclude that †*Eohiodon* should be regarded as a synonym of *Hiodon*. Significant strides have been made recently in our understanding of hiodontid anatomy and systematics (e.g. Li & Wilson 1996a, 1999; Li et al. 1997; Hilton 2002). However, further study needs to be made to clarify the systematic interrelationships of all species within Hiodontidae, including the redescription of Chinese taxa such as †*Plesiolycoptera* and †*Yanbiania*.

It is our pleasure to contribute this paper to this volume in honor of Peter Forey, our mentor, colleague, and friend. Peter was a member of EJH's doctoral committee and had a great influence on his early interest and studies of fossil and living fishes. Both of us have enjoyed our collaborations and interactions with him, and the times we have spent in discussion, often over a lunchtime pint or an after-work gin and tonic.

We are grateful for access to and loan of specimens by W. E. Bemis (UMA), M. V. H. Wilson (UALVP), A. Neuman and J. Gardiner (TMP), and J. Maisey and I. Rutzky (AMNH). M. V. H. Wilson encouraged our studies through thoughtful discussion and sharing of his knowledge of fossil hiodontids, and facilitated visits to Edmonton by EJH. We thank A. Murray and M. V. H. Wilson for constructive and thorough criticisms of the original manuscript, although we may have differing views and conclusions. J. Weinstein and K. Bean provided photographic assistance and line drawings were rendered by L. Grove. This work was initiated while EJH was at FMNH as a Lester Armour and William A. and Stella Rowley Graduate Fellow and a doctoral candidate in the Graduate Program in Organismic and Evolutionary Biology at UMA. This work benefited from the financial support of the NSF (DEB-0073066, to Bemis for Hilton; DEB-0128929, to Hilton, Grande & Bemis; DEB-0414552, to Hilton & Grande), the Jane H. Bemis Fund for Research in Natural History, the Lester Armour and William A. and Stella Rowley Graduate Fellowships (FMNH), a Visiting Scientist Scholarship (FMNH), the Graduate School at the University of Massachusetts Amherst (UMA), and the Graduate Program in Organismic and Evolutionary Biology (UMA). This paper is contribution number 2895 of the Virginia Institute of Marine Science, The College of William and Mary.

References

BRINKMAN, D. B. & NEUMAN, A. G. 2002. Teleost centra from uppermost Judith River Group (Dinosaur Park Formation, Campanian) of Alberta, Canada. *Journal of Paleontology*, 76, 138–155.

BROWN, B., BENVENISTE, L. M. & MOLLER, P. 1996. Basal expansion of anal-fin rays: a new osteological character in weakly discharging electric fish (Mormyridae). *Journal of Fish Biology*, 49, 1216–1225.

BRUNER, J. C. 1992. A catalogue of type specimens of fossil fishes in the Field Museum of Natural History. *Fieldiana (Geology) new series*, 23, 1–54.

CAVENDER, T. 1966. Systematic position of the North American Eocene fish, '*Leuciscus*' *rosei* Hussakof. *Copeia*, 1966, 311–320.

CHANG, M.-M. 1999. 'Mid'-Cretaceous fish faunas from northeast China. *In*: ARRATIA, G. & SCHULTZE, H.-P. (eds) *Mesozoic Fishes 2 – Systematics and Fossil Record*. Dr. F. Pfeil, Munich, 469–480.

CHANG, M.-M. & CHOU, C. 1976. The discovery of *Plesiolycoptera* from Song Liao Basin, with notes on the origin of osteoglossomorph fishes. *Vertebrata PalAsiatica*, 14, 146–153.

CHANG, M.-M. & MIAO, D. 2004. An overview of Mesozoic fishes in Asia. *In*: ARRATIA, G. & TINTORI, A. (eds) *Mesozoic Fishes 3 – Systematics, Paleoenvironments and Biodiversity*. Dr F. Pfeil, Munich, 535–563.

CUVIER, G. 1816. *Le Règne Animal distribué d'après son organisation pour servir de base à l'histoire naturelle des animaux et d'introduction à l'anatomie comparée. Les reptiles, les poissons, les mollusques et les annélides.* (1st Edn.)

DINGERKUS, G. & UHLER, L. D. 1977. Enzyme clearing of alcian blue stained whole small vertebrates for demonstration of cartilage. *Journal of Stain Technology*, 52, 229–232.

GRANDE, L. 1979. *Eohiodon falcatus*, a new species of hiodontid (Pisces) from the late early Eocene Green River Formation of Wyoming. *Journal of Paleontology*, 53, 103–111.

GRANDE, L. 1984. Paleontology of the Green River Formation, with a review of the fish fauna. *Bulletin of the Geological Survey of Wyoming*, 63, 1–333.

GRANDE, L. 1987. Redescription of †*Hypsidoris farsonensis* (Teleostei: Siluriformes), with a reassessment of its phylogenetic relationships. *Journal of Vertebrate Paleontology*, 7, 24–54.

GRANDE, L. 1994. Studies of paleoenvironments and historical biogeography in the Fossil Butte and Laney members of the Green River Formation. *Contributions to Geology*, 30, 15–32.

GRANDE, L. 2001. An updated review of the fish faunas from the Green River Formation, the world's most productive freshwater lagerstätten. *In*: GUNNELL, G. F. (ed.) *Eocene Biodiversity: Unusual Occurrences and rarely sampled habitats*. Kluwer Academic/Plenum Publishers, New York, 1–38.

GRANDE, L. & BEMIS, W. E. 1998. A comprehensive phylogenetic study of amiid fishes (Amiidae) based on comparative skeletal anatomy. An empirical search for interconnected patterns of natural history. *Society of Vertebrate Paleontology Memoir*, 4, 1–690.

GRANDE, L. & BUCHHEIM, H. P. 1994. Paleontological and sedimentological variation in Early Eocene Fossil Lake. *Contributions to Geology*, 30, 33–56.

GRANDE, L. & CAVENDER, T. M. 1991. Description and phylogenetic reassessment of the monotypic Ostariostomidae (Teleostei). *Journal of Vertebrate Paleontology*, 11, 405–416.

HILTON, E. J. 2002. Osteology of the extant North American fishes of the genus *Hiodon* Lesueur, 1818 (Teleostei: Osteoglossomorpha: Hiodontiformes). *Fieldiana (Zoology) new series*, 100, 1–142.

HILTON, E. J. 2003. Comparative osteology and phylogenetic systematics of fossil and living bony-tongue fishes (Actinopterygii, Teleostei, Osteoglossomorpha). *Zoological Journal of the Linnean Society*, 137, 1–100.

HUSSAKOF, L. 1916. A new cyprinid fish *Leuciscus rosei*, from the Miocene of British Columbia. *American Journal of Science*, 42, 18–20.

ILES, R. B. 1960. External sexual differences and their significance in *Mormyrus kannume* Forskal 1775. *Nature*, 188, 516.

JORDAN, D. S. & BEAN, T. 1877. Hyodontidae. *In*: JORDAN, D. S. (ed.) Contributions to North American Ichthyology, Based on the Collections of the United States National Museum. *Bulletin of the United States National Museum*, 10, 67–68.

KIRTLAND, J. P. 1847. Descriptions of the fishes of Lake Erie, the Ohio River, and their tributaries. *Boston Journal of Natural History*, 5, 330–344.

LAVOUÉ, S. & SULLIVAN, J. P. 2004. Simultaneous analysis of five molecular markers provides a well-supported phylogenetic hypothesis for the living bony-tongue fishes (Osteoglossomorpha: Teleostei). *Molecular Phylogenetics and Evolution*, 33, 171–185.

LESUEUR, C. A. 1818. Descriptions of several new species of North American fishes. *Journal of the Academy of Natural Sciences of Philadelphia*, 1, 359–368.

LEIDY, J. 1873. Contributions to the extinct vertebrate fauna of the western territories. *Report of the United States Geological Survey of the Territories*, 1–358.

LI, G.-Q. 1987. A new genus of Hiodontidae from Luozigou Basin, East Jilin. *Vertebrata PalAsiatica*, **25**, 91–107.

LI, G.-Q. 1994. *New osteoglossomorphs (Teleostei) from the Upper Cretaceous and Lower Tertiary of North America and their phylogenetic significance.* Unpublished PhD dissertation, University of Alberta, Canada.

LI, G.-Q. & WILSON, M. V. H. 1994. An Eocene species of *Hiodon* from Montana, its phylogenetic relationships, and the evolution of the postcranial skeleton in the Hiodontidae (Teleostei). *Journal of Vertebrate Paleontology*, **14**, 153–167.

LI, G.-Q. & WILSON, M. V. H. 1996a. Phylogeny of Osteoglossomorpha. *In*: STIASSNY, M. L. J., PARENTI, L. R. & JOHNSON, G. D. (eds) *Interrelationships of Fishes*. Academic Press, San Diego, 163–174.

LI, G.-Q. & WILSON, M. V. H. 1996b. The discovery of Heterotidinae (Teleostei: Osteoglossidae) from the Paleocene Paskapoo Formation of Alberta, Canada. *Journal of Vertebrate Paleontology*, **16**, 198–209.

LI, G.-Q. & WILSON, M. V. H. 1999. Early divergence of Hiodontiformes sensu stricto in East Asia and phylogeny of some Late Mesozoic teleosts from China. *In*: ARRATIA, G. & SCHULTZE, H.-P. (eds) *Mesozoic Fishes 2 – Systematics and Fossil Record*. Dr F. Pfeil, Munich, 369–384.

LI, G.-Q., WILSON, M. V. H. & GRANDE, L. 1997. Review of *Eohiodon* (Teleostei: Osteoglossomorpha) from western North America, with a phylogenetic reassessment of Hiodontidae. *Journal of Paleontology*, **71**, 1109–1124.

LINNAEUS, C. 1758. *Systema naturae per regna tria naturae, secundum classes, ordines, genera, species, cum characteribus, differentiis, synonymis, locis. Tome 1. Editio decima, reformata.* Holmiæ: Laurentii Salvii. [1956 facsimile reprint; London, Trustees of the British Museum (Natural History).)]

MA, F. C. 1983. Early Cretaceous primitive teleosts from the Jiaohe Basin of Jilin Province, China. *Vertebrata PalAsiatica*, **21**, 17–31.

MONOD, T. 1968. Le complex urophore des poissons téléostéens. *Mémoires de l'Institut Fondamental d'Afrique Noire*, **81**, 1–705.

MÜLLER, J. 1848. Fossil Fische. *In*: VON MIDDENDORFF, A. T. (ed.) *Sibirische Reise. Reise in den aussersten Norden und Osten Sibiriens während der Jahre 1843 und 1844.* vol. 1, 260–262.

NELSON, G. J. 1968. Gill arches of teleostean fishes of the division Osteoglossomorpha. *Journal of Linnean Society (Zoology)*, **47**, 261–277.

NELSON, G. J. 1969. Infraorbital bones and their bearing on the phylogeny and geography of osteoglossomorph fishes. *American Museum Novitates*, **2394**, 1–37.

NEWBREY, M. G. & WILSON, M. V. H. 2005. Recognition of annular growth on centra of Teleostei with application to Hiodontidae of the Cretaceous Dinosaur Park Formation. *In*: BRAMAN, D. R., THERRIEN, F., KOPPELHUS, E. B. & TAYLOR, W. (eds) *Dinosaur Park Symposium*. Royal Tyrrell Museum, Drumheller, 61–68.

NEWBREY, M. G., WILSON, M. V. H. & ASHWORTH, A. 2005. Growth characteristics of North American

Hiodontidae (Teleostei) from the Late Cretaceous to Recent. *Journal of Vertebrate Paleontology*, **25**, 96A.

NEWBREY, M. G., WILSON, M. V. H. & ASHWORTH, A. 2007. Centrum growth patterns provide evidence for two small taxa of Hiodontidae in the Cretaceous Dinosaur Park Formation. *Canadian Journal of Earth Science*, **44**, 721–732.

OKEDI, J. 1969. Observations on the breeding and growth of certain mormyroid fishes of the Lake Victoria Basin. *Revue de Zoologie et de Botanique Africaines*, **79**, 34–64.

RAFINESQUE, C. S. 1818. Discoveries in natural history, made during a journey through the western region of the United States. *American Monthly Magazine and Critical Review*, **2**, 354–356.

RAFINESQUE, C. S. 1819. Prodrome de 70 nouveaux genres d'animaux découverts dans l'intérieur des Etats-Unis d'Amérique durant l'année 1818. *Journal de Physique, Paris*, **88**, 417–429.

RAFINESQUE, C. S. 1820. *Ichthyologica Ohioensis, or Natural History of the Fishes Inhabiting the River Ohio and its Tributary Streams, Preceded by a Physical Description of the Ohio and its Branches.* W. G. Hunt, Lexington.

ROBERTS, W. 1989. The mooneye in Alberta. *Alberta Naturalist*, **19**, 134–140.

SCHAEFFER, B. 1949. A teleost from the Livingston Formation of Montana. *American Museum Novitates*, **1427**, 1–16.

SCHULTZE, H.-P. & ARRATIA, G. 1988. Reevaluation of the caudal skeleton of some actinopterygian fishes: II. *Hiodon, Elops*, and *Albula. Journal of Morphology*, **195**, 257–303.

SCOTT, W. B. & CROSSMAN, E. J. 1973. Freshwater Fishes of Canada. *Bulletin of the Fisheries Research Board of Canada*, **184**, 1–966.

SHEN, M. 1989. *Eohiodon* from China and the distribution of osteoglossomorphs. *Vertebrata PalAsiatica*, **10**, 237–247. [In Chinese, with an English summary.]

SYTCHEVSKAYA, E. K. 1986. Palaeogene freshwater fish fauna of the USSR and Mongolia. *Transactions of the Joint Soviet-Mongolian Paleontological Expedition*, **29**, 1–157. [In Russian, with an English abstract.]

TAVERNE, L. 1977. Ostéologie, phylogénèse et systématique des Téléostéens fossiles et actuels du super-ordre des ostéoglossomorphes. Première partie. Ostéologie des genres *Hiodon, Eohiodon, Lycoptera, Osteoglossum, Scleropages, Heterotis* et *Arapaima. Mémoires de la Classe des Sciences, Académie Royale de Belgique*, **42**, 1–235.

TAVERNE, L. 1979. Ostéologie, phylogénèse et systématique des Téléostéens fossiles et actuels du super-ordre des ostéoglossomorphes. Troisième partie. Évolution des structures ostéologiques et conclusions générales relatives à la phylogénèse et à la systématique du super-order. Addendum. *Mémoires de la Classe des Sciences, Académie Royale de Belgique*, **43**, 1–168.

TAVERNE, L. 1998. Les ostéoglossomorphes marin de l'Éocène du Monte Bolca (Italie): *Monopteros* Volta 1796, *Thrissopterus* Heckel, 1856 et *Foreyichthys* Taverne, 1979. Considérations sur la phylogénie des téléostéens ostéoglossomorphes. *Studie e Ricerche sui Giacimenti Terziari di Bolca*, **7**, 67–158.

TOOMBS, H. A. & RIXON, A. E. 1959. The use of acids in the preparation of vertebrate fossils. *Curator*, **2**, 304–312.

WILSON, M. V. H. 1977. Middle Eocene freshwater fishes from British Columbia. *Life Sciences Contributions Royal Ontario Museum*, **113**, 1–61.

WILSON, M. V. H. 1978. *Eohiodon woodruffi* n. sp. (Teleostei, Hiodontidae) from the middle Eocene Klondike Mountain Formation near Republic, Washington. *Canadian Journal of Earth Sciences*, **15**, 679–686.

WILSON, M. V. H. & WILLIAMS, R. R. G. 1992. Phylogenetic, biogeographic, and ecological significance of early fossil records of North American freshwater teleostean fishes. *In*: MAYDEN, R. L. (ed.) *Systematics, Historical Ecology, and North American Freshwater Fishes*. Stanford University Press, Stanford, California, 224–244.

ZHANG, J.-Y. 2006. Phylogeny of Osteoglossomorpha. *Vertebrata PalAsiatica*, **44**, 43–59.

Osteoglossomorphs of the marine Lower Eocene of Denmark – with remarks on other Eocene taxa and their importance for palaeobiogeography

NIELS BONDE

Institute of Geography and Geology, Øster Voldgade 10, DK-1350 Copenhagen K and Fur Museum, DK-7884 Fur, Denmark (e-mail: nielsb@geol.ku.dk; niels.bonde@mail.tele.dk)

Abstract: The geological, faunal and palaeoecological conditions of the marine deposits from lowermost Eocene in North Jutland are briefly reviewed as background for the descriptions of six species of osteoglossiform fishes from the Stolle Klint Clay and the overlying Mo-clay (Ølst and Fur Formations respectively). Four of these primitive teleosteans are referred to new genera and species (one based on an almost complete skeleton, three others on skull material, one very incomplete), and the two most fragmentary specimens are referred to *Brychaetus* sp. and an indeterminate osteoglossiform. The phylogenetic relationships of these fossils are evaluated in the framework of two different models of osteoglossomorph phylogeny provided earlier by Taverne and Hilton. Despite differences in both data bases, methodologies and results given by the two models (the former based on *c.* 300 characters in an intuitive, qualitative phylogenetic parsimony analysis, the latter on 72 characters in a critical, rigorous, quantitative cladistic analysis) the phylogenetic positions of four of the fossil species are very similar in the two models concerning the relations to the recent forms. The other two species, rather fragmentary, but similar in many ways to the Eocene phareodonts (paraphyletic group), end up very differently in relation to extant forms in the two models. The phylogenetic systematics of all the marine, fossil osteoglossiforms (including *Brychaetus*, *Opsithrissops* and Monte Bolca forms) is evaluated as background for interpretation of their (palaeo-)biogeographic significance as marine members of a group, Osteoglossomorpha (of which the recent forms are prime examples of 'primary division freshwater fishes', and of which the extant osteoglossiforms have a classical 'Gondwana distribution'. There are 9 marine, Eocene taxa (plus an otolith from the Maastrichtian of USA) and none of the 9 appear more closely-related to any other marine form in either model: they might constitute 9 separate migrations from freshwater into the sea. The phylogenetic results strongly suggest instead, that the extant osteoglossiforms have independently entered freshwater from the sea on two, perhaps even three occasions. This may have happened as late as the Eocene, and phareodonts could be yet another independent invasion of freshwater in the Late Cretaceous. The mormyriforms most likely had an independent invasion into freshwater (in one model even with notopterids as a separate migration from the sea by Mid or Early Cretaceous). Because all the closest outgroups of the Osteoglossomorpha are marine, the group obviously originated in the sea, probably by the Late Jurassic, and it is not impossible that Hiodontiforms in NE Asia and North America underwent another independent freshwater invasion very early in the Cretaceous. What then is wanting? The expected Cretaceous, marine osteoglossomorphs are not found (but note the above otolith).

Geology, 'ash-series' and faunas

This 'ash-series' comprises the main series of ash falls of the Palaeogene of NW Europe. The Palaeocene–Eocene ash falls were recognized as three distinctive 'phases' (Knox 1996, 1997; Knox & Morton 1988, 1990) of which the second one constitutes the main phase (phase 2.1–2.2b in Knox 1996, 1997 correction sheet p. 10x), which was deposited in the Danish Stolle Klint Clay (of the Ølst Clay facies, Heilmann-Clausen 1996) and the overlying Mo-clay (Fur Formation proper, Pedersen & Surlyk 1983 as modified by Heilmann-Clausen *et al.* 1985; Bonde 1997; Heilmann-Clausen

2006). These two deposits are well exposed only in NW Jutland round the western Limfjorden region, but tiny exposures of 'Mo-clay like' layers with ash can be found in a few places further south in East Jutland, and Stolle Klint Clay seems to correspond to the basal part of the Ølst Clay Formation exposed south of Limfjorden and in East Jutland (Andersen 1937; Nielsen 1994), NW Sealand (Petersen 1973) and also to the lower part of the Sele Formation in the North Sea (Schiøler *et al.* 2007).

Prinz & von Ermengen (1883) described and figured the so-called 'black sand' from limestone boulders of the Mo-clay as volcanic ash (tuffs),

From: CAVIN, L., LONGBOTTOM, A. & RICHTER, M. (eds) *Fishes and the Break-up of Pangaea.*
Geological Society, London, Special Publications, **295**, 253–310.
DOI: 10.1144/SP295.14   0305-8719/08/$15.00 © The Geological Society of London 2008.

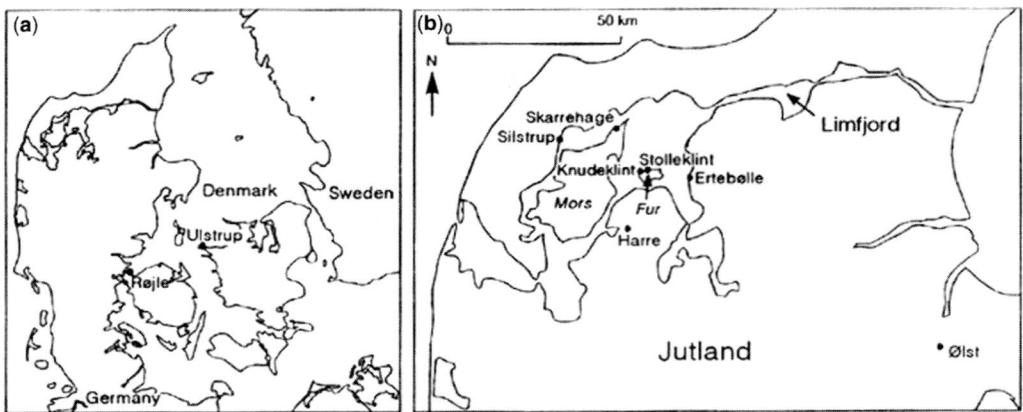

Fig. 1. Localities of the Mo-clay region (modified from Bonde 1997).

which, however was only recognized in Denmark by 1902. Professor N.V. Ussing immediately sent the young O.B. Bøggild to all known localities with such layers in Jutland (Bøggild 1903). Ussing also numbered the upper part of the ash series from +1 to +140 in a footnote to his major work on end moraines in Jutland (1907). After Ussing's death in 1910, Bøggild took over both the professorship and the investigation of the ash layers, which, after some delay, was published as his famous monograph in 1918. In this he continued the numbering of the ash layers downwards from −1 to −39 in the lower half of the Mo-clay (in which the ash layers are much less frequent). In those days many of the now-conspicuous sea cliffs were covered by scree and grass, due to less coastal erosion in the Limfjorden, and the industrial exploitation of the Mo-clay in the many clay pits had hardly begun early in the century, the initiation being the founding of 'Skarrehage Molérværk' (now 'Skamol') by 1912 on the Isle of Mors (see Bonde 1987 at the 75th anniversary of Skamol; Pedersen et al. 1994). It is estimated from measurements made on Isle of Fur in the 1920s of the horizontal mine shaft into the Stolle Klint (= cliff; originally dug about 1800 in search for coal, the black volcanic ashes) that, since then, at least 50 m of the seaward face of the cliff has eroded away. The Knudeklint, now type locality of Fur Formation (Pedersen & Surlyk 1983), was early in the 20th century mostly covered by grass and had a wide low foreland protecting part of the cliff from the sea.

Stolle Klint Clay (bottom of Ølst Fm)

Stolle Klint Clay (= SKC; which was informally named by Heilmann-Clausen 1996) is a blackish-greyish, laminated mudstone with a few thin, hardened and silicified beds, and it contains a few of the earliest and numbered ash layers −34 to −39 (Bøggild 1918; Pedersen & Surlyk 1983; Heilmann-Clausen et al. 1985; Nielsen 1994). The 10–15 cm thick and whitish ash layer −33 is at the upper boundary of SKC. The fossils, plant debris, fishes, shrimps and insects are found mainly in the hardened layers, locally called 'shale' (Danish: 'skifer'; and therefore likely to be confused with the silicified layers in the Mo-clay originally called 'skifer' by Gry (1940) from around the level of ash layer −20, low in the Fur Formation; see Bonde 1997; Andersen & Sjørring 1997). The SKC contains few, if any, diatoms (Homann 1991). The fish fauna in North Jutland is clearly from open marine water (Bonde 1997), but Köthe (1990) indicates that this basal part of the ash series, at least in the North German region, seems to show a brackish influence as based upon the dinoflagellates.

No doubt the North Sea basin at this time (corresponding to the lower part of Sele Formation in the central North Sea, see Heilmann-Clausen 1985; Schiøler et al. 2007) was very restricted and nearly or completely landlocked by the 'Thulean land-bridge' (in the SW from Greenland via the Faroes to Scotland) combined with the closed 'Channel' and by the Spitzbergen-Barents shelf (in the north) in the narrow region between Greenland and the 'Scandinavian Continent' (Fig. 2; Bonde 1979, 1997; Schmitz et al. 1996; Ziegler 1990). This closure of the basin may be due to a combination of low global sea level and upheaval of the Thulean land-bridge area above the 'Icelandic hot spot' (Heilmann-Clausen 2006). Some indicate that the entire rift zone along the East Greenlandic coast and the Mohn Ridge may have been about one km above sea level (Larsen 1988) before the

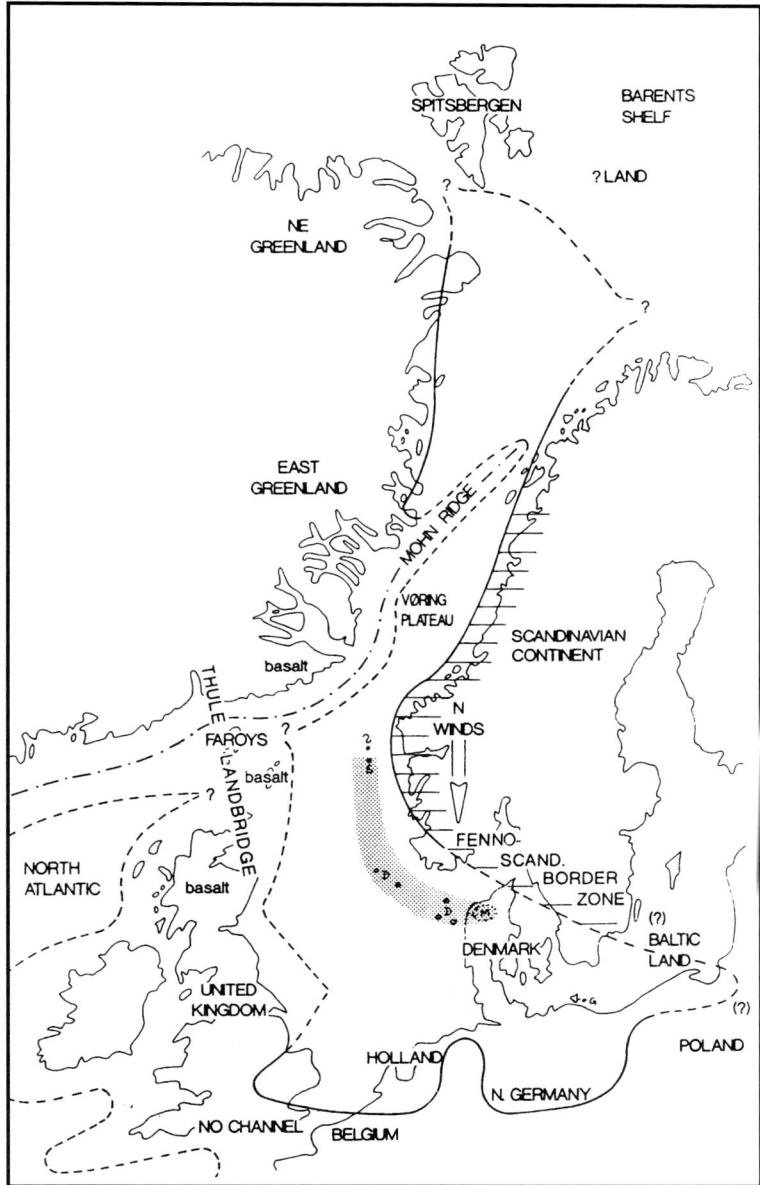

Fig. 2. Palaeogeography of the Mo-clay Basin modified from Bonde 1997. At the deposition of Stolle
Klint Clay the basin was even more restricted, presumably a totally landlocked sea. Diatomite stippled.

sea floor spreading with its gigantic volcanism collapsed the rift zone beginning about 55.5 ma.

It is notable that the few complete fish which have been found in cores from the ash series below the central North Sea (Bonde 1979, 1982, 1987, 1997) are all preserved in dark, hardened, laminated mudstones very similar to the shales of the SKC. Only one is from the upper part of the

ash series corresponding to Balder Fm, while the others are from the underlying Sele Fm (though not necessarily from its lower part). Apparently this hardened mudstone is the normal facies in the main ash series of the North Sea (e.g. Frodesen *et al.* 1981; Thomsen & Danielsen 1994).

In these dark mudstones most fishes are preserved as extremely detailed imprints (Bonde

1997, fig. 4; this *Sardinella*-like clupeid was the only species well-known from the 'shales' until collection began more intensively in the 1990s), but larger fish may be preserved with parts of the skeleton intact and apparently little changed apart from becoming dark and brownish to more or less disintegrated as a dark, crumbling, carbonaceous material (see *Xosteoglossid* below). In some cases the bone and teeth may be preserved with a bluish to whitish colour, presumably due to silicification or opalisation of the skeleton (e.g. cf. *Brychaetus*, below).

Mo-clay (Fur Fm)

The so-called 'Mo-clay' (Danish: 'Molér') is a true diatomite about 50 m thick composed of diatom skeletons mixed with about 30% clay and 10% volcanic dust (Pedersen *et al.* 2004) and for much of especially its lower part well-laminated (Pedersen 1981), thereby indicating anoxic conditions at the bottom (Bonde 1973). This is probably combined with a wind driven and coast parallel upwelling zone producing the rich plankton (diatoms, silicoflagellates and radiolaria; while calciferous microplankton was dissolved in the slightly acidic bottom water; see Bonde 1973, 1979). The predicted extent of the diatomaceous facies further towards the NW below the North Sea was confirmed by Thomsen & Danielsen (1994). The main part of the ash series is intercalated in this diatomite, constituting the Fur Formation proper (Pedersen & Surlyk 1983, as modified by Heilmann-Clausen *et al.* 1985). The basin is much expanded due to a high stand in the global oceans probably increasing the depth of the basin by some 150 m (Heilmann-Clausen 2006), but Bonde (1997) estimated 'a few hundred metres', perhaps 500 m (see below, e.g. the 'deep sea fish'), in order to explain how new, more oceanic fishes could invade the basin (Bonde 1997). This depth estimate is not unlikely, since the Holmehus Clay below the SKC (Heilmann-Clausen 2006) has a similar estimate, and the overlying Røsnæs Clay has benthic foraminifera indicating up to 600 m depth or more (Schmitz *et al.* 1996) even though the North Sea was on the continental shelf. In the North Sea drillings the Mo-clay corresponds to the upper part of the Sele Fm and the lower part of the Balder Fm (Heilmann-Clausen 1985; Michelsen *et al.* 1998; Schiøler *et al.* 2007).

Bøggild (1918) described, correlated and numbered the ash beds from +140 at the top, to −33 at the bottom (Fig. 3; also Andersen & Sjørring 1997, fig. 12), and at most localities the basal part below ash layer −17 is much more dark and clayey, and there seems to be a rather gradual

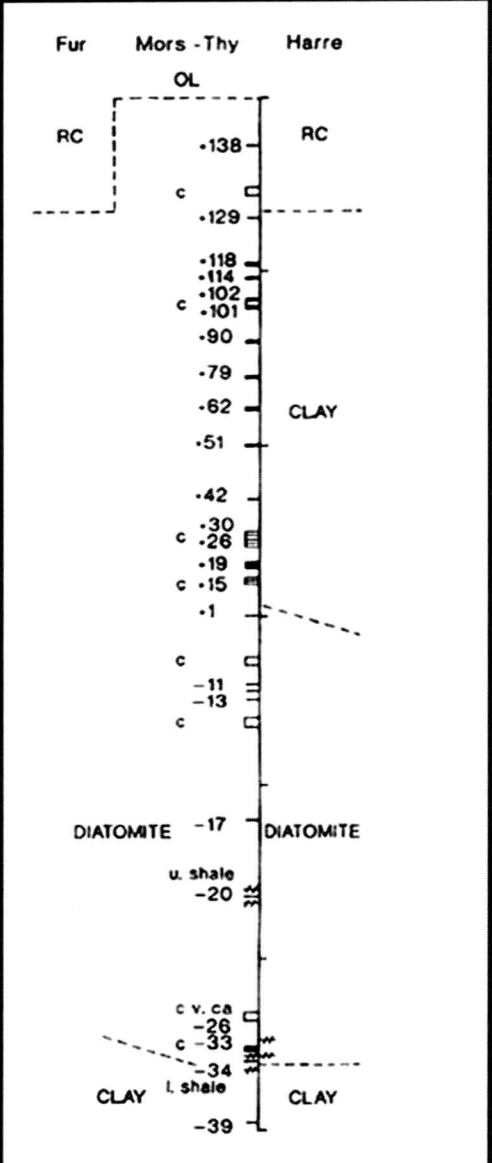

Fig. 3. Stratigraphy of the ash series modified from Bonde 1997. Numbers of the most significant ash layers, thickness per 10 m at right and cementstone levels as small boxes and the two levels for the hardened 'shales' are indicated. Harre is a borehole. OL, Oligocene; RC, Røsnæs Clay; l. shale is SKC (Stolle Klint Clay).

transition from the SKC into the Mo-clay (pers. obs.) above the thick ash layer −33. The thickest ash layer +19 is nearly 20 cm thick in NW Jutland and can be recognized in all of the North

Sea region, west of Ireland, in the Bay of Biscay and even in Austria (Egger *et al.* 2000). Bonde (2003*a*) and Egger & Brückl (2006) have estimated the amount of ash from that eruption to be thousands of cubic kilometres – an order of magnitude larger than any known from the recent historical period. The light colour of the soft diatomite, Mo-clay, is obviously a diagenetic feature due to weathering. Originally the sediment must have been an organic-rich, dark grey or black mud.

The diatomite is now light coloured (whitish to yellowish to beige/light grey) and porous with no lime, but in a few narrow horizons calcite has precipitated as lens-shaped limestone boulders, so-called cementstones, less than one metre thick (Fig. 3). Only in one level round ashes +101 and +102 was a continuous limestone bed formed, while, for example, the boulders containing −33 are far spread with perhaps 50–100 m between them and only known from the type locality for Fur Fm, Knudeklint, Fur (e.g. *Furichthys*, below). The precipitation of lime is probably conditioned by bacterial activity (Pedersen & Buchardt 1996), and would have taken place less than one metre below the sea floor. Therefore this makes a lot of difference in terms of preservation of the sediments and the fossils. The cementstones are dark grey (preserving much more of the original colour of the dark, anoxic mud) and the ash grains in them are almost perfectly fresh and they contain un-weathered glasses and mineral grains (Bøggild 1918; Larsen *et al.* 2003) and the diatoms are perfect and beautiful opal skeletons (Møller 1892; Pedersen 1981; Bonde 1987, Homann 1991; Pedersen *et al.* 1994). Chitinous skeletons of insects are preserved as a dark matter, and often colour marks can be seen as dark spots on the wings (Rust 1999; Madsen & Rust 2000; Bonde *et al.* 2007) and sometimes also on the fins of fishes (Bonde 1987, p. 21, 41).

Skeletons of vertebrates are preserved in the cementstones as calcium phosphate and can therefore be prepared out by weak acetic acid (sometimes the remaining, sticky clay can be nearly impossible to remove from the bones when the latter are small and fragile) resulting in extremely well-exposed fossils, especially of birds with skulls preserved in 3D (Bonde 1987; Kristoffersen 2002*a*, *b*). In one level of cementstones containing ash +15 sometimes the fishes (and fish coprolites) are preserved not completely flattened, but with the interior of the body between the scales from left and right with a perfect skeleton that is not filled by sediment or secondary calcite (see Bonde 1987; Pedersen *et al.* 1994) and with the skull not entirely crushed but showing a braincase with only very limited secondary calcite in its cavities. A large near complete tarpon over 1 m long was

found recently in a cementstone and has the braincase preserved in 3D, which has been removed by acetic acid (Bonde *et al.* 2007).

In the soft diatomite, the Mo-clay, insects are rarely preserved and all the fish skeletons and invertebrates like snails, bivalves, starfish and brittle stars (Rasmussen 1972) are completely dissolved leaving, however, in general perfect imprints (Bonde 1987, 1997, figs 5–6). Only rather large and strong bones may be partly-preserved in the diatomite, but most often as a dark, crumbling, carbonaceous material, which should rather be removed to expose the fine imprints (like *Heterosteoglossum*, below). Moulds in silicone or latex material of the fine imprints is a distinct possibility for the larger fossils, but with the many overlapping layers or sheets of imprints, there is obviously a risk of damaging the fossils by removing important details (if the rubber material penetrates below the thin sheets and into deep cavities in the fragile clay matrix.)

Ages

The stratigraphic age of the ash series and the Mo-clay has been controversial since 1900, sometimes recognized as Upper Paleocene, sometimes as lowermost Eocene, the problem being the lack of calciferous microplankton and correlation to the standard Palaeogene zonation (Heilmann-Clausen 1982). This was apparently overcome by Knox (1984), who could correlate the ash series to the nanoplankton zonation in the Eastern Atlantic to show that the main part of the ash series corresponds to lower part of the NP 10 zone, while part of the negative numbered ashes and SKC correlate to the Sele Formation and most of NP 9 (Schiøler *et al.* 2007). The very distinctive ash layer −17 is close to the base of NP 10 and has a radiometric age of *c.* 54.5 ma (Knox 1997), lately revised to 55.1 ma by Storey *et al.* (2007) with SKC beginning about 0.5 ma earlier. Recently it has been decided, by a stratigraphic sub-commission, that the lower boundary of the Eocene is defined as the base of the temperature optimum to be globally recognized (see below Crouch *et al.* 2001; Auby & Ouda 2003; Gradstein *et al.* 2004) and implying that the stratigraphic age of the Stolle Klint Clay is the very earliest Eocene date. The positive ash series (ash +1 − 140) correlates to lower Balder Fm in the North Sea and the total duration of the ash series (phase 2.1–2.2b) is about 1.5 ma (Knox 1997; Beyer *et al.* 2001), with the intensive ash falls of the positive series distributed over a period of about 300000 years (Knox 1997) between 54–55 ma. The ash series also marks the initiation of the volcanism and the seafloor spreading along the

East Greenlandic coast, which can be precisely correlated with these ash falls (Heister *et al.* 2001).

Faunas

Both of these deposits, Stolle Klint Clay and Mo-clay contain rich marine fish faunas (Nielsen 1960; Bonde 1987, 1997; Bonde *et al.* 2007), very poor faunas of marine invertebrates (Bonde 1979), but abundant faunas of insects – presumably blown out from the northern Scandinavian continent (described by Willmann (1990) and several of his students subsequently in Meyniana, summarized by Rust's thesis (1999); in total over 20000 specimens according to Madsen & Rust (2000); see also Andersen (1998) and Archibald & Markarkin (2006)). The Mo-clay has further provided a few planktonic crustacea (Garassino & Jakobsen 2005) and marine reptiles (Nielsen 1963; Hoch 1975) and quite a number of land birds (Kristoffersen 1999, 2002*a*, *b*; Dyke *et al.* 2004; Leonard *et al.* 2005; Lindow & Dyke 2006; Bonde *et al.* 2008).

Environments at the Paleocene–Eocene boundary

Between SKC and the underlying Holmehus Clay there is a small hiatus, some places are partly infilled by a few metres of grey, more sandy clay indicating reduced depth (Nielsen & Heilmann-Clausen 1986; Beyer *et al.* 2001). The significance of this period of (almost) non-deposition is difficult to evaluate. Perhaps the 'Proto-Icelandic hot spot dome' elevated the entire North Sea region above sea level (Heilmann-Clausen 2006). Corresponding shallow water sediments could be Woolwich Beds and freshwater deposits could be the English Reading Clay and French–Belgian Sparnacian (see Beyer *et al.* 2001).

A similar, mostly small hiatus above the Mo-clay and below the Røsnæs Clay (e.g. on Fur) is equally difficult to interpret – in the westernmost Mo-clay localities this hiatus is enormous as the diatomaceous clay conformally overlying the Mo-clay is of Late Oligocene age (Heilmann-Clausen 1997) about 30 ma younger.

SKC was deposited as an anoxic, laminated mud in a much reduced and entirely closed basin (Bonde 1979, 1997; Ziegler 1990; Heilmann-Clausen 2006, figs 10-2, even smaller than in Fig. 2) during a short period beginning nearly 56 ma ago (based on Storey *et al.* 2007) and lasting around 200000 years (according to Röhl *et al.* 2000) of increased temperature as indicated by carbon isotope studies (Norris & Röhl 1999; Heilmann-Clausen & Schmitz 2000; Crouch *et al.* 2001; Zachos *et al.* 2003; Wing *et al.* 2005). This basin seem to have

a marine, pelagic fish fauna enclosed with no clear cut representatives from a freshwater environment. However, a single fossil of a possible 'percopsiform' (listed with doubts by Bonde 1997) and some rare finds of the very osteoglossomorphs to be discussed below, obviously cannot entirely be excluded as being transported from rivers running into the basin. This basin was, according to Heilmann-Clausen & Schmitz (2000) and Heilmann-Clausen (2006, fig. 10-2), less than 200 m deep. Plant material in SKC must have been transported from land, presumably mainly by rivers. However, the general impression of the fish fauna is of a marine one comprising about 25 forms with only a few among these indicating possible affinities to benthic or near coastal fishes: a muraenid, an ariid (?) and some perhaps among the five species of clupeids and small aulostomoids, although one of each of these two groups survive into the Mo-clay basin (Bonde 1997, 2003*a*).

After this brief temperature optimum (increase 5–10°C, Wing *et al.* 2005) the warmth decreased a little during the deposition of the Mo-clay, perhaps from tropical to subtropical climate (Heilmann-Clausen 2006, fig. 10-2), and the basin increased in size and water depth. The transition to this larger and deeper basin, still almost landlocked, seems gradual as judged from the diatomaceous sediment, which, in the lower half of the Fur Fm, is dominated by periods of laminated mud deposition under anoxic conditions at the bottom (Bonde 1979; Pedersen 1981), where the stagnant and acid water was poisoned by hydrogen sulphide preventing all life but bacteria. In contrast to this, the planktonic life at the surface was rich especially in a zone paralleling the coast and governed by wind driven upwelling along the low Scandinavian continent (Bonde 1973, 1979, 1987, 1997; Thomsen & Danielsen 1994). Such upwelling in the upper 100–200 m (moving south into the closed basin by frequent and strong northern winds, as indicated by the distribution of the ash falls), was combined with a deeper counter current and below this the stagnant water was locked. The entire system probably demanded at least 500 m of water, but possible connections to the neighbouring basins may have been very narrow (through the Channel, between the Faroes and Scotland, along the Norwegian NW coast, and perhaps between NE Greenland and Spitsbergen; see Fig. 2).

Supported at the surface was a rich life of abundant oceanic, pelagic fishes, some of which ended as more or less complete skeletons in the laminated mud, undisturbed by scavengers and under very slow putrefaction, leaving the fossils sometimes with colour markings on the fin membranes (Bonde 1987). Upwards in the sedimentation, laminated periods became less frequent due to the infilling of the basin low and therefore fewer periods with stagnant water according to Pedersen (1981). Usually no lime was precipitated because of the subacidity, but sometimes for short periods the chemical environment, controlled by bacterial activity a short distance below the surface, allowed calcite to precipitate as large, flat and lens shaped concretions, or cementstones, (Pedersen & Buchardt 1996).

The change in the fish fauna between SKC and Mo-clay indicates that some connection to the surrounding oceans was established allowing more oceanic, pelagic fish to enter the basin, which, however, for most of the time may have been nearly land locked (fig. 2; Bonde 1997). The more permanent opening of the Atlantic connection through the Channel later in Early Eocene introduced southern and warmer ocean currents, even with nummulite immigration, and probably this influx destroyed at least the southern region of the upwelling zone and thereby the deposition of diatomaceous sediment in the Danish region (Bonde 1979, 1987). After this only the finest clay particles (smectite, indicating that it is a result of weathering volcanic material) reached the centre of the basin to deposit the extremely fine grained so-called 'plastic clays' of Denmark, first Røsnæs Clay then followed by Lillebælt Clay into Middle Eocene and finally the Søvind Marl ending the Eocene sedimentation in the Danish region (Fig. 4; Heilmann-Clausen et al. 1985; Graversen 1993; Heilmann-Clausen 1996, 2006; Michelsen et al. 1998).

Fish faunas and marine osteoglossomorphs

The fish faunas of the Stolle Klint Clay and the Mo-clay were mapped by Bonde (1997) indicating,

as mentioned above, that although fishes from both deposits are marine and pelagic in general, those from the Mo-clay appear much more oceanic with a tarpon, a paralepidid relative like *Holosteus*, 2–3 small zeiforms, a polymixiid, several lampridiforms, *Exellia*, probably two species of stromateoids, many scombrids, palaeorhynchids, a gempylid (euzaphlegid) and one carangid species, and a single 'true' deep sea fish, a *Rondeletia*-like cetomimiform (Bonde et al. 2007).

Apart from scales of the tarpon, none of these have been found in SKC: but, on the other hand, it has yielded such pelagic fishes as *Mene*, not occurring in the Mo-clay, and a small *Antigonia*-like fish (of which the occurrence in the negative series of the Mo-clay is a little uncertain) as well as another carangid species and a *Vomeropsis*-like species, presumably fully marine and pelagic fish. A few fishes from SKC might be considered more shallow water fishes, such as the three types of aulostomoids (two very small, the larger is also found in the Mo-clay) and the muraenid eel (and above was mentioned the dubious 'percopsi-form', a freshwater group apart from a Cretaceous relative), but the fauna does not have strong littoral affinities.

The occurrence of several osteoglossid-like species (about 6) in the two near-contemporaneous, marine faunas is therefore remarkable, as all species of this group today live in freshwater and on the southern continents with a typical Gondwanan biogeographic distribution (cf. Darlington 1948, 1957): from South America (two genera: *Osteoglossum*, (2 species and *Arapaima gigas*) via Africa (*Heterotis* [=*Clupisudis*]) and *Pantodon* – both genera monospecific) to Australia and Indonesia (*Scleropages* with 6 species or subspecies [Pouyeaud et al. 2003]). Mostly these few species are referred to one family, Osteoglossidae, with *Pantodon* closest

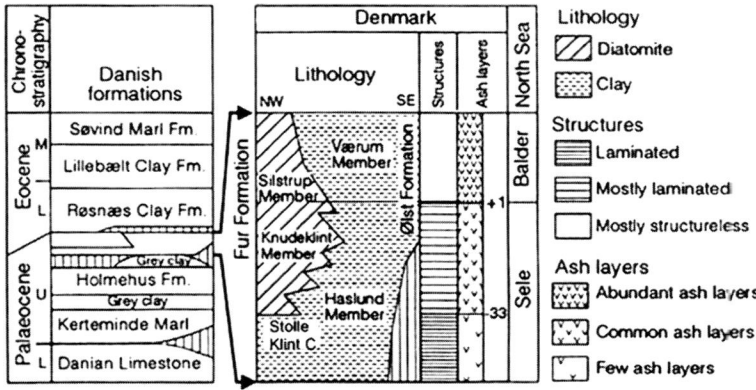

Fig. 4. Stratigraphy of Danish Eocene. Modified from Thomsen & Danielsen 1994 (with permission of the authors). Fur Fm. proper does not include Stolle Klint Clay, and both are considered Lower Eocene.

to Osteoglossinae (=*Osteoglossum* + *Scleropages*), but sometimes *Pantodon* is placed in its own family as sister-group to osteoglossids (see Taverne 1979, 1998; Nelson 1994; Li & Wilson 1996*a*, *b*; Li, Grande & Wilson 1997; Li, Wilson & Grande 1997, in contrast to Nelson 1968, 1969). Greenwood (1971) initially only specified that *Pantodon* is related to osteoglossids, and in 1973 placed Pantodontidae as sister-group to Osteoglossidae in osteoglossoids, and with all other osteoglossomorphs in its sister-group notopteroids. These remaining osteoglossomorph fishes (mormyrids, notopterids and hiodontids) today occur in respectively Africa, Africa plus South Asia and North America, and are sometimes indicated as a monophyletic sister-group to osteoglossids (Greenwood 1971, 1973). Or mormyrids plus notopterids are considered as related to osteoglossids, and hiodontids form the primitive sister-group of all the others (Li, Grande & Wilson 1997*a*; Taverne 1998 Nelson 1969) very tentatively held mormyrids and osteoglossids as closely-related and the sister-group to notopterids plus hiodontids. For this reason, the author remained uncertain concerning the placement of mormyrids (1996, fig. 4).

The last reviews of osteoglossomorphs that still consider that notopterids and/or mormyroid are most closely-related to hiodonts were by Patterson (1993) and Nelson (1994). Since the mid 1990s there seems to be general agreement that Hiodontiforms is the (plesiomorph) sister-group to all other osteoglossomorphs, constituting a large monophyletic taxon (Li & Wilson 1996*a*; Taverne 1998 and Hilton 2003), that is in need of a name. This group is called 'Osteoglossi' here (p. 296).

By the mid 1990s hiodontid-like fishes were known from middle Cretaceous (*Yanbiania*, Li 1987) and could have probably been established by mid Early Cretaceous (*Chetungichthys*, Chang & Chou 1977, accepted by Taverne 1979, and perhaps *Plesiolycoptera*, Chang & Chou 1976). Later Li, Wilson & Grande (1997) only accepted *Yanbiania* and *Plesiolycoptera* as hiodontids (and did not mention *Chetungichthys*). Cretaceous notopterids were known only from otoliths (Rana 1988), but have later acquired a better fossil record with *Palaeonotopterus* from late Early Cretaceous in Morocco (Forey 1997; Taverne & Maisey 1999), while mormyrids are generally believed to hardly have a fossil record at all. Ironically, *Palaeonotopterus* turns out perhaps to be a mormyrid relative than related to the notopterids (Cavin & Forey 2001; Hilton 2003, fig. 5), although the evidence is not that convincing, as Hilton left it unresolved (2003, p. 19, fig. 6).

Optimistically (1996, fig. 4), and probably wrongly (p. 280), I considered *Kipalaichthys* from mid Cretaceous in Congo (see Taverne 1976) as a possible relative of *Pantodon* based on very little evidence (scale similarity), as the *Pantodon* lineage has little fossil record. This changed dramatically with Hilton's analysis (2003) resulting in both most parsimonious trees showing *Singida* as sister of *Pantodon*, and *Phareodus* as sister of those two. However, the support for this was meagre, (only homoplasies, four parallelisms and two reversals), (2003, p. 24). Such fragmentary mid Cretaceous fish, as *Paradercetis* (Taverne 1976) and *Chanopsis* (Taverne 1984), if they are osteoglossomorphs at all, could well be in the stem-group of *Pantodon* and osteoglossids. The same counts for the complete and very primitive looking *Laeliichthys* from Brazil (as judged by the reconstruction by Silva Santos 1985; here right spelling contrary to Bonde 1996, fig. 4; Taverne 1998, 136 ff; Hilton 2003, fig. 2), as I stated earlier (1996). It has sometimes been placed close to heterotines (Li 1996) or even as sistergroup of only *Heterotis* (Taverne 1979), despite its Early Cretaceous age (Aptian - and Brazilian colleagues now tell, that it is not even obvious that it is an osteoglossomorph, and indicate that the reconstruction is not so easy to reproduce from the many small fossils). Freshwater osteoglossids have been reported from the French Campanian (Sige *et al.* 1997).

Phareodontines, an extinct group of osteoglossids known from Late Cretaceous to Eocene (Taverne 1979; Grande 1984; Li, Grande & Wilson 1997) is usually, and firmly, based on several characters and placed in a stem-group position as closely related to Osteoglossinae. This is interesting because the phareodontines contain a marine member, *Brychaetus*, originally described from Early Eocene London Clay (Woodward 1901; Casier 1966; Roellig 1974; Taverne 1974); and, as indicated below, it probably occurs also in the Stolle Klint Clay. It is known from the Eocene Moroccan phosphates (Arambourg 1952), from Nigeria (Capetta 1972), and Taverne (1978) referred a caudal skeleton from the Paleocene (?) of Cabinda, Congo, to the same taxon as jaw fragments of a second species of *Brychaetus*. Later Weems & Horman (1983) identified jaw fragments from Maryland as *Brychaetus*, and Longbottom (1984) mentioned *Brychaetus* from Mali (enormous jaws, pers. obs. in NHM). All jaw fragments with teeth seem fairly trustworthy, because the large bony pedicles for the oval and pointed teeth, are smooth and conical with a small, distinct 'cap' closely set in the jaws seem very characteristic of *Brychaetus*.

Eocene marine otoliths from NW Europe have been referred to *Brychaetus* by Taverne (1978), but they do look more like heterotine than osteoglossine otoliths, and Nolf (1978) has described osteoglossid otoliths from Belgian Paleocene. Considering the number of different osteoglossid-like taxa in the Danish lowermost Eocene it seems unwise to assign such otoliths to specified genera.

Late Cretaceous (Maastrichtian) marine osteoglossid otoliths have been described as *Osteoglossidarum taverni* by Nolf & Stringer (1996). It should also be noted that a tiny premaxilla from the marine Fish Clay (basal Danian at Stevns Cliff, Sealand) has been described as an osteoglossid (Bonde *et al.* 2008). The referrals of 'squamules' to *Brychaetus* (parts of reticulate scales when fragmented along the un-mineralised zones; see Meunier 1984) by, for example, Gayet & Meunier (1983) from Morocco are very uncertain. Slightly different squamules from continental Paleocene and Eocene of India and Pakistan are *Phareoides*, the genus known from the Australian mid Tertiary (Taverne 1978), but neither *Brychaetus* nor *Phareoides* has ever had their scale-structure analysed in any detail, and the former was generally, but incorrectly described with non-reticulate scales (see Bonde 1996). *Phareoides* (Li, Grande & Wilson 1997) is synonymized with *Phareodus*, as they do for *Brychaetus* (and Li [1996] has a similar suggestion for *Musperia* [Sanders 1934] from the Palaeogene of Sumatra). Li (1996) also described the oldest phareodontine, Late Cretaceous *Cretophareodus*, as primitive sister-group of all other taxa in the group (for more details about 'phareodontines', squamules and otoliths, see Taverne [1998, pp. 128–129, 136]). Recently, a *Brychaetus*-like phareodontine skull has been described as *Tavernichthys* from freshwater Paleocene in India (Kumar *et al.* 2005).

The synonymizing by Li, Grande & Wilson 1997 of five (or more) species within *Phareodus* is not necessarily the most informative, as there is a clear hierarchical structure indicating that the species *P. encaustus* and *P. queenslandicus* (Taverne's *Phareoides* [1973]) form a monophyletic group *Phareodus* with *Brychaetus* (2 spp.) as sister-group, and *Dapedoglossus testis* as sister-group of all the others (*Musperia* has not been reanalysed in this connection). So, here, I retain the generic name *Brychaetus* for the London Clay species and *B. muelleri* and the central African *B. caheni* (Taverne 1969). Two species are known to retain a small supramaxillary, *B. muelleri* (pers. obs.) and *P. ('Phareoides') queenlandicus*, presumably a primitive feature lost several times in osteoglossid evolution; (as it is also known from one of the Mo-clay species, from *Opsithrissops* (below), *Laeliichthys* and most outgroups to osteoglossomorphs – most of which actually have two supramaxillae). To imply that the presence of a second supramaxilla is an 'apomorph reversal' five times (Taverne 1998, trait no. 223; see Fig. 5) does not seem well justified. Loss of supramaxillae has occurred independently many times in teleostean evolution. 'Dollo's law' should be obeyed here: a lost organ does not reappear.

Another marine osteoglossomorph contemporary with the forms in the ash series is *Opsithrissops* (Danil'chenko 1968; described as 'chirocentrid' meaning an ichthyodectid) from Danatinsk Series in Turkmenistan from the basal Eocene (Tyler & Bannikov 1992): it is a large osteoglossid (as pointed out by Patterson [1975] and Bonde [1975]). Taverne (1979) placed it in phareodontines near *Brychaetus*, although no phareodontine synapomorphies among the three that are claimed by Taverne (which *Brychaetus* also possesses) were demonstrated in *Opsithrissops*. Taverne (1979, fig. 13) gave a new and certainly better reconstruction based soley on Danil'chenko's reconstruction of the entire fish and his published photo of the skull. No further documentation appears to have been published about these big fish reaching 122 cm in length and known from three specimens (Danil'chenko 1968; 130 cm in length quoted by him in 1980).

Danil'chenko's drawings are not trustworthy in detail. They are very schematic, not showing nearly as much skeletal details, e.g. in the skulls, as can be observed in the fossils (I have closely scrutinized some lampridiforms from the Danatinsk deposits kindly brought to Copenhagen by Dr V. Fedotov). His reconstructions of caudal fins are usually unrealistic, even concerning the number of fin rays and his description (1968 in translation) and figure of *Opsithrissops* do not correspond, (the reconstruction has 23 principal caudal rays, which is very unlikely). None-the-less Taverne's interpretation is not unlikely – just unvalidated by facts.

Taverne recently (1998) completely abandoned his earlier views on *Phareodus* and other species by looking at the phylogeny of osteoglossomorphs from a non-quantitative, cladistic angle with arguments turning especially around parsimony and investigating around 300 features in a characterization of monophyletic groups in the entire osteoglossomorph hierarchy. He dissolved his subfamily phareodontines entirely (although it is also supported by Li & Wilson 1996*a* and Li, Wilson & Grande 1997 – which are, however, only briefly mentioned in Taverne's Appendices 1 & 2, not really discussed), distributing them as two paraphyletic groups of osteoglossiforms, one in stem-group position, the other more derived and related to *Pantodon* plus osteoglossines. The greatest difference concerns the genus *Phareodus* itself, which, instead of being an advanced relative of osteoglossines, now has a position as a very primitive, even paraphyletic, stem-group to crown-group osteoglossids (Taverne 1998, fig. 22; Fig. 5) as the

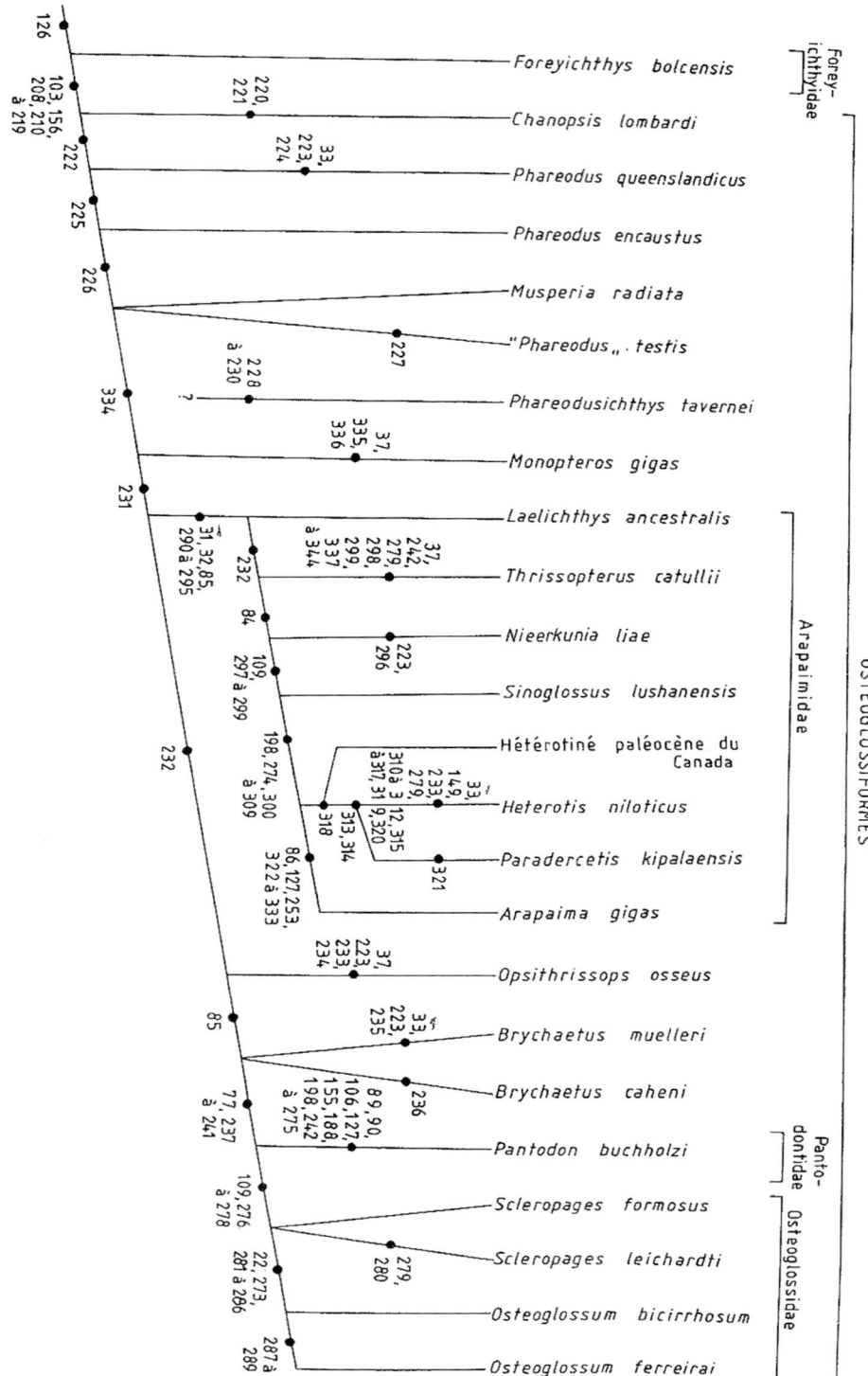

Fig. 5. Osteoglossiform phylogeny/'cladogram' from Taverne (1998, fig. 22 – permission from the author).
Concerning *Foreyichthys* it should be moved to a position as most advanced member of the Osteoglossid (+*Pantodon*)
stem-group above *Brychaetus*. Numbers are traits; e.g. 223: supramax. present ('reversal').

first splits within Osteoglossiformes after the very incomplete, dubious and mid Cretaceous genus, *Chanopsis* (cf. my doubts in 1996). Now only *Opsithrissops* and *Brychaetus* are placed successively as relatives to osteoglossines (in his 1998 paper considered a family like its extant sister-group, Arapaimidae, earlier called 'heterotines'). Hilton's analysis (2003) gave the untraditional result, that *Phareodus* was closest to *Pantodon* (and *Singida* – see below), but he unfortunately did not include *Brychaetus* in his analysis (neither did he include *Opsithrissops, Phareoides, Musperia* nor other Eocene forms known from complete fossils like *Foreyichthys, Monopteros* and *Sinoglossus*).

Taverne's analysis (1998) was prompted by the description of three more marine ostoglossomorphs, all from the Monte Bolca fish fauna of Mid Eocene age, *c.* 5 younger than the Mo-clay. Of these forms the big and high-bodied *Monopteros* specimens are very poorly-preserved, hardly showing the precise outline of any skull bones (Taverne 1998, fig. 3 & pl. I; pers. obs.) nor any details of the caudal base. But it can be accepted as an osteoglossomorph with: its huge pectoral fins, tiny pelvic fins, 17 principal caudal rays, dorsal fin placed opposite the anal fin, many vertebrae and very long ribs, as well as cycloid scales of which some show superficial reticulation with tuberculated 'squamulae' (Taverne 1998, fig. 5), and they also have pores (pers. obs.). Although not well-preserved and fragmentary known *Monopteros* can be precisely placed (according to Taverne) as the most advanced member of the stem-group to crown-group osteoglossiforms (arapaimids + pantodontids + osteoglossids), based on the large number of vertebrae slightly more derived than *Dapedoglossum ['Phareodus'] testis* (by Cope 1877; Taverne 1998, fig. 22; Fig. 5).

Foreyichthys

The small Bolca fossil *Foreyichthys bolcensis* (first named with a reconstruction and an overview of its description by Taverne 1979, before being mentioned in Forey's thesis (1970) as cf. *Platinx macropterus*) was finally described in detail (Taverne 1998, 91 ff. and photos of the only specimen having no counterpart, pl. VI & VII; NHM P 16.821). There is also an improved reconstruction (*ibid.*; fig. 12), and more details from the skull, caudal skeleton and part of a scale (*ibid.*; figs 13–15). I here add some details from notes and drawing made 1974 and 1992 and some checked in 2005: Taverne has shown one tooth at the symphysis of the lower jaw, although two seem preserved, and furthermore the proximal premaxilla with part of the ascending process and with two stout teeth can be seen even in his photo, pl. VI. The process nearly

reaches the tip of the nasal (presumably near the midline), of which the posterior boundary is difficult to see. There is a frontal with a laterally placed sensory canal and no indication of an anterior broad lappet. The proximal 'maxilla' fragment indicated by Taverne seems to be placed too far up and could instead be part of the premaxilla. Behind it, however, there appear to be more of a slim maxilla (dental margin not seen) reaching nearly to what seem to be traces of the quadrate below the posterior part of the orbit, although, admittedly, it is difficult to be sure of the exact position of the articulation and therefore the length of the lower jaw. This has consequences for estimating the length of the horizontal branch of the preopercular (not preserved) which I would estimate longer (and, therefore, more primitive) than reconstructed by Taverne. The posterior part of the endopterygoid shown by Taverne with a deep notch is perhaps metapterygoid (as in *Osteoglossum*), and in front of this a tooth patch of the endopterygoid (right) can be seen paralleling the parasphenoid. On the latter, just above the metapterygoid notch, there seems to be a weak trace of the basipterygoid process partly hidden by some lime. The bones limiting the orbit are not so clear, and I believe the anteroventral part of Taverne's orbithosphenoid is rather the parethmoid (Taverne, pers. com. 2007, does not agree) while his small 'lateral ethmoid' could as be the mesethmoid. Behind the orbit only the inner side of one large (right) infraorbital can be seen in between remains of crushed bone, while further down, level with the 'quadrate' (?) and the missing horizontal preopercular, another inner surface of a large flat bone seems exposed, perhaps part of a very large and deep infraorbital 3 (as in extant osteoglossiforms). There seems to be a trace of a narrow anterior infraorbital just below the parethmoid (like in osteoglossids). A pterotic with a canal/groove is seen with a subquadratic parietal above it and the temporal foramen, as indicated by Taverne, but between epiotic, parietal and supraoccipital there is also a matrix infill, which might hide a foramen or depression. Behind the epiotic a tiny triangular fragment perhaps, with a canal indicated is seen which might be a small supratemporal, and behind this is a large posttemporal (or perhaps extrascapular). The tiny subopercular is seen merely as an imprint on the inner side (not on the outside) of the opercular, which is large and D-shaped. The preopercular has striations on the narrow dorsal branch and near the corner, and a horizontal ledge hiding the slime canal, but the horizontal branch is not preserved and therefore of unknown length. Below the ventral arm of the large cleithrum the coracoid is seen, perhaps with a large foramen indicated. There are about 70 vertebrae, half of these abdominal with a supraneural above each neural spine in front of the long, low dorsal fin opposed to a slightly shorter anal fin. Epineurals are seen in the anterior abdominal region, with no epipleurals, but very long, strong ribs. It cannot be said with certainty that hypural 3–5 are fused to each other and to ural 2, and it is difficult to see the free hypural 6, and to me parhypural and the hemal arch of preural 2 are probably autogenous – altogether a more primitive caudal fin than described by Taverne. The most remarkable feature, rightly reconstructed by Taverne, is the large path of very big and stumpy teeth in the bottom of the mouth, which must have been placed on the 'tongue'.

My conviction is that, *Foreyichthys*, despite its more primitive caudal fin, is a little more osteoglossine-like than indicated by Taverne (who concluded that a monotypic family Foreyichthyidae is sister-group of all Osteoglossiformes [1998, fig. 22; Fig. 6], based on one synapomorphy the lack of basisphenoid, a feature

very difficult to confirm in a small, crushed, fossil braincase [and it might stay cartilaginous in that size of fish]). Of 13 features said certainly to link *Foreyichthys* to osteoglossiforms plus mormyriforms (Taverne 1998, p. 143) I find only 3 of them (characters (ch.) 1, 3, 35) somewhat doubtful, and the same counts for 3–4 of the 13 'probable characters' (ch. 41 [especially if Taverne's boundary between the upper infraorbitals is correct], 45, 57 and perhaps 63), while character 44, the notch in endopterygoid, probably is in metapterygoid instead as mentioned above. On the other hand, three of the six osteoglossiform + mormyriform characters said to be missing cannot easily be checked in *Foreyichthys* (ch. 103, 212, 216) and character 222 is a bit dubious being involved in a reversal. More advanced features found in *Foreyichthys* are large nasals meeting (ch. 226 – therefore reduced dermethmoid), a long, low body (ch. 232), high number of vertebrae, c. 70 (ch. 334), and – if Taverne is right, which I doubt – a caudal skeleton with fused ural 2 + hypural 3–5 (ch. 5), further loss of frontal expansion (ch. 237) and open (reopened in Taverne's model) interorbital septum (ch. 238).

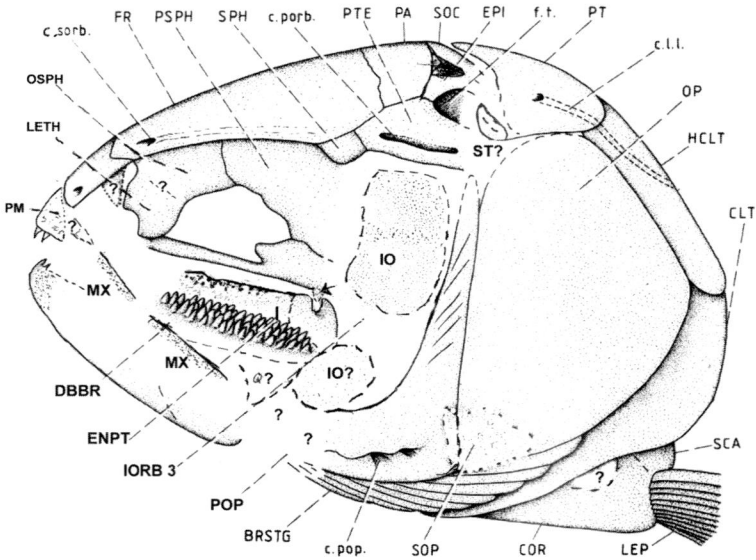

Fig. 6. An improved reconstruction of the skull of *Foreyichthys*, modified from Taverne 1998. BRSTG, branchiostegal ray; c.l.l., lateral line sensory canal; c.pop., preopercular sensory head canal; c.porb., postorbital sensory head canal; c.sorb., supraorbital sensory head canal; CLT, cleithrum; COR, coracoid; DBBR, dermobasibranchial; ENPT, entopterygoid (= endopterygopid); EPI, epiotic (= epioccipital); f.t., fosse temporale; FR, frontal; HCLT, hypercleithrum (= supracleithrum); IO, infraorbital; IORB, infraorbitals; LEP, lepidotrichia; LETH, lateral ethmoid; MX, maxilla; OP, opercular; OSPH, orbitosphenoid; PA, parietal; PM, premaxilla; POP, preopercular; PSPH, pleurosphenoid; PT, posttemporal; PTE, pterotic; Q, quadrate; SCA, scapula; SOC, supraoccipital; SOP, subopercular; SPH, sphenotic (= autosphenotic); ST, supratemporal (= extrascapular). Arrow, ?basipterygoid process.

The latter two traits, both reversals, place *Foreyichthys* after *Brychaetus* at the base of *Pantodon* plus Osteoglossidae. Accordingly it should be placed in Taverne's implied classification (1998, figs 21, 22) as described below.

Osteoglossomorpha
  Hiodontiformes
    †Ostariostomidae [*Ostariostoma*]
    †Lycopteridae [2–3 gen.]
    Hiodontidae [incl. 3–4 extinct genera]
  †Huashiidae [2 gen.]
  †*Kipalaichthys* [? – family unnecessary]
  †*Singida* [ditto]
  Mormyriformes
    †*Palaeonotopterus* [added in this study]
    Notopteridae
    Mormyroidei
      Mormyridae
      Gymnarchidae
  Osteoglossiformes [†*Foreyichthys* more advanced, moved downwards]
    †*Chanopsis* [?]
    †'*Phareodus*' [= †*Phareoides*]
  †*Phareodus*
    Taxon A
      †'*Phareodus*' [= †*Dapedoglossum*] mut.
    †*Musperia* mut.
      †*Phareodusichthys* mut.
    Taxon B mut.
      †*Monopteros*
      Arapaimidae
        †*Laeliichthys* [?]
        †*Thrissopterus*
        †*Nieerkunia*
        †*Sinoglossus*
        Arapaima
      Heterotinae
        †*Joffrichthys* [= Taverne's 'Paleocene Heterotine, Canada']
        †*Paradercites* [?]
        Heterotis
      †*Opsithrissops*
      †*Brychaetus* [2 species]
      †*Foreyichthys* [placed here by me]
      Pantodon[-tidae]
      Osteoglossidae
        Scleropages
        Osteoglossum

† = extinct, 'mut.' means *mutabilis mutandis*, that those taxa can be interchanged due to lack of precise knowledge; [..] are author's changes or remarks, e.g. if the extinct taxa (†) have more than one species. This classification is strictly cladistic (phylogenetic) and without unnecessary absolute ranking, the convention being that in a monophyletic group a taxon (fossil or recent) is sister-group to all groups listed (sequenced) below it at the same relative rank (here marked by identical indentation). If a taxon name is needed for mormyriforms plus osteoglossiforms, those two groups should just be given 'lower rank' by extra indentation. This system could be made entirely non-Linnaean, if terminal taxa (species) were given only one name (e.g. the generic name without capitalizing – see Bonde & Westergaard 2004). If the very dubious taxa marked [?] (see also below) are removed from this classification, there remains very little inconsistency concerning stratigraphic age of the remaining taxa – and, therefore, there is no need for extremely long 'ghost lineages' (Norell 1992), apart from in Mormyriformes, in which very few fossils are known (there is an Eocene–Oligocene notopterid and the mid Cretaceous *Palaeonotopterus* [perhaps a mormyrid?] and undescribed notopterids of the Early Cretaceous [Taverne, pers. comm. 2007]).

The third Bolca osteoglossomorph, the very slim *Thrissopterus*, has never been studied by me. It seems well described and analysed by Taverne (1998), who concludes that it is a primitive relative of his arapaimids (*Arapaima* plus *Heterotis*). It is slightly more advanced than mid Cretaceous *Laeliichthys* based on one synapomorphy shared with 'higher' arapaimids (reduced height of the body; and increase of vertebral number should be added – further critique in the phylogenetic discussion below). It has eight other apomorphies shared with arapaimids, three of which are reversals, one convergent, and one further, which *Thrisopterus* reverses together with three more reversed features. So its position is not so clear cut. The position of *Laeliichthys*' is equally tenuous, being based on just the same features but one, although without the four last reversals, simply because it is so primitive. In 1996 I doubted its position as arapaimid, and I still do (see further sceptical remarks above). The only arapaimid stem-group member I have studied is the Eocene *Sinoglossus* (in prep.) and that may well be an arapaimid sharing the important fusion of antorbital and infraorbital 1 with such fishes, but, when checked against Li & Wilson's character lists from 1996*a*, and correcting their coding for wrong and 'unlikely' observations, it was discovered that it might equally be placed in osteoglossids, and is, therefore, of rather uncertain phylogenetic position.

Hilton's new cladistic analysis and classification (2003, fig. 7; Fig. 7) has notopterids as sister-group of osteoglossids (instead of mormyrids), and it comprises only few fossil taxa, but these, especially the osteoglossids, are placed in

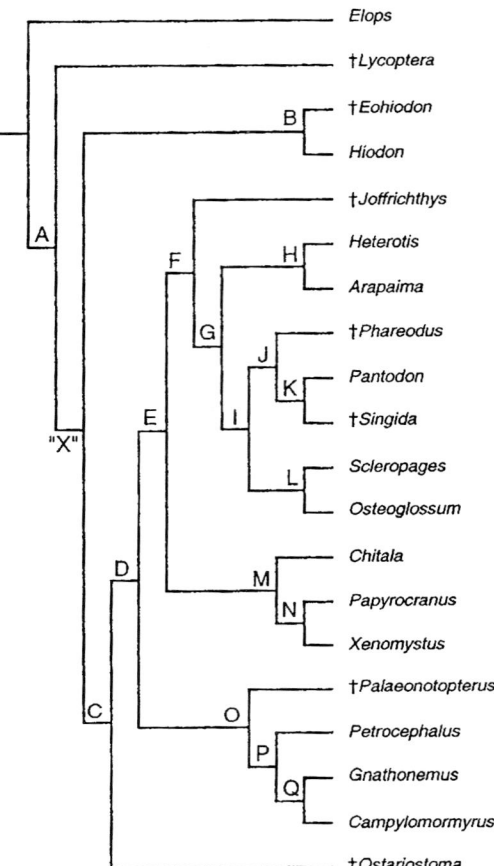

Fig. 7. Hilton's cladogram (2003, fig 4B) (reproduced with permission of the author). A, Osteoglossomorpha; X, its crown group; C, Osteoglossiformes, its crown group; D, unnamed; F, Osteoglossidae, its crown group; G, unnamed; H, Heterotinae; I, Osteoglossinae (B, E, J–L, see pp. 299–300).

very different relationships from those indicated by Taverne. *Joffrichthys* is sister-group of all other osteoglossids, and within these *Phareodus* and *Singida* are placed in osteoglossines related to *Pantodon* and *Osteoglossum* plus *Scleropages*. Further *Ostariostoma* is most closely-related to all crown-group osteoglossiformes, not to hiodontids. This analysis is based on 72 characters from 19 terminal taxa and one outgroup (*Elops*) with a consistency index of about 0.6, which is difficult to compare with Taverne's analysis. But the latter comprises 37 terminal taxa with three outgroups (Ichthyodectiforms, Elopomorphs and Clupeocephalans), and one can count about 50 parallelisms (= same number repeated) in his two trees (Figs 21, 22) based upon changes in about 300

different characters (somewhat difficult to count), presumably meaning 50 parallelisms out of 350 steps, which is about about 15%. To this should be added at least the same number of 'reversals' (even more difficult to count precisely, and mormyriform and hiodontiform features not scrutinized in detail), adding up to at least 30–35% homoplasies in total. That is about same level as in Hilton's analysis (about 40%) – so the two may be 'equally good' in terms of parsimony.

Descriptions of Osteoglossomorphs

Heterosteoglossum foreyi n. gen. & sp.
(Figs 8–14)

The generic name is a hybrid of *Heterotis* and *Osteoglossum*, alluding to its similarity to *Heterotis* in the shape of the short jaws and high mandible, the corresponding shape of the long ventral branch of the preopercular, the slight bend of the parasphenoid which may be toothless, the small pelvic fin and the position of the mesocoracoid, while the upturned mouth, the profile of the head, the very elongate body and the many vertebrae, the large pectoral fins, and to some degree the relation between dorsal and anal fins are more *Osteoglossum* like. The specific name is in honour of my friend and colleague Dr Peter Forey, Natural History Museum, London, UK, who for over three decades has enriched us with detailed descriptions and cladistic analyses of primitive teleosts, including osteoglossomorphs.

Diagnosis and phylogenetic relations are given below. (Diagnoses are here understood as [probable] autapomorphies and placed *after* their respective descriptions, because logically the diagnoses follow from the descriptions. The diagnoses are here not just abbreviated descriptions mixing plesiomorp and apomorph features. In fact it could well be argued that diagnoses are not possible before the phylogenetic analyses are finished, because from such analyses follows which features are accepted as autapomorphies).

Holotype MGUH 28.904 (DK 255; Danekræ, see note p. 305). From laminated diatomite (Mo-clay) in the 'negative' ash series of the central mo-clay pit near the highest point, Stendal Høje, on the Isle of Fur, North Jutland, DK. Found *in situ* between the ash layers −13 and −17 in the wall of the quarry in 1997. Almost complete, lacking the posterior caudal region and fin and part of the dorsal fin, with less complete counterpart plate lacking more of the postero-dorsal body region.

Fig. 8. *Heterosteoglossum foreyi*, holotpe, MGUH 28.904 (DK 255), right side of the nearly complete fish. Imprint in diatomite, Mo-clay, between ash layers −17 and −13 in the lower part of Fur Formation. Mo-clay pit at Stendal Hills, Fur. Fish as preserved 89 cm.

Over one metre long. Illustrated also in Bonde *et al.* 2008. Age: Earliest Eocene, about 55 ma.

Referred material. The holotype is the only more or less complete specimen and comprises the only known skull. Two smaller caudal regions with the tail fin appear to be of the same species, NHM P.23946/47, (figured by Taverne [1998, fig. 17–18, Fig. 12] as an indeterminate osteoglossiform) found in 1938 by Walter Kühne around ash layer −18 in Skarrehage (northern) pit, northern Mors, N-Jutland, DK, and a corresponding specimen, also from the Skarrehage Quarry (southern pit at the time) found in the 1980s by Bent Søe Mikkelsen. Both caudal regions are with counterparts and preserved as imprints in laminated diatomite from the 'negative' ash series. They can be referred to this species entirely due to the reticulate scales (all other osteoglossiform fishes from the ash series have scales that are much less reticulated or not at all). Hundreds of isolated scales, rounded and oval, in the Mo-clay and cementstones as well as in Stolle Klint Clay are of this reticulate type, the largest nearly 5 cm high, many unregistered and several in the I. P. Andersen collection in Geological Museum, Copenhagen, registered under 1954.469, some in the W. Kühne collections in GMC (registered under 1938.67) and four collected by him in NHML (one figured by Taverne 1998, fig. 16) and large numbers in Fur Museum and Molermuseet, Mors – this species must have been quite common despite the find of only the above three specimens of well articulated fossils. There is also a single scale from London Clay division B at Aveley, NHM P.65206, which on the label is referred to *Brychaetus*, but it seems to be fundamentally like scales of *Heterosteoglossum*, and not like those of the big skulls in the phosphatic concretions (derived from division D – see King 1981 and Beyer *et al.* 2001). Div. B (now Walton Mb.) is very low in the London Clay, just above division A comprising the Harwich ash layers, now the Harwich Fm, corresponding to part of ash series in

the Mo-clay, so this scale is probably not much younger than the Danish specimens). Ages: *c.* 55.5 ma to *c.* 54 ma (or possibly slightly younger).

Description. The holotype (Figs 8–11) is an almost-complete fish, lacking part of the dorsal fin and the posterior caudal region with the caudal fin.

Measurements. The standard length is estimated about 100 cm, total length just over one metre. As it is preserved in several pieces the fossil is about 89 cm long, and missing probably *c.* 10 cm of the caudal vertebrae and hypurals, indicating about 100 cm standard length (which, with a caudal fin estimated over 10 cm, gives a total length around 110 cm). The precaudal region is about 70 cm and, of this, *c.* 18 cm would be the head. Maximal body height is 16–17 cm, slightly more than the head (*c.* 15 cm). Orbit length 2.5–3 cm, postorbital skull *c.* 9 cm, and opercular width and height *c.* 5 × 7 cm. Scales are oval, a little higher than wide and from 1–1.5 cm high. Lower jaw length is *c.* 6.5 cm.

Summary of meristics. About 100 vertebrae (*c.* 87 preserved) of which *c.* 56 are abdominal.

Fins: Dorsal, about 35 rays, *c.* 16 cm base. Anal *c.* 45 rays, *c.* 22 cm base. Ventral, 7–8 rays, 4 cm long. Pectoral, 1 large plus 15, *c.* 10 cm long. Caudal (from referred specimen), 9 + 9 principal rays.

Skull (Figs 9–11). As preserved the left side imprint seems a little more distinct than that of the right side. Little detail of the mesethmoid-vomer may be distinguished and no teeth be seen, and in some parts of the right preorbital region the surface with the imprint and a few millimetres of sediment laminae have split off leaving no anatomical structure to be seen. The same has happened to part of the skull roof on the right side. The parethmoid is broad and obvious on the left side (almost destroyed on the right), but details are difficult to distinguish on its lateral face. Whether a dermal

Fig. 9. *Heteroseoglossum foreyi* holotype, fragmentary counterpart to the skull preserved as a more detailed imprint than the main plate. Skull length *c.* 15 cm.

antorbital component is present, perhaps fused to the surface, seems uncertain as there is no trace of a sensory canal. There is a dorsally placed, distinct, oval structure, which may represent the ophthalmic foramen. The basal part appears wide laterally and perhaps also at the medial end close to or at the parasphenoid, and to what degree a mesethmoid part is involved cannot be seen; that region appears low and smooth. Neither can the relation of the parethmoid to the infraorbitals be determined.

The parasphenoid is gently bent down in front, probably jointly with the (pre-)vomer, which however, may not be clearly distinguished (no teeth on either bone are seen). The parasphenoid is a rather straight and slim rod between the orbits, which are not closed by an interorbital septum or down-growths from the pleuro- and orbithosphenoids. The posterior, ascending part of parasphenoid, although impossible to outline in detail, bends up about 135°, and just above the bending there is a deep imprint of what has to be

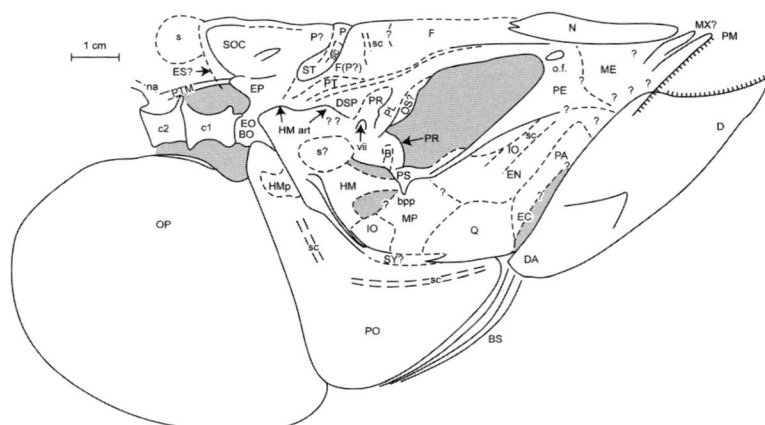

Fig. 10. *Heterosteoglossum foreyi*, reconstruction of the skull combined from both slabs, but based mainly on a camera lucida drawing of the left slab. Abbreviations used in the text and figures (excluding Figures 6 and 12): bpp, BP, basipterygoid process; c (1, 2), centra (no. 1, 2); na, neural arch; o.f., ophthalmic foramen; s, scale; sc, sensory canal; AN, angular; AR, articular; ASP, autosphenotic; B, basisphenoid; BH, basihyal; BO, basioccipital; BR, branchial element; BS, branchiostegal; D, dentary; DA, dermarticular; DSP, dermosphenotic; EC, ectopterygoid; EN, endopterygoid; EO, exoccipital; EP, epioccipital; ES, 'extrascapular scale'; F, frontal; HM, hyomandibular; HMart, hyomandibular articulation; HMp, hyomandibular process; IO, infraorbital; L, left; ME, mesethmoid; MP, metapterygoid; MX?, maxilla?; N, nasal; OP, opercular; ORB, orbit; OS, orbitosphenoid; P, parietal; PA, palatine; PE, parethmoid (lateral ethmoid); P–E, palato-ectopterygoid; PL, pleurosphenoid; PM, premaxilla; PO, preopercular; PR, prootic; PS, parasphenoid; PT, pterotic; PTM, posttemporal; Q, quadrate; R, right; RAR, right articular; SO, subopercular; SOC, supraoccipital crest; ST, supratemporal; SY, symplectic; V, vomer; VII, facialis foramen.

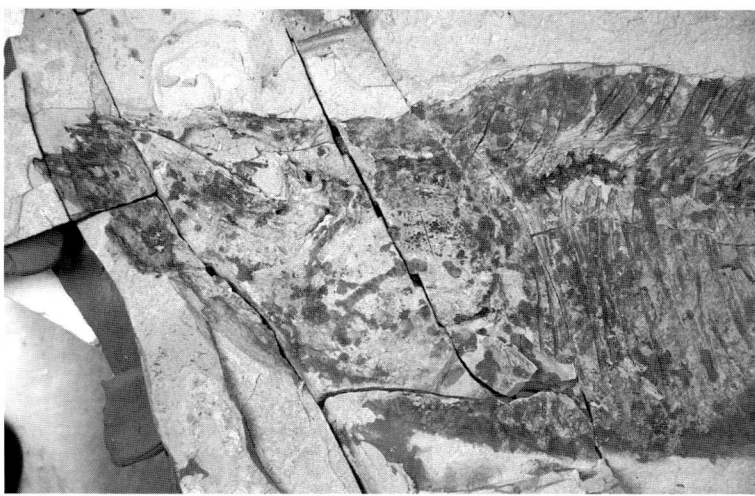

Fig. 11. *Heterosteoglossum foreyi*, holotype, anterior region of the main plate. Skull length 15 cm.

the basipterygoid process pointing lateral and a little downwards. In the medium plane between the anterior edge of the ascending processes and/ or that of the prootic is seen a subrectangular and smooth imprint of what most likely is a small vertical basisphenoid. This configuration would imply a rather high posterior myodome, and perhaps traces of the prootic bridge above it are visible. Above this ascending process is seen the lateral surface of the prootic with a dorsal depression, which is probably the foramen for the hyoid branch of the facialis. A little behind this the surface appears reticulate as if it (and possibly the anterior head of hyomandibular) were covered by a scale (or the bone surface has cracked?). Above the facialis foramen is a strong lateral process, which must be the dermosphenotic. In front of the prootic it is lined by pleurosphenoid, which has the anterior edge set off, or this part might be the orbithosphenoid in a very posterior position – if not, there seem to be no obvious trace of an ossified orbithosphenoid, neither in the dorsal nor the anterior part of the orbit. Dorsally the orbit is covered by a long frontal of which the lateral edge gives a deep near perpendicular depression into the diatomite without showing any evidence of a supraorbital. A large and long nasal is pressed up in vertical position anterior to the frontal, and has a zig-zag suture against frontal rather than a straight one. Broad anterior frontals seem unlikely.

Below the orbit is a large and smooth (dorsal) surface of the endopterygoid adjacent to the parasphenoid, and darkened by the colour from the eye ball. In the anterior part of the endopterygoid a patch with small teeth is indicated on the right

counterpart plate. Imprinted into its surface a distinct, squarish depression apparently is continued backwards with sub parallel edges, widening a little, then tapering off, and it is difficult to interpret, although it may be one of hypo- plus ceratohyals displaced into a very high position (see branchiostegals below). The remaining palate is difficult to distinguish, apart from the quadrate of the right side with its posterior process forming an angle about 100° with its anterior edge, along which the ectopterygoid area is weakly indicated and probably in continuation forward with the palatine, but no teeth are visible. A symplectic cannot be safely outlined. While the border between the metapterygoid and quadrate is vaguely distinguishable, the dorsal and anterior limits of the metapterygoid is very uncertain. The infraorbitals should cover this palatal region, but cannot be distinguished unless a rather straight groove on the right plate is the upper edge with the canal from the anterior of these bones, which in that case cannot have been very deep.

Above the sphenotic a long lateral edge of the pterotic is seen, and medial to that the broader posterior part of the frontal showing traces of the supraorbital sensory canal, perhaps with a branch toward the midline (unless this part is really the fairly long parietal [?] reaching the midline). Behind this is a nearly oval area apparently with an arched sensory canal also reaching the midline. This element most likely is a flat supratemporal, perhaps with the canal continued at the posterior edge of a small parietal (so the size of parietal is uncertain). The pterotic buts against the epi- and exoccipital area at its posterior end, and the former has a strong posterolateral point. Above that is a very flat, vertical area close to the dorsal outline of the skull, presumably a quite high supraoccipital crest, and in the region between this crest and epioccipital are impressions of what is most likely the dorsal branch of the posttemporal. The exoccipital area meets or combines with the basioccipital to form the articulation for the first vertebral centrum, and the latter dorsally caries a forward pointing process reaching the exoccipital. Finally one should note that behind and above the supraoccipital crest is a narrow rim of what may be a large element like a huge, lateral, extrascapular scale covering most of the area behind the skull roof as in *Osteoglossum, Heterotis* and *Arapaima* figured by Taverne (1977).

On the left side in the postorbital region it is possible by a fine distinction between smooth and ornamented surfaces (pitted imprints) to differentiate between endo- and exoskeletal bones. In this way the smooth, long, triangular process on the anterior edge of hyomandibular can be seen pointing towards and just below the basipterygoid process on both plates. With a regular ornament of tiny tubercles a part of the large infraorbital behind the eye is vaguely outlined at a level slightly deeper, that is, lateral to the smooth process. While the anterior edge of the ventral branch of the hyomandibular is a strong deep imprint, the dorsal head is missing on the left plate and is only vaguely indicated by the shape of the articular areas of the pterotic behind and sphenotic (and pterotic?) in front. But the divided head is well indicated on the right plate just behind the deep print of dermosphenotic, and the opercular process is seen as a distinct imprint in the surface of the dorsal branch of the preopercular. This branch is rather narrow and smooth and continues ventrally bending slightly backwards along the opercular, then turning forward by a rounded posteroventral corner (seen best on left side), which has some few and weak ridges converging away from it indicating direction of growth, as also occur on the substantial and rather long horizontal branch, that reaches forward to the lower jaw. It seems as if the openings of the sensory canal are pushed back from the anterior edge by a broad, smooth bone lamella. The opercular is large, measuring *c*. 7 cm in height, and it is 5 cm wide and nearly oval, but with an almost straight anterior edge and fine ridges on the surface radiating from the articular area, again in the direction of growth. Sub- and interoperculars are not visible, and the region below the opercular most likely is occupied by the smooth surfaces of the anterior parts of cleithrum and coracoid (below).

On both sides the lower jaws are preserved with the articular region far posterior and a very short retroarticular process, and perhaps the outline of a rather short dermarticular (here used as a term for the combined articular, retroarticular and angular, which cannot be seen as separate elements in these Eocene fishes – but cf. *Furichthys* below). The two posterior pores for the mandibular canal can probably be seen as well as one pore in the anterior half of the dentary. The lower jaw length is just above 6 cm, and the height of the posterior region is 2 cm and it is slightly higher in front. The anterior edge is strongly curved downwards and then forwards (in a very clupeid-like way) to a low and pointed symphyseal region, that is split open, and along the edge it carries small, pointed teeth in a single row. On the left side a shallow, elongate premaxillary is seen pointing forward with small teeth in a row on its ventral edge, and no dorsal ascending process to be seen. Just above it another slim bone points forward, presumably the anterior process of the maxilla, while the distal end of this bone is impossible to outline and no teeth are seen, perhaps the maxilla was quite small and more or less covered from the lateral side.

Imprints on the surface of the ventral part of the preopercular of a few long and slender branchiostegals perhaps make the interpretation of the very high position of the ceratohyals (above) less likely. Little is seen of the tongue and branchial skeleton, namely two elongate, near horizontal fragments just below the posterior orbit on the left plate; they must be epibranchials, and a small oval tooth plate seems attached to these elements.

Girdles and fins. There is a strong cleithrum of which the broad ventral branch can vaguely be seen on the right counterpart plate below the opercular that covers its dorsal edge as well as the anterior edge of its broad dorsal branch, which does not quite reach the level of the vertebral column. The dorsal end is overlapped by an elongate supracleithrum, apparently with a sensory canal indicated. The dorsal part of the bone is difficult to outline, probably being partly hidden by the opercular and partly obscured by the vertebrae. The posterior part of a strong, broad coracoid is seen on the left plate showing a distinct, oval fenestra near the posterior border where it meets the small, triangular scapula along the edge where its round foramen appears to be placed. At the anterodorsal part of the scapula is a deep and distinct, ovoid impression near the anterior edge of cleithrum; it must be the mesocoracoid arch in an anterior position as in *Heterotis* (Greenwood & Thomson 1960, fig. 2; Taverne 1977, fig. 111). Four radials seem mainly supported by the scapula, and they articulate against the strongly downward-bent bases of the pectoral fin rays. The anterior or upper fin ray is very large with the shaft c. 6 mm wide, unbranched but distally segmented, the second ray is not quite as big and this and the remaining c. 14 rays are branched and decrease in size. The length of the fin is c. 10 cm.

Although the pelvic (ventral) fin is not very big the pelvis is substantial, triangular-shaped, about 4 cm long and quite high, c. 2.5 cm near the posterior border where there is a strong ridge from the fin articulation reaching the dorso-lateral corner. Furthermore there is a flat, smooth structure 'blurring' two sets of rib-imprints distally just behind the pelvis; probably this indicates an extensive, near vertical postpelvic process 2 cm long and 1.5 cm high. The pelvic fin is rather small for such a very long fish, the longest ray is only c. 4 cm long, and there are 7–8 fin rays, the lateral one segmented and unbranched and much stronger than the other branched rays, of which the internal one is branching nearly from the base. The fin articulation is placed below the 44th vertebral centrum.

The anal fin begins below centrum number 63 and has the anterior radial (pterygiophore) touching the hemal spine of number 57. There are c. 33 segmented rays preserved, but with 6–7 rays missing in front, and probably a few are missing at the posterior end. Only 21 rays are preserved in the referred specimen P. 23946 (Taverne 1998, fig. 17), but the two referred specimens show that the last anal ray is below preural centrum 7, and the posterior dorsal ray above preural 8. So the type must have had nearly 45 anal rays (and in front on first radial most likely were further 2–3 tiny unsegmented rays). The holotype shows the dorsal fin beginning above centrum no. 71, and with the strong first radial pointing to the neural spine of no. 66, which is the first one without a supraneural connected, so there are 65 of these. Only 3 tiny unsegmented rays and ca. seven longer rays are preserved as the unsegmented bases of c. 2 cm length (indicating rays about twice as long). A few radials are preserved above centrum no. 83, and combining P. 23946 with the estimated lack of about 10 vertebrae in the holotype, indicates that the dorsal fin probably had about 35 rays (26 are preserved in P. 23946). So both fins have a rather high number of rays compared to most osteoglossiforms (but there are more in *Osteoglossum*), but the fins are rather short and retreated in relation to the length of the fish because of the extended abdominal region.

Axial skeleton (Figs 8, 12a, b). The anterior vertebra articulates with the basioccipital and apparently has dorsal contact (zygapophyses?) on the exoccipital. The anterior centra are c. 1 cm long and almost as high, and in total about 87 vertebrae are preserved, and 10–12 posterior caudal vertebrae seem to be missing. So a total count of c. 100 vertebrae is most likely with c. 56 being abdominal,

which means a very long abdominal region. The centra are 'primitive' with many thin ridges as horizontal, lateral lamellae and not very deep excavations (Fig. 12a). The ribs are very long and strong reaching the ventral border, and the first pair appears to articulate on the second centrum itself, while the following ribs are attached to parapophyses at the anterior end of the centra. There are 'bunches' of epineurals at the anterior 31 vertebrae, 6–8 cm long and starting from the first vertebra, probably its neural arch, which is difficult to see, however. There are no epineurals in the caudal region, and no epipleurals are ossified. There are thin supraneurals with a slight backward bend in the dorsal end and approaching to the first 65 neural spines. Epineurals did not reach below the dorsal fin, and accordingly none of these bones can be seen on the referred caudal regions (Fig. 12; Taverne 1998, fig. 17).

The posterior caudal vertebrae are only preserved on the two referred caudal regions, P. 23946 (Fig. 12a) has 22 centra plus the separate second ural (U2; Fig. 12b), its counterpart P. 23947 has a few more vertebrae, but in very poor state of preservation, and the fossil from Molermuseet has only about 14 vertebrae. Taverne's description (1998, fig. 17–18) is mostly confirmed (Fig. 12b): a separate second ural centrum (U2) is fused to a plate of 'fused hypurals 3-5' (H 3–5, if interpreted as by Taverne); the dorsal part of this element (H6?) appears separate, but the proximal 'dividing line' is perhaps only caused by the edge of a scale. But if this is interpreted as by Hilton (2003, 80) the two probable bones would be H3 and H4 (with no 'fusions', but U2 + H3), and a pattern like *Pantodon* (fig. also in Greenwood 1967). The narrow element above it in the first case could be a separate uroneural (UR? – or, as it seems unpaired, an epural; less likely according to Hilton [2003, 74–77]). The broad H1 and H2 are separate, the parhypural with a strong proximal head is autogenous like the hemal arches with long spines in front of it. The neural arches with long spines are fused to the centrum of a separate U1 (?) and to the posterior preural centra (PU1, etc.). Arrows (Fig. 12b) are pointing to the fin rays likely to be the outer, unbranched principal rays giving a count of 18 principal rays (9 + 9). Branched elements are not actually preserved, and the shape of the fin is unknown.

Scales (Figs 12–14). The scales of the holotype are very characteristic and of a type found very often as isolated scales in both Mo-clay (Fig. 14) and Stolle Klint Clay in many different sizes from 0.5 to c. 5 cm in diameter. Those of the holotype (Fig. 13) vary from less than 1–1.5 cm in height, and they are rounded or oval (height greater than width/

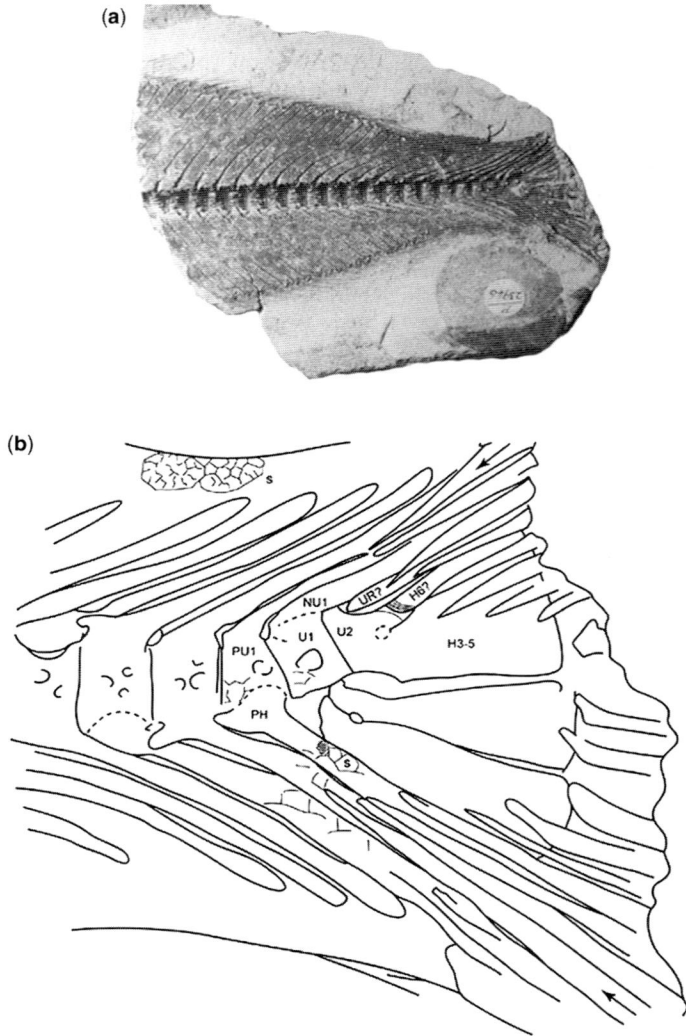

Fig. 12. (**a**) *Heterosteoglossum foreyi*, NHM P. 23946, caudal region, right plate. Skarrehage Mo-clay Pit, North Mors, near ash layer −18; (**b**) NHM P. 23946, camera lucida drawing and interpretation of caudal base and scales (s), with the four last preural centra measuring *c*. 1 cm, H, hypural; NU, neural arch of ural vertebra; PH, parhypural; PU, preural centrum; U, ural centrum; UR, uroneural.

length); accordingly 5 cm scales indicate a much bigger fish, perhaps over three metres long. At the nucleus (centre) the scales are clearly reticulate as in most living osteoglossiforms, that is divided into small irregular and angular squamules by narrow, unossified fissures lined on the inner surface of the scale by thin ridges, so that each squamule forms an angular dish with the edges turned in. Further there are tiny pores through the squamules ending on the inside surrounded by a small hill or tubercle on an otherwise smooth surface apart from the very fine concentric circuli (growth lines) crossing over the borders of the squamules. When the scale is just a few millimetres wide (<5 mm) the typical reticulation tends to disappear at the posterior, free margin (but the pores remain for a few millimetres), while the pattern of unossified zones changes to become irregular radial at

Fig. 13. *Heterosteoglossum foreyi*, holotype, scales from the ventral border. Scales *c.* 1.5 cm high.

the anterior (basal or covered) end. The external surface of the scales shows a very fine tuberculation and very fine circuli, while the same pattern of unossified zones show up as very narrow grooves. When preserved as imprints in Mo-clay the external surface has fine pits and a pattern of very narrow ridges, while the inner surface has a central area with small pits and reticulate grooves transforming into irregular fissures with very fine growth lines crossing them. The posterior (apical or free) area is covered by ornamentation of very fine tuberculation and only little reticulation if any.

On the referred specimens a few small scales (*c.* 3 mm long) are very evidently reticulate with very fine circuli. Two such scales are clearly seen above the posterior preural vertebrae at the dorsal margin of P. 23946 (Fig. 12b), and furthermore such reticulation is clearly visible imprinted onto the surface of many of the bones (in Fig. 12b only shown on parhypural). So I cannot at all agree with Taverne (1998, p. 101) that the scales are poorly preserved and show no reticulation. These small, reticulate scales are the sole reason for referring the two caudal specimens to the same species as the holotype, because the small scales correspond to the central fields of the larger scales – and no other form of osteoglossiform in the Mo-clay shows this typical reticulation of the scales. The closest match today would be *Pantodon* and mormyrids as described by Hilton (2003, fig. 39) although not identical.

Diagnosis. Characteristics of the new taxon *Heterosteoglossum foreyi*, that is its autapomorphies, are the body proportions with *c.* 100 vertebrae and a very long abdominal region (far distal retreat of the anal and dorsal fins), the scales with central reticulation transformed through growth to a radiating pattern in the anterior field and tending to disappear in the posterior, free area. Probably also the large number of pectoral rays and possibly the very wide parethmoid (unless a feature of distortion?) and the bending down of the anterior parasphenoid. The gently angled preopercular with fine ridges, and probably the extremely short retroarticular process are also diagnostic features, as are the tiny teeth in the

Fig. 14. Two isolated scales of *Heterosteoglossum*, inside imprints in diatomite, from W. Kühne collection MGUH 1938.67, and one scale, external face, in cementstone MGUH 1935.32 (scale in mm).

jaws and the shape of the lower jaw (somewhat like *Heterotis*).

Relationships. The phylogenetic relations are discussed below. Features showing osteoglossiform affinities are the large first pectoral ray, the long ribs without epipleurals, and the large number of vertebrae with only epineurals. Likewise the reticulations of the juvenile scales, and remnants of dividing the scale into squamules with fine external tuberculation, and pores through to the inside ending on small hills. Further the basipterygoid process and the anterior hyomandibular process, as well as the possibly fused palato-ectopterygoid, and the large opercular and preopercular are typical for osteoglossiforms.

Brief remarks on way of life. Heterosteoglossum is a large fish, the holotype is over one metre long, and isolated scales indicate size over three metres with diminutive teeth. Today some osteoglossiforms take prey (fish, amphibians, insects and other invertebrates) by jumping out of the water after it (*Osteoglossum*, the arawana captures amphibians and insects both in and above the water, *Pantodon* perhaps also has similar behaviour). Such food objects must have been also targets for four of the Danish extinct species that had large teeth. Extant *Heterotis* with small teeth in the jaws and with short and high lower jaw is a plankton feeders with a suprabranchial organ forming a spiral over the slit between fourth and fifth branchial arches (see Taverne 1977, fig. 110). Here slime and plankton is concentrated before being swallowed. There is no trace of the posterior branchial arches preserved in *Heterosteoglossum*, so a similar way of feeding would be unsupported guesswork. On the other hand, this type of jaws and teeth found in *Heterosteoglossum* are hardly those of a piscivorous fish, and the gape of the mouth seems rather big. With the extremely rich plankton from an upwelling zone (Bonde 1979, 1996) as the source of the diatomite, life as an oceanic plankton feeder is a distinct possibility (perhaps supported by its very large size).

Furichthys fieldsoei *n. gen. & sp. (Figs 15–19)*

Named for the island Fur and the late Erik Fjeldsø Christensen (deceased 1996), palaeobotanist, once director of Fur Museum, collector of the larger part of the holotype and later the referred specimen; he traced the German finder of the holotype and borrowed it for the museum (that later bought this specimen through funding by 'Statens Museumsnævn'); he was a staunch supporter of the concept 'danekræ' (Bonde *et al.* 2008: 7, 204) since the 1980s (see note, p. 305).

Holotype FUM-N 1440. The large fish, with skull and scattered fragments of the abdominal region, found by a German collector in the 1980s on the beach at Knudeklint, Fur. It is preserved with counterpart in a cementstone containing ash layer −33 in Fur Museum. Referred specimen, FUM-N 1848A, also in Fur Museum, posterior skull and anterior abdominal region in 'striped cementstone' including the ash layers around −25, at Stolle Klint, Fur; no counterpart.

Age. Earliest Eocene, about 55 ma. Illustrated also by Bonde (1987), Christensen (1994), Bonde *et al.* (2008: 7).

Description. The holotype is preserved in a large cementstone *c.* 85 cm in diameter (Fig. 15). It exposes almost all the bones of the flattened skull as exposed in the fossil, which means that in general the surfaces of the bones are not visible, making their precise identification difficult and outlines sometimes impossible to indicate with any certainty. The entire opercular region and pectoral girdle is not visible, some of it is hidden in the matrix. The better part of the skull with most of the thickness of the braincase is in the smaller right side counterpart of the stone (Figs 16–17). There are scattered vertebral centra, ribs and scales, but no indication of the shape of the body. The referred specimen is in a 72 cm long block, cut in two a little behind the pectoral girdle (and with a third small fragment). It shows the postorbital part of the skull, the pectoral region and part of the abdominal region with *c.* 35 vertebrae. Although incomplete both at the dorsal and ventral line the fossil confers the distinct impression of a rather high-bodied fish with a gentle arch to the dorsal profile and a deeper ventral profile (perhaps somewhat like *Phareodus*, but with a more horizontal skull roof and pointed snout). Its vertebrae indicate a fish that is probably about the same size as the type specimen, and it is estimated that the two fishes were between 1.5 and 2 m long.

Skull (Figs 15b–18). Lower jaw is *c.* 25 cm long and the skull roof *c.* 25 cm long (length of skull and braincase is difficult to estimate, but perhaps 30–35 cm long plus 7–8 cm opercular), height of the skull *c.* 25 cm (Figs 15–16). As preserved the braincase is about 5–6 cm wide, and although crushed by the sediment, it is difficult to escape the impression that the skull roof has been comparatively narrow, which seems somewhat at odds with the very heavy premaxillary (see below). As the braincase is split right through the skull roof, the sutures cannot be seen and the precise shape of the bones remains uncertain. There is, however, a

(a)

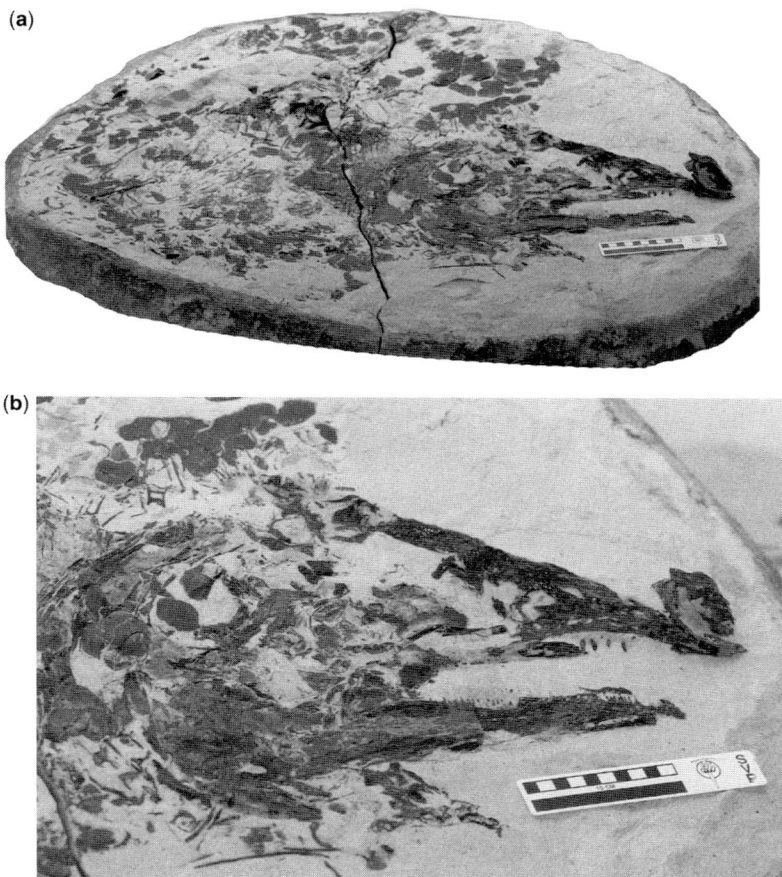

(b)

Fig. 15. (**a**) *Furichthys fjeldsoei*, holotype, Fur Museum, main block of cementstone *c*. 85 cm wide with left side; (**b**) *Furichthys fjeldsoei*, holotype, left side skull region with four strong teeth from left maxilla, and right premaxilla in original position. Scale = 10 cm.

strong ethmoid-vomer complex (Figs 15b–17) with a large path of tiny teeth on the vomer forming an elongate, oval tooth field (Fig. 17a, c). The extent of mes- and parethmoid is not obvious. Borders between nasal, frontal and parietal elements cannot be determined. Dermosphenotic and auto-sphenotic are indicated above the orbit, which is of very moderate size, and the remaining elements of the braincase cannot be outlined.

From the palate only the quadrate and the metap-terygoid are partly-preserved. The parasphenoid may be represented by a toothpath of tiny teeth behind and a little above the vomer, but otherwise cannot be seen. A large part of endopterygoid is pre-served (no visible teeth), and there is an excavation for the basipterygoid process, which is itself cut

through. Much of the large palato-ectopterygoid is preserved with a part of its dentition of fine teeth seen in the posterior end. It seems uncertain where the quadrate is preserved. Some fragments of one may be seen on the right plate near the articu-lar surface of the left jaw. On the same plate a triangular bone pressed on top of the lower jaw in front of the right articular may be the right quad-rate – or perhaps rather a high 'coronoid process' of the angular (Fig. 16b, Q?).

Of the upper jaw only part of the very strong right premaxilla is seen, it was acid prepared after being chiselled out of the block (Fig. 17), and its distal end has eroded away, so there must have been a few more teeth than preserved now (actually this heavy, black, eroded premaxilla was the bone

276 N. BONDE

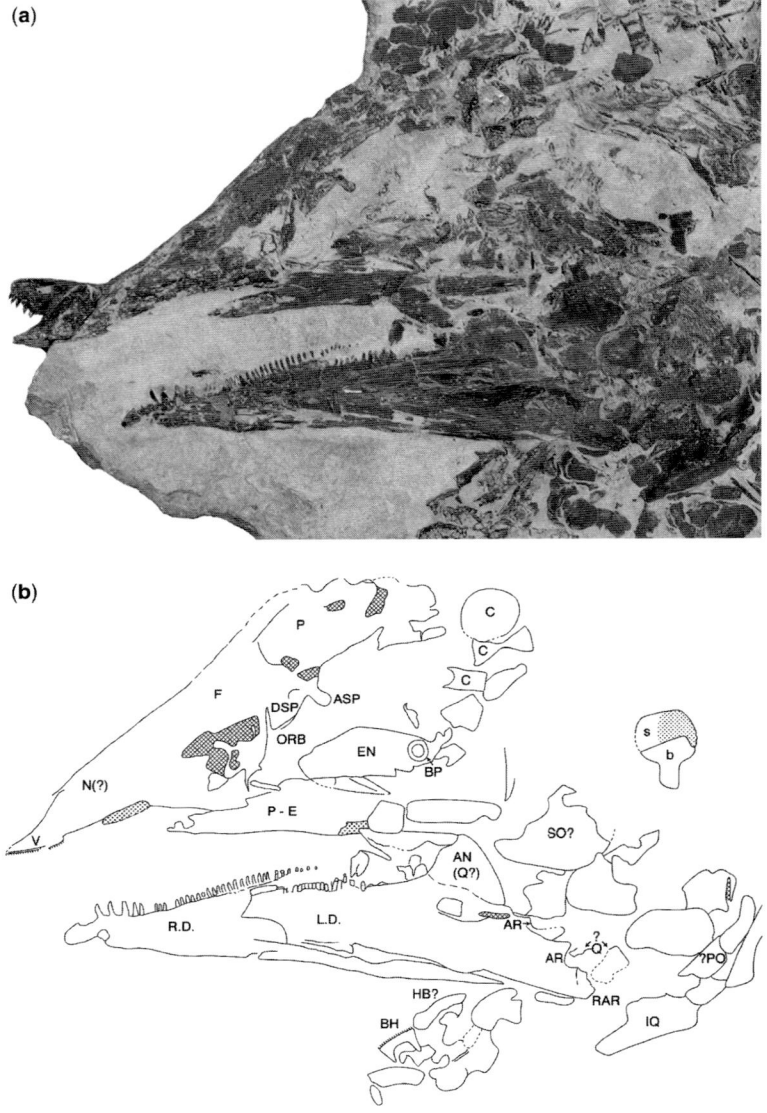

Fig. 16. (**a**) *Furichthys fjeldsoei*, holotype, Fur Museum, skull region, right side; (**b**) interpretative drawing of skull, right side. Lower jaw *c*. 25 cm long. HB?, perhaps hypobranchial; IO, interopercular; b, bone fragment; other abbreviations p. 268.

spotted by the collector on the surface of the stone). The proximal end is stuck into the large left plate, but not much can be hidden, so it is remarkable that this very heavy bone shows no traces of an ascending process. The thick body of the bone as preserved leans on a sloping surface of a strong ethmoid ossification, which appears fused to the vomer. The thickness of premaxillary as seen from above is near 4 cm, and the width of the dentigerous edge is 2 cm, about the same as the height

of the bone, which is not compact, but hollow. The two premaxillae must have formed a very strong 'rostrum' on the snout supported by a heavily ossified ethmoid, and here preserved a few centimetrs above its natural position in relation to the vomer (Fig. 17). The premaxilla has a very heavy dentition with four smaller teeth in front (one [or more] still in the large block) increasing in size backwards, then follow three much stronger teeth, the largest *c*. 13 mm high and 9 mm wide at the base, and the

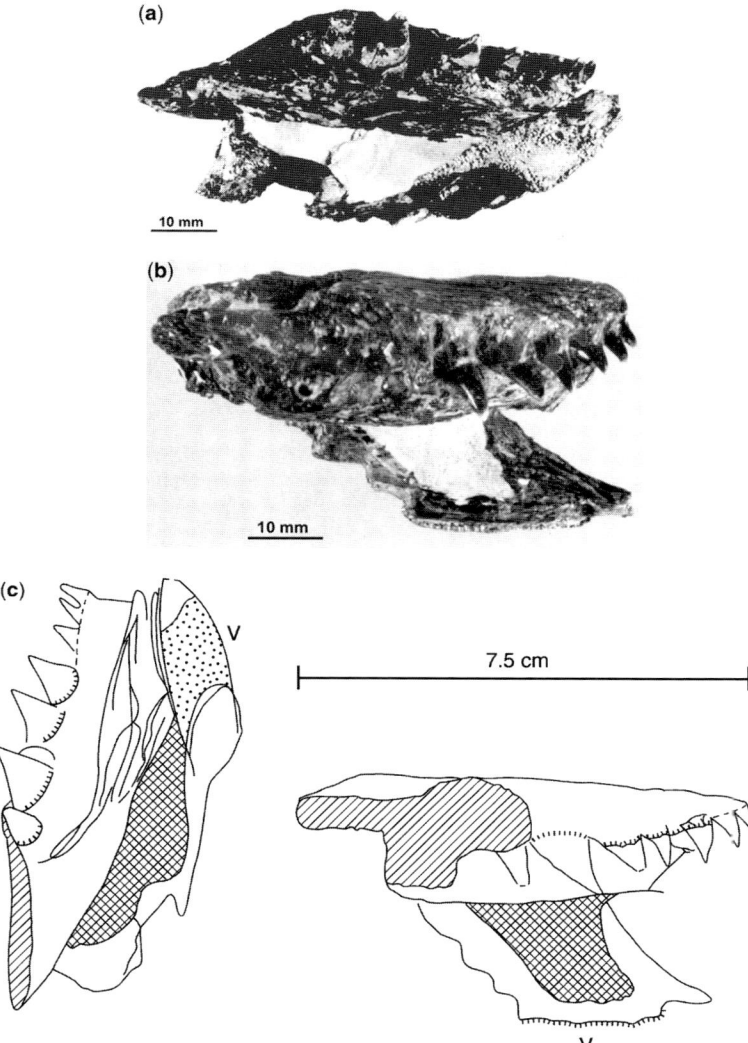

Fig. 17. (a) *Furichthys fjeldsoei*, holotype, right premaxilla and mesethmo-vomer ventral sight with vomerian tooth plate; (b) same, seen from right side; (c) interpretation of (a, b). V, vomerian toothplate; diagonal shading indicates sectioned bone; cross-hatching, matrix.

last to be seen is smaller again, but a few more (2–3?) are likely to have been lost by erosion. These teeth are robust, conical with smooth surface and indication of a cap-like point. They are carried on low bony pedicles. The tooth row is almost straight and its angle with the median plane (as defined by the elongate vomerian tooth field) is near 45°, and the incomplete premaxillary extends *c.* 4 cm lateral from the median plane. This means that when this right premaxillary-vomer complex is fitted onto the left plate and its vomer at the same time touches the right plate on its lateral face, the

angle at the symphysis would be about 90° making the snout quite broad, at least 10 cm at the posterior end of the bone, not narrow as expected from the skull roof. Four strong conical teeth of the left maxilla are visible, smaller and slimmer than the big premaxillary teeth, but nothing of the hidden bone itself can be seen as prepared at present.

Both branches of the lower jaw (Figs 15–16) are well-preserved and some of the lateral surface of the right dentary is seen. The bone appears quite thin and narrow, and the lower jaws rather fit the

(a)

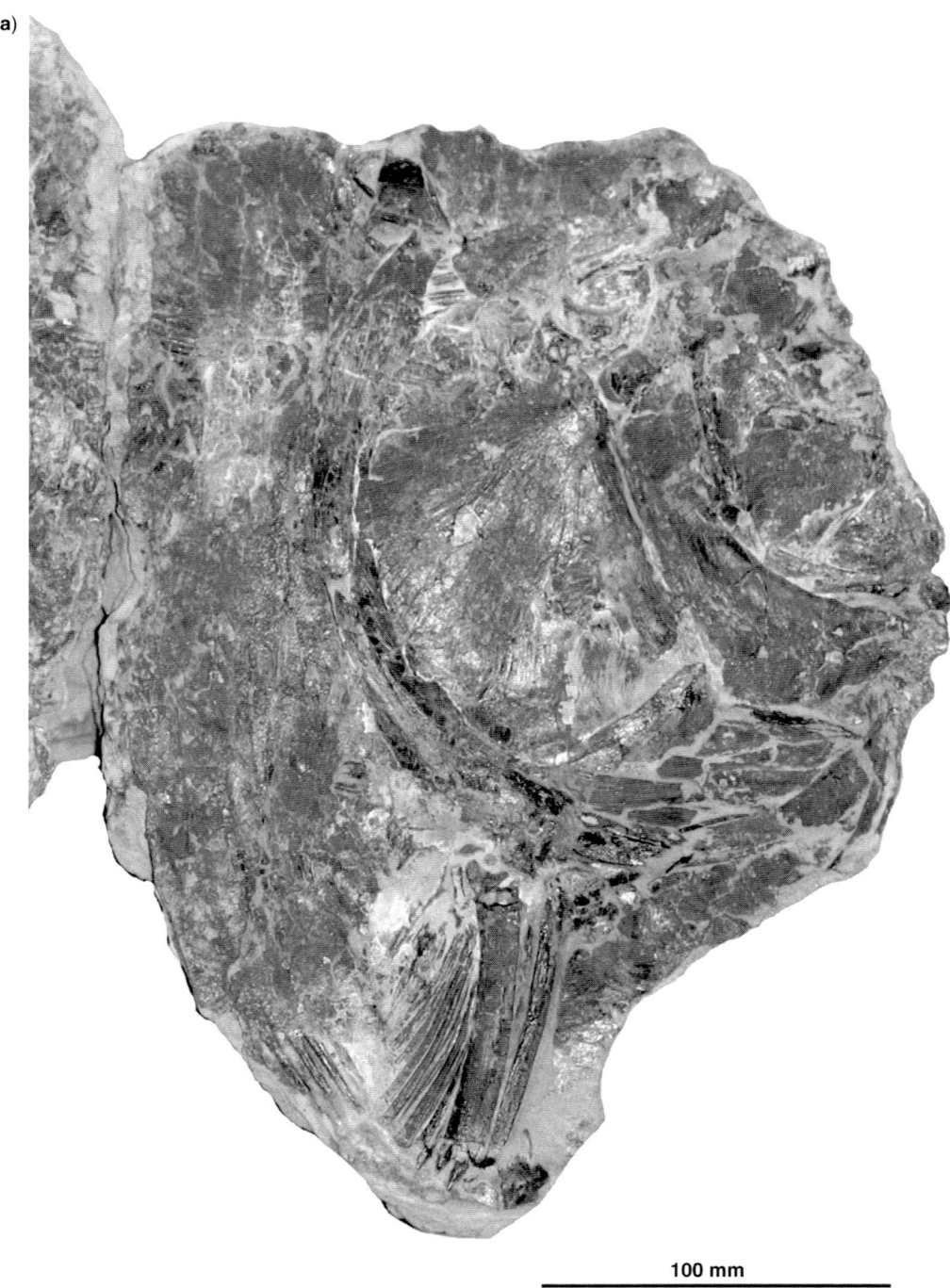

100 mm

Fig. 18. (**a**) *Furichthys fjeldsoei*, referred specimen, Fur Museum, in 'striped cementstone', right lateral face of entire specimen; (**b**) interpretation (made from transparent paper on top of specimen) of (a) anterior part, opercular and pectoral region. CL, cleithrum; CO, coracoid; HY, hyoid arch; P1, first pectoral fin ray; SC, scapula; SCL, supracleithrum; other abbreviations p. 268.

(b)

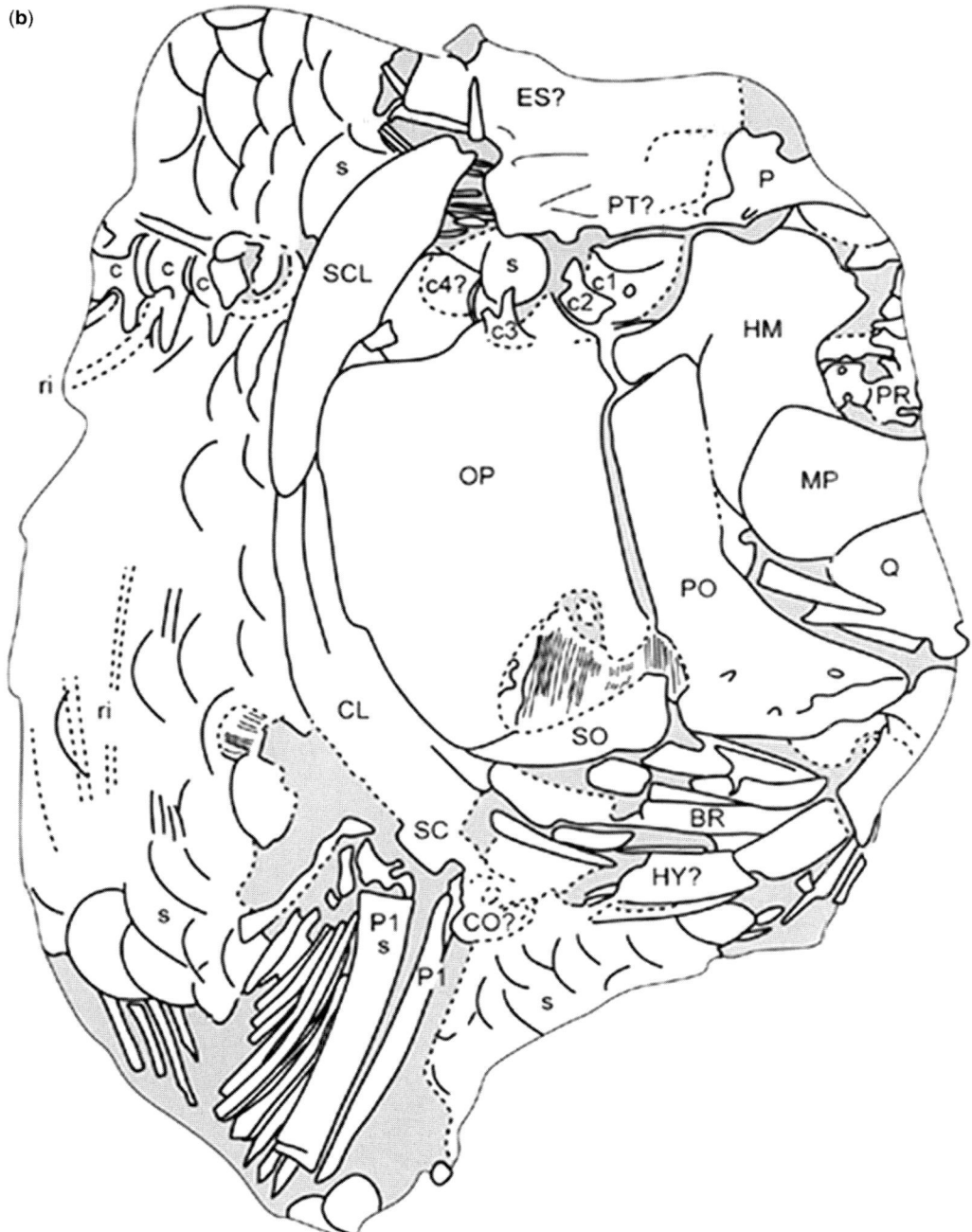

Fig. 18. (**b**) (*Continued*).

picture of a narrow snout. The dentaries appear to have the symphyseal region preserved in front, and they are long, *c.* 25 cm, and low, *c.* 5 cm high, with numerous teeth in one row (about 40 teeth 7–8 mm high in the middle of the jaw, slightly decreasing in size backwards). All of these are sub-cylindrical with a distinct pointed 'cap', and they are attached directly to the jawbone without

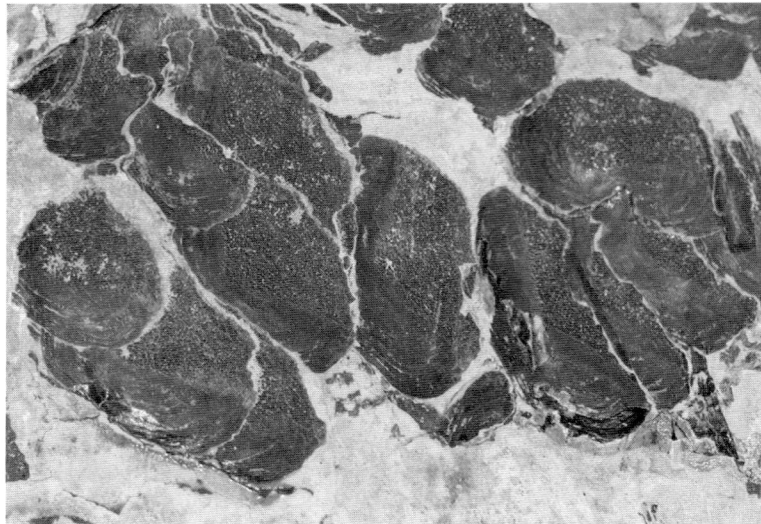

Fig. 19. *Furichthys fjeldsoei*, holotype, scales, anterior left. The larger scales *c*. 4 cm high.

pedicles. There is a strong retroarticular process and a 'half-open' suture from the bottom of the posterior part of the articulation, indicating that the bone is only partly fused into the dermarticular. The 'glenoid' is directed backwards and upwards, curving nearly 180°. On both plates it is evident that the lower jaws are preserved in a position, where they cannot reach the tip of the upper jaw. They have to be moved forward *c*. 10 cm to close the gape.

Part of the tongue can be seen below the lower jaw, but which bones are represented seems very uncertain. One of them with many small teeth on its dorsal surface perhaps is a basihyal. A few thin bones below the articular end of the lower jaw presumably are branchiostegals. Of the cheek only few fragments are visible, probably part of a large rounded infraorbital, and perhaps fragments of preopercular and interopercular. Most of the bones of the right side could still be hidden in the stone, however, and part of a large bone has been prepared free. Several detached vertebral centra are scattered in the region behind the skull. They are *c*. 25 mm high and very short, only *c*. 13 mm long. Some rib fragments are seen, but none of the postcranial bones are in articulation.

The postorbital region is well exposed on the referred specimen, it has been cut just in front of the quadrate articulation and a little behind the eye, and apparently (nearly) all elements preserved are seen from the lateral, right side (Fig. 18a, b; the entire thickness of the fish being hidden in the stone). Part of the prootic is visible with some foramina difficult to interpret.

Above it the dermosphenotic region is not well delimited, but with the anterior articulation for hyomandibular, and the posterior part of the parietal (P – or frontal) grading into the pterotic, which forms the posterior hyomandibular articulation. Above the pterotic is a very large bone, probably an extrascapular which is incomplete towards the dorsal midline. A small narrow fragment on its surface might be part of a posttemporal, which is close to the upper end of a long rather narrow supracleithrum.

The hyomandibula is well exposed with a broad two headed articular end, a triangular flat process meeting the metapterygoid, a large process articulating against the opercular and a strong shaft supporting the upper end of preopercular. The symplectic is a rather small and narrow bone wedged into the quadrate. The preopercular is a strong rather narrow and vertical bone, 11 cm high, 2.5 cm wide, with a short ventral branch carrying a horizontal flange over the sensory canal, and apparently with a small, triangular process below the end of the hyomandibular shaft. There is a large, almost semi-rectangular opercular bone, 8 cm wide, with the subopercular appearing along the ventral border and not very reduced. Below the pre- and subopercular several ventral elements of the branchial arches are visible, probably with the broad and most ventral ones being ceratohyals (hyoid arch?), and there are fragments of some branchiostegals.

Pectoral girdle and fin. The long supracleithrum overlaps the dorsal and equally narrow end of the cleithrum. This increases in width towards the scapular and coracoid region, which is not well exposed, and the ventral part of cleithrum is eroded away. Between the scapular articulation and the large anterior pectoral ray, fragments of the radials are seen. The coracoid may show traces of a foramen near its posterior end, but only a little of the bone is visible. The first pectoral ray is very strong and broad, *c.* 13 mm wide, and its two halves seem slightly separated. Behind it are seen 10–12 much thinner rays, but none of the rays are preserved in their full length.

Axial skeleton (Fig. 18). Between opercular, hyomandibular and pterotic in the referred specimen are seen the anterior three or probably four vertebral centra slightly disarticulated (and a scale; Fig. 18b), and behind the supracleithrum another three to four centra are exposed between the scales of the anterior block. The second part of the block with part of the abdominal region shows 26 articulated vertebral centra, which 'fade out' at the posterior end. There are about 35 vertebrae preserved in total. The centra are *c.* 13 mm long and partly covered by the heavy squamation, but one centrum is turned to show that the height is *c.* 25 mm. The ventral ends of four long ribs can be seen behind the pectoral fin, and many long ribs are visible further back. The neural spines gently bend backwards, and at the end of some of them supraneurals are indicated. There are long, thin epineurals, and several of them, nearly horizontal, can be seen crossing the fissure between the two parts of the block.

Squamation (Fig. 19). The scales of the referred specimen are big, *c.* 3–4 cm in diameter, thick, rounded to oval with a distinct ornamentation of small tubercles on the exposed field. They are smooth on the anterior part and show no reticulation. They appear similar to those of the holotype, and also here these scales are the sole reason for referring the two specimens to the same taxon. A large, round scale is well exposed besides some ribs on the small third fragment of the referred specimen and the ornamentation on its 'free' posterior region seems slightly weaker than on the scales of the holotype. There are somewhat more than 15 scales (perhaps near 20) in a vertical row behind the pectoral girdle. Where the maximal height is *c.* 15 cm above the vertebral column, the depth below the latter is probably *c.* 30 cm, indicating a body *c.* 0.5 m deep.

Diagnosis. Furichthys is a large-sized and deep-bodied osteoglossiform with large, non-reticulate scales. It has a pointed snout with long, slim lower jaws and very heavy premaxillaries with a strong and differentiated dentition on very low pedicles with the three middle teeth the largest, conical, slightly bent, almost 1.5 cm high and 1 cm wide. The maxillary teeth are slimmer, *c.* 1 cm high, and the dentary teeth in front are a little smaller and decreasing backwards. There are tiny teeth covering (at least) vomer, palato-ectopterygoid and the tongue, and probably the (anterior) parasphenoid. The first pectoral ray is very large. Perhaps the heavy ethmo vomer complex is also characteristic.

The knowledge of *Furichthys*' anatomy is somewhat fragmentary, and known characteristic osteoglossomorph features are rather few. Most indicative is the dentition with the strong, conical to subcylindrical teeth on pedicles. although the differentiation of sizes does not occur in most relatives (some comparative remarks on osteoglossiform teeth below). But also the fused palato-ectopterygoid, the strong basipterygoid process, the shape and pores of the preopercular (like phareodonts), and the shape of the opercular point in that direction. The same counts for the huge first ray of the pectoral fin and the large number of the very short vertebrae, as well as the very long ribs and the lack of epipleurals – perhaps also for the fine tuberculation of the scales.

Osteoglossiform teeth

Because *Furichthys* and the following three 'bony tongue' fishes have quite characteristic teeth, a few remarks on such teeth seems relevant here. The typical osteoglossiform, *Osteoglossum bicirrhosum* is illustrated here (Fig. 20) for comparison with the fossils. Note that in this large adult specimen, almost 1 m long (precise length not known) from 'Danmarks Akvarium' near Copenhagen, the teeth are relatively much smaller than those of the smaller specimen (19 cm) figured by Taverne (1977, fig. 42). All the teeth of the jaws are placed on bony pedicles, and each has a quasi-cylindrical (slightly oval section perpendicular on the edge of the jaw), high, slim and hollow basal part of smooth dentine (this is called 'socle conique' by Taverne, 1977, 84) ending in an offset, small and slightly narrower, pointed and in-curved cap (Taverne: 'pointe très acérée'), nearly translucent, of acrodin (a hyper-mineralised dentine characteristic of actinopterygians). The pedicles here are about one fourth of the height of the teeth, and they are also hollow and somewhat 'bulbous'. Taverne paid only some little attention to details of the teeth, and he called them all 'grandes' (1977, pp. 84, 95) and even compared them to the huge teeth of *Brychaetus*, but called those of *Osteoglossum* 'exagéré à l'extrême' and 'encore plus évolué' with a 'socle énorme'. This is somewhat misleading, because it seems obvious

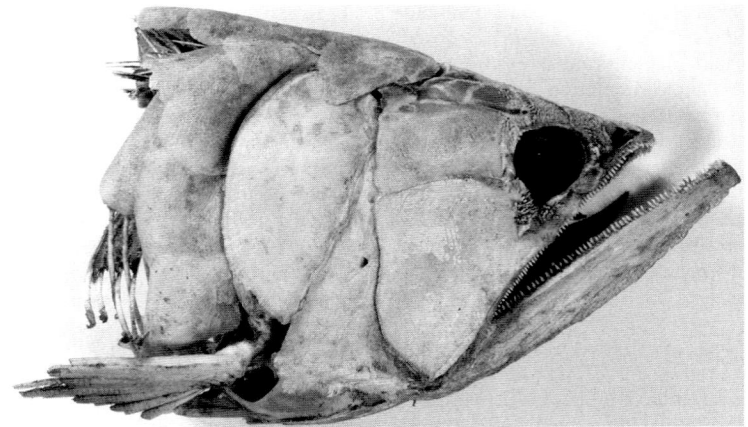

Fig. 20. Arawana, *Osteoglossum bicirrhosum*, skull and pectoral region of a *c.* 1 m long adult specimen.

that it is *Brychaetus* having the most extreme teeth (well shown by Taverne [1978, fig. 20] and Casier [1966] and Woodward [1901] and see the Danish jaw below), very large and with enormous bony pedicles, but such is now by Taverne (1978, p. 39) called 'très haut socle rugueux' [rough]. And the remainder of the tooth is described as 'une pointe cylindrique lisse' [smooth], and it is repeated that in *Osteoglossum* and *Scleropages* the 'socle' is more developed than in *Brychaetus*.

This is not true, in *Brychaetus* the pedicle/socle is up to almost half of the tooth, but much less in *Osteoglossum*. In the skull figured here the teeth are not 'grandes' at all, but quite small, and though both Taverne's small specimen and my specimen has about 10 teeth in the premaxilla, the numbers are very different in the maxilla (Taverne's about 50 positions, mine about 60, counting also positions with teeth fallen out) and dentary (Taverne shows about 50, mine has about 80). It seems that Taverne (1977, fig. 48) in section shows a smaller tooth inside the outer row in premaxilla, without mentioning it. On the contrary, in my specimen in the dentary there is a row of a dozen smaller teeth inside the external row at the symphysis (very similar in *Brychaetoides*, below). Nothing about two rows is mentioned by Taverne although in *Scleropages* he clearly shows two rows of teeth in the dentary (figs 82, 83), and seemingly also in the maxilla (fig. 71). Whether the difference in relative size of the teeth is simply age related, is not known, but the differences in numbers especially in the dentaries can hardly be explained in that way. The pedicle size is positively age correlated as shown by the London Clay *Brychaetus* and the huge jaws from

Malawi (Casier 1966, pl. 17 and pers. obs. in NHM, London).

The typical osteoglossiform jaw tooth thus has a hollow bony pedicle, a quasi-cylindrical/-conical, smooth dentine tooth with a small, pointed, offset tip or cap of clear acrodine. Differentiation in size of the teeth is not so evident in the extant ones as in some of the fossils.

Xosteoglossid rebeccae *n. g. & sp.*
(Fig. 21a, b)

The generic name alluding to the somewhat uncertain or imprecise relation to other osteoglossids/osteoglossiforms (X = 'mystery' plus 'bony tongue'), and the specific name honouring the finder of this Danekrae no. 71 (see note, p. 305), Rebekka Madsen, Sejerslev, Mors, DK.

One specimen identified so far, the holotype DK 71 (MGUH 28.905 in counterparts), found in so-called 'shale', hardened (slightly silicified), laminated, dark grey mudstone of the Stolle Klint Clay on the beach at Stolle Klint, Fur. Collected in 1994. Length of the specimen *c.* 20 cm.

Age. Lowermost Eocene, at the bottom of the ash series, probably derived from the upper few metres below ash −33 (cf. Fig. 3 and Bøggild 1918; Bonde 1987, 1997). The fossil is briefly described and figured also by Bonde *et al.* (2008: 92).

Description. Incomplete fish (14 cm preserved) comprising the skull with anterior part of dentary missing, and the pectoral girdle and fin as well as some vertebrae, ribs and scales. The length of the skull is *c.* 10 cm (snout slightly disarranged). It is compressed to 2–5 mm thickness and preserved mainly as a very sharp and detailed imprint in the

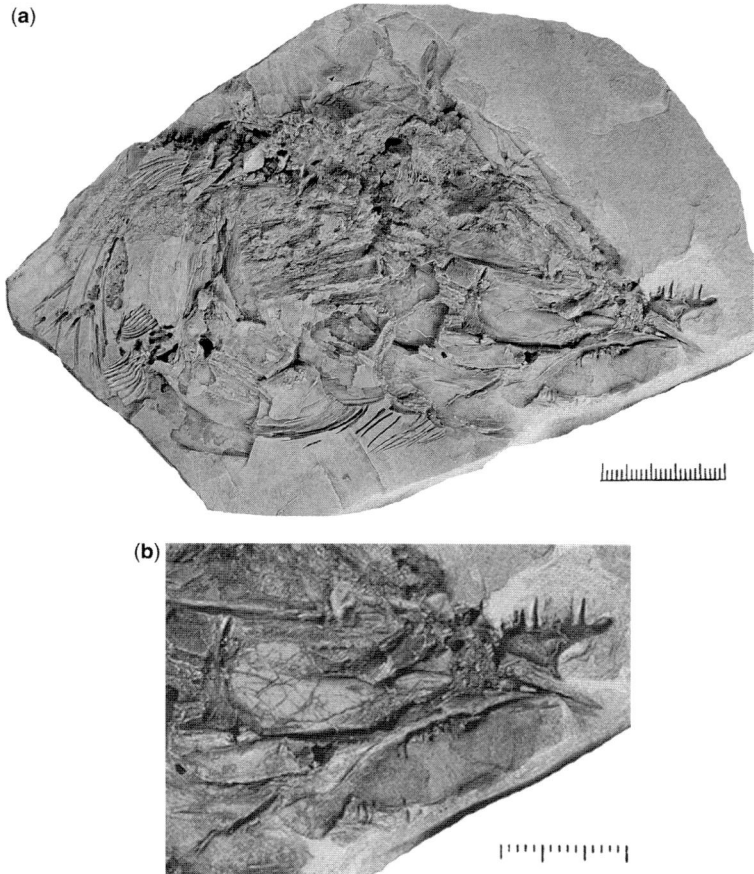

Fig. 21. (**a**) *Xosteoglossid rebeccae*, holotype, MGUH 28.905 (DK 71), skull and anterior abdominal region as partly imprint in hardened Stolle Klint Clay. Slight ammonium chloride dusting and 'reverse light direction' (from lower right); (**b**) upper jaw region to expose details of the state of preservation and the 'cracked' bones. Scales in mm.

ventral region, but with the crushed bones beautifully-preserved in most of the dorsal region with the braincase and some vertebrae. The branchial basket is a crumbling mass of disintegrating bone, difficult to interpret. The well-preserved bones appear as brittle, lamellar bone and airfilled spongiosa, perhaps as unchanged mineralization but for the dark brown colour. Bones of the braincase and branchial region are, unfortunately, split right through the bones leaving almost no external or internal surfaces visible on either part or counterpart. Imprints of the completely dissolved bones are left as empty cracks between hardened laminae of mud only fractions of a millimetre thick. The left and right surfaces of any bone are seen on the left and right counterparts respectively, and medial, horizontal structures like some tooth plates and the skull roof are squeezed into the vertical plane.

Roughened surfaces of endoskeletal bone, where they met cartilage can generally be recognized by their irregular structure, e.g. at the anterior end of the dermopalatine where it continues as the autopalatine, which may have been more or less completely cartilaginous (Fig. 21b).

Skull. The skull is *c.* 10 cm long (the rostral end is a little disturbed, the anterior half of the dentary is missing), the height (flattened) is 6–7 cm, in life probably a little less. The precrbital snout is *c.* 3 cm, the orbit *c.* 2 cm, and the opercular is *c.* 2.5 × 5 cm (lower edge not well defined). Snout to quadrate distance is *c.* 5 cm, approximately corresponding to jaw length, and height of the lower jaw is just over 1 cm. The skull roof comprises large frontals *c.* 4 cm long, which have been compressed by breaking them along the median suture (now forming the 'dorsal line'), and the splitting of the fossil went through the sensory canal inside the left frontal of which the external table is on the left slab, the internal table on the right plate with most of the bone preserved as a spongy mass. Although difficult to judge, there is no indication that the anterior part of the frontals were very wide: rather, the contrary. The central division of the sensory canal is visible. The anterior and posterior borders against parietal and nasal are not obvious. The parietal is probably rather small and short, and a very deep, broad and arched imprint on the left slab is probably made by the transverse edge where the parietal bends down from the roof towards the occipital region. One of the nasals is displaced forward and down between the rotated premaxilla and the maxilla, and it appears to be a narrow, straight and flat bone presumably meeting its fellow and with a broad, open sensory canal and a bifid anterior point. A small, oval supratemporal with a sensory canal is displaced above the skull in the parietal region. Behind this is a smooth bone, which may be a supraoccipital crest, and at a level lateral to this is a large bone which most likely is a large 'extrascapular scale' (as in *Osteoglossum*).

The braincase is preserved partly as spongy bones split through, so that they are somewhat difficult to interpret, but preserved best on the left slab. There seem to be a closed interorbital septum mainly formed by the orbithosphenoid, but with a posterior component from the pleurosphenoid and a ventral part from the parasphenoid. The latter is a very straight bone but the ventral surface seems hidden, so a possible dentition cannot be observed. The parasphenoid shape may look like that of *Heterotis* (which lacks teeth). On both plates its basipterygoid processes can be seen pointing backwards near a dorsal indentation in the metapterygoid (right slab), and the posterior parasphenoid does not seem to bend upwards in this region, while its ascending process is difficult to outline. In the mesh of spongy bone the sutures can be distinguished between orbito-, pleuro-, autosphenotic and pro- and pterotic, but no surface details of those bones are visible, and the latter's contact with epioccipital seems hidden. The latter clearly forms a posterolateral corner of the skull, and below it is a mesh of bone which must comprise ex- and basioccipital and possibly intercalar, but no sutures can be seen, apart from that between the latter two and the pterotic and prootic. The basioccipital (and perhaps exoccipital) is in contact with the first vertebral centrum, which has been displaced relative to the articulated row of other anterior centra preserved (see below).

In the snout region the parasphenoid seems to pass below the parethmoid and end rather abruptly a short distance in front of it or be hidden below the anterior endopterygoid and palatine and a small subtriangular (?dermal) bone of uncertain affinities. The mesethmoid-vomer complex and a nasal has been moved down and a little forward, while the left premaxilla was rotated upwards and backwards 180° from the anterior maxillary process. The vomerian small and rounded tooth patch is turned 90° to make imprints from the small teeth into the right plate, and the bone just above it with 'cartilaginous structure' is from the ethmoid complex, probably the mesethmoid. The parethmoid shows no signs of having a lateral dermal bone attached to it. Unless the subtriangular bone or a smooth, oval surface below it and behind the mesethmoid (which most likely is part of endopterygoid) is part of the infraorbitals, no such bones are visible in this anterior region – they must have been quite small bones.

Palate, jaws and visceral arches. The length of the lower jaw is measured indirectly by the quadrate to snout length at 5–6 cm the anterior half of which is not preserved. Only *c.* 1.5 cm of the dentigerous edge of the dentary is preserved showing 3 mm high, upright and densely set teeth with small bony pedicles in one row. There are 14–15 teeth in the 15 mm jaw, indicating about 20 more teeth in the missing 2 cm in front in the left jaw, and the number hidden by maxilla can be estimated to about 10 teeth by comparison with the right jaw. So in total perhaps there were about 45–50 teeth in a lower jaw. There is a distinct retroarticular process behind the articulation, but it is difficult to judge whether it is a separate bone or fused into the dermarticular, which may occupy about half of the jaw. The lower jaw is not much over 1 cm high giving the impression of a narrow gape. While the two lower jaws almost precisely overlap each other, the upper jaws and the palate have been squeezed asymmetrically, so that the left parts are seen about 1 cm below and in front of the corresponding right part. The left premaxilla has been turned 180° backwards with the nine strong teeth now pointing up. They are about 4 mm high including about 1 mm pedicles, and a few imprints expose the pointed cap. The premaxilla is *c.* 2 cm long with a 7 mm high process in the middle, and the posterior end slimmer than the symphyseal part. The thin posterior branch should rest firmly against and below the 1 cm long and thin anterior process of the maxilla. In the right premaxilla one small replacement tooth is preserved as a thin cylinder with pointed cap of dentine (? acrodine) – the only tooth that has not been dissolved. The more distal 2.5 cm of maxilla has teeth a little weaker than the other jaw bones, only *c.* 2 mm high on little, if any, pedicles. About 10 teeth are visible on the anterior centimetre, but even smaller teeth reach the posterior part of the bone, which is flattened and 7 mm broad. All teeth are relatively slim, sub conical with oval section basally (longer axes perpendicular to jaw length) and are pointed with a little cap. There is a large drop-shaped supramaxilla with a sharp point pointing forward. The arched maxilla and the way the upper jaw has been destroyed indicate some mobility, probably that this jaw could swing forward, when the mouth was opened allowing the gape to be bigger – presumably more so than as preserved. With the long, slim nasals and (apparently) frontals the fish must have had a narrow, pointed snout with large fangs in front in a much inclined and some-what prognathous gape.

From the palate the large endopterygoids are well exposed, both left and right ones from their dorsal, smooth surfaces, which at the posterior edges are shaped as strong vertical and slightly arched ridges. Imprints of their covering of tiny teeth are seen on the opposite counterpart. The small vomerian toothplate is exposed on the right slab in front of endopterygoid and above the dense dentition of the anterior process of the pala-tine. The left endopterygoid is lined by a rather narrow palatine(-ectopterygoid, the latter hardly visible) covered with small teeth and with a distinct row along the lateral edge. It appears (though a parasphenoid dentition cannot be confirmed) that all of the palatal surface is covered by tiny teeth. The dermopalatine has a rostral process well ossi-fied medially (right side is partly preserved as bone), but apparently covered by a cartilaginous autopalatine on its (dorso-)lateral face. The quad-rate is well-exposed on both sides, and the articula-tion can be seen on the right side, where also the symplectic and a large metapterygoid are seen, the latter having a notch approached by both the basip-terygoid process and the large triangular flange from the hyomandibula. The latter bone is well exposed on the right slab with some of its bone partly preserved and a large single headed articula-tion for the braincase and a very strong opercular process. Its long ventral shaft and a strong lateral ridge supporting the dorsal branch of preopercular is preserved.

In this region all four epibranchials of both sides seem to be preserved as straight and parallel rods lying just behind each other, and only partly over-lapping number one of the left side onto number four of the right. Small fragments of a few pharyn-gobrachials are also seen, one is placed above epi-branchial 2; all of these preserved as very crumbling bone, but all epibranchials remarkably uniform and slim in shape. Only number 4 may have a small postero-dorsal expansion, and above this a small, elongate bone in position as a pharyngobranchial – perhaps it is a toothplate of the fourth arch (in modern relatives, Taverne [1977, 1978] found such toothplate in Osteoglossi-dae and some notopterids). Some of the ventral branchial elements are also visible as a jumble of bones exposed in a space between the right supra-maxilla and endopterygoid. There is both a right and left hypobranchial and apparently some basi-branchials with small parts of toothplates indicated, but no large bony tongue. The large ceratohyals of both sides are seen with the posterior ossifications squeezed on top of each other – mainly visible on the left slab. Two small hypohyals are seen on both plates, and a small basihyal is indicated on the left slab. There are 17 branchiostegals, the anterior 13 are very slim, but the four posterior ones increase in width and probably all join the posterior ceratohyal.

Infraorbitals and operculars. Very little is seen of the infraorbitals, only part of a large right one on the left slab preserved as a smooth imprint of the medial face surrounding the two posterior cerato-branchials mentioned above (perhaps infraorbital 3). Part of the external surface of the same large bone may be seen on the right plate between the quadrate and metapterygoid, but the shape of this infraorbital cannot be determined. The large pre-opercular is only partly visible on the right plate with a high dorsal branch indicated by its anterior edge, and only the short anterior part of the ventral branch preserved with a clear indication of three to four large pores for the horizontal part of the sensory canal. The large right opercular has been detached from the hyomandibular articulation and has slid down on the outside to be placed partly below the skull (and with the ventral end out of the block). It has a vertical break in the middle, but its shape is well exposed with a rounded dorsal rim and sub parallel anterior and posterior edges. Although the ventral edge cannot be seen, the bone must have been about twice as high as wide, and it has a strong ridge on the inside supporting the articula-tion for hyomandibular. Sub- and interoperculars are not visible.

Pectoral girdle and fin. The broad anterior plate of the right cleithrum sutured to the coracoid is visible as imprint of the medial surface on the left plate, and further down is seen the lateral surface of the left coracoid. The inside of the cleithrum is contin-ued upwards as a very broad vertical branch, cut off by imprints of the internal abdominal cavity, appar-ently filled with small fish debris from the last meal. On the right side the dorsal arm of cleithrum is approaching the vertebral column, where it overlaps the elongate and rather narrow supracleithrum. The right coracoid clearly shows a large fenestra close to the posterior prong where it meets the deep imprint of the small, triangular scapula which has a small central foramen. Above the coracoid fenestra a strong, elongate mesocoracoid is placed in a vertical and anterior position. About five radials have been slightly disarranged between scapula and the bases of the pectoral fin rays, which evidently are from the right fin showing about 14 rays (crossing under the ribs on the right plate), while the left fin is pointing the opposite way exposing only 8 of the rays. The anterior ray is strongest, but not very much so, and the decrease in size of the rays backwards is even.

Axial skeleton. 11–12 vertebral centra are preserved with the two anterior ones displaced onto the top of the fourth and fifth centra. Very long ribs running all the way to the ventral line are seen beginning from the fourth centrum directly without parapophyses. Parapophyses start from about the sixth centrum and are quite large and pointed. Only 5–6 of the neural arches are visible due to imprints of large dorsal scales. Whether the neural arches are paired is uncertain and one rod may be the anterior supraneural, but there is an indication of some horizontal epineurals low down near the centra. The centra are *c.* 5 mm long and 6–7 mm high with 1–2 rather strong lateral ridges, and are clearly hour glass shaped with just one of the chordal intercentral spaces filled in by calcite. It is estimated that, with the narrow, pointed snout and no indication of a deep abdomen, this fish had a long, low and compressed body of a fast hunter – and perhaps a 'jumper' – somewhat like *Osteoglossum* in shape and maybe in behaviour.

Scales. On the left slab a small patch of large oval scales is preserved on the nape. One scale behind the supraoccipital crest is seen in its entirety from its external surface. It is 17 mm high and *c.* 10 mm long with an even ornamentation of small, irregular tubercles on the 'free', posterior field, while the anterior, basal field is more smooth (but in reality is covered by the tiniest tubercles tending to be slightly elongated and arranged in a radiating pattern mirroring the growth direction). There are some well-spaced, very thin and crossing lines as indication of a possible reticulation on much of the scale, while other and stronger fissures must be cracks, especially on one scale around a puncture hole made by a bone fragment (apparently from the outside). The posterior (apical) field shows a number of pores in the surface. This scale shows part of its inside on the right counterpart, but while the broader cracks are clearly seen, the traces of reticulation and pores are not so convincing (which is unusual; they should be more

evident on the inside). One smaller scale, 5 × 5 mm, just below the left pectoral fin does, however, show a clearer reticulation by fissures, especially on the inside of the posterior field, while pores are only weakly indicated on the anterior field. The external ornamentation is of the same type, but the stronger ornamentation on the posterior part only occupies about one third of the scale. When evaluating these indications of reticulation it is worth noting, that many of the bones show an irregular pattern of sediment filled fissures which surely are cracks (Fig. 21b) and usually more 'straight lined' than proper reticulation – this is an obvious difficulty when looking for reticulation in the scales, which also seem to be cracked. The conclusion is that the scales show some weak indications of reticulation and pores as well as ornamentation typical of osteoglossiform scales.

Diagnosis. Complete interorbital septum of orbitho-, pleuro- and parasphenoid. Rather narrow and high opercular and preopercular with short ventral branch with four large pores for the sensory canal. Marked supraoccipital crest and notch in metapterygoid (for basipterygoid process and/or hyomandibular process?). Probably tiny teeth all over the mouth cavity (parasphenoid teeth unknown). Ribs beginning only from the fourth centrum without parapophyses (which start from about the sixth centrum). Differentiated dentition with the teeth on the premaxilla much bigger than the other jaw teeth.

The presence of a supramaxilla is an unusual feature among osteoglossiforms, but it is probably plesiomorphic – see text on marine forms above, and the phylogenetic analysis below. The latter shows *Xosteoglossid* to have many osteoglossomorph synapomorphies. Furthermore, there are nearly half of the characteristics present of the new 'Osteoglossi' (Mormyriformes plus Osteoglossiformes), and several features to place it among osteoglossiforms and even high in the stem-group of the extant members of the group.

Brychaetoides greenwoodi n. gen. & sp. *(Fig. 22)*

Meaning *Brychaetus*-like due to some superficial similarity to *Brychaetus* from the London Clay (Casier 1966), and named in honour of Dr P. H. Greenwood, late colleague in the Fish Department, Natural History Museum, London, a great connoisseur of osteoglossomorph fishes both extant and extinct. In 1973 he published his knowledge of the group, after the Linnaean Society meeting in 1972, which seriously introduced cladistics into fish systematics (see Bonde 1974, 1999, 2003b).

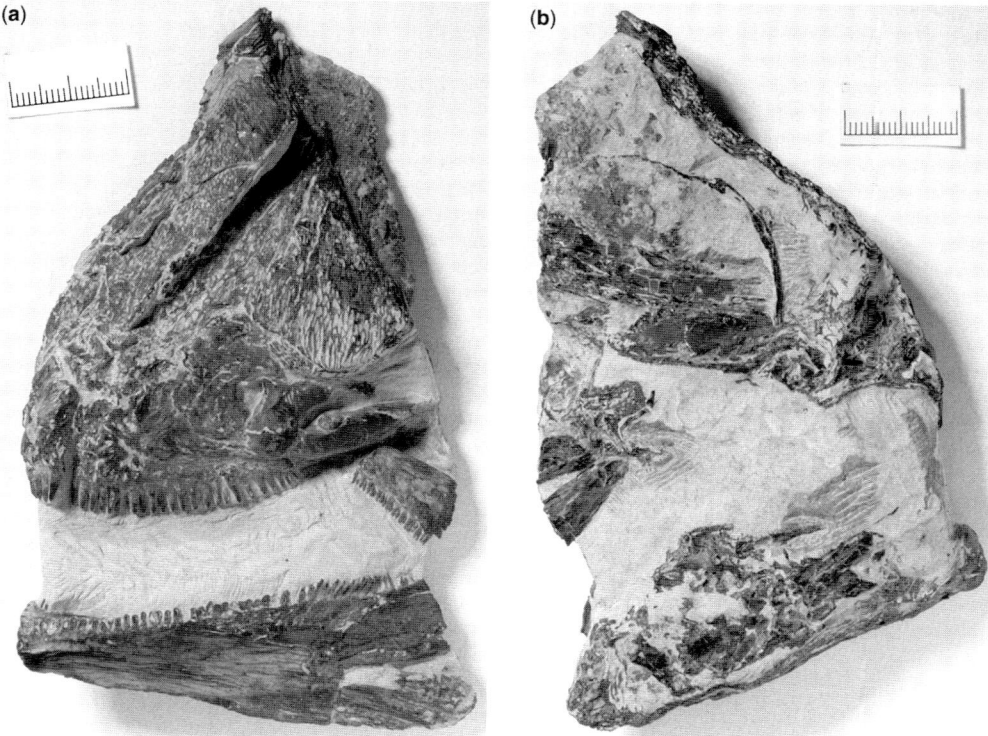

Fig. 22. (**a**) *Brychaetoides greenwoodi*, holotype, MGUH 28.906 (1954.469). Snout part in cementstone, left side; (**b**) right side of snout sectioned through the oral cavity exposing palate and tongue. Scales 2 cm.

Holotype (only known specimen) MGUH 28.906 (former 1954.469). Originally described by Bonde (1965, unpublished 'Gold Medal' thesis; summary 1966) a very fragmentary skull, pectoral bones and scales in a cementstone from the Fur Formation found in 1947 at the eastern part of Knudeklinten, Fur, presumably on the beach, by the late I. P. Andersen, Viborg. Four pieces said to be from the same fossil, preserved in a cementstone, light grey with some weak lamination. The level is unknown, but the limestone looks like the one having ash −33 through it from the very base of Fur Fm (same level and locality as the large *Furichthys* described above, although it was recorded by this author [1997, p. 47], as 'Ost. 3', as level +25−30? from the upper part of the formation). The specimens consists of: (a) mainly the snout part with anterior end of the lower jaw and most of the orbital region, part of the palate and tongue: (b) part of a large flat skull bone, apparently an opercular with some crushed branchial arches attached to its inner surface, and some bony struts at one end of the elongate specimen could be the distal ends of branchiostegals: (c) a piece with strongly overlapping scales from both sides of the

fish with fragments of ribs in between and apparently part of a vertebral centrum and parts of bones from possibly the shoulder girdle. Those three parts of the fossil do not fit exactly onto each other. There is a fourth much smaller fragment (d) with some scales of just one side pressed together and a fragment of a rib – not even that fragment can be convincingly fitted onto one of the other parts. All fragments have sharp, freshly-broken edges, but apparently no more of the fossil was in I. P. Andersen collection, when the Geological (then Mineralogical) Museum acquired the collection (registered in 1954), which contains a large number of isolated scales, many of them osteoglossoid of the reticulate type known from *Heterosteoglossum*.

Skull (Fig. 22a, b). The skull (snout) of specimen 'a' has been laterally compressed and split in a near mid sagittal plane with most of the right half missing while exposing some of the palatal and tongue region. The frontals are broken through the orbital region, the posterior part (and the rest of skull roof and braincase) is missing, the left frontal is squeezed down into the left orbit, and the anteromedial part of the right frontal is pre-served. The antorbital is displaced forward, and the maxilla is broken in two and the distal end is missing. Most of left dentary and the rostral end of dermarticular are preserved.

The snout part is *c*. 14 cm high and can probably be oriented by keeping the line from the vomer and the parasphenoid approximately horizontal, indicating that the fish did not have a near horizontal skull roof to snout line (like *Osteoglossum*, *Scleropages*, *Heterosteoglossum*), but rather a profile like that of *Heterotis* or *Phareodus* (with a falling snout-line (a little over 45°) and an upward pointing dentary (less than 45°)). If the skull roof is kept horizontal and the mouth slit/upper jaw turned upward about 45°, the exposed dermarticular would be unlikely long or the jaw (dentary *c*. 8 cm) very short compared to the entire fish.

Of the lower jaws (Fig. 22a) almost only the left dentary is preserved with a small part of the anterior point of dermarticular mainly seen on the inside of dentary. The anteriormost few millimetres at the rather thick, and somewhat expanded, symphysis are missing. There is an inner row of about five small, cylindrical teeth, *c*. 2 mm high, one of which was actually pointing its cap the wrong way, outwards (but this cap was lost years ago). The main row of teeth numbers over 45 teeth and a few are missing at the symphysis and perhaps also distally, so around 50 teeth is a fair estimate. The teeth are 3–4 mm high, upright with a distinct, rounded cap pointing lingually, but with near paral-lel sides in labial view, but basally oval, almost twice as wide (linguo-labially) as long (meso-distally). The crowns are set on small bony pedicles comprising about one fourth of the height. They are hollow with 0.5 mm thick walls and height slightly decreasing distally, where they are inclined a little backwards. About 8 of the teeth have much thinner walls and are newer replacement teeth. The dentary is almost complete, *c*. 8 cm long, and *c*. 3 cm high distally, but the ventral border is broken off. Close to this the sensory canal runs at the lower bent-in edge with one anterior, narrow pore pointing downwards and the posterior pore to the side. Little can be observed of the anterior part of the exposed dermarticular, but the sensory canal can be seen cut at the posterior end of the edge where the medial lamella bends in. The inside of the jaw is mostly hidden by parts of the tongue and a fragment of the medial side of the right dentary.

The premaxilla, nearly 4 cm long, has larger teeth *c*. 5 mm high and slightly more conical, upright with a cap, and set on pedicles 20–25% of the height. The teeth slightly decrease in size dis-tally. The thickness of the dentine is only 0.3 mm in the largest teeth. There are 24 teeth in one row (a

full grown possible replacement tooth, pointing through from an inner position, is seen in fifth pos-ition in both sides, but the section of the right pre-maxillary after the seventh position does not show two rows of teeth – two other replacement teeth are in 16th and 23rd position). Quite differently, the broken off middle part of the maxillary dentition distinctly shows two rows of teeth, about 2.5 mm high, oval at the bases and set on very low pedicles in an alternate pattern, where the inner teeth point out between the outer teeth, so that all the pointed caps are in nearly one line.

Twenty-three teeth of both rows combined are preserved in a fragment less than 2 cm long so, if the upper and lower dentitions were approxi-mately equally long, the maxillary may have had nearly twice that amount. The dentigerous part of the bone is narrow and only *c*. 1 cm high, with a dorsal edge indicating no attachment to the infraorbitals, and tapering in front, where it is broken from a strong anterior part, that has a big articular 'knob' for the antorbital (stronger than in osteoglossids). Behind this it has teeth pointing into the matrix and exposed on the reverse side of the slab. The most proximal end is a thinner process closely attached to the dorso-medial side of the slim posterior process of the premaxilla. The latter takes up about half the length of the bone, while its proximal half is much higher, nearly 2 cm, and has a blunt, dorsal process passing up between the nasal and the mesethmoid region.

In between the two premaxillae at the dorsal part of the symphysis a small part of a cartilage bone is visible, probably a hypethmoid ossification ('hypoethmoïde ventral' by Taverne 1977–1979, which may be fused to vomer). Between this region and the nasals/frontals is exposed a rim of the mesethmoid ossification of which the dorsal surface is ornamented like a dermal bone ('hypoeth-moïde dorsal', Taverne). Between this and the ante-romedial flanges of the frontals is a small, round supraethmoid bone. Lateral to the mesethmoid is a much bigger and oval nasal with a large lateral embayment for a nostril, and the bone has a small mid-ventral pore and probably receives the sensory canal at the postero-medial edge from the indentation, where it fits into the frontal. The nostril on its postero-lateral side is limited by a strongly ossified, pillar-like antorbital with a rounded ventral surface presumably to meet the 'knob' a little further back on maxilla, and the broader dorsal end meets the frontal. This antorbital distinctly appears to be an endoskeletal bone, and it is not obvious that it has a lateral, dermal com-ponent. There are some small, dorsal superficial pores and a small ventrally placed pore at a horizon-tal break in the bone, and another tiny one at the ventral edge, but they do not really look like those from a sensory canal. The bone is no doubt what is called 'antorbital' by Taverne (1977–1979) in the fossil *Phareodus* and *Brychaetus*, where it, as in the present fossil, does not appear like the antorbitals of the recent osteoglossids, although the bone in *Osteoglossum*, *Scleropages* and *Pantodon* does have the same relation with an articulation onto the maxilla. The last two fossils mentioned and *Opsithrissops* (Danil'chenko 1968; Taverne 1979, 1998) may perhaps lack this dermal component or it may be fused completely into what looks more like some sort of (par-)ethmoid ossification. On the reverse side of the fossil (Fig. 22b), however, under the right nasal and lining the nasal cavity is seen the mesethmoid ossification in conjunction with a near vertical ridge, that must be part of the true parethmoid. This continues toward the orbital side as thick, spongy bone. These strong ethmoids seem not to be co-ossified with the thin vomerian tooth plate, which closely follows their ventral surface.

The frontal, to accommodate the supraethmoid, nasal and antorbital has a wavy anterior border, which continues laterally in a broad and ornamented lappet, behind which the snout is cut off. It appears likely that this lappet is wider than the frontals, in general similar to the condition in *Brychaetus* and *Phareodus*, and the lappet has been pressed down into the left orbit and onto the side of the orbitosphenoid with a thin sclerotic ossification squeezed in between the two. The course of the sensory canals is not very evident in these dermal bones, although it perhaps can be traced in the right frontal as a slit near the broken edge, and in the left bone as a narrow slit in a near symmetrical position, and it appears to end at the notch into which the nasal fits. At the top end of the right frontal is a fragment of a more posterior bone, presumably the pterotic, and if so, approximately indicating the width of the skull roof at this region, namely much narrower than the anterior frontal lappets.

On the reverse side of the fossil where it is cut through the right frontal, nasal and premaxilla, the section cuts through the mouth cavity (Fig. 22b) and the visceral arches. In the snout the mesethmoid is cut, and below it is attached a thin plate, perhaps Taverne's ventral hypethmoid. Closely below the latter is a very thin plate of vomer, totally covered by tiny teeth. Behind the mesethmoid is an upright strut or wall, presumably the mentioned parethmoid with a postero-ventral extension butting against some dermal bone, either endopterygoid or dermopalatine. Part of two plates of the sclerotic ring is cutting down behind this region, and a flat bone posterior to this is likely to be the

dorsal part of endopterygoid (dorsal surface of right side), while the straight bone cut below it carrying tiny teeth on its ventral surface is probably the corresponding toothplate (or could it be the parasphenoid with a displaced endopterygoid border above it?). Above this 'endopterygoid' is another flat bone with indistinct borders above and a nearly straight border below within the orbit that might be the parasphenoid with a dorsal lamella partly closing the interorbital fenestra. It seems uncertain whether the said 'parasphenoid' carried teeth although none is seen in the section of its ventral rim.

In the dorsal region of the mouth cavity is a stout cartilage bone with thin dermal plates, presumably dorsal elements of the first gill arch, and ventrally in the mouth cavity some unidentified element of the tongue is sectioned showing tiny teeth on two surfaces. A large endoskeletal bone is pressed into the innerside of left dentary, presumably the ceratohyal, and it is worth noting, that it carries tiny toothplates on the lateral side facing the lower jaw. Such dentition is not described by Taverne (1977–1979) for any of the living osteoglossiforms, and it may be unique within teleosteans. So perhaps most of the cavities in the mouth were lined with thin tooth plates covered with tiny teeth.

Specimen 'b' shows a fragment of a strong, flat dermal bone, most likely an opercular, or perhaps an infraorbital, with a rather smooth surface, but no edges of the bone exposed. The 'pieces c and d' have many large and fragmented scales tightly squeezed together, so that limits of individual scales are difficult to observe. They appear laminated with 3–4 thin layers penetrated by pores which end in small, very low raised areas on the inside of the scales as in many osteoglossiforms. No very obvious reticulation is visible, but the squeezed scales have thin and sometimes wider breaks forming a pattern reminiscent of squamulae, and the external surface is ornamented with fine tubercles and ridges upon which is overprinted a larger pattern of low, crossing grooves also a bit reticulation like.

Specimen 'c' has a vertebral centrum c. 2 cm in diameter (therefore probably between 1–2 cm in length) and somewhere between 50–100 centra can be estimated for the vertebral column, so its body length would be 0.5–2 m. Specimen 'a' has over 6 cm long frontals, and accordingly would have a braincase over 10 cm, meaning a total length of the fish (with tail) would be between 70 cm and (if elongate like *Osteoglossum* or *Heterosteoglossum*) 2 m.

Diagnosis. Premaxilla with a large number of strong, closely set teeth, over 20 teeth in one row, decreasing in size distally, and a plumb ascending process near the midline touching the mesethmoid. Maxilla with similar, but smaller teeth closely set rather in two rows with alternating teeth. The dentary has numerous closely set teeth, around 50 in number, of the same type in one row with a short inner row of about five small, pointed, cylindrical teeth near the expanded symphysis. The larger teeth set on strong bony pedicles, which are relatively very low for the smaller teeth. This specific pattern of differentiated dentition of osteoglossiform-like teeth is characteristic of this taxon, and the tooth plates apparently on the ceratohyal seems unique. Scales are thin, laminar with many pores each ending on a tubercle on the inside (inner surface otherwise smooth), and dense ornamentation of tiny tubercles and ridges are present on external surface, also where they overlap in three or four layers. No, or very little, typical reticulation. Both the scales and the specific pattern of dentition of typical osteoglossiform teeth may well be autapomorphic for *Brychaetoides*. The medium large rounded nasals fitting into rounded excavations of the frontals, and not meeting in midline, as well as the dermal supraethmoid visible between nasals and frontals, and the mesethmoid exposed between nasals and premaxillaries, may well be autapomorphies also.

The following features have a somewhat wider, but still narrow distribution among osteglossomorphs (see below): Frontals very broad in front of the orbit (a phareodont feature); sclerotic ossifications present; antorbital (perhaps), without a dermal component, but it has a very strong articulation for the proximal maxillary process; all exposed bones of the mouth cavity may have small, densely set teeth (not known with certainty for parasphenoid), and there is a rather large, separate vomerine tooth plate with tiny teeth.

cf. Brychaetus *sp. (Figs 23, 24)*

Several parts of (probably) the same individual of a large osteoglossiform fish. Some of these have been valuated as Danekræ, namely part and counterpart of a fragment of the symphyseal part of lower jaw and premaxilla with huge teeth Danekræ 177 (MGUH 28.907) and several fragments of strong, segmented fin rays and many large scales Danekræ 181 (MGUH 28.908a–h). All preserved in hardened (silicified), dark grey to black mudstone found on the beach near Stolle Klint, Fur, that is from Stolle Klint

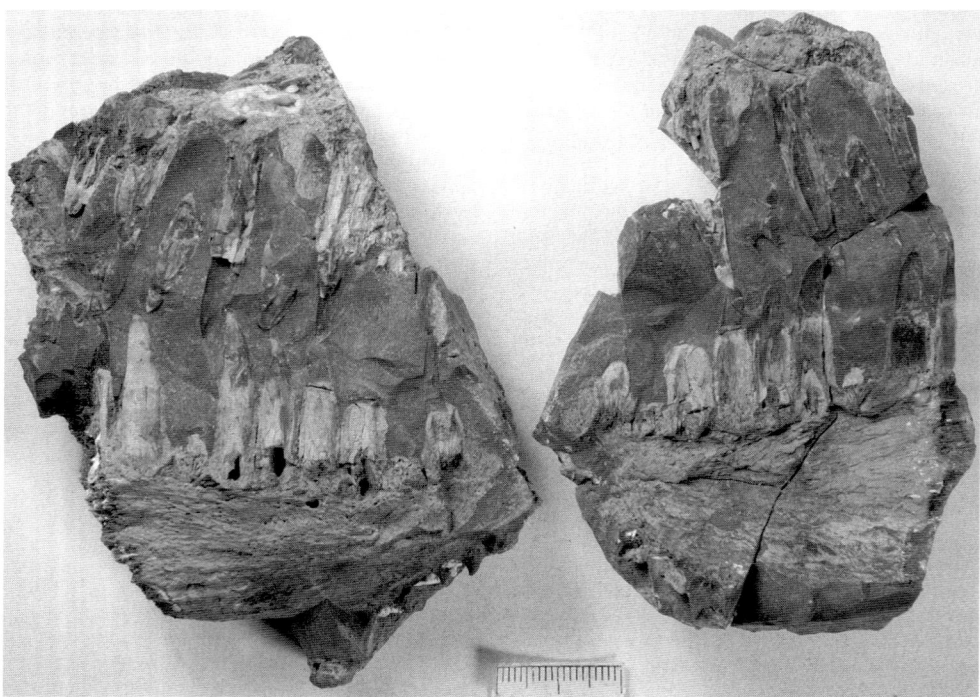

Fig. 23. cf. *Brychaetus* sp. in hardened Stolle Klint Clay, MGUH 28.907 (DK 177), near symphyseal parts of right upper and lower jaw, part and counterpart. Scale 2 cm.

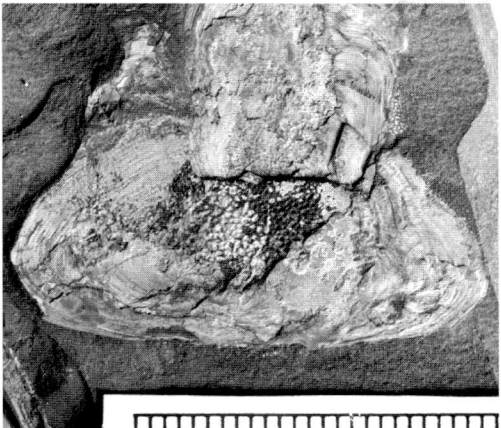

Fig. 24. cf. *Brychaetus* sp., part of same specimen as Figure 23. MGUH 28.908 (DK 181), large scales seen from the lateral side. Scale in mm.

Clay, age earliest Eocene. Found by C. Sönderby and N. Christensen; some fragments in Molermuseet, Mors and other fragments said to be in private collections. The bone is preserved in both jaw bones, teeth, fin rays and scales with the spongy bone often filled with secondary chert (opal?) of a whitish-bluish colour. These fossils are not here described in any detail, the two figures are just referred to. The teeth indicate a very large fish when compared to the big skulls known from the London Clay (Casier 1966), probably over 2 m long. In the *Brychaetus* sp. from Mali, mentioned by Longbottom (1984) some jaw fragments have even bigger teeth (pers. obs. in NHM).

Jaws and teeth (Fig. 23). The 7 cm long lower jaw fragment is only 3 cm high at the end cut off furthest away from the symphysis, and it has 3 cm high teeth. This indicates a rather low and slim lower jaw. The teeth in the premaxilla are about 4 cm high, and all the big jaw teeth have pedicles covering about half their height and the dentine continues inside the pedicles.

Scales (Fig. 24). The scales have a fine external ornamentation of irregular tubercles and small ridges with tiny pores penetrating the laminated scale in the posterior area and ending on small protuberances on the otherwise smooth internal surface. There are no clear signs of proper reticulation, despite some cracks giving such impression.

Characteristics. The huge teeth with very high bony pedicles are typical for *Brychaetus*. The same counts for the comparatively weak and low mandible, despite its large teeth. Perhaps also the scales are characteristic with pores only through the posterior, ornamented part of the scale, but without reticulation (*B. muelleri* scales seem to be weakly reticulate [Bonde 1996], but Taverne disagrees [1978, p. 45–46] although his Figure 25 appears to show squamulae). The difference in scale structure may indicate different species. Considering the age difference from earliest Eocene to late Early Eocene in the North Sea Basin, it is a bit surprising that *Brychaetus* has not been found in the Mo-clay of intermediate age – but perhaps *Brychaetus* was simply rare in the earliest Eocene North Sea. This genus is known from Eocene deposits in Europe, eastern USA and northern and central Africa.

Osteoglossiform indet.

A small fish comprising part of the abdominal region and part of the skull, that is cut off in front of the hyomandibular. It is preserved in a cementstone without counterpart, probably at the level of ashlayer +15 in the upper half of Fur Formation. The fragment is 43 mm long, and the height of the body and the skull is 13 mm. About 3 cm of the abdominal region is preserved behind the opercular,

Fig. 25. Small osteoglossiform indet. MGUH 28.909. Opercular and anterior abdominal region of juvenile (?) fish. Fossil 43 mm long.

and apparently nothing of the caudal region. Only a few details of this fish will be described.

Skull. Very little detail is visible of the braincase and the large hyomandibular. The preopercular is incomplete, the rostral part of the horizontal branch is missing, but it appears to have been about as long as the vertical branch, which is *c.* 8 mm high, the angle of the bone being about 100°, and its maximal width is 3 mm. The large, rounded opercular is 10 mm high and 8 mm wide and has both a rough radiating ornamentation and very evident concentric growth lines. A small sub-opercular is visible at the preopercular corner. The missing snout is due to a break in the stone, the skull of the fossil may well have been complete and *c.* 3 cm long.

Pectoral girdle and fin. A rather broad cleithrum, broken at the dorsal end, and a strong, horizontal coracoid – probably with a hole near the posterior border – frame the opercular behind and below. The supracleithrum is not well preserved and the small scapular shows no details. The pectoral fin is 10 mm long and appears to be folded, because only about 8 rays can be seen. The upper ray is large, but not extremely so.

Abdominal region. Only the anterior part of the abdominal region is preserved, and there is no trace of the unpaired fins. Thirty-six vertebrae are visible behind the opercular, and 32 pairs of *c.* 10 mm long and strong ribs reach the ventral border, and they attach directly to the centra behind quite well-developed parapophyses at least in the anterior part. The neural spines of the anterior 20 or so vertebrae are strongly backwards inclined, and neither supra-neurals nor epineurals are seen above them, so the dorsal musculature must have been very low. The posterior part of the vent has been entirely torn away, leaving the ribs near the end bent away from each other, and the last four vertebrae are without ribs. It may well be that the hind end of the animal was bitten off before the cadaver ended in the diatomaceous ooze. All the vertebral centra are as high as they are long, and vertebral column, ribs, opercular region etc. are well ossified, so perhaps only the lack of ossification of supra- and epineurals as well as the small size indicates, that the animal is in fact a juvenile. The pelvic region is not preserved, which suggests that the fish may well have had twice the number of vertebrae as preserved.

Scales. The scales are small, smooth and round with concentric growth lines and no trace of reticulation, which might also be a juvenile feature. It appears unlikely, however, that this little fish is a juvenile *Heterosteoglossum.*

Relations. The huge opercular, large preopercular, very long ribs and rather strong first pectoral ray and elongate body with (presumably) many vertebrae are features found in most 'higher' osteoglossomorphs. Although not strictly diagnostic of these fishes, there seems no better alternative. The little that can be performed of comparative analysis (below) tends to place it rather high in the osteoglossiforms, but obviously this is very tentative.

Stratigraphic distribution of the Danish fossils

Two of the six Danish osteoglossomorph taxa, *Xosteoglossid* and *Brychaetus*, are known exclusively from the Stolle Klint Clay, that is from a low stand and landlocked marine basin. Two other taxa, *Furichthys* and *Brychaetoides*, have so far been found only in the very earliest Mo-clay (between ash layers −33 and −25). The indeterminate little osteoglossiform is known only from near the middle of the Mo-clay, and only *Heterosteoglossum* is found in both deposits and is quite common as judged by the many finds of scales (in fact also found in the lower London Clay).

Relationships of the Danish fossils

The relationships of the Danish Eocene osteoglossomorphs will be discussed in the framework of the recent reviews by Taverne (1998) and Hilton (2003) with some remarks also on the paper by Li & Wilson (1996*a*). I will accept these ideas as different models of the evolutionary history of osteoglossomorphs discussed in phylogenetic systematic or cladistic terms (for a distinction see Bonde 1977) to scrutinize what they mean for the phylogenetic positions of the Danish fossils. The fossils shall first be interpreted within Taverne's model, which is based on more than 300 characters, and which included all known fossils.

The discussion below is not 'quantified' by including the Danish taxa in a matrix, because there are serious problems with the many missing characters. It is more reasonable to confront the features themselves as they are used in the phylogenetic models by Taverne (1998) and by Hilton (2003) based on very different methodologies. Quantifications, in my opinion, tend to hide the real problems about comparing the single features, because whatever the data there are always some consensus models appearing according to some mathematical considerations and assumptions, which may have little to do with the empirical (real) world. So this study checks every feature among the postulated synapomorphies.

Heterosteoglossum

It is an osteglossomorph possessing the following features of Taverne (1998, p. 104, character number indicated by *; see Fig. 5): interbuccal dentition – only a little is visible on several bones (1*); no supraorbital (4*); reduced number of epurals, perhaps none (10*); complete npu1 (11*); 18 (or less) principal caudal ray (12*); Dorsal fin inserted very distally (ibid, p. 105); perhaps has no interhyal (7*) – at least none is observable.

Like forms more 'advanced' than Hiodontiforms it has: large opercular, nearly oval (24*); only 6 hypurals or less (29*); complete nu1 (28*); probably also no 'free' epural (27*); reduced subopercular (25*) – none seen.

Of those features shared also by *Singida* and more advanced forms it has: large nasals sutured to frontals (40*); large infraorbital 3 & 4 (42*) and quite likely also only four infraorbitals (41*); Further enlarged coracoid and pectoral fin (46*); less than two uroneurals (47*), and it seems to show notch in endopterygoid for basipterygoid process (44*); it definitely has neither short ventral branch of preopercular (long ventral arm as a reversal in Taverne's model) (45*) nor less than 18 principal caudal rays (48*); (the 18 rays in Taverne's model would represent a reversal from a more advanced osteoglossiform stage to a more primitive one).

Of Osteoglossiform plus Mormyriform synapomorphies it has: u2 with 3 dorsal hypurals fused in (65*); scales partly reticulated with ornamented squamules (66*); it probably also shows epineurals not fused to neural arches (63*); only one uroneural (64*); it seems not to have large ossified orbithosphenoid (58*); retroarticular excluded from the articulation (60*) – a debatable feature.

Because of the above two supposed reversals by Taverne it shares apomorphies with mormyroids caudal with 18 principal rays (12*); long ventral arm of preopercular (32*). It is more disturbing, however, that the few osteoglossiform synapomorphies, which can be checked, are not present: supracleithrum witout sensory canal (103*); lack of basisphenoid bone (126*); interorbital septum (156*); paired orbitosphenoid bones (208*); teeth with pedicles (211* – but teeth too small to judge) and another characteristic trait not mentioned by Taverne: premaxilla with a broad, medial, ascending process. Several of these features are, admittedly, not found in one or another 'advanced' osteoglossiform, especially in *Pantodon*, and neither in its close relatives *Osteoglossum* and *Scleropages*. Furthermore *Heterosteoglossum* seems also to be lacking the few controllable apomorphies shared by phareodonts and the more advanced osteoglossiforms: it probably has neither the broad antero-lateral expansion of frontals (214*); nor lack of membraneous supratemporal (219*); and it is uncertain whether it lacks teeth on the middle part of parasphenoid (215*). On the other hand it does have large nasals which presumably meet in the midline (226*), a feature of more advanced osteoglossiforms (and some 'phareodonts'). It also has a feature shared by *Opsithrissops* and more 'advanced forms': a longer and lower body with more vertebrae (232*); and, like *Brychaetus* it has dorsal hypurals 3–5 fused to u2 (if the caudal skeleton referred to is really from *Brychaetus*).

Even more important are the advanced traits shared with the extant osteoglossiforms of which one lineage comprises the Osteoglossidae: *Osteoglossum*, *Scleropages* and *Pantodon*. With those three the fossil shares no bony interorbital septum (reversal; 238*); and possibly derm- and retroarticular fused (79*; several parallelisms), while it does not have the elongation of lower jaw (239*). There are no important similarities specifically with *Pantodon*, but one with the lineage of *Osteoglossum/Scleropages* (277*: orbitosphenoid not ossified), which is countered by the lack of 109* (reduced number of principal caudal rays). Significant similarities with *Osteoglossum* alone could be very long body with more than 80 vertebrae (282*), possibly coupled with elongation of the dorsal (283*) and anal fin (284*), and also long first pelvic fin ray (285*). Primitive retentions are the lack of: lateral ethmoid loss (281*); 5 hypurals or fewer (22*); fewer than 10 branched caudal rays (286*).

There are also apomorphies jointly with fossil and Recent Arapaimidae, namely two coupled features: short mandible (31*); and long ventral arm of preopercular (reversal) (32*); while others are lacking: deep infraorbital 1–2 (291*); nu1 thin or short (294*); and uroneurals are small ridges on top of hypural 6 (295*). Shared with Eocene *Sinoglossus* and living arapaimids it has elongate dorsal (298*) and anal (299*) fins, but it lacks reduced caudal fin (109*), and probably also the unique fusion of antorbital and infraorbital 1 (297*). With the crown-group *Arapaima* plus *Heterotis* it shares further elongation of the body and dorsal and anal fins (307–309*); and probably retroarticular as part of the articulation (274*); while it seems not to have reduced myodome (302*); and there is no indication of a descending lamina on nasals (303*). Important traits shared with *Heterotis* alone are: reduced teeth in the short, rather high mandible (318*); but there are no traces of apomorphies like suprabranchial organ (316*); epipleurals (233*); or very large haemal arches (320*). A slim body, short upturned mouth with a short, high lower jaw, rather weak teeth and preopercular with a long ventral arm is also characteristic of the primitive arapaimid *Thrissopterus* (and for that matter also for the mid Cretaceous *Laeliichthys*, should it really be a very primitive arapaimid, which is doubtful [Bonde 1996]).

Arapaima specializations are lacking and there are only vague similarities with the two large Eocene, marine osteoglossiforms from Monte Bolca, *Monopteros* and *Thrissopterus*, those are reduced pelvis and pelvic fins (37*); and long dorsal and anal fins (298–299*). Likewise the only specific similarity with *Foreyichthys* seems insignificant, only one uroneural (64*).

Summing up these comparisons, there are significant similarities with advanced osteoglossiforms, but this concerns features combined from Osteoglossidae and *Heterotis* (of Arapaimidae), so *Heterosteoglossum* should probably be placed in Taverne's 'cladogram' as an advanced member of the stemgroup for Osteoglossidae plus Arapaimidae, that is about the same position as *Foreyichthys* was given above, especially due to the open interorbital fenestra, but with no special relationship with *Heterotis* and *Heterosteoglossum*. In the corresponding classification as outlined below *Heterosteoglossum* could be placed as the most advanced stem-group member of the Osteoglossidae (if it has unossified orbitosphenoid this might even place it as sister-group to the Osteoglossinae, because *Pantodon* has a pair of medium-sized orbitosphenoid ossifications in the anterior part of the orbit, which otherwise has cartilage almost closing the interorbital fenestra). Only a very conservative standpoint would place it as *sedis mutabilis* with the two families because of the character-conflict relating it to those two groups, which would imply that the just mentioned special similarities with crown-group osteoglossids would be due to convergence.

Furichthys

Furichthys, as presently preserved and prepared, is difficult to relate precisely to other osteoglossiforms due to the lack of information. Of its osteoglossomorph features only (1*) the interbuccal dentition can be assumed – but it is probably a primitive feature. Of 'higher osteoglossomorph' traits (non *Hiodon*-like) it has a large opercular (24*); and perhaps subopercular (slightly) reduced (25*); There seem also to be large nasals meeting (40*); and presumably a notch in endopterygoid for the basipterygoid process (44*); and preopercular with short ventral branch (45*). Likewise it has a large pectoral fin combined with some enlargement of the coracoid (46*).

It may have osteoglossiform–mormyriform specialisations such as strongly ossified ethmoid region (56*); and fused palato-ectopterygoid (59*), but it seems to lack retroarticular exclusion from the articulation (60*), and it probably has an ossified basihyal (contra 61*) and shows no reticulation of the scales (part of 66*).

The only osteoglossiform features shown by *Furichthys* is pedicles of the teeth (211*), but only small ones and only in premaxilla, which seems to lack the characteristic ascending process. And given the symmetrical shape of the possible basihyal with its tooth plate the bone is hardly fused to several more posterior elements forming a long bony tongue (218*). *Furichthys* does not have a long and low body like *Opsithrissops* and most advanced osteoglossiforms (232*), and the *Brychaetus* autapomorphies which can be checked (33*, 235*, 236*) are not present.

It does have a few of the osteoglossid synapomorphies, such as 239* long lower jaw and 79* articular fused to angular (a dermarticular), but none from the subdivisions of the group, nor from arapaimids including fossils.

In conclusion *Furichthys* seems to be a primitive relative of Osteoglossiformes plus Mormyriformes. It does not have very convincing features of osteoglossiforms, and apparently has no feature of any constituent subgroup apart from the 'long lower jaw' (osteoglossid-like), and there is no indication of close relationship to any of the known fossils. According to Taverne's model (1979, 1998) it occupies, based on one or two synapomorphies, a position just above *Singida* as an advanced member of the stem-group for the Osteoglossiformes/Mormyriformes, but it seems to lack 1–3 (?) specializations of this crown-group (Osteoglossi – named below).

Xosteoglossid

This fossil exhibits some more details, especially from the skull, and it can easily be recognized as a 'non-Hiodont', that is as more advanced osteoglossomorph having about 10 of the about 18 synapomorphies characteristic of the level, where *Singida* branches off in the stem-group of the osteoglossiform–mormyriform crown-group. (It only lacks one trait, the presumed loss of the last supramaxilla, which demands several reversals of this bone reappearing later in the history – see the introduction). It has about six of the about 14 further synapomorhies of this crown-group, but of these two features seem not to be present: the lack of ossification of the basihyal (60*) and the ventral hypohyal (61*) and it is, as mentioned above, not obvious that the scales are divided into squamules (reticulate; 66*). All three are features with difficulties of interpretation.

It does have a few of the osteoglossiform specialisations: 'divided' teeth on pedicles (211*), interorbital septum (156*) and the latter may not leave space for a separate basisphenoid (126*). But it appears not to have features of phareodonts (paraphyletic) and more advanced forms, neither antero-lateral expansion of frontals (214*), nor large, fused toothplate on the tongue (218*; it should have been visible in this type of detailed preservation), nor supratemporal without membrane bone (219*). It shows the questionable 'reversal' of a large supramaxillary (223*), but it is believed to be primitive. Of more advanced osteoglossiform traits it shares large meeting nasals (226*) placing it above *Phareodus sensu stricto*, and the diminished, more narrow ascending process on the premaxilla (231*), indicating a position at or above *Opsithrissops* and *Brychaetus*. If the lack of frontal expansion is really a loss (237*; a reversal), this might indicate an even higher position as an advanced member of the stemgroup of living (crown group) Osteoglossiformes. (The inferred body and likely fin proportions would agree with such position – and here *Laeliichthys* should be left out of the discussion at this level, as almost none of its claimed shared specialisations [290–295*] can be checked with certainty in these only 5 cm long fishes).

There is a character conflict between the long, prognathous jaws of osteoglossids (239*) and the free, movable maxilla of arapaimids (290*), the only features it possesses from these crown-group members. So it could be placed *sedis mutabilis* alongside Osteoglossidae and Arapaimidae. The alternatives are such, that if it is really an arapaimid relative, then it is quite primitive in this lineage. If it is an osteoglossid, it must be close to the split between *Osteoglossum/Scleropages* and *Pantodon*, and therefore also close to *Foreyichthys*, which shows a partly open interorbital septum (238*) perhaps only as a juvenile feature. But *Xosteoglossid* seems to share no important apomorphies with any of the fossils close to this position, neither to *Opsithrissops*, *Brychaetus*, *Foreyichthys* itself, nor *Heterosteoglossum* (with which it might share the inferred long, narrow body and head profile, but with a very different lower jaw).

Brychaetoides

This fragmentary fossil only shows a few features to indicate its relationships: extensive interbuccal dentition (1*) and no indication of supraorbital (4*) indicate its osteoglossomorph status. Another clue might be a large opercular (? 24*), and the *Singida*-level is indicated by large nasals meeting frontals (40*), and perhaps some partly open sensory canals (?43*). The ossification pattern of the ethmoids could be of a type (56*) found in the osteoglossiform–mormyriform group, while it is very uncertain whether there is a reticulate scale pattern (66* – but there are pores through the tubercles on the inner surface).

The teeth are clearly osteoglossiform (211*), and perhaps the parasphenoid part of an interorbital septum is visible (? 156*), and it has the broad,

medial ascending proces of primitive osteoglossiforms (and therefore not the *Opsithrissops* level; 231*). Frontals are evidently with lateral expansion like phareodonts (214*; therefore not 237* the more advanced loss of this trait, a reversal), but another feature is the lack of nasals meeting (226*) as they do in advanced osteoglossiforms. It probably has a long lower jaw as in living Osteoglossidae (239*; but has not lost the ossified parethmoid like *Osteoglossum*; 281*). The maxilla was not attached firmly to infraorbitals, and it may have had some mobility (290* partly) like in arapaimids, but with a longer mandible (not 31*). Its own specializations, e.g. the pattern of dentition, would lead to the conclusion that it seems to be a primitive osteoglossiform branch at the level below *Phareodus sensu stricto*.

The relations of cf. *Brychaetus* are quite obviously based on the characteristic and huge teeth, while its scales are not entirely similar to the London Clay species. The small indeterminate 'osteoglossiform' has the large rounded opercular of advanced osteoglossomorphs (24*), and large coracoid of even more advanced forms (46*). However, it does not have the concomitant very large pectoral fin, neither short ventral arm of preopercular (45*; characterizing the level above *Singida*, but reversed in arapaimics), and it lacks the reticulate scales (66*) as do most of the Danish osteoglossiforms. Its most significant feature may be its apparently long, low body (232*) with almost 40 vertebrae seemingly in front of the pelvic region (perhaps twice that number in total). This could indicate a level of *Opsithrissops* or higher on the osteoglossid lineage, and the above number is exceeded only by *Osteoglossum* and *Heterosteoglossum*. If the long ventral arm of the preopercular is interpreted as a reversal, it is an arapaimid characteristic (32* – but on the other hand also shared with *Heterosteoglossum*), and these also have rather long bodies (307*) with a similar number of vertebrae, c. 80, in *Arapaima*. The conclusion must be that this fossil probably is a 'higher' (derived) osteoglossiform, but very imprecise as *sedis mutabilis* (with perhaps a tendency for the arapaimid lineage, which only more complete fossils can test).

Finally it should not be overlooked, that in Taverne's model both *Opsithrissops* and *Brychaetus* are placed on the osteoglossid stemlineage based on very weak arguments, namely two consecutive apomorphies (elongate body, 232* and hypural 3–5 fused to u2, 85*), which are paralleled immediately during the first two steps of the arapaimid lineage. Only because the very dubious *Laeliichthys* is placed as a primitive arapaimid (based on 9 synapomorphies of which three are reversals, two or perhaps three are parallelisms with Hiodonts and Early Cretaceous Huashiidae, and the remaining three traits are impossible or very unlikely to be observed with certainty in such tiny fossils [5 cm fish, cf. my scepticisms above]), the aforementioned features 232* and 85* are not reconstructed already for the morphotype (last common ancestor) of arapaimids and osteoglossids. If this ancestor was supposed to have those features *Opsithrissops* and *Brychaetus* should be placed either with uncertainty at, or even below, this ancestor in the osteoglossiform stem-group. And in the same way also *Foreyichthys* and *Heterosteoglossum* should be placed near this ancestor, but presumably still as stem-group osteoglossids. The net result would be that the osteoglossiform crown-group would be characterized by some extra synapomorphies, namely the above 232* and 85*, but further also the reduction of the lateral expansion of frontals (237*) and the loss of supra-maxilla (23*; see p. 261). With this bone 'retained' in all of *Opsithrissops*, *Brychaetus* and *Xosteoglossid* around the level of this common ancestor, and also in *Phareoides* as the most primitive osteoglossiform stem-group member (actually also *Laeliichthys* has a supramaxilla), then it is much more likely to be a plesiomorph feature, and not several reversals, violating 'Dollo's law'. The supramaxilla undoubtedly has instead been lost in many osteoglossomorph lineages, as it is the case in many other groups of fishes.

Summary of interrelationships based on Taverne's model

All of the Danish Early Eocene bony tongues seem in the framework of Taverne's model (1998, which is almost unchanged since 1979, only the fossil Icthyodectiforms have been left outside Osteoglossomorpha following Patterson & Rosen 1977) to be osteoglossomorphs more 'advanced' than Hiodontids or rather related to the recent sister-group of the latter (that is Osteoglossi relatives, below). Only *Furichthys* is so primitive as to be an advanced member of the stemgroup of Osteoglossi, all the others are osteoglossiforms. *Brychaetoides* may belong in the osteoglossiform stem-group as a non-Mormyriform, while the four others are possibly crown-group members (or nearly so) with *Xosteoglossid* and the small form in uncertain positions between the two recent subgroups Arapaimidae and Osteoglossidae. *Brychaetus* and *Heterosteoglossum* are in advanced positions in the osteoglossid stem-group (where *Foreyichthys* should also be placed), but none appear to be truly a member of the crown-group Osteoglossidae. Only one species is known in many details including postcranium, namely *Heterosteoglossum foreyi*, but it does not seem to be especially closely-related to any of the other fossil marine forms, while it has a few

Heterotis-like features in the jaws, which might suggest behaviour as plankton feeder like the extant *Heterotis*.

A new name: Osteoglossi

As is readily seen in the above discussion, there is an obvious need of a name for the monophyletic group of Osteoglossiformes and Mormyriformes (= mormyroids plus notopteroids), which Taverne did not include in his 1979 classification, neither in 1998. Here it is suggested that taxon name is Osteoglossi for that clade, which seems to be recognized in all of the more comprehensive recent reviews (despite disagreements over the precise interrelationships within this group). Taverne (1998) and Li & Wilson (1996*a*, *b*) suggest the relation above, while Hilton (2003) is the first to argue that notopterids are most closely-related to the osteoglossiform (his osteoglossid) group with the sister-group of the being mormyroids (Mormyridae plus Gymnarchidae). Hilton calls this larger group [Mormyrids [Notopterids + Osteoglossids]] characterised at his node 'D' (see 2003, figs 4 and 7 – and here his fig. 4B is used as Fig. 7) an 'unnamed group', but it is quite obvious that this crown-group should have a name as sister-group to extant *Hiodon*, a crown-group containing two living species.

This taxon, Osteoglossi, is not identical to Hilton's Osteoglossiformes, which also contains fossil *Ostariostoma* (a problematic relationship) and therefore is a 'stem-based' taxon as opposed to the crown-group Osteoglossi (a 'node based' taxon – see de Queiroz & Gauthier 1992 and Bonde & Westergaard 2004). It is remarkable that Hilton, a neontologist, nearly always names taxa inclusive of stem-group fossils (2003), while he refrains from giving formal names to the corresponding, well-established living crowngroups. Is this the 'Simpsonian' legacy? Evolutionary tradition may destroy proper biological systematics by always insisting on fossils and 'ancestors' in order to make phylogenies and their reflected classifications more objective (or 'less hypothetical' as it was claimed – see Bonde 1977). The same story is behind the eternal quarrels over the 'true meaning' of birds, the taxon Aves, and this has very important consequences for discussing the age and origin of a group, whether one talks about the crown-group or the crown- plus stem-group – or somewhere in-between (as is usually done by palaeontologists, e.g. in the case of Aves or *Hiodon*).

New classification of the Osteoglossomorphs

Below is a classification of Osteoglossomorpha, based on the cladogram from Taverne (1998, fig. 22); but changed for *Foreyichthys*, here placed after *Brychaetus* at the base of *Pantodon* plus Osteoglossidae, as above. Also *Palaeonotopterus* and the six Danish osteoglossiforms have been introduced (underlined in the classification below) in their proper positions, and *Joffrichthys* has been moved to conform with Li & Wilson (1996*b*). The taxon name Osteoglossi is coined for crown-group of osteoglossiforms plus mormyriforms. Here also (minimum) ages are added to give an immediate idea of the minimum ages of the nodes (splits, speciations), which can, in fact, be used as both a relative and absolute rank, especially if ages are given as millions of years (see Bonde & Westergaard 2004).

The most dubious taxa, marked [?] in the above classification of Taverne's trees (1998, figs 21, 22; Fig. 5) have been removed (they could perhaps be reinstalled as Osteoglossomorpha *incertae sedis*), and superfluous taxon names are avoided, like monotypic families (e.g. †*Singida* instead of †Singidae). On the other hand a few intermediate taxa are indicated as taxon A, B etc., they are not all strictly necessary as formal taxa. 'Taxon D' is a total group, that is, crown-group Osteoglossidae plus its entire stem-group (back to the split from Arapaimidae), and a taxon name seems necessary to express that this taxon is interchangeable (shown as mut.) at the same level with Arapaimidae (total group), and the two Danish fossils, *Xosteoglossid* and the 'small indet osteoglossiform'. In the same way 'taxon B' needs a name for expressing that at a higher level in the hierarchy this group is interchangeable with *Musperia, Phaerodusichthys* and *Dapedoglossum* (all indicated mut.) at this level. But 'taxon A' is not strictly necessary, as it only gives a name to the latter level where all members have a certain synapomorphy, in this case character 226, although unknown for *Phaerodusichthys*, which is known only from jaw fragments. The latter has been placed here by Taverne (1998, 131) only due to its strong ascending process of premaxilla, which thus is similar to phareodonts (see also Gayet *et al.* 2001 – and like *Brychaetoides*). It is, however, problematic at which stage this heavy process at the symphysis was developed because, in the mormyriform sister-group there is such process on the rather small premaxillae in notopterids (Taverne 1978), but the premaxilla is not known for the next more basal branches, *Singida* and *Kipalaichthys* (Greenwood & Patterson 1967; Taverne 1976), and the small Huashiidae have reduced upper jaws and the premaxilla of Hiodonts is a thin bone without an ascending process (Taverne 1977; Hilton 2002). So the strong ascending process may have been characteristic even in the stem-group of Osteoglossi, and does not indicate a very precise level for the position of *Phaerodusichthys*. Whether it belongs exactly at this level or not does not change the fact, that the mutually interchangeable groups could just have been sequenced between *Phareodus* and *Monopteror* without creating a name for taxon A.

It is obvious, that because the three more dubious osteoglossiform genera from Lower to mid. Cretaceous, marked [?] in the classification p. 265, are removed, then the need of very long 'ghost lineages' (Norell 1992) is greatly diminished, the only ones being those between *Plesiolycoptera* and *Eohiodon* from Early Cretaceous to mid Eocene (*c.* 70 ma), for *Palaeonotopterus* to Notopteridae from mid-Cretaceous to Eocene–Oligocene (*c.* 65 ma), for *Ostariostoma* from Early to latest Cretaceous (*c.* 60 ma), and those for *Arapaima* Paleocene to Pliocene (*c.* 55 ma), and for Mormyroidei, *Pantodon* and *Osteoglossum*, all Eocene-Oligocene to Recent (*c.* 40 ma). It is seen that all known fossil or recent genera of Osteoglossiforms (of the crown-group) are not older than Paleocene (minimum ages), contrary to the implications of Taverne's placement of *Paradercetis* as sister-group to *Heterotis* giving both that lineage and that of *Arapaima* (both actually comprising only one species) a minimum age about 100 ma.

The relative high ages of Recent genera also in this phylogenetic classification with the mentioned lower to mid Cretaceous fossils removed to an uncertain position (perhaps as stem-group osteoglossiforms as discussed by Bonde 1996), namely Paleocene for *Heterotis* and accordingly also for *Arapaima*, and mid-Eocene for *Hiodon* (indicated as minimum ages by *Joffrichthys* and *Eohiodon* respectively), may be an artifact of the traditional way of naming such monophyletic taxa including part of their stemgroup as 'genera.' If taxon names were instead only used for crown-groups (since last common ancestor of extant members), then the two extant species of *Hiodon* alone would define that name for the (crown) genus, which might be very young, perhaps from the Pleistocene, as defined by their speciation (node or separation from each other).

Only a fossil referred to one of those two extant species would indicate min. age of that speciation, and therefore of *Hiodon* in the restricted sense. The *Hiodon consteniorum* from Lower Eocene is in a stem-group position, and therefore of no relevance for the age of the *Hiodon* crown-group. Furthermore, lineages with only one species today like *Heterotis* and *Arapaima*, cannot really give an estimate of the age of their respective 'crown group lineages' because no splits (or nodes) are known (and a single species is at the limit of usual definitions of a [monophyletic] group). There may well have been some so far unknown and extinct species split away from these lineages

New classification of Osteoglossomorpha, including all marine fossils

Osteoglossomorpha
  Hiodontiformes
    †*Ostariostoma*, L. Cretaceous/E. Paleocene
    †Lycopteridae [3+ gen.], E. Cretaceous
    Hiodontidae [*Hiodon*, L. Eocene & 3–4 extinct genera, since E. Cretaceous, with *Eohiodon*, M. Eocene]
    †Huashiidae [2 gen.], L. Cretaceous
    †*Singida*, Eocene
    †*Furichthys*, Eocene
  Osteoglossi, new crown-group
    Mormyriformes (total group)
      †*Palaeonotopterus* [added here], M. Cretaceous
      Notopteridae, Eocene-Oligocene
      Mormyroidei
        Gymnarchus
        Mormyridae [*c.* 14 gen.], Pliocene
    Osteoglossiformes (total group)
      † *Brychaetoides*, Eocene
      †*Phareoides* [= †'*Phareodus*'], Eocene
      †*Phareodus*, Paleocene
      Taxon A
        †*Dapedoglossus* [=†'*Phareodus*'], Eocene, mut.
        †*Musperia*, Eocene/Oligocene, mut.
        †*Phaerodusichthys*, Paleocene, mut.
      Taxon B mut.
        †*Monopteros*, Eocene
        Taxon C
          †*Xosteoglossid*, Eocene, mut.
          †'small indet. osteoglossiform' (Mo-clay), Eocene, mut. (aff. Arapaimidae?)
          Arapaimidae, mut.
            †*Joffrichthys*, Paleocene
            †*Trissopterus*, Eocene
            †*Sinoglossus*, Eocene
            Arapaima, Pliocene?
            Heterotis
        Taxon D, mut. (total group)
          †*Opsithrissops*, Eocene
          †*Brychaetus* [2 spp.], Paleocene – Eocene
          †*Foreyichthys*, Eocene
          †*Heterosteoglossum*, Eocene
          Osteoglossidae (s.l.)
            Pantodon
            Scleropages (? Paleocene/Eocene)
            Osteoglossum

Symbols, abbreviations and position of †*Foreyichthyus* as in the classification on p. 265. The most dubious taxa from Taverne's classification (1998) removed. †*Joffrichthyus* placed according to Li & Wilson (1996*b*) and Taverne (1998, Addendum 1). Danish taxa underlined. [. . .] remarks about content of a taxon, synonyms and diversity of fossil taxa. Taxon C represents the Osteoglossiformes crown group with two Danish fossils in uncertain position; they may be in the stem group as listed, but could be inside the proper crown group (Arapaimidae plus Osteoglossidae).

and having evolved characteristics to indicate a different species and thereby a (crown) group (to be referred to by a generic name if such fossils were found) of minimum age as the fossil taxa.

The possible Pliocene scales (Taverne 1979) might do the trick for *Arapaima*. The same arguments count for *Pantodon* and osteoglossids, the latter comprising two crown-group genera each with two species, but there are no fossils to indicate their ages, which for all of them might be very young (even a Pleistocene distribution pattern – across the 'Wallace line' – might well be a possibility for the species of *Scleropages*) – completely in disagreement with the molecular analyses by Kumazawa & Nishida (2000), which are said to indicate the split among the species of *Scleropages* in SE Asia and New Guinea–North Australia (*S. formosus* and *S. leichardti* respectively) to be of Early Cretaceous age (Pouyaud *et al.* 2003 recognised six 'species' within *S. formosus*!). From a palaeontological viewpoint this age appears to be very unlikely, even if one accepts that some scales can actually be identified with confidence as *Scleropages* from Eocene–Oligocene on Sumatra (Sanders 1934) or otoliths and fragments from Palaeocene in Belgium (Taverne *et al.* 2007) (see the biogeographical discussion).

Relationships in Hilton's model

If Hilton's hypothesis of osteoglossomorph interrelationships is accepted as a framework for interpreting the Danish fossils it remains to be seen if it makes a significant difference for the position of those fossils (specifically if any group of the marine genera should emerge as a clade). This could have some bearing upon their (palaeo-) biogeographic significance, because in the extreme case that all marine genera formed a single monophyletic group, this would facilitate the hypothesis that at least the Osteoglossi is a 'primary freshwater group' with a Gondwana origin and spreading only by freshwater routes – apart from that single excursion into marine waters.

Hilton's model(s) from 2003 (Fig. 7) are based on very thorough discussions of every single character used to generate his cladograms. It is one of the largest osteoglossomorph datasets to be employed in a cladistic analysis based upon 19 terminal taxa (and only one outgroup, *Elops*) and 72 characters carefully selected (several of those used in Taverne's analysis [1998 and above] were discarded for reasons stated in detail). Unfortunately only few fossils were included (*Lycoptera, Eohiodon, Ostariostoma, Joffrichthys, Phareodus, Brychaetus, Palaeonotopterus* and a fossil species of *Notopterus*, *N. primaevus* but the latter and *Brychaetus* do not appear in Hilton's trees).

The latter taxon was considered synonymous with *Phareodus*, and that genus alone (then based on three species, two of which are from freshwater deposits) was coded (e.g. Hilton 2003, p. 57 and App. I). A surprising number of features were considered unknown for *Phareodus*, actually the most well-known of all fossil osteoglossiforms, of

which even-acid prepared specimens exist. It is also unfortunate that Hilton used only one outgroup, although many primitive teleosteans were discussed, and a few of those from clupeocephalans and/or euteleosts or perhaps Jurassic teleosts could easily have been added to the matrix. It is also a little disturbing that state 0 is not always the most plesiomorph state, even when that information is well established.

The comparisons below refer to Hilton's (2003, p. 25–27) characterizations of the nodes of his tree, fig. 4B (Fig. 7) by listing the relevant character number, which are described in detail by Hilton (p. 27–82). The states are only given, when they are different from [1] and advanced (i.e., if the state is not given with the character number then it is advanced and assumed to be [1]).

Heterosteoglossum fits node A, Osteoglossomorpha, by possessing characters 20, 22, 28 [0] (perhaps primitive), 56 [0] (quite likely a primitive trait), 65, 68, 69 [0] out of the 15 features listed for this node. From node X (all taxa but *Lycoptera*, based on 4 traits) it possesses 37, probably 36, but not 7. Of six hiodontid features, node B, it may have something like the postpelvic bone (62). From node C, Osteoglossiformes [including *Ostariostoma* plus the recent crown-group (much more inclusive than Taverne's taxon name)], it possesses 60, 66 and 71 [2] and of the 17 features it may also show 5[0] and possess several, which are not preserved, but it does not have 7 [2], 43 and 58. Of the five traits for D, above called Osteoglossi, it has 68 [2], but probably not 41.

Among 7 features for node E, Hilton's new 'Osteoglossoidei' (=Osteoglossidae plus Notopteridae) it possesses only 6 [2] and 67, but not 37 [0] and 65 [2], and perhaps not 32 [2] and 2. (This lack of many synapomorphies seems odd here). From Hilton's 10 characters of his *sensu lato* Osteoglossidae, node F, it possesses 7 [3], 29, 41 [0] and perhaps 24 [0] and 25, but apparently does not show 2 [2], 21 [0] and 49. Node G (unnamed, corresponds to his Osteoglossidae crown-group, should clearly have a name as above), with three traits sharing 9 [0] with *Heterosteoglossum*, but not 72 [2] (the fully reticulate scales), and 35 (subopercular size) is uncertain. Hilton's node H, Heterotinae (= Taverne's Arapaimidae, above) has 10 features, of which *Heterosteoglossum* may have 32 [0] and 43 [0] (both primitive), while it lacks 23, 28 and probably 42 [2]. From the sister-group at node I, Osteoglossinae (Taverne's Osteoglossidae plus Pantodontidae), with 4 traits it has 61, 63 and probably 3, but not 33. From node J, unnamed, with 6 traits 'shared' by *Pantodon, Phareodus* and *Singida* (most are unknown for one or both fossils) it has 58 [0] ('presumably plesiomorph' Hilton, p. 71) and uncertainty about all others. With node

K (unnamed for *Pantodon* plus *Singida*, for the latter only one trait is known), having 8 features, it only may be said to share 72 (the scales with both reticulate and radial furrows), but does not have 29 [0], other features uncertain. Node L is Hilton's unnamed group for *Scleropages* plus *Osteoglossum* (Taverne's Osteoglossidae) with five synapomorphies and only sharing 12 and 37 with *Heterosteoglossum*, others unknown.

Summing up this distribution of features which are recognizable in *Heterosteoglossum* the pattern in Table 1 appears. But how can we interpret this pattern in terms of relationships? *Heterosteoglossum* clearly has some basic osteoglossomoph features, although two of them are primitive teleostean traits, and some evidence for the next level on the tree. There are also several special similarities with specific subgroups such as *Osteoglossum* plus *Scleropages* (Osteoglossidae of the preceeding discussion) and the next higher level (Hilton's Osteoglossinae including *Pantodon*). But between this level and the basic level there is a suspicious lack of supporting characters, (actually more characters are known *not* to be present [17] than supporting ones [13]). This implies a lot of homoplasy because of the missing synapomorphies at several levels, if *Heterosteoglossum* is placed within Hilton's framework. Although *Heterosteoglossum* appears best interpreted as related to Hilton's osteoglossines based on 5 synapomorphies, the lack of 20 synapomorphies (from the *c.* 50 that are possible to verify in the fossil) is troublesome. Also some of the 'synapomorphies' at different levels are really primitive retentions (e.g. the two heterotine 'synapomorphies'), made possible in Hilton's analysis due to the lack of more outgroups. One should note, that the conclusion here for *Heterosteoglossum* is exactly the same as when using Taverne's model, and almost 100 features were checked.

Furichthys shares the following traits with Hilton's nodes:

Node A: 20 (no supraorbital) and all others unknown.

Node X: 37 (only slightly developed proc. asc. on premaxilla), but not 7.

Node B; Hiodonts: none known.

Node C: Osteoglossiformes: perhaps 30 (palato-ectopterygoid), but probably not 43, others unknown.

Node D: Osteoglossi (new name): not 41, others unknown.

Node E: probably 6 [2] (nasals meeting), but not 37, the rest unknown.

Node F: Osteoglossidae: 41 [0] (primitive), probably 7 [3] (nasals flat, broad) and 21 [0] (primitive), but not 44.

Node G: 9 [0] (? primitive), but not 72 [2].

Table 1. Heterosteoglossum *features 'mapped' on Hilton's model*

Node	Number of characters *Heterosteoglossum* possesses / does not have		My comments in parentheses; Hilton's taxonomy	Total number of 'node-apomorphies'	My systematic conclusion
A	6	0	(two traits plesiomorphic)	15	Osteoglossomorph
X	2	1	Osteoglossomorpha excl. stem	4	Osteoglossomorph crown-group
B	1	3	(dubious homology: postpelvic)	6	not hiodont
C	3	1	Osteoglossiformes	17	? Osteoglossiform
D	1	4	Osteoglossiformes crown-group	5	? Osteoglossi new
E	2	4	new Osteoglossoidei	7	?
F	4	1	'Osteoglossidae'	10	?
G	1	3	Osteoglossidae crown-group	3	?
H	2	1	'Heterotinae'	10	? not related
I	3	0	'Osteoglossinae'	4	Osteoglossin/-id
J	1	1	*Pantodon* + 2 fossils	6	(primitive feature)
K	1	0	*Pantodon* + *Singida*	8	(parallelism)
L	2	1	Osteoglossinae + *Scleropages*	5	? closely-related
Total	29	20		100	

Node H: apparently 43 [0] (primitive), but not 42 [2] and 47.

Node I: Osteoglossinae: perhaps 3 (equal frontal width).

Node J: *Pantodon* plus fossils, nothing is known.

Node K: only 43 [0] (primitive), the rest unknown.

Node L: 37, but the lack of an ascending proces on the huge, very specialized premaxilla in *Furichthys* is probably not the same as the lack of such process on the tiny premaxilla in osteoglossines; nothing else known.

Comparison with notopterids and mormyroids is of no relevance, *Furichthys* appears to be a very primitive osteoglossid (*sensu* Hilton), with synapomorphies no higher than node F, or perhaps even no higher than node E in the stem-group of his new clade, combined notopterids + osteoglossids. This corresponds approximately to the position in the stem-group of Osteoglossi in the analysis based upon Taverne's model (where also mormyriforms are included in the crown-group), where the level would correspond to node D.

There are many characters of *Xosteoglossid* to relate to the Hilton model – it has the following characterizing his nodes:

Node A: 20, 22, 28 [0], 31, but not 40 (lack of supramaxilla, which is coded incorrectly anyway).

Node X: it probably has 36, but not 7.

Node B: it shows no hiodontid features.

Node C: it has 5 and 66, and probably 30, but not 7 [2] and probably not 43.

Node D: those five features are unknown in the fossil.

Node E: it has 10 and 37 [0], but not 32 [2] and probably not 2.

Node F: it has 7 [3], 21 [0], 25, 29, 41, but not 2 [2] and probably not 49.

Node G: it has 9 [0].

Node H: it has 32 [0] and probably 39, but not 23 and 28.

Node I: it has 61 and probably 3 and 33.

Node J: it has no information on those features.

Node K: it may have 72 (the reticulate scale character weakly developed), but not 29 [0].

Node L: it does not have 12 and 37; Node M etc, notopterids and mormyrids, are not relevant.

Concluding remarks. *Xosteoglossid* has some features up to the levels of node I (osteoglossines) and node H, (heterotines) but it lacks a few from the latter group. Concerning the lower nodes *Xosteoglossid* shows most of the characteristic features (with only one or two traits lacking at some levels), but it has no hiodontid traits. Again, as in Taverne's model, the conflicting features from osteoglossines and heterotines (osteoglossids and arapaimids in his terms) gives an uncertain position

(*sed. mut.*) between those two groups. So it may belong to the crown-group osteoglossids (osteoglossiforms for Taverne) or just outside as an advanced member of the stem-group.

The few characters that can be checked for *Brychaetoides* indicate that from node A it has character 6 and perhaps 44. From node X it lacks 7, and it has none of the hiodontid features of node B. From node C it has 6 [0], but may lack 44 [0]. It does not give information on node D features, but from node E it has 37 [0], but not 6 [2]. From node F it can only be seen to show 41 [0], while it lacks 7 [3]. Node G features are unknown, and from node H it just lacks 23 with the rest unknown. It gives no information on node I and J characters, but from node K (*Pantodon*) it has 6 and perhaps 21. It is unknown for node L traits.

It can thus be confirmed for *Brychaetoides* that it shows a few traits related to the *Pantodon* group and thereby to osteoglossines, but shows no features from heterotines. From more basal nodes, if it shows any of the characters, it generally has one and lacks another at each level, and it shows two features of the most basal osteoglossomorph node. To conclude, *Brychaetoides* should (in accordance with its advanced features) be placed near *Pantodon*. This seems quite different from the more basal position indicated in Taverne's model. But one should note that in Hilton's model, not very surprisingly, *Phareodus* is closely-related to *Pantodon* (and *Singida*), causing *Brychaetoides* to shift up into the crown-group of osteoglossiforms/-glossids past *Xosteoglossid*. In the original description of *Singida*, and shortly after (Greenwood & Patterson 1967; Nelson 1969; Murray & Wilson 2005), a relationship to *Pantodon* was seriously discussed, and in the analysis of *Phareodus* by Li *et al.* (1997) phareodonts (including *Brychaetus*), *Pantodon* and *Singida* appear as consecutive branches on the way towards *Osteoglossum/Scleropages* with only 1–2 steps between those branches. Li *et al.* (1997) conclude their research with a model of the osteoglossomorph interrelationships that, for the recent forms, is exactly the same as Taverne's model.

Brychaetus is synonymized with *Phareodus* in the Hilton model, as done by Li *et al.* (1997), and it would therefore also be moved in the system. The small indet. osteoglossiform can only be related to a few characters in Hilton's scheme. It probably has 56 of node A (epipleurals absent) and 60 from node C (coracoid fenestra), and it does not have the osteoglossine feature of a very deep opercular (no. 33 of node I). Accordingly it should be placed somewhere between node C and node I. This is also where it ended up with a little more precision in Taverne's model, namely at the node leading to heterotines and osteoglossines, or as an osteoglossid *incerta sedis* (using Hilton terms corresponding to node G).

Also with Hilton's model as framework the six Danish fossils are distributed over the cladogram from the stemgroup of non-Hiodont osteoglossomorphs (*Furichthys*) to inside the crowngroup of the osteoglossines/osteoglossids proper (*Heterosteoglossum*) or just high in their stemgroup, and with none of them closely related to each other or to other marine osteoglossiforms (the latter, however, 'hidden' under synonymy in Hilton's model).

Hilton (2003) found after profound discussion several severe problems in the phylogenetic analysis by Li & Wilson (1996*a*), which could otherwise also have been used for comparisons with the Danish fossils, so although the latter included as much as 14 fossil taxa and three living outgroups plus the Jurassic fossil *Leptolepis*, I refrained from using their model. My own experience (in prep.) trying to relate *Sinoglossus* from the Chinese Eocene to their model is also that there are many problems with both their interpretation and coding of characters, so their model of relationships is not very easy to use.

The more recent quantitative, cladistic analysis of osteoglossomorph interrelationships by Zhang (2006; acquired after submitting this paper) is based on 65 characters and has exactly the same relation between the living forms as in Taverne's model. Zhang includes many Chinese fossils, not in the models mentioned above, but has no other Asian fossils, none of the European, marine forms apart from *Brychaetus*, no African fossils but *Singida*, and none from South America. Zhang keeps the phareodonts including *Brychaetus* together with *Singida* as a sister-group to osteoglossids including *Pantodon*, and those two groups combined as sistergroup to arapaimids. Therefore comparison with the Danish fossils is unlikely to give a result very different from the above comparison with Taverne's model, apart from the obvious one that *Brychaetus* is placed in a monophyletic phareodont group.

Phylogeny and distribution

The marine, fossil osteoglossomorphs are of special interest to zoogeographers because they are related to one of the groups of fishes, which today comprises only so called 'primary freshwater fish' (Myers 1949, also used in biogeographic texts like Darlington 1948, 1957, 1965), which appear to be completely intolerant of saltwater, so that their present distribution cannot be explained by migrations via seawater. To reconstruct past distributional history of a group in any reasonable way, a secure phylogenetic background is mandatory

with precise knowledge of the interrelationships of the members of the group and of the group to its most closely-related taxa (Nelson 1969, 1976; Patterson 1975, 1981; Gayet 1987; Grande & Bemis 1999). During the period of these studies the concept 'vicariance biogeography' was developed by Nelson and his colleagues (see Rosen 1978; Nelson & Platnick 1981; Nelson & Rosen 1981) as a method which corresponded better to a world knowledgeable of continental drift.

The experience of using Taverne's (1998) and Hilton's (2003) respective phylogenetic models, which have been constructed in different ways, perhaps to be characterized as 'qualitative-intuitive' and 'quantitative-rigorous' respectively, has shown the following. For the position of the six taxa of Danish fossils within osteoglossiforms the results are very similar for four of these taxa, the three with most information present, *Heterosteoglossum Xosteoglossid* and *Furichthys*, and the small indeterminate form: *Heterosteoglossum* is just inside the crown-group Osteoglossidae (Taverne's taxonomy) on the lineage to *Osteoglossum/Scleropages*, or just outside as an advanced member of the stemgroup. *Xosteoglossid* can be placed best in an uncertain relationship with the two families Osteoglossidae and Arapaimidae, and be classified *sedis mutabilis* with these families. *Furichthys* seems much more primitive, and belongs in the stem-group for Osteoglossi (Osteoglossiforms plus Mormyriforms including notopterids; Taverne's terms) as an advanced member more derived than the *Singida* branch, although in Hilton's model it tends to be placed slightly 'higher' in the stem of a less inclusive clade, his new Osteoglossoidei, or even in the stemgroup of his Osteoglossidae (osteoglossines plus heterotines). On the contrary the small osteoglossiform seems placed with greater precision in Taverne's model, namely at the node for crown osteoglossiforms, perhaps even near the base of the branch to arapaimids. In Hilton's model it can, due to the very few (only 3) of his characters that can be observed, only be placed somewhere between node C and I (six splits – that is as an osteoglossiform no more advanced than a stem-group osteoglossine in his terms).

There is a greater difference concerning *Brychaetus* (by Hilton coded as *Phareodus*) and *Brychaetoides*. In Taverne's model *Brychaetus* is an advanced member of the osteoglossid *sensu stricto* stem-group far 'above' *Phareodus*, while in Hilton's model the two are coded together and end up 'one step higher' inside the osteoglossine crown-group as closely-related to *Pantodon* (and *Singida*). The difference is much more drastic for *Brychaetoides*, in Taverne's model placed in the stem-group of osteoglossiforms (= Hilton's osteoglossids) just 'below'

Phareodus sensu stricto. But, because the latter in Hilton's model has moved many 'steps up' (six nodes higher), into the lineage of *Pantodon*, then *Brychaetoides* apparently moves with it. In this model this new genus is placed very close to *Brychaetus/Phareodus*.

Hilton's model comprises no marine forms, but by the addition of the Danish fossils in six (at least five) different positions in the osteoglossiform part of the tree, each of these positions in an evolutionary context will constitute separate excursions into the sea. The same is true for Taverne's model, which already included five marine forms, all at different branches of the osteoglossomorph tree. By adding the Danish marine fossils there will be yet six more marine branches on the tree (or at the very least four, if both *Xosteoglossid* and the small form here placed near the split between arapaimids and osteoglossids could be shown to join another marine lineage).

This demands a closer analyses of the implication for the minimum number of osteoglossomorph excursions into the sea because, in the most parsimonious model for the ecological preferences and changes of habitats of these fishes, several neighbouring marine branches could be interpreted as first one migration into the sea with several consecutive branches living there, and then one (or more) later re-invasion(s) of freshwater.

Before these Danish additions, the tree by Taverne (Fig. 5) – especially if *Laeliichthys* is removed from its uncertain position as a basal arapaimid – implies that the last common ancestor of his arapaimids and osteoglossids (including *Pantodon*) is most likely to have been marine. This is because on all sides of this ancestor node there are exclusively marine branches (*Monopteros*, *Thrissopterus*, *Opsithrissops* and *Brychaetus* and it is suggested that *Foreyichthys* is more derived than *Brychaetus*). So the most parsimonious solution for the habitat of this ancestor of the two families is the sea, which was invaded before the *Monopteros* branch. The arapaimids then re-invaded freshwater after the *Thrissopterus* split, and *Joffrichthys* gives the minimum date of that as Paleocene. The osteoglossids did the same after the split with *Foreyichthys* (or *Brychaetus*) and, if there really are *Scleropages* scales in the Eocene of Sumatra (Sanders 1934) and otoliths and skeletal fragments in the Belgian Palaeocene (Taverne *et al.* 2007), it would have had to be earlier than that.

Even if the criticism above is not acceptable concerning the position of *Opsithrissops* and *Brychaetus* on the osteoglossid lineage, and they should be relegated down to just above *Monopteros* in the top of the stem-group for osteoglossiforms, this would make no difference for the two families. They would still have marine forms at their bases (*Thrissopterus* and *Foreyichthys* respectively),

and several marine forms in the top of their stem-group.

It is quite clear, that the addition of the Danish marine forms to the tree makes this hypothesis much more evident, because both *Xosteoglossid* and the small form are placed somewhere near this ancestral node. Furthermore *Heterosteoglossum* is placed near the top of the osteoglossid stemgroup, if not inside the crowngroup on the *Osteoglossum/Scleropages* lineage. The latter position would imply that both that lineage and *Pantodon* were separate re-invasions of freshwater. These invasions may not be older than Eocene, in fact they might well be younger (unless it is really a *Scleropages* [stem group, presumably] described by Taverne *et al.* 2007 – above).

Furichthys and *Brychaetoides* are not so well known anatomically and therefore probably not quite as safely placed in the phylogeny, but most likely they occupy positions near and probably below respectively above the 'common ancestor node' for the two lineages of osteoglossiforms and mormyriforms (including notopterids). *Furichthys* is 'high' in the stem-group, and *Brychaetoides* near the base of the osteoglossiform lineage. The implication of this is clearly that the common ancestor of those two lineages was also marine. This would be even much more evident if it were right that *Phareodus sensu lato* is a natural group comprising both *Phareoides* and *Dapedoglossum* (whether *Brychaetus* and perhaps *Musperia* are included or not is unimportant for this argument – it may complicate the model a little though). In that case this genus, *Phareodus* (*sensu lato*) may constitute just one branch and one re-invasion of freshwater by Late Cretaceous, and the entire stem-lineage for osteoglossiforms would evidently have been marine including the node from which it originated by splitting from mormyriforms by the mid Cretaceous or earlier.

If we look at the base of the osteoglossomorph tree it is clear that all the closest outgroups of this clade are marine, whether one prefers the Patterson & Rosen model (1977) with osteoglossomorphs as sistergroup of all other living teleosts, or Arratia's model (e.g. 1997, 2000) with elopomorphs in that basal position. All the early teleosts from the Jurassic at the top of their stem-group are also marine (Arratia 1997, 2000; Patterson & Rosen 1977), so osteoglossomorphs originated in the sea, we just have not yet found or recognized the earliest osteoglossomorphs. This carries the implication that also the hiodontiforms might be a separate migration from sea- to freshwater (by Early Cretaceous), especially because of the somewhat uncertain position of the other early freshwater branches in the tree, such as Huashiids, *Kipalaichthys* and *Singida*. If they were placed differently, either on the hiodontiform lineage or on that of the mormyriforms (or if one or more of them are not ostoglossomorphs at all), then the simplest model could well be, that the entire stem-lineage from the root of the tree and up to the node for osteoglossids was better interpreted as marine. Such interpretation is entirely dependent on the phylogenetic positions of the many new marine members of the group.

When there was only one anomaly, *Brychaetus*, one could almost forget about it (or raise questions about its relations like Nelson 1969), and in Patterson's model (1975) a single marine form did not make much difference. But by now when there are 9 marine taxa placed in as many different positions in the tree, they cannot be ignored (unless they were all members of just one or two marine clades). They paint the entire picture in very different colours than before, and we will have to re-think the history of the bony-tongues, and wonder why they are all today so intolerant of salt water as Myers (1949) would claim (and which perhaps is not entirely true according to Taverne *et al.* 2007).

After the findings and/or reinterpretations of all the Eocene marine osteoglossiforms, there are evidently good arguments for abandoning the classical idea of osteoglossiform fishes as primary freshwater fishes clearly of Gondwanan origin with a potential of linking widespread continental areas in a comprehensive vicariance biogeographic model. Early on this was done exclusively in 'dispersalist' models like Darlington's (1948, 1957, 1965) or other 'evolutionists'. But this was not very different from 'progression' models by Hennig (e.g. 1966) and Brundin (1966) both in a phylogenetic systematic framework criticising Darlington and his 'school'. Today much historical biogeography is done with a background in vicariance theory as developed by Nelson, Rosen, Platnick and others firmly based in cladistic theory (Nelson 1969; Patterson 1981; Nelson & Platnick 1981; Nelson & Rosen 1981). In such analyses precise phylogenetic models are required in the attempts to reconstruct ancient distribution patterns of many different natural groups.

In fact, looking at a single group is not optimal, unless there are several subgroups which can complement each other. The classical single group approach, like here, as done both by 'evolutionists' of the Mayr–Simpson–Darlington school and the early 'hennigians' is often open for interpretations in terms of dispersal. As done early on also by Nelson (1975), it is dependent on the tendency of the organisms to move, migrate and disperse. One attempts to reconstruct the simplest possible migrations from one area to another, often assuming a 'need' to expand the area of occupation. A vicariance approach suggests that the land (or sea for that matter) moves or become divided with the organisms passively moving with their habitats. Seen in a worldview of known continental drift and origin of physical dispersal barriers, this makes one less assumption about behaviour of the organisms.

But most of these models should 'face the real world', that is be tested by data, and here fossil distributions force themselves upon the interpreter in unexpected and sometimes inexplicable ways. We did not know this great diversity of marine osteoglossomorphs before testing. In an analogous way, a scientific study gave us the disturbing fact that there appears to be an Eocene anteater in Europe (Storch 1981, 1984). Should that number increase to several Old World anteaters, the history of the edentates would certainly have to be drastically rewritten – like that of the osteoglossomorphs, which should now be given up as primary freshwater fish.

Conclusion

The description of several new marine osteoglossiforms of the Danish Eocene dramatically increases the diversity of this group. The phylogenetic positions of these marine forms on the phylogenetic tree necessitates total re-evaluation of the biogeographic history of the group, because they make it quite clear that Osteoglossomorpha is not a primary freshwater fish group with osteoglossiforms having a typical Gondwana distribution and vicariance history. Instead several subgroups of the osteoglossomorphs are separate invaders into freshwater from the sea. Both the osteoglossids (perhaps at two occasions) and the arapaimids are separate invasions, and the same may be true for the mormyriforms and probably even the hiodontiforms.

Without the findings of these many marine fossils such interpretations would never have been possible. But where would the missing marine, (Late Jurassic–) Cretaceous osteoglossiforms have been? Perhaps in the Pacific round 'Pacifica' (Melville 1966), the mythical and disintegrating continent in the middle of the ocean (which Gayet [1987] also invoked to explain osteoglossomorph distribution) from which slivers of land were squeezed into the surrounding continents mainly by subduction, so much of these marine deposits have been lost forever (including their fossils). Search in Andean Cretaceous to Palaeogene sediments and perhaps corresponding rocks in Japan or Alaska might produce some answers (and one should remember that the North American Maastrichtian has produced marine 'osteoglossid' otoliths [Nolf & Stringer 1996]).

Note: Danekræ comprise exceptional Danish natural objects (meteorites, fossils, minerals etc.) which when found must, following a law of 1990, be offered to the state (Hald 1993). If approved by the Geological Museum as a danekræ the finder receives a reward. The large *Furichthys* described herein, found by a German collector in about 1985, was instrumental in the process of convincing politicians to pass this legislation through the Danish parliament. The story of the danekrae and descriptions and photographs of the 200 most important danekrae (*c.* 500 approved since 1990) are given in Bonde *et al.* 2008.

Many thanks to P. Forey for many discussions over the years about primitive teleosteans, phylogenetic systematics and – what we shall never agree upon – classification conventions; I have learned a lot (I hope). And thanks for his staunch support to those cladistic principles also 30 years ago, when it was not quite so simple, but actually very controversial. We have won in the long run it appears – but still not in many palaeontological circles, especially in Scandinavia, East Europe and Germany. And many thanks to the three editors for their invitation to contribute to this volume – and for their gentle patience during the process. Thanks also to all three for generous help during visits to NHM over the last few years – to Alison and Peter actually for help during 30 years or so. My thanks for discussions since the 1960s on osteoglossids should also be extended to our late colleagues, C. Patterson and H. Greenwood, they were an invaluable inspiration for many years when also G. Nelson and the late D. Rosen were involved in those discussions, which gradually ended in cladistics taking over among ichthyologists, especially because of those four persons. I am grateful to preparators Z. Fihl and S. L. Jakobsen in Geological Museum for skilful preparation of the fragile and difficult *Heterosteoglossum*, for photographic help with all the illustrations and for discussions about our 'pet-fossils' the beautiful and important Danekræ. For the latter my thanks also go to our co-worker on the Danekræ-book and former chairman of the 'Danekræ-committee', N. Hald. Thanks to Danmarks Akvarium for arawana material, and to the Zoological Museum, especially J. Nielsen, for access to their fish collections. The drawings were finished from my *camera lucidas* by B. Munch and C. Hagen in my institute, and I am also grateful to this institution for support to many trips to Jutland, London and Paris to study and collect fossil fish. Not the least I owe many thanks to the local museums in the Mo-clay area for permission to study their valuable fossil collections: in Molermuseet, Mors to the former and present leaders and ardent fossil collectors, B. Søe Mikkelsen since 1980, whose private collection is the basis for that museum, and more recently H. Madsen and to their families also for hospitality and friendship. In Fur Museum to its former leaders, the late M. Breiner on whose collection that museum was founded in the 1950s and the late E. Fjeldsø Christensen, palaeobotanist, and the last few years the present leader B. Schultz, geologist, and his co-workers. Back in the 1960s and 1970s it was most often the Carlsberg Foundation that supported the excursions to the Mo-clay, early on by my teacher, the late Dr E. Nielsen.

Institutions: FUM, Fur Museum; MGUH, Geological Museum, Copenhagen; NHM, Natural History Museum, London.

References

ANDERSEN, N. M. 1998. Water striders from the Paleogene of Denmark with a review of the fossil record and evolution of semiaquatic bugs (Hemiptera, Gerromorpha). *Det kongelige danske V.denskabernes Selskab, Biologiske Skrifter*, **50**, 1–157.

ANDERSEN, S. & SJØRRING, S. (eds) 1997. *Geologisk set: Det nordlig Jylland.* Naturstyrelsen & Geografforlaget (Brenderup).

ANDERSEN, S. A. 1937. Volcanic ashlayers in the road-cutting at Ølst and their distribution in Denmark. *Danmarks geologiske Undersøgelser*, **59**, 1–53. [In Danish, with an English summary.]

ARCHIBALD, S. B. & MARKARKIN, V. N. 2006. Tertiary Giant Lacewings (Neuroptera: Polystoechotidae): Revision and description of new taxa from Western North America and Denmark. *Jounal of Systematic Palaeontology*, **4**, 119–155.

ARAMBOURG, C. 1952. Les Vertébrés fossiles des Gisements de Phosphates (Maroc-Algérie-Tunisie). *Service Géologique, Maroc, Notes et Mémoires*, **92**, 1–372.

ARRATIA, G. 1997. Basal teleosts and teleostean phylogeny. *Palaeo Ichthyologica*, **7**, 5–168.

ARRATIA, G. 2000 Remarkable teleostean fishes from the Late Jurassic of southern Germany and their phylogenetic relationships. *Mitteilungen, Museum für Naturkunde, Berlin, Geowissenschaftlische Reihe*, **3**, 137–179.

AUBRY, M.-P. & OUDA, K. 2003. Introduction. *In*: OUDA, K. & AUBRY, M.-P. (eds) *The Upper Paleocene–Lower Eocene of the Upper Nile Valley: Part 1, Stratigraphy. Micropaleontology*, **49**, Supplement 1.

BEYER, C., HEILMANN–CLAUSEN, C. & ABRAHAMSEN, N. 2001. Magnetostratigraphy of the Upper Paleocene–Lower Eocene deposits in Denmark. *Newsletters of Stratigraphy*, **39**, 1–19.

BONDE, N. 1966. The fishes of the Mo-clay Formation. *Meddelelser fra dansk geologisk Forening*, **16**, 198–202.

BONDE, N. 1973. Fish fossils, diatomites and volcanic ashlayers. *Dansk Geologisk Forening*, **Årsskrift for 1972**, 136–143. [In Danish.]

BONDE, N. 1974. Review of 'Interrelationships of Fishes' (eds, Greenwood, Rosen & Patterson, 1973). *Systematic Zoology*, **23**, 562–569.

BONDE, N. 1975. Origin of 'higher groups': viewpoints of phylogenetic systematics. *Colloque International du Centre National de la Recherche Scientifique, Paris*, **218**, 293–324.

BONDE, N. 1977. Cladistic classification as applied to vertebrates. *In*: HECHT, M. K., GOODY, P. C. & HECHT, B. M. (eds) *Major Patterns in Vertebrate Evolution.* Plenum Press, New York, 741–804.

BONDE, N. 1979. Palaeoenvironment in the 'North Sea' as indicated by the fish bearing Mo-clay deposit (Paleocene/Eocene) Denmark. *Mededelungen, Werkgruppe Tertiär Kwartär Geologie*, **16**, 3–16.

BONDE, N. 1982. Teleostei (bony fish) from the Paleocene of the Norwegian North Sea drillings. *Norsk Geologisk Tidsskrift*, **62**, 59–65.

BONDE, N. 1987. *Moler – its origin and its fossils, especially fishes*. SKAMOL, Nykøbing Mors. 53pp.

BONDE, N. 1996. Osteoglossids (Teleostei: Osteoglossomorpha) of the Mesozoic. Comments on their interrelationships. *In*: ARRATIA, G. & VIOHL, G. (eds) *Mesozoic Fishes – Systematics and Paleoecology*. Dr F Pfeil, Munich, 273–284.

BONDE, N. 1997. A distinct fish fauna in the basal ash-series of the Fur/Ølst Formation (U. Paleocene, Denmark). *Aarhus Geoscience*, **6**, 33–48.

BONDE, N. 1999. Colin Patterson, a major palaeontologist of this Century. *Geologie en Mijnbouw*, **78**, 255–260.

BONDE, N. 2003*a*. The Mo-clay – a shrine of ancient life. *Geografisk Orientering*, **33**, 90–96. [In Danish.]

BONDE, N. 2003*b*. Introducing phylogenetic systematics – Advance of cladistics in Denmark and other countries. *Dansk Naturhistorisk Forening, Aarsskrift*, **13**, 8–34. [In Danish.]

BONDE, N. & WESTERGAARD, B. 2004. Progress in hominid classification: cladistic approaches. *In*: BAQUEDANO, E. & RUBIO JARA, S. (eds) *Miscelanea en homenaje a Emiliano Aguirre vol. III, Paleoantropologia, Zona Arqueologica, No. 4*. Museo Arqueologico Regional, Alcala de Henares, Madrid, Spain, 37–57.

BONDE, N., ANDERSEN, S., HALD, N. & JAKOBSEN, S. L. 2008. *Danekræ* – The best fossils from Denmark [In Danish.]

BRUNDIN, L. 1966. Transantarctic relationships and their significance as evidenced by chironomid midges. *Kungliga Svenska Vetenskaps Akademiets Handlinger*, **11**, 1–472.

BØGGILD, O. B. 1903. Vulkansk Aske i Moleret. *Meddelelser fra Dansk Geologisk Forening*, **2**, 1–12. [In Danish.]

BØGGILD, O. B. 1918. Volcanic ashes in the Mo-clay *Danmarks Geologiske Undersøgelser*, **33**, 1–84. [In Danish; French Summary.]

CAPETTA, H. 1972. Les poissons crétacés et tertiaires du bassin des Iullemmeden (Rep. di Niger). *Palaeovertebrata*, **5**, 179–251.

CASIER, E. 1966. *Faune Ichthyologique du London Clay*. British Museum (Natural History). London, 1–496.

CAVIN, L. & FOREY, P. L. 2001. Osteology and systematic affinities of *Palaeonotopterus greenwoodi* Forey 1997 (Teleostei, Osteoglossomorpha). *Zoological Journal of the Linnean Society*, **133**, 25–52.

CHANG, M.-M. & CHOU, C. C. 1977. On late Mesozoic fossil fishes from Zhejiang Province, China. *Memoirs of Institute of Paleontology and Paleoanthropology, Akademia Sinica (Beijing)*, **17**, 1–60. [In Chinese, English summary].

CHANG, M.-M. & CHOU, J.-J. 1976. Discovery of *Plesiolycoptera* in Songhuajiang–Liaoning Basin and origin of Osteoglossomorpha. *Vertebrata Palasiatica*, **14**, 146–153. [In Chinese.]

CHRISTENSEN, E. Fjeldsø 1994. Hunting large fish in the Mo-clay *Museerne i Viborg Amt*, **14**, 5–18. [In Danish.]

COPE, E. D. 1877. New fossil fishes from Wyoming. *American Naturalist*, **11**, 570.

CROUCH, E. M., HEILMANN–CLAUSEN, C. *ET AL*. 2001. Global dinoflagellate event associated with the Late Paleocene thermal maximum. *Geology*, **29**, 315–318.

DANIL'CHENKO, P. G. 1968. The fishes of the Upper Paleocene of Turkmenistan. *In*: OBRUCHEV, D. V. (ed.) *Phylogeny and Systematics of Fossil Fishes and Agnathans*. Nauka Press, Moscow, 113–156. [In Russian.]

DANIL'CHENKO, 1980. Clupeiformes. *In*: NOVITSKAJA, L. J. (ed.) *Iskolaembe kostistbe ryby SSSR*. Akademia Nauk SSSR., Trudy Paleont-Inst. (Moskva), **178**, 7–26. [In Russian.]

DARLINGTON, P. J. 1948. The geographical distribution of cold-blooded vertebrates. *Quarterly Review of Biology*, **23**, p1–26 & 105–123.

DARLINGTON, P. J. 1957. *Zoogeography. The Geographical Distribution of Animals*. Wiley & Sons, New York.

DARLINGTON, P. J. 1965. *Biogeography of the Southern End of the World*. Harvard University Press, Cambridge, MA.

DE QUEIROZ, K. & GAUTHIER, J. 1992. Phylogenetic taxonomy. *Annual Review of Ecology and Systematics*, **23**, 449–480.

DYKE, G. J., WATERHOUSE, D. M. & KRISTOFFERSEN, A. V. 2004. Three new fossil landbirds from the early Paleogene of Denmark. *Bulletin of the Geological Society of Denmark*, **51**, 47–56.

EGGER, H. & BRÜCKL, 2006. Gigantic volcanic eruptions and climatic change in the Early Eocene. *International Journal of Earth Science (Geologische Rundschau)*, **95**, 1065–1070.

EGGER, H., HEILMANN-CLAUSEN, C. & SCHMITZ, B. 2000. The Paleocene/Eocene boundary interval of a Tethyan deep-sea section and its correlation with the North Sea Basin. *Societé Géologique de France, Bulletin*, **217**, 243–264.

FOREY, P. L. 1970. *A revision of the order Elopiformes (Pisces: Teleostei)*. University of London, PhD thesis.

FOREY, P. L. 1997. A Cretaceous notopterid (Pisces, Osteoglossomorpha) from Morocco. *South African Journal of Science*, **93**, 564–569.

FRODESEN, S., MOL, A., OFSTAD, K., ORMAASEN, E., SJULSEN, S. E. & ULLEBERG, K. 1981. The Balder Area. *Norwegian Petroleum Directorate, Paper*, **28**, 1–30.

GARASSINO, A. & JAKOBSEN, S. L. 2005. *Morscrangon acutus* n. gen. n. sp. (Crustacea, Decapoda, Caridea) from the Fur Formation (Early Eocene) of the Islands of Mors and Fur (Denmark). *Atti Societa italiana di Scienze naturali, Museo civico di Storia naturale, Milano*, **146**, 95–107.

GAYET, M. 1987. *Conciderationes preliminares sobre la paleobiogeografia de los Osteoglossomorpha*. IV Congresso Latinoamericana Paleontologia, Bolivia, (1987) I, 379–398. La Paz. [In Spanish.]

GAYET, M., MARSHALL, L. G. *ET AL*. 2001. Middle Maastrichtian vertebrates (fishes, amphibians, dinosaurs and other reptiles, mammals) from Pajcha Pata (Bolivia). Biostratigraphic, palaeoecological and palaeobiogeographic implications. *Palaeogeography, Palaeoclimatology, Palaeoecology*, **169**, 39–68.

GAYET, M. & MEUNIER, F. 1983. Écailles actuelles et fossiles d'Osteoglossiformes (Pisces, Teleostei). *Comptes Rendus de l'Academie des Sciences, Paris*, **297**, Série II, 867–870.

GRADSTEIN, F. M., OGG, J. & SMITH, A. (eds) 2004. *A Geologic Time Scale.* Cambridge University Press, Cambridge, UK.

GRANDE, L. 1984. Paleontology of the Green River Formation with a review of the fishfauna, 2nd ed. *Bulletin of the Geological Survey of Wyoming*, **63**, 1–333.

GRANDE, L. & BEMIS, W. E. 1999. Historical biogeography and historical paleoecology of Amiidae and other halecomorph fishes. *In*: ARRATIA, G. & SCHULTZ, H.-P. (eds) *Mesozoic Fishes 2 – Systematics and the fossil record.* Dr F. Pfeil, Munich, 413–424.

GRAVERSEN, P. 1993. Collecting Fossils in South Scandinavia and North Germany. Goldschneck-Verlag, Weinstadt, 1–248. [In German.]

GREENWOOD, P. H. 1967. The caudal fin skeleton in osteoglossoid fishes. *Annals and Magazine of Natural History, series 13*, **9**, 581–597.

GREENWOOD, P. H. 1971. Hyoid and ventral gill arch musculature. *Bulletin of the British Museum (Natural History), Zoology*, **22**, 1–5.

GREENWOOD, P. H. 1973. Interrelationships of osteoglossomorphs. *In*: GREENWOOD, *ET AL.* (eds), *Interrelationships of Fishes.* Zoological Journal of the Linnean Society, London, **53**, Suppl. 1. London, Academic Press, 307–331.

GREENWOOD, P. H. & PATTERSON, C. 1967. A fossil osteoglossoid fish from Tanzania East Africa. *Zoological Journal Linnean Society, London*, **47**, 211–223.

GREENWOOD, H. P. & THOMPSON, K. S. 1960. The pectoral anatomy of *Pantodon buchholzi* Peters (a freshwater flying fish) and the related Osteoglossidae. *Proceedings of the Zoological Society of London*, **135**, 283–301.

GRY, H. 1940. Glacial tectonics in the Mo-clay. *Meddelelser fra dansk geologisk Forening*, **9**, 586–626. [In Danish.]

HALD, N. 1993. Three years with Danekrae. *Fossilien*, **6**, 346–350. [In German.]

HEILMANN-CLAUSEN, C. 1982. The Paleocene–Eocene boundary in Denmark. *Newsletter of Stratigraphy*, **11**, 55–63.

HEILMANN-CLAUSEN, C. 1985. Dinoflagellate stratigraphy of the uppermost Danian to Ypresian in the Viborg 1 borehole, central Jutland, Denmark. *Danmarks Geologiske Undersøgelser, Serie A*, **7**, 1–39.

HEILMANN-CLAUSEN, C. 1996. Paleogene above the limestone. *Aarhus Geokompendier*, **1**, 69–114. [In Danish.]

HEILMANN-CLAUSEN, C. 1997. How one diatomite led to the formation of another diatomite – the Oligocene section at Silstrup, NW–Denmark. *Tertiary Research*, **18**, 31–34.

HEILMANN-CLAUSEN, C. 2006. Coral limestone and muddy sea. *In*: LARSEN, G. (ed.) *Geologien, Naturen i Danmark.* Gyldendal, København, 78–81, 87–120. [In Danish.]

HEILMANN-CLAUSEN, C., NIELSEN, O. B. & GERSNER, F. 1985. Lithostratigraphy and depositional environments in the Upper Paleocene and Eocene of Denmark. *Bulletin of the Geological Society of Denmark*, **33**, 287–323.

HEILMANN-CLAUSEN, C. & SCHMITZ, B. 2000. The Late Paleocene thermal maximum δ13C excursion in Denmark. *Geologiska Föreningens I Stockholm Förhandlinger*, **122**, 70.

HEISTER, L. E., O'DAY, P. A., BROOKS, C. K., NAUHOFF, P. S. & BIRD, D. K. 2001. Pyroclastic deposits within the East Greenland Tertiary flood basalts. *Journal of the Geological Society, London*, **158**, 269–284.

HENNIG, W. 1966. *Phylogenetic Systemctics.* University of Illinois Press. Chicago.

HILTON, E. J. 2002. Osteology of the extant North American fishes of the genus *Hiodon* Lesueur 1818 (Teleostei: Osteoglossomorpha: Hiodontiformes). *Fieldiana, Zoology, new series*, **100**, 1–142.

HILTON, E. J. 2003. Comparative osteology and phylogenetic systematics of fossil and living bony-tongue fishes (Actinopterygii, Teleostei, Osteoglossomorpha). *Zoological Journal of the Linnean Society of London*, **137**, 1–100.

HOCH, E. 1975. Amniote remnants from the eastern part of the Lower Eocene North Sea Basin. *Colloque International du Centre National de la Recherche Scientifique, Paris*, **218**, 543–562.

HOMANN, M. 1991. Die Diatomeen der Fur Formation. *Geologisches Jahrbuch*, A **123**, 1–285.

KING, C. 1981. *The stratigraphy of the London Clay and associated deposits.* Tertiary Research, Special Paper 6. Backhuys, Rotterdam.

KNOX, R. W. O'B. 1984. Nannoplankton zonation and the Paleocene/Eocene boundary beds of NW Europe: An indirect correlation by means of volcanic ash layers. *Journal of the Geological Society, London*, **141**, 993–999.

KNOX, R. W. O'B. 1996 *Correlation of the Early Paleogene in northwest Europe: an overview.* Geological Society, London, Special Publications, **101**, 1–11.

KNOX, R. W. O'B. 1997. The Late Paleocene to Early Eocene ash layers of the Danish Mo-clay (Fur Formation): Stratigraphic and tectonic significance. *Aarhus Geoscience*, **6**, 7–11.

KNOX, R. W. O'B. & MORTON, A. C. 1988. *The record of early Tertiary N. Atlantic volcanism in the sediments of the North Sea Basin.* Geological Society, London, Special Publications, **39**, 407–419.

KNOX, R. W. O'B. & MORTON, A. C. 1990. Geochemistry of late Paleocene and early Eocene tephras from the North Sea Basin. *Journal of the Geological Society, London*, **147**, 425–437.

KRISTOFFERSEN, A. V. 1999. Lithornid birds (Aves, Palaeognathae) from the lower Paleogene of Denmark, *Geologie en Mijnbouw*, **78**, 375–381.

KRISTOFFERSEN, A. V. 2002a. *The avian diversity in the latest Paleocene-earliest-Eocene Fur Formation.* Ph.D. dissertation, Denmark, Geological Institute, University of Copenhagen, 95pp. (unpublished).

KRISTOFFERSEN, A. V. 2002b. An Early Paleogene trogon (Aves: Trogoniformes) from the Fur Formation, Denmark. *Journal of Vertebrate Paleontology*, **22**, 661–666.

KÖTHE, A. 1990. Paleogene dinoflagellates from Northwest Germany, biostratigraphy and environment. *Geologische Jahrbuch*, A **118**, 1–111.

KUMAR, K., RANA, R. S. & PALIWAL, B. S. 2005. Osteoglossid and lepidosteid fish remains from the Paleocene Palana Formation, Rajasthan, India. *Palaeontology*, **48**, 1187–1209.

KUMAZAWA, Y. & NISHIDA, M. 2000. Molecular phylogeny of osteoglossoids: A new model for Gondwanian origin and plate tectonic transportation of the Asian arowana. *Molecular Biology and Evolution*, **17**, 1869–1878.

LARSEN, H. C. 1988. A multiple and propagating rift model for the NE Atlantic. *In*: MORTON, A. C. & PARSON, L. M. (eds) *Early Tertiary Volcanism and the Opening of the NE Atlantic*. Geological Society, London, Special Publications, **39**, 137–138.

LARSEN, L. M., FITTON, J. G. & PEDERSEN, A. K. 2003. Paleogene volcanic ash layers in the Danish Basin: compositions and source areas in the North Atlantic Igneous Province. *Lithos*, **71**, 47–80.

LEONARD, L., DYKE, G. J. & VAN TUINEN, M. 2005. A new specimen of the fossil palaeognath *Lithornis* from the Lower Eocene of Denmark. *American Museum Novitates*, **3491**, 1–11.

LI, G.-Q. 1987. A new genus of Hiodontidae from Luozigou Basin, East Jilin. *Vertebrata PalAsiatica*, **25**, 91–107. [In Chinese with English summary.]

LI, G.-Q. 1996. A new species of Late Cretaceous osteoglossid (Teleostei) from the Oldman Formation of Alberta, Canada, and its phylogenetic relationships. *In*: ARRATIA, G. & VIOHL, G. (eds) *Mesozoic Fishes – Systematics and Palaeoecology*. Dr F. Pfeil, Munich, 285–298.

LI, G.-Q. & WILSON, M. V. H. 1996a. Phylogeny of Osteoglossomorpha. *In*: STIASSNY, M. L. J., PARENTI, L. R. & JOHNSON, G. D. (eds) *Interrelationships of Fishes*. Academic Press, San Diego, 163–174.

LI, G.-Q. & WILSON, M. V. H. 1996b. The discovery of heterotidinae (Teleostei, Osteoglossomorpha) from the Paleocene Paskapoo Formation of Alberta, Canada. *Journal of Vertebrate Paleontology*, **16**, 198–209.

LI, G.-Q., GRANDE, L. & WILSON, M. V. H. 1997. The species of *Phareodus* (Teleostei: Osteoglossidae) from the Eocene of North America and their phylogenetic relationships. *Journal of Vertebrate Paleontology*, **17**, 487–505.

LI, G.-Q., WILSON, M. V. H. & GRANDE, L. 1997. Review of *Eohiodon* (Teleostei: Osteoglossomorpha) from western North America, with a phylogenetic reassessment of Hiodontidae. *Journal of Paleontology*, **71**, 1109–1121.

LINDOW, B. & DYKE, G. J. 2006. Bird evolution in the Eocene: climate change in Europe and a Danish fossil fauna. *Biological Reviews*, **81**, 483–499.

LONGBOTTOM, A. 1984. New Tertiary pycnodonts from the Tilemsi Valley, Republic of Mali. *Bulletin of the British Museum (Natural History), Geology*, **38**, 1–26.

MADSEN, H. & RUST, J. 2000. World's oldest butterfly – insects from Mo-clay and Stolle Klint Clay; *Varv, København*, **2000**, 9–18. [In Danish.]

MELVILLE, R. 1966. Continental drift, Mesozoic continents and the migration of the angiosperms. *Nature*, **211**, 116–120.

MEUNIER, F. 1984. Spatial organization and mineralization of the basal plate of elasmoid scales in osteichthyans. *American Zoologist*, **24**, 953–964.

MICHELSEN, O., THOMSEN, E., DANIELSEN, M., HEILMANN-CLAUSEN, C., JORDT, H. & LAURSEN, G. V. 1998. Cenozoic sequence stratigraphy in the eastern North Sea. *In*: GRACIANSKY, P. C., JACQUIN, T. & VAIL, P. R. (eds) *Mesozoic and Cenozoic Sequence Stratigraphy of European Basins*. SEPM Special Publications, **60**, 91–118.

MØLLER, J. D. 1892. Catalogue of tables of diatomes by Møller. Wedel, Holstein. [In German.]

MURRAY, A. M. & WILSON, M. V. H. 2005. Description of a new Eocene osteoglossid fish and additional information on †*Singida jacksonoides* Greenwood & Patterson 1967 (Osteoglossomorpha), with an assessment of their phylogenetic relationships. *Zoological Journal of the Linnean Society, London*, **144**, 213–228.

MYERS, G. S. 1949. Salt tolerance of fresh-water fish groups in relation to zoogeographical problems. *Bijdragen Dierkunde*, **28**, 315–322.

NELSON, G. J. 1968. Gill arches of teleostean fishes of the division Osteoglossomorpha. *Zoological Journal of the Linnean Society, London*, **47**, 261–277.

NELSON, G. J. 1969. Infraorbital bones and their bearing on the phylogeny and geography of osteoglossomorph fishes. *American Museum Novitates*, **2394**, 1–37.

NELSON, G. J. 1975. Historical biogeography: an alternative formalization. *Systematic Zoology*, **23**, 555–558.

NELSON, G. J. 1976. Reviews: Biogeography, the vicariance paradigm, and continental drift. *Systematic Zoology*, **24**, 490–504.

NELSON, G. J. & PLATNICK, N. 1981. *Systematics and Biogeography. Cladistics and Vicariance*. Columbia University Press, New York.

NELSON, G. J. & ROSEN, D. E. (eds) 1981. *Vicariance biogeography: a critique*. Columbia University Press, New York.

NELSON, J. S. 1994. *Fishes of the World*. 3rd ed. Wiley & Sons, New York.

NIELSEN, E. 1960. A new Eocene teleost from Denmark. *Meddelelser fra Dansk Geologisk Forening*, **14**, 247–252.

NIELSEN, E. 1963. On the postcranial skeleton of *Eosphargis breineri* Nielsen. *Meddelelser fra Dansk Geologisk Forening*, **15**, 281–328.

NIELSEN, O. B. 1974. Sedimentation and diagenesis of Lower Eocene sediments at Ølst, Denmark. *Sedimentary Geology*, **12**, 25–44.

NIELSEN, O. B. 1994. Lithostratigraphy and sedimentary petrography of the Paleocene and Eocene sediments from the Harre borehole, Denmark. *Aarhus Geoscience*, **1**, 15–35.

NIELSEN, O. B. & HEILMANN-CLAUSEN, C. 1986. Lithology and stratigraphy of the Tertiary section. *In*: NIELSEN, O. B. ET AL. (eds) *Tertiary deposits in Store Bælt*. Geoskrifter (Aarhus University), **24**, 235–253.

NOLF, D. 1978. Les otolithes de téléostéens des formations de Landen et de Heers (Paléocène de la Belgique). *Geologica et Palaeontologica, Marburg*, **12**, 223–234.

NOLF, D. & STRINGER, G. L. 1996. Cretaceous fish otoliths – a synthesis of the North American record. *In*: ARRATIA, G. & VIOHL, G. (eds) *Mesozoic Fishes – Systematics and Paleoecology*. Dr. F. Pfeil, Munich, 433–459.

NORELL, M. A. 1992. The effect of phylogeny on temporal diversity and evolutionary tempo. *In*: NOVACEK, M. & WHEELER, Q. D. (eds) *Extinction and Phylogeny*. Columbia University Press, New York, 89–118.

NORRIS, R. D. & RÖHL, U. 1999. Carbon cycling and chronology of climate warming during the Paleocene/Eocene transition. *Nature*, **401**, 775–778.

PATTERSON, C. 1975. The distribution of Mesozoic fresh water fishes. *Mémoires, Musée Nationale d'Histoire Naturelle, Série A, Zoologie*, **88**, 156–174.

PATTERSON, C. 1981. Methods of paleobiogeography. *In*: NELSON, G. & ROSEN, D. E. (eds) *Vicariance biogeography: a critique*. Plenum Press, New York, 446–500.

PATTERSON, C. 1993. Teleostei. *In*: BENTON, M. J. (ed.) *The Fossil Record 2*. Chapman & Hall, London, 619–654.

PATTERSON, C. & ROSEN, D. E. 1977. Review of ichthyodectiform and other Mesozoic teleost fishes and the theory and practice of classifying fossils. *Bulletin of the American Museum of Natural History*, **158**, 81–172.

PEDERSEN, G. K. 1981. Anoxic events during sedimentation of a Paleogene diatomite in Denmark. *Sedimentology*, **28**, 487–504.

PEDERSEN, G. K. & BUCHARDT, 1996. The calcareous concretions (cementstone) in the Fur Formation: isotopic evidence of early calcite precipitation. *Bulletin of the Geological Society, Denmark*, **43**, 78–86.

PEDERSEN, G. K., PEDERSEN, S. A. S., STEFFENSEN, J. & SCHACK, C. 2004. Clay content of a clayey diatomite, the Early Eocene Fur Formation, Denmark. *Bulletin of the Geological Society, Denmark*, **51**, 159–177.

PEDERSEN, G. K. & SURLYK, F. 1983. The Fur Formation, a Late Paleocene ash-bearing diatomite from northern Denmark. *Bulletin of the Geological Society, Denmark*, **32**, 43–65.

PEDERSEN, S. A. S., PEDERSEN, G. K. & NOE, P. 1994. *Moler på Mors*. Nykøbing Mors, 1–48.

PETERSEN, K. S. 1973. Some features in clay with tuff-beds from Lower Eocene on Røsnæs, Denmark. *Danmarks Geologiske Undersøgelser*, **1972**, 69–78.

POUYEAUD, L., SUDARTO, A. & TEUGELS, G. G. 2003. The different colour varieties of the Asian arowana *Scleropages formosus* (Osteoglossidae) are distinct species: morphologic and genetic evidence. *Cybium*, **27**, 287–305.

PRINZ, M. W. & VON ERMENGEN, E. 1883. Recherches sur la structure de quelques diatomées continues dans le 'cementsten' du Jutland. *Annales de la Société Belgique de Microscopie*, **8**, 7–74.

RANA, R. S. 1988. Fresh water fish otoliths from the Deccan Trap associated sedimentary (Cretaceous-Tertiary transition) beds of Rangapur, Hyderabad District, Andhra Pradesh, India. *Geobios*, **21**, 465–493.

RASMUSSEN, H. V. 1972. Lower Tertiary Crinoidea, Asteroidea and Ophiuroidea from northern Europe and Greenland. *Royal Danish Academy of Sciences, Biology*, **19**, 1–83.

ROELLIG, H. F. 1974. The cranial osteology of *Brychaetus muelleri* (Pisces, Osteoglossidae) Eocene, Isle of Sheppey. *Journal of Paleontology*, **48**, 947–951.

RÖHL, U., BRALOWER, T. J., NORROS, G. & WEFER, G. 2000. New chronology for the Late Paleocene thermal maximum and its environmental implications. *Geology*, **28**, 927–930.

ROSEN, D. E. 1978. Vicariant patterns and historical explanation in biogeography. *Systematic Zoology*, **27**, 159–188.

RUST, J. 1999. Biologie der Insekten aus dem ältesten Tertiär Nordeuropas. Bd. 1 & 2. Göttingen, Georg-August-Universität. (Unpublished Ph.D. thesis).

SANDERS, M. 1934. Die fossilen Fische der Alttertiären Süsswasserablagerungen aus Mittel-Sumatra. *Verhandelingen van het Geologisch-Mijnbouwkundig Genotschap voor Nederländ enKolonien, Gravenhage, Geologische Serie*, **11**, 1–144.

SCHIØLER, P., ANDSBJERG, J. *ET AL*. 2007. Lithostratigraphy of the Paleogene–lower Neogene siliciclastic sediments in the Danish sector of the North Sea. *Geological Survey of Denmark and Greenland, Bulletin* (in press).

SCHMITZ, B., HEILMANN-CLAUSEN, C *ET AL*. 1996. *Stable isotope and biotic evolution in the North Sea during the Early Eocene: Albæk Hoved section, Denmark*. Geological Society, London Special Publications, **101**, 275–306.

SIGE, B., BUSCALIONI, S., DUFFAUD, S, GAYET, M., ROTH, J.-C. & SANZ, J. L. 1997. Etat des données sur le gisement crétacé supérieur continental de Champ-Garimont (Gard, Sud de la France). *Münchener Geowissenschaftlische Abhandlungen, A*, **34**, 111–130.

SILVA SANTOS, R. DA 1985. *Laeliichthys ancestralis*, novo genero e especie de Osteoglossiformes do Aptiano da Formacao Aredo, Estado de Minas Gerais, Brasil. Coletanea de Trabalhos Paleontologicos, Congresso Brasileiro de Paleontologia 1983. *Geologia, Paleontologia e Estratigrafia* nc. 2, 161–167. Departamento Nacional da Producao Mineral, Brasilia.

STORCH, G. 1981. *Eurotamandua joresi*, ein Myrmecophagide aus dem Eozän der 'Grube Messel' bei Darmstadt (Mamalia: Xenarthra). *Senckenbergiana Lethaea*, **61**, 247–289.

STORCH, G. 1984. The Early Tertiary Mammalian Fauna of Messel – a palaeobiogeographic puzzle. *Naturwissenschaften*, **71**, 227–233. [In German.

STOREY, M., DUNCAN, R. A. & SWISHER, C. 2007. Paleocene-Eocene thermal maximum and the opening of the North East Atlantic. *Science*, **316**, 587–589.

TAVERNE, L. 1969. Sur un squelete caudal d'Osteoglossomorphe (*Brychaetus?*) dans le Paléocéne (Montien) de Landana (Enclave de Cabinda). *Revue de Zoologie et Botanique Africaine*, **79**, 125–131.

TAVERNE, L. 1973. Établissement d'un genre nouveau, *Phareoides*, pour *Phareodus queenslandicus* Hills, E.S. 1934 (Pisces, Osteoglossiformes) du Tertiaire d'Australie. *Bulletin de la Société Belge de Géologie, Paléontologie et Hydrologie*, **82**, 497–499.

TAVERNE, L. 1974. A propos de *Brychaetus* Woodward, A.S., 1901 (Éocène d'Afrique et Europe) et de ses rapports avec les Ostéoglossidae actuels et fossiles (Pisces Osteoglossomorphes). *Revue de Zoologie Africaine*, **88**, 724–734.

TAVERNE, L. 1976. Les téléostéens fossiles du Crétacé moyen de Kipala (Kwango, Zaire). *Annales du*

Musée Royal de l'Afrique Centrale, Tervuren, Série in 8°, Sciences Géologiques, **79**, 1–50.

TAVERNE, L. 1977. Ostéologie, phylogénèse et systématique des téléostéens fossiles et actuels du super-ordre des Ostéoglossomorphes. Première partie. Ostéologie des genres *Hiodon, Eohiodon, Lycoptera, Osteoglossum, Scleropages, Heterotis* et *Arapaima*. *Mémoires, Académie Royale de Belgique, Classe des Sciences, Coll. in 8°, Série 2*, **42**, 1–235.

TAVERNE, L. 1978. Ostéologie, phylogénèse et systématique des téléostéens fossiles et actuels du super-ordre des Ostéoglossomorphes. Deuxième partie. Ostéologie des genres *Phareodus, Phareoides, Brychaetus, Musperia, Pantodon, Singida, Notopterus, Xenomystus* et *Papyrocranus*. *Mémoires, Académie Royale de Belgique, Classe des Sciences, Coll. in 8°, Série 2*, **42**, 1–213.

TAVERNE, L. 1979. Ostéologie, phylogénèse et systématique des téléostéens fossiles et actuels du super-ordre des Ostéoglossomorphes. Troisième partie. Évolution des structures ostélogiques et conclusions générales relatives à la phylogénèse et à la systématique du super-ordre. Addendum. *Mémoires, Académie Royale de Belgique, Classe des Sciences, Coll. in 8°, Série 2*, **43**, 1–168.

TAVERNE, L. 1984. A propos de *Chanopsis* Lombardi du Crétacé inférieur du Zaïre (Teleostei, Osteoglossiformes). *Revue Zoologique Africaine*, **98**, 578–590.

TAVERNE, L. 1998. Les ostéoglossomorphes marins de l'Éocène du Monte Bolca (Italie): *Monopteros* Volta 1796, *Thrissopterus* Heckel 1856 et *Foreyichthys* Taverne, 1979. Considérations sur la phylogénie des téléostéens ostéoglossomorphes. *Studie e Ricerche Giacimenti Terziari di Bolca, Miscellanea Paleontologica*, **7**, 67–158.

TAVERNE, L. & MAISEY, J. G. 1999. A notopterid skull (Teleostei, Osteoglossomorpha) from the continental Early Cretaceous of southern Morocco. *American Museum Novitates*, **3260**, 1–12.

TAVERNE, L., NOLF, D. & FOLIE, A. 2007. On the presence of the osteoglossid fish genus *Scleropages* (Teleostei, Osteoglossiformes) in the continental Paleocene of Hainin (Mons Basin, Belgium). *Belgian Journal of Zoology*, **137**, 89–97.

THOMSEN, E. & DANIELSEN, M. 1994. Transitional Paleocene-Eocene ash-bearing diatomite in the eastern North Sea. *Tertiary Research*, **15**, 111–120.

TYLER, J. & BANNIKOV, A. 1992. A remarkable new genus of Tetraodontiform fish with features of both balistids and ostraciids from the Eocene of Turkmenistan. *Smithsonian Contributions to Paleobiology*, **72**, 1–14.

USSING, N. V. 1907. Om Floddale og Randmoræner i Jylland. *Kongelige danske Videnskabernes Selskab, Forhandlinger*, **1907** (4), 161–213. [In Danish.]

WEEMS, R. E. & HORMAN, S. R. 1983. Teleost fish remains (Osteoglossidae, Blochiidae, Scombridae, Triodontidae, Diodontidae) from the Lower Eocene Nanjemoy Formation of Maryland. *Proceedings of the Biological Society of Washington*, **96**, 38–49.

WILLMANN, R. 1990. Insects of the Fur Formation, Denmark. Allgemeines. *Meyniana*, **42**, 1–14. [In German.]

WING, S. L., HARRINGTON, G. J. *ET AL*. 2005. Transient floral change and rapid global warming at the Paleocene-Eocene boundary. *Science*, **310**, 993–996.

WOODWARD, A. S. 1901. *Catalogue of the Fossil Fishes in the British Museum (Natural History), Part IV*, British Museum (Natural History), London, 1–636.

ZACHOS, J. C. *ET AL*. [10 persons] 2003. A transient rise in tropical sea surface temperature during the Paleocene-Eocene thermal maximum. *Science*, **302**, 1151–1154.

ZHANG, J.-Y. 2006. Phylogeny of Osteoglossomorpha. *Vertebrata Palasiatica*, **44**, 43–59.

ZIEGLER, P. A. 1990. *Geological Atlas of Western and Central Europe*. 2nd ed. Shell Internationale Petroleum Maatschappij, Holland.

New information on the cranial anatomy of the eel genus *Echelus* Rafinesque, 1810 (Ophichthidae: Anguilliformes) from the Early Eocene

SALLY V. T. YOUNG[1] & R. J. WILLIAMS[2]

[1]*Department of Palaeontology, Natural History Museum, Cromwell Road, London, SW7 5BD, UK (e-mail: s.young@nhm.ac.uk)*

[2]*40 Bruce Avenue, Hornchurch, Essex, RM12 4JE, UK (e-mail: bobfosswilliams@hotmail.com)*

Abstract: Two neurocrania of the eel genus *Echelus* Rafinesque, 1810 were collected from the London Clay Formation, Eocene, from Aveley, Essex. They are identified herein as *E. branchialis* Woodward, 1901. One specimen retains an incomplete premaxillary ethmo vomerine plate, normally lost in fossil specimens, and provides further anatomical information and taxonomic characters for this species.

The geographical range of the species is extended and localities of fossil species of *Echelus* and other fossil taxa believed by various authors to be closely-related to *Echelus* species are depicted on a map of the distribution of continental crust in the northern hemisphere during Oligocene times. The distribution of such eel taxa is consistent with the supposed extent of the Eocene sea within Europe. It would appear that modern species of *Echelus* now occupy areas that are more cosmopolitan than the fossil species. During the break-up of Pangaea and the subsequent expansion of the Atlantic and Indo-Pacific Oceans species of *Echelus* have ventured beyond their original provenance of continental sea and now occupy habitats along margins of the eastern Atlantic and of the western and eastern Indo-Pacific Oceans.

The examination of industrial excavations (being carried out on an area of land to prepare it for use as a landfill site) in Aveley, Essex, yielded two eel neurocrania. The fossil specimens were collected by Mr R. J. Williams in 1998 and in 2005 he presented them to the Natural History Museum, London. A number of horizons of the Early Eocene, London Clay were exposed in the landfill site. The neurocrania were collected from an exposure of clay in the horizon of Division B2 of the London Clay Formation.

The specimens were compared with neurocrania from the Early Eocene of the Isle of Sheppey, Kent and from the Middle Eocene of Barton-on-Sea, Hampshire and are identified as *Echelus branchialis*. The geographic extent of this species is thus extended. One specimen retains the premaxillary ethmo vomerine complex, not normally preserved or poorly-preserved, and provides further characters for the species.

The site at Aveley (Figs 1a–b, 2) has been known since the 1960s, when site ownership was with the 'Tunnel Cement' company and clay was extracted commercially for use in the production of cement. In 1964 the site received attention in the national media following the discovery of two prehistoric elephant skeletons (*Mammuthus*

rogontherii and *Palaeoloxodon antiquus*) found in glacial deposits that overlie the London Clay. They were recovered by, and are currently displayed at, the Natural History Museum, London. The glacial deposits, of sands and gravels, were also of commercial value and were subsequently removed. In the early 1960s a number of works were undertaken at the site and involved glacial deposits (e.g. Blezard 1966; Cooper 1972) but the London Clay received little attention (Kirby 1974).

In 1976 when 'Tunnel Cement' ceased operations the site fell into disuse and became somewhat overgrown and derelict. In the late 1980s the site was acquired for development as a landfill site to be used for the disposal of nonindustrial and domestic waste and excavations of clay commenced. The manner of excavation enabled the recovery of the specimens that are the subject of this paper. At the turn of the 21st century planning permission for extension of the site was refused. Excavation activities ceased and the site has been backfilled and landscaped following the termination of its commercial life. The collecting area is now covered over, London Clay is no longer exposed at the location and collecting is no longer possible.

From: Cavin, L., Longbottom, A. & Richter, M. (eds) *Fishes and the Break-up of Pangaea.*
Geological Society, London, Special Publications, **295**, 311–336.
DOI: 10.1144/SP295.15   0305-8719/08/$15.00 © The Geological Society of London 2008.

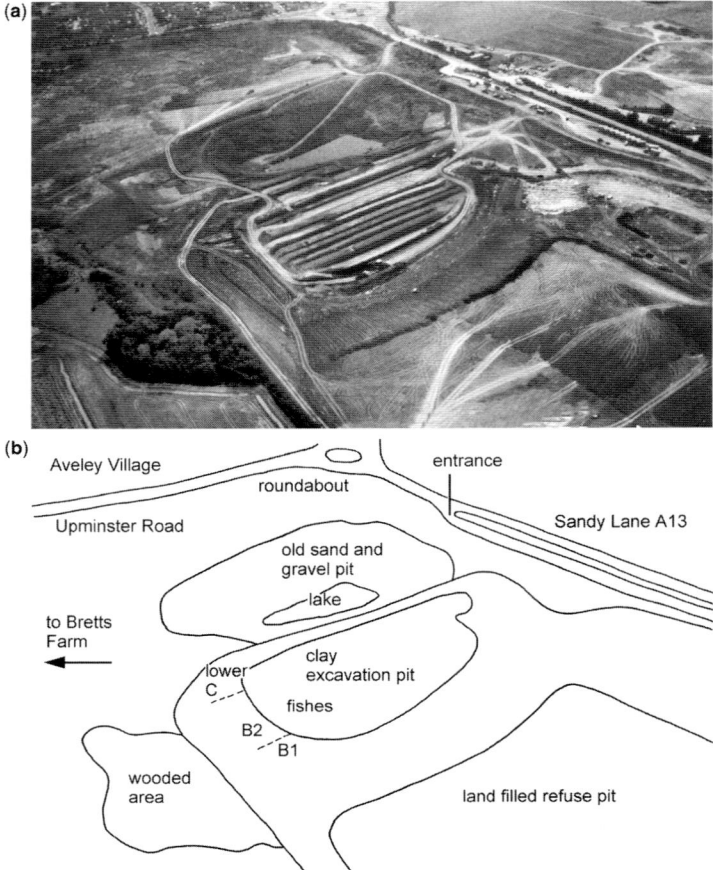

Fig. 1. (**a**) Photograph from the air of the layout of the former landfill site, 'Greenways' landfill site at Sandy Lane, Aveley, Essex, RM15, OS grid reference TQ 556 809, where horizons of London Clay are exposed and in which the two fossilised neurocrania of *Echelus branchialis* (Woodward 1901) described herein were collected; (**b**) Sketch drawing of layout of former landfill site at 'Greenways' landfill site to indicate main features of area as indicated in photograph, Fig. 1a. Approximate positions of Divisions B1, B2 and lower part of C of the London Clay Formation are indicated as well as location of collection of fish fossils.

Fig. 2. Photograph of detail of 'Greenways' landfill site taken from ground level and indicating terraces in the London Clay. Divisions B1, B2 and the lower part of C were exposed at various times as indicated. Division B1 is in the foreground at a lower topographical level and the lower part of C is in the background in the photograph at a higher topographical level.

This site when active provided the largest artificial exposure of the Early Eocene London Clay deposit in the United Kingdom at the time and is now permanently gone.

Abbreviations used in the figures and/or text

BMNH, Natural History Museum, London, England.
IRSNB, Institut Royal des Sciences Naturelles de Belgique, Belgium.
MNHNP, Muséum National d'Histoire Naturelle, Paris, France.

af	adductor fossa on the dentary for attachment of muscles
afahm	anterior facet for articulation of hyomandibular with neurocranium
ba	basioccipital
bs	basisphenoid
de	dentary
enfssc	entry foramen for the supraorbital sensory canal
eo	exoccipital
ep	epiotic
epp	epiphysial pore
exfssc	exit foramen for the supraorbital sensory canal
fm	foramen magnum
fprof	foramen for the profundus nerve
fr	frontal
frcr	frontal crest
fV + VII + j	foramen for main branches of the trigeminal nerve, for the ramus buccalis and palatine branches of the facial nerve and of the jugular vein
fVro	foramen for the ramus ophthalmicus of the trigeminal nerve
mx	maxilla
pa	parietal
pacr	parietal crest
pfahm	posterior facet for articulation of the hyomandibular with the neurocranium
pmv	premaxillary ethmo vomerine plate
pr	prootic
ps	parasphenoid
psp	pterosphenoid
pt	pterotic
ptfoss	posttemporal fossa
rlm	lateral extension or ridge on pmv for the attachment of a ligament to the maxilla
scp	sensory canal pores
so	supraoccipital
soc	supraoccipital crest
sp	sphenotic
ssc	supraorbital sensory canal
tskt	sockets for teeth

Materials and methods

Echelus branchialis (Woodward 1901). Two neurocrania (BMNH P65201, BMNH P65205) from the Early Eocene exposure of London Clay, Division B2, at 'Greenways' landfill site, Sandy Lane, Aveley, Essex, RM15. Ordnance Survey grid reference TQ556 809. BMNH P65201 is 31 mm in length from the posterior margin of the supraoccipital (so) to the anterior margin of the fractured frontal (fr). BMNH P65205 is 58 mm in length from the posterior margin of the supraoccipital (so) to the anterior margin of the fractured premaxillary of the premaxillary ethmo vomerine plate (pmv).

Four neurocrania BMNH P1746, BMNH P1746a, BMNH P163 and the holotype P633 and about sixteen further BMNH specimens of neurocrania, from the Early Eocene, Ypresian Stage, London Clay Formation, Isle of Sheppey, Kent.

- BMNH P1746 a poorly preserved neurocranium is 83 mm in length from the posterior margin of the supraoccipital to the anterior of the ethmoid part of the premaxillary ethmo vomerine plate.
- BMNH P1746a is 59 mm from the posterior margin of the supraoccipital to the front part of the broken ethmoid part of the premaxillary ethmo vomerine plate.
- BMNH P163 is a poorly-preserved neurocranium and is 44 mm in length from the posterior part of the supraoccipital to the remaining part of the anterior of the premaxillary ethmo vomerine plate.
- BMNH P633 is a poorly-preserved neurocranium 24 mm in length from the posterior margin of the supraoccipital to the anterior margin of the fractured frontal.
- BMNH P62749 is a neurocranium, from Middle Eocene, Barton Formation, Barton-on-Sea, Hampshire. BMNH P62749 is 29 mm from the posterior margin of the so to the anterior margin of the fractured frontal.

Goslinophis acuticaudus (de Zigno 1874). One skull and vertebral column, BMNH P3880, a small specimen with the head and post-cranial skeleton. The spinal column is 79 mm in length and the head is 10 mm in length. (The holotype of *Goslinophis acuticaudus* MNHNP BOL 0040-0041 (+10994-10995) from the Middle Eocene, Lutetian Stage, Monte Postale, Bolca, Verona, Italy was not studied.)

Echelus dolloi (Storms 1896). One neurocranium, IRSNB P651 holotype from the Middle Eocene, Lutetian Stage, Wemmelian Sand, Wemmel, NW of Brussels, Belgium, the only known specimen. It is *c.* 29 mm from the posterior margin of the supraoccipital to the anterior margin of the premaxillary ethmo vomerine plate.

Echelus myrus (Linnaeus 1758). Skull and post-cranial skeleton from two extant specimens of adults. Fusion of the component bones of the neurocrania suggests that the individuals were adults. Numbers BMNH 1988.12.16.1 and 1988.12.16.2. The specimens were incomplete and fragmented in places but the total length of each specimen from anterior of snout to tip of tail was estimated to be *c.* 20–25 cm. The length from the posterior margin of the so to the anterior margin of the premaxillary ethmo vomerine plate of the neurocranium is *c.* 48 mm.

Drawings of specimens were achieved with a *camera lucida*.

Preparation of specimens

The fossil specimens from Aveley were preserved in a matrix of fine-grained clay with silt and, in some areas, were obscured by iron pyrites. Matrix and iron pyrites were removed by using a steel dental probe, an air abrasive or a rotary hand tool with a variety of diamond burrs and finer details of the skeleton were thereby revealed. Preparation of modern specimens of *Echelus myrus* to reveal the internal skeletal anatomy would have been carried out originally by one of two methods. One method involved using a scalpel to remove soft tissues; the second method involved placing the whole fish in an environment into which beetles of the genus *Demestes* were introduced. The soft tissues were then eaten by the beetles, leaving the hard skeleton preserved.

Physical, geographical and palaeogeographical notes about the exposure

Details of the exposure of quarries and the stratigraphic sequence in the London Clay at Aveley are provided by King (1981). The exposure of sediment at the Aveley site has revealed a depth of between 30–35 metres of Early Eocene clay, which is *in-situ*. The depth varies according to the commercial activity taking place at the time. The exposure was excavated to form a series of terraces which were worked in a vertical consecutive pattern. Removal of the clay allowed examination of one terrace at a time allowing collection of fossil material from identifiable horizons.

Examination of these deposits has established that clay horizons from Divisions B1, B2 and part of Division C of the succession (King 1981) have been exposed (Figs 1a–b, 2). The specimens described herein from Aveley are from Division B2. Clay horizons from Division B of the London Clay Formation are believed to represent an environment of deep water sea or ocean, which was widespread at the time of deposition.

Specimens of *E. branchialis* have been collected from the London Clay Formation of Isle of Sheppey and from either Division D or F of the Barton Clay Formation from Barton-on-Sea, Hampshire Basin (Young 1993). The discovery of specimens of *E. branchialis* at this locality in the London Clay at Aveley therefore extends the geographical range of the species.

Flora and fauna of the London Clay, comments and comparisons with modern taxa and implications of palaeoenvironment and palaeoclimate

The London Clay at Aveley and its flora and fauna have been discussed by several authors such as: Blezard (1966); Kirby (1974); King (1981); Paul (1992); Williams (2002).

The flora, fauna and stratigraphy of the London Clay have been discussed generally by a number of authors. Some examples of particular relevance include: Britton (1960); Casier (1966, 1967); Collinson (1983); Davis & Elliott (1957); King (1981, 1984); Reid & Chandler (1933); Stinton (1966, 1975–1984); Venables & Taylor (1963). The presence and nature of flora and fauna described, or mentioned in these papers are believed to give indications of the environment and climate at the time of deposition of the London Clay. From comparisons with modern forms an environment of deep water, low energy marine shelf with a relatively warm temperature is indicated.

Fossil floras indicate a range of climate zones. Some are similar to modern floras from Malaya while others are similar to those that are typical of regions with a more temperate climate. Several climate zones have been recognised among the floras of the London Clay and include tropical and temperate. The Recent analogue believed to be most similar to the environment of the London Clay is the 'para-tropical' rain forest along coastal lowlands of NE Asia, although it is not the same environment. A study of sand-sized grains within the London Clay indicates that the London Clay is predominantly composed of grains from sources in Scotland. This suggests the presence of currents flowing from north to south and which could transport material including plant debris from a provenance a long distance to the north. This could account for the presence of both temperate and tropical flora within the London Clay.

Modern eels of the family Ophichthidae comprise *c.* 260 species distributed among 58 genera (McCosker *et al.* 1989; McCosker pers. comm., August, 2006). They range from elongate burrowing forms to deeper bodied shallow-water forms. A few species occur in mid-water regions to depths of 800 m but most are benthic burrowers ranging from inter-tidal regions to over 1000 m (McCosker, pers. comm., August 2006) and are the subject of his current research.

Modern species of *Echelus* live in the eastern Atlantic, Mediterranean and Indo-Pacific from East Africa to Australia and Japan (McCosker, pers. comm., August 2006; see p. 317 for details).

Modern eel environments may range between temperate and tropical conditions including deep to shallow water on the continental shelf (McCosker, pers. comm., August 2006). Thus a comparison of fossil flora and fauna with modern forms suggests that the depositional environment of London Clay may have ranged between temperate and tropical marine conditions with deep to moderately shallow water, low energy and on a marine shelf.

Stratigraphical and geographical distribution of fossil eels of the genus *Echelus* and taxa believed to be closely-related to *Echelus*

The genus *Echelus* extends back to the Early Eocene and species of *Echelus* are recorded from Early Eocene, Middle Eocene, Oligocene to Miocene, Early Miocene, Middle Miocene sediments and from Recent environments.

An outline map is depicted in Figure 3a–b (re-drawn from Owen 1983) and indicates regions of continental crust that were present during the Oligocene epoch and marked as continuous lines with margins of modern landmasses indicated as dotted lines (A separate map for the Eocene epoch was not available and distribution of Oligocene continental plates is almost similar to those of Eocene for the purpose used in the present paper. Owen, H. G. pers. comm., 2006).

The present day geographic distribution of the fossil eel taxa as given on the map Figure 3b of the distribution of continental crust during the Eocene/Oligocene is consistent with the

approximate position of the Early Eocene marine areas and shoreline as depicted by e.g. Collinson (1983, text figure 2). According to the map by Collinson, the position of a marine shoreline is close to the western margin of the Hampshire Basin, which is the provenance of a specimen of *Echelus branchialis* from the Middle Eocene.

The skeletal cranial elements of *Echelus myrus* have been described by Storms (1896) and by Gosline (1952) with further information added by McCosker (1977) and Young (1993). The genus which seems to be most similar to *Echelus* and *Goslinophis* is *Ophichthus* according to McCosker (1977, figs 2, 3) but *Ophichthus* differs in details of the anatomy (see e.g. McCosker 1977).

The fossil eel specimens depicted on the map (Fig. 3b) include species of *Echelus* and of taxa that are believed to be closely-related to *Echelus* and further details are given below.

The material described as *E. branchialis* (Woodward, 1901) is represented mainly by isolated neurocrania which are from the Early Eocene, Isle of Sheppey, Kent (BMNH P633 holotype, P163, P1746, P1746a plus about sixteen further neurocrania) from Aveley, Essex (P65201, P65205) and from the Middle Eocene, Barton-on-Sea, Hampshire (BMNH P62749).

A single neurocranium, the only known specimen, of *E. dolloi* (Storms 1896) is from the Middle Eocene, Wemmel, near Brussels, Belgium (IRSNB P651, holotype). Material described as *Goslinophis acuticaudus* (de Zigno 1874) mentioned herein is of a skull and postcranial material from Middle Eocene, Bolca, Verona, Italy (BMNH P3880).

Specimens of poorly-preserved skulls and postcranial material also from the same locality and same age as *Goslinophis* were described by Cadrobbi (1962), Eastman (1905) and Blot (1978, 1980, 1984). They include three genera, *Voltaconger*, *Bolcyrus* and *Paracongroides*, which were referred by these authors to the family Congroidae. However, the specimens seem unlike the neurocrania of *Echelus* or of *Goslinophis* (see Young (1993) for anatomical details). Another taxon, *Proteomyrus ventralis* (Agassiz) from the same age and locality was said by Blot (1984) to be intermediate between Ophichthidae and Congridae. Material described as *Paranguilla* Bleeker, 1864, type: *Enchelyopus tigrinus* Agassiz nom. gen. praeocc. (one species) from the Eocene of Italy was ascribed to the family Echelidae by Obruchev.

Figures and descriptions of species of *Eomyrus* and *Ophichthus* from Bolca, Italy, are provided by Eastman (1905) and Cadrobbi (1962) and mentioned by Leriche (1906). The specimens seem to be small and not well-preserved and it is not easy

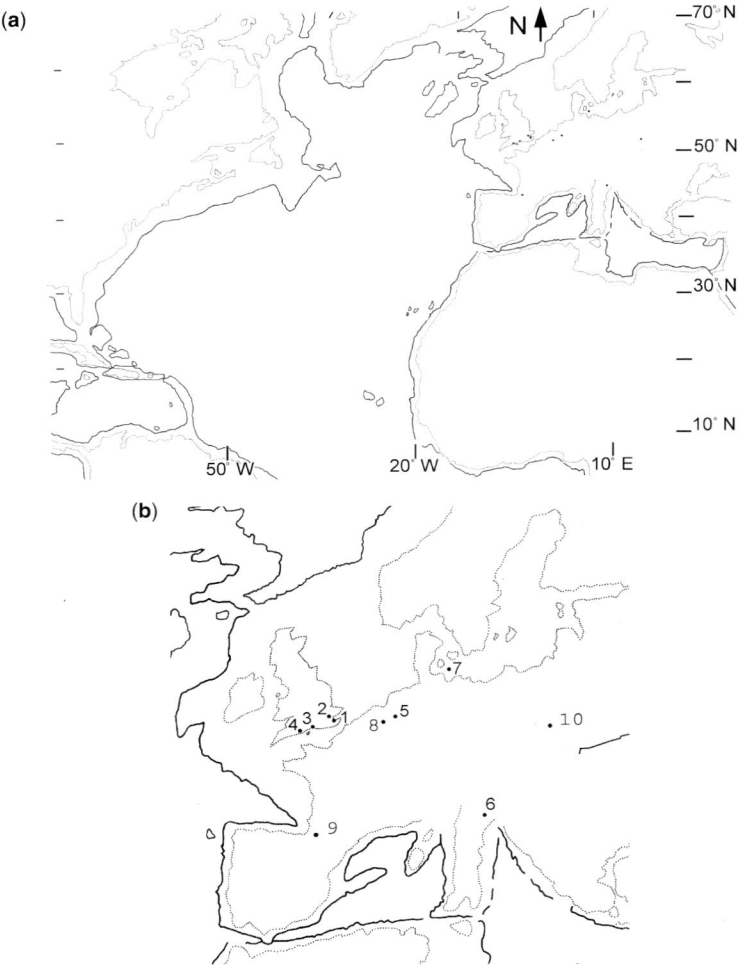

Fig. 3. (**a**) Outline map of part of the northern hemisphere indicating regions of continental crust during the time of the Oligocene epoch marked as continuous line with positions of margins of modern landmasses indicated as dotted line. Map re-drawn from Owen (1983). Map 65 Anomaly 9 (29 Ma) Oligocene with modern dimensions. The 1000 metre isobar was selected by Owen (1983) to indicate the depth in the ocean at margins of continents; (**b**) A map of Europe enlarged from (a) giving the distribution of fossil species of *Echelus* and presumed closely related taxa. Numbers indicated on the map and below relate to localities and taxa as follows (see text for further details): (1) *Echelus branchialis* (Woodward 1901). Neurocrania from the Early Eocene, Isle of Sheppey, Kent; (2) *Echelus branchialis* (Woodward 1901). Two neurocrania from the Early Eocene, Aveley, Essex; (3) *Echelus branchialis* (Woodward 1901). A neurocranium from the Middle Eocene, Barton-on-Sea, Hampshire; (4) *Echelus contractus* Stinton (1975). An otolith from Middle Eocene, East Wittering, West Sussex; (5) *Echelus dolloi* (Storms 1896). A neurocranium from Middle Eocene, Wemmel, NW of Brussels, Belgium; (6) *Goslinophis acuticaudus* (de Zigno, 1874) and other taxa which may be closely-related to *Echelus* from Middle Eocene, Bolca, Verona, Italy; (7) Specimens from Early Eocene of Katherinenhof, Fehmarn Island, Schleswig–Holstein, North Germany; (8) Otoliths of *E.* sp. and of *E. myrus* (Linnaeus 1758) from the Sables d'Edegem, Lower Miocene, Edegem, near Anvers, Belgium; Nolf & Smith (1983); (9) Otoliths of *E.* aff. *myrus* described by Steurbaut (1984) from the Miocene, Saint Géours d'Auribat, and Moulin de Couillautres, Aquitaine, SW France; (10) *E. arcuatus* Radwánska (1984) was described from otoliths from Middle Miocene, Badenian, Mount Lysa, Korytnica, 24 km, SW of Kielce, southern Holy Cross Mountains, Central Poland.

to interpret details of their anatomy. They may be closely-related to *Echelus* but a detailed study of the specimens would be required to verify this and such a study is beyond the scope of the present paper.

Several neurocrania of eels which belong to the family Ophichthidae from the Early Eocene of Katherinhof, Fehmarn Island, Schleswig–Holstein, North Germany, were described by Casier (1967) as *Palaeomyrus franzi* and *Micromyrus fehmarnensis* and were referred by Casier (1967) to the family Echelidae. The majority of species previously placed in the Echelidae are now referred to the Ophichthidae (Gosline 1952; McCosker 1977). The specimens show some similarities to neurocrania of *Echelus* and may be closely-related. However, they also show some differences (for comparison between the taxa see Young 1993, p.185). The remaining neurocrania of Anguilliformes which Casier (1967) described and figured include new species: *Parechelus prangei* which Casier referred to a new family, the Parechelidae, said to be inter-mediate between Ophichthidae and Muraenidae and *Eomuraena sagittidens*, which he referred to the family Muraenidae. These taxa seem unlike *Echelus* and *Goslinophis* (see Young 1993 for discussion). The specimens are stored in the Geologisches Land-esamt Schleswig–Holstein and the Geologisches–Paläontologisches Institut Universität, Kiel.

Otoliths of *Echelus* sp. and of *E. myrus* (Linnaeus 1758) were described from the Lower Miocene, Belgium by Nolf (1985); Nolf & Smith (1983). *E.* aff. *myrus* was described by Steurbaut (1984) from otoliths from the Oligo-Miocene of Aquitaine, SW France. An otolith of *E. contractus* Stinton, 1975 was described from the Middle Eocene of East Wittering, West Sussex. *E. arcuatus* Radwańska, 1984 was described from otoliths from Middle Miocene, Badenian, Mount Lysa at Korytnica, (24 km SW of Kielce, southern Holy Cross Mountains, Central Poland). Stinton (1975) described an otolith from the Middle Eocene, Barton-on-Sea, Hampshire, as *Echelus crenulatus*. It is possible that this otolith belongs to *E. branchialis*, but Nolf (1985, p. 117) commented that the specimen is a '... doubtful specimen ...' (For details and descriptions of otoliths see Nolf [1985]; Nolf & Smith [1983]; Stinton, [1966, 1975–1984]).

Modern species of *Echelus*

Modern species of *Echelus* include *E. myrus* (Linnaeus 1758), *E. pachyrhynchus* (Vaillant 1888) and *E. uropterus* (Temminck & Schlegel 1846).

The following information relating to their dis-tribution and environment is provided by McCosker, J. E. (pers. comm., August, 2006, and is the subject of his research in process of publication). *E. myrus* (Linnaeus 1758) lives in the Mediterranean and Bay of Biscay to the Congo at a depth of between 3–60 m. *E. pachyrhynchus* (Vaillant 1888) described from external morphology and dentition by, for example, Blache (1968) lives along the coast between Morocco and Namibia and including the Cape Verde Islands at a depth of between 200–500 m. *E. uropterus* (Temminck & Schlegel 1846) described by Karrer (1982) lives along the coast of East Africa to Australia and Japan at a depth of between 120–380 m. All species are benthic and burrow in sand or mud.

Anatomical description of the two eel neurocrania from Aveley

The ventral surfaces of each of the two neurocrania from Aveley (BMNH P65201, BMNH P65205) are virtually obscured by a matrix of sediment contain-ing isolated fragments of skeletal elements includ-ing teeth, which may or may not belong to these specimens. Other surfaces of the neurocrania including dorsal, posterior, left and right lateral and anterior, including the premaxillary ethmo vomerine plate in specimen BMNH P65205, are partially obscured by sediment. Sediment was removed where possible.

The dorsal surface of the neurocranium is smooth, convex in transverse plane, gently concave longitudinally. The posterior end of the neurocranium is truncated vertically with a ledge of bone dorsally formed by a continuation of the convex surface of the epiotic extending beyond the neurocranium. This surface together with the dorso-lateral part of the pterotic forms a concave surface, the posttemporal fossa, on the posterior surface of the neurocranium. The supraoccipital extends towards the posterior to form a medial rounded point.

A medial crest is present extending from the posterior margin of the so to the anterior margin of the frontal and is more pronounced on the supraoccipital and the parietal. Short sections and faint traces of suture lines of specimens from Aveley are occasionally preserved on each neuro-cranium and indicate boundaries in places between some of the bones, although it is often dif-ficult to distinguish boundaries between bone elements. Several apertures for blood vessels and nerves are preserved on each specimen.

One specimen, BMNH P65205 retains the premaxillary ethmo vomerine plate, which although poorly-preserved and cracked, provides some information. The premaxillaries, ethmoid and remaining poorly-preserved portion of the vomer seem to be fused to form a single structure, the premaxillary ethmo vomerine plate. The premaxillary area of the premaxillary ethmo vomerine plate is widened anteriorly. Individual cranial elements are described below for the specimens from Aveley.

Frontal (Figs 4, 5, 8, 9, 14, 15, 16 & 17)

Although the paired frontals are cracked along the midline there seems to be no sign of a suture. The frontals would seem to be ankylosed to form a single fused bone. This is a character of the family Ophichthidae, McCosker (1977), McCosker *et al.* (1989). The frontal is thus a medial bone that forms part of the central area of the dorsal surface of the neurocranium and tapers towards the anterior. The frontal also contributes to the antero-lateral surface of the neurocranium. At its ventro-lateral margin, it contributes to the dorsal margin of the interorbital fenestra.

On the dorsal surface of the neurocranium the frontal forms a straight suture with the pterotic laterally and a zigzag suture with the parietal posteriorly. The medial crest is abraded and is hardly preserved on either specimen from Aveley.

On specimen BMNH P65205 the medial crest becomes divided towards the anterior of the frontal to form a backwardly directed V-shaped flat surface for the posterior, V-shaped margin of the premaxillary ethmo vomerine plate to fit over the frontal. The margins of the V-shape on the frontal are slightly raised to become gently convex and may indicate the site of a bony tube which unites the supraorbital sensory canals. The epiphysial pore is not evident on the Aveley specimens.

Paired foramina for the exit for the supraorbital sensory canal are situated on the dorso-lateral surface of the frontal immediately anterior to the anterior margin of the pterotic. The paired foramen for the ramus ophthalmicus of the trigeminal nerve is not apparent on either specimen from Aveley. This foramen may possibly be present as a tiny aperture on specimen BMNH P65205 just ventral to exit for the supraorbital sensory canal, but this is unclear.

Parietal (Figs 4, 5, 6, 8, 9, 14, 15, 16 & 17)

The paired parietal is roughly pentagonal in shape, situated on the dorsal surface of the neurocranium

Fig. 4. *Echelus branchialis* (Woodward 1901). BMNH P65025. Neurocranium. Stereo-pair photograph of dorsal view. Scale bar = 10 millimetres.

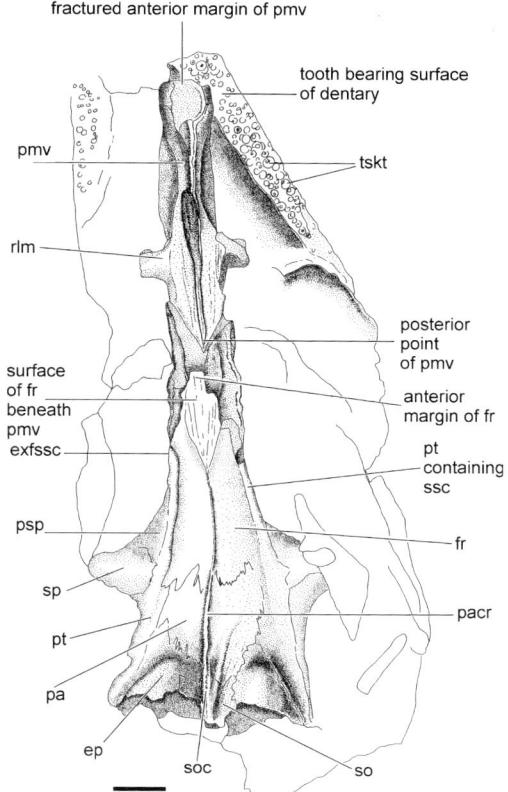

Fig. 5. *Echelus branchialis* (Woodward 1901). BMNH P65205. Neurocranium. *Camera lucida* drawing of dorsal view. The dorsal view of the neurocranium is drawn in detail with an outline of the concretion in which it is contained (in order to facilitate recognition of the specimen). Scale bar = 5 millimetres.

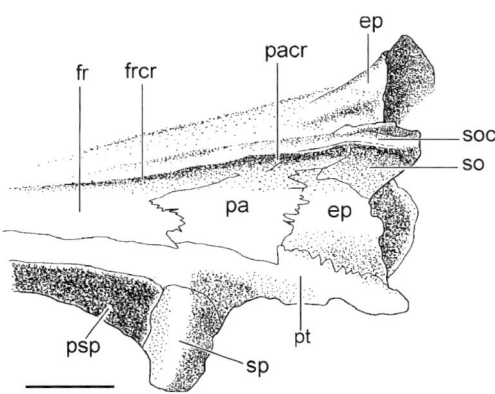

Fig. 6. *Echelus branchialis* (Woodward 1901). BMNH P65205. Neurocranium. *Camera lucida* drawing of postero-dorsal view to show details of suture lines and relative positions of bones. Scale bar = 5 millimetres.

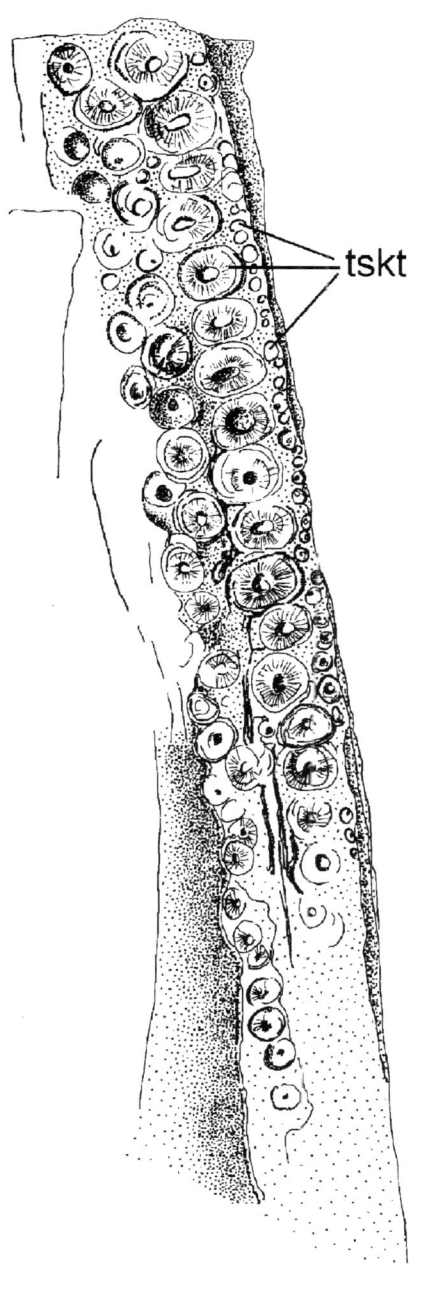

Fig. 7. *Echelus branchialis* (Woodward 1901). BMNH P65205. Neurocranium. *Camera lucida* drawing of tooth-bearing surface of incomplete posterior portion of right dentary to show details of circular tooth sockets. Larger sockets towards anterior and on central area of surface; minute tooth sockets align outer margin of surface of dentary. Scale bar = 5 millimetres.

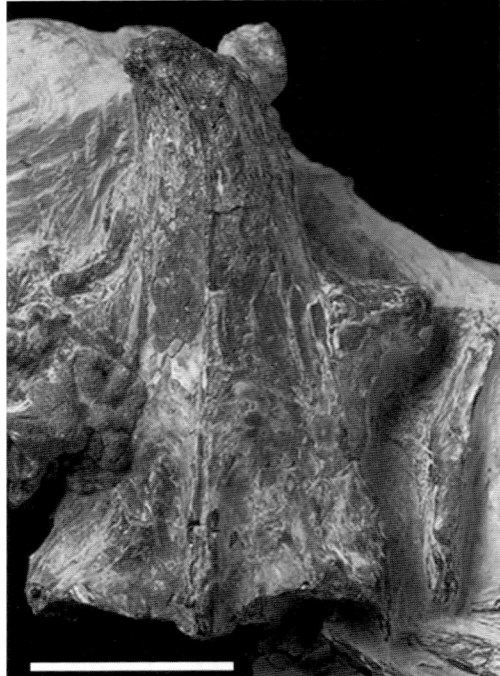

Fig. 8. *Echelus branchialis* (Woodward 1901). BMNH P65201. Neurocranium. Photograph of dorsal view. Scale bar = 10 millimetres.

and they each meet in the midline and form a mid-dorsal crest. Remnants of suture lines seem to be indicated between the two parietals in the midline. The paired parietal separates the supraoccipital from the frontal.

The anterior margins of the parietal with the frontal form a suture which varies from sinuous to zig-zag, although the exact course is not clear. Part of the frontal seems to extend back between the paired parietals to form an elongate outline in the midline region. The parietals meet the pterotics on the lateral margins, the epiotics on the postero-lateral margins and the supraoccipitals on the posterior margins in sutures which vary from sinuous to zig-zag.

The mid-dorsal crest extends back to join the supraoccipital crest. The parietal crest is quite pronounced, becoming deeper towards the posterior to the supraoccipital crest. The parietal crest joins the mid-frontal crest towards the anterior.

Epiotic (Figs 4, 5, 6, 8, 9, 10, 11, 12, 13, 14, 15, 16 & 17)

The paired epiotic is separated by the supraoccipital and meets the parietal and the supraoccipital in sinuous to strongly zig-zag sutures, and the pterotic in sinuous sutures. The epiotic forms a strongly convex dorsal surface of the neurocranium, which extends towards the posterior beyond the posterior surface of the neurocranium. The posterior surface of the epiotic is concave and contributes to the posttemporal fossa of the posterior surface of the neurocranium (Figs 10, 11) where it meets the exoccipital in a gently sinuous suture.

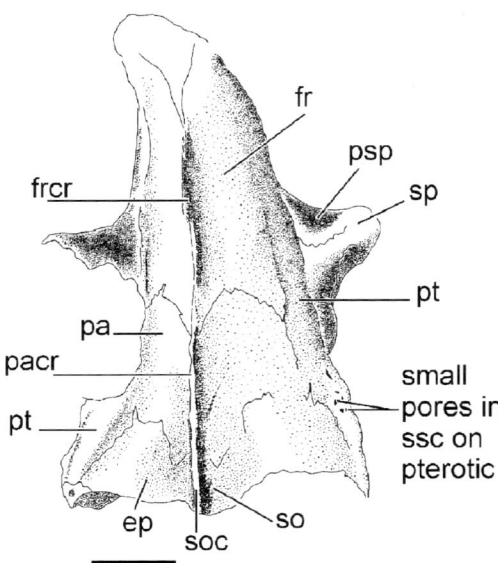

Fig. 9. *Echelus branchialis* (Woodward 1901). BMNH P65201. Neurocranium. *Camera lucida* drawing of dorsal view. Scale bar = 5 millimetres.

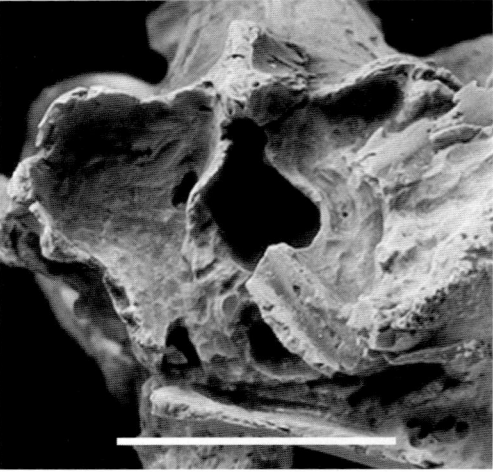

Fig. 10. *Echelus branchialis* (Woodward 1901). BMNH P65205. Neurocranium. Photograph of posterior view. Scale bar = 10 millimetres.

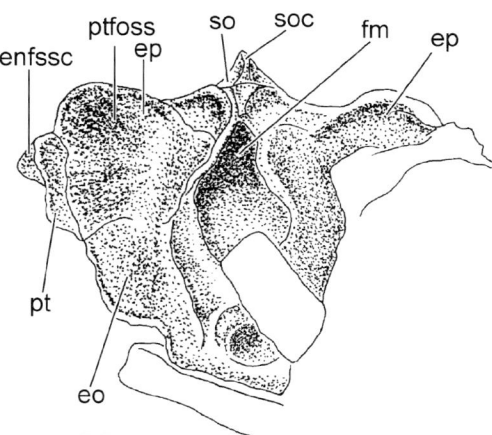

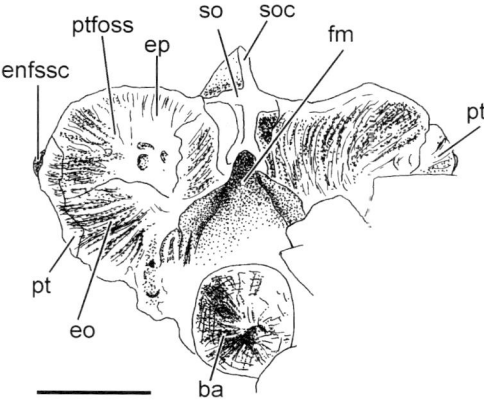

Fig. 11. *Echelus branchialis* (Woodward 1901). BMNH P65205. Neurocranium. *Camera lucida* drawing of posterior view. Scale bar = 5 millimetres.

Fig. 13. *Echelus branchialis* (Woodward 1901). BMNH P65201. Neurocranium. *Camera lucida* drawing of posterior view with occipital condyle in place ventral to the foramen magnum. Scale bar = 5 millimetres.

Supraoccipital (Figs 4, 5, 6, 8, 9, 10, 11, 12, 13, 14, 15, 16 & 17)

The supraoccipital is a median bone which separates the epiotics and is bordered towards the anterior by the parietals. The supraoccipital

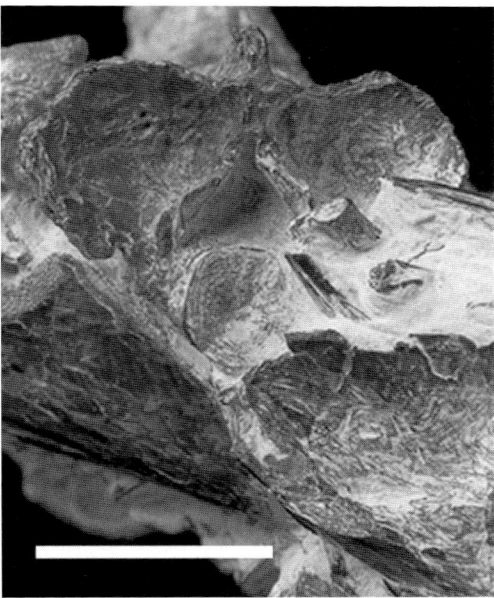

Fig. 12. *Echelus branchialis* (Woodward 1901). BMNH P65201. Neurocranium. Photograph of posterior view with occipital condyle in place ventral to the foramen magnum. Scale bar = 10 millimetres.

extends posteriorly to a mid-point approximately level with the pterotics and beyond the posterior level of the neurocranium. The medial crest of the supraoccipital is somewhat abraded in the two specimens. The so forms the dorsal margin of the foramen magnum.

Pterotic (Figs 4, 5, 6, 8, 9, 14, 15, 16, 17, 18 & 19)

The pterotic is a paired bone which forms part of the dorsal and dorso-lateral surfaces of the neurocranium. The pterotic forms sutures dorsally with the frontal, parietal, epiotic, laterally with the pterosphenoid and sphenotic, posteriorly with the exoccipitals and epiotic where it contributes to a small area of the posttemporal fossa on the extreme outer dorso-lateral margin of the posttemporal fossa. Other margins with bones are not clear. Towards the antero-lateral margin of the dorsal surface of the neurocranium the pterotics are extended to form paired, elongate, slender, tube-like structures to contain the supraorbital sensory canal. The entry foramen of the canal is situated at the extreme postero-lateral margin of the pterotic. Several tiny pores are present along the postero-lateral margin of the supraorbital sensory canal. The exit foramen for the supraorbital sensory canal is situated on the frontal immediately anterior to the most anterior margin of the slender, anterior component of the pterotic.

The pterotic meets the frontal and the pterosphenoid in straight sutures, it meets the parietals postero-dorsally in sinuous or more zig-zag sutures and it meets the sphenotics laterally in gently sinuous sutures.

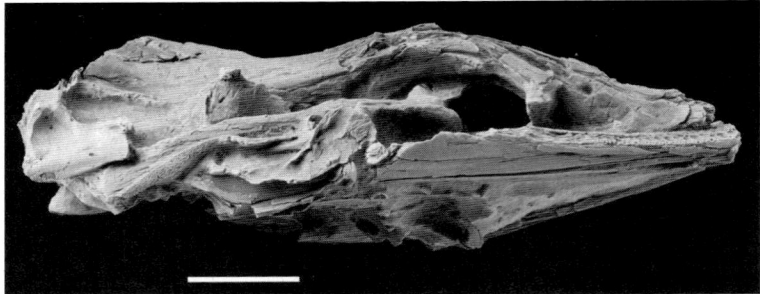

Fig. 14. *Echelus branchialis* (Woodward 1901). BMNH P65205. Neurocranium. Photograph of right lateral view. Scale bar = 10 millimetres.

A small, elongate, oval, shallow depression is evident on specimen BMNH P65205 on the postero-lateral margin of the pterotic, immediately ventral to the dorsal surface of the neurocranium and is particularly distinct on specimen BMNH P65201 and is the posterior facet for the articulation of the hyomandibular.

Pterosphenoid (Figs 4, 5, 6, 8, 9, 14, 15, 16 & 17)

The paired pterosphenoid is situated on the dorso-lateral margin of the neurocranium. Margins of the pterosphenoid and sutures between it and neighbouring bones are not clear except for a straight suture dorsally with the pterotic on the dorso-lateral surface of the neurocranium. The foramen for the main branches of the trigeminal nerve, for the ramus buccalis and for the palatine branches of the facial nerve and of the jugular

vein (fV + VII + j) seems to open within or mainly within the pterosphenoid of specimen BMNH P65205 and within a groove filled with iron pyrites. On the dorsal side of fV + VII+j on specimens BMNH P65201 and BMNH P65205 is a ledge-like structure having an even margin. The anterior extent of the ledge is not clear on either specimen.

Sphenotic (Figs 4, 5, 6, 8, 9, 16 & 17)

The sphenotics are not well-preserved and are incomplete. The suture with the pterotic is apparently straight to sinuous although it is not distinct. The dorsal surface of the paired sphenotic is smooth and convex. On the dorso-lateral surface of the neurocranium the sphenotic contributes to the anterior facet for the articulation of the hyomandibular with the neurocranium.

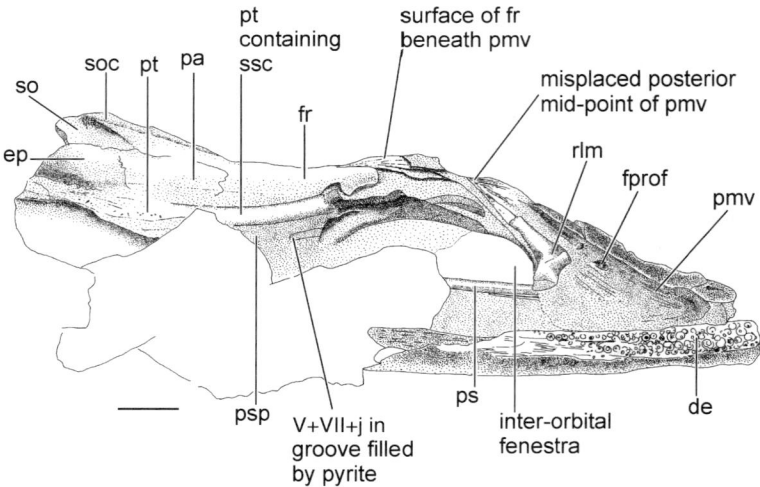

Fig. 15. *Echelus branchialis* (Woodward 1901). BMNH P65205. Neurocranium. *Camera lucida* drawing of right lateral view. Dotted line indicates approximate boundary between vomer and rock matrix. Scale bar = 5 millimetres.

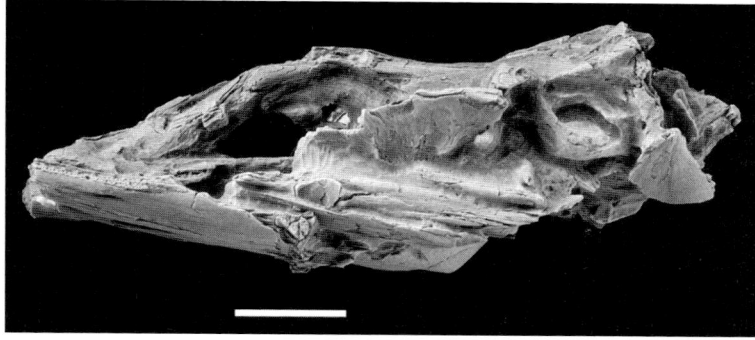

Fig. 16. *Echelus branchialis* (Woodward 1901). BMNH P65205. Neurocranium. Photograph of left lateral view. Scale bar = 10 millimetres.

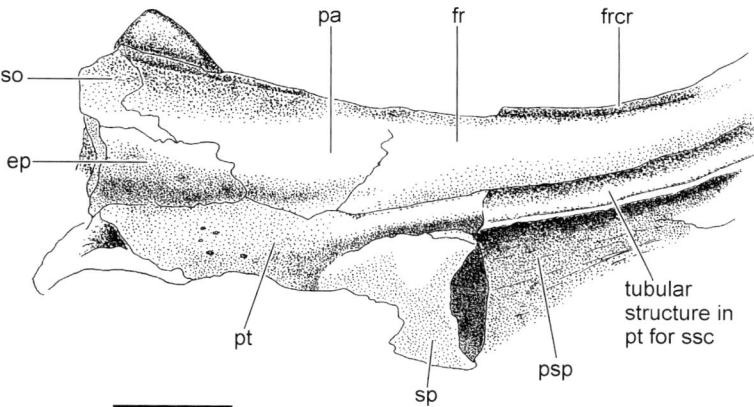

Fig. 17. *Echelus branchialis* (Woodward 1901). BMNH P65201. Neurocranium. *Camera lucida* drawing of right lateral view. Scale bar = 5 millimetres.

Auditory bullae (Fig. 19)

The paired auditory bullae composed of the prootic, the exoccipital and the basioccipital are evident on the specimens from Aveley and although fractured are obviously strongly convex structures. The component bones meet in strongly zig-zag sutures which perhaps help to form a particularly strong link over the distinctly convex surface of the bulla. The bullae converge gently towards the posterior. The fractured surface of the bulla of specimen BMNH P65205 reveals the remains of a white-coloured, opaque otolith.

Prootic (Fig. 19)

Only a tiny extent of the paired prootic is evident on Aveley specimen BMNH P65205. It contributes to the auditory bulla where it meets the basioccipital and the exoccipital in a strongly zig-zag suture.

Exoccipital (Figs 10, 11, 12 & 13)

The paired exoccipital is evident on specimens BMNH P65201 and BMNH P65205 on the posterior surface where it forms part of the post temporal fossa (ptfoss) and meets the epiotic in a somewhat sinuous suture. The exoccipital forms the lateral and much of the ventral margin of the foramen magnum. On the ventro-lateral surface of specimen BMNH P65205 the exoccipital is preserved as a component of the fractured auditory bulla on the surface of which it meets the basioccipital and the prootic in strongly zig-zag sutures to form a strongly convex auditory bulla.

Basioccipital (Figs 12, 13 & 19)

Little of the paired basioccipital is evident on the specimens from Aveley and is probably mainly obscured by matrix; however, a small area is present on BMNH

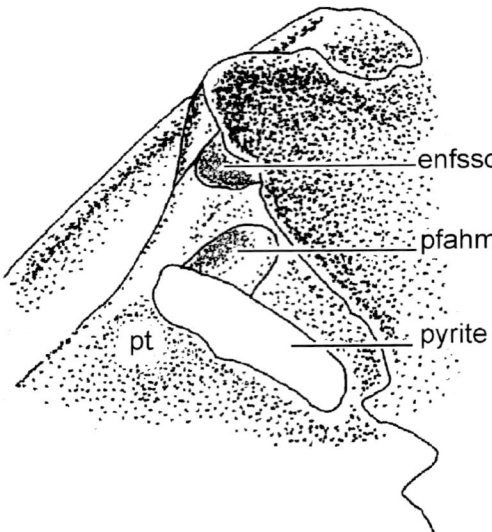

Fig. 18. *Echelus branchialis* (Woodward 1901). BMNH P65201. Neurocranium. *Camera lucida* drawing of postero-dorsal view of left side of neurocranium to show positions of enfssc and pfahm on pterotic. Scale bar = 5 millimetres.

P65205 where it contributes to the auditory bulla and meets other bones in strongly zig-zag sutures. The basioccipital is also present on the posterior surface of BMNH P65201 and forms the occipital condyle in place immediately ventral to the foramen magnum and is partially obscured by a matrix of sediment and fragments of bone. The basioccipital of specimen BMNH P65201 also contributes to the central part of the ventral margin of the foramen magnum together with the exoccipital.

Parasphenoid (Figs 14, 15 & 16)

The parasphenoid is a slender, medial bone forming the central part of the ventral surface of the neurocranium. Little of the parasphenoid is evident although a small portion is evident on specimen BMNH P65205 as a thin limb of bone extending towards the anterior margin of the ventral surface of the neurocranium. It lies between this margin and the ventral surface of the premaxillary ethmo vomerine plate, where it seems to overlie the vomer portion of the premaxillary ethmo vomerine plate. Other details of the parasphenoid are not clear or are hidden by a matrix of sediment and bone.

Basiphenoid

Details of this bone are not clear.

Premaxillary ethmo vomerine plate
(Figs 4, 5, 14, 15, 16, 20, 21 & 22)

The premaxillary ethmo vomerine plate (pmv) is preserved on specimen BMNH P65205. It seems to be a single medial, fused structure formed from the fused premaxillaries, ethmoid and incompletely preserved vomer (see above) and is situated immediately anterior to the frontals forming the snout.

The pmv is elongate, slender and fragile and is rarely-preserved or poorly-preserved on specimens of *Echelus*. It is preserved on specimen BMNH P65205 from Aveley, although it is fractured and incomplete on the dorsal and anterior surfaces. It has become misplaced in relation to the frontal and is somewhat anterior to its original position. The premaxillary part of the pmv is expanded to become wider laterally, then it becomes narrower towards the posterior ethmoid region of the pmv. The tooth-bearing surface of the pmv is hidden from view and is not well-preserved and teeth and tooth sockets are not evident on the pmv. The pmv forms the anterior part of the interorbital fenestra.

The pmv is supported on the ventral margin by the anterior component of the parasphenoid, which forms the ventral margin of the interorbital fenestra. The postero-dorsal margin of the pmv forms a backwardly directed V-shaped point which would overlie the anterior margin of the dorsal surface of the frontal.

A short distance towards the anterior from the posterior margin of the pmv and laterally on each side of the pmv of BMNH P65205 is a paired structure, which is a distinct, robust, bony, short extension or ridge (rlm) probably for the attachment of a ligament to support the maxilla. The ridge extends at right angles on each side of the pmv from the ethmoid region and appears to be continuous with the ethmoid, although this area is cracked and is not distinct. The dorsal surface of the rlm is smooth, and convex antero-posteriorly. Just anterior to the rlm on each side of the pmv of the Aveley specimens is a small, paired foramen for the profundus nerve. The dorsal surface of the anterior margin of the pmv of specimen BMNH P65205 is fractured to reveal two sets of paired canals which lie within the bone. Their function is not clear but they may be for paired rostral sensory canals or they may have an olfactory function (Figs 21 & 22).

Maxilla

A fractured piece of the paired maxilla is preserved on specimen BMNH P65205 and because of its size and position would seem to belong to the same individual as the neurocranium. The maxilla is a sinuous, curved bone with some of the

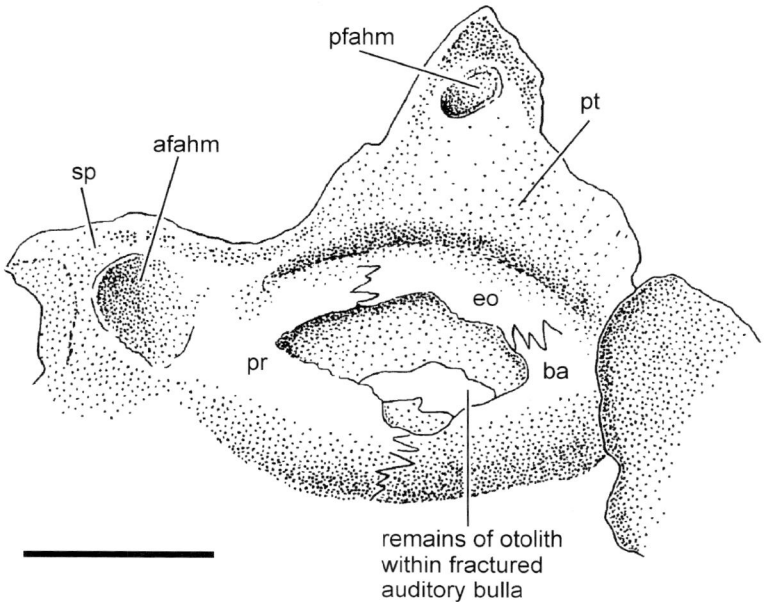

Fig. 19. *Echelus branchialis* (Woodward 1901). BMNH P65205. Neurocranium. *Camera lucida* drawing of oblique postero-lateral view of left side of neurocranium showing afahm on sphenotic, pfahm on pterotic, auditory bulla composed of pr, ba, eo, fractured and reveals internal remains of otolith. Remnants of suture lines over bulla are indicated. Scale bar = 5 millimetres.

tooth-bearing surface retained at the posterior end. The surface is covered with a multitude of minute, equally-sized, circular sockets for teeth, and which become slightly larger towards the anterior

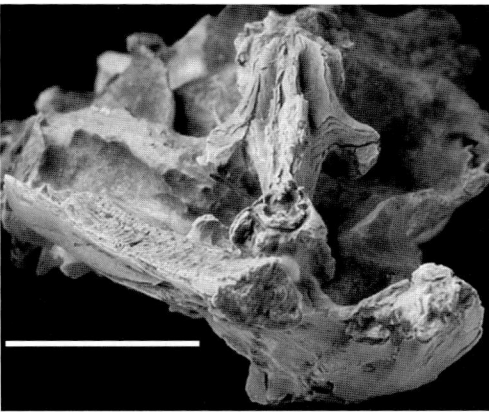

Fig. 20. *Echelus branchialis* (Woodward 1901). BMNH P65205. Neurocranium. Photograph of anterior view of snout to show details of premaxillary ethmo vomerine plate (pmv). Dorsal and anterior surfaces of fractured pmv. Scale bar = 10 millimetres.

of the maxilla, although hardly any tooth-bearing surface is visible nearer the anterior end of the maxilla.

Lower jaw (Figs 4, 5, 7, 14, 15, 16, 21, 23 & 24)

Incomplete portions of the lower jaw are preserved on specimen BMNH P65205, and include an incomplete portion of the left dentary and a larger, incomplete portion of the right dentary. The inner surface of the dentary is recessed in the coronoid region to form the adductor fossa, a depression on the dentary for the mandibular muscles and to accommodate the articular. Incomplete tooth-bearing surfaces are present on each dentary and only tooth sockets remain, but teeth are not present. The tooth sockets provide some information about the nature of the teeth. Tooth sockets occupy all the space over the tooth-bearing surface and there would seem to be no gaps between teeth. Most of the sockets are circular, some are slightly oval and all seem to have a central canal. Tooth sockets are larger along the central part of the tooth-bearing surface and towards the anterior end. Tooth sockets become smaller towards the posterior end and along the inner margins. A row of tiny tooth sockets aligns the outer margin of the tooth-bearing

Fig. 21. *Echelus branchialis* (Woodward 1901). BMNH P65205. Neurocranium. Photograph of dorsal view of anterior area of specimen showing details of premaxillary ethmo vomerine plate (pmv) and incomplete, tooth bearing surface of dentary with tooth sockets. Dorsal and anterior surfaces of pmv fractured and reveal internal tubes possibly for sensory canals as discussed in the text. Paired, bony ridges (rlm) extend from each side of the pmv. Premaxillary part of pmv is widened compared with remainder of pmv. Scale bar = 10 millimetres.

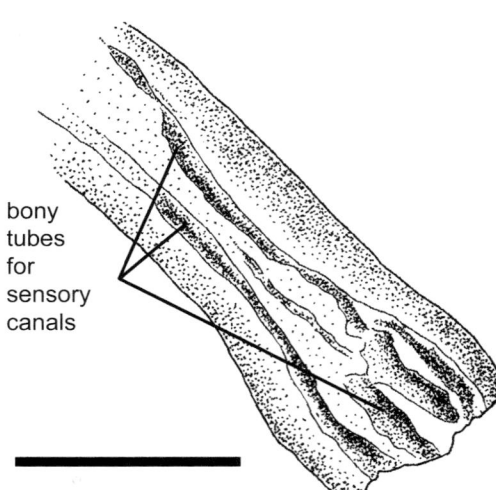

bony tubes for sensory canals

Fig. 22. *Echelus branchialis* (Woodward 1901). BMNH P65205. Neurocranium. *Camera lucida* drawing of dorsal view of anterior region of premaxillary ethmo vomerine plate (pmv) fractured on dorsal and anterior surfaces to reveal internal tubes possibly for sensory canals (as in Fig. 22). Scale bar = 5 millimetres.

surface of the dentary. An incomplete piece of dentary is preserved on specimen BMNH P65201 and part of the tooth-bearing surface remains. The surface is crowded with numerous irregularly arranged tooth sockets which are circular and generally small. Many, very tiny sockets are present on the posterior surface and become slightly larger towards the anterior and the central area of the bone.

Isolated teeth, which are not *in-situ* are scattered within the matrix of specimens BMNH P65205, BMNH P65201. They are small to medium sized, conical, sometimes becoming almost tubular, circular in section, bluntly pointed and larger teeth are sometimes gently curved inwards.

The outer surface of the incomplete dentary of BMNH P65205 is smooth and shiny and has a row of three elongate sensory canal pores remaining (Figs 23 & 24). The total number of sensory pores for this specimen is unknown.

Remains of other bones are present within the matrix of the two specimens from Aveley and include fragments of bone belonging to the opercular series and also individual vertebrae. However, the bones are incomplete and are disarticulated and may or may not belong to the specimens described herein.

Fig. 23. *Echelus branchialis* (Woodward 1901). BMNH
P65205. Neurocranium. Photograph of ventral view with
outer surface of right, incomplete dentary and three of
the series of sensory canal pores. Scale
bar = 10 millimetres.

General comments and comparisons between the two eel neurocrania from Aveley and presumed closely related taxa

(For taxonomic discussions of members of the
family Ophichthidae including *Echelus* and/or
descriptions and illustrations see particularly
Storms (1896), Regan (1912), Gosline (1952),
Blach (1968), McCosker (1977), Karrer (1982)
and McCosker *et al.* (1989).

Illustrations and descriptions of two modern
species of *Echelus*: *E. uropterus* and *E. pachyrhynchus*
have been provided by, for example, Karrer (1982) and
Blache (1968) respectively, and comparative comments are made below on the basis of their illustrations
and descriptions of the dentition.

Descriptions and illustrations of the cranial
region of *E. myrus*, *E. branchialis*, *E. dolloi* and
G. acuticaudus and their anatomical comparisons
are given in Young (1993). Dentition is often used
as an essential diagnostic character to define
members of the family Ophichthidae as well as
other eels (McCosker 1977). Important diagnostic
features of dentition include the identity
and nature of the bone which has tooth-bearing surfaces. Diagnostic features of teeth include: their
location, distribution, density of numbers of individual teeth, arrangement, size, shape and any
distinct features.

Tooth-bearing surfaces are present on the
ventral surfaces of the premaxillaries, ethmoid
and vomer of the premaxillary ethmo vomerine
plate and on lower surfaces of the maxilla and
upper surfaces of the dentary of species of
Echelus. Some of these structures are preserved or
partially preserved in the fossil specimens described
herein and further details and comparative comments between taxa are given below.

The two neurocrania BMNH P65201 and
BMNH P65205 from Aveley show an overall
general similarity in the arrangement, main proportions, position, shapes of bones and of other anatomical features, to those of the modern eel,
E. myrus (Linnaeus, 1758) and the fossilised eels
E. branchialis (Woodward 1901) from the Hampshire and London basins, *E. dolloi* (Storms 1896)
from Wemmel, NW of Brussels, Belgium, and
Goslinophis acuticaudus (de Zigno 1874) from
Bolca, Verona, Italy.

In BMNH P65205, *E. myrus*, *E. dolloi*, apparently in *E. branchialis* (where it is partly preserved)
in BMNH P1746a and in *Goslinophis acuticaudus*
the neurocranium is elongate, slender and has an
interorbital fenestra which is longer than high.
This feature is typical of the genus *Echelus* according to Gosline (1952).

The premaxillaries, ethmoid and vomer are
fused to form the pmv in BMNH P65205, in
E. myrus and in *E. dolloi*. The pmv is incomplete
in *E. branchialis* and *G. acuticaudus* and little of
the component bones are preserved. The neurocrania from Aveley, as well as those of *E. branchialis*, *E. myrus*, *E. dolloi* and *G. acuticaudus* are
truncated at the posterior margin. A surface is
formed by the posterior extension of the epiotic
and the supraoccipital and extends beyond the posterior margin of the neurocranium in the specimens
from Aveley, *E. branchialis*, *E. myrus*, apparently

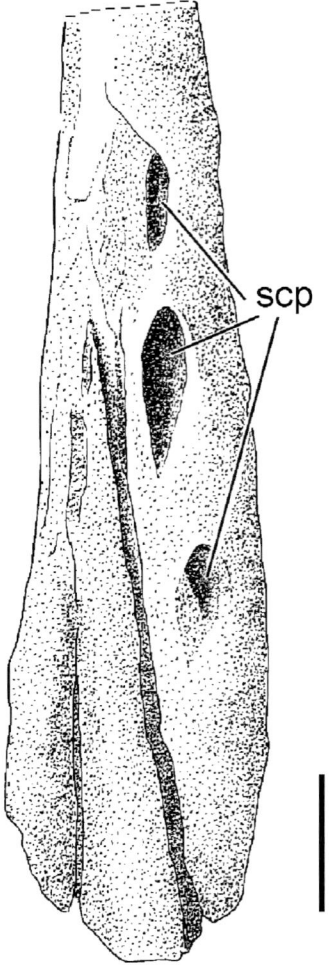

scp

Fig. 24. *Echelus branchialis* (Woodward 1901). BMNH P65205. Dentary. Camera lucida drawing of outer surface of right, incomplete dentary and three of the series of sensory canal pores (scp). Scale bar = 5 millimetres.

features are characteristic of the genus *Echelus* according to Gosline (1952).

Individual cranial elements of the neurocrania from Aveley are of a generally similar shape and occupy a similar relative position to those of *E. dolloi*, *E. branchialis*, *E. myrus* and *G. acuticaudus*. In *E. myrus*, *E. branchialis*, *E. dolloi* and in the specimens from Aveley, the paired epiotics are separated by the supraoccipital, and the paired parietal separates the supraoccipital from the frontal. The supraoccipital forms the dorsal margin of the foramen magnum in *E. branchialis*, *E. myrus*, the specimens from Aveley and apparently in *E. dolloi* and so this may be a taxonomic character of *Echelus*. The foramen for the main branches of the trigeminal nerve, for the ramus buccalis and palatine branches of the facial nerve and of the jugular vein (fV + Vll + j) lies mainly within the pterosphenoid in the specimens from Aveley as it does in *E. myrus* and in the fossil species of *Echelus* and this feature may have taxonomic significance among species of *Echelus*. Specific differences between these taxa, as well as features of possible taxonomic interest, are discussed below.

Frontal (Figs 4, 5, 6, 14, 15, 16 & 17)

Although the frontals of the specimens from Aveley are cracked along the midline there seems to be no sign of a suture. They seem to be fused along their entire length to form a single bone similar to those of *E. myrus*, *E. dolloi* and *E. branchialis* (unknown in *G. acuticaudus*). Regan (1912) in his classification divided the eels into groups according to the fusion/separation of the frontals and this feature has continued to be generally accepted as a natural taxonomic character. The specimens from Aveley, as well as *E. branchialis*, *E. myrus* and *E. dolloi* would belong to the group of eels that have frontals which are fused along their entire length. This is a character of the family Ophichthidae McCosker (1977) (McCosker *et al.* [1989]).

The medial crest on the frontal of specimen BMNH P65205 from Aveley as well as *E. dolloi*, *E. branchialis* and *E. myrus* (unknown in *G. acuticaudus*) becomes divided towards the anterior to form a posteriorly directed V-shaped, smooth surface for the pmv to fit over the frontal. In these taxa the margins of the V-shaped area are slightly raised to become gently convex and may indicate the site of a transverse canal within the frontal which unites the paired supraorbital sensory canal of each side. This is believed to be a character of the family Ophichthidae, McCosker (1977) (McCosker *et al.* [1989]).

An epiphysial pore, not evident on the specimens from Aveley, is present on *E. myrus* and

in *G. acuticaudus* and unclear in *E. dolloi* because of poor preservation.

In all these taxa a mid-dorsal crest is present along the ankylosed frontals, parietals and to varying extents on the supraoccipitals. The posterior margin of the ethmoid of these taxa is extended to form a V-shape which fits over the anterior surface of the fused frontals. Each of these taxa has a well developed auditory bulla on the ventral surface of the neurocranium, although this feature is not evident in *G. acuticaudus* because of insufficient preservation. All these

E. dolloi, although not clear on *E. branchialis* or *G. acuticaudus*. On specimen BMNH P65025 from Aveley one remaining paired foramen for the exit for the supraorbital sensory canal (exfssc) is situated on the dorso-lateral surface of the frontal immediately anterior to the anterior margin of the pterotic. The exfssc occupies a similar position in *E. branchialis*. The paired exfssc of *E. myrus* and of *E. dolloi* is situated on the frontal some significant distance anterior to the anterior margin of the pterotic. The relative positions of the exfssc and the anterior margin of the pterotic are unknown in *G. acuticaudus* because the specimen is too poorly preserved in that area.

A foramen fVro was not identified on the specimens from Aveley. The fVro on *E. myrus* is situated postero-ventral to the exfssc and on *E. dolloi* and *G. acuticaudus* the fVro is just below exfssc. The fVro in *E. branchialis* seems to be approximately ventral to the exfssc (although the exact position is not clear because of damaged bone).

Parietal

The paired parietal separates the frontal from the supraoccipital and from the epiotics and a distinct medial crest is present in the neurocrania from Aveley as well as in *E. myrus*, *E. branchialis* and *E. dolloi* and is unclear in *G. acuticaudus*.

Epiotic

The epiotic of *E. myrus*, *E. branchialis* (BMNH P1746a and BMNH P65201, BMNH P65205) is strongly convex on the dorsal surface of the neurocranium and is extended towards the posterior beyond the margin of the neurocranium to form a ledge. This is unknown in *E. dolloi* and *G. acuticaudus* because of incomplete preservation.

Supraoccipital

The supraoccipital extends towards the posterior to a rounded, medial point approximately level with the pterotics in the specimens from Aveley, *E. branchialis* (BMNH P1746a) and in *E. myrus*. This is unknown in *G. acuticaudus* and in *E. dolloi*. The so forms the dorsal margin of the foramen magnum in the specimens from Aveley as well as in *E. branchialis* and *E. myrus*, appears to do so in *E. dolloi*, and is unknown in *G. acuticaudus*. This feature seems to have taxonomic significance and may be a character of *Echelus*.

Pterotic

In the specimens from Aveley, as well as in *E. branchialis*, the slender anterior component of the pterotic on the dorsal surface of the neurocranium extends beyond the anterior margin of the pterosphenoid to a point just posterior to the exfssc on the frontal.

In *E. myrus* and *E. dolloi* the anterior margin of the pterotic is some distance posterior to exfssc. In *E. myrus* the anterior component of the pterotic extends to a point approximately level with the anterior margin of the pterosphenoid. The relative positions of these features are not clear in *G. acuticaudus*.

Pterosphenoid

In specimens of *E. myrus*, *E. branchialis*, *E. dolloi*, and *G. acuticaudus* the foramen for the main branches of the trigeminal nerve, for the ramus buccalis and for the palatine branches of the facial nerve and of the jugular vein (fV + VII + j) seems to open within, or mainly within, the pterosphenoid and within a groove, as it does in the specimens from Aveley. In specimen BMNH P65205 this groove is filled with pyrite.

On the dorsal side of fV + VII+j (on specimens BMNH P65201, BMNH P65205), is a ledge-like structure with an even margin, similar to that of *E. branchialis*, *E. dolloi* and *G. acuticaudus* and unlike *E. myrus*, where the ledge is frilled. The ledge on the pterosphenoid of *E. myrus* and of *G. acuticaudus* extends to a point within it, while in *E. dolloi* the ledge extends to a point within the frontal. The ledge on the pterosphenoid of *E. branchialis* extends to the junction of the pterosphenoid with the frontal, apparently similar to that of the specimens from Aveley, although it is not easy to interpret.

Auditory bullae

Auditory bullae composed of the prootic, the exoccipital and basioccipital, are present on *E. myrus*, *E. dolloi*, and *E. branchialis* although not identified on *G. acuticaudus*. They are generally similar to those of the specimens from Aveley, however there are differences. Auditory bullae of *E. branchialis* are strongly convex, distinct structures, similar to the specimens from Aveley and unlike those of *E. myrus* and *E. dolloi* (where they are more slender, far less distinct and more weakly developed).

Premaxillary ethmo vomerine plate

The pmv is elongate, slender and fragile and is rarely preserved on fossil specimens of *Echelus*. It is partially preserved on specimen BMNH P1746a of *E. branchialis*, although the anterior end is fractured and incomplete and much of it is obscured by iron pyrites.

The pmv seems to be an ankylosed structure formed by the maxillaries, ethmoid and vomer in *E. myrus*, *E. dolloi* and *E. branchialis* and specimen BMNH P65205. Little of the pmv is preserved in *G. acuticaudus*, although the ethmoid part seems to overlie the anterior margin of the frontal, as in *E. myrus*, *E. dolloi* and *E. branchialis* and in BMNH P65205, where the posterior margin of the ethmoid portion of the pmv is a V-shaped medial point.

The premaxillary part of the pmv is enlarged and widened in BMNH P65205, *E. myrus*, and *E. dolloi* and becomes narrower towards the ethmoid region of the pmv, unknown in *E. branchialis* and *G. acuticaudus*. The premaxillary part of the pmv is expanded in most ophichthids, McCosker (1977) and this feature may have taxonomic significance.

The ventral surface of the premaxillary and ethmoid parts of the pmv form a surface with the vomer to which they are fused and the continuous surface so formed bears teeth in *E. myrus* and *E. dolloi*. Teeth appear to be generally similar in distribution and approximate size in *E. myrus* and *E. dolloi* as indicated by the teeth on *E. myrus* and the remaining tooth sockets on *E. dolloi*. This tooth-bearing surface is either not preserved or insufficiently preserved to be identifiable in specimen BMNH P65205, *E. branchialis* or *G. acuticaudus* and the nature of the tooth-bearing surface of the pmv and of teeth from the pmv is unknown in these taxa. The pmv forms the anterior margin of the interorbital fenestra of *E. myrus*, *E. dolloi*, BMNH P65205, apparently in *G. acuticaudus* and not clear in *E. branchialis*.

The tooth-bearing surface of the components of the pmv (premaxillaries, ethmoid, vomer) of *E. myrus*, *E. dolloi*, *E. uropterus*, and *E. pachyrhynchus* seems to be continuous and there seems to be no demarcation between the component bones of the pmv or in type of teeth on these taxa. Teeth on this surface of *E. myrus* and tooth-sockets of *E. dolloi* are numerous, are arranged in an irregular manner over the surface and are not arranged in rows. In *E. myrus* teeth seem to be of a more uniform size than on *E. dolloi*, where sockets of different sizes are sometimes in close proximity. However, in both taxa, teeth tend to be largest on the tooth-bearing surface of the premaxillary and also on medial areas of the vomer. Small teeth are present on *E. myrus* medially at the posterior end of the vomer, which is not preserved on *E. dolloi*. Small, scattered, circular tooth-sockets are present on lateral and anterior margins of the ventral surface of the pmv of *E. dolloi*.

The teeth of *E. myrus* are conical, sometimes narrow and almost tubular, although often relatively wide based, short, bluntly pointed, circular in section, sometimes straight, and sometimes gently curved towards the posterior. Teeth on the premaxillary surface of the pmv tend to be a little more curved backwards than teeth on the vomer.

The ridge (rlm) on the ethmoid region of BMNH P65205 appears to be identical in appearance and comparable position to an incomplete structure on the ethmoid region of specimen BMNH P1746a, *E. branchialis* (see for example Young 1993, fig. 9). In each specimen the structure is of bone and seems to be continuous with the ethmoid although neighbouring areas are cracked, so interpretation is not easy. The function of the structure is believed to be for the attachment of a ligament to the maxilla to provide support for the maxilla. The structure seems to be comparable with a preorbital strut or antorbital strut mentioned by Gosline (1952). He commented that such paired structures are often developed in eels to support the maxilla where maxillaries are used for biting or crushing and a preorbital or antorbital strut may be a functional adaptation related to feeding.

The rlm seems to be partly comparable in function to a ridge on the pmv of *E. myrus* and which is believed to be for the attachment of a ligament to the maxilla. Gosline (1952) commented that the preorbital strut of *E. myrus* is apparently cartilaginous and its origin is not clear. The presence, nature and position of this kind of structure are variable among ophichthids. The small, paired foramen for the profundus nerve is situated in a relatively more posterior position in the specimens from Aveley compared with that of *E. myrus*, and *E. dolloi* in both of which it is situated towards the anterior of the ethmoid This is unknown in *E. branchialis* and *G. acuticaudus*.

Maxilla

Fragments of the maxilla are preserved on *E. branchialis* specimens BMNH P163, BMNH P1746a, BMNH P1746 and *G. acuticaudus* and bear teeth similar to those described for other surfaces of bones which bear teeth of *G. acuticaudus*, *E. myrus*, *E. branchialis* and described Young (1993).

An incomplete fractured piece of the right and left maxilla of *E. branchialis* (BMNH P1746a) is preserved on each side as a thin, sinuous bone. The right maxilla is preserved as an incomplete bone the remaining part of which is about 22 mm in length and the remaining part of the left maxilla is about 36 mm in length. Each bone has a tooth-bearing surface with tooth-sockets and some teeth remaining. Many very tiny sockets cover the posterior tooth-bearing surface of the maxilla, with no space between the sockets, and become larger medially and towards the anterior of the bone.

Tiny teeth or sockets are present along the outer margin of the surface. Some teeth are preserved and are short, conical, circular in section, with a bluntly pointed to rounded tip, occasionally gently curved medially and with sometimes narrow but usually quite a wide base. Teeth, where preserved, are similar in shape on other specimens of *E. branchialis*. The largest teeth on the maxilla were about 1.3 mm high.

Teeth on the maxilla of *E. myrus* are arranged in an irregular manner over the tooth-bearing surface and do not seem to form rows. Teeth are largest centrally becoming smaller towards the posterior and anterior ends of the bone. Teeth are conical, circular in section, short, bluntly pointed.

A tiny fragment of the maxilla remains on *G. acuticaudus* and a few extremely small teeth are present. Although they are extremely small, they are similar in shape to those of *E. branchialis* and *E. myrus*. They are conical, circular in section, bluntly pointed, sometimes very slightly curved medially and cover the tooth-bearing surface with no apparent space between individual teeth.

Lower jaw (Figs 7, 14, 15, 16, 23 & 24)

An incomplete part of the dentary of specimen BMNH P65205 is preserved and is similar in general appearance to that of *E. myrus*. In both taxa the inner surface is recessed in the coronoid region to form the adductor fossa (a depression on the dentary for the mandibular muscles and for the articular). The outer surface of the dentary of specimens of *E. branchialis*, *G. acuticaudus*, *E. myrus* and BMNH P65205 is smooth and bears a number of elongate sensory canal pores. The dentary of BMNH P65205 is incomplete; only three pores remain and the total number is unknown.

The number of sensory canal pores of specimen number BMNH P1746a, *E. branchialis*, is seven; six pores were present on *E. myrus* and five on *G. acuticaudus*. The most anterior pores in each case are very small. The number of sensory canal pores may vary between different species of ophichthids. Gosline (1952) commented that *Echelus* appears to differ both from the congridae and from other ophichthids in having a reduced number of external pores of the lateral line system of the head.

Tooth sockets are present on the tooth bearing surface of the dentary of specimen BMNH P65205. The sockets indicate that teeth are arranged in an irregular manner, not in rows on the dentary, and are similar to that of *E. myrus*. The size of tooth sockets, and presumably the size of teeth, on the Aveley specimen varies over the surface of the dentary such that larger teeth occupy the central area of the surface with tiny sockets for teeth along the inner and outer margins, similar to those

of *E. myrus*. The anterior portion of the dentary of BMNH P65205 is missing. Some replacement teeth are evident within larger sockets. Teeth on the dentary of *E. myrus* seem generally to be more even in size, although larger in the central part of the surface and smaller towards the anterior and posterior margins, becoming very tiny at the posterior end of the bone. Teeth of the dentary of *E. myrus* are conical, small, circular in section, bluntly pointed and sometimes gently curved towards the posterior end of the bone.

Teeth are preserved on the dentary of *G. acuticaudus* and are smaller towards the posterior and larger towards the anterior of the jaw, but still remain extremely small. Many teeth are crowded on the surface of the dentary and apparently cover the whole tooth-bearing surface. Teeth are conical, circular in section, short, bluntly pointed, some gently curved towards the medial area of the jaw.

Where preserved, isolated teeth from matrix containing specimens from Aveley are similar in size and shape to those of *Echelus branchialis* and *E. myrus*. The two remaining species of *Echelus* that are hardly discussed so far are Recent species. They include: *E. pachyrhynchus* (Vaillant, 1888) and *E. uropterus* (Temminck & Schlegel, 1846). Descriptions and illustrations of the cranial bony skeleton involve details of the tooth-bearing surfaces of the pmv, maxillae and dentary and of the teeth and are provided for *E. pachyrhynchus* by Blache (1968) and for *E. uropterus* by Karrer (1982).

Comparisons between the species of *Echelus* described herein and the modern species are based on descriptions and illustrations of the nature of the tooth-bearing surfaces of the bones and on the dentition provided by Blache (1968) and by Karrer (1982). The premaxillary part of the pmv of *E. uropterus* and of *E. pachyrhynchus* is expanded as it is in *E. myrus*, *E. dolloi*, in specimen BMNH P65205 and as in most ophichthids (McCosker 1977). This surface becomes narrower backwards towards the surface of the vomer, which widens and then tapers to a posterior medial point. The tooth-bearing surface of the premaxillary ethmo vomer is relatively short and wide in *E. pachyrhynchus*, when compared with the more slender and elongate surface of *E. uropterus*, *E. myrus* and apparently *E. dolloi*, in which the posterior section of this surface is not preserved. This surface is not evident in specimen BMNH P65205 and not preserved on *E. branchialis* or *G. acuticaudus*. The upper and lower jaws of *E. pachyrhynchus* are relatively wider than those of *E. myrus* and *E. uropterus* and the maxillae form a relatively wider angle at the anterior end of the vomer. Tooth-bearing surfaces of *E. pachyrhynchus* are those on the ventral surface of the pmv and the maxilla and the upper surface of the dentary. The surface of the pre maxillary part of the pmv continues with the ethmo vomer part of the surface without a separation.

Teeth on the tooth-bearing surfaces of *E. pachyrhynchus* are generally conical, short, gently arched or straight with a pointed, sharp tip: unlike teeth of *E. myrus, E. branchialis* or *G. acuticaudus.* They vary significantly in size and in some aspects of the shape over the individual tooth-bearing surfaces. Teeth on the premaxillary ethmo vomer surface are very massive and strongly curved on their anterior surface with a steeply sloping posterior face and a small, sharp point directed towards the posterior on the dorsal tip between the two faces. Teeth on the pmv are spread out in a somewhat irregular manner and with space between the teeth according to the figure by Blache (1968, fig. 8). The largest teeth tend to occupy the central area of the surface of the pmv with smaller teeth aligning lateral margins of the surface.

The maxillae of *E. pachyrhynchus* are covered with a high concentration of numbers of teeth, particularly at the posterior ends of the surface where teeth are extremely small. Blache commented that they are blunter than the anterior teeth. Towards the anterior of the maxilla teeth are larger, particularly on the inner margin, and are more sparsely arranged with spaces between teeth. Teeth generally on the maxilla are more conical in shape than those on the pmv, and all are sharply pointed on the outer tip. The teeth of the dentary of *E. pachyrhynchus* are present over the tooth-bearing surface of each of the paired components of the dentary as well as on the medial area: the mandibular symphysis, and as with the upper jaw, posterior teeth are very small and are more blunt than the anterior teeth. Teeth on the dentary are quite sparsely arranged in an irregular arrangement with spaces between teeth. Individual teeth on the dentary are large, although not quite as large as those on the vomer.

The dentition of *E. pachyrhynchus* differs from that of *E. myrus* and the fossil species of *Echelus* and *Goslinophis* in the shape and nature of the teeth particularly and the concentration of numbers of teeth on the tooth-bearing surfaces. The outline and relative size and shape of the tooth-bearing surfaces differs among the different species. The tooth-bearing surface of the pmv of *E. myrus* and of *E. dolloi* is far more slender and elongate than that of *E. pachyrhynchus.* However, the maxillae of *E. pachyrhynchus* are relatively more slender than of *E. myrus.* The maxilla of *E. branchialis* is slender and a high concentration of numbers of teeth is present.

The upper and lower jaws of *E. uropterus* are slender and the maxillae and dentaries each form a more acute angle at the anterior end of the jaw than those of *E. pachyrhynchus* with the result that the head of *E. uropterus* is relatively more slender than that of *E. pachyrhynchus.* Tooth bearing surfaces of *E. uropterus* are present on the ventral surfaces on the pmv, maxilla and the upper surface of the dentary. The surface of the premaxillary part of the pmv continues with the ethmo vomer part of the surface without a separation.

Teeth on the tooth-bearing surfaces are of a similar form but become narrower towards the rear. Teeth are small, conical becoming blunt and are gently curved with sharp points. The largest teeth are on the vomer, where they are more wide than deep and the teeth with the greatest depth are on the premaxillary. The tooth-bearing surface of the pmv is slender and elongate, contrasting with that of *E. pachyrhynchus*, which is relatively a little more short and wide. The tooth-bearing surface of the maxillae of *E. uropterus* is also elongate and slender. The head and jaws are narrow and the upper and lower jaws taper towards the narrow snout.

Teeth on the maxilla are quite small, particularly at the posterior end, where they are more numerous. Teeth on the dentary are very small externally becoming larger towards the interior margin. The height diminishes towards the rear, but the teeth become more numerous. Teeth are not present on the mandibular symphysis of *E. uropterus.*

Thus *E. uropterus, E. pachyrhynchus* and *E. myrus* differ in the relative width of the jaw, the angle of the maxilla with the pmv, the angle formed by the two sides of the dentary and the lack of teeth on the mandibular symphysis of *E. uropterus*, (present on *E. pachyrhynchus*). Teeth of *E. pachyrhynchus* and *E. uropterus* are conical with a sharp, pointed tip and are larger and massive on the vomer of *E. pachyrhynchus* and differ in shape from those of *E. myrus, E. branchialis, G. acuticaudus* and specimen BMNH P65205 in which they are conical, sometimes almost tubular, quite narrow, sometimes slightly curved, circular in section, with a bluntly pointed to rounded tip and do not have a sharp, pointed tip.

The specimens BMNH P65205, BMNH P65201 from Aveley, Essex, show anatomical features which are generally similar to the genus *Echelus* and to *Goslinophis*, a genus believed to be closely related to *Echelus* (see Young 1993). In particular they share several features with *E. branchialis* which seem to be specific to *E. branchialis* and may be taxonomic characters. The features are as follows: the exfssc is situated on the frontal and immediately anterior to the anterior margin of the pterotic; auditory bullae are strongly convex and distinct; a paired, strong, distinct ridge (rlm) for the attachment of a ligament to support the maxilla is situated near the posterior margin of the ethmoid of the pmv. On the basis of the similar characters described above it is concluded that the two specimens from Aveley, Essex (numbers BMNH P65201, BMNH P65205) are similar to *Echelus branchialis* and are identified herein as this species.

Systematics, diagnoses and additional characters for species of *Echelus*

Order Anguilliformes [Apodes]
Sub-order Congroidei
Family Ophichthidae Dumeril
Sub-family Ophichthinae Jordan & Everman
Genus *Echelus* Rafinesque, 1810
Myrus Kaup, 1856
Eomyrus Storms, 1896
Rhynchorhinus Woodward, 1901

Type species. Echelus punctatus Rafinesque, 1810 [=*Muraena myrus* Linnaeus, 1758].

Diagnosis. see McCosker, 1977 p. 75; see Gosline, 1952, for description; additional skull characters: Young, 1993 p. 170.

Echelus branchialis (Woodward, 1901). Figures 4– 24.
1844 *Rhynchorhinus branchialis* Agassiz, p. 139 (nom nud)
1844 *Rhynchorhinus branchialis* Agassiz, p. 308 (nom nud)
1901 *Rhynchorhinus branchialis* Woodward, p. 342, pl. 18, fig. 4
1901 *Rhynchorhinus major* Woodward, p. 343
1940 *Rhynchorhinus* Berg, p. 277, 451
1958 *Rhynchorhinus* Grasse, p. 2321
1966 *Rhynchorhinus branchialis* Casier, p. 168
1966 *Rhynchorhinus major* Casier, p. 169.
1967 *Rhynchorhinus branchialis* Obruchev, p. 427
1993 *Echelus branchialis* Young, p. 171,

Diagnosis (emended: see Young, 1993, p. 171). Additional characters based on skeletal cranial elements: On each side of the pmv and a short distance towards the anterior from the posterior margin of the pmv is a short, pronounced lateral extension (rlm) for the attachment of a ligament to the maxilla; immediately anterior to the rlm on each side of the lateral surface of the pmv is a small foramen for the profundus nerve (fprof); the exit foramen for the supraorbital sensory canal (exfssc) on the frontal is situated immediately anterior to the anterior margin of the pterotic; the premaxillary portion of the pmv is widened in relation to the vomer and the ethmoid portions of the pmv. See above for details of holotype and other material described herein.

Echelus myrus *(Linnaeus 1758)*

Synonymy. See e.g. McCosker (1977); Young (1993).

Diagnosis. See McCosker (1977); Young (1993). Descriptions and illustrations mainly of the external morphology, cranial and post-cranial skeleton, tooth-bearing bones and dentition are provided by Gosline (1952). Additional characters based on skeletal cranial elements: On each side of the pmv and a short distance towards the anterior from the posterior margin of the pmv is an indistinct paired ridge (rlm) for the attachment of ligaments to the maxilla; a small foramen for the profundus nerve (fprof) lies on each side of the pmv at the anterior end of the recessed lateral surface of the pmv; the exit foramen for the supraorbital sensory canal (exfssc) on the frontal is situated at a significant distance anterior to the anterior margin of the pterotic; the premaxillary portion of the pmv is widened in relation to the vomer and the ethmoid portions of the pmv.

Material. Skulls from two specimens BMNH 1988.12.16.1 & 2. See above for further information about specimens.

Echelus dolloi *(Storms, 1896)*

Synonymy. See Young (1993).

Diagnosis (emended). See Young (1993, p. 171). Additional characters based on cranial elements: A small foramen for the profundus nerve (fprof) is situated towards the anterior of the ethmoid area of the pmv; the exit foramen for the supraorbital sensory canal (exfssc) on the frontal is situated at a significant distance anterior to the anterior margin of the pterotic; the premaxillary portion of the pmv is widened in relation to the vomer and the ethmoid portions of the pmv.

Material. See above for details of material described herein.

Echelus pachyrhynchus *(Vaillant 1888)*

Synonymy. See e.g. Blache (1968). Descriptions and illustrations mainly of the external morphology, post-cranial skeleton, tooth-bearing bones and dentition are provided by Blache, 1968.

Echelus uropterus *(Temminck & Schlegel 1846)*

Synonymy. See *Karrer (1982).* Descriptions and illustrations mainly of the external morphology, post-cranial skeleton, tooth-bearing bones and dentition are provided by Karrer (1982).

Goslinophis acuticaudus *(de Zigro 1874)*

Synonymy. See e.g. Cadrobbi (1962); Blot (1980).

Diagnosis. See Cadrobbi (1962); Blot (1980).

Remarks. The species *Goslinophis acuticaudus* seems to share some similarities of features with *Echelus* and may be a species of *Echelus*. However, there is insufficient basis for comparison because of poor preservation of the specimen. Additional characters as discussed above are not clear on specimen BMNH P3880.

Discussion

Two specimens of neurocrania of Eocene eels were collected from division B2 of the London Clay Formation at Aveley, Essex, SE England. The specimens have characters which define the family Ophichthidae, and also have characters which are found among genera belonging to the family Ophichthidae. The frontals of the specimens lack an obvious suture and seem to be fused for their entire length. A transverse commissure is present at the anterior end of the fused frontal and unites the paired supraoccipital sensory canal of each side. These two features are characters of the family Ophichthidae.

The specimens from Aveley have a general similarity to neurocrania of members of the genus *Echelus* in the shapes, positions and distribution of the individual bones and in other anatomical details.

The size and shape of tooth-bearing surfaces of bones; dentition, nature, size, shape, distribution and concentration of numbers of teeth, have important taxonomic significance among eels. Shapes of tooth-bearing bones and arrangement, shape and size of teeth of the specimens from Aveley have some similarities with those of fossil and modern species of *Echelus* although there are differences in the shapes of bones and the shape, size and distribution of teeth among species of *Echelus*. The teeth of *E. branchialis*, the specimens from Aveley, *E. myrus* and *G. acuticaudus* do not have a sharp pointed tip as is present in the teeth of the modern species *E. pachyrhynchus* and *E. uropterus*. Teeth of the specimens from Aveley are similar to those of *E. myrus* and of *E. branchialis*.

Several characters of the Aveley specimens are similar to those of *E. branchialis* and involve in particular the position of exfssc immediately anterior to the pterotic; the anterior extent of the pterotic beyond the anterior margin of the pterosphenoid and the strongly convex nature of the auditory bullae. These features would seem to be taxonomic characters.

The pmv is preserved on one of the specimens from Aveley. This structure is not normally preserved in fossil specimens or is poorly-preserved because it is fragile and is probably lost easily. It is possible that in ontogenetically young individuals at least part of the pmv may have been composed of cartilage, and would not be preserved easily as a fossil.

The pmv provides further anatomical information and further characters of the species. A robust, bony, paired, lateral ridge-like structure is preserved on each side of the ethmoid of the Aveley specimen. It is identified as a ridge for the attachment of a ligament to the maxilla to add strength to the maxilla in relation to feeding. The structure is similar in shape and position to a remaining portion preserved on an incomplete part of the pmv that is preserved on a specimen of *E. branchialis* from Sheppey and would seem to be a taxonomic character of the species *E. branchialis* as well as a functional character.

The rlm of *E. branchialis* may serve a similar function to that of the preorbital or antorbital strut on the ethmoid of certain eels such as *E. myrus*, (which is cartilaginous) and may be present or absent among eels according to their mode of feeding. A very small ridge of bone is present on the ethmoid of *E. myrus* and is identified as a ridge for the attachment of a ligament to the maxilla apparently via a cartilaginous preorbital or antorbital strut rather than directly to the maxilla. Thus the ridge on the ethmoid of *E. myrus* would contribute support for the maxilla. It is possible that the more robust rlm of *E. branchialis* may itself provide the function of a preorbital or antorbital strut on its own. However, this is unknown.

A further character that may have taxonomic significance and that is present on the pmv concerns the relative position of the foramen for the profundus nerve on the ethmoid. On the specimen from Aveley the foramen for the profundus nerve is situated relatively close to the posterior margin of the ethmoid compared with *E. myrus* and *E. dolloi* where it is situated further forward (unknown in other taxa).

Ratios of relative distances between structures on the neurocranium may have taxonomic significance but variations in such relative distances may be related to ontogenetic changes. Further fossil material is needed for further studies to estimate their taxonomic value including if possible ontogenetic ranges of specimens. Ratios which may have taxonomic significance could involve relative distances between the entry foramen for the supraorbital sensory canal (enfssc) on the pterotic to other points on the neurocranium. Other points include exfssc on the frontal; the junction of the three bones, pterotic, sphenotic and pterosphenoid; the anterior margin of the pterotic; the antero-medial point of the frontal where the frontal ridge divides; the postero-medial point of the pmv.

Although the pmv is fractured on its dorsal and anterior surfaces further anatomical details and taxonomic characters of *E. myrus*, *E. branchialis* and *E. dolloi* are identified herein as a result of study of the premaxillary ethmo vomerine plate (pmv) On the basis of similarities between specific characters of the specimens from Aveley and of *E. branchialis* the specimens from Aveley are identified as *Echelus branchialis*.

This species was previously found in the Early Eocene of Sheppey, Kent and the Middle Eocene of Barton-on-Sea, Hampshire. So the discovery of the specimens from the Eocene of Aveley extends the geographic provenance of this species and supports the ideas of the extent of the Eocene sea in Europe.

The localities of fossil specimens of *Echelus* and of taxa believed to be closely-related to *Echelus* are illustrated and give some indication of areas occupied by the Eocene and Miocene sea in relation to regions of continental crust and of the emerging Atlantic Ocean in part of the northern hemisphere. Modern species of *Echelus* seem now to occupy areas that are more cosmopolitan than the fossil species. It seems that during the break-up of Pangaea and the creation of new ocean species of *Echelus* have ventured beyond their original provenance of continental sea and now occupy margins of the eastern Atlantic and of the western and eastern Indo-Pacific Oceans.

We wish to thank the following staff of the Natural History Museum, London for their help in various ways: Mr P. Crabb, and Mr P. Hurst of the Photographic Unit for their excellent photographs. Mr S. Moore–Fey for his careful preparation of specimen BMNH P65205. Dr H. G. Owen for permission to use the map, Owen (1983) and for helpful discussions relating to the map (Fig. 3a, b). We wish to thank Dr J. McCosker, California Academy of Sciences, for permission to use data as cited and acknowledged in the text. This information is the subject of his current research in process of publication. We are grateful to our reviewers for a number of useful references, and whose valuable comments have helped to make many improvements in the manuscript. Finally I would like to thank Dr P. Forey for providing help on many occasions over many years with work associated with fishes.

References

AGASSIZ, L. 1833–1844. *Recherches sur les Poissons fossiles*. Text, vol. 1. Introduction. i–xlix, p. 1–188. Text, vol. 2. De l'ordre des Ganoides en general. i–xii, p. 1–338. Text, vol. 3. Des ichthyodorulites. i–viii, p. 1–390. Text, vol. 4. Des Cténoides. i–xvi, p. 1–296. Text, vol. 5. Des Cycloides. i–xii, p. 1–160. Neuchâtel.

BERG, L. S. 1940. Classification of fishes both recent and fossil. *Trudy Zoologicheskogo Instituta Academiya Nauk SSSR, Leningrad*, **5**, 346–517. [English translation.]

BLACHE, J. 1968. Contribution à la connaissance des Poissons anguilliformes de la côte occidentale d'Afrique. Huitième note: la famille des Echelidae. *Bulletin de l'Institut Fondamenta' de l'Afrique Noire, Dakar*, **30**, 1501–1539.

BLEEKER, P. 1864. *Atlas ichthyologique des Indes orientales néerlandaises: public sous les auspices du gouvernement: colonial neerlandaises. Tome IV. Murènes, Synbranches, Leptocéphales*. F. Muller, Amsterdam, 1–150.

BLEZARD, R. G. 1966. Field meeting at Aveley and West Thurrock. *Proceedings of the Geologists Association, London*, **77**, 273–276.

BLOT, J. 1978. Les Apodes fossiles du Monte Bolca. *Studi e Richerche sui Giacimenti Terziari di Bolca, Verona*, **3**, 1–260.

BLOT, J. 1980. La faune ichthyologique des gisements du Monte Bolca (Province de Vérone. Italie). *Bulletin du Muséum d'Histoire Naturelle, Paris*, **4** (ser 2), 339–386.

BLOT, J. 1984. Les Apodes fossiles du Monte Bolca. *Studi e Richerche sui Giacimenti Terziari di Bolca, Verona*, **2**, 61–238.

BRITTON, E. B. 1960. Coleoptera of the London Clay (Eocene) from Bognor Regis. *Bulletin of the British Museum (Natural History), London*, **4**, 29–50.

CADROBBI, M. 1962. Gli Anguilliformi fossili di Monte Bolca conservati nel Museo dell'Istituto di Geologi dell'Universita di Padova. *Memorie degli Istituti di Geologia e Mineralogia dell'Universita di Padova, Padova*, **22**, 1–91.

CASIER, E. 1966. *Faune ichthyologique du London Clay*. British Museum (Natural History), London, 1–496.

CASIER, E. 1967. Poissons de L'Eocene Inférieur de Katharinenhof-Fehmarn (Schleswig–Holstein). *Bulletin Institut royal des Sciences naturelles de Belgique, Bruxelles*, **43**, 1–23.

COLLINSON, M. E. 1983. Fossil plants of the London Clay. *Palaeontological Association Field Guides to Fossils*, **1**, 1–121.

COOPER, J. 1972. Last Interglacial (Ipswichian) non-marine mollusca from Aveley, Essex. *The Journal of the Essex Field Club, Stratford, London*, **33**, 9–14.

DAVIS, A. G. & ELLIOTT, G. F. 1957. The palaeogeography of the London Clay sea. *Proceedings of the Geologists, Association, London*, **68**, 255–277.

EASTMAN, M. C. R. 1905. Les types de poissons fossiles du Monte Bolca au Muséum d'Histoire Naturelle de Paris. *Mémoires de la Société Géologique de France, Paléontologie Mémoire*, **34**, 5–33.

GOSLINE, W. A. 1952. Notes on the systematic status of four eel families. *Journal of the Washington Academy of Sciences, Washington*, **42**, 130–134.

GRASSÉ, P. P. 1958. Traité de zoologie, anatomie, systématique, biologie. *Agnathes et Poissons*, **13**, 1813–2758.

KARRER, C. 1982. Anguilliformes du Canal de Mozambique (Pisces, Teleostei). Faune Tropicale. *Editions de l'Office de la Recherche Scientifique et Technique outre Mer*, **23**, 1–116.

KAUP, J. J. 1856. *Catalogue of apodal fishes in the British Museum*. British Museum, London, 1–163.

KIRBY, R. I. 1974. Report of project meeting and field meeting to Aveley, Essex. *Tertiary Times*, **2**, 53–67.

KING, C. 1981. The stratigraphy of the London Clay and associated deposits. *Tertiary Research Special Paper*, **6**, 1–158.

KING, C. 1984. The stratigraphy of the London Clay Formation and Virginia Water Formation in the coastal sections of the Isle of Sheppey (Kent, England). *Tertiary Research*, **5**, 121–160.

LERICHE, M. 1906. Contribution à l'étude des poissons fossiles du nord de la France et des régions voisines. *Mémoires de la Société Géologique du Nord, Lille*, **5**, 430.

LINNAEUS, C. 1758. *Systema Naturae. Regnum Animalie.* Guilielmi Engeleman, Lipsiae. 824.

MCCOSKER, J. E. 1977. The osteology, classification and relationships of the eel family Ophichthidae. *Proceedings of the California Academy of (Natural) Sciences*, **41**, 1–123.

MCCOSKER, J. E., BÖHLKE, E. B. & BÖHLKE, J. E. 1989. Family Ophichthidae. *In*: BÖHLKE, E. B. (ed.) (1989). *Fishes of the Western North Atlantic.* Orders Anguilliformes and Saccopharyngiformes. 254–412.

NOLF, D. 1985. Otolithi piscium. *In*: SCHULTZE, H.-P. (ed.) *Handbook of Palaeoichthyology*, Stuttgart, 1–145.

NOLF, D. & SMITH, R. 1983. Les otolithes de téléostéens du stratotype des Stables d'Edegem (Miocène Inférieur de la Belgique). *Bulletin de la Société Belge de Géologie, Bruxelles*, **92**, 89–98.

OBRUCHEV, D. V. 1967. Fundamentals of Palaeontology. Agnatha, Pisces. *In*: ORLOV, Y. A. (ed.) *Osnovy paleontologii*, 1–825. [Israel Program for Scientific Translations, English translation.]

OWEN, H. G. 1983. Atlas of continental displacement 200 million years to the Present. *Cambridge Earth Sciences Series, Cambridge*, 1–159.

PAUL, C. 1992. Amphorometra (Crinoidea, Echinodermata) from the London Clay of Aveley, Essex. *Tertiary Research*, **13**, 117–124.

RADWAŃSKA, U. 1984. Some new fish otoliths from the Korytnica Clays Middle Miocene; Holy Cross Mountains, Central Poland. *Acta Geologica Polonica, Warszawa*, **34**, 299–321.

RAFINESQUE, C. S. 1810. *Caratteri di Alcuni Nuovi Generi e Nuove Species di Animali e Piante della Sicilia, con varie osservazioni sopra i medesimi*, Palermo.

REGAN, C. T. 1912. The osteology and classification of the teleostean fishes of the order Apodes. *The Annals and Magazine of Natural History, London*, **10**, 377–387.

REID, E. M. & CHANDLER, M. E. J. 1933. *The London Clay Flora.* British Museum, Natural History, London.

STEURBAUT, E. 1984. Les otolithes de téléostéens de l'Oligo-Miocène d'Aquitanien (sud-oest de la France). *Palaeontographica, Abteilung A*, **186**, 1–162.

STINTON, F. C. 1966. Appendix: Fish otoliths from the London Clay. *In*: CASIER, E. *Faune ichthyologique du London Clay Including Appendix: Fish Otoliths from the London Clay.* British Museum (Natural History), London, 404–464.

STINTON, F. C. 1975–1984. Fish otoliths from the English Eocene. *Palaeontographical Society Monographs, London.* (1), 1–56 (1975); (2), 57–126 (1977); (3), 127–189 (1978); (4), 191–258 (1980); (5), 259–320 (1984).

STORMS, R. 1896. Première note sur les poissons Wemmeliens (Eocène supérieur) de la Belgique. *Bulletin de la Société Belge de Géologie, Paléontologie et Hydrologie, Bruxelles*, **10**, 198–240.

TEMMINCK, C. H. & SCHLEGEL, H. 1846. *In*: SIEBOLD, P. F. *Fauna Japonica IV. Pisces.* Lugduni, Batavorum, 173–269.

VENABLES, E. M. & TAYLOR, H. E. 1963. An insect fauna of the London Clay. *Proceedings of the Geologists, Association, London*, **73**, 273–279.

VAILLANT, L. 1888. *Expéditions Scientifiques du Travailleur et du Talisman pendant les années 1880, 1881, 1882, 1883.* Paris, 1–406.

WILLIAMS, R. J. 2002. Observations of the London Clay excavation at Aveley, Essex. *Tertiary Research*, **21**, 95–111.

WOODWARD, A. S. 1901. Catalogue of the fossil fishes. *British Museum (Natural History)*, London, 4.

YOUNG, S. V. T. 1993. A neurocranium of the eel genus *Echelus* Rafinesque, (Ophichthidae, Anguilliformes) from the Eocene of the Hampshire and London Basins and a review of the genera *Echelus* Rafinesque, *Rhynchorhinus* Woodward, *Eomyrus* Storms and *Goslinophis* Blot. *Darmstadter Beitrage zur Naturgeschichte*, **2**, 163–194.

ZIGNO, A. DE 1874. Annotazioni paleontologiche. Pesci fossili nuovi del calcare eocene de: Monte Bolca e Postale. *Memorie del Real Istituto Veneto di Scienze, Lettere ed Arti*, **18**, 287–301.

Fossil Cypriniformes from China and its adjacent areas and their palaeobiogeographical implications

MEE-MANN CHANG[1] & GENGJIAO CHEN[1,2,3]

[1]Institute of Vertebrate Paleontology and Paleoanthropology, Chinese Academy of Sciences, P. O. Box 643, Beijing 100044, People's Republic of China
(e-mail: zhangmiman@pa.ivpp.ac.cn)

[2]Natural History Museum of Guangxi Zhuang Autonomous Region, Nanning 530012, Guangxi, People's Republic of China

[3]Graduate School of Chinese Academy of Sciences, Beijing 100039, People's Republic of China

Abstract: Fossil cypriniforms are abundantly represented in China and its adjacent areas, with the described taxa approximating to a total of 80 genera and 100 species and subspecies. They are known mainly from the Eocene, Miocene and Pliocene deposits. The Oligocene and Quaternary materials are relatively rare. These fossil cypriniforms represent three of the five Recent families: the Catostomidae, Cobitidae and Cyprinidae. Comparison of the Eocene catostomids from mainland East Asia with those from western North America points to an obvious transpacific distributional pattern, whereas there is only one species in Asia and more than 70 species in North America at present. Fossil cobitids are comparatively rare. Cyprinids are the most diverse and widespread group among the three families. The Miocene and Pliocene taxa shared by east mainland Asia and the Japanese Islands indicate that the fishes from these areas must have belonged to the same ichthyofauna during the Neogene. At the same time, some of them are quite similar to those from Europe, which is indicative of a closer connection between the two areas than previously thought.

The Cypriniformes is a widespread and very diverse freshwater group today. The group contains five families, 279 genera and approximately 3268 species (Nelson 2006). They have a very interesting history both in evolution and distribution (Bănărescu 1990, 1992; Cavender 1991). Diverse views exist on the interrelationships among and between the subgroups within the Cypriniformes, the division of the Cyprinidae, and the relationships of the subsets of the family (Fink & Fink 1981; Wu *et al.* 1981; Cavender & Coburn 1992; Nelson 2006).

Recent cypriniforms are the largest group of freshwater fishes in China and its adjacent countries, namely, Kazakhstan, Mongolia, Siberia, and Japan. Both Recent and fossil cypriniforms are abundantly diverse in these areas. They consist more than 70% of the total numbers of the Recent freshwater fish species in China, and a comparable percentage in its adjacent countries. Fossil cypriniforms so far known from these areas represent three of the five Recent families: the Catostomidae, Cobitidae and Cyprinidae. No fossils have been found up to now from the Gyrinocheilidae and Homalopteridae (Balitoridae).

Fossil cypriniforms from these areas are discovered mainly from the Eocene, Miocene,
Pliocene deposits. Those from the Oligocene and Quaternary are relatively rare. Many of the fossils are well-preserved and allow detailed morphological studies and thus provide important information for discussion on the origin, evolutionary history, and distribution of the group and its subgroups.

Fossils of the group from these areas were first discovered and studied in 1933 (Tchang 1933). Yet only sporadic collections were made and preliminarily studied during a long period of many decades. The main reasons for neglecting the cypriniform fossils probably are: (1) fossils of the group mostly occurred in the often easily weathered Cenozoic deposits, which do not provide favorable conditions for good preservation of fossils; and (2) the fossils are not sensational enough so as to attract researchers' attention.

Lately, with the attention of scientists to the global changes and especially the modern geological events' major impacts on the welfare of human society, more interest is shifted to fossils of younger age. Moreover, the disposition of the land and sea has reached its recent configuration in the Cenozoic, and it is easier to trace back what happened in the near past than in the more distant past.

From: CAVIN L., LONGBOTTOM, A. & RICHTER. M. (eds) *Fishes and the Break-up of Pangaea.*
Geological Society, London, Special Publications, **295**, 337–350.
DOI: 10.1144/SP295.16   0305-8719/08/$15.00 © The Geological Society of London 2008.

This paper provides a preliminary review of the fossil cypriniforms from China and its adjacent areas in reference to the group's systematic position and distributions. Their palaeobiogeographical implications are also discussed.

Fossils of the three families and their palaeobiogeographical implications

Catostomidae

Fossil catostomids are very abundant from the Eocene of China. Thousands of complete specimens have been collected from localities ranging from Inner Mongolia in the north, to the Sanshui Basin, Guangdong Province in the south (Fig. 1). The earliest described fossil catostomid was collected by the Central Asiatic Expeditions of The American Museum of Natural History from the Ulan Shiren Formation of Shara Murun, Inner Mongolia. The material consists only of three detached opercles, two subopercles and a few vertebrae, and was referred to the genus *Catostomus* (Hussakof 1932). Many more materials were discovered since the end of the 1950s. Those from Linli, Hunan Province were assigned to a living cyprinid genus *Osteochilus* (Tang 1959), and described as a new species *O. linliensis*. Later researchers followed Tang's suit in their work on the Eocene fishes from other localities of southern China and allocated similar fishes to the same genus, i.e. *Osteochilus hunanensis* (Cheng 1962), *O. hubeiensis* (Lei 1977), and *O. sanshuiensis*, *O. longipinnatus* and *O. laticorpus* (Wang *et al.* 1981). Their opinion was based mainly on the comparison of that the fish

fauna from the area as a whole, including associated forms of the Perciformes and Siluriformes etc., with that from the slaty marl ('Mergelschifer', then referred to the Eocene) of Middle-Sumatra, Indonesia, described by Sanders in 1934 (Liu *et al.* 1962). The 'cyprinid' fish was assigned to *Osteochilus*, whereas the siluriform was assigned to *Aoria*, Bagridae (Cheng 1962), and the perciform was described as a new genus *Tungtingichthys* and thought to be similar to *Toxotes beauforti* from Sumatra (Cheng 1962; Liu *et al.* 1962; Lei 1977; Wang *et al.* 1981). Lei (1987), while working on the fossil fishes from Xiadong, Dangyang, Songzi and Hubei Province, noticed that the fish from these localities are distinguished from *Osteochilus* and cyprinids as a whole in: (1) the premaxilla is triangular in shape, not excluding the maxilla from the lateral margin of the mouth; (2) the 2nd and 3rd vertebrae are not fused, and the transverse process of the 2nd vertebra divides into dorsal and ventral branches; (3) the sphenotic is not covered by the frontal; and (4) the dentary is high and short. He gave a new genus name *Jianghanichthys* (family *incertae sedis*) for the materials from the Hubei localities, replacing the genus name of *Osteochilus hubeiensis* that he had previously given in 1977.

After a nearly complete pharyngeal bone with teeth (Fig. 2) was found from Huadian, Jilin Province, and hundreds of specimens from southern China were examined we finally realized that all these described species, formerly thought of belonging to *Osteochilus*, were, in fact, catostomids. They are extremely similar to the North American *Amyzon* (Wilson 1977; Grande *et al.* 1982) and thus were referred to that genus (Chang

Fig. 1. Map of distribution of living catostomids (shaded area) and main localities of Eocene fossil suckers, modified from Nelson (1984). 1, Zaissan Basin, East Kazakhstan; 2, Mongolia; 3, Shara Murun, Inner Mongolia; 4, Huadian, Jilin, China; 5, Primorye, East Siberia; 6, East Sihote-Alen, Russia; 7, Changle; 8, Longkou, Shandong; 9, Songzi, Hubei; 10, Linli; 11, Xiangxiang; 12, Hengyang; 13, Hengnan, Hunan; 14, Sanshui Basin, Guangdong; 15, Zhangshu, Jiangxi, China; 16–22, localities in western USA; 23–25, localities in Canada.

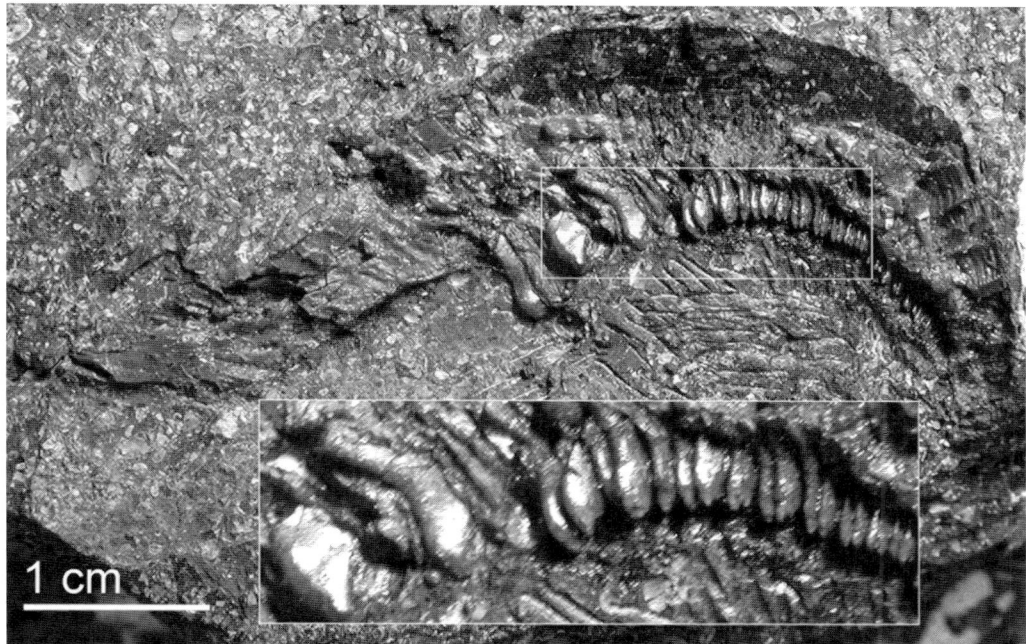

Fig. 2. Catostomidae indet. from the middle Eocene of Huadian, NE China, pharyngeal bone with teeth (V12572.2, Institute of Vertebrate Paleontology and Paleoanthropology). After Zhang *et al.* (2001), fig. 3.

et al. 2001). As in *Amyzon* from North America there are certain variations among the specimens collected from different localities of China, e.g. in the proportion of the body, the number of rays in the dorsal fin (see Fig. 3a, b) etc. However, it remains to be further studied whether all of the materials from China belong to the same species, or even to the same genus. They are in need of more detailed comparisons with those from North America, and their exact phylogenetic relationships to those from North America are also to be reassessed.

Another fossil catostomid based on complete skeletons was described from the late Eocene–early Oligocene deposits of Artem lignite locality, north of Vladivostok, Primorye Province, East Siberia by Sytchevskaya (1986) and named as *Vasnetzovia artemica*. As the Chinese catostomids, it is also of the *Amyzon*-type, similar to those from the Eocene–Oligocene of western North America. Isolated catostomid pharyngeal teeth were also reported from the Eocene and Oligocene deposits of Zaissan Basin of East Kazakhstan, East Siberia, and Mongolia. The materials were described by Sytchevskaya (1986) as *Amyzon gosiutensis* Grande *et al.* (1982), two new species of *Amyzon* (*A. interruptus* and *A. zaissanicus*), and new species of extant genera: *Carpiodes brevidens*, *Cycleptus robustus*, *Catostomus columnaris*,

Erimyzon luxus, *Minytrema shevyrevi*, *Xyrauchen rotundus* and *Moxostoma fungiaens*. We agree with Smith (1992) that it is difficult to verify the detailed identifications based on isolated pharyngeal teeth alone, and yet past presence of catostomids in those areas seems beyond any reasonable doubt.

Comparison of the Eocene catostomids from the mainland East Asia with those from western North America points to an obvious transpacific distributional pattern (Fig. 1). If we look at their present distribution we see enormous difference (Nelson 1984). On the western side of the Pacific there is only one species of catostomids (*Myxocyprinus asiaticus*) surviving in the Yangtze River and Minjiang River (Fujian Province), China and another one (*Catostomus catostomus*) in East Siberia, whereas there are around 70 species in North America on the eastern side of the Pacific (Chang *et al.* 2001; Harris & Mayden 2001). This picture is congruent with the distribution of other groups of the Eocene fishes from the mainland East Asia and those from western North America. Fishes of eight families (Dasyatidae, Amiidae, Osteoglossidae, Hiodontidae, Paraclupeidae, Clupeidae, Catostomidae, Esocidae) and seven genera (*Amia*, *Phareodus*, *Eohiodon*, *Diplomystus*, *Knightia*, *Amyzon*, *Esox*) from the families so far

Fig. 3. †*Amyzon hunanensis* (Cheng) from the middle Eocene of Xiawanpu, Xiangxiang, Hunan Province (V12571.1, IVPP) (**a**) and a newly collected complete catostomid fish from Hubei Province; (**b**) China.

known are shared by East Asia and western North America during the Eocene (Zhang *et al.* 1985; Chang & Chow 1986; Shen 1989; Chang & Zhou 1993; Zhang 2003). In other words, the Eocene fishes from both areas might have belonged to a single fauna. This distribution pattern started to emerge in the mid-Cretaceous, reached its maximum in the mid-Eocene, blurred afterwards, and becomes hardly recognizable at present (Chang & Chen 2000). The transpacific distribution of the Eocene freshwater fishes was also noticed by Sytchevskaya (1986) and Grande (1982), based on the discoveries of *Amia*, *Eohiodon* and catostomids in Kazakhstan and Mongolia by the former and *Diplomystus* in northern China and osteoglossids (*Phareodus* and *Musperia*) in west North America, Sumatra and Australia by the latter.

Bănărescu (1992) also mentioned the 'faunal exchanges' between Siberia/East Asia and North America during the Cretaceous or Palaeogene age, based on several groups of freshwater animals.

Cobitidae

Fossil cobitids are comparatively rare. Only one fossil cobitid, namely *Cobitis longipectoralis* Zhou, 1992 (Fig. 4) was found from the late early Miocene of Shanwang, Shandong Province, eastern China.

Several new species and subspecies of *Cobitis* (*C. zaisanica*, *C. zaisanica orientalis*, *C. ichberchae*, *C. centralasiae*) and *Sabanejewia* (*S. shargaensis*) were described by Sytchevskaya (1989), based on isolated suborbital spines, from

(a)

(b)

10 mm

Fig. 4. *Cobitis longipectoralis* Zhou 1992, part (**a**) and counterpart (**b**) of H 11.082, Shandong Provincial Museum, from Shanwang, Linqu, Shandong Province.

the middle-late Miocene and Pliocene of Zaissan Basin in East Kazakhstan and Mongolia. The suborbital spines of special type are sufficient to provide evidences for the presence of cobitids but may not be adequate for establishing new species.

Cyprinidae

Fossil cyprinids are the most diverse and widespread group among the three families. They were mainly uncovered from the localities in East Kazakhstan, South Siberia, Mongolia, China and Japan. Most of them are from the Miocene and Pliocene.

Most researchers accept that the Cyprinidae can be divided into two subgroups: Leuciscini and Barbini (Chen *et al.* 1984; Cavender & Coburn 1992), although different opinions exist concerning the subdivisions of the family Cyprinidae into subfamilies (Wu *et al.* 1964, 1977; Bănărescu 1990; Chen *et al.* 1998; Yue *et al.* 2000; Nelson 2006). The subfamilies we use in this paper are mainly according to the Chinese authors.

Earliest cyprinids. A single specimen of nearly complete skeleton collected from a drilling (no. Wei 40) of the Zhongyuan Oil Field (Fanxian County, Henan Province, China) at the depth of 2823.79 m from the ground surface, was described by Zhou (1990) as a new genus and species of the Gobioninae, *Palaeogobio zhongyuanensis.* The fish is from the early middle Eocene Member IV of the Shahejie Formation. It thus far represents the earliest known cyprinid from China. Newly collected cyprinid materials from the Eocene Hetaoyuan Formation of the nearby Nanyang Oil

Field are awaiting study. Complete skeletons of the Early Tertiary gobionins were also found from the late Eocene to early Oligocene deposits in Primorye Province, East Siberia. The fish was described as a new species of an extant genus, *Rostrogobio maritima* (Sytchevskaya 1986).

A barbin, *Parabarbus mynsajensis*, from the early and middle Oligocene of Turgai Basin, Central Kazakhstan was named by Sytchevskaya (1986), based on six pharyngeal bones and a few dozens of detached pharyngeal teeth. Isolated pharyngeal teeth from the early-middle Eocene of Zaissan Basin, East Kazakhstan were also mentioned and referred to the genus *Parabarbus* (Sytchevskaya 1986). In the section discussing 'the history of the Catostomidae and the problem on the differentiation of the amphipacific region' in the same paper, the author stated that the oldest finds of cyprinids were the early-middle Eocene *Parabarbus* from East Kazakhstan, though neither description nor figures of these particular pharyngeal teeth were given in the paper. This view was reassumed in Popov *et al.* (2001). Were this indeed the case, *Parabarbus* would represent the earliest cyprinid known from Asia and perhaps even in the world. The specimens from the Buxin Formation, referred to Paleocene, of Sanshui Basin, Guangdong Province, China, described by Wang *et al.* (1981) as belonging to living genera of cyprinids, i.e. *Barbodes, Varicorhinus, Zacco, Aphiocypris, Rasbora* and Leuciscinae *incertae sedis* do not show any reliable characters of cyprinids. Additional excavations and investigations in this area are still needed for the clarification of the problem.

Although an age of Miocene was assigned to *Cyprinus maomingensis* Liu (1957*a*) from the upper part of the Youganwo Formation of Maoming, Guangdong Province, China, the authors of its associated testudinid *Anosteira maomingensis* (Chow & Liu 1955; Chow 1956) suggested that the age should be late Eocene. *Cyprinus maomingensis* was found from a drilling, 48 m below the ground surface. The fish is not well preserved, showing its ventral view. Yet both its dorsal and anal fins bear a robust, unbranched ray with posterior edge serrated. This character demonstrates that it is undoubtedly the earliest known cyprinin.

Oligocene cyprinids. The Oligocene fossil fishes in general and cyprinids in particular are very rare in China. The cyprinids are mainly represented by isolated pharyngeal teeth. Those include a *Ctenopharyngodon*-like pharyngeal tooth from the Dongying Formation of Anci, Hebei Province in the area of Dagang Oil Field, and numerous pharyngeal teeth, not yet identified to genera and species, from the same Formation along the coastal region of the Bohai Gulf, and all are from drillings (Fig. 5; Zhang *et al.* 1985; Li *et al.* 1992). Some of them were referred to the Leuciscinae by Zhang *et al.* (1985). From northwestern China, a pharyngeal bone and isolated pharyngeal teeth were studied by Chen & Liu (2006) and referred to the Barbinae.

In the areas adjacent to China, known Oligocene cyprinids are also scarce. Sytchevskaya (1986) described nine genera (four of them are new) and five new species from Central and East Kazakhstan, Mongolia, and Primorye, East Siberia. They can be referred to four subfamilies: (1) Leuciscinae, including *Rutilus* sp., *Paleotinca turgaica* gen. et sp. nov. from the early–middle Oligocene of Central Kazakhstan, *Tribolodon* sp. from the middle Oligocene of East Kazakhstan, and *Zaissanotinca cristidens* gen. et sp. nov. from the early–middle Oligocene of East and Central Kazakhstan; (2) Gobioninae, including *Rostrogobio maritima* sp. nov. from the late Eocene–early Oligocene of Primorye and *Pseudorasbora* sp. from the middle–late Oligocene of Mongolia; (3) Barbinae, including *Parabarbus mynsajensis* gen. et sp. nov. from the early–middle Oligocene of Central Kazakhstan and *Parabarbus* sp. from the early–middle Eocene and early Oligocene of East Kazakhstan; and (4) Schizothoracinae, including *Schizothorax* sp. from the early–middle Oligocene, *Eodiptychus longidens* gen. et sp. nov. from the early Oligocene, and *Eodiptychus* sp. from the middle Oligocene, of East Kazakhstan. Thus, Leuciscinae, Barbinae and Schizothoracinae are found in Kazakhstan and Mongolia, whereas

Gobioninae is found in East Siberia. Most taxa are identified or established only on the basis of isolated pharyngeal teeth, few (*Parabarbus mynsajensis* and *Eodiptychus longidens*) are known by pharyngeal bones, and only one (*Rostrogobio maritima*) has a complete skeleton. Incidentally, pharyngeal teeth are sometimes quite similar, not only in their shape but also in their number and rows, in different genera of the same subfamily, or, in a few cases, even across different subfamilies. To identify or establish new genera and species only on the basis of isolated pharyngeal teeth or incomplete pharyngeal bones is not always reliable. In spite of all this, we can still see that during the Oligocene there were gobionins in eastern Asia, whereas barbins, schizothoracins and leuciscins occurred in the western part of Asia.

Miocene and Pliocene cyprinids. The Miocene and Pliocene cyprinids are very abundant in the areas under discussion (Fig. 6). Thousands of complete skeletons with details have been unearthed along with rich fossil mammals since the 1930s from the early Miocene diatomite Shanwang Formation of Shanwang, Linqu city, Shandong Province. Young & Tchang (1936) first studied the fishes and referred them to Recent genera, such as *Leuciscus*, *Barbus* and *Pseudorasbora*. Unfortunately, the specimens studied by Young & Tchang were all lost during the Second World War. Zhou (1990) collected new specimens from Shanwang and studied part of the collections. She found that those identified by Young & Tchang as barbins are, in fact, cyprinins for the reason that both their dorsal and anal fins all bear robust serrated fin rays. She referred most fishes to new fossil genera and species rather than extant ones, e.g. *Lucyprinus*, *Platycyprinus*, *Qicyprinus* for cyprinins, *Plesioleuciscus* for *Leusiscus miocenicus* Young and Tchang, 1936 and established a new genus *Miheichthys* for a danionin. Recently, we collected more specimens from Shanwang (Fig. 7) and based on our preliminary examination some of the fishes might bear a closer relationship to the contemporary ones from Europe than previously thought. For example, *Lucyprinus* might be correlated to *Palaeocarassius* from many European localities. Recent dating (Deng *et al.* 2003) suggests the age of the Shanwang Formation as 18 Ma, and thus it can be correlated to zone MN4 in the European chronology. An early xenocyprinin *Eoxenocypris liui* was described from the Miocene Daotaiqiao Formation of Huanan, Heilongjiang Province (Chang *et al.* 1996). *Ecocarpia ningmingensis* was recently discovered from the early Miocene or late Oligocene Ningming Formation of Ningming Basin, Guangxi Zhuang Autonomous Region, and was regarded as the sister group of cultrinins + xenocyprinins

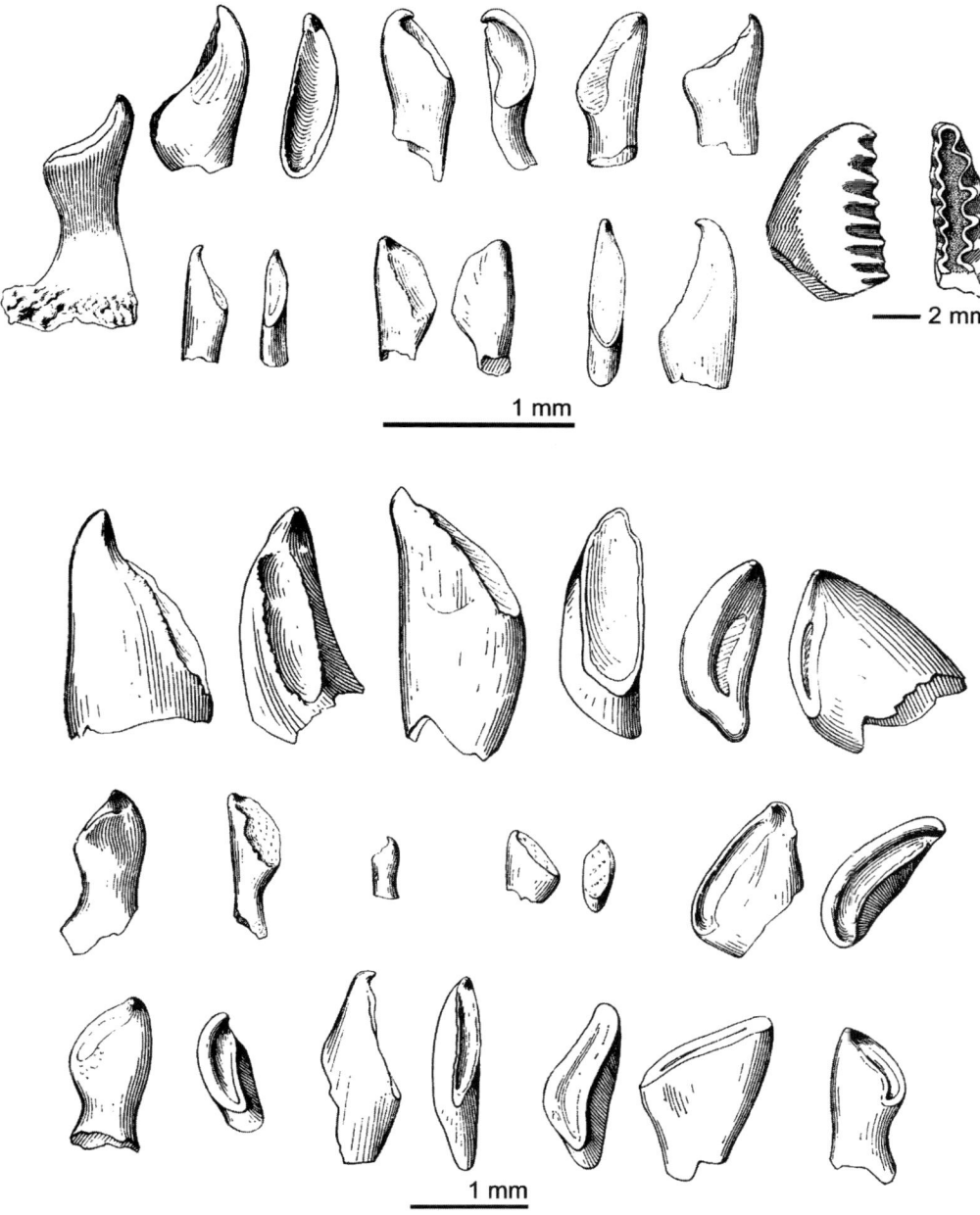

Fig. 5. Isolated pharyngeal teeth of Cyprinidae from the coastal region of Bohai Gulf, China; Dongying Formation, Oligocene. After Zhang *et al.* (1985), figs 26 and 34.

(Chen *et al.* 2005). Wu & Chen (1980) set up a new fossil genus and species of the Cyprinidae close to schizothoracins, *Plesioschizothorax macrocephalus* from the late Miocene–early Pliocene Dingqinghu Formation of northern Tibet.

Pharyngeal bones and teeth are often found in the Miocene deposits of eastern as well as northwestern parts of China. From the eastern part, specimens were mainly obtained from the drilling cores of the oil fields around the Bohai Gulf,

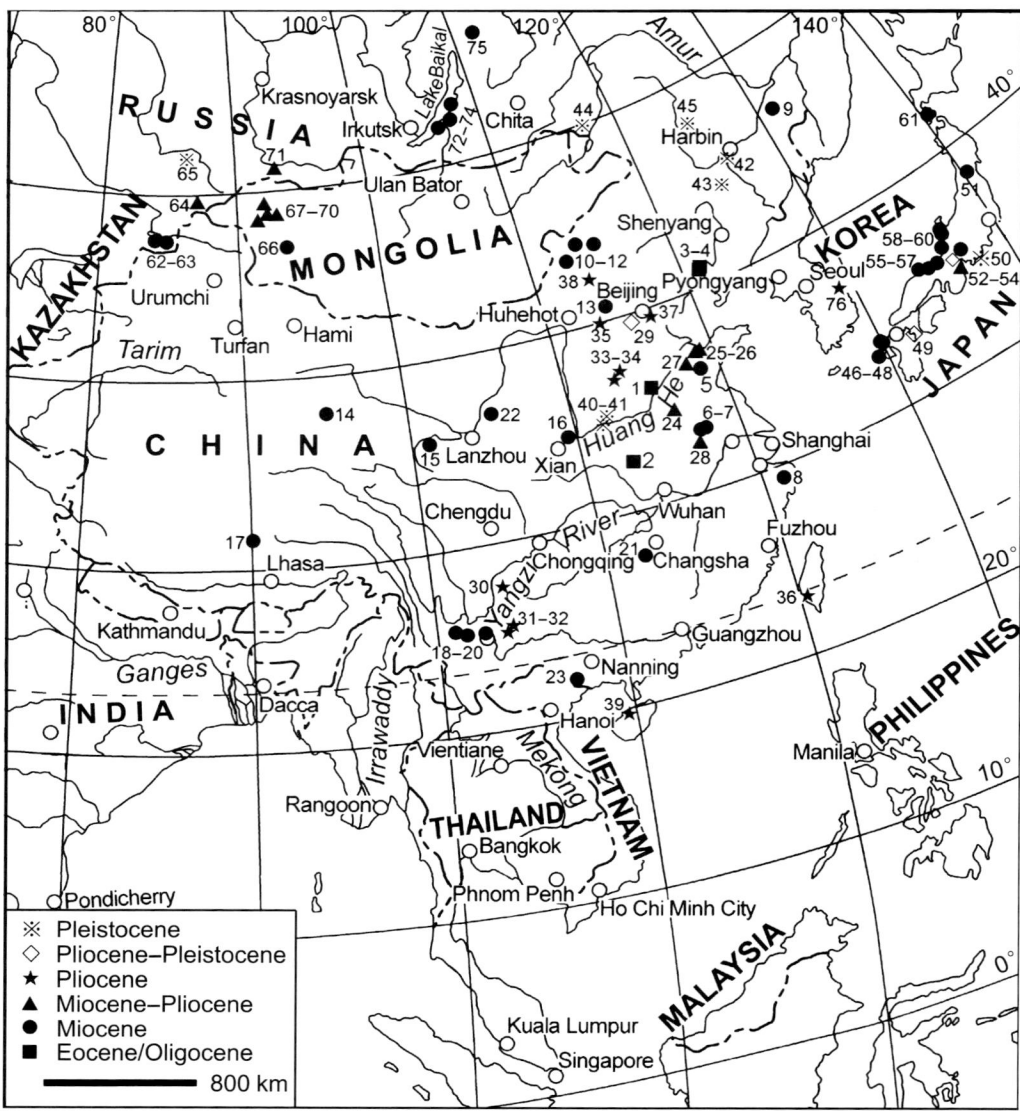

Fig. 6. Map of the cyprinid localities in China and its adjacent areas. 1, Fanxian; 2, Nanyang, Henan; 3, Panshan; 4, Dawa, Liaoning; 5, Linqu, Shandong; 6, Sihong; 7, Huaiyun, Jiangsu; 8, Ninghai, Zhejiang; 9, Huanan, Heilongjiang; 10, Tunggur; 11, Baogeda Ula; 12, Abagaqi, Inner Mongolia; 13, Zhangbei, Hebei; 14, Delingha; 15, Huangzhong, Qinghai; 16, Lantian, Shannxi; 17, Bange, Tibet; 18, Yuanmou; 19, Lufeng; 20, Xianfeng Coal Mine, Yunnan; 21, Xiangxiang, Hunan; 22, Haiyuan, Ningxia; 23, Ningming, Guangxi; 24, Fengxian, Jiangsu; 25, Binxian; 26, Kenli; 27, Jiyang, Shandong; 28, Liuhe, Jiangsu; 29, Zhoukoudian, Beijing; 30, Zhaotong; 31, Qujin; 32, Yiliang, Yunnan; 33, Yushe; 34, Taigu, Shanxi; 35, Yangyuan, Hebei; 36, Tainan, Taiwan; 37, Anci, Hebei; 38, Bilike, Inner Mongolia; 39, Hainan Island; 40, Pinglu, Shanxi; 41, Sanmenxia, Henan; 42, Harbin, Heilongjiang; 43, Nong'an, Jilin; 44, Zhalannor, Inner Mongolia; 45, Fuyu, Heilongjiang, China; 46, Hirato Island; 47, Iki Island; 48, Mastu-ura; 49, Oita, Kyushu; 50, Shizuoka; 51, Yamagata; 52, Mie; 53, Shiga; 54, Gifu; 55, Oki-Dogo Island; 56, Kasumi; 57, Kyoto; 58, Fukui; 59, Ishikawa; 60, Noto Peninsula, Hongshu; 61, Yoshioka, Hokkaido, Japan; 62–63, Zaisan Basin, East Kazakhstan; 64, Altai Mountains; 65, Altai region; 66, Schargain Gobi; 67–70, West Mongolia; 71, Southern Tuva; 72–74, East Prebaikalia; 75, Vitim, Plateau, Russia; and 76, Bukpyeong Basin, South Korea.

Fig. 7. A nearly complete cyprinin from Shanwang, Linqu, Shandong Province, China; Shanwang Formation, early Miocene.

from the Miocene Guantao Formation and Pliocene Minghuazhen Formation. They were identified as ?*Mylopharyngodon*, leuciscins and xenocyprinins (Fig. 8; Zhang *et al.* 1985; Li *et al.* 1992). Pharyngeal teeth were often found from other localities of East China, e.g. the middle Miocene of Inner Mongolia, Shaanxi, Jiangsu and Zhejiang Provinces. Most of the teeth were recognized as belonging to the Xenocyprininae, Leuciscinae and Cyprininae. From the western part, a pharyngeal tooth from the early Miocene Xiejia Formation, Huangzhong, Qinghai Province was described and referred to *Ctenopharyngodon* sp. (Fig. 8; Zhang *et al.* 1985). Schizothoracin or barbin pharyngeal bones with teeth and numerous other bones were also found from the Miocene of Qaidam Basin, Qinghai Province. Barbins and cyprinins are found from Yunnan Province (Liu 1985).

Thus, during the Miocene, the cyprinids from the eastern part of China include members of the Leuciscinae, Xenocyprininae, Cyprininae, Gobioninae and ?Danioninae, whereas those from the western part include Cyprininae, Barbinae and Schizothoracinae.

Many complete skeletons of cyprinids were also collected from the early Pliocene Gaozhuang Formation of Yushe, Shanxi Province since the 1930s. Tchang made a preliminary study in 1933. More extensive study by Liu & Su (1962) found that most of the fishes are Recent genera and species, such as *Cyprinus carpio*, *Carassius auratus*, *Mylopharyngodon piceus*, *Ctenopharyngodon idellus*, *Hypophthalmichthys molitrix*, *Culter* cf. *mongoliensis*. Some of the fishes were referred to Recent genera with new species established, e.g. *Xenocypris yüshensis* (Fig. 9, showing the state of preservation of the specimens from the locality), *Hemiculterella longicephalus*, *Pseudorasbora changtsunensis*. The Gaozhuang Formation falls within the Gilbert reversed palaeomagnetic chron, thus constraining its age to 5.2–3.4 Ma and being correlated to zones MN14 + 15 in the

European chronology (Qiu & Qiu 1995). Pharyngeal teeth of *Cyprinus carpio*, *Mylopharyngodon piceus* and *Aristichthys nobilis* recently were also discovered from the Pliocene of Tainan, Taiwan (Tao & Hu 2001). The Pliocene fish locality near the Peking Man site, Zhoukoudian, Beijing, produces several species of barbins referred to the extant genera *Barbus* and *Matsya* (Chang 1936–1937; Liu 1954).

The Miocene and Pliocene cyprinid remains from Japan are also rich and widespread (Fig. 6). Many researchers (Tomoda 1979; Nakajima 1984, 1986; Yasuno 1986, 1989, 1991, 1992, 2000, 2001, 2003; Nakajima & Yamasaki 1992; Nakajima & Yue 1995) have studied these cyprinids. Most studied materials consist of pharyngeal teeth. Complete skeletons from Iki Island, NW of Kyushu, and elsewhere are still under study. The teeth were described as belonging to Cyprininae, Xenocyprininae, Cultrinae, Leuciscinae, Gobioninae and Hypophthalmichthyinae.

The Miocene and Pliocene fish faunas from East China and Japan, to a great extent, resemble each other in their compositions, whereas the Recent fish faunas from the two areas are noticeably different (Bănărescu 1990). The Shanwang Miocene fish fauna is quite similar to the fish fauna from a series of early Miocene localities of Honshu and Hokkaido, e.g. Kyoto, Fukui, Gifu, Ishikawa, Yamagata, southern Hokkaido, etc. (Fig. 6). The Pliocene fishes from China and Japan belong to exactly the same subfamilies, which are still common in the East Asian freshwater fish fauna today. All this indicates that the fishes from the eastern part of mainland Asia and the Japanese Islands must have belonged to the same ichthyofauna during the Neogene (Yasuno 1986; Nakajima & Yamasaki 1992; Chang *et al.* 1996; Chang & Chen 2000). The overwhelming percentage of extant genera and species in the Pliocene fish fauna of East Asia led Chang *et al.* (1996) to suggest that the Recent freshwater ichthyofauna

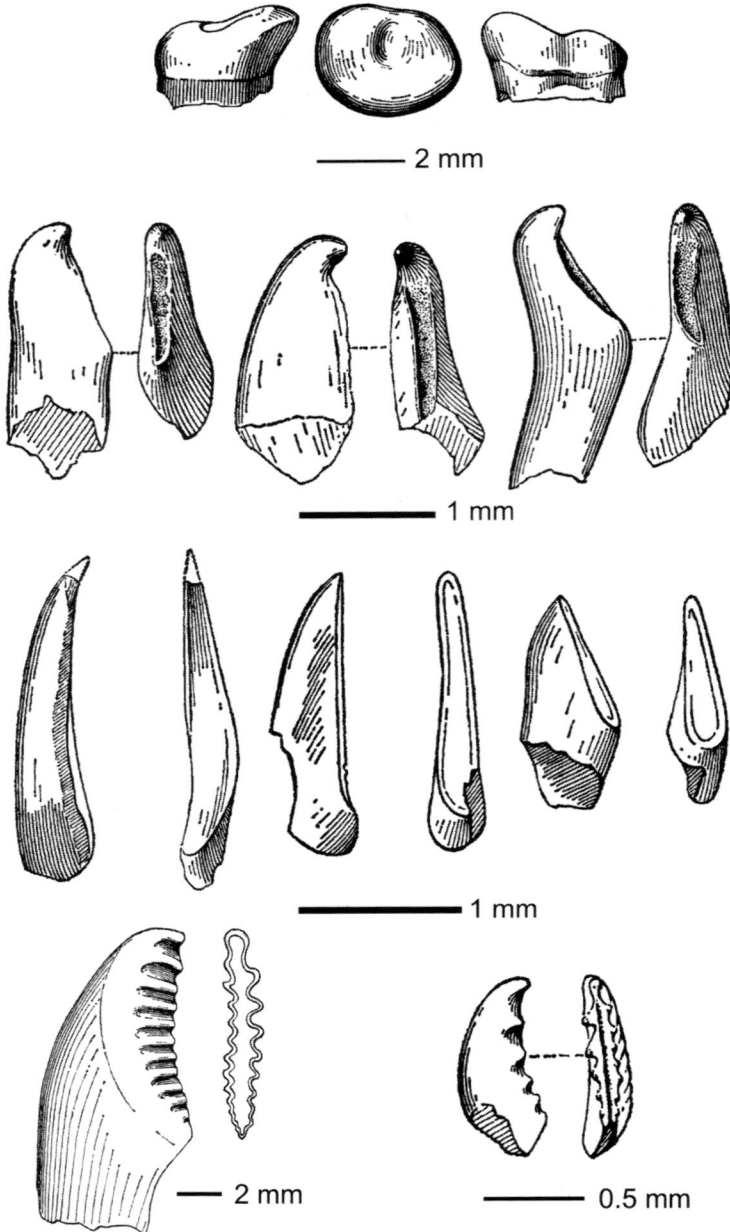

Fig. 8. Isolated pharyngeal teeth of Cyprinidae from Binxian and Kenli, Shandong, China; Guangtao and Minghuazhen Formation, Miocene and Pliocene, and, at the left lower corner of the figure, a pharyngeal tooth of *Ctenopharyngodon* sp. from Huangzhong, Qinghai Province, China; Xiejia Formation, early Miocene. After Zhang *et al.* (1985), figs 27–31.

from this area basically took its shape in the early Pliocene.

The Miocene and Pliocene fishes are also abundant and diverse in the northern neighbouring areas of China, i.e. Zaissan Basin of East Kazakhstan, Altai Mountains, Southern Tuva, West Mongolia, Schargain Gobi, Mongolia, Vitim Plateau and East Prebaikalia (Fig. 6). The fossils

Fig. 9. †*Xenocypris yūshensis* from Yūshe, Shanxi Province, China; Gaozhuang Formation, Pliocene (V.2442).

from these areas have been studied by many researchers, e.g. Schtylko (1934), Lebedev (1959), Yakovlev (1961), Sytchevskaya (1986, 1989). Among them Sytchevskaya (1989) did the most extensive and thorough work. Materials from the Miocene consist mostly of isolated pharyngeal teeth, occasionally of pharyngeal bones and other skull bones, and rarely of complete or incomplete skeletons. In this case, the morphological and taxonomic work must be rather difficult. From the Pliocene or sometimes even the upper Miocene deposits complete and/or incomplete skeletons are often preserved. For instance, the new species *Carassius intermedius* Sytchevskaya, 1989 was based on 50 complete and incomplete skeletons, a few hundreds of skull bones, and countless pharyngeal teeth. Consequently, the work seems more reliable and results are easier to use for comparison. Sytchevskaya described from these areas 32 genera, more than 40 species and subspecies, belonging to Leuiscinae, Gobioninae, Cyprininae, Barbinae and Schizothoracinae. Among them nine new fossil genera and 34 new fossil species were named by Sytchevskaya and earlier researchers.

Many of the Neogene, and some of the Oligocene, taxa from Asia, especially those from Central and East Kazakhstan and West Mongolia, are comparable to their contemporaneous ones from Europe (Obrhelová 1970, 1971; Sytchevskaya 1986, 1989; Cavender 1991; Bănărescu 1992; Gaudant 1997). Further detailed work will clarify the relationships between the fishes, as well as the relationship between the areas.

Quaternary cyprinids. Among our discussions of the cypriniform fossils from China and its adjacent areas, the least can be said about the Quaternary cyprinids. The deposits of this age have always yielded fragmentary bones. Almost no new species, let alone new genera, are found so far.

Therefore, few people have the interest to work on them, although they might not be as insignificant as one tends to think.

From China, a few Quaternary localities (Fig. 6) have yielded fragmentary bones and detached pharyngeal teeth. Even fewer materials have been studied. Known from the Pleistocene of Zhoukoudian, Beijing (Bian 1934), Dingcun, Shanxi (Liu 1958), Sanmenxia, Henan (Huang 1957), Zhalannor, Inner Mongolia (Liu 1951) and the Holocene of Yichang, Hubei (Liu 1957b) are all extant species, most commonly occurring in the water system of the area today, such as *Cyprinus carpio*, *Ctenopharyngodon idellus*, *Mylopharyngodon piceus*, *Hypophthalmichthys* sp., *Culter* sp. etc.

Uyeno (1965) and Tomoda (1979) mentioned *Distoechodon* cf. *tumirostris* from the middle Pleistocene of Shizuoka Prefecture, Honshu, Japan. From the middle–late Pleistocene and 'Eopleistocene' of Altai region, new subspecies *Rutilus rutilus pleistocaenicus* ssp. nov. and *Cyprinus carpio altaicus* ssp. nov. were described by Sytchevskaya (1989).

Conclusions

Fossil cypriniforms are very abundant from China and its adjacent areas. At present, approximately a total of 80 genera and 100 species and subspecies of fossil cypriniforms have been described from these areas. However, their morphological and phylogenetic studies remain largely preliminary. Many of them await more in-depth revisions, especially in the light of many newly collected and more interesting materials. Still more are being collected now. However, this brief review represents an overall picture of our current knowledge about fossil cypriniforms in those areas.

Among the fossil cypriniforms currently known from these areas, most of them are from the Eocene, Miocene and Pliocene deposits, a few from the Oligocene, and due to the collecting/studying bias, even fewer from the Quaternary. They represent three of the five Recent families: the Catostomidae, Cobitidae and Cyprinidae, although cobitids are comparatively rare. No fossils have been found so far of the Gyrinocheilidae and Homalopteridae (Balitoridae). Comparison of the Eocene catostomids from the mainland East Asia with those from western North America points to an obvious transpacific distributional pattern, in a sharp contrast to the family's current disjunct distributions.

Fossil cyprinids are the most diverse and widespread group among the three families. The majority of fossil cyprinids found so far from the Miocene and Pliocene of the eastern part of the mainland Asia and the Japanese Islands shows that the freshwater fishes from these two areas most probably belonged to the same ichthyofauna during the Neogene. The rich Miocene and Pliocene fossil cyprinids from Kazakhstan, Mongolia and Siberia appear to link the fish faunas from Europe and Asia, although they are still in need of the most work.

We hope that this paper provides a launching pad for further conducting a detailed study of the newly-collected materials and more thorough revisions of the old ones. In so doing, we believe that a clearer picture of their morphology, phylogeny, and palaeobiogeographical implications should emerge in a not-too-distant future.

We thank D. Miao for discussions and stylistic improvement of the manuscript, E. Sytchevskaya and Y. Yabumoto for discussions and providing literature, J. Zhang for help in preparation of the illustrations. We also thank J. Gaudant and an anonymous reviewer for their well-informed and constructive opinions. This work is supported by the National Natural Science Foundation of China (Grant No. 40432003, 40662001), Chinese Academy of Sciences (Grant No. KZCX3-SW-126), Ecocarp project (European Commission, INCO-DEV programme, contract number ICA4-CT-2001-0024), and Cypriniformes Tree of Life, NSF grant no. EF0431326 to R. Mayden.

References

BĂNĂRESCU, P. 1990. Zoogeography of Freshwaters. Vol. 1. General Distribution and Dispersal of Freshwater Animals. AULA Verlag, Wiesbaden, 48–170, 499–510.

BĂNĂRESCU, P. 1992. Zoogeography of Freshwaters. Vol. 2. Distribution and Dispersal of Freshwater Animals in North America and Eurasia. 524–531, 860–1091.

BIAN, M. N. 1934. On the fossil Pisces, Amphibia and Reptilia from Choukoutien Localities 1 and 3. Palaeontologica Sinica (Series C), 10, 5–32.

CAVENDER, T. M. 1991. The fossil record of Cyprinidae. In: WINFIELD, I. L. & NELSON, J. S. (eds) Cyprinid Fishes. Chapman & Hau, London.

CAVENDER, T. M. & COBURN, M. M. 1992. Phylogenetic relationships of North American Cyprinidae. In: MAYDEN, R. L. (ed.) Systematic, Historical Ecology and North American Freshwater Fishes. Stanford University Press, Stanford, 293–327.

CHANG, H. C. 1936–1937. Fossil fishes from Choukoutien. Bulletin of Geological Society of China, 8, 432–448.

CHANG, M.-M. & CHEN, Y. Y. 2000. Late Mesozoic and Tertiary ichthyofaunas from China and some puzzling patterns of distribution. Vertebrata PalAsiatica, 38, 161–175.

CHANG, M. M. & CHOW, C. C. 1986. Stratigraphic and geographic distributions of Late Mesozoic and Cenozoic fishes of China. In: UYENO, T., ARAI, R., TANIUCHI, T. & MATSUURA, K. (eds) Indo-Pacific Fish Biology. Proceedings of the Second International Conference of Indo-Pacific Fishes. Ichthyological Society of Japan, Tokyo, 529–539.

CHANG, M. M., CHEN, Y. Y. & TONG, H. W. 1996. A new Miocene Xenocyprinine (Cyprinidae) from Heilongjiang Province, Northeast China and succession of Late Cenozoic fish faunas of East Asia. Vertebrata PalAsiatica, 34, 165–183 [Chinese 165–176; English 176–183].

CHANG, M. M., MIAO, D. S., CHEN, Y. Y., ZHOU, J. J. & CHEN, P. F. 2001. Suckers (Fish, Catostomidae) from the Eocene of China account for the family's current disjunct distributions. Science in China (Series D), 44, 577–586.

CHANG, M. M. & ZHOU, J. J. 1993. A brief survey of the Chinese Eocene ichthyofauna. Kaupia, 2, 157–162.

CHEN, G. & LIU, J. 2006. First fossil barbin (Cyprinidae, Teleostei) from Oligocene of Qaidam Basin in Northern Tibetan Plateau. Vertebrata PalAsiatica, 45, 330–341 [in Chinese with English summary].

CHEN, G. J., FANG, F. & CHANG, M. M. 2005. A new cyprinid closely related to cultrins + xenocyprinins from the mid-Tertiary of Southern China. Journal of Vertebrate Paleontology, 25, 451–461.

CHEN, X. L., YUE, P. Q. & LIN, R. D. 1984. Major groups within the family Cyprinidae and their phylogenetic relationships. Acta Zootaxonomica Sinica, 9, 424–440 [in Chinese with English summary].

CHEN, Y. Y., CHU, X. L., LUO, Y. L. ET AL. (eds) 1998. Fauna Sinica, Osteichthyes, Cypriniformes II Science Press, Beijing [in Chinese with English summary].

CHENG, C. C. 1962. Fossil fishes from the early Tertiary of Hsiang-Hsiang, Hunan, with discussion of age of the Hsiawanpu Formation. Vertebrata PalAsiatica, 6, 333–343 [in Chinese with English summary].

CHOW, M. C. 1956. Supplementary notes on Anosteira maomingensis. Acta Palaeontologica Sinica, 4, 233–238 [in Chinese with English summary].

CHOW, M. C. & LIU, C. L. 1955. A new anosterine turtle from Maoming, Kwangtung. Acta Palaeontologica Sinica, 3, 275–282 [in Chinese with English summary].

DENG, T., WANG, W. M. & YUE, L. P. 2003. Recent advances of the establishment of the Shanwang stage in the Chinese Neogene. Vertebrata PalAsiatica, 41, 314–323 [in Chinese with English summary].

FINK, S. V. & FINK, W. L. 1981. Interrelationships of the ostariophysan fishes (Teleostei). *Zoological Journal of Linnean Society*, **72**, 297–353.

GAUDANT, J. 1997. A new species of the genus *Palaeocarassius* Obrhelová in the lacustrine upper Miocene of Alissas (Ardèche, France). *Géologie de la France*, **1997**, 29–37.

GRANDE, L. 1982. A revision of the fossil genus †*Diplomystus*, with comments on the interrelationships of clupeomorph fishes. *American Museum Novitates*, **2728**, 1–34.

GRANDE, L., EASTMAN, J. T. & CAVENDER, T. M. 1982. *Amyzon gosiutensis*, a new catostomid fish from the Green River Formation. *Copeia*, **1982**, 523–532.

HARRIS, P. M. & MAYDEN, R. L. 2001. Phylogenetic relationships of major clades of Catostomidae (Teleostei: Cypriniformes) as inferred from mitochondrial SSU and LSU rDNA sequences. *Molecular Phylogenetics and Evolution*, **20**, 225–237.

HUANG, W. L. 1957. Early Pleistocene fish remains from Sanmen Area, Henan. *Vertebrata PalAsiatica*, **1**, 313–319 [in Chinese with English summary].

HUSSAKOF, L. 1932. The fossil collected by the Central Asiatic expedition. *American Museum Novitates*, **1932, 553**, 1–19.

LEBEDEV, V. D. 1959. Neogene fauna of freshwater fishes from Basin in West-Siberian Lowland. Issues of Ichthyology, **1959**, 28–69 [in Russian].

LEI, Y. Z. 1977. Vertebrates. *In*: Hubei Institute of Geological Science, Bureau of geology of Henan Province (eds) *Atlas of Fossils from Central-Southern China*, **3**, 133–136. Geological Publishing House, Beijing [in Chinese].

LEI, Y. Z. 1987. Fish. *In*: Yichang Institute of Geology, Mineral Resources, Ministry of Geology, Mineral Resources (eds) *Biostratigraphy of the Yangtze Gorges Area (5): Cretaceaous and Tertiary*, **104**, 191–194. Geological Publishing House, Beijing [in Chinese with English summary].

LI, L. L., YAO, Y. M. & XIANG, W. D. 1992. The Tertiary 'Miscellaneous Fossils' from Jiyang Depression, Shandong Province. Shangdong Science and Technology Press, Jinan [in Chinese with English summary].

LIU, H. T. 1951. Fossil fish from Zhalannor, Inner Mongolia. *Geological Review*, **16**, 33 [in Chinese].

LIU, H. T. 1954. Fossil fish from Locality 14 of Choukoutien. *Palaeontologica Sinica*, New Series C, **14**, 1–7 [in Chinese with English abstract].

LIU, H. T. 1957a. A new fossil cyprinid fish from Maoming, Kwangtung. *Vertebrata PalAsiatica*, **1**, 151–153 [in Chinese with English summary].

LIU, H. T. 1957b. Fish bones from Neolithic Lijiahe site, Yichang Hubei. *Archeology Correspondence*, **3**, 78–80.

LIU, H. T. 1958. Description of fish bones. *In*: PEI, W. C. (ed.) Report on the excavation of Palaeolithic sites at Tingtsun, Hsiangfenghien, Shansi province, China. *Memoires of Institute of Vertebrate Paleontology and Paleoanthropology, Academia Sinica*, **2**, 77–79 [in Chinese with English summary].

LIU, H. T. & SU, T. T. 1962. Pliocene fishes from Yushe basin, Shansi. *Vertebrata PalAsiatica*, **6**, 1–47 [in Chinese with English summary].

LIU, T. S., LIU, H. T. & TANG, X. 1962. A new percoid fish from south China. *Vertebrata PalAsiatica*, **6**, 121–129 [in Chinese and English].

LIU, X. T. 1985. Fish fossils from the Homonoids bearing locality at Shihuiba Lufeng, Yunnan. *Acta Anthropologica Sinica*, **4**, 109–112 [in Chinese with English abstract].

NAKAJIMA, T. 1984. A new species of cyprinid fish, *Hypophthalmichthys okuyamai*, from the Early Pliocene Iga Formation of the Kobiwako Group. *Bulletin Mizunami Fossil Museum*, **11**, 69–72 [in Japanese with English summary].

NAKAJIMA, T. 1986. Pliocene cyprinid pharyngeal teeth from Japan and East Asia Neogene cyprinid zoogeography. *In*: UYENO, T., ARAI, R., TANIUCHI, T. & MATSUURA, K. (eds) *Indo-Pacific Fish Biology. Proceedings of the Second International Conference of Indo-Pacific Fishes*. Ichthyological Society of Japan, Tokyo, 502–513.

NAKAJIMA, T. & YAMASAKI, H. 1992. Temporal and spatial distributions of fossil cyprinids in East Asia and their paleogeographic significance. *Bulletin of the Mizunami Fossil Museum*, **19**, 543–557.

NAKAJIMA, T. & YUE, P. Q. 1995. A new species of the fossil cyprinid fish, *Cyprinus* (*Mesocyprinus*) *okuyamai*, from the Pliocene Ueno Formation of the Kobiwako Group in the Ueno Basin. Mie Prefecture, central Japan. *Earth Science*, **49**, 221–226.

NELSON, L. S. 1984. *Fishes of the World*. 2nd edn. Wiley, New York.

NELSON, L. S. 2006. *Fishes of the World*. 4th edn. Wiley, New York.

OBRHELOVÁ, N. 1970. Fische aus dem Süßwassermolasse im Süden von Cechy. *Geologie*, **19**, 967–1001.

OBRHELOVÁ, N. 1971. Vergleichende Osteologie der Gattung *Leuciscus* (Pisces) aus tertiären Schichten der nördlichen und westlichen ČSSR. *Paläontologische Abhandlungen, Abteilung A Paläozoologie*, **4**, 549–660.

POPOV, S. V., AKHMETIEV, M. A., BUGROVA, E. M. ET AL. 2001. Biogeography of the Northern Peri-Tethys from the Late Eocene to the Early Miocene: Part 1. Late Eocene. Supplement to *Paleontological Journal*, **35**, 1–68.

QIU, Z. X. & QIU, Z. D. 1995. Chronological sequence and subdivision of Chinese Neogene mammalian faunas. *Palaeogeography, Palaeoclimatology, Palaeoecology*, **116**, 41–70.

SANDERS, M. 1934. Die Fossilen Fische der altertertiären Süsswasserablagerungen aus Mittel-Sumatra. *Verhandelingen van het Geologisch-Mijnbouwkundig Genootschap voor Nederland en Kolonien. Geologische Serie*, **11**, 1–144.

SCHTYLKO, B. A. 1934. A Neogene fauna of freshwater fishes from western Siberia. *Trudy Geologo-Razvedochnovo Ob'edinenia*, **359**, 1–94 [in Russian].

SHEN, M. 1989. *Eohiodon* from China and the distribution of osteoglossomorphs. *Vertebrata PalAsiatica*, **27**, 237–247 [in Chinese with English summary].

SMITH, G. R. 1992. Phylogeny and biogeography of the Catostomidae, freshwater fishes of North America and Asia. *In*: MAYDEN, R. L. (ed.) *Systematics, Historical Ecology, and North American Freshwater Fishes*, Stanford: Stanford University Press, 778–826.

SYTCHEVSKAYA, E. K. 1986. Paleogene freshwater fish fauna of the USSR and Mongolia. *Joint Soviet-Mongolian Paleontological Expedition Transactions*, **29**, 1–157 [in Russian with English summary].

SYTCHEVSKAYA, E. K. 1989. Neogene freshwater fish Fauna of Mongolia. *Joint Soviet-Mongolian Palaeontological Expedition Transactions*, **39**, 77–82 [in Russian].

TANG, X. 1959. A new fossil fish from Linli, Hunan. *Vertebrata PalAsiatica*, **1**, 211–213 [in Chinese].

TAO, H. J. & HU, C. H. 2001. Cyprinidae fossil fishes of Tainan Hsien, Taiwan. *Geology*, **21**, 51–64.

TCHANG, T. L. 1933. Notes on a fossil fish from Shanxi. *Bulletin of the Geological Society of China*, **12**, 467–468.

TOMODA, Y. 1979. Discovery of the late Cenozoic Xenocypridinae (Cyprinidae) fishes from Tokai and Kinki Districts. *Memoirs of National Science Museum*, **12**, 93–101 [in Japanese].

UYENO, T. 1965. On a cyprinid fish from a Pleistocene bed in Shizuoka Prefecture, Japan, and 'fossil species' problem. *Reports of Japanese Society of Systematic Zoology*, **1**, 27–29 [in Japanese with English summary].

WANG, J. K., LI, G. F. & WANG, J. S. 1981. The early Tertiary fossil fishes from Sanshui and its adjacent basin, Guangdong. *Palaeontologia Sinica, (Series C)*, **22**, 1–90 [in Chinese with English summary].

WILSON, M. V. H. 1977. Middle Eocene freshwater fishes from British Columbia. *Contributions in Life Science, Royal Ontario Museum*, **113**, 1–61.

WU, X. W. *ET AL.* 1964. *The Cyprinoid Fishes of China*, Vol. **1**. People's Press of Science and Technology, Shanghai [in Chinese].

WU, X. W. *ET AL.* 1977. *The Cyprinoid Fishes of China*, Vol. **2**. People's Press, Shanghai [in Chinese].

WU, X. W., CHEN, Y. Y., CHEN, X. L. & CHEN, J. X. 1981. A taxonomical system and phylogenetic relationship of the families of the suborder Cyprinoidei (Pisces). *Scientia Sinica*, **24**, 563–572 [in Chinese with English summary].

WU, Y. F. & CHEN, Y. Y. 1980. Fossil cyprinid fishes from the late Tertiary of North Xizang, China. *Vertebrata PalAsiatica*, **18**, 15–20 [in Chinese with English summary].

YAKOVLEV, V. N. 1961. Distribution of freshwater fishes of the Neogene of Holarctic and zoogeographic zonation. *Issues of Ichthyology*, **1**, 209–220 [in Russian].

YASUNO, T. 1986. Paleontological studies of the fossil cyprinids from the Cenozoic deposits in Japan. *Bulletin of High School, Fukui Prefecture*, **4**, 61–81 [in Japanese with English summary].

YASUNO, T. 1989. Fossil cyprinid discovered from the early Miocene Hiramaki Formation, Gifu Prefecture, Central Japan. *Bulletin of Mizunami Fossil Museum*, **16**, 121–124 [in Japanese with English summary].

YASUNO, T. 1991. Fossil pharyngeal teeth from the early Miocene Atsumi Formation, Yamagata Prefecture, north east Japan. *Bulletin of Japan Sea Research Institute of Kanazawa University*, **23**, 51–58 [in Japanese with English summary].

YASUNO, T. 1992. Miocene cyprinid from Yoshioka in the Oshima Peninsula southwest Hokkaido, Japan. *Bulletin of Mizunami Fossil Museum*, **19**, 459–464 [in Japanese with English summary].

YASUNO, T. 2000. Miocene freshwater fish fossils firstly discovered from the Oki-Dogo Island, Shimane Prefecture, Japan (Preliminary report). *Bulletin of Fukui City Museum of Natural History*, **47**, 1–13 [in Japanese with English summary].

YASUNO, T. 2001. First discovery of Miocene cyprinid fossils from the Noto Peninsula, Ishikawa Prefecture central Japan and its implication. *Bulletin Fukui City Museum Natural History*, **48**, 1–15 [in Japanese with English summary].

YASUNO, T. 2003. Early Miocene pharyngeal teeth (Cyprinidae) fossils from northwestern Shan-in and Kyushu, Japan (1). *Bulletin Fukui City Museum of Natural History*, **50**, 1–8 [in Japanese with English summary].

YOUNG, C. C. & TCHANG, T. L. 1936. Fossil fishes from the Shan-wang Series of Shantung. *Bulletin of the Geological Society of China*, **15**, 179–206.

YUE, P. Q., SHAN, X. H., LIN, R. D. *ET AL.* (eds) 2000. Fauna Sinica, Osteichthys, Cypriniformes III. Beijing: Science Press, 273–390 [in Chinese].

ZHANG, J. Y. 2003. First Phareodus (Osteoglossomorpha: Osteoglossoidae) from China. *Vertebrata PalAsiatica*, **41**, 327–331.

ZHANG, M. M., ZHOU, J. J. & QING, D. R. 1985. Tertiary fish fauna from coastal region of Bohai Sea. *Memoirs of Institute of Vertebrate Palaeontology and Palaeoanthropology, Academia Sinica*, **17**, 1–60 [in Chinese with English summary].

ZHOU, J. J. 1990. The Cyprinidae fossil from middle Miocene of Shanwang Basin. *Vertebrata PalAsiatica*, **28**, 95–127 [in Chinese with English summary].

ZHOU, J. J. 1992. A new cobitid from the middle Miocene of Shanwang, Shandong. *Vertebrata PalAsiatica*, **30**, 71–76 [in Chinese with English summary].

Can the comparative study of the morphology and histology of the scales of *Latimeria menadoensis* and *L. chalumnae* (Sarcopterygii: Actinistia, Coelacanthidae) bring new insight on the taxonomy and the biogeography of recent coelacanthids?

FRANÇOIS J. MEUNIER[1,2], MARK V. ERDMANN[3], YVES FERMON[1] & ROY L. CALDWELL[4]

[1]*UMR CNRS 5178 Biodiversité et dynamique des communautés aquatiques, Département des Milieux et Peuplements aquatiques, Muséum National d'Histoire Naturelle, 43 rue Cuvier, 75231 Paris cedex 05, France (e-mail: meunier@mnhn.fr)*

[2]*UMR CNRS 7179, Mécanismes adaptifs – squelette des vertébrés, UPMC, case 7077, 2 place Jussieu, 75251 Paris cedex 05, France*

[3]*Conservation International Indonesia, Jl. Dr. Muwardi No. 17, Bali 80235, Indonesia (e-mail: mverdmann@attglobal.net)*

[4]*Department of Integrative Biology, University of California, Berkeley, CA 94720, USA (e-mail: 4roy@socrates.berkeley.edu)*

Abstract: SEM (Scanning electron microscopy) and photonic microscopy (ground sections) studies confirm that the scales of the coelacanth *Latimeria menadoensis* have strong morphological and histological similarities with the scales of *L. chalumnae*. They are both elasmoid scales, the external layer of which is made of radial ridges that are overlaid, on the posterior field, by odontodes. The odontodes of *L. menadoensis* are made of the typical mineralized tissues described for teeth of the coelacanth and their width is similar to that of *L. chalumnae* odontodes. Globular corpuscles are found in the isopedine contact with the external layer. Their mineralization seems to be inotropic as in the Mandl's corpuscles of teleost elasmoid scales. Scale organisation in *L. menadoensis* does not show any characteristics that may support significantly, in the absence of additional evidence, two different species in the extant coelacanths.

The discovery in 1938, of a living coelacanth, *Latimeria chalumnae* Smith 1939*a*, shocked not only the world's icthyological community, but also all students of vertebrate evolution (Smith 1939*b*, *c*, 1953). Coelacanths belong to a very ancient group of Crossopterygii, since the oldest ones have inhabited the oceans for more than 360 my (Forey & Cloutier 1991; Forey 1998), and they were thought to have become extinct 70–75 my ago (Forey 1998; Cavin *et al.* 2005). But, in fact, their descendants survived five major extinction crises (Fricke 2001). So for the half century following the description of *L. chalumnae* (Smith 1939*a–c*), this animal was considered as a 'living fossil' with a geographic range limited to the Comoran Islands (Forey 1998; de Vos & Oyugi 2002). More than 170 specimens of *L. chalumnae* were captured from the Comoros between 1952 and 1995 (Bruton & Coutouvidis 1991;

Bruton 1999), and 'Old Fourlegs' (= 'Gombessa') was the subject of a most intensive series of biological investigations on its morphology, anatomy, histology and a range of other topics (see Locket 1980; Bruton *et al.* 1991).

Though the subsequent discovery of coelacanths off the coast of Mozambique (Bruton *et al.* 1992) and SW Madagascar (Heemstra *et al.* 1996) generated significant excitement amongst ichthyologists, these findings were soon eclipsed by the announcement in 1998 of the discovery of 2 individuals of living coelacanths in north Sulawesi, Indonesia – nearly 10,000 km away from the nearest known population in the Comoros (Erdmann *et al.* 1998; Erdmann 1999; Erdmann *et al.* 1999). Even before detailed morphological and genetic analyses were completed for the single preserved Indonesian specimen, several authors (e.g. Springer 1999) were speculating on the biogeography of these apparently

From: CAVIN, L., LONGBOTTOM, A. & RICHTER, M. (eds) *Fishes and the Break-up of Pangaea.*
Geological Society, London, Special Publications, **295**, 351–360.
DOI: 10.1144/SP295.17   0305-8719/08/$15.00 © The Geological Society of London 2008.

widely disjunct populations and predicting that Indonesian fish would prove to be a distinct species.

Shortly thereafter, these predictions were upheld as Pouyaud *et al.* (1999) described the new species *Latimeria menadoensis*, and differentiated it from *L. chalumnae* primarily upon genetic differences. Though they pointed out some serious flaws in the genetic analysis reported by Pouyaud *et al.* (1999), Holder *et al.* (1999) also suggested that the level of sequence divergence in selected mitochondrial DNA between *L. chalumnae* and *L. menadoensis* (4.1% difference for a 4 823 base pair sequence) would indeed seem to justify the description of a new species. Analyses by Erdmann *et al.* (1999) and Pouyaud *et al.* (1999) also provided some indication of slight morphological and meristic differences between *L. chalumnae* and the Indonesian specimen, but these analyses were severely hampered by the lack of comparative specimens of the putative species *L. menadoensis*.

Unfortunately, there have been no further reported coelacanth specimens collected from Indonesia since 1998. Though this time period has seen a rash of new discoveries of *L. chalumnae* occurrences in the western Indian Ocean, including in South Africa (Venter *et al.* 2000), Kenya (de Vos & Oyugi 2002) and Tanzania (Verheij, pers. comm.), the only additional coelacanth sightings in Indonesia were those of Fricke *et al.* (2000), (who observed two additional specimens *in situ* in North Sulawesi). Though this sighting helped verify the existence of a viable Sulawesi population of extant coelacanths, the lack of further specimens has made it impossible to further define the variability of the morphological and meristic characters of the Indonesian coelacanth and evaluate the consistency of the purported differences with *L. chalumnae*.

In the absence of further specimens of *L. menadoensis*, it is imperative to maximize comparative analyses of the one existing museum specimen with the wealth of data existing on *L. chalumnae*. Indeed, Holder *et al.* (1999) urged more detailed comparative morphological analyses of *L. menadoensis* in order to verify its status as a distinct species. Those authors specifically mentioned the importance of a detailed investigation of scale morphology: one of the potential differences noted for *L. menadoensis* was the gold-flecked appearance of the scales (not previously reported in the literature for *L. chalumnae*), which apparently created a prismatic effect of light reflecting off the odontodes of the scales. Erdmann *et al.* (1998) had previously suggested that this apparent difference in appearance may belie an underlying difference in scale morphology between the Indonesian fish and *L. chalumnae*.

The present study is focused upon a detailed comparison of the morphology and histology of the scales of *L. menadoensis* and *L. chalumnae*. The body of extant and fossil coelacanths is covered by numerous scales, several of which can easily be sampled without noticeable damage to preserved museum specimens (Millot & Anthony 1958; Millot *et al.* 1978; Forey 1998). In *L. chalumnae*, the morphology and the structure of the scales are well-known (Roux 1942; Smith *et al.* 1972; Castanet *et al.* 1975; Miller 1979; Giraud *et al.* 1978a; Millot *et al.* 1978; Smith 1979; Meunier 1980; Meunier & Zylberberg 1999). Conversely, only Hadiaty & Rachmatika (2003) have previously published a study on the scales of *L. menadoensis*, with their results focused on describing the morphology of scales from different locations on the body (without specifically focusing on a comparison between the scales of *L. menadoensis* and *L. chalumnae*). The present study aims to bridge the work of the previous authors and provide an explicit comparison of the morphological and histological characteristics of the scales of *L. menadoensis* and *L. chalumnae*, using both scanning electron microscopy (SEM), photonic microscopy and microradiography of ground sections.

Material and methods

Material

Latimeria menadoensis. Nine scales were sampled from the second known Indonesian coelacanth specimen (MZB10003; N° CCC 175; female 29.2 kg, 124 cm TL) captured off Manado Tua, Sulawesi Island. These scales were originally fixed with formalin, and then stored in alcohol. After measurements of the odontodes, some scales were studied with SEM and others were used for ground sections.

Latimeria chalumnae. The morphology (SEM) and the structure (ground sections) of the scales have been examined predominantly from two main specimens: (a) the scales overlying the basis of the pelvic fin of (N° CCC 67; female 78 kg, 163 cm TL) have been sampled and fixed in neutral formalin and kept in ethanol 70 degrees; and (b) several scattered scales of specimen MNHN 1989–806 (N° CCC 117; 105 cm TL) have also been sampled. The morphometric study has been completed with the measurement of the odontodes of one or two scales belonging to each of the following Comoran coelacanths: N°s CCC 6, CCC 22, CCC 36a, CCC 61 and CCC 64 (see Bruton & Coutouvidis 1991).

Institutional abbreviations. MZB = Museum Zoologicum Bogoriense (Indonesian National Zoological Museum in Bogor, Indonesia); MNHN = Muséum national d'Histoire naturelle (Paris, France).

Methods

For the SEM observations, the scales were steeped in 6 or 12% sodium hypochloride solution at room temperature (in order to strip the surface of the scales and to destroy the unmineralized collagenous fibres to allow for cleaning of the mineralized front of the basal plate). The scales were then washed in distilled water, dehydrated in absolute ethanol, air-dried, glued and coated with evaporated gold. The upper and deep surfaces of the scales were examined in a JEOL-SEM-35 scanning electron microscope.

Results

Our morphological and histological studies show that the scales of the two species are extremely similar and show only a few minute differences. Below our findings are described for both *L. chalumnae* and *L. menadoensis*; except where otherwise noted, these descriptions apply equally to the scales of both species.

Morphology

SEM examination shows that the whole outer surface of the scale of *Latimeria* is ornamented with radial ridges. These ridges are present on the surface of the anterior field (which is inserted within the dermis and covered by the neighbouring scales) as well as on the surface of the uncovered posterior field, where odontodes are located (Fig. 1a–e).

The odontodes that characterize *Latimeria* scales are found only on the posterior field of the scales and are generally isolated from each other (Fig. 1a–c), though they are occasionally found in close association to form odonto-complexes (Fig. 1d–e). An odontode is composed of two parts (Fig. 1f–i): a spiny denticle made of dental tissues and a basis that is composed of bony tissue (see below). The sharp apical extremity of the odontodes is orientated posteriorly and its proximal region shows thin ridges parallel to the axis of the odontode (Fig. 1j–k). The bony basis is in close contact with the ridges of the scale surface (Fig. 1c–e, i). Some apertures scattered on the margin of the bony basis correspond to the openings of vascular canals crossing this bony tissue (Fig. 1d, i). A vascular network composed of vascular cavities and canals, revealed by histological studies, is associated with the odonto-complexes. Thin globular structures are observed in the basal part of the odontode in contact with the bony base (Fig. 1j).

The odontodes found on *Latimeria* scales display a range of sizes and morphologies, both between scales and even on the same scale (Fig. 1a–b). Some odontodes are relatively short (Fig. 1c) whereas others are long and occasionally display two points (Fig. 1g). The apices of certain odontodes are exposed to erosive processes (Fig. 1h) that can eventually lead to the disappearance of the whole crown (Fig. 1e, l); in these cases, the bony basis is preserved and will generally support the growth of a new odontode, the basis of which fuses with the old one (Fig 1e) and then forms an odonto-complex.

Importantly, our comparison of the measurements of the odontodes on the scales of *L. menadoensis* and *L. chalumnae* does not show significant or consistent differences between the two species. Though significant variation was observed in the size of the odontodes examined, these differences seem to be closely linked with the size of the scale upon which the odontodes were found, rather than varying consistently between species.

Histology

The scales of the two species are composed of two main parts: an upper one called the 'external layer' (also known as the 'superficial layer' or 'ornamented layer') that is well-mineralized; and a lower (or deeper) one, the 'basal plate' that is stratified and nearly totally deprived of mineralized elements (Fig. 2a–c). The examination of the ground sections with transmitted natural light, polarized light and microradiography, clearly shows the histological characteristics of the two layers (Fig. 3a–c). Attention will be specifically focused on the posterior field of the scale.

In the posterior field, the odontodes overlie the stratified basal plate (Fig. 3a–b) from which they are separated by the thin ridges of the external layer (Fig. 3c). Each odontode is made of a cone of dentine around a pulpar cavity (Fig. 3c–e). Their crown is covered by a thin layer of enamel. On extant specimens, the largest odontodes can penetrate the epidermis.

The bony basal pad anchors the odontode to the underlying external layer (Fig. 3c, e). When the odontodes fuse together to form an odonto-complex, the bony pads are frequently superimposed (Fig. 3f). A thin cementing line is present between the older odontodes and the more superficial newly formed ones in the odonto-complexes (Fig. 3f).

The basal plate is composed of multiple strata, each of which is composed of thick collagen fibrils (Fig. 3a, b, g). Between two collagenous layers there are star-shaped cells: the elasmocytes (not illustrated), with their cytoplasmic processes that insert between the collagenous fibres. The collagenous fibres of the basal plate are set in a complex network. They form successive strata in which fibres are parallel to each other, with their

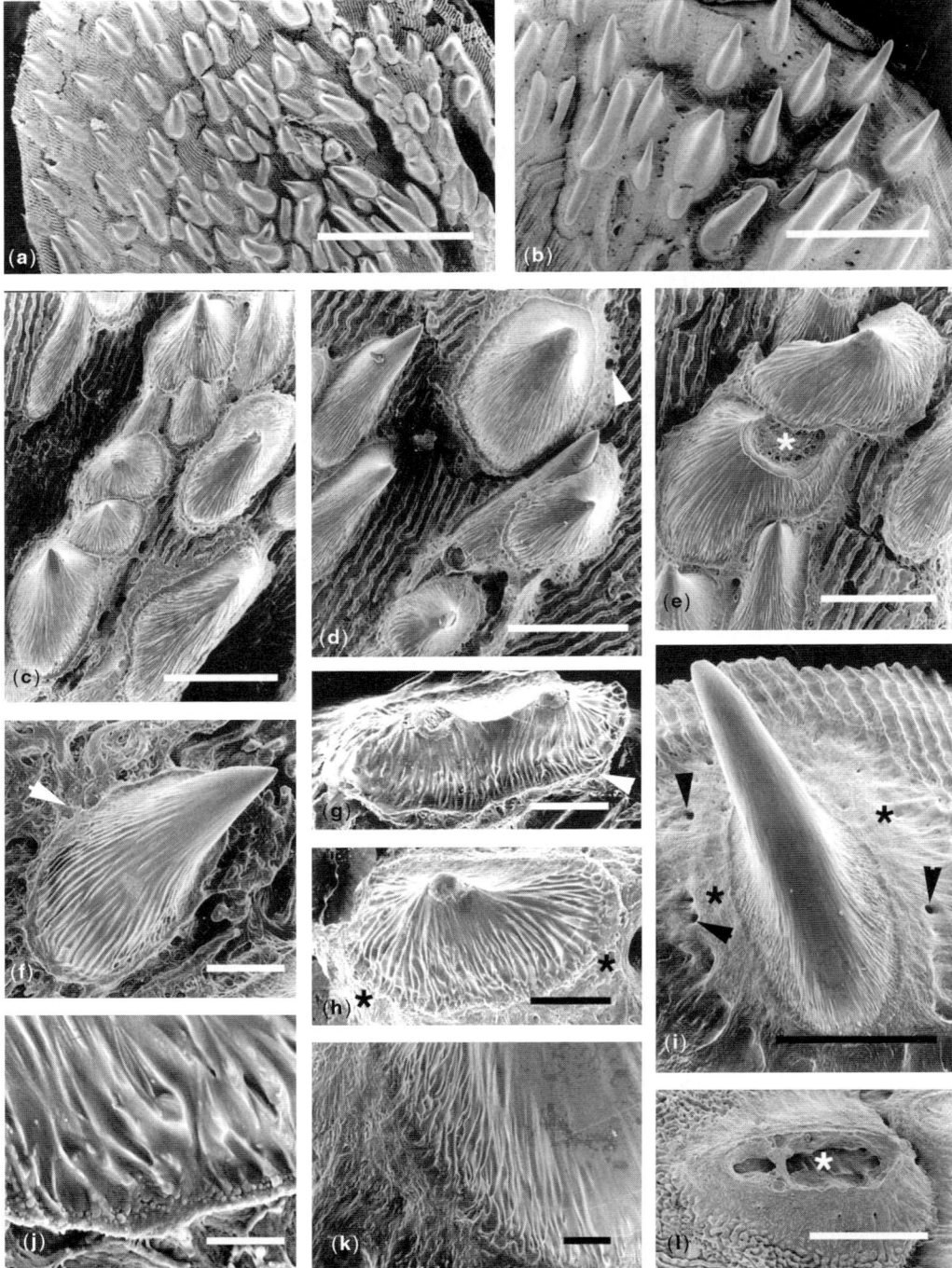

Fig. 1. SEM. Posterior field of scales. (**a**) *Latimeria menadoensis* (MZB 10003). General view of the odontodes. The posterior margin of the scale is on the upper left. The radial ridges of the external layer are clearly seen between the odontodes (Bar = 1 mm); (**b**) *Latimeria chalumnae* (MNHN 1989–806). General view of the odontodes. The posterior margin of the scale is on the upper right. The radial ridges of the external layer are clearly seen

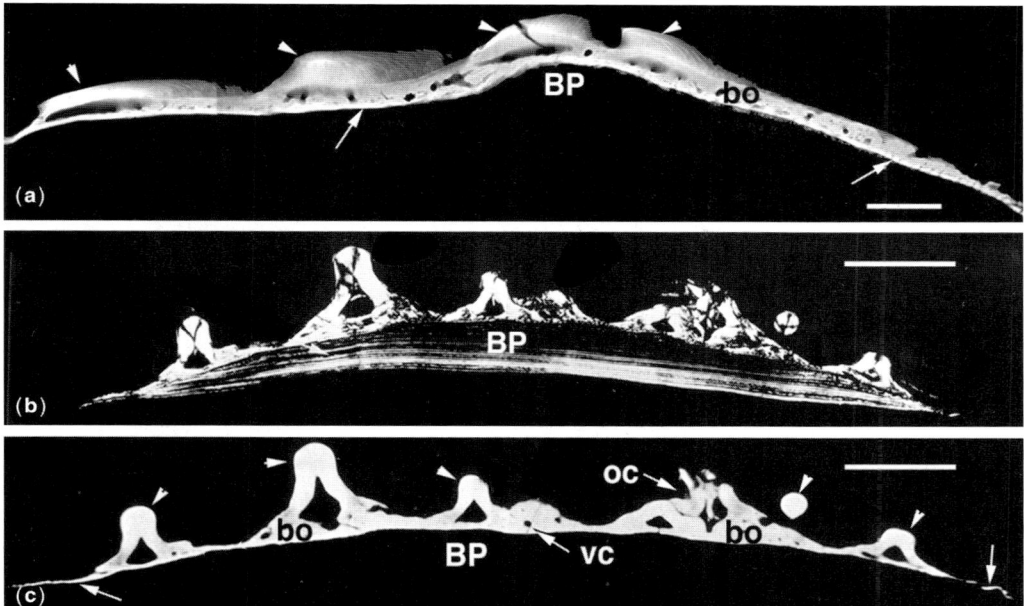

Fig. 2. (a) *Latimeria menadoensis* (MZB 10003). Longitudinal section of the posterior field, with the anterior part on the right; microradiography. The ornamented superficial layer (arrow) and four odontodes (arrowheads) only are seen. The whole basal plate (BP) lacks mineral and so is black (bo = bone) (Bar = 1 mm); (b) *Latimeria chalumnae* (CCC 67). Transversal section of the posterior field; polarized light. The ornamented superficial layer and the odontodes overlie the laminae (arrow) of basal plate (BP). Some vascular canals are seen in the bony pads of the odontodes (Bar = 1 mm; from Castanet *et al.* 1975); (c) *Latimeria chalumnae* (CCC 67). Same section as part (b); microradiography. The ornamented superficial layer (arrow) and the odontodes (arrowheads) only are seen. The whole basal plate (BP) lacks mineral and is therefore black (bo = bone; oc = odonto-complex; vc = vascular canal) (Bar = 1 mm; from Castanet *et al.* 1975).

direction changing from one layer to the next layer (Fig. 3h). In *L. chalumnae*, previous work has shown that the direction of fibres changes regularly between strata; this regular organisation is the result of a specific spatial arrangement termed 'twisted plywood' by Giraud *et al.* (1978*a, b*). The rotation from one layer to the next in each scale examined has a mean angle of 27° (Giraud *et al.* 1978*a*). Scales broken in liquid nitrogen allow measurements of angles between fibre directions of

between the odontodes (Bar = 1 mm); (c) *Latimeria menadoensis* (MZB 10003). Detail of several odontodes, inserted above the ridges of the ornamented layer (Bar = 200 μm); (d) *Latimeria menadoensis* (MZB 10003). Detail of two superimposed odontodes. The arrowhead points to an aperture where blood vessels penetrate (Bar = 200 μm); (e) *Latimeria menadoensis* (MZB 10003). Detail of two superimposed odontodes; the apical part of the lower one (*) is eroded. The ridges of the external layer are obvious (Bar = 200 μm); (f) *Latimeria menadoensis* (MZB 10003). Detail of a sharp odontode, the surface of which is delicately ridged in its basal half. The ridges of the external layer are masked by superficial ossifications that correspond to the bony base of the odontodes (arrowhead) (Bar = 25 μm); (g) *Latimeria menadoensis* (MZB 10003). Detail of a double spined odontode and its bony base (arrowhead) (Bar = 25 μm); (h) *Latimeria menadoensis* (MZB 10003). Detail of a short spiny odontode, the tip of which is weakly eroded; its base is obviously ridged. The asterisks indicate the basal bony tissue that joins the odontode to the ornamented layer (Bar = 25 μm); (i) *Latimeria chalumnae* (MNHN 1989–806). Detail of a sharp relatively long odontode the surface of which is delicately ridged in its basal part. The asterisks indicate the basal bony tissue that joins the odontode to the ornamented layer. The arrowheads point to apertures where blood vessels penetrate (Bar = 250 μm); (j) *Latimeria menadoensis* (MZB 10003). Detail of the basal ridges of an odontode. Some minute spheritic granules are seen at the base of the odontode (Bar = 10 μm); (k) *Latimeria chalumnae* (MNHN 1989–806). Detail of the basal ridges of an odontode (Bar = 25 μm); (l) *Latimeria chalumnae* (MNHN 1989–806). Detail of a partly eroded odontode, the pulpar cavity of which is clearly seen (*) (Bar = 200 μm).

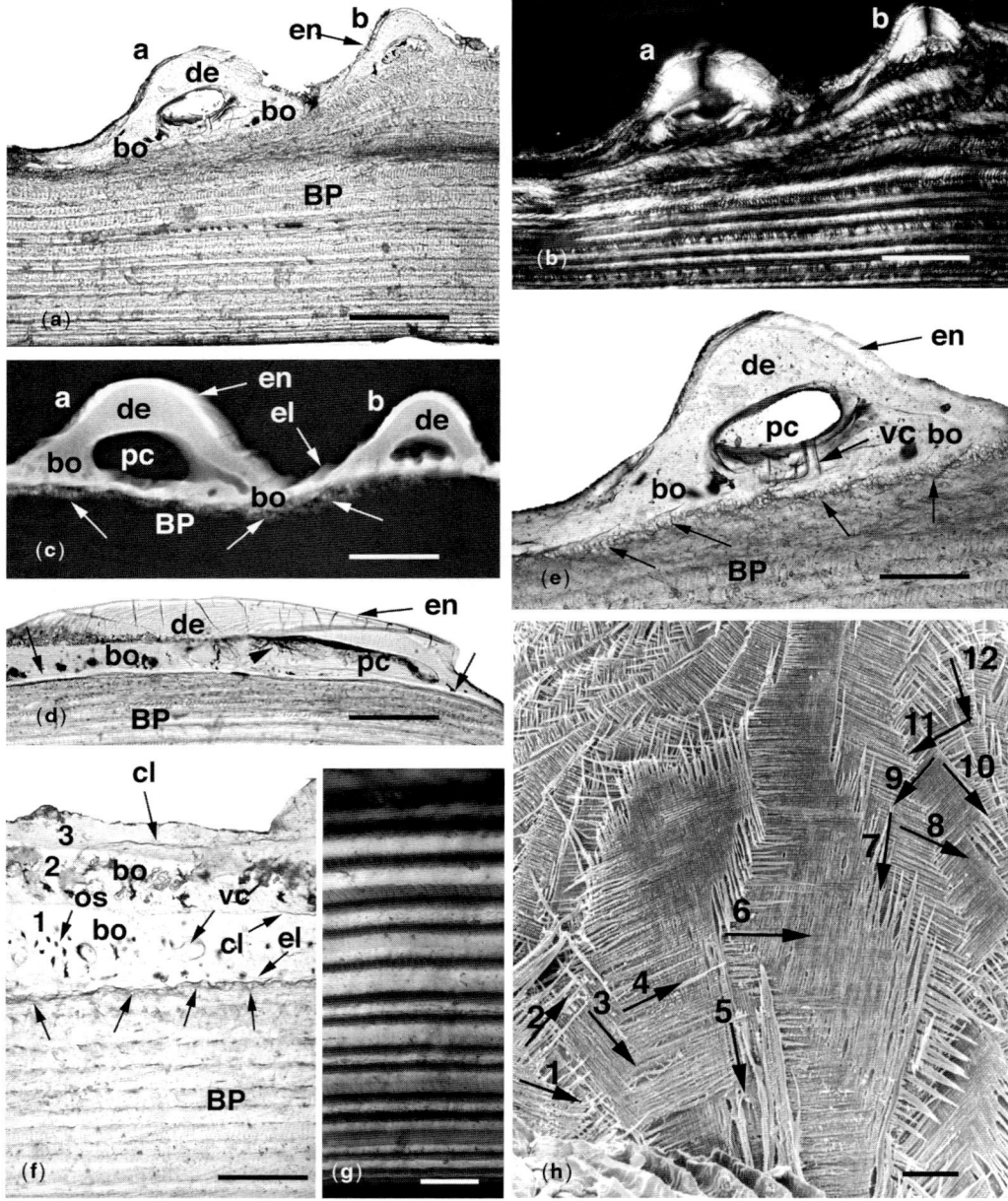

Fig. 3. (**a**) *Latimeria menadoensis* (MZB 10003). Transversal section of the posterior field; transmitted natural light. Two sections of odontodes (a, b) are seen above the successive layers of the basal plate (BP). These layers are finely striated, revealing the collagenous fibre packing in each strata (bo = bone; de = dentine; en = enamel) (Bar = 500 μm); (**b**) *Latimeria menadoensis* (MZB 10003). The same section as part (a) observed with polarized light. The striated aspect due to the thick collagenous fibres is reinforced. (Bar = 500 μm); (**c**) *Latimeria menadoensis* (MZB 10003). The same section as part (a) observed with X-rays. The basal plate is deprived of mineralization; but at the vicinity of the external layer the greyish aspect (arrows) is given by small mineralised granules localized in the first lamina of the basal plate just below the external layer (bo = bone; BP = basal plate; de = dentine; el = external layer; en = enamel; pc = pulpar cavity) (Bar = 500 μm); (**d**) *Latimeria menadoensis* (MZB 10003). Longitudinal section of the posterior field. Transmitted natural light. Detail of an odontode that

successive layers. As in *L. chalumnae*, the organization of collagenous fibrils in *L. menadoensis* forms a plywood-like model with two imbricated systems, odd and even (Fig. 3h), but in *L. menadoensis*, this rotation seems slightly less regular as shown with polarized microscopy.

Another peculiarity of the basal plate is its almost complete lack of mineralization. However, at the point where the superficial layer and the basal plate join, one can see numerous spheritic mineralized granules that extend into the very first layers of the basal plate (Fig. 3c, e, f). There, the mineralization front is ornamented with numerous spherical mineralized corpuscles very similar to the granules described in the scales of *L. chalumnae* (Meunier & Zylberberg 1999); they must not be mixed up with the granules of the base of the odontodes that are over the external layer (Fig. 1g, l).

Discussion

The morphology and histology of scales in *L. chalumnae* are well known. The body of the fish is covered with numerous large imbricated scales (Millot & Anthony 1958) which agree with the concept of elasmoid scales (Smith *et al.* 1972; Miller 1979; Castanet *et al.* 1975; Meunier 1980, 1984) as defined by Bertin (1944) in the Teleostei. Indeed, the scales of *L. chalumnae* are: (1) thin and flexible plates; (2) imbricated, their anterior part deeply inserted within the dermis and their posterior part overlapping the lateral and the anterior fields of the neighbouring scales; and (3) composed of two parts, a thin mineralized and ornamented superficial layer topping a thick basal plate made of cellular isopedine (*sensu* Meunier 1987 = 'elasmodin' of Schultze 1996) which is almost entirely unmineralized. Nevertheless, the upper part of the basal plate mineralizes at the contact of the external layer by mean of granules that can be homologous to Mandl's corpuscles of the teleostean

scales (Zylberberg *et al.* 1992). The results that are reported herein, as well as those of Hadiaty & Rachmatika (2003), suggest that the above description of *L. chalumnae* scales applies equally well to the scales in *L. menadoensis* (Fig. 3a–h).

In *L. chalumnae*, the isopedine is made of thick collagen fibrils (from 100–130 nm in diameter; Castanet *et al.* 1975; Giraud *et al.* 1978a; Meunier 1980) that form bundles (Giraud *et al.* 1978a) which are arranged in a twisted plywood fashion and the progressive rotation of the fibril directions is right-handed (Giraud *et al.* 1978a, b). Again, our results show that this description applies equally to scales of *L. menadoensis* even if the rotation seems less regular but this assertion needs confirmation for this taxa. Moreover, the presence of numerous odontodes scattered on the radial ridges of the posterior field (Smith *et al.* 1972; Castanet *et al.* 1975; Smith 1979) is characteristic of the coelacanth scales; the morphology of these odontodes does not show any consistent significant differences between the two species. Taken together, our results suggest that scale organization (including morphology and histology) in *L. menadoensis* does not show any valuable characteristics that may support, in the absence of further evidence, the existence of two different species in the extant coelacanths.

Our results support the assertions of previous authors (Erdmann *et al.* 1999; Holder *et al.* 1999) that the morphology and allometry of *L. menadoensis* is nearly identical to that of *L. chalumnae*. Indeed, Erdmann *et al.* (1999) showed that (of the 15 categories of lengths and meristic data measured and proportions calculated by McAllister & Smith (1978) in their comparison of known *L. chalumnae* specimens) only the proportional lengths of the gular plate and the pectoral fins to the specimen's standard length and the number of fin rays in the left pectoral fin of *L. menadoensis* fell outside of the range reported for *L. chalumnae*. Though Pouyaud *et al.* (1999) reported nine morphological

lies over the external layer (arrows); star shaped melanocytes (arrowhead) are seen in the pulpar cavity (pc); (bo = bone; BP = basal plate; de = dentine; en = enamel) (Bar = 500 μm); (**e**) *Latimeria menadoensis* (MZB 10003). Detail of the left odontode of part (a) transmitted natural light. At the basement of the odontode, numerous spheritic concretions are seen (arrows) just above the upper layers of the basal plate (BP) (bo = bone; de = dentine; en = enamel; pc = pulpar cavity; vc = vascular canal) (Bar = 250 μm); (**f**) *Latimeria menadoensis* (MZB 10003). Transmitted natural light. Detail of the superficial layer showing three successive bases (1 to 3) of odontodes separated by cementing lines (cl). These bases are constituted of vascularized bone (bo). Just below the ornamented external layer (el), in the basal plate (BP), thin mineralised spherules are seen (arrows) (os = osteocytes; vc = vascular canals) (Bar = 250 μm); (**g**) *Latimeria menadoensis* (MZB 10003). Polarized light. Detail of the basal plate. The successive laminae are dark, lightened or near grey according to the orientation of the collagenous fibres relatively to the section plane. The thickness of the plies decreases from the oldest (on the top) to the more recent (below) (Bar = 150 μm); (**h**) *Latimeria menadoensis* (MZB 10003). Fracture of frozen material (SEM). The progressive right handed rotation of the collagenous fibres in the successive plies is obvious. The two imbricated systems, odd and even, form 12 successive directions that are reinforced (1–12) (Bar = 200 μm).

measurements that they claimed differentiate *L. menadoensis* from *L. chalumnae*, Holder *et al.* (1999) have shown that five of these reported differences are in fact spurious, while the remaining four reported differences are difficult to assess for accuracy because they are based on measurements that have not been reported widely in the literature that describe *L. chalumnae* specimens. Nonetheless, it is important to note that one would perhaps not expect large morphological differences between these two putative species, given that the coelacanth lineage has shown surprisingly few morphological changes throughout its 360 my history (Forey 1998).

Given the miniscule morphological differences used to differentiate the two species (and these based upon a single specimen of *L. menadoensis*), it is clear that the final assessment of the validity of *L. menadoensis* as a separate and distinct species will rely upon the eventual collection of additional specimens, enabling a more accurate assessment of the consistency of these small differences. Currently, the most convincing data supporting the idea that the separate species status of *L. menadoensis* is genetic; the 4.1% sequence divergence reported between *L. menadoensis* and *L. chalumnae* for 4823 base pairs of mitochondrial DNA suggest a date of their most recent common ancestor to be nearly 5.5 my (Holder *et al.* 1999). This genetic analysis would also benefit greatly from additional samples from *L. menadoensis*; if this strong genetic difference is confirmed in multiple specimens (especially in additional specimens obtained from the intervening areas between the Comoros and Sulawesi), the validity of *L. menadoensis* would be firmly established and the lack of large morphological differences between the species could simply be attributed to an exceedingly low rate of morphological evolution in *Latimeria* and coelacanthids in general.

Whatever the truth between two species (*L. chalumnae* and *L. menadoensis*) or two ecotypes of the same species, the biogeographical link between the Indonesian coelacanth and the west of India coelacanth is a question that has been shelved. The coelacanth is absolutely known to not be a transoceanic migrating fish (Fricke *et al.* 1991; Fricke & Hissmann 1994). The geographical limits of the various populations of Gombessa (*L. chalumnae*) have spread through the whole Mozambique Channel (Mozambique and North of South African coasts, west Madagascar coast, Comoros) and extend in the north until the Kenyan coast and in the south until East London (de Vos & Oyugi 2002). The settlement of these various sites from one centre of dispersal (?Comoros) does not raise any basic problem even if the western coelacanth is known to have a high site fidelity and to be a poor swimming fish; yet it may extend over several kilometres of coastline (Fricke & Hissmann

1994). The discovery of the Indonesian coelacanth, off the coast of Sulawesi, is still recent (Erdmann *et al.* 1998). Is this population unique in the Indonesian area or is it more widespread, like the Comoran one that appeared half a century after its first discovery? If applied habitats are probably present in some other Indonesian islands coasts, until now no coelacanths have been reported anywhere else, but some have been observed *in situ*, 360 km SW to Manado Tua (Fricke *et al.* 2000). Moreover, the frequent tectonic major events that regularly affect this active geological region may have lethal consequences on eventual unknown coelacanth populations, even if these events can also build volcanic habitats favourable to coelacanth life. Whatever the real range of the Indonesian coelacanth, there is a very wide gap between the two extreme actual coelacanth sites: west of India versus Indonesian. The tops of the ridges that stretch along the Indian Ocean between Madagascar and the Indonesian Archipelago are too deep to house coelacanths, which are known to live at depths about 100–200 metres (Fricke *et al.* 1991; Fricke & Hissmann 1994; Fricke *et al.* 2000). Moreover, the coelacanth seems to prefer habitats that are in the vicinity of raised lands (Fricke *et al.* 1991). Until now, no ocean search has revealed a refuge with coelacanths, e.g. in Mascarene Islands and Plateau, Chagos Archipelago, South of India and Sri Lanka, etc. that could represent geographical links between the two extreme coelacanth populations.

A final question concerns the offspring. The number of coelacanths under 100 cm in length is very small (Bruton & Armstrong 1991). Is it possible that the juveniles play a more positive part in dispersal activity than the adults do?

We are grateful to C. Chancogne (MNHN) for her technical assistance for SEM studies, and to the Indonesian Institute of Sciences, particularly M. K. Moosa, A. Tjakrawidjaja, R. Hadiaty and I. Rachmatika, for their assistance with the Indonesian coelacanth specimen from which the *L. menadoensis* scales were collected.

References

BERTIN, L. 1944. Modifications proposées dans la nomenclature des écailles et des nageoires. *Bulletin de la Société Zoologique de France*, **69**, 198–202.

BRUTON, M. N. 1999. Alterations and additions to the coelacanth inventory: IV. *Environmental Biology of Fishes*, **54**, 458–461.

BRUTON, M. N. & ARMSTRONG, M. J. 1991. The demography of the coelacanth *Latimeria chalumnae*. *Environmental Biology of Fishes*, **32**, 301–311.

BRUTON, M. N. & COUTOUVIDIS, S. E. 1991. An inventory of all known specimens of the coelacanth *Latimeria chalumnae*, with comments on trends in catches. *Environmental Biology of Fishes*, **32**, 371–390.

BRUTON, M. N., COUTOUVIDIS, S. E. & POTE, J. 1991. Bibliography of the living coelacanth *Latimeria chalumnae*, with comments on publication trends. *Environmental Biology of Fishes*, **32**, 403–433.

BRUTON, M. N., CABRAL, A. J. P. & FRICKE, H. 1992. First capture of a coelacanth *Latimeria chalumnae* (Pisces, Latimeriidae), off Mozambique. *South African Journal of Sciences*, **88**, 225–227.

CASTANET, J., MEUNIER, F., BERGOT, C. & FRANÇOIS, Y. 1975. Données préliminaires sur les structures histologiques du squelette de *Latimeria chalumnae*. I Dents, écailles, rayons de nageoires. *In: Problèmes actuels de Paléontologie. Evolution des Vertébrés.* Colloques Internationaux du CNRS, **1**, 159–168.

CAVIN, L., FOREY, P. L., BUFFETAUT, E. & TONG, H. 2005. Latest European coelacanth shows Gondwanan affinities. *Biology Letters*, 10.1098/rsbl.2004.0287: 1–3.

DE VOS, L. & OYUGI, D. 2002. First capture of a coelacanth Smith, 1939 (Pisces: Latimeriidae), off Kenya. *South African Journal of Sciences*, **98**, 345–347.

ERDMANN, M. V. 1999. An account of the first living coelacanth known to scientists from Indonesian waters. *Environmental Biology of Fishes*, **54**, 439–443.

ERDMANN, M. V., CALDWELL, R. L., JEWETT, S. L. & TJAKRAWIDJAJA, A. 1999. The second recorded living coelacanth from north Sulawesi. *Environmental Biology of Fishes*, **54**, 445–451.

ERDMANN, M. V., CALDWELL, R. L. & MOOSA, M. K. 1998. Indonesian 'king of the sea' discovered. *Nature*, **395**, 335.

FOREY, P. L. 1998. *History of the Coelacanth Fishes.* Chapman and Hall (ed.), London.

FOREY, P. L. & CLOUTIER, R. 1991. Literature relating to fossil coelacanths. *Environmental Biology of Fishes*, **32**, 391–401.

FRICKE, H. 2001. Coelacanths: a human responsibility. *Journal of Fish Biology*, **59** (Suppl. A), 332–338.

FRICKE, H. & HISSMANN, K. 1994. Home range and migrations of the living coelacanth *Latimeria chalumnae*. *Marine Biology*, **120**, 171–180.

FRICKE, H., HISSMANN, K., SCHAUER, J., REINICKE, O., KASANG, L. & PLANTE, R. 1991. Habitat and population size of the coelacanth *Latimeria chalumnae* at Grand Comoro. *Environmental Biology of Fishes*, **32**, 287–300.

FRICKE, H., HISSMANN, K., SCHAUER, J., ERDMANN, M., MOOSA, M. K. & PLANTE, R. 2000. Biogeography of the Indonesian coelacanths. *Nature*, **403**, 38.

GIRAUD, M. M., CASTANET, J., MEUNIER, F. J. & BOULIGAND, Y. 1978a. Organisation spatiale de l'isopédine des écailles du coelacanthe (*Latimeria chalumnae*, Smith). *Comptes Rendus de l'Académie des Sciences*, **287**, 487–489.

GIRAUD, M. M., CASTANET, J., MEUNIER, F. J. & BOULIGAND, Y. 1978b. The fibrous structure of coelacanth scales: a twisted 'plywood'. *Tissue and Cell*, **10**, 671–686.

HADIATY, R. K. & RACHMATIKA, I. 2003. Morphological study of the scales of *Latimeria menadoensis* Pouyaud *et al.*, 1999. *Treubia (Journal on Zoology of the Indo-Australian Archipelago)*, **33**, 1–11.

HEEMSTRA, P. C., FREEMAN, A. L., WONG, H. Y., HENSLEY, D. A. & RABESANDRATANA, H. D. 1996. First authentic capture of a coelacanth off Madagascar. *South African Journal of Sciences*, **92**, 150–151.

HOLDER, M. T., ERDMANN, M. V., WILCOX, T. P., CALDWELL, R. L. & HILLIS, D. M. 1999. Two living species of coelacanths? *Proceedings of the National Academy of Sciences*, **96**, 12616–12620.

LOCKET, N. A. 1980. Some advances in coelacanth biology. *Proceedings of the Royal Society of London*, **B 208**, 265–307.

MCALLISTER, D. E. & SMITH, C. L. 1978. Mensurations morphologiques, dénombrements méristiques et taxonomie du coelacanthe, *Latimeria chalumnae*. *Naturaliste Canadien*, **105**, 63–76.

MEUNIER, F. J. 1980. Les relations isopédine-tissu osseux dans le post-temporal et les écailles de la ligne latérale de *Latimeria chalumnae* (Smith). *Zoologica Scripta*, **9**, 307–317.

MEUNIER, F. J. 1984. Spatial organization and mineralization of the basal plate of elasmoid scales in Osteichtyans. *American Zoologist*, **24**, 953–964.

MEUNIER, F. J. 1987. Os cellulaire, os acellulaire et tissus dérivés chez les Osteichtyens: les phénomènes de l'acellularisation et de la perte de minéralisation. *L'Année Biologique*, **26**, 201–233.

MEUNIER, F. J. & ZYLBERBERG, L. 1999. The structure of the external layer and of the odontodes of scales in *Latimeria chalumnae* (Sarcopterygii, Actinistia, Coelacanthidae) revisited using scanning and transmission electron microscopy. *In*: SÉRET, B. & SIRE, J.-Y.(eds) Proceedings of the 5th Indo-Pacific Fish Conference, Nouméa. 1997, Société Française d'Ichthyologie, Paris, 109–116.

MILLER, W. A. 1979. Observations on the structure of mineralized tissue of the coelacanth, including scales and their associates odontodes. *In* The Biology and Physiology of the Living Coelacanth. *Occasional Papers of the Californian Academy of Sciences*, **134**, 68–78.

MILLOT, J. & ANTHONY, J. 1958. Anatomie de *Latimeria chalumnae*. 1. Squelette et muscles et formations de soutien. CNRS (ed.), Paris.

MILLOT, J., ANTHONY, J. & ROBINEAU, D. 1978. Anatomie de *Latimeria chalumnae*. 3. Appareil digestif, appareil respiratoire, appareil urogénital, glandes endocrines, appareil circulatoire, teguments, écailles, conclusions générales. CNRS (ed.), Paris.

POUYAUD, L., WIRJOATMODJO, S., RACHMATIKA, I., TJAKRAWIDJAJA, A., HADIATY, R. K. & HADIE, W. 1999. Une nouvelle espèce de coelacanthe, preuves génétiques et morphologiques. *Comptes Rendus de l'Académie des Sciences*, **322**, 261–267.

ROUX, G. H. 1942. The microscopic anatomy of the latimeria scale. *South African Journal of Medical Sciences*, **7**, 1–18.

SCHULTZE, H. P. 1996. The scales of Mesozoic actinopterygians. *In*: ARRATIA, G. & VIOHL, G. (eds) *Mesozoic Fishes – Systematics and Palaeoecology*, Dr F. Pfeil, Munich, Germany, 83–93.

SMITH, J. L. B. 1939a. A living fish of the Mesozoic type. *Nature*, **143**, 455–456.

SMITH, J. L. B. 1939b. A living coelacanthid fish from South Africa. *Transactions of the Royal Society of South Africa*, **28**, 1–106.

SMITH, J. L. B. 1939c. The living coelacanthid fish from South Africa. *Nature*, **143**, 748–750.

SMITH, J. L. B. 1953. The second coelacanth. *Nature*, **171**, 99–101.

SMITH, M. M. 1979. Scanning electron microscopy of odontodes in the scales of a coelacanth embryo, *Latimeria chalumnae* Smith. *Archives of Oral Biology*, **24**, 179–183.

SMITH, M. M., HOBDELL, M. H. & MILLER, W. A. 1972. The structure of the scales of *Latimeria chalumnae*. *Journal of Zoology, London*, **167**, 501–509.

SPRINGER, V. G. 1999. Are the Indonesian and western Indian ocean coelacanths conspecific: a prediction. *Environmental Biology of Fishes*, **54**, 453–456.

VENTER, P., TIMM, P., GUNN, G., LE ROUX, E., SERFONTEIN, C., SMITH, P., SMITH, E., BENSCH, M., HARDING, D. & HEEMSTRA, P. 2000. Discovery of a viable population of coelacanths (*Latimeria chalumnae* Smith, 1939) at Sodwana Bay, South Africa. *South African Journal of Sciences*, **96**, 567–568.

ZYLBERBERG, L., GÉRAUDIE, J., MEUNIER, F. J. & SIRE, J. Y. 1992. Biomineralization in the integumental skeleton of the living lower vertebrates. *In*: HALL, B. K. (ed.) *Bone. Volume 4*. CRC Press, Boca Raton, FL, 171–224.

Index

Please note: Page numbers denoted in *italics* refer to figures and page numbers denoted in **bold** refer to tables.